SECOND EDITION

FINANCIAL INSTITUTIONS AND MARKETS

Meir Kohn
Dartmouth College

New York   Oxford
OXFORD UNIVERSITY PRESS
2004

Oxford University Press

Oxford   New York
Auckland   Bangkok   Buenos Aires   Cape Town   Chennai
Dar es Salaam   Delhi   Hong Kong   Istanbul   Karachi   Kolkata
Kuala Lumpur   Madrid   Melbourne   Mexico City   Mumbai
Nairobi   São Paulo   Shanghai   Taipei   Tokyo   Toronto

Library of Congress Cataloging-in-Publication Data

Kohn, Meir G.
  Financial institutions and markets / Meir Kohn.—2nd ed.
      p. cm.
  Includes bibliographical references and index.
  ISBN 0–19–513472–9 (hardcover : alk. paper)
  1. Financial institutions—United States. 2. Capital market—United
States. 3. Money market—United States. 4. Banks and banking—United
States. I. Title.
  HG181 .K64 2003
  332.1'0973—dc21
                                                      2002154594

Printing number: 9 8 7 6 5 4 3 2 1

Printed in the United States of America
on acid-free paper

TO ADAM, DANIEL, AND LEAH

CONTENTS

PREFACE

W hy? That is the question I have tried to answer in this book. Why do financial institutions and markets have the structure they do? Why is that structure changing?
Existing texts are long on description, but short on explanation and intuition. This book
provides the student with the facts, but it places those facts in a context that makes sense
of them. Facts get old quickly—but an understanding of the forces that lie behind the facts
will stand the student in good stead many years after the facts themselves have changed.

Understanding requires a conceptual framework. Recent advances in finance and
economics—the economics of information, principal–agent theory, and the theory of market microstructure—provide just such a framework. The book uses these ideas—in an intuitive rather than in a formal way—to explain what financial institutions and markets do and
how they do it.

Understanding also requires perspective—both historical and international. Institutions and markets do not exist in a vacuum. They have developed over time in response to
changing economic needs and changing regulatory constraints. The book explains how
today's institutions and markets have evolved and compares institutions and markets in the
United States with those of other countries.

This book is intended for courses in financial institutions, financial markets, or a combination of institutions and markets at either the undergraduate or master's level. The book
is designed to be self-contained, but students will benefit from having taken introductory
economics and basic corporate finance.

I have tried to make the book accessible to students of all levels. It is easy to read and,
I hope, even enjoyable. Nonetheless, there is enough substance to satisfy even the best students. By varying the pace and the level of discussion, the book should be suitable for a
wide range of schools.

ORGANIZATION OF THE BOOK

The organization and coverage of the book is innovative in a number of ways:

- Part I stresses the role of the financial system in facilitating payments and trade
  in risk (insurance and forward transactions) as well as in borrowing and lending.
  Accordingly, the treatment of payments in Chapter 8 and of insurance in Chapter 9 are more extensive than is customary.

- Chapter 3 provides a framework for the discussion of government intervention and regulation in later chapters. It looks at why intervention might be justified (market failure) and why it might be unsuccessful (government failure).
- Part II and Part III open with chapters that explain the basic principles, respectively, of intermediaries and markets; they treat specific institutions and markets in subsequent chapters.
- Financial management is covered twice. Chapter 6 introduces the basic ideas needed for the ensuing discussion of financial intermediaries in Part II. Then Chapter 18 provides a more complete treatment, drawing on what has been learned about institutions and markets in the intervening chapters.
- Chapter 10 discusses pension funds and mutual funds together in the general context of long-term saving.
- After Chapters 12 through 16 have discussed individual financial markets, Chapter 17 explores how financial markets themselves are organized—the different arrangements for trading and settlement—as well as the powerful economic forces that are transforming the "market industry."

This book represents a major reworking of my earlier *Financial Institutions and Markets* (New York: McGraw-Hill, 1994). The major changes include the following:

- The coverage of banking has been condensed considerably, reflecting changes in U.S. banking regulation that have reduced the importance of some of the traditional issues—interstate banking, separation of commercial and investment banking, deposit insurance.
- This has allowed a considerable expansion of the coverage of financial markets, with separate chapters on corporate debt and equity, a chapter on market organization, and a chapter on securities regulation.
- The discussion has been broadened, wherever possible, to compare the U.S. financial system with those of other major economies. This comparative perspective complements the historical perspective that characterized the earlier book and remains in this one.

PEDAGOGY

Each chapter begins with a list of study objectives and ends with a summary. A marginal glossary defines key terms as they occur (there is a list of key terms at the end of each chapter). End-of-chapter questions are intended as a stimulus for discussion.

ACKNOWLEDGMENTS

My thanks to Paul Donnelly of Oxford University Press for bringing this project to fruition. I am grateful too to the reviewers of the book. Their comments and suggestions have been of much help.

INTRODUCTION

When an industry is evolving rapidly, it is mistaken and potentially dangerous to understand it in terms of its existing products and structure. Products and structure can change. For example, IBM understood the computer industry in terms of mainframe computers and the integrated production of processors, peripherals, and software. Thinking in this way, IBM missed the boat. Today, the computer industry's principal product is the PC; processors, peripherals, and software are each produced by specialized firms.

Like the computer industry, the financial industry is evolving rapidly. A course that merely describes its existing institutions and markets—however up to date the course is—will not prepare you for the changes to come. To see why, imagine you had taken a course in financial institutions and markets some 30 years ago. Here are a few of the things you might have learned:

- The U.S. financial system is divided into distinct segments—commercial banks, securities firms, insurance companies, and so on. The business of each is distinct, and the segments rarely compete with one another.
- Instability of the financial system is a thing of the past. Deposit insurance has eliminated bank failures and bank runs. Stock market crashes are a historical curiosity.
- Financial institutions and markets in most countries are closed to foreign competition. There is little international lending or international trade in securities.
- Futures markets, which deal in things like corn and hog bellies, are of little consequence to the financial system.
- Life insurance is the principal vehicle of long-term saving.
- Thrifts are an up-and-coming industry and account for most mortgage lending.

How well would this course in financial institutions and markets have prepared you for the developments of the subsequent 30 years? Here are just some of the things that have happened over that period:

- The segmentation of the financial system has largely disappeared. The largest financial institutions today combine banking with the securities business and insurance.
- Instability is not a thing of the past. Bank failures reached epidemic proportions in the 1980s, and the collapse of the deposit insurance funds cost taxpayers over $200 billion. The stock market crash of October 1987 was the most severe in his-

tory, and the rise and fall of the dot-coms in the 1990s was as dramatic as anything the market has ever seen.

- Financial institutions and markets have become globalized. Foreign banks account for an increasing share of U.S. banking, and U.S. banks do much of their business overseas. Cross-border trading in stocks is huge. In 1998, nearly half of individual stock owners in the United States had some exposure to non-U.S. companies.
- Financial futures now dwarf commodity futures in importance. The amount outstanding of financial futures and related instruments worldwide is well over $100 trillion.
- The principal vehicle of long-term saving today is pension funds. Total pension assets of Americans in 1999 added up to about $13 trillion. Life insurance companies now do more business serving pension funds than selling life insurance.
- The thrift industry has declined in importance. It now accounts for little more than 20% of mortgage originations. Today, some 100 mortgage websites account for almost as much business as the thrifts. Most mortgages, however they originate, are packaged and sold on the bond market.

Financial institutions and markets will continue to change in the future. To be ready for these changes, and, if possible, to anticipate them, you must do more than just familiarize yourself with the institutions and markets of today. You must understand *why* they are the way they are, and why they are changing. This book is designed to provide you with that understanding.

THE PLAN OF THE BOOK

PART I. PRINCIPLES

Chapter 1. LENDING, PAYMENTS, AND TRADE IN RISK

Chapter 2. THE FINANCIAL SYSTEM AND ITS TECHNOLOGY

Chapter 3. EFFICIENCY, STABILITY, AND GOVERNMENT INTERVENTION

Chapter 4. INTEREST RATES, EXCHANGE RATES, AND SECURITY PRICES

When an industry is changing we cannot define it simply in terms of existing products and structure. We need a deeper understanding of what the industry does—the needs it serves and the technology it uses. Chapter 1 looks at the needs the financial system serves. Individuals and businesses gain from trading with one another, but there are obstacles that stand in the way of trade. The financial system helps to overcome those obstacles. Specifically, it facilitates lending, payments, and trade in risk. Chapter 2 looks at the technology the financial system uses to do this.

In addition to needs and technology, there is a third factor that shapes the products and structures of industries—government intervention. For example, the phone company is eager to bring you TV and movies, and the cable company is equally eager to provide you with telephone service. The needs are there, the technology is there, but government regulation stands in the way. Compared to most industries, the financial system is highly regulated. In Chapter 3 we investigate why this is so, when such regulation is justified, and when it is harmful.

To understand the technology of the financial system, we need some elementary financial theory. Chapter 4 describes how the value of a security depends on interest rates and exchange rates.

Parts II, III, and IV are the core of the book. Part II looks at financial intermediaries, Part III at financial markets, and Part IV at the safety and stability of the financial system.

The goal throughout is to understand why institutions and markets take the form they do and why this form is constantly changing. To achieve this goal we look at each institution or market from three perspectives:

Economic Function. We apply the principles we have learned in Part I to understand the needs an institution or market fills, the technology it uses, and the regulatory constraints it faces.

Historical Context. Existing institutions and markets are just one stage in a continuing evolutionary process. To see where that process is going, it helps to know where it has come from. We examine the historical development of institutions and markets for lessons about the process of change.

International Comparison. We examine financial institutions and markets in other countries. One reason for this, of course, is the growing globalization of financial institutions and markets. Your knowledge of our own financial system would be seriously incomplete without a familiarity with its international connections. But a second, no less important, reason is that we have much to learn from a comparison of our financial system with those of other countries. Other financial systems often do things differently. Why? Is it better the way they do it?

PART II. INTERMEDIARIES

Chapter 5. UNDERSTANDING FINANCIAL INTERMEDIARIES

Chapter 6. WHAT IS A BANK?

Chapter 7. THE BANKING INDUSTRY

Chapter 8. PAYMENTS AND FOREIGN EXCHANGE

Chapter 9. INSURANCE

Chapter 10. PENSION PLANS AND MUTUAL FUNDS

Chapter 5 takes a look at what is involved in managing a financial intermediary—the factors that affect profitability, the basics of risk and liquidity management.

Chapters 6 through 8 look at banking from various points of view. Chapter 6 explores the nature of a bank. What types of institution have evolved into the modern commercial bank? How has the business done by banks evolved over time? What is the scope of that business today, and how does it differ across countries? Chapter 7 looks at banking as an industry, both within individual countries and internationally. Chapter 8 looks at the different way financial systems—ours and others—facilitate the making of payments. Payments across national boundaries involve foreign exchange, so we take a look here at the foreign exchange market.

Chapter 9 looks at insurance. The treatment here is more extensive than is customary. There are two reasons for this. If we define the financial system in terms of needs served and technology used, then insurance merits equal treatment. Insurance companies facilitate risk shifting much as banks facilitate lending, and they use much the same technology in doing so. Second, the structural boundary between insurance companies and other financial institutions is absent in some countries and is being eroded in the United States.

Chapter 10 looks at two types of institution that serve the needs of long-term saving—pension funds and mutual funds.

PART III. FINANCIAL MARKETS

Chapter 11. UNDERSTANDING FINANCIAL MARKETS

Chapter 12. THE MARKET FOR GOVERNMENT SECURITIES

Chapter 13. THE MORTGAGE MARKET

Chapter 14. DEBT MARKETS

Chapter 15. THE EQUITY MARKET

Chapter 16. THE DERIVATIVES MARKET: FUTURES, OPTIONS, AND SWAPS

Chapter 17. THE ORGANIZATION OF FINANCIAL MARKETS

While different financial markets involve different securities, they all perform the same basic functions and face the same fundamental problems. Chapter 11 opens Part III by examining the nature of these common functions and problems. It then takes a look at the securities firms whose activities make financial markets work.

Chapter 12 takes a close look at the market for government securities—in many ways the pivotal securities market. It examines carefully the business of being a government securities dealer as an example of securities dealing in general.

Chapter 13 looks at the market for residential mortgages and at the problems that have shaped it. It includes an extensive discussion of mortgage securitization—the conversion of mortgage loans into tradable securities.

The key to understanding corporate debt in all its forms is the need for the lender to control risk. Chapter 14 begins by examining the various methods lenders use to control risk. It then reviews the various debt markets to see how these methods are put into practice.

Chapter 15 discusses the equity market—the market for shares in the ownership of corporations. It looks at the mechanisms that have evolved to assure equity holders a fair return on their investment. It examines both the public equity market and the market for private equity finance.

Chapter 16 looks at a set of financial instruments, known collectively as derivatives, that are used to "trade" various types of risk. The chapter discusses how each instrument is used and how it is traded.

Chapter 17 looks at what is involved in organizing a securities market: how exactly trading takes place; how securities markets ensure that buyers receive their securities and sellers their money; and how the "market industry" is being rocked by powerful economic forces.

PART IV. SAFETY AND REGULATION
Chapter 18. MANAGING LIQUIDITY AND RISK
Chapter 19. BANK SAFETY AND REGULATION
Chapter 20. SECURITY MARKET REGULATION AND STABILITY

Part IV looks at the safety and stability of financial intermediaries and markets and at what regulation can do to enhance safety and stability.

Chapter 18 opens Part IV with a discussion of how individual financial institutions manage liquidity and risk. The discussion is concentrated in a single chapter, rather than being treated piecemeal for each type of intermediary. This is to bring out the similarities in the problems that different types of intermediary face and in the common methods they use to address these problems.

Chapter 19 extends the discussion of liquidity and risk from the individual intermediary to the system as a whole. It looks at how government can intervene to improve safety and stability of the system by regulation by being a lender of last resort, and by providing guarantees (in particular deposit insurance). The limits of government intervention and its harmful side effects are discussed too.

Chapter 20 looks at security market regulation. Securities markets face two major problems—cheating and instability. The chapter examines the nature of these problems and asks what regulation can do to mitigate them.

When you reach the end of the book and complete this course of study, you will be well prepared both for the dangers that lie ahead and for the opportunities.

ABOUT THE AUTHOR

Meir Kohn (Ph.D., M.I.T.) is a Professor of Economics at Dartmouth. He has also taught at the Hebrew University, University of California at Berkeley, Boston University, the University of Western Ontario, and UCLA. His professional work focuses on the financial system and on monetary theory and macroeconomics. He has published extensively in professional journals.

PART I

PRINCIPLES

CHAPTER I

LENDING, PAYMENTS, AND TRADE IN RISK

When you finish this chapter, you will understand:

- Why people trade and how they benefit from it
- Why lending, insurance, and forward transactions are all forms of trade
- The underlying motivation for lending, insurance, and forward transactions
- The obstacles to these various forms of trade.

The financial system is changing rapidly. That change is driven by innovation. There are two main types of innovation. The first serves existing needs in new ways. An example is the credit card: this provided a new way to pay for goods and services. The second type of innovation uses existing technology to serve new needs. An example is the financial futures contract: this takes an instrument originally designed to serve the needs of grain dealers and adapts it to serve the needs of financial institutions.

To participate in this process of innovation and change, and perhaps to profit from it, you must understand the needs the financial system serves and the technology it uses. This chapter focuses on the needs; Chapter 2 focuses on the technology.

We must be careful not to define the needs too narrowly. If we do, innovation will leave us behind. So here is a broad definition: *The financial system makes it easier to trade.* Our goal in this chapter is to understand why there is a need to make trade easier.

The first part of the chapter looks at the nature of trade. We start with simple trade in goods and services and go on to more complicated forms—lending, insurance, and forward transactions. The second part of the chapter looks at the problems that stand in the way of trade—problems that the financial system can address.

TRADE AND THE GAINS FROM TRADE

To understand the nature of trade, let us consider a simple example. Imagine that you and twenty others have just arrived at a national park where you will work as rangers for the summer. As you line up to be issued uniforms, you are surprised that no one asks you your size. Uniforms are handed out seemingly at random. However, trade soon sets things right. A frantic half-hour of comparing and swapping leaves everyone dressed in clothes that more or less fit. The gains from trade are obvious to see. As this example shows, people trade because they differ in what they have and in what they want. The basis of trade is diversity.

An important advantage of trade is that it allows specialization. The grassy meadows of New Zealand are a perfect place to raise sheep and cattle. So, New Zealand trades wool and cheese for automobiles and computers. Were it unable to trade, New Zealand would have to produce everything it needs itself. It would have to switch resources from raising sheep and cattle to producing automobiles and computers. But this would be highly inefficient. Because New Zealand is a small country, producing the limited number of cars and computers it needs would be very expensive. Without specialization and trade, New Zealanders would have less of everything.

Although self-sufficiency sounds appealing, it makes no economic sense. Many of your needs can be provided for more cheaply by others; what you have in abundance or can produce easily is often scarce and valuable for someone else. Trade benefits everyone.

SAVING, INVESTMENT, AND LENDING

Lending is a form of trade. When you lend, you give up purchasing power now in exchange for purchasing power in the future. For example, when you put $1,000 into a savings account for a year, you give up what the $1,000 could buy today in exchange for what the $1,000 plus interest will buy one year from now.

As with trade in uniforms in our first example, the basis for this type of trade is diversity. Some people have purchasing power now but want purchasing power later. Others expect to have purchasing power later but want purchasing power now. Let us look at some of the reasons for this diversity.

Saving and Wealth

Life-Cycle Saving.   You are probably looking forward to the day when you put aside your textbooks and start to earn a regular paycheck. Exhibit 1.1 shows the path your income will probably take over your lifetime. Initially it will rise rapidly, reaching a plateau in middle age. Then it will drop when you retire.

EXHIBIT 1.1   The Life-Cycle Pattern of Saving

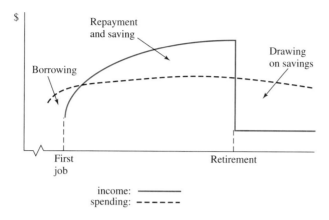

Exhibit 1.1 also shows the path your spending will take over your lifetime. As you can see, it differs substantially from the path of your income. You will likely spend more than your income while you are young, borrowing the difference. During your peak earning years you will repay what you have borrowed and save for your retirement. After you retire, you will spend more than your income, drawing on your savings. This pattern of borrowing, saving, and drawing on savings, which is very typical, is called the **life-cycle pattern of saving**.

life-cycle pattern of saving
Pattern of borrowing and repayment, saving and dissaving, over a lifetime.

Turning Wealth into Income.   Saving is not the only way to acquire wealth. You may win the state lottery. Or you may inherit a fortune from a long-lost uncle. Universities and museums acquire wealth through the gifts of alumni and benefactors. However wealth is acquired, it represents a command over purchasing power. Typically, the owners of wealth do not wish to exercise that purchasing power immediately. Rather, they wish to convert it into a flow of purchasing power over time. You will want to preserve most of your winnings or most of your inheritance to provide you, and perhaps your children, with income for a long time to come. The university or museum will want to preserve its endowment and use the income to fund its yearly operations.

precautionary reserve
Assets held as protection against fluctuations in income or spending.

Precautionary Reserves.   While you can expect your income and spending to behave as shown in Exhibit 1.1, there may be setbacks. You may lose your job, or you may get sick. To protect yourself against such contingencies, you will probably want to accumulate a **precautionary reserve**. When times are good you will set aside some of your income for a "rainy day".[1] A precautionary reserve has other advantages. Ready access to purchasing power allows you to take advantage of unexpected opportunities—for example, a "special" on a European vacation.

---

[1] Insurance is an alternative way of dealing with certain kinds of emergency. We will have more to say about insurance later in the chapter.

Even more than households, businesses need precautionary reserves. Their income is more uncertain. A temporary fall in income can force a firm under if it has no reserves to rely on. Businesses need ready access to purchasing power to be able to exploit profit opportunities as they come along.

Investment

Savers and holders of wealth are potential lenders. Potential borrowers are businesses and households that need purchasing power now in order to invest.

Business Investment.   To understand why businesses need to borrow, let us look at an example. You decide to fulfill your lifelong dream and open a bike shop. You rent some premises and hire some help—a sales assistant and a mechanic. You order a range of bikes and an assortment of accessories like helmets and clothing. All this is expensive. You must lay out a substantial sum of money—perhaps $100,000—before you see any sales revenue. Even if the store is a great idea and it ultimately proves to be highly profitable, you cannot get started unless you have the $100,000 to begin with.

Your problem is typical. All businesses make substantial outlays before they see any revenue. This is true even after a business has started. Revenue coming in pays for past production, but there are always new expenses for current production. The basic problem is that businesses incur expenses before they can sell their products. The funds required to finance the current expenses of producing and selling a product or service are known as **working capital**. The need for working capital is one reason why businesses borrow.

Meanwhile, back at your bike shop, talking to customers has given you a great idea for a new product—an automatic gear shifter, the EZ-Shift. Working with an engineer, you have developed a design. To produce the EZ-Shift, you need a small factory—a building and some machinery. Such a factory would cost about $1 million. Even if the EZ-Shift is just what the market has been waiting for and future profits are sure to be enormous, you will be unable to go into production unless you can find the $1 million.

Again, your situation is typical. Production often requires long-term investment in equipment and facilities. The resources required are known as **fixed capital**. The need for fixed capital is a second reason businesses borrow.

Your investment in working capital and your investment in fixed capital are both productive. They will add to your future income more than they cost today. However, both investments involve a timing problem. Without the purchasing power now, you will be unable to make the investment, and you will not be able to reap the rewards.

Household Investment.   Individuals and households make investments too. Some, like those of business, are productive. For example, your investment in a college education will increase your future income by substantially more than the cost of the investment.

Other types of household investment, like the purchase of a house or a car, are not productive in the sense of increasing future cash flow. Rather, they provide a stream of consumption services over time. That stream of services may be less expensive or preferable in other ways to what could be achieved otherwise. For example, it may be cheaper to buy a house than it is to rent, and the choice of houses may be better.

---

working capital
Finance needed to cover the expense incurred in the production and sale of a product or service.

fixed capital
Finance needed for investment in machinery or buildings.

Households face the same timing problem in making investments as do businesses. Going to college or buying a house may be eminently worthwhile: the benefits in the future may well exceed the cost now. But unless you can obtain the necessary funds, you will be unable to make the investment.

Gains to Trade in Borrowing and Lending

On the one hand, we have savers and wealth holders with an excess of purchasing power now that they wish to trade for purchasing power in the future. On the other, we have businesses and households needing purchasing power now to finance investments. Both groups stand to gain from trade.

The gain to borrowers is obvious. Borrowing allows you to open your bike shop and to set up a factory to produce the EZ-Shift. If these investments are sufficiently productive, you will be happy to pay interest on the loan—to pay back in the future more purchasing power than you received at the time you took out the loan.

Lenders, too, gain from trade. The interest you pay gives the lender a better return than he could achieve otherwise. What are his alternatives? He could hold cash, but this earns no interest at all. He could make a productive investment himself. But finding productive investments is difficult. Some people are much better at it than others. The typical saver does better by lending his money to someone with a highly productive use for it than by making an investment himself.

TRADE IN RISK

The world is an uncertain place: businesses and households face a variety of risks. Trade can reduce significantly the economic burden of many of these risks. There are two principal forms of trade in risk—insurance and forward transactions.

Insurance

Insurance is particularly useful in dealing with such events as accidents, illnesses, and natural disasters. Some examples will illustrate.

Reciprocal Insurance. In agricultural communities, mutual aid is common. If a farmer's barn burns down, neighbors contribute materials and labor to rebuild it. In primitive hunter-gatherer societies, a family's food supply is highly uncertain: a family that has more than it can eat one day may face starvation the next. A common way to deal with this uncertainty is gift exchange. A family with a surplus gives it away to the other members of the community; in return, it will at other times receive its share of the surplus of others.

reciprocal insurance
An agreement whereby those facing a particular risk agree to share their losses.

Mutual aid and gift exchange are examples of **reciprocal insurance**. Those facing a particular kind of risk agree to share the losses. Reciprocal insurance is a form of trade. The farmer makes the relatively small sacrifice of helping neighbors as necessary if they lose their barns in exchange for a large amount of help from them in the less likely event that his own barn is lost. With gift exchange, a family gives up some of its food when it has plenty in exchange for food from others when it may have little.

External Insurance.   Some types of natural risk do not lend themselves to reciprocal insurance—for example, the risk that a ship will strike a reef or that a satellite will be destroyed on launch. In both cases, the number of potential participants in a scheme of reciprocal insurance is too small relative to the size of the potential losses.

In such cases it may be possible to make an arrangement with others who are not themselves inherently at risk. For example, a shipowner can pay a small amount to each of many individuals not themselves exposed to the risk of shipwreck. If the ship founders, these individuals will compensate the owner for the loss.

We could call such an arrangement **external insurance**. External insurance too is a form of trade. The shipowner pays, and the insurers receive, a relatively small sum with certainty. In exchange, the insurers pay, and the shipowner receives, a large sum with relatively low probability if the ship is lost.

external insurance
An agreement whereby those who do not face a particular risk agree to share the losses of those who do.

Diversity and Gains from Trade in Insurance.   As with other forms of trade, the basis for insurance is diversity. With reciprocal insurance, some will be lucky after the event and others will not. With external insurance, the diversity lies in the *exposure* to risk. Those not inherently exposed are willing, in exchange for payment, to accept a small share of the exposure.

All parties gain from this trade in risk. For the participant in reciprocal insurance or the purchaser of external insurance, the insurance softens the blow of the loss. This benefit is worth more than the cost of the insurance. For the external insurer, the payment received for providing insurance is worth more than the expected cost of covering a loss.

Forward Transactions

A second form of trade in risk is the forward transaction. The type of risk it addresses and how it does so are best illustrated with an example.

Imagine that you own a copper mine. You find that you can expand the mine to increase output over the coming year by one million pounds of metal. The cost of the additional output works out at about $1.00 per pound. If you can sell the copper for more than $1.00 you will make a profit. The price today is $2.00, but the market price of copper fluctuates widely. It may be substantially lower over the next year.

price risk
The risk of an adverse change in market prices.

This sort of risk—call it **price risk**—is common in business. Some course of action requires the commitment of resources today. Its profitability depends on the value of some market price or prices in the future.

forward transactions
Transactions in which two parties agree in advance on the terms of a trade to be carried out at a specified future time.

Price risk can be mitigated by a form of trade called a forward transaction. In a **forward transaction**, a price is set today for delivery and payment at a specific time in the future. For example, you can mitigate the price risk of your mine expansion by agreeing with someone today to deliver your copper to that person next year at a price of, say, $1.80.

Who would want to help you in this way by guaranteeing you a price for your copper? There are two possible candidates. The first is someone who will have to buy copper next year and is worried about the risk of the price rising. For example, American Electric wants to be able to quote prices for its electric motors for the coming year. It does not want to have to annoy its customers by changing prices in the middle of the year to compensate for a change in the price of copper. By buying the copper it will need from you in a forward transaction, American Electric can protect itself from fluctuations in the market price of copper.

speculator
Traders who take a position in an asset solely to profit from a change in price.

Another potential buyer of your copper is a speculator. A **speculator** is someone who neither has copper nor needs it, but is willing nonetheless to take a position in the hope of profiting from it. For example, a trader who expected the price of copper to increase to $3.00 next year might be willing to buy your output forward for $1.80 in the hope of reselling it at a profit. A speculator is like an external insurer. He is not inherently exposed to price risk, but he is willing to take on some exposure in the hope of profiting from it.

GAMBLING AND LOTTERIES

Outlays on all forms of legal gambling in the United States represent about 2% of personal income—comparable in amount to spending on restaurant meals. Net revenue to the industry, after winnings are paid, is about 0.4% of personal income—comparable in amount to spending on tobacco or newspapers and magazines.

Why do people gamble? Gambling that involving small prizes, like local bingo games, seems to be mainly for entertainment. Gambling that involves large prizes—state lotteries, for example—seems to have a more serious purpose—getting rich. The attraction of this type of gambling is that it offers people a chance, however small, of a significant move upward. The marked increased in popularity of gambling in times of social and economic upheaval, such as the Great Depression, seems to support this view.

Governments, while generally limiting commercial gambling, have not been above harnessing it to their own uses. Nero used a lottery to finance the rebuilding of Rome after the great fire. In the eighteenth and nineteenth centuries, European governments used lotteries extensively as a means of financing public works and of raising general revenue. In colonial America, governments used lotteries to finance the building of fortifications, churches, and colleges (Harvard, Yale, Princeton, and the future University of Pennsylvania among them).

By 1832, 420 regular lotteries in eight states grossed some $66 million—five times the federal budget of that year. Trade in lottery tickets was a big business. Lottery contractors managed the lotteries. Brokers bought blocks of tickets at a discount and resold them to the public nationwide. Many of these lottery brokers later developed into banks, investment banks, and stockbrokers.

Lotteries, and most other forms of gambling, became illegal in the late nineteenth century, but they have made a comeback in recent years. New Hampshire, in 1963, was the first to reintroduce a state lottery. By 1985, nearly 60% of the U.S. population lived in a state with some form of legal lottery.

Source: Brenner and Brenner (1990).

Diversity and Gains from Trade in Forward Transactions.   You can see that here too diversity is the basis for trade. You are worried about a fall in the price of copper. American Electric is worried about a rise. The speculator is not worried at all, unless he takes a position.

All of you will benefit from trade. You reduce your risk by selling your copper forward. American Electric reduces its risk by buying your copper forward. The speculator reduces your risk by taking it on himself; for him, the potential gain of this position outweighs the potential loss.

Of course, not all trade in risk is driven by the desire to reduce risk. See "Gambling and Lotteries" for a different perspective.

THE DIFFICULTIES OF TRADE

Trade is beneficial. We have seen how trade in goods and services, as well as lending and trade in risk, all confer benefits on those involved. There are, however, obstacles. The role of the financial system is to overcome these obstacles. To understand how it does so, we need first to understand the nature of the obstacles. Let us begin with simple trade in goods and services.

Trade and Trust

Our financial system is so good at facilitating trade in goods and services that we find it hard to imagine what the problems might be. You want to buy something? Write a check or hand over a credit card. But, of course, that is begging the question: the check and the credit card are two of the solutions the financial system has found to the problems of trade. To understand the nature of those problems, we need to look at trade in a society that lacks a sophisticated financial system. The republics of the former Soviet Union are in just such a position. Let us take as our example an imaginary composite, which we will call the Republic of Ruthenia.

The White Star furniture factory—formerly the Red Star furniture factory—is located in the small provincial city of Novograd. Boris, the manager of White Star, faces a problem. Hyperinflation has destroyed the value of the Ruthenian ruble, and his workers are no longer willing to be paid in rubles. Boris offers to pay them in furniture, but they are not interested. Bartering their "wages" for the food and clothing they need would take up so much time they would be unable to work. So Boris arranges a deal with a neighboring clothing factory. His workers will receive credit there for clothes; the garment workers will receive credit at White Star for an equivalent amount of furniture. He arranges similar deals with a farmers' cooperative and with a number of other large enterprises.

This arrangement requires trust. When White Star hands over furniture to someone as part of the agreement, the firm receives nothing immediately in exchange. All it gets is a promise that a White Star worker will be compensated at some time in the future. If that promise is not kept, White Star will take a loss. For example, what is to stop the clothing factory from running up a significant tab at White Star and then reneging on the agreement? Given the chaos in the judicial system, taking the owner of the clothing factory to court is not an option.

Boris is not too worried about this, however, because he realizes the clothing factory has a strong interest in honoring its debts. The business community of Novograd is small and close-knit. Everyone knows everyone else. If the clothing factory reneges, its reputation will suffer, and no one will want to trade with it in the future.

Novograd's system of reciprocal credit works reasonably well, but it includes only the town's largest enterprises and covers only a small range of goods. Smaller businesses are excluded: their credit is not good enough, and the potential volume of trade does not justify the cost of setting up the credit agreement.

Smaller transactions are excluded too. Transactions in the reciprocal credit system involve a lot of paperwork to keep track of who owes what to whom: it is just too costly to handle the purchase of a newspaper or the payment of a bus fare in this way. Therefore, many transactions outside the reciprocal credit system are handled by barter or by payment in cash. With the ruble worthless, "cash" usually means foreign currency—primarily U.S. dollar bills.

The reciprocal credit system is limited in other ways too. White Star's machinery is breaking down and needs to be replaced. Boris cannot buy spare parts or new machines locally, so he travels to the capital, Borodino. In the big, impersonal market of the capital, reciprocal credit is not available. Boris's reputation counts for little: no one there has even heard of White Star. To buy new machinery, Boris must pay in dollars. Unfortunately, Boris has no dollars. Since White Star's business is mostly local, it has no opportunity to acquire foreign currency. So Boris returns to Novograd disappointed.

credit trading
The exchange of value for a promise.

Our little parable illustrates some of the important principles and problems of trading goods and services. We see that there are basically two possible ways to trade—credit trading and cash trading. **Credit trading** involves the exchange of value for a promise—for example, the Novograd reciprocal credit system. **Cash trading** involves the exchange of value for value—for example, barter or payment in U.S. dollars. Credit trading is limited by the need for trust and by large setup costs. Cash trading requires no trust or setup costs, but trade is impossible if prospective buyers do not have the cash.

cash trading
The exchange of value for value.

In Chapter 2 we shall see how the financial system addresses the problems of trade by providing means of payment that make trade easier.

The Problems Involved in Lending

While trade in goods and services may or may not involve promises, lending always does. A lender gives up purchasing power today in exchange for a promise of purchasing power tomorrow. The basic problem is that the promise may not be kept. The borrower may default.

The Need for Information. The risk of default need not deter you from lending. If the chance of default is small, and if the potential reward is great, you may want to go ahead anyhow. The key to your decision is information. You need to know exactly what the risks and prospects are.

For example, suppose you are considering lending some money to Origen, a promising biotech company. Before you hand over your money, you will want to know something about the company. Has it ever defaulted in the past? What are its prospects? What other debts does it owe? Will its earnings enable it to service its loans? If it does default, what are the assets that can be liquidated to repay its debts?

Getting answers to these questions is costly. Origen will have to prepare accounts for you to see and write up a prospectus explaining its plans. You will have to digest this information and check its reliability. You may have trouble believing everything you are told: you expect Origen to stress the positive. On the other hand, Origen may be reluctant to tell you everything. For example, it will not wish to disclose to you its ideas for new products for fear they will fall into the hands of its competitors.

Writing a Contract.   These problems notwithstanding, suppose you have the information you need and decide to go ahead with the loan. You will need to work out an agreement with Origen's owner, Joanna Jones. The agreement will be a formal contract that can, if necessary, be enforced in a court of law. Negotiating and drawing up this contract will be expensive in time and in lawyers' fees.

Incentive Effects of Debt and Equity Contracts.   You will need to be careful about the terms of the contract. They may change Joanna's incentives in ways that harm your own interests. For example, suppose you write an **equity contract**: you put up $1 million in exchange for a 50% share of Origen's profits. From Joanna's point of view, this arrangement imposes a "tax" of 50% on every extra dollar the company earns. As a result, she may not work as hard as you had expected, and the firm's profits—and your return— may suffer. Moreover, she may get herself a bigger office and take more trips on her expense account. Because of the "tax" on profits, each dollar of expenses costs her only $0.50. If she responds to these incentives, Joanna will not be alone: see "Ownership Stakes and Executive Perks."

An alternative to an equity contract that avoids these particular incentive problems is a **debt contract**. For example, you put up $1 million now in exchange for a fixed payment of $5 million in 10 years' time. The "tax" effect is gone: every dollar Origen earns beyond the $5 million is Joanna's to keep. This contract gives her an incentive to work hard and to keep costs down.

However, this type of contract has incentive problems of its own. They are illustrated in Exhibit 1.2. Suppose Joanna is pondering two business strategies. At the end of 10 years, strategy A pays off either $5 million or $8 million, each with equal probability. Strategy B pays off either zero or $10 million, again each with equal probability. From your point of view, strategy A is preferable: it guarantees that Origen's debt to you will be paid. From Joanna's point of view, strategy B is preferable. With strategy A, she gets either zero or $3 million. With strategy B, she gets either zero or $5 million.

Safeguards and the Costs of Monitoring.   Because all lending contracts—debt and equity—create undesirable incentives of one kind or another, they typically include provisions that safeguard the interests of the lender. In the case of equity, the contract might give you some say in how Joanna runs the company. This would enable you to monitor her effort and perhaps to veto wasteful expenditures. In the case of debt, the contract

equity contract
Contract representing a claim to a share in the net income and in the assets of a business.

debt contract
Contract stating agreement by the borrower to pay the lender fixed dollar amounts.

EXHIBIT 1.2   Payoffs from Two Alternative Business Strategies

		Total payoff	Payoff to you	Payoff to Joanna
Strategy A	50%	$5 million	$5 million	Zero
	50%	$8 million	$5 million	$3 million
Strategy B	50%	Zero	Zero	Zero
	50%	$10 million	$5 million	$5 million

loan covenants

Clauses in a loan contract that restrict the borrower's behavior in various ways.

might include clauses, called **loan covenants**, that impose certain conditions. For example, the contract might prohibit Origen from taking on any more debt until the debt to you has been repaid.[2]

Such interference with the management of the company may be necessary to protect the interests of the lender. But it does have its costs. First, outside interference and restrictions may prevent Joanna from doing some things that would be of benefit both to the company and to you. For example, the loan covenant prohibiting Origen from taking on any additional debt might prevent it from exploiting a promising new discovery.

A second cost of these safeguards is the time and effort of monitoring. Once the contract has been signed, you cannot just assume that its conditions will be fulfilled. You will be obliged to check periodically to make sure. Origen will have to hire accountants to audit its books. You will have to read their reports and, perhaps, attend board meetings.

Liquidity.   These incentive problems are not the only way in which your interest's and Joanna's may diverge. Suppose that soon after you lend Origen the $1 million, something comes up and you need your money back in a hurry. You could deal with such a contingency by writing into the contract a clause that requires Joanna's company to repay you on demand. But Origen needs the money to invest in new equipment. Once the money has been spent, the company cannot easily repay it ahead of schedule. If you require that it does so, the loan will be of little use and Joanna will not take it.

liquid

Describing an asset that can be turned into cash rapidly without loss.

You would like your loan to be as **liquid** as possible—as easy as possible to turn back into cash. On the other hand, Origen needs the funds to be committed for a reasonable period of time. As a result, you may have to make a loan that is less liquid than you would like. Of course, you might be willing to accept less liquidity if you were offered a higher return. Origen, on the other hand, may have to take a loan that is more liquid than Joanna would like, or you may ask for a return so high that the whole proposition becomes unattractive.

[2] The reason for such a covenant is that the claims of the new lenders might compete with your own if the company got into trouble.

OWNERSHIP STAKES
AND EXECUTIVE PERKS

Two extreme examples of the incentive effects of a small ownership stake are provided by Armand Hammer, CEO of Occidental Petroleum until his death in 1990, and F. Ross Johnson, CEO of RJR Nabisco until its buyout in 1988. Hammer, although he had once owned nearly half the company, held less than 0.5% of the stock of Occidental. Johnson held 0.02% of the stock of RJR Nabisco.

Armand Hammer managed Occidental seemingly more for his own glory than for the profits of the shareholders. He pursued a variety of grandiose money-losing ventures in the Soviet Union and China, hobnobbing with generations of Communist leaders. He had Occidental fund the construction of the Armand Hammer Museum of Art in Los Angeles to house his personal art collection at a cost of $120 million. In the 1980s, while oil company shares on average tripled in value, Occidental's value fell by a third.

F. Ross Johnson was known as a lavish spender even before he rose to the top at RJR Nabisco. As head of Standard Brands, he had provided executives—including himself—with company apartments, a private box at Madison Square Garden, and multiple country club memberships. The pattern continued when he took over RJR Nabisco. He gave away $1,500 watches. He hired former U.S. president Gerald Ford to play in a company-sponsored golf tournament and Frank Sinatra and Bob Hope to entertain guests. He provided executives with chauffeured Cadillacs, Mercedes Benzes, and Rolls-Royces. He hired 36 pilots for the company's fleet of corporate jets—the "RJR Air Force." All this, of course, at company expense.

Source: Milgrom and Roberts (1992).

The difficulties involved in your lending to Origen are quite typical of lending in general. As we have seen, these difficulties include:

- the cost of acquiring and processing information
- the costs of negotiating and writing a contract
- the incentive problems inherent in all lending arrangements
- the costs of establishing safeguards and of monitoring borrower compliance
- conflicting interests over liquidity

In Chapter 2, we shall see how the financial system addresses these difficulties by reducing the costs of lending and by improving the liquidity of loans.

The Problems of Trade in Risk

Trade in risk has many of the same problems as lending, because it too inevitably involves promises. Let us look in turn at the problems of insurance and those of forward transactions.

The Problems of Insurance.   We looked at three simple insurance arrangements—mutual aid among farmers, gift exchange among hunter-gatherers (both examples of reciprocal insurance), and simple marine insurance (external insurance). In all three cases, promises are involved. Farmers provide assistance in exchange for a promise that they too will receive help if they need it. Tribesmen give away their surplus on the understanding that they will receive gifts from others. The owner of a ship makes payments to other merchants in exchange for a promise that if a shipwreck occurs, they will cover the loss.

As we have seen, the problem with promises is that they may not be kept. In our simple examples of reciprocal insurance, this problem is dealt with informally and at relatively low cost. Everyone knows everyone else, and social pressure ensures that promises are kept. Initially, simple marine insurance, too, relied on reputation: the insurers and the insured were all members of a small circle of merchants who knew each other well.

Limiting insurance to a small circle of acquaintances reduces the costs associated with promises, but it also limits the effectiveness of the insurance. For example, as ships grew in size and value it became increasingly difficult to purchase external insurance from a small circle of insurers of limited means. Insurance is more effective and cheaper if the risk can be broken down among a larger group with greater total resources. The problem with a larger group, however, is the cost of dealing with the promises of strangers. As we have seen, this requires costly information gathering, contracting, and monitoring.

Like lending, insurance creates incentive problems. There are two types of problem. The first is **moral hazard**. This is the tendency of an insured to take greater risks because he is insured. For example, a shipowner may face the choice between two routes—one safe but slow, the other fast but risky. Without insurance, the shipowner chooses the safe route; with insurance, he chooses the fast route.

The second type of incentive problem associated with insurance is **adverse selection**. This is the tendency of worse risks to buy insurance and better risks not to. For example, suppose the price of insurance is the same for all ships. Then owners of ships that are in poor shape will find insurance more attractive, and will be more likely to purchase it, than owners of sound ships.

Moral hazard and adverse selection are problems because they raise the cost of claims to the insurer. Dealing with them, like dealing with the incentive problems of a loan, requires safeguards. For example, the insurance contract might require the ship to take the safe route; insurers might inspect a ship before writing insurance. Of course, safeguards are costly, and they require costly monitoring.

In Chapter 2 we shall see how the financial system addresses the problems of insurance and reduces its cost.

Forward Transactions.   A forward transaction is an exchange of one promise for another: one party promises to buy, the other promises to sell. The danger, of course, is default. Either party might fail to keep its promise. The nature of default risk in such a two-sided promise differs from that in a one-sided promise such as a loan. To see why, let us return to our example of a forward transaction in copper.

You have promised to supply one million pounds of copper to American Electric next December; it has promised to pay you $1.8 million. Suppose American Electric defaults: it goes out of business and cannot accept delivery. You must now find a new buyer for your copper. What is your loss? That depends on how much you get for your copper. If you sell

---

moral hazard

The tendency of an insured to take more risk because he has insurance.

adverse selection

The tendency of worse risks to buy insurance and better risks not to.

it for $1.6 million, your loss is the amount you were promised less the amount you actually received: $1.8 million − $1.6 million = $200,000. However, you might be able to sell it for $2 million. In this case, you actually *gain* $200,000 from the default.

Your loss from American Electric's default, therefore, is not generally the full $1.8 million it has promised to pay you. The reason is that American Electric's default on its promise to you automatically releases you from your promise to it. Consequently, your cost is the cost of replacing American Electric as your trading partner. The risk associated with default on a forward transaction is therefore known as **replacement risk**.

replacement risk
The risk that a counterparty to a forward transaction will default and have to be replaced.

The risks of a forward transaction are mutual. American Electric, too, faces replacement risk. If you default on your promise to deliver the copper, it will have to fill its needs elsewhere. If the cost turns out to be more than $1.8 million, American Electric will take a loss.

Because each party to a forward transaction is exposed to replacement risk by the potential default of the other, each party must take the necessary precautions. These are much like the precautions required in making a loan—information gathering, contracting, and monitoring. These precautions are, of course, costly.

A forward transaction involves a commitment. Changing circumstances may make it desirable for one of the parties to escape that commitment. For example, suppose the finance required for the expansion of your mine falls through. Unable to expand your mine, you will be unable to produce the copper you have promised to deliver. You would like to cancel your agreement with American Electric. American Electric, on the other hand, is counting on the firmness of the deal.

There is the same conflict here that we saw in connection with the liquidity of a loan. Each side would like to be able to get out of its commitment if circumstances change. But the forward transaction is worthless unless the commitment is firm.

In Chapter 2, we shall see how the financial system reduces the costs of forward transactions and improves their liquidity.

The Common Pattern

We have looked at three different types of trade—trade in goods and services, lending, and trade in risk. We have seen that they face similar problems. We can group these problems into three categories—reliance on promises, incentive problems, and illiquidity. Exhibit 1.3 shows for each type of trade the problems it involves.

Reliance on Promises.   In all cases except cash trading in goods and services, trade involves promises. Promises are a problem because they may not be kept. So before a promise can be accepted, information must be gathered on the promiser's credit. Then a contract must be drawn up specifying the exact nature of the promise.

Incentive Problems.   The terms of the contract may create undesirable incentives that alter the behavior of one party to the detriment of the other. This is true for all lending contracts and for insurance. Dealing with these undesirable incentives requires that specific safeguards be built into the contract. It also requires monitoring to ensure compliance.

EXHIBIT 1.3   The Problems with Different Types of Trade

	PROBLEMS			
Type of Trade	Promises	Incentive Problems	Liquidity	Other
Goods and services				
Credit trading	Yes	No	No	
Cash trading	No	No	No	Restrictive
Lending				
Equity	Yes	Reduced effort	Yes	
Debt	Yes	Excessive risk-taking	Yes	
Trade in risk				
Insurance	Yes	Moral hazard; Adverse selection	No	
Forward transactions	Yes (two-sided)	No	Yes	

Liquidity.   Lending and forward transactions involve commitments. In each case, commitment is an essential feature of the transaction: a loan is more useful if it assures a borrower the use of the funds for a definite period; a forward transaction is valuable because it relieves the contracting parties of price risk. However, because of a change of circumstances, parties may want to be relieved of their commitments. The lender may want his money back; the forward transactor may want to cancel the transaction. The ability or inability to undo commitments affects greatly the appeal of the transaction.

Transactions Costs.   Dealing with all these problems is costly. The steps that must be taken before a promise can be accepted, the measures necessary to control incentive problems, the arrangements required to provide liquidity or to accommodate illiquidity—all these take time and effort.

These costs, as well as the problems themselves, are an obstacle to trade. A trade may be mutually beneficial. However, if the problems are too serious or the costs of dealing with them too high, the trade will not be worthwhile, and it will not take place.

Think of the economy as an engine. The potential gains from trade are the fuel that drives it. The obstacles to trade and the costs of dealing with them are friction. As we shall see in Chapter 2, the financial system provides the lubrication.

SUMMARY

- Innovations serve existing needs in new ways or use existing technology to serve new needs. This chapter looks at the needs that the financial system serves. Chapter 2 looks at the technology.
- People trade because they differ in what they have and in what they want. The basis of trade is diversity.
- Lending, insurance, and forward transactions are all forms of trade. As with simple trade in goods and services, the basis for these forms of trade is diversity, and all involved gain from trade.

- The difference between the typical profile of income over a lifetime and the typical profile of spending gives rise to the life-cycle pattern of spending.
- Owners of wealth lend to convert their command over purchasing power today into a stream of income in the future.
- Households and businesses accumulate precautionary reserves to protect themselves against fluctuations in income or spending.
- Businesses and households borrow to finance investment. Businesses invest in working capital and in fixed capital. Households invest in education, housing, and durables.
- Insurance provides protection against the risk of losses due to accidents, illnesses, and natural disasters. Insurance can be reciprocal or external.
- Forward transactions provide protection against adverse changes in future market prices. Users include those wishing to protect themselves against a rise or a fall in price and speculators.
- There are two ways of trading goods and services—credit trading and cash trading. Credit trading is limited by the need for trust and by large setup costs. Cash trading requires no trust or setup costs, but it is limited by the availability of cash.
- Because of the danger of default, lenders need to gather and process information on the borrower, negotiate and write a contract, and monitor compliance.
- Lending contracts may create incentives for the borrower to behave in ways that harm the interests of the lender. Safeguards built into the contract can help, but they may also hinder the operations of the borrower.
- Lenders prefer their loans to be as liquid as possible. Borrowers prefer the funds to be committed as solidly as possible.
- Trade in risk involves promises and so suffers from many of the same problems as lending.
- Insurance involves two types of incentive problem—moral hazard and adverse selection.
- Like loans, forward transactions are subject to default risk (replacement risk), and they involve the same sort of conflict over liquidity.
- Dealing with the difficulties of trade is costly. The difficulties and the costs of dealing with them may make otherwise beneficial trades unattractive. The financial system mitigates the difficulties and reduces the costs of dealing with them. In so doing it increases the extent of trade and the benefits therefrom.

DISCUSSION QUESTIONS

1. Both partners to a trade gain from it. Explain the gains from trade in the different types of trade: trade in goods and services, borrowing and lending, and trade in risk. In each case, how would people manage in the absence of trade? How are things better as a result of trade?

2. Insurance involves incentive problems. Suppose you were offering automobile insurance. What clauses would you write into the contract to protect yourself? How would these clauses address the incentive problems?

3. Compare the incentive problems in lending to those in insurance. How are they similar? How do they differ?

4. You need to accumulate assets for your retirement, and you also need assets as a precautionary reserve. Would you want the same type of assets for both purposes? For example, how important would the return be in each case? Liquidity?

5. Suppose you wished to save for your retirement but lived in an economy where lending was impossible. What sort of assets could you accumulate? Why might this be less desirable than lending?

6. From what you know of the financial system already, describe some of the ways in which it deals with the problems of lending, insurance,

and forward transactions mentioned in the chapter.

7. It would seem that a simple way to deal with the incentive problems of lending and insurance would be to monitor closely the actions of the borrower

or the insured. Why might this not be a perfect solution?

8. List and explain five situations in which forward transactions would be beneficial.

BIBLIOGRAPHY

Brenner, Reuven, and Gabrielle A. Brenner. *Gambling and Speculation: A Theory, a History, and a Future of Some Human Decisions*. Cambridge, U.K.: Cambridge University Press, 1990.

Milgrom, Paul, and John Roberts. *Economics, Organization, and Management*. Englewood Cliffs, NJ: Prentice-Hall, 1992.

KEY TERMS

life-cycle pattern of saving
precautionary reserve
working capital
fixed capital
reciprocal insurance
external insurance

price risk
forward transaction
speculator
credit trading
cash trading
equity contract

debt contract
loan covenants
liquid
moral hazard
adverse selection
replacement risk

CHAPTER 2

THE FINANCIAL
SYSTEM AND ITS
TECHNOLOGY

When you finish this chapter you will understand:

- How banks make payments easier and how they create money
- How financial markets and banks make it easier to lend
- How insurance companies and futures markets operate
- The four basic techniques that all financial institutions and markets use

To understand the changes taking place in the financial system, you need to understand what the financial system does and how it does it. In Chapter 1, we saw what it does: the financial system makes it easier to trade. We saw that there are various types of trade—trade in goods and services, lending, and trade in risk (insurance and forward transactions). These different types of trade face similar obstacles—the problems associated with promises and with incentives, and illiquidity. The financial system addresses these problems. In this chapter, we shall see how.

The chapter looks in turn at lending, payments, and trade in risk. In each case, we review the key institutions and the methods they use. The final section highlights the similarities in these techniques. Our goal in this chapter is to understand basic principles: we shall have much more to say about specific institutions later in the book.

PAYMENTS

In Chapter 1, we saw that there are two general methods of trading—*credit trading* and *cash trading*. We looked at some examples in the fictional Republic of Ruthenia. The system of mutual credit, in which factories provide each other's workers with goods, was an example of credit trading. Payment in U.S. dollars was an example of cash trading. As we saw, both methods had their problems. Let us see how Ruthenia's emerging financial system addresses these problems.

Reducing the Costs of Payment in Cash

In Borodino, the capital of Ruthenia, trade is mostly in cash. The anonymity of the big city, and the large number of traders, make promises of payment unacceptable. This exclusive reliance on cash is costly and cumbersome. People need to hold large amounts of cash and guard them against theft. Large payments require secure transportation, the counting of large amounts of currency, and authentication of each bill (counterfeiting is widespread).

Ruthenia's new entrepreneurs see these problems as a profit opportunity. They are sure that if they can offer a service that reduces the transactions costs of cash payment, they will attract plenty of business and make a good profit.

warehouse bank
A bank that keeps depositors' cash in storage.

Warehouse Banks.   Several entrepreneurs set up **warehouse banks**. In exchange for a fee, warehouse banks offer security and ease of payment. They accept deposits of cash, count and authenticate the currency, and store it in a solid and well-guarded vault. They allow depositors to make payments by transferring title to deposited cash rather than by transferring the cash itself.

For example, Yuri has a deposit at Svoboda Bank. He needs to pay Natasha $100,000. Rather than having to go to the trouble and expense of transferring to Natasha a large amount of U.S. currency, Yuri simply writes an order to his bank to pay her that amount. Such an order is called a **check**. If Natasha, too, has a deposit at Svoboda Bank, the institution simply credits the deposit with an extra $100,000 and debits Yuri's for that amount.

check
An order to a bank to make payment from a deposit.

The Clearinghouse.   What if Natasha has a deposit at a different bank? She could cash the check at Svoboda and carry the cash to her own bank, Narodny, for deposit. But that would be risky and inconvenient. Happily, the banks have an arrangement that makes such a physical transfer of cash unnecessary. The arrangement is called **clearing**.

clearing
Collection process for checks in which checks drawn on one bank are offset against checks drawn on another.

Clearing works like this. On a typical day, each bank receives many checks drawn on other banks. So each afternoon, messengers from all the banks get together at an agreed location, trade checks, and settle the net amounts owed. For example, suppose Svoboda has $10,000,000 of checks drawn on Narodny and Narodny has $9,600,000 drawn on Svoboda. Instead of Narodny paying Svoboda $10,000,000 and Svoboda paying Narodny $9,600,000, they net the two amounts: Narodny pays Svoboda the difference: $10,000,000 − $9,600,000 = $400,000.

Narodny could pay this amount by physically delivering cash. However, there are less costly alternatives. Svoboda could simply agree to hold a $400,000 deposit at Narodny: it may well have to use it the next day to settle with Narodny. Or the two banks could keep

A HISTORY OF CLEARING

London in the eighteenth century was a center of financial innovation. One of the most successful new ideas was the check. As the use of checks increased, banks began to send "walks clerks" to other banks to collect payment. This meant having hundreds of clerks walking across town carrying large sums of cash, with all the attendant dangers.

The clerks themselves eventually established an informal, unsanctioned meeting, usually at a local coffeehouse. There, they traded checks with one another, settling net balances only. This required less walking and reduced the need to carry cash—probably making the lives of the clerks much safer.

By 1770, the banks formally recognized the clearing and established an official meeting place. By the 1850s, they were settling with deposits at the Bank of England rather than with cash.

The first clearinghouse in the United States was established in New York City in 1854. By the end of the century most large cities had a clearinghouse.

clearinghouse
An association of banks to facilitate clearing.

clearing deposits at a third bank, on which each could write checks to the other.[1] The clearing of payments among banks is organized through an association called a **clearinghouse**. Clearing and clearinghouses have a long history (see "A History of Clearing").

So, Natasha signs over Yuri's check to her own bank, Narodny. Narodny credits her deposit with an extra $100,000 and collects from Svoboda through the clearinghouse.

Bank Deposits as Money.   Notice that "payment in cash" has taken on a new meaning. For large payments, it is deposits that are now used as money, rather than the underlying cash. When a payment is made, it is the ownership of a deposit, rather than the underlying cash, that changes hands.

The cash in the banks' vaults is rarely touched. There is no need to move cash, to count it, or to authenticate it. Since physical cash rarely changes hands for large payments, the cost of such payments is greatly reduced.

Fractional Reserve Banking

Noticing that the cash backing the bank's deposits is rarely touched, the owner of Svoboda Bank has an interesting idea. How about *creating* "deposits" and lending them? The borrowers would have "deposits" without ever having deposited any cash with the bank.

Here is how it works. Ivan applies for a $1 million loan. If the loan is approved, Svoboda creates for him a $1 million deposit and accepts his IOU in exchange. Ivan can

---

[1] We shall have much more to say about checks and clearing in Chapter 8.

draw on this $1 million "deposit" to make payments in precisely the same way he could draw on a regular deposit.

When Ivan draws on his deposit, checks clear through the clearinghouse and Svoboda loses some of its cash to other banks. Since the cash legally belongs to the regular depositors, the bank must have their agreement to use it in this way. To win their agreement, it offers them "free checking" and waives the fees they have been paying on their deposits. It also assures them that they can still withdraw their deposits whenever they wish.

Svoboda's innovation has a number of far-reaching implications.

Bank Deposits Become IOUs.   Once it creates these new deposits, Svoboda Bank ceases to be a warehouse bank. The deposits of a warehouse bank are claims to specific dollars left in safekeeping—in the same way that a cloakroom check is a claim to a specific coat or umbrella. There is a one-to-one correspondence between deposits and cash in the bank's vault.[2]

With the creation of deposits through lending, the nature of the bank deposit and so the nature of the bank changes. A deposit at Svoboda becomes no more than an IOU of the bank—a promise by the bank to pay on demand a certain sum of dollars. It is a claim on the bank's assets in general, rather than on any particular sum of vault cash in particular. The cash in the bank's vault becomes a general reserve that helps ensure that the promise to pay can be met. Since the amount of this reserve is only a fraction of the amount of deposits, this new type of bank is called a **fractional reserve bank**.

fractional reserve bank
A bank that holds reserves of cash equal to only a fraction of its deposit liabilities.

Adding to the Quantity of Money.   While warehouse banking does not alter the total quantity of money in the economy, fractional reserve banking increases it. To see why, let us begin with the situation before Svoboda's innovation.

If the total quantity of currency in Ruthenia is $100 million, this is also the total quantity of money. Warehouse banking does not change this total. The deposits of warehouse banks *are* money: we have seen that people make payments by transferring ownership of their deposits. So we must include the quantity of warehouse bank deposits in the total quantity of money. However, for each dollar of warehouse bank deposit, one dollar of currency is "retired" by being locked up in a bank's vault. For example, if there is $30 million of warehouse bank deposits, there is also $30 million of currency in bank vaults. Therefore,

$$\underset{(\$100m)}{\underset{\text{of money}}{\text{total quantity}}} = \underset{(\$100m)}{\underset{\text{currency}}{\text{total}}} + \underset{(\$30m)}{\underset{\text{deposits}}{\text{bank}}} - \underset{(\$30m)}{\underset{\text{bank vaults}}{\text{currency in}}} \qquad [2.1]$$

When Svoboda creates and lends a "deposit" to Ivan and becomes a fractional reserve bank, this arithmetic changes. The loan creates an additional $1 million of money in the

---

[2] However, since dollar bills are more interchangeable than umbrellas, the bank does not keep specific dollar bills associated with specific deposits. When a depositor makes a withdrawal, he receives an equivalent amount of dollar bills, rather than the very same ones deposited originally.

form of bank deposits, *without* any addition to the amount of currency in bank vaults. So the total quantity of money increases by $1 million. Now,

$$
\begin{array}{ccccc}
\text{total quantity} & & \text{total} & \text{bank} & \text{currency in} \\
\text{of money} & = & \text{currency} + \text{deposits} - \text{bank vaults} & & \\
(\$101m) & & (\$100m) & (\$31m) & (\$30m)
\end{array} \qquad [2.2]
$$

A New Method of Trading.   Remember our two methods of trading. Credit trading involves the exchange of value for promise: the seller provides the buyer with value in exchange for the buyer's promise. Cash trading involves the exchange of value for value: there is no promise, and, therefore no trust is required.

Payment with warehouse bank deposits is cash trading. Such payment is easier and less costly than the physical transfer of cash, but the two are essentially equivalent. The seller receives title to cash rather than physical cash, but no trust is involved (assuming that warehouse banks are run honestly).

Payment with the deposits of fractional reserve banks, however, represents a fundamentally new method of trading. When the seller receives payment in the form of a claim on a fractional reserve bank, he receives not value, but a promise. However, the promise is not the promise of the buyer: it is the promise of a third party—the bank. For example, suppose the seller receives payment in the form of $100 of bank deposits. As we have seen, the deposits of a fractional reserve bank are IOUs. The $100 in deposits is a promise of the bank to pay $100 in cash on demand.

The new method makes trade easier because the promise of the bank is more readily acceptable to the seller than is the promise of the buyer himself. One reason is better credit. The bank is better known, and it has an interest in maintaining its reputation by honoring its promises. A second reason is that the bank's promise is money: the seller can pass it on to someone else in payment. The seller could not, in general, do this with a promise from the buyer.

Because it relies on the credit of a bank rather than on the credit of the buyer, this new method of trading extends the potential scope of credit trading enormously. The exchange of value for promise becomes possible not only in a small community of mutual trust, but also in the larger community of anonymous traders.

We have seen some of the things financial systems can do to make payment easier. Modern financial systems have developed many refinements of the simple payments process described here—for example, credit cards, debit cards, electronic payments, and foreign exchange. We shall discuss these in detail in Chapter 8.

LENDING

We saw in Chapter 1 that lending is difficult. Generally, it involves risk. To manage the risk, you need to acquire and process information, to draw up a contract with the borrower—with due attention to the incentives this creates—and to monitor compliance. Liquidity too may be a problem: circumstances may change, and you may want your money back. The financial system addresses these difficulties and so makes lending easier.

The best way to see how the financial system does this is through an example. You have $50,000 you would like to save. Origen, the promising biotech company we encountered in Chapter 1, needs $10 million to invest in a new project. There is potential here for a trade. If the difficulties can be overcome, you can lend your $50,000 to Origen to the mutual benefit of yourself and the firm.

Direct Lending and Financial Markets

Financial markets are organized to make it easier for you to lend. Let us see how.

Market Institutions That Make It Easier to Lend.   The first step in making a loan is gathering and digesting information. A variety of institutions exist to satisfy your need for information:

- The financial press—*The Wall Street Journal, the New York Times, Business Week*, and other publications—gathers and disseminates news about individual companies and about the economy as a whole.
- Accounting firms audit a firm's books. Firms that borrow from the public must make the results of these audits publicly available.
- Investment information services such as Standard & Poor's, Moody's, and Value Line gather and publish information and analysis on individual companies and industries.

loan indenture (trust deed)
A loan contract.

The next step is to negotiate and write a loan contract called a **loan indenture** (or **trust deed**). Fortunately, you do not have to do this yourself. New securities are usually sold to the public through an **underwriter**, generally a securities firm. The underwriter negotiates the terms of the loan contract with the issuer and appoints a **trustee** to monitors compliance. In the United States, the trustee is usually a commercial bank.[3]

underwriter
Someone who purchases new securities from an issuer with the intention of reselling them.

When the contract is written and the trustee appointed, the underwriter usually buys the whole issue from the borrower and resells it to the public.[4] In doing so, the underwriter incurs a legal obligation to provide purchasers with accurate information about the risks involved.

These market institutions greatly reduce the cost to you of lending to Origen. Relying on the information they provide, you decide to go ahead with your loan. You make the loan by buying Origen's securities from the underwriter. Over the life of the loan, your legal interests are represented by the trustee. Rather than you, and hundreds of other lenders like you, having to do all the necessary work individually, it is done for you by these market institutions.

trustee
Someone granted the legal power to manage property for someone else.

These institutions—underwriters, trustees, accountants, and information sources—have an interest in doing their work well. Their reputations will affect how much business

---

[3] This function used to be performed by specialized *trust companies*, but the distinction between such companies and banks eventually disappeared. The word "trust" still appears in the names of many banks as a hint of their origins as trust companies—for example, Bankers Trust, Morgan Guaranty Trust. In Canada, trust companies remain distinct from banks.

[4] We will look at underwriting in detail in Chapter 11.

they get in the future. For example, an underwriter that gets the reputation of floating issues that turn out to be lemons will find it hard to sell new issues in the future. As a result, issuers will not hire the firm as an underwriter.

The reduction in cost to you comes at a substantial cost to Origen. It must pay the accountants to prepare the required information; it must pay lawyers to draw up the contract and the trustee to administer it; it must pay the underwriter to organize and to sell the issue to the public (see "The Cost of a Public Issue").

Many of the costs of a public issue are indivisible. That is, they are incurred whether the sum borrowed is large or small. For example, the legal fees and the costs of providing information will be much the same whether Origen borrows $1 million or $100 million. These indivisibilities make it very expensive—and so unattractive—to raise small sums in this way. A public issue will make sense only when the amount to be raised is substantial.

Liquidity and the Secondary Market.   Once you have made your loan, Origen has your $50,000 and you have some securities acknowledging its obligation to you. If the securities are bonds (debt securities), Origen's obligation is to pay you interest periodically and to repay the $50,000 at a specified time—say in 20 years. If the securities are equities, its obligation is to pay you dividends (a share in the firm's profits); it has no obligation to repay you the $50,000.

THE COST OF A PUBLIC ISSUE

To float a $1 million issue, Origen would incur something like the following costs:

Underwriter's fee (2% of face value plus $15,000 expense allowance)	$ 35,000
Legal fees	75,000
Accounting fees	65,000
Printing costs	50,000
Debt rating by Moody's or Standard & Poor's	25,000
Assorted fees (includes stock exchange, state "blue sky" law, SEC registration, and registrar's fees)	18,000
Total	$268,000

The cost is nearly 27% of the total amount raised.

To raise $10 million in this way would cost $215,000 in underwriter's fees (2% of $10 million, plus $15,000). The other costs would be roughly the same. The total cost would be $448,000—only 4.5% of the amount raised.

Sources: Jennings and Marsh (1987) and Soderquist (1982).

transferable security
A security that may be transferred from one person to another.

secondary market
Financial market in which previously issued securities are traded.

primary market
A market for newly issued securities.

dealer
Someone who makes a market by standing ready to buy or sell at quoted prices.

brokers
Someone who arranges trades but is not a party to them.

bid price
The price at which a market maker is willing to purchase.

asked price
The price at which a market maker is willing to sell.

over-the-counter (OTC) market
Physically dispersed market in which market makers are in communication by phone or electronically.

exchange
A market at a specific location, in which traders trade face to face.

What if circumstances change and you would like your money back immediately? Origen is under no obligation to give you back your money. As we saw in Chapter 1, for the money to be of use, Origen needs to be able to rely on having the use of it for a specified period.

Financial markets have developed a solution to this problem—a way for you to get your money *without* Origen having to give it up. In principle, the solution is simple: sell the security to someone else. That way, you get your money, but from someone other than Origen. Origen's obligation of future payment to you is transferred to the purchaser of the security. If the loan contract allows you to do this, the security is described as being **transferable**.

Of course, being *allowed* to sell the security is not enough: you have to be *able* to sell it. But selling securities is just another form of trade. We know that trade is difficult and costly. You will be able to sell your securities relatively easily and at a fair price only if there is an organized market there to help you. Such a market in existing securities is called a **secondary market**. For example, the principal secondary market for equities in the United States is the New York Stock Exchange. A market for new issues is called a **primary market**.

A secondary market will exist only if someone creates it. Market creators come on two types—dealers and brokers. **Dealers** stand ready to buy and sell at posted prices. You could sell your Origen securities immediately by contacting the appropriate dealer and accepting his posted price. The dealer would hold onto the securities until someone else came along wishing to buy them.

Brokers differ from dealers in that they bring buyers and sellers together but do not themselves buy or sell the securities. For example, you would probably sell your Origen securities through a stockbroker. The stockbroker, rather than buying the securities from you, would find someone willing to buy them (perhaps a dealer).

To help you remember the distinction between dealers and brokers, think of used car dealers and a real estate brokers. Used car dealers buy and sell cars and keep an inventory of cars on display with prices posted. Real estate brokers simply help people selling houses find buyers; they do not buy houses themselves for resale.

Dealers make a profit from the difference between the price at which they buy—their **bid price**—and the price at which they sell—their **asked price**. Brokers usually charge a commission for their services.

A secondary market for securities typically consists of many brokers and dealers in communication with one another. Where the organization is loose and communication mainly over the telephone (or over a computer network), the market is called an **over-the-counter (OTC) market**. Where the organization is more structured and communication is often face to face, the market is known as an **exchange**. As examples, we shall see in later chapters that the secondary market for government securities is an OTC market and the secondary market for corporate equities consists of both OTC markets and exchanges.[5]

Making a market in a security is costly. Apart from the actual transactions costs of trading, the broker or dealer must invest time in learning about the company and about the market. A dealer must invest in an inventory of the security and accept the risk of capital loss if the value of the security falls. Many of the costs of making a market are indivisible:

---

[5] We shall learn in detail about securities markets in Chapter 11.

they do not depend on the volume of trading. It will therefore be worthwhile to make a market only if trading volume in a given security is large.

A existence of a good secondary market is of benefit to borrowers as well as to lenders. The existence of a good secondary market makes the loan more liquid and therefore more attractive to lenders. The more attractive the loan, the lower the return the borrower will have to pay.

Indirect Lending and Financial Intermediaries

direct lending
Lending by ultimate lender to ultimate borrower with no intermediary.

financial intermediary
Institution that borrows by issuing its own securities and relends the funds it raises.

indirect lending
Lending by ultimate lender to financial intermediary that then relends to ultimate borrower.

We have seen how financial markets make it easier for you to lend to Origen directly. The financial system also offers you an alternative to such **direct lending**. You could lend your $50,000 to First National Bank and First National could lend to Origen. First National is acting as a **financial intermediary** in this transaction: it is borrowing in its own name to relend to others. The process is called **indirect lending**.

You are still the ultimate source of the loan: it is you who is giving up purchasing power now in exchange for a promise of purchasing power in the future. However, now the promise to you is First National, not from Origen. As a result, you face no risk from Origen's defaulting. Indeed, you may not even know to whom First National is lending your money. If Origen defaults, the bank's promise to you is unaffected. Any loss on the loan is First National's problem, not yours.

As a result, all that matters to you is the reliability of First National's promise to you. You should be able to satisfy yourself relatively easily that First National is a reasonable risk. Since banks are in the business of borrowing money and relending it, they have an interest in being safe and in having customers know they are safe. To encourage depositors to trust them with their money, banks reduce the information and monitoring costs of lending to them.[6]

While Origen's creditworthiness is now of no concern to you, it is of great concern to the bank. So the costs of making the loan are passed on to First National. However, its costs will be much lower than yours would have been. Let us look at some of the reasons.

Informational Advantages.   First National can obtain a wealth of information about its customers that is not available to the public at large. For example, from observing transactions in Origen's checking account, the bank will have direct access to information on Origen's cash flow. Origen may also be more willing to provide information to its bank in private than to the public at large because it doesn't carry as much risk that valuable secrets will be revealed to its competitors.

Pooling to Make Large Loans.   We have seen that because many of the costs of a loan are indivisible, making large loans is relatively less expensive than making small ones. Compared to individual investors, banks make very large loans. For example, the loan First National makes to Origen might be for $10 million. To make a loan of this size,

---

[6] In many countries, small deposits are wholly or partly guaranteed by the government. This effectively reduces the information and monitoring costs of depositors to zero. Of course, the insurer of the deposits is faced with substantial information and monitoring costs. We shall have much to say about this in Chapter 19.

First National will put together your $50,000 with money it receives from many other depositors. On average, bank loans are much larger than individual deposits.

Gains from Specialization.

Banks are specialists in assessing the creditworthiness of borrowers and in monitoring their performance. Because of this specialization, they tend to be better at it than the average small lender. Banks are good at reading between the lines of financial statements, and they are less likely to be misled. Experience helps them detect early signs of impending trouble that a small lender might not recognize. This is not to say that banks make no mistakes: in later chapters we shall learn of some doozies.

The Value of a Continuing Relationship.

When Origen borrows from First National, it expects to come back to the bank repeatedly for additional loans. It therefore cannot afford to jeopardize its ability to borrow by failing to honor the terms of its current loan. If Origen does default and is cut off by First National, the biotech firm cannot simply switch banks. Being cut off by one bank is hardly a recommendation to others. This strong incentive for a borrower to behave makes monitoring less expensive.

Diversification.

The amount of money you, as a single individual, can lend is small compared to the average amount that borrowers like Origen want to borrow. Therefore, if you lend directly, you will not have the resources to lend to more than a few borrowers. If one of your borrowers defaults, you are likely to lose a large portion of your assets.

A bank like First National pools the deposits of thousands of people like you, giving it a very large amount to lend. It can therefore make many loans, each of which is small relative to the size of its total portfolio. Splitting up one's lending in this way is called **diversification**. With a diversified portfolio, if a few borrowers default, only a small part of the total amount will be lost.

diversification
Spreading of an invested sum over many independent assets (not putting all one's eggs into one basket).

To illustrate the advantages of diversification, let us look at an example. Suppose the typical loan is for $1 million. The borrower pays 15%, but there is a 1-in-20 chance of default; in this case, the whole amount is lost. The expected return is

$$0.95 \times 15\% + 0.05 \times (-100\%) = 9.25\%$$

If First National has a total of $1 billion to lend, it can make 1,000 loans to 1,000 different companies. The law of large numbers translates the 1-in-20 chance of default on a single loan into a fairly reliable 50 defaults among the 1,000 loans. The chance of more than 70 defaults is only 1 in 1,000. The chance of *all* the loans defaulting is less than 1 in $10^{1,700}$, a truly infinitesimal number. As a result, for First National, the 9.25% expected return is fairly reliable. There is only a 1-in-1,000 chance of the return falling below 6.95% (if there are more than 70 defaults).[7]

Diversification works this well only if the chances of default on the various loans are unrelated. There is little reduction in risk to be gained, for example, from making 1,000

---

[7] According to the law of large numbers, the total number of defaults has a Normal distribution with a mean of 50 and a standard deviation of 6.9. The chance of an outcome 3.1 standard deviations above the mean (3.1 × 6.9 = 21 defaults) or more is 1 in 1,000. The probability of all the loans defaulting is 0.05 to the power 1,000.

loans, all to real estate developers in the same region. If there is a slump in the local real estate market, all the borrowers will tend to default together. In this case, in terms of risk, the 1,000 loans are really like a single big loan.

Because of diversification, First National can promise a sure return on its deposits, 5% say. This leaves enough to cover expenses, unusual losses, and a modest profit. As a saver, you may prefer to put your $50,000 in a bank deposit for a sure 5% rather than gambling on a direct loan that pays 15% if things go well but has a 1-in-20 chance of being a total loss.

Liquidity.   The bank deposit also offers you superior liquidity. First National promises to pay what it owes you whenever you ask for it. How can the bank do this, given that its loans are illiquid? The loan to Origen, for example, may be for several years, and it is not easy for the bank to sell it.

It is pooling that enables First National to offer liquid deposits despite the illiquidity of its loans. The behavior of any single depositor—the timing and size of additional deposits, the timing and size of withdrawals—is fairly unpredictable. However, First National has not one but 100,000 depositors. The behavior of 100,000 depositors is much easier to predict.

First National has $1 billion in deposits. Suppose withdrawals vary between $20 million and $80 million each day, and new deposits also vary between $20 million and $80 million. Withdrawals and new deposits will tend to offset one another: only rarely will a day of many withdrawals also be a day of few new deposits. As a result, the chance that withdrawals will exceed new deposits by more than, say, $50 million is quite small. Therefore, by making sure it can readily lay its hands on $50 million in cash, First National can meet most demands for liquidity on the whole $1 billion of its deposits.[8]

Occasionally, of course, net withdrawals *will* exceed $50 million, and the bank will have to have a way to deal with this. Of course, the magic of pooling works only when withdrawal by one individual is unrelated to withdrawal by another. If all depositors want to withdraw their money at once (a **bank run**), the bank will be in serious trouble.[9]

bank run
A simultaneous withdrawal of funds from a bank by many depositors.

Direct or Indirect Lending?

We see, then, that the financial system offers two different solutions to the problems of lending: financial markets make it easier to lend directly; financial intermediaries offer the alternative of lending indirectly. What are the relative merits of the two solutions?

Indirect lending generally promises lenders less risk and more liquidity. Consequently, it also promises a lower average return. Of course, less risk is not always a plus. It means a lower chance of loss, but it also means a lower chance of gain. You may get rich with a clever—or lucky—investment in the stock market, but you will never get rich putting your money in the bank.

---

[8] The law of large numbers assures that total new deposits and total withdrawals each have a Normal distribution. Assume that the mean of each is $50 million and the standard deviation, $15 million. There is a 95% chance that each will be within two standard deviations of the mean—between $20 million and $80 million. Assuming they are independent, the mean value of the difference between new deposits and withdrawals is zero, and the standard deviation is $\sqrt{2} \times \$15$ million = $21 million. There is therefore a 99% probability that withdrawals will exceed new deposits by more than 2.3 standard deviations, or $48 million.

[9] We will discuss bank runs thoroughly in Chapter 19.

Indirect lending has advantages too for borrowers. The bank's edge in gathering information and in monitoring allows the borrower to avoid many of the costs of a public issue. Because of the indivisibility of many of these costs, indirect borrowing is usually cheaper for small or short-term loans. Most borrowers, however, have little choice: their lack of credit standing rules out direct borrowing.

Borrowers who *do* have the option of going to the direct market may find it cheaper to raise large sums on that market. In fact, it may not even be possible to borrow *very* large sums of money indirectly: the capacity of the direct financial markets is much larger than that of even the largest intermediaries.

Direct and indirect lending differ with respect to their flexibility in dealing with repayment problems. The reasons a borrower may be having difficulty repaying a loan may be permanent or temporary. If they are permanent—the result of bad management, for example—**bankruptcy** may be in the lender's best interests. Letting the borrower continue in business will only mean more losses and fewer assets to pay its debts. However, if the problem is temporary—a slow economy, for instance—bankruptcy may not be such a good idea. Bankruptcy is costly, in terms of lawyers' fees, and destructive, in terms of disruption of the firm's normal operations (see "Bankruptcy"). When the problems are temporary, lenders may do better by simply giving the borrower more time to repay the debt.

bankruptcy
A legal process, supervised by a court, that settles claims against a corporation or individual in default.

With direct lending, rescheduling a loan is difficult. The relationship between the borrower and the many, relatively uninformed, lenders is necessarily arm's-length and legalistic. Typically, the lenders do not monitor the borrower closely, and they have no idea whether the problems are permanent or temporary. Because they are so many, it is hard for the lenders to agree on new terms for the loan. As a result, when there are problems, the

BANKRUPTCY

A corporation that is unable to pay its debts may file for bankruptcy. If it does not, its creditors may be able to force it into bankruptcy. Bankruptcy is a legal process, supervised by a court, that settles all claims against the bankrupt to the extent possible. The idea is to ensure that debts are paid in an orderly and equitable fashion, rather than there being a mad scramble among creditors to be paid first. In 2001 some 40,000 businesses filed for bankruptcy.

There are two basic types of bankruptcy—*liquidation* (under Chapter 7 of the bankruptcy code) and *reorganization* (under Chapter 11). About two-thirds of filings are for liquidation; the rest are for reorganization. In a liquidation, the corporation ceases to exist. Its remaining assets are sold. Creditors are paid off to the extent possible from the proceeds. In a reorganization, the corporation, its creditors, and the court agree on a plan for future payment of all or part of its debts. The corporation continues in operation, under court supervision, until the plan is executed.

We shall look at bankruptcy again in Chapter 14.

EXHIBIT 2.1   **Direct and Indirect Lending Compared**

	DIRECT LENDING	INDIRECT LENDING
Example	Stock Market	Bank
Gathering and evaluating information	Information published by borrower; investment information services; media.	Lender needs information only on bank; bank checks up on borrower
Negotiating and writing loan contract	Underwriter	Bank
Monitoring compliance	Trustee	Bank
Liquidity	Secondary market	Pooling of deposits
Dealing with default	Formal bankruptcy proceedings	Private renegotiation or bankruptcy

terms of the contract tend to be enforced rigidly—regardless of whether this is in the best interests of the lenders.

With indirect lending, the bank is in a much better position to know whether the problem is permanent or temporary. As a sole lender, it can alter the terms of the loan without having to obtain the agreement of others. It can reschedule payments, waive loan covenants, or even make new loans to help the borrower through a temporary bad spot.

Exhibit 2.1 summarizes the main differences between direct and indirect lending.

Exhibit 2.2 shows the relative importance of different types of direct and indirect lending in the United States. Note that indirect lending dominates.

EXHIBIT 2.2   **Amounts of Direct and Indirect Lending Outstanding June 30, 2001 (Billions of Dollars)**

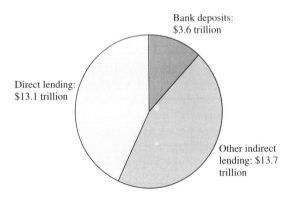

Bank deposits: $3.6 trillion

Direct lending: $13.1 trillion

Other indirect lending: $13.7 trillion

Direct lending includes credit market instruments and other corporate equities; other indirect lending includes mutual fund shares, life insurance reserves, and pension fund reserves.

Source: Federal Reserve Bulletin *(2001).*

Countries differ significantly in their reliance on direct and indirect lending. Exhibit 2.3 shows the split for a number of countries in 1985. Notice that developed countries relied relatively more on direct lending (although France was an exception). Notice, too, that banks were less important in the United States than they were in most other countries—developed or less developed. We shall see some of the reasons for these differences in later chapters.

TRADE IN RISK

As we saw in Chapter 1, trade in risk is subject to many of the same problems that affect lending. Let us see how the financial system addresses the problems of the two main types of trade in risk—insurance and forward transactions.

Insurance

In Chapter 1, we looked at some simple forms of reciprocal insurance that did not involve the financial system in any way. For example, under a system of mutual aid, a farmer who

EXHIBIT 2.3   Direct and Indirect Lending—An International Comparison

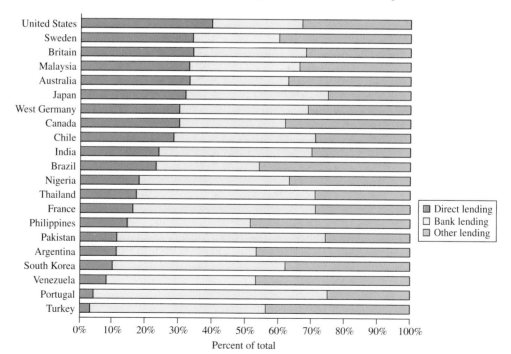

Source: The World Bank (1989); data are for 1985.

assessment
A share of a loss to be paid by a member of an insurance pool.

loses his barn receives help from his neighbors to rebuild it. In exchange, he must provide whatever help is necessary (an **assessment**) to help others in the same predicament.

Let us compare this with the alternative offered by the financial system—an **insurance policy** with an insurance company, Gibraltar Property and Casualty. This is how the policy works. Each year, on January 1, the farmer pays Gibraltar a **premium** of $1,200. In exchange, if his barn burns down during the year, Gibraltar pays him the replacement cost—$100,000.

insurance policy
A contract with an insurance company under which the insured pays a premium in exchange for coverage of specified losses.

How an Insurance Company Works.   How can Gibraltar accept this risk? It can do so because it pools the risks on some 200,000 farmers. Pooling this large number of risks converts the 1-in-100 chance of an individual claim into a near certainty of about 2,000 claims out of the 200,000. Gibraltar takes in $240 million in premiums and pays out about $200 million in claims. Thanks to the law of large numbers, there is less than a 1-in-1,000 chance that claims will exceed this amount by more than $14 million.[10]

Gibraltar can increase its profits by investing the premiums it collects. Gibraltar receives the premiums at the beginning of the year and pays claims at a steady rate throughout the year. That means it pays claims on average half a year *after* it receives premiums. So Gibraltar can earn half a year's interest, say 3%, on its $240 million in premiums—a total of $7.2 million.

premium
The amount an insured pays for coverage under an insurance policy.

Notice that by investing the premiums, Gibraltar acts as a financial intermediary: it raises funds by issuing claims on itself and uses the proceeds to make loans. In this respect, it differs from a bank only in that the claims it issues are insurance policies rather than deposits.

property-liability insurance
Insurance that covers damage to property.

The Advantages of an Insurance Policy.   What are the advantages to the farmer of an insurance policy over reciprocal insurance? First, the assessments required under reciprocal insurance are themselves a source of risk. Neither their size nor their timing can be known in advance. The farmer may be called upon to provide a lot of help just when it is particularly costly for him to do so. In contrast, the premiums on the insurance policy are fixed and certain.

Second, the reciprocal insurance is based a much smaller pool, so there is a greater chance that it will fail. A severe storm, or an arsonist, could cause more damage than the participants could handle. In contrast, the insurance policy is based on a much larger and better diversified group. And, in addition, it is backed by the capital of the insurance company itself: if losses exceed premiums, Gibraltar promises to cover the difference.

life insurance
Insurance that covers "damage" to individuals.

actuarial risks
Risks experienced by large populations and therefore of known probability.

In much the same way that Gibraltar covers the loss of the farmer's barn, insurance companies cover a variety of risks. These include risks to homes, automobiles, and commercial property (collectively called **property-liability insurance**) as well as medical expenses or death due to illness or accident (**life insurance**). These various categories of insurance are based on the pooling of many similar risks of known probability (**actuarial risks**).

---

[10] The calculations are similar to those in footnote 9. The mean number of claims is 2,000 and the standard deviation is $\sqrt{200,000 \times 0.99 \times 0.01} = 44.5$. The chance of an outcome 3.1 standard deviations above the mean ($3.1 \times 44.5 = 138$ claims) or more is 1 in 1,000.

Nonactuarial Risk and External Insurance. Many risks are not actuarial—for example, the risk that a satellite launch will fail. In such cases, the probability of loss is not known as it is with actuarial risks. Moreover, the pool of those exposed to the risk is small. So it is impossible to organize insurance for this sort of risk in the same way as for actuarial risks.

For nonactuarial risks, the financial system offers external insurance. Insurers not inherently exposed to the risk agree to bear part of it for a premium. If there is a loss, they pay their share of the loss; if not, they are ahead by the amount of the premium. External insurers cope with the risk through diversification: they take on many unrelated risks, each small relative to their capital.

Actuarial insurance is generally offered by insurance intermediaries, but there is an important *market* for external insurance—**Lloyd's of London**. This is an exchange where groups of wealthy individuals bid to accept nonactuarial risks for a premium.[11]

> **Lloyd's of London**
> An exchange comprising groups of wealthy individuals who bid to accept non-actuarial risks for a premium.

Dealing with Incentive Problems. As we saw in Chapter 1, insurance faces the twin problems of moral hazard and adverse selection. These problems are more serious for an insurance company than they are for a system of mutual aid. With mutual aid, the farmer himself faces considerable costs if his barn is lost: he too must work on its reconstruction. This gives him an incentive to take care, reducing moral hazard.

The insurance company can replicate this incentive structure by offering only partial coverage. With a **deductible**, an initial amount, say, $1,000 of a loss is not covered. With **coinsurance**, the insurer pays only a part of the loss, say 90%. With a deductible or coinsurance, the insured still faces a cost if there is a loss, and therefore has an incentive to exercise care. The insurance company can also *require* care as a condition for coverage. For example, a condition of coverage might be that no combustible materials (except hay, of course!) be stored in the barn.

> **deductible**
> Initial amount of a loss to be paid by the insured.

Adverse selection is not much of a problem for mutual aid, because participation is not voluntary. All members of the community are expected to participate. However, it is a problem for the insurance company. High-risk farmers will find the insurance a bargain and will buy a policy; low-risk farmers, finding the insurance too expensive, will not buy it. As a result, the frequency of claims will rise, and the insurance company may lose money. The best it can do is to gather as much information as possible to distinguish high-risk farmers from low, and to try to tailor its premiums to reflect risk.

> **coinsurance**
> Percentage of a loss to be paid by the insured.

Forward Transactions. Like lending, forward transactions involve promises. They are therefore subject to the same kinds of problem. As with lending, the financial system helps in two ways: the first is to make direct trading easier; the second is to offer indirect trading through intermediaries. Direct forward transactions are made easier by futures markets—the analog of markets for stocks and bonds. Indirect forward transactions are offered by banks, much as they offer indirect lending.

Futures Markets. Let us return to the forward transaction example we used in Chapter 1. Remember, you were thinking of expanding your copper mine, but were concerned about taking on the consequent price risk. If the price of copper were to fall, you

---

[11] See Chapter 9 for more on Lloyd's of London.

would take a loss. We saw that you could reduce this risk by selling your copper forward to American Electric. We saw, too, that such promises to buy and to sell in the future are subject to default risk (replacement risk). Dealing with this risk imposes significant costs on both parties to the transaction.

The financial system offers you an alternative to selling forward to American Electric. You could instead protect yourself from a fall in the price of copper by trading in the **futures market**. For example, you could sell copper futures on COMEX, a commodities exchange in New York that specializes in metals. Each contract commits you to deliver for an agreed price a certain quantity of copper at a specified time—say, next December. Your broker goes onto the floor of the exchange and finds traders willing to buy contracts for the 1 million pounds you wish to sell. The price, determined by supply and demand, is $1.80 a pound.

futures market
A market in standardized contracts for future delivery of various goods.

Both parties to a futures contract are guaranteed against default by the exchange. If, a buyer fails to keep his part of the bargain, COMEX will buy the copper from you at the contract price. If you default, the exchange will provide the buyer with copper at the contract price. While this arrangement makes things much easier for buyer and seller, it does expose the exchange itself to risk. We shall see in Chapter 16 that the exchange handles this risk by requiring traders to post collateral and by organizing trading in ways that minimize the risk.

The futures exchange solves another problem of forward transactions—the difficulty and cost of finding trading partners. It does this by providing an organized market in which buyers and sellers can easily find one another. To increase the number of potential traders, contracts are standardized. Each contract specifies a standard amount of a standard grade of the commodity, to be delivered at a standard time and place. The large number of traders and the large volume of trading ensure that you get a fair price for your contracts and that transactions costs are low.

Continuous trading in each contract up to the date of delivery provides you with liquidity. For example, suppose the financing for your planned mine expansion falls through, so that you will not have the copper to sell after all. You would like to get out of your contract. No problem. All you need do is ask your broker to *buy* contracts for 1 million pounds of copper to offset the contracts you have already sold. Since you will then be obliged both to deliver and to accept delivery of 1 million pounds of copper next December, your original obligation is effectively canceled.[12]

Futures contracts exist not only in metals, but also in agricultural commodities, oil products, foreign currencies, and a variety of financial instruments. We shall discuss the futures market in detail in Chapter 16.

Forward Intermediaries.   To illustrate how banks act as forward intermediaries, let us look at another example. Valley Motors of Los Angeles imports Kamikaze cars from Japan. It does not have to pay for each shipment immediately: it has 90 days to pay. Although this credit is useful, it exposes Valley to a type of price risk.

---

[12] If the price of December contracts has changed since you sold them, you will make a gain or a loss. For example, suppose the price has fallen to $1.75. You are obliged under the new contracts to pay $1.75 million for 1 million pounds of copper in December. Under the contracts you sold earlier, you are to receive $1.80 million for 1 million pounds of copper. Your profit in this case is $50,000. If the price of copper had risen, you would have taken a loss.

To understand the nature of this risk, suppose that Valley has just received a shipment of cars. Each car costs ¥2.5 million, which is $20,000 at the current exchange rate of 125¥/$. Over the next 90 days, Valley sells the cars to dealers for $22,000 each. At the end of 90 days, Valley's treasurer goes to the bank to arrange payment. He is stunned to find that the yen has risen to 105 to the dollar (the fewer yen to the dollar, the higher the value of the yen). For each car, Valley now has to pay ¥2.5 million/105 = $22,900. The rise in the value of the yen has turned an expected profit of $2,000 per car into an actual loss of $900. This type of price risk, due to a change in the exchange rate, is called **exchange rate risk**.

exchange rate risk
Risk associated with fluctuations in exchange rates.

Valley can avoid exchange rate risk by buying yen forward. Fortunately, its bank, First National, offers to buy and sell foreign exchange forward. So next time Valley receives a shipment of cars, the treasurer goes to First National and buys forward the yen Valley will need 90 days later. For example, suppose First National's 90-day forward price is 123¥/$. By buying forward, Valley can lock in a price per car of ¥2.5 million/123 = $20,325. If the cars sell for $22,000, this guarantees Valley a profit of $1,675 per car whatever happens to the exchange rate over the next 90 days.

But doesn't this just pass on the risk to First National? Not at all. First National is acting as an intermediary. While some customers, like Valley, want to buy yen forward, others—say, exporters who are owed payment in yen—want to *sell* yen forward. So First National can offset its forward commitments to sell yen with forward commitments to buy yen.

As is the case with lending, trading with an intermediary lowers the costs to buyers and sellers. Rather than check each other's credit, all they have to worry about is the credit of the bank. Because the bank has an interest in being safe and in being seen to be safe, its credit is relatively good and easily verified.

Of course, the bank must check the credit of buyers and sellers of its forward exchange. However it has many of the same advantages here as it did in the case of lending:

- It has good information about its customers (the same information it gathers when making loans).
- It is a specialist in assessing credit and in monitoring performance.
- It has a continuing relationship with its customers that gives them an interest in meeting their obligations.

Because of pooling, the bank is able to offer its customers liquidity. For a fee, it will allow them to cancel forward commitments.

THE TECHNOLOGY OF THE FINANCIAL SYSTEM

We have seen how the financial system makes different types of trade easier. Looking back, some common patterns emerge that shed light on the basic technology of the financial system. This technology consists of a number of techniques that are used in various combinations in everything the financial system does. These basic techniques are:

- Delegation
- Credit substitution
- Pooling
- Netting

Delegation

To trade you need to find a trading partner and negotiate terms. If the trade involves a promise, you must gather and process information, write up a contract, and monitor compliance. It may be less costly to delegate this work than to do it all yourself.

delegation
Appointing of someone to act for others in a transaction.

The most obvious example of **delegation** is indirect lending: a depositor delegates to a bank or some other intermediary the work of making a loan. But there is delegation too in direct lending: lenders delegate to an underwriter the task of setting up a loan and to a trustee the task of monitoring compliance with the contract. With insurance, the insured delegates to the insurance company setting up the risk pool and dealing with moral hazard and adverse selection. With forward transactions, traders delegate to futures exchanges and to forward intermediaries the work of dealing with promises.

Delegation reduces transactions costs for a number of reasons. For concreteness, we discuss them in terms of delegated lending, but they apply to other forms of delegation as well.

1. Many of the costs of a transaction are *indivisible*. A loan of $10,000 involves much the same work as a loan of $10 million. When many lenders lend to a single borrower, the delegate can do the work once for all of them, rather than each having to do the work independently.
2. Delegation allows *specialization*. An individual lender may lend only occasionally, and so acquire little expertise. The delegate, representing many lenders and lending often, acquires experience and know-how.
3. The delegate is in a *stronger bargaining position*. Because lending is concentrated in his hands, the delegate can negotiate better terms. Because the borrower is more likely to do repeat business with the delegate than with a single small lender, the borrower has more of an incentive to behave well.
4. *Revealing information* to a single delegate may be more acceptable to the borrower than a more general disclosure to the public at large.

bonding
The putting up of assets to guarantee performance.

Of course, delegation involve a fundamental problem of its own: *How is the delegate to be trusted?* There are two possible solutions—**bonding** and **reputation**.

A delegate can post a surety or performance bond. For example, banks fund a part of their lending with their own capital. If loans go bad, the bank is first to bear the loss. Having its own money at stake gives the bank an incentive to do its work well.

reputation
The general estimation in which someone is held by the public.

Reputation is valuable. A bank with a reputation for soundness attracts more deposits and has to pay less for them. An underwriter with a reputation for floating only sound issues, finds it easier to sell a new issue and attracts more business from borrowers. The value of its reputation gives the delegate an incentive to be conscientious. A violation of trust damages its reputation and costs it business in the future (see "Adam Smith on Reputation").

credit substitution
Replacement of the credit of one party to a transaction with the (superior) credit of a financial institution.

Credit Substitution

In many cases delegation is combined with **credit substitution**. A bank substitutes its own credit for the credit of the borrower: depositors lend to the bank rather than to the ultimate borrower. An insurance company substitutes its own credit for the credit of members of the

ADAM SMITH ON REPUTATION

"Of all the nations in Europe, the Dutch, the most commercial, are the most faithful to their word. The English are more so than the Scotch, but much inferior to the Dutch. . . . This is not at all to be imputed to national character, as some pretend; there is no natural reason why an Englishman or a Scotchman should not be as punctual in performing agreements as a Dutchman. It is far more reducible to self-interest, . . . [which] is as deeply implanted in an Englishman as a Dutchman. A dealer is afraid of losing his character, and is scrupulous in observing every engagement. When a person makes perhaps twenty contracts a day, he cannot gain so much by endeavoring to impose on his neighbours, as the very appearance of a cheat would make him lose. When people seldom deal with one another, we find that they are somewhat disposed to cheat, because they can gain more by a smart trick than they can lose by the injury which it does their character."

Source: Smith (1964).

risk pool. The futures exchange substitutes its own credit for the credit of individual traders.

Delegation and credit substitution do not always go together. Underwriters do not guarantee the issues they float: there is delegation but not credit substitution. When bank money is used in payment, the bank substitutes its own credit for the credit of the buyer: there is credit substitution but no delegation.

Credit substitution works because the promise of the bank, insurance company, or futures exchange is more acceptable than the promise of the ultimate trading partner. This is so for two reasons. The first is reputation: the financial institution's reputation for keeping its promises is essential to its business. The second reason is that the financial institution may be better *able* to keep its promises. The principal reason for this is pooling.

pooling
Combination of assets or liabilities in ways that reduce risk or improve liquidity.

Pooling

Pooling makes the liabilities of a financial intermediary (the promises it makes) safer and more liquid than its assets (the promises to it). For example, we have seen how pooling makes bank deposits safer and more liquid than bank assets. One reason pooling works is *diversification*. Another is netting.

netting
Offsetting of one transaction against another to reduce the number of transactions that actually need be executed.

Netting

Executing a transaction is costly. **Netting** lowers costs by offsetting one transaction against another, so that fewer transactions need actually be executed. The clearing of checks is an

EXHIBIT 2.4   Institutions, Technologies, and Types of Trading

		TECHNIQUES			
Type of Trade	Institution	Delegation	Credit Substitution	Pooling	Netting
Payments					
Cash trading	Warehouse bank			✓	✓
	Clearinghouse				✓
Credit trading	Fractional reserve bank		✓	✓	✓
Lending					
Direct	Underwriter	✓			
	Trustee	✓			
	Secondary market (dealer, broker, exchange)				✓
Indirect	Lending intermediary (bank and others)	✓	✓	✓	✓
Trade in risk					
Insurance	Insurance company	✓	✓	✓	
Forward transactions	Futures exchange	✓	✓		✓
	Forward intermediary (bank and others)	✓	✓	✓	✓

example. The physical transfer of currency is costly: the netting of banks' obligations to one another reduces the need for physical transfer and so reduces costs.

Netting also creates liquidity. For example, a bank can hold relatively illiquid assets because it can meet withdrawals out of new deposits, without having to liquidate the underlying assets. By netting new deposits and withdrawals, it reduces the need to buy and sell the underlying assets.

Secondary markets function in much the same way. A security is a claim on an illiquid asset (a factory, say). The holder can liquidate the claim by selling it to someone else. In this way, the market nets sales of claims against purchases of claims, providing liquidity without touching the underlying asset.

How Different Institutions Use the Basic Techniques

Exhibit 2.4 shows how different financial institutions apply the basic techniques to make the different types of trade easier.

SUMMARY

- Warehouse banks reduce the costs of cash payment.
- Fractional reserve deposits are IOUs rather than claims on specific amount of cash. Fractional reserve banks create additional money. Payment with the deposits of a fractional reserve bank is a form of credit trading, relying on the credit of the bank.

- Organized financial markets make direct lending easier. Different institutions provide information, negotiate and write the loan contract, and monitor compliance. These institutions have a reputational stake in doing their work well.
- Dealers and brokers create secondary markets to provide liquidity for direct loans.
- Financial intermediaries offer the alternative of indirect lending. Their credit is good and easy for lenders to check, and they have advantages in dealing with borrowers. Pooling enables them to offer lenders improved liquidity.
- Indirect lending has advantages for borrowers, too—lower costs for small loans and better treatment of re-payment problems.
- The advantages of an insurance policy over private arrangements such as mutual aid include sure premiums and greater reliability. The reason for these advantages is pooling over a larger number of insureds.
- Futures markets and forward intermediaries make forward transactions easier. They offer low transactions costs, guaranteed delivery, and greater liquidity.
- All these different institutions rely on the same four basic techniques—delegation, credit substitution, pooling, and netting.

DISCUSSION QUESTIONS

1. A fractional reserve bank creates money. Are there any limits to how much it can create? Does a large bank face the same limits as a small bank? What would be the limits for a large bank that was the only bank in the country?

2. How do financial markets and financial intermediaries provide liquidity. What are the differences from the point of view of the lender? The borrower? In each case, could the mechanism providing liquidity fail? What would happen if it did?

3. What are the risks of being a dealer? A broker? Which would you expect to charge a larger fee?

4. A bank, an underwriter, a securities dealer—what are the similarities in what they do? What are the differences?

5. Describe the different ways that pooling is used by various financial intermediaries.

6. Give three examples of actuarial risks not mentioned in the chapter. Give three examples of nonactuarial risks. Does insurance exist for each? If it does not, why not?

7. Find five types of contract from the list of traded futures contracts in *The Wall Street Journal*. Against what type of price risk does each provide protection? Who are the potential traders in each type of contract?

8. Gambling is a form of trade in risk.
   a. What is the nature of gambling transaction? How does it differ from insurance?
   b. What are the obstacles to this form of trade? What institutions exist to overcome these obstacles? Compare their methods with those of financial intermediaries (say, insurance companies).

BIBLIOGRAPHY

Federal Reserve Bulletin, September 2001, Table L. 100.
Jennings, R. W., H. March. *Securities Regulation: Cases and Materials*. 6th ed. Mineola, NY: Foundation Press, 1987.
Smith, Adam. "The Influence of Commerce on Manners." In *Lectures On Justice, Police, Revenue,* *And Arms*. Edited by Edwin Cannan. New York: Augustus M. Kelley, 1964, pp. 253–254.
Soderquist, Larry D. *Securities Regulation: A Problem Approach*. Mineola, NY: Foundation Press, 1982.
The World Bank. Quoted in *The Economist*, August 18, 1989.

KEY TERMS

warehouse bank

check

clearing

clearinghouse

fractional reserve bank

loan indenture (trust deed)

underwriter

trustee

transferable security

secondary market

primary market

dealer

broker

bid price

asked price

over-the-counter (OTC) market

exchange

direct lending

financial intermediary

indirect lending

diversification

bank run

bankruptcy

assessment

insurance policy

premium

property-liability insurance

life insurance

actuarial risks

Lloyd's of London

deductible

coinsurance

futures market

exchange rate risk

delegation

bonding

reputation

credit substitution

pooling

netting

CHAPTER 3

EFFICIENCY, STABILITY, AND GOVERNMENT INTERVENTION

When you finish this chapter you will understand:

- How inefficiencies in the financial system provide opportunities for profit
- Why there are banking panics, stock market crashes, and inflations
- Why financial institutions face so many rules and regulations

Our ultimate goal is to understand why the financial system is organized the way it is, and why it is changing. To this end, we have looked at the needs the financial system serves (Chapter 1) and at the technology it uses (Chapter 2). The picture, however, is not yet complete. Much of what we see cannot be understood purely in terms of needs and technology. There is a third factor—the government.

The government plays an important role in creating the environment in which the financial system operates. The government provides the legal system. The government controls the level of interests rates and the behavior of the price level through its control of monetary and fiscal policy. The failure of government in any of these areas can be fatal to the development of the financial system.

In addition to creating a suitable environment for the financial system, the government may intervene directly in its operation. It may set the rules for financial institutions and markets, and it may intervene in other ways that affect the financial system. This chapter provides a general framework for the discussion of different types of government intervention. We focus here on the basic principles; later chapters will go into the specifics.

In general, the justification for government intervention is market failure. If the free market fails to perform satisfactorily, there are calls for the government to do something about it. Market failures can be divided into two categories—those that impair the efficiency of the financial system and those that impair its stability.

We begin with efficiency. We explore what efficiency might mean, why a free-market financial system might sometimes be inefficient, and how intervention might promote efficiency. Next we consider why a free-market financial system might be unstable and how intervention might help. We then look briefly at some other reasons for government intervention, including consumer protection and social policy. We conclude with a discussion of the limitations of government intervention. Government, too, is subject to failure.

EFFICIENCY

Before we can discuss how government intervention in the financial system might promote efficiency, we need to understand what efficiency might mean. In general, efficiency means doing something as well as possible. We have seen what the financial system does: it makes lending, payments, and trade in risk easier. Our first task, then, is to understand what it might mean for the financial system to do its work "as well as possible."

Initially, we discuss efficiency in terms of lending alone. Once we have the basic ideas, it will be easy to generalize them to include the other forms of trading.

The Potential Gains from Lending

You have $1 million dollars you wish to save for your retirement. You could lend the money or you could invest it yourself by building a new house and renting it out. The net yearly income from this investment would be $80,000 a year.[1] When you weigh alternative ways of lending your money, this investment is your benchmark. If lending would earn you a better return (adjusting for risk and liquidity), you will prefer to lend.

Origen, our biotech company from Chapters 1 and 2, would like to borrow your $1 million to invest in a new lab. The new lab would add $200,000 a year to Origen's net income.[2]

If we assume for the moment that there are *no* transactions costs in making the loan, then there seems to be a good basis for trade here. If you lend your money to Origen, you

---

[1] Net income is rent plus appreciation, less expenses, taxes, and the value of you own time in managing the property.

[2] The risk and the liquidity of this investment are comparable to your investment in a rental property.

give up the $80,000 a year you could have earned by investing yourself in the rental property. If Origen invests your money instead in the new lab, it will earn $200,000 a year. The difference between the return on your own investment in the rental property and the return on Origen's investment of your money in the new lab, $120,000 a year, is the potential **gain from lending**. Column 1 of Exhibit 3.1 summarizes the numbers.

gain from
lending

The increase in
total return made
possible by
lending.

It is not clear how you will divide this gain with Origen. You are willing to lend for any return higher than $80,000; it is willing to pay you up to $200,000 for your money. How you split the difference depends on bargaining. Suppose you split the $120,000 gain 50-50, so that Origen gets $60,000 and you get $60,000. Then Origen will pay you $140,000 a year for your money—$60,000 more than you would have earned from the rental property—and it will be left with the remaining $60,000.

Not only do both you and Origen gain from the loan, but the economy as a whole gains, too. From the point of view of the economy, an investment that would have earned $80,000 is replaced by one that earns $200,000. As a result, there is a net addition of $120,000 to the total income of the economy. No matter how that additional amount is divided, the economy as a whole is better off by $120,000 a year.

The Effect of Transactions Costs.   Now let us be more realistic. We know that making a loan is difficult and that overcoming the difficulties is costly. Information must be gathered and processed; a contract must be negotiated and written; the borrower's behavior must be monitored; and incentive effects may remain that distort the borrower's behavior and reduce the return on the investment.

Consider first the costs if you and Origen arrange the loan yourselves, without any help from the financial system. The transactions costs—information, monitoring, and so on—turn out to be equivalent to $150,000 a year. Since the $200,000 return on the lab does not cover the sacrifice of the $80,000 return on the rental property plus the $150,000 in transactions costs, the loan is not worthwhile.

EXHIBIT 3.1   The Gains from Lending

	Lending with No Transactions Costs (1)	LENDING WITH TRANSACTIONS COSTS	
		With *No* Help from Financial System (2)	*With* Help from Financial System (3)
Return on borrower's investment	$200,000	$200,000	$200,000
Less: Return on lender's best alternative to the loan	80,000	80,000	80,000
Gross gain from lending	120,000	120,000	120,000
Less: Transactions costs to borrower and lender	—	150,000	50,000
Less: Transactions costs to financial system	—	—	40,000
Net gain from lending	$120,000	$−30,000	$ 30,000

An alternative way to see this is to compare the transactions costs, $150,000, with the potential gains from lending, $120,000. Since the former exceed the latter by $30,000, the *net* gain from lending is negative. Taking transactions costs into account, you are worse off making the loan. Column 2 of Exhibit 3.1 summarizes the numbers.

Consequently, if no help were available from the financial system, you would not make the loan. Instead, you would invest in the rental property, and Origen would not be able to build in lab.

The Contribution of the Financial System.   As we know, the financial system reduces the transactions costs of lending. You and Origen take advantage of its help by using a financial intermediary. You lend your money to First National Bank, and First National lends to Origen.

Although using the bank as an intermediary reduces the transactions costs, costs remain. While your costs of checking out the bank are negligible, Origen must still provide information and bear the other costs of being a borrower. These costs add up to $50,000 a year. This is much less than the $150,000 transactions cost of a do-it-yourself loan, but it is still substantial.

Of course, First National does not provide its services for free. It too has transactions costs. Borrowing from you, it must bear certain costs of being a borrower. Lending to Origen, it must bear the costs of being a lender. The total cost to the bank of acting as an intermediary in this transaction add up to $40,000 a year.

The *total* transactions costs of the loan are therefore the $50,000 cost that remains to the ultimate borrower and lender, plus the $40,000 cost to the bank—$90,000 in all. If we subtract the total transactions costs from the gross gains from lending, $120,000, the net gains are $30,000. Column 3 of Exhibit 3.1 summarizes the numbers.

The net gains will now be split three ways. Some will go to you, some to Origen, and some to the bank. How you divide the $30,000 is once again a matter of bargaining. For example, you might split the difference among you equally. In this case:

* First National pays you $90,000 for your deposit, $10,000 more than you would have earned from the rental property.
* First National charges Origen $140,000 for the loan, covering the $90,000 it pays you plus its own $40,000 in transactions costs, and leaving it with a gain of $10,000.
* Origen pays $140,000 to the bank plus $50,000 in transactions costs, leaving Origen with a gain of $10,000.

All the parties to the transaction benefit.

How the parties divide the gain does not affect the net benefit to the economy. The economy gives up an investment that would earn $80,000, spends a total of $90,000 on transactions costs, and gains an investment that earns $200,000. The net gain is $30,000. No matter how that gain is divided, the economy as a whole is better off by $30,000 a year. This is the net contribution of the financial system to the economy from helping to arrange this particular loan.

The contribution of the financial system (in terms of lending) is the *sum* of all the gains from all the loans it helps to arrange. The financial system is **efficient in lending** when the sum of all the gains from lending is as large as possible.

efficient in lending
The sum of all the gains from lending is as large as possible.

Conditions for Efficiency in Lending

If lending is to be efficient, three conditions must be satisfied:

- Pricing must be competitive.
- Transactions costs must be minimized.
- The financial system must be integrated.

Competitive Pricing. The way the gains from a given transaction are divided depends on the relative bargaining power of the parties. Suppose First National is the only bank in town, so that its bargaining power is considerable. It will exploit this power to boost its profits.

The best First National could do would be to take all of the gains on each of the loans it intermediates. For example, for intermediating your loan to Origen, it would charge its $40,000 cost plus the $30,000 gain. The deal is still barely worthwhile for you and for Origen, and the bank gets the most it can. If it did the same for all the loans it intermediates, its profit would be as high as possible. Such a scheme, however, is impractical: the bank simply does not know what the gains are from each individual deal.

Not knowing the gains from each deal, the bank has to offer the same terms on all of them. In deciding how much to charge, it faces a trade-off. The higher the price of its services, the greater its profit on each deal. However, the higher the price, the fewer deals there will be. For example, if First National charges more than $70,000 for intermediating your loan to Origen, it will not be worth your while, and there will be no loan.

Taking this trade-off into account, First National will set a price it believes will yield the maximum profit. This price will certainly be higher than the $40,000 cost of providing the service. If First National charges exactly $40,000, its profit is zero. As it raises its price, its profit will increase up to some point; beyond that point, its profit will start to decline. The trick, of course, is to find the point. Suppose that First National believes its profit to be maximized at a price of $80,000. It will lose some business, including yours, but what it earns on the business it keeps will more than make up for the loss.

While this solution is best for First National, it is not best for the economy as a whole. The outcome is not efficient: the sum of the gains from lending is not as large as possible. Loans that could yield positive gains, like yours to Origen, are not being made. Efficiency requires that First National set a price equal to cost—that is, $40,000. If it does this, all potential loans with positive gains will be made.

Note that we must calculate the cost to include a fair return on *all* the resources the bank employs. That is, it must include a fair return on the capital invested in the bank and on the time of its owners. So cost, by this definition, includes a fair profit.[3]

Left to its own devices, First National will set its price too high from the point of view of efficiency. At this price it will earn more than a fair profit. Fortunately, there is a powerful force that will cause it to lower its price—competition. For example, suppose Broad Street Bank opens for business across town. Broad Street has the same technology as First

---

[3] This is the *economic* cost, rather than the accounting cost. The difference is that the economic cost includes the cost of resources provided by the owner. If price is above economic cost, the firm is said to earn an *economic rent*.

National: it too can intermediate a loan for $40,000. If Broad Street charges less for its services than the $80,000 First National charges, it will attract away some of First National's business, and still do very well.

First National will respond by lowering its own price. The more vigorous the competition between the banks, the closer will their prices approach the $40,000 cost of providing the service. Because of the role of competition in bringing it about, we call the condition that price equal cost, **competitive pricing**.

competitive pricing
Pricing that covers the cost of all resources used to produce a good or service, but no more.

Throughout the book we shall see that this scenario is played out over and over again. High prices and excessive profits create profit opportunities; exploitation of the profit opportunities reduces market power and brings prices down. Some examples:

- Competition from money market mutual funds has caused banks to raise the rates they pay on deposits.
- Competition from the futures markets and from other trading systems has led to a fall in commissions on the New York Stock Exchange.
- Competition from nonbank issuers of credit cards like AT&T, GM, and Ford has forced banks to lower the interest rates they charge on their cards.

The first condition for efficiency, then, is competitive pricing. If pricing is not competitive, the financial system is inefficient because some loans that offer positive net gains are not being made.

Minimum Transactions Costs.   For lending to be efficient, the financial system must minimize transactions costs. Obviously lowering transactions costs is desirable for its own sake: transactions costs absorb resources that could be put to better use. But lowering transactions costs has another, even more important benefit. The lower the transactions costs of making a loan, the larger the number of worthwhile loans, and the greater the sum of the net gains from lending. If transactions costs are unnecessarily high, some potentially worthwhile loans will not be made and the economy as a whole will be the poorer as a result.

Let us look at the forces that tend to bring transactions costs down. Given current methods, it costs a bank $40,000 to arrange your loan to Origen. If pricing is competitive, that is what First National will charge. In making the loan, it earns a fair profit, but no more.

However, if the bank could find a way to arrange the loan at lower cost, it could make a larger profit. Suppose some smart young MBAs come up with a new method that lowers the cost to $35,000. If the bank charges you the same $40,000, it will increase its profit by $5,000. It can do even better by lowering its price a little, say to $38,000. That way it will attract a lot of business away from its cross-town rival.

By lowering its price, First National puts enormous pressure on Broad Street. Broad Street searches frantically for ways to cut its costs and manages to lower them to $32,000. It cuts its price to $34,000, and now the shoe is on the other foot. First National must scramble to catch up.

There are two lessons here. First, one way to attract more business and to increase profits is to find a way of arranging transaction at lower cost. Second, the search for lower costs and for higher profits is driven by competition.

The second condition for efficiency, then, is that transactions costs be minimized. If they are not, the financial system is inefficient because loans that would offer positive net gains at minimum transactions costs are not being made.

Integration.   Even if pricing is competitive and transactions costs are minimized, the financial system may still fail to be efficient if it is not integrated. To see why, let us compare what is happening in your hometown, York, to what is happening across the country in San Miguel.

While York is quiet and sedate, San Miguel is a boomtown. Because there are so many good investment opportunities, competition for loans is intense and loan rates are high. As a result, some very good investments are not being made. For example, Genius, a software company, would like to borrow $1 million to expand its operations. The net return on this investment would be $250,000 a year. However, loans in San Miguel are so expensive that it doesn't pay Genius to borrow to fund this investment.

In San Miguel, Genius passes up an investment that would earn $250,000. Back in York, you are lending to Origen to make an investment that earns only $200,000. This is not efficient. Exhibit 3.2 shows why. It compares the gain from arranging a loan your loan to Origen with the gains that could be achieved from arranging a loan from you to Genius. (The costs of the latter are a little higher because of the physical distance involved.) You can see that the gains from the loan to Genius are substantial higher than the gains from the loan to Origen.

The cause of the inefficiency is a lack of integration in the financial system. Borrowing and lending in York are separated from borrowing and lending in San Miguel. Lenders in York fund loans to borrowers in York. Lenders in San Miguel fund loans to borrowers in San Miguel.

The economy as a whole would be better off if Origen's investment were canceled and your funds were used instead to finance the investment by Genius. The economy would give up the net gain from the loan to Origen in exchange for the net gain form the loan to Genius. The total gain from lending for the economy as a whole would therefore increase by the difference in the gains from the two loans: $75,000 − $30,000 = $45,000.

Fortunately, the inefficiency creates incentives for its own removal. The inefficiency is a profit opportunity. To see why, imagine that San Miguel Bank opens a branch in York. Since the potential gain from a loan to Genius is greater than the potential gain from a loan to Origen, San Miguel Bank can offer you a better deal than can First National. You earn more on your deposit, San Miguel makes a nice profit, and the economy as a whole is richer by $45,000 a year.

EXHIBIT 3.2   A Comparison of Two Loans

	Loan to Origen	Loan to Genius
Return on borrower's investment	$200,000	$250,000
Less: Return on lender's best alternative to the loan	80,000	80,000
Gross gains from lending	120,000	170,000
Less: Transactions costs to borrower and lender	50,000	50,000
Less: Transactions costs to financial system	40,000	45,000
Net gains from lending	$ 30,000	$ 75,000

By borrowing in York and lending in San Miguel, San Miguel Bank improves the integration of the financial system. Borrowers in San Miguel can now borrow from lenders in York. As a result of better integration, funds move to where the return is higher. With more funds available in San Miguel and less available in York, loans become cheaper in San Miguel and more expensive in York. Eventually, equivalent loans should cost the same in both places.

integration
A financial system is integrated if similar loans are made on similar terms everywhere.

Generalizing from this example, we say that a financial system is **integrated** if similar loans are made on similar terms everywhere. Integration is the third condition for efficiency. If the financial system is not integrated, it is not efficient, since loans that offer smaller net gains are being made at the expense of loans that offer greater net gains.

Many of the changes in the financial system that we shall discuss in the following chapters are driven by the same forces that motivate San Miguel Bank. Some examples:

- U.S. banks are expanding outside their home states and outside the country.
- Home mortgages are increasingly funded in the national bond market rather than by a local bank or S&L.
- A device called a swap gives corporate borrowers access to bond markets that would otherwise be closed to them.

In all of these cases, a lack of integration created profit opportunities. And the profit opportunities stimulated action that improved integration and so efficiency.

Efficiency in Payments and in Trade in Risk

We have talked about efficiency in terms of lending. However the financial system also plays an important role in payments and in trade in risk (insurance and forward transactions). Efficiency in these other activities can be understood in terms that parallel those we have used to understand efficiency in lending.

Consider payments first. Suppose there are two countries that do not trade with each other. The sum of their national incomes is $100 billion. Were they to trade, each could specialize and become more productive, and the sum of their incomes would rise to $110 billion—a gain of $10 billion.

However, trade involves payments, and arranging payments is costly. Without the help of the financial system, the resulting transactions costs would amount to $20 billion. Taking into account these transactions costs, trade is not worthwhile. However, the financial system can lower transactions costs to $2 billion. The net gain from trade, after transactions costs, is $8 billion. This is also the net contribution of the financial system in its role of arranging payments.

Now consider trade in risk. Imagine a small country with a primitive financial system that provides no help with either insurance or forward transactions. There are some private arrangements, but that is all. National income of this country is $50 billion.

What happens when a modern financial system develops? Insurance companies and futures markets open, and banks begin to offer forward transactions. Because of improved trade in risk, firms undertake new, profitable activities that before they had thought too risky. As a result, national income rises to $55 billion. The net contribution of the financial system, and the net gain from trade in risk, is the $5 billion increase in national income less the $1 billion in extra transactions costs—$4 billion.

The conditions for efficiency in payments and in trade in risk are exactly the same as those for efficiency in lending—competitive pricing, minimum transactions costs, and integration. If these conditions are not fulfilled, the financial system is not efficient. Examples of inefficiencies in payments and in trade in risk might include the following:

- Banks charge more for credit cards than the cost to them of providing the service (pricing not competitive).
- Commissions in futures markets are high because exchanges are slow to introduce computer technology (costs not minimized).
- Adjusting for differences in risks, automobile insurance costs more in New York than in London (lack of integration).

efficiency of the financial system
A situation in which the sum of all gains from lending, payments, and trade in risk are as large as they can be.

The *total* contribution of the financial system is the sum of *all* the gains from lending, from payments, and from trade in risk. The financial system is **efficient** when the sum of all these gains is as large as possible.[4]

Market Failure and Inefficiency

A lack of efficiency of the financial system is undesirable because it reduces our national income. The free market, left to itself, may fail to produce efficiency. If this is so, there *may* be a case for government intervention. Successful intervention will rectify the faults of the free market, improve the efficiency of the financial system, and increase national income.

A major reason why the free market might fail to produce efficiency is insufficient competition. We have seen the vital role of competition in promoting efficiency. It promotes competitive pricing; it spurs the financial system to reduce costs; and it promotes integration. If competition is lacking, inefficiencies may persist. There are two common reasons why the free market may fail to produce sufficient competition—economies of scale and natural monopoly.

economies of scale
Declining average cost of operation as the scale of operation is increased.

Economies of Scale.   An industry exhibits **economies of scale** if large producers can produce at lower cost than small ones. As a result of economies of scale, large firms can lower their prices below the costs of small ones, driving smaller firms out of business. Economies of scale can cause an industry to become **concentrated**—dominated by a few large firms. In a concentrated industry, collusion to restrain competition becomes easier, and efficiency suffers.[5]

For example, because of economies of scale, the automobile industry in the United States became highly concentrated after World War II. By the 1960s, the "big four" dominated the market. Tacit collusion allowed these automakers to raise their prices, and they had little incentive to lower costs or to offer new products.

concentrated industry
One in which a small number of firms account for most of the business.

Normally, if prices are above costs, this will attract new firms into the industry. However, economies of scale are a **barrier to entry**. If the entering firm is small, its cost

barrier to entry
An obstacle to new firms entering an industry.

---

[4] To keep the story as simple as possible, we have considered only gains to the economy that take the form of increases in income. In addition, there are gains to individual welfare that do not take this form. For example, a consumer loan does not raise your lifetime income. But it does increase your enjoyment of it by allowing you to time your spending in the way you desire.

[5] We shall have more to say about economies of scale in Chapter 5.

will be high relative to those of existing firms, and it will find it hard to compete. To compete successfully, a new entrant must match the existing firms in size. For example, Kaiser-Frazer attempted to enter the automobile industry in 1946, but it could not compete with the larger companies and eventually gave up.[6]

Economies of scale are widespread in the financial system (we shall see why in Chapters 5 and 11). As a result, many parts of the financial system are highly concentrated. For example:

- In many countries, the 10 largest life insurance companies account for over half the market.
- In many countries, the five largest banks account for over half the market.[7]
- In the United States, the 10 largest underwriters account for nearly 90% of the business. Even worldwide, the top 10 underwriters account for nearly 70% of the business.

With such a high degree of concentration, there is a danger of insufficient competition and of inefficiency.[8]

natural monopoly
An industry in which costs would be minimized if the industry consisted of a single firm.

Natural Monopoly.   Another enemy of competition is natural monopoly. An industry is a **natural monopoly** if costs would be minimized if the industry consisted of a single firm. The local supply of electricity is a common example: it is obviously less expensive to bring electricity to homes on the same street with a single network rather than having adjacent houses served by rival networks. If an industry is a natural monopoly, it will eventually become very concentrated. As a result, the remaining firms, or firm, will be able to raise prices and will be under little pressure to further lower costs.

Cases of natural monopoly are common in the financial system. A clearinghouse is an obvious example: it makes no sense to have more than a single clearinghouse in a given city. To some extent, securities exchanges are natural monopolies.[9] We shall encounter other examples in later chapters.

market failure
The failure of a free market to produce efficiency.

Economies of scale and natural monopoly are reasons for **market failure**—the failure of a free market to produce efficiency. When the market fails to produce efficiency, there *may* be a case for government intervention.

Intervention to Promote Competition

When competition is lacking, and the inefficiencies become obvious, there are calls for the government to do something. There are a number of possible approaches the government may take.

antitrust laws
Laws that prohibit monopolistic or anticompetitive practices.

One approach is to prevent firms from exploiting their market power to raise prices. The U.S. government does this under **antitrust laws** administered by the Department of Justice. Examples of practices that these laws prohibit include

---

[6] Beginning in the 1970s, competition was reestablished in the U.S. automobile market by the entry of large foreign producers of automobiles (mainly Japanese producers).

[7] The United States is an exception. We shall see why in Chapter 7.

[8] Because concentration is conducive to monopoly profits, there are potential gains to creating a cartel or "trust." Therefore, an industry can become concentrated even if there are no economies of scale.

[9] We shall discuss this in Chapter 17.

- Collusion to fix prices or divide up markets
- Charging different prices to different customers for the same product

Antitrust laws can be applied and are applied to the financial system. At one time, for example, brokers in the stock market had agreed not to compete with one another over the commissions they charged customers for buying and selling stock. The antitrust laws were used to prohibit this practice.

Another approach to promoting competition is to attack excessive concentration. The idea is that an industry composed of many small firms should naturally be competitive. The government has the power to reduce concentration by breaking up existing large firms in an industry. It also has the power to prevent concentration by blocking mergers and acquisitions. For example, proposed bank mergers and acquisitions must be approved by regulators before the plans can be implemented.

Preventing firms from getting larger may be desirable in terms of promoting competitive pricing. But it may also be bad in terms of another of our conditions for efficiency—cost minimization. If mergers and acquisitions are driven by economies of scale, blocking them keeps costs higher than they might otherwise be. Regulators therefore face a trade-off. They must take both these effects into consideration in deciding whether a given merger or acquisition will increase or decrease overall efficiency.

In the case of a natural monopoly, the cost advantages are overwhelming, so preventing the monopoly from being formed is not an option. One way to keep the monopoly from exploiting its market power to raise prices is to regulate the prices it can charge. For example, power companies are allowed to be monopolies, but public utility commissions regulate their rates. Such industries are known as **regulated monopolies**.

regulated monopoly
A legal monopoly whose prices are regulated.

Another way to prevent the abuse of market power by a natural monopoly is for the customers to own it. A monopoly owned by its customers has no reason to set its price above cost. For example, clearinghouses are generally owned by the banks they serve; exchanges are usually owned by the traders who use them.

nationalization
A government takeover of a firm or industry.

This idea of changing ownership to change incentives is also the idea behind **nationalization**—government takeover of a firm or industry. In principle, the government should run the firm or industry in the public interest rather than trying to extract monopoly profits. For example, the French government in 1981 and the Mexican government in 1982 nationalized their countries' major commercial banks in the belief that government could manage them more effectively in the public interest.

Unfortunately, however, both regulated monopoly and nationalization have problems. Although they prevent monopoly pricing, neither leaves much incentive for cutting costs. For example, the costs of the U.S. Postal Service are much higher than those of private competitors such as UPS and FedEx. Neither France nor Mexico was very happy with the results of its nationalization, and both are in the process of reprivatizing their banks.

Intervention to Lower Costs

All these forms of intervention are designed to promote efficiency by encouraging competitive pricing. Sometimes, government intervention can promote efficiency directly by lowering costs.

We have seen that if transactions costs are too high, a given trade will not be worthwhile, and it will not take place. The financial system lowers transactions costs, but it may not lower them to the point where trade becomes worthwhile.

For example, the free market does not provide certain types of insurance. Sometimes the problems of moral hazard and adverse selection are too great. Unemployment insurance is an example. Sometimes, too, the risks of simultaneous large losses make private insurance difficult. Insurance against natural disasters such as floods, earthquakes, and hurricanes is an example.

In some cases, a government can be more successful than the private market at overcoming problems and at lowering transactions costs. Governments have means not available to private insurers. They can eliminate adverse selection by forcing *everyone* to buy the insurance—for example, with unemployment insurance. They can use the tax system to spread risk widely. For example, when a government provides disaster relief, it covers the cost by levying an "assessment" on all taxpayers.

STABILITY

We have seen how important a financial system is for the functioning of an economy. Developed modern economies are so dependent on the proper functioning of their financial systems that a breakdown can be disastrous. For example, financial breakdowns in the United States and in Europe in the early 1930s led to the worldwide economic slump known as the Great Depression. In the United States, unemployment reached 25%, and output fell by a quarter. Economic collapse in Germany helped the Nazis to power, paving the way for World War II.

The stability of the financial system is therefore a vital concern of government policy. Before we see what the government can do to promote stability, let us review the three principal types of instability—panics, crashes, and price-level instability.

Bank Runs and Banking Panics

Financial intermediaries create liquidity through pooling and netting claims. We saw in Chapter 2 that although the underlying assets are illiquid, claims on those assets can be made liquid by netting one against the other. This technology breaks down, however, if all claimants wish to liquidate at once. No netting is possible, and claims cannot be met.

The primary example of such a breakdown is a bank run. Problems at a bank undermine depositor confidence, and depositors rush to withdraw their money. Since the rule is first come, first served, everyone wants to be first. When reserves—a fraction of total deposits—are exhausted, the bank can no longer honor its promise of liquidity, and it must close its doors.

banking panic
A simultaneous run on many banks.

A bank run is obviously bad for the bank involved, but it need not have much effect on the economy. However, a **banking panic**—a run on the banking system as a whole—is another matter. When depositors lose faith in banks in general, the financial system can be paralyzed, and the consequences for the economy can be severe.

In the Great Depression, widespread bank runs developed into a general banking panic. Widespread default on loans caused many banks to fail. Depositors rushed to withdraw deposits from all banks, including those that were still sound. As a result, many sound banks were unable to meet the demands of their depositors, and they too failed. As banks failed, many small and medium-sized firms found themselves without credit and were forced to scale back their operations and lay off their workers. The resulting fall in spending caused more business to default on their loans and more banks to fail. Of an original 24,000 banks in the United States 9,000 failed; the combined assets of the banking system shrank by a third.

We shall take another, closer, look at bank runs and banking panics in Chapter 19. For a more recent example of a bank run, see "The New England Banking Crisis of 1991."

Securities Market Crashes

Secondary markets provide liquidity for holders of direct securities. We saw in Chapter 2 that they do this through pooling and netting, just like a bank. A pool of investors holds claims to illiquid underlying assets. The secondary market nets the sales of those wishing to liquidate their claims against the purchases of those wishing to acquire claims. As with banks, however, if everyone wishes to liquidate at once, netting becomes impossible. If this happens in a secondary market, prices of securities drop precipitously. There is a **crash**.

(securities market) crash
A large and sudden drop in securities prices.

The stock market crash of 1929 is an example. The "Roaring Twenties" saw an unprecedented boom. The Dow Jones Industrial Average (a measure of stock prices) rose from 200 in January 1928 to 381 in September 1929. However, in October, the market faltered. Investors, fearing a fall in prices, rushed to sell. In the week of October 23–29, the market crashed. By the end of the year, stock prices had fallen by over a third, and they fell by a third again in 1930. By 1932 the Dow had fallen to 58, about 15% of its 1929 high.

THE NEW ENGLAND BANKING CRISIS OF 1991

In November 1990, depositors of Heritage Loan and Investment Co., a small Rhode Island bank, learned of the mysterious disappearance of the bank's president. Worried about the safety of their deposits, they ran on the bank. The bank's failure wiped out the small private insurance fund that insured its deposits, and on January 1, 1991, the governor of Rhode Island closed the 45 other small banks and credit unions that relied on the fund for deposit insurance.

Depositors could not gain access to their deposits. Businesses, unable to pay their suppliers or meet their payrolls, were forced to close. Individuals had to borrow from relatives to pay for groceries. A year later, many depositors were still waiting for their money.

The events in Rhode Island shook public confidence in banks throughout New England. A few days later, Bank of New England, one of the largest banks in Massachusetts, announced a fourth-quarter loss of $450 million. Depositors rushed to withdraw their money, lining up at tellers' windows and emptying cash machines. Bank of New England lost nearly $1 billion in deposits in two days.

The effects on the economy of the Great Crash are still being debated. There can be little doubt, however, that the great loss of wealth contributed to the fall in spending, and that the collapse of the stock market made it harder for firms to sell new equity.

We shall look at stock market crashes in greater detail in Chapter 20. For a more recent example of a stock market crash, see "The Crash of '87."

inflation

Continuing rise in prices over a substantial period of time.

deflation

Continuing fall in prices over a substantial period of time.

Price-Level Instability

Price-level instability can take either of two forms. A continuing rise in prices is called an **inflation**. A continuing and sustained fall is called a **deflation**. Both are harmful.

In both inflation and deflation, lending suffers. A loan is an exchange of money now for a promise of money in the future. Inflation reduces the value of the promised money in

THE CRASH OF '87

The Dow rose steadily during the 1980s, from 1,000 points in 1982, to 1,500 in 1985. The rise then accelerated, and by the morning of Wednesday, October 17, 1987, the Dow stood at over 2,500. That day bad economic news led to heavy selling, and the Dow fell 95 points on volume of over 200 million shares (normal daily volume at the time averaged 150 million shares). Fearing a further decline, investors sold heavily on Thursday and Friday, bringing the Dow down to 2,250 by the end of the week. That weekend, worried investors flooded their brokers with sell orders.

On Monday morning, prices dropped at first, but then recovered towards noon. Alan Greenspan, the chairman of the Federal Reserve Board, was on a flight to Texas for most of the afternoon. When he landed, his first concern was for the market. "It's down five-o-eight," he was told. Believing the market was down only 5.08 points for the day, he breathed a sigh of relief. In fact, it had fallen 508 points—a 22.5% decline—on volume of over 600 million shares. This decline far exceeded the previous record for a single day—the 12.8% decline on October 28, 1929 that had ushered in the Great Depression.

The crash in New York was mirrored in stock exchanges around the world. Stock prices fell by 22% in London, by 18% in Frankfurt, by 8% in Tokyo, and by 45% in Sydney.

Many feared the crash would lead to an economic collapse like the one that followed the Great Crash of 1929, but there seemed to be little effect on the U.S. and world economies. The effect on Wall Street, however, was substantial. With investors scared away from the market, trading volume dropped, and brokers' earnings plummeted. Some 45,000 employees of securities firms were laid off.

Source: *Report of the Presidential Task Force on Market Mechanisms,* January 1988.

terms of what it will actually buy; deflation increases it. As a result, unexpected inflation hurts lenders and benefits borrowers; unexpected deflation has the opposite effect. Uncertainty about possible future inflation or deflation makes loans riskier both for borrowers and for lenders and therefore makes lending less attractive.

Deflation played a major role in the Great Depression. The general level of prices fell by a quarter; farm prices fell by a half. The fall in prices made repayment of debt more difficult, and borrowers defaulted in large numbers. Widespread defaults contributed significantly to the general economic decline, not least by causing large numbers of banks to fail.

hyperinflation
A very rapid inflation (prices increasing by more than 50% a month).

The effects of inflation can be just as dramatic. Between 1921 and 1923, prices in Germany doubled every two weeks. Inflation at such a rate is called **hyperinflation**. Workers demanded to be paid twice daily, so their wages would not lose all value before they received them. Payment for a bag of groceries could take half an hour because of the need to recalculate prices—which had risen since the last customer had paid—and the need to count bundles of next-to-worthless bills. People in the towns went hungry while food rotted in the fields because farmers refused to accept money in payment. The economy eventually ground to a halt as transactions costs rose so high that trade became impossible.

Hyperinflation had a devastating effect on the economies of Latin America in the 1980s, and it continues to be a problem in Argentina. It continues to be a threat to the success of economic reform in the countires of the former Soviet Union.

Less severe inflation is not as dramatic in its effects, but it still increases transactions costs and makes trade more difficult. We shall see in coming chapters how rising inflation in the United States, beginning in the 1960s, led to momentous changes in the structure of the financial system.

Inflations and deflations are the result of changes in the quantity of money. When the quantity of money increases more rapidly than the quantity of goods and services available, prices rise. When the quantity of money increases less rapidly than the amount of goods and services available, or even declines, prices fall.

Changes in the quantity of money can be the result of the actions of the banks. As we saw in Chapter 2, bank deposits are money and fractional reserve banks create deposits when they lend. An increase in the rate of creation of money by banks can cause inflation; a decrease can cause deflation. For example, the collapse of the banking system during the Great Depression destroyed a large part of the bank deposits in existence. The fall in the quantity of money caused prices to drop.

Market Failure and Instability

We have seen that instability of the financial system can devastate an economy. Why are financial systems subject to instability?

composition problems
Problems that arise out of behavior that is sensible for a single individual but harmful if pursued by all individuals.

Composition Problems.
The three types of instability—banking panics, stock market crashes, and price-level instability—all involve **composition problems**. In every case, behavior that makes sense for each individual separately leads to an outcome that is damaging to all.

In a banking panic, fearing the banks will fail, individuals rush to ensure their liquidity by withdrawing their deposits. The result of their actions is the very failure they fear.

The crash of an asset market is very similar: fear of a collapse in prices prompts massive selling. Massive selling leads to a collapse in prices.

Price-level instability, too, involves a composition problem. When a single bank increases or decreases its lending, and creates or destroys money, it has little effect on prices. But when all banks do this together, the general increase or decrease in the quantity of money leads to an inflation or deflation. The result is harmful, not least to the banks themselves.

In each of these cases, the market fails to provide individuals with the incentives to act in a way that produces the best outcome for all.

Excessive Risk Taking.   There is another incentive problem that may contribute to instability. Banks make risky loans. If the loans go bad, a bank may fail. If the bank bears all the losses that result from its failure, it will presumably take these losses into account when making loans (the expected return will reward it adequately for the risk it bears[10]).

Suppose though that the failure of the bank triggers a banking panic, which in turn results in a collapse of the economy. Then the losses due to the bank's failure greatly exceed those borne by the bank itself. When these losses are taken into account, the bank's loans are too risky from the economy's point of view. The expected return does not compensate the economy as a whole for the risks it bears. It would be better from the economy's point of view if the bank made loans that were less risky.

The Role of Externalities.   Both composition problems and excessive risk taking are examples of a type of market failure known as an externality. An **externality** exists when the costs of an individual's actions are not all borne by the individual himself.[11] Externalities create an incentive problem. Because the interests of the individual are not aligned with those of the economy as a whole, the individual will behave in ways that harm the general good.

The role of externalities in financial instability may justify government intervention to promote stability.

externality

An externality exists when all the costs of an individual's actions are not all borne by the individual himself.

Intervention to Promote Stability

Financial instability is a serious threat to the economy. It is, to some extent, the result of market failure. What can the government do to help? There are basically two approaches—regulation to promote stability and the creation of institutions that enhance stability.

Regulation to Promote Stability.   Government regulation can combat instability by restricting the individual behavior that causes it. For example, the government can reduce the chance of bank failure and banking panic by limiting the freedom of banks to

---

[10] If deposits are not insured, depositors too share some of the risk. The return they receive must compensate them for this risk. So the return depositors require on their deposits depends on the riskiness of the bank's loans. The bank will take this dependence into account when it makes risky loans.

[11] This is the definition of a negative externality. There are also examples of positive externalities. In these cases the individual's actions have beneficial effects on others for which he is not compensated.

bear risk. It can do this by prohibiting banks from holding certain classes of asset or from engaging in certain types of activity.

We shall see throughout the following chapters that banks and other financial institutions face an enormous number of such restrictions. Many of these restrictions are the response of legislators to specific episodes of financial instability. In the 1930s, the Great Depression gave rise to a wave of financial legislation that radically altered the U.S. financial system. In the 1980s, the collapse of the S&L industry and the cost of the public bailout led to a host of new regulations.

The Great Depression saw a collapse of the financial system and of the economy that was unprecedented. This collapse prompted a wave of financial legislation that transformed the structure of the financial system and froze it for many years. This legislation was guided by the popular view of what had caused the collapse. People believed that excessive competition among banks had pushed them into financing stock market speculation. This had contributed to the stock market boom, which ended, inevitably, in a stock market bust. Because of the involvement of banks in the stock market, the stock market bust had caused a collapse of the banking system, and this in turn had caused a collapse of the economy.

The legislative response was twofold—to exclude commercial banks from the securities markets and to restrict competition among them. To keep banks out of danger, the financial structure was rigidly segmented. The **Glass–Steagall Act of 1933** decreed that commercial banks were to be restricted to payments and intermediation; the securities business was to be limited to **investment banks**. Commercial banks were required to divest themselves of existing securities operations. Institutions wishing to engage in the securities business (investment banking) were to divest themselves of their commercial banking operations. Segmentation was reinforced by later legislation, such as the **Bank Holding Company Act of 1956**, which restricted the affiliation of banking and nonfinancial corporations ("the separation of banking and commerce").

The second goal of the Depression era legislation was to restrict competition among banks. For example, for many years, the rates banks could pay on deposits were limited to prevent them from competing with one another for deposits. Banks and securities firms were prohibited from competing in each others' lines of business. The rationale for these restrictions was that "excessive" competition had led to too much risk taking and so to instability.

Institutions that Enhance Stability.   In promoting stability, government intervention can go beyond regulation of individual behavior to the creation of institutions that enhance stability.

In a bank run or banking panic, many depositors simultaneously wish to convert their deposits into cash. Banks, with limited reserves of cash, cannot meet this demand. One solution is a source of liquidity *outside* the regular banking system to which banks can turn in case of need—a **lender of last resort**. In most countries this function in performed by the **central bank**.

The central bank is an institution either set up by the government or sponsored by it. The central bank of the United States is the **Federal Reserve (the Fed)**. Other central banks include the Bank of Japan, the Bank of England, and the European Central Bank. A central bank typically performs a number of functions:

investment banks
Financial institutions specialized in the securities business.

lender of last resort
Financial institution that stands ready to lend to banks in times of crisis.

central bank
Official institution with broad responsibilities for a nation's monetary system.

Federal Reserve (the Fed)
The central bank of the United States.

- It is the lender of last resort, responsible for the stability of the financial system.
- The central bank typically acts as the government's banker and financial agent.
- It is usually the central bank that is given the responsibility of controlling the creation of money.
- The central bank shares the responsibility of regulating the financial system with other government agencies. In most countries, however, it is the principal regulator.
- Ordinary banks hold deposits at the central bank, which they use both as reserves and as a medium for clearing payments among them.

One way a lender of last resort can enhance stability is by reassuring depositors. Knowing there is a lender of last resort, they have less reason to make a run on the bank. A more direct way of reassuring depositors is for the government simply to guarantee deposits. Depositors have no reason at all to make a run on their bank because whatever happens, they know their money is safe. In the United States, deposits are guaranteed by

Federal Deposit Insurance Corporation (FDIC)
A government agency that insures bank deposits.

the **Federal Deposit Insurance Corporation (FDIC)**. The establishment of the FDIC was another part of the wave of Depression era legislation.

Government guarantees of bank deposits creates problems of its owns. Because deposits are guaranteed, depositors have little incentive to monitor the behavior of their banks. As a result, the banks can take greater risks without losing the confidence of their depositors and so their deposits. Banks fail more often, and this imposes increasing costs on the insurer of deposits—the government. (This is an example of the moral hazard problem in insurance that we studied in Chapter 1.) To protect itself from these losses, the government has to impose restrictions on the risk taking of banks. Protecting the government is another reason, perhaps the dominant reason, for banking regulation. We shall discuss deposit insurance and its problems in detail in Chapter 19.

THE TRADE-OFF BETWEEN STABILITY AND EFFICIENCY

There is something of a trade-off between stability and efficiency. Anticompetitive policies designed to promote stability can come into conflict with procompetitive policies to promote efficiency. For example, in 1968 the Department of Justice accused stockbrokers of illegal collusion to fix commissions on stock trades. It believed that such noncompetitive pricing harmed efficiency. The collusion had, in fact, occurred with the full knowledge and blessing of another government agency—the SEC. The SEC believed that healthy profits made it less likely that stockbrokers would behave in a fashion likely to cause instability.[12]

deregulation
A process of easing or removal of regulations that affect an industry.

The U.S. financial system and the financial systems in other countries are undergoing a process of **deregulation**. Many restrictive regulations are being removed, and financial institutions are gaining more freedom than they have had in many years. The motivation for deregulation is to promote efficiency. However, it should come as no surprise if it also reduces stability. At some point, the efficiency gain from increased competition may be more than offset by the potential cost of increased instability.

---

[12] The conflict was resolved on the side of competition when the Securities Acts Amendments of 1975 prohibited further collusion and paved the way for discount brokerage and a general lowering of commissions.

Regulation and Innovation

Regulation that restricts the freedom of financial institutions and markets, for whatever reason, creates inefficiencies. We have seen that inefficiencies represent profit opportunities, and that the pursuit of these profit opportunities is one of the driving forces of innovation.

We shall see repeatedly in coming chapters that a very large part of the innovation that has taken place in the financial system is the result of attempts to get around restrictive regulations. For example, restrictions on U.S. banks were the driving force behind the development of Eurodollar banking and of money market mutual funds (we discuss these in Chapters 7 and 10, respectively).

OTHER TYPES OF GOVERNMENT INTERVENTION

There are reasons for government intervention in the financial system other than the promotion of efficiency and stability. These include consumer protection and social policy.

Consumer Protection

asymmetric information
The situation that exists when one party to a transaction is better informed than the other.

The idea that trade is beneficial rests on the assumption that buyers and sellers know what they are doing. This assumption fails when one of the parties is much better informed than the other—that is, when there is **asymmetric information**. Asymmetric information may be the result of differences in expertise: for example, consumers are at an informational disadvantage when they purchase services from a physician, lawyer, or accountant. Or it may be the result of deception or fraud: one party deliberately conceals information or misleads the other.

Information asymmetries of both kinds are present in the financial system. The average consumer is less well informed and less financially sophisticated than large financial institutions and is therefore at a disadvantage in buying their services. For example, individual borrowers may not understand fully the terms of the obligations into which they are entering. Traders in securities markets may have access to inside information before it is available to the general public. In such cases, some sort of government intervention may be justified to inform and to protect consumers.

There exist extensive regulations designed to protect unsophisticated investors. Securities laws require issuers of new securities to disclose all relevant information and prohibit trading on inside information. We shall discuss these laws in detail in Chapter 20.

There are also regulations to protect the small borrower. The most important ones are contained in the **Consumer Credit Protection (Truth-in-Lending) Act of 1968**, which requires lenders to provide borrowers with accurate information on the cost of credit. The Fed is charged with administering this law.[13]

Another way to protect consumers is to guarantee them against loss. Deposit insurance has this effect, although that was not its principal motivation, at least in the United

---

[13] Other consumer protection laws include the Real Estate Settlements and Procedures Act, the Fair Credit Reporting Act, and the Fair Credit Billing Act, the Electronic Fund Transfer Act, the Home Mortgage Disclosure Act, and the Truth-in-Savings Act. Other legislation contains sections dealing with consumer protection.

States. The government also guarantees many private pensions (we shall learn about this in Chapter 10).

Social Policy

Some government intervention in the financial system is motivated by the desire to improve the access of disadvantaged groups and individuals to insurance and credit.

One way government does this is through regulation such as the following laws:

- The **Equal Credit Opportunity Act of 1974** prohibits discrimination in the granting of credit on the basis of race, age, national origin, or dependence on public assistance.
- The **Community Reinvestment Act of 1977** prohibits lenders from refusing loans purely on the basis of area of residence (a practice known as "redlining").

In addition, the federal government itself acts as a financial intermediary to provide loans to certain groups. Such programs include loans to low-income students and to minority businesses. The government also guarantees private loans to students.

GOVERNMENT FAILURE

government failure
The failure of government action to produce efficiency.

We have treated government intervention as though it were always executed flawlessly, costlessly, and in the public interest. In reality, execution is imperfect and expensive, and intervention often serves special interests rather than the public good. Perfect government is as much a dream as perfect markets. So when we consider government intervention to correct market failure, we must recognize **government failure**.

Intervention Often Serves Special Interests

Government action often serves special interests rather than the public interest. Legislators are beholden to groups and to individuals who support them with votes and money, and they will find ways to show their gratitude. Their favors include laws that limit competition and direct and indirect subsidies at taxpayer expense.

The anti–competitive banking legislation of the 1930s provides a good example. Although the promotion of stability did play a role, it was certainly not the only motivation. Many small banks were delighted to see their profits increased and their lives made easier by the restriction of competition.

More recently, a 1991 proposal that would have allowed banks to sell insurance was blocked by insurance agents who did not want the competition. The Independent Insurance Agents of America is a potent lobby and an important contributor to campaign finance.

Administrators, too, frequently serve special interests rather than the public. Employees of regulatory agencies often go on to lucrative careers in the industries they had regulated. They therefore have a strong incentive to please their future employers. For example, lax regulation by the federal agencies charged with regulating the savings and loan industry contributed to the cost of the S&L collapse.

The government itself is a special interest. It is a major customer of the financial system. Regulation can be used to bias the system in the government's favor at the expense of other customers. For example, banks can be required to buy government securities. Or the central bank can use its control over the quantity of money to keep interest rates low, which in turn reduces the cost of financing the government debt.

Intervention Is Costly

Even when government acts in the public interest, intervention is costly. Government is not an abstract disembodied force but a large organization employing millions of people to produce a particular set of services. The administration of additional regulations requires additional bureaucracies whose employees can number in the thousands or even tens of thousands.

Government bureaucracies have little incentive for efficiency: there is no competition, and accountability is limited. Consequently, the cost of having government perform a given task is generally much higher than the cost of having the private market perform it.

Government intervention also imposes costs on the financial system. Complying with regulations involves considerable work: tens of thousands of people are employed filling out all the forms required by the different regulations.

For example, the British government introduced a host of new regulations to protect investors under the Financial Services Act of 1986. A subsequent study found that the direct costs to the government of administering these regulations came to about £20 million per year. Compliance by the financial system cost another £100 million a year. In comparison, the total losses to investors from the sort of failures the act was designed to prevent had averaged roughly £2 million a year in the eight years before the act became law.

Intervention Often Does Not Work

Intervention often does not achieve its goal. We can set up a bureaucracy to perform a particular task. But there is no guarantee that it will be successful. Regulations may be ignored because they are not effectively enforced. As we shall see, when regulations are onerous and costly, there is a strong incentive to find ways around them. The financial system is particularly good at doing this. The behavior that results from trying to get around a regulation may ultimately be more harmful than the original problem the regulation was designed to address. Not only does intervention often fail to make things better, in some cases it can make things worse. We shall see many examples in the coming chapters.

Because intervention is costly and its effect uncertain, it simply may not be worthwhile. For example, suppose the loss to the economy from a particular type of market failure is $100 million a year. Costless and effective intervention could rectify the failure and add $100 million of value to the economy. However, suppose the intervention is only partly effective, reducing the loss to $50 million, and that the cost of intervention is $200 million. Then intervention leaves the economy $150 million the poorer. In this case, we would be better off living with the market failure rather than trying to correct it.

A balanced approach to government intervention weighs government failure against market failure: only when the cost of intervention is small and the benefit large is interference with the free market a good idea. The basic rule for government intervention is the same as the basic rule for medicine: first, do no harm.

SUMMARY

- A loan benefits both the parties to the transaction and the economy as a whole. However, if the costs of making the loan exceed the gain, the loan is not worthwhile and will not be made.
- The financial system reduces transactions costs and increases the number of worthwhile loans. It is efficient, in terms of lending, if the sum total of the gains from lending is as large as possible.
- Three conditions must be satisfied if lending is to be efficient: pricing must be competitive; transactions costs must be minimized; and the financial system must be integrated.
- Inefficiencies create profit opportunities, which provide an incentive for actions that tend to remove the inefficiencies.
- The meanings of efficiency in payments and efficiency in trade in risk parallel the meaning of efficiency in lending. The same three conditions must be satisfied to attain efficiency.
- The financial system is efficient when the sum of all the gains from all the system's activities is as large as possible.
- Economies of scale and natural monopoly are forms of market failure that can lead to insufficient competition.
- Government intervention to promote competition and to lower costs may be possible.
- Financial systems are subject to three forms of instability—panics, crashes, and price-level instability. Composition problems play a role in all of them.
- Composition problems and excessive risk-taking are a form of market failure known as an externality. The existence of externalities may justify government intervention.
- Governments may promote stability through regulation. They may also promote it by setting up institutions that strengthen the financial system.
- There may be a trade-off between efficiency and stability.
- The government also intervenes in the financial system for reasons of social policy and to protect poorly informed consumers.
- Government action, too, is subject to failure. Governments often serve special interests including their own. Intervention is costly, and often ineffective.

DISCUSSION QUESTIONS

1. Here are the average rates on bank loans in various cities in the 1890s:

Boston	3.8%	New York	4.4%
Richmond	6.0%	Atlanta	8.0%
Chicago	5.7%	Kansas City	6.9%
Denver	10.0%	San Francisco	6.2%

What are some possible explanations for these differences? What do they say about the efficiency of the U.S. financial system at the time? What sort of profit opportunities do these numbers represent? How might someone exploit such opportunities?

2. Michael Milken was instrumental in setting up a market for "junk bonds" (high-yield, high-risk bonds) in the 1980s. This market provided finance to many new companies otherwise unable to raise long-term funds. Milken became notorious for the hundreds of millions of dollars a year he earned for doing this, and he eventually went to prison for violations of securities laws. Can you make an argument to justify his earnings?

3. Russia is in the process of building a financial system along Western lines. What general advice

would you give the Russians in doing this? What should they expect to be the benefits of a good financial system?

4. Consider the example in the chapter in which San Miguel Bank helps to integrate the financial system by opening a branch in York. Who benefits from this? Who loses? Do the gains outweigh the losses? How might the losers use the political process to prevent the move? What arguments would you expect them to make? Discuss the merits of these arguments.

5. Based on our discussion in Chapter 2 of financial technology, can you think of reasons why economies of scale are widespread in the financial system? How might such economies of scale create barriers to entry?

6. Financial instability is partly the result of externalities. Can you think of any private arrangements that could be made, without government help, to deal with some of these problems?

KEY TERMS

gain from lending
efficiency in lending
competitive pricing
integration
efficiency of the financial system
economies of scale
concentrated industry
barrier to entry
natural monopoly
market failure
antitrust laws
regulated monopoly
nationalization

banking panic
securities market crash
inflation
deflation
hyperinflation
composition problems
externality
Glass–Steagall Act of 1933
investment banks
Bank Holding Company Act of 1956
lender of last resort
central bank

Federal Reserve Banks (the Fed)
Federal Deposit Insurance Corporation (FDIC)
deregulation
asymmetric information
Consumer Credit Protection (Truth-in-Lending) Act of 1968
Equal Credit Opportunity Act of 1974
Community Reinvestment Act of 1977
government failure

CHAPTER 4

INTEREST RATES,
EXCHANGE RATES,
AND SECURITY PRICES

When you finish this chapter you will understand:

- How to calculate the value of a security
- How to compare yields on different securities
- How changes in market interest rates or exchange rates can be the source of loss or gain

Much of what banks, futures markets, and other financial institutions do involves prom- ises of future payment. They accept promises, make promises, and trade promises. Changes in the value of these promises are therefore of great consequence to them. A fall in values can be a danger: for example, a fall in values led to the collapse of the savings and loans. A rise in values can be a boon: a rise in values had much to do with the im- provement in the situation of the commercial banks in the early 1990s.

The value of promises of future payment depends on interest rates and on exchange rates. Therefore, to understand the risks financial institutions face, we need to understand how the value of promises of future payment change in response to changes in interest rates, changes in exchange rates, and changes in the value of money. That is what we shall learn in this chapter.

We begin by examining the relationship between interest rates and the value of promises of future payment. We look first at promises of a single payment and then at promises of multiple payments. We then see how fluctuations in interest rates affect their value. We then look at how exchange rates affect the value of promised payments. We conclude by examining how changes in the value of money affect the value of promised payments

PRICING SECURITIES PROMISING A SINGLE PAYMENT

present value
Value today of an amount due in the future.

We begin with a promise of a single payment. The **present value** of such a promised payment is the amount you would give up now for the right to receive it. For example, consider a bank CD that promises to pay $10,000 in one year's time. How much is it worth? How much would you give the bank today in exchange for it?

Suppose that banks are offering 10% on 1-year CDs. If you deposit $1,000 now, at the end of a year you will receive

$$\$1,000 \times (1 + 0.10) = \$1,100$$

That is, the $1,000 is multiplied by 1 (for repayment of the principal) plus 0.10 (for the interest).

In general, if you put the amount P into the bank and the annual interest rate is i, at the end of the year you will have

$$A = P(1 + i) \qquad [4.1]$$

future value
Value at a time in the future, including accumulated interest, of an amount invested earlier.

The amount you receive at the end of the year, A, is called the **future value** of the amount P at an annual interest rate of i.[1]

We can rearrange Equation 4.1 to read

$$P = \frac{A}{(1 + i)} \qquad [4.2]$$

The amount P is the amount you would have to put in the bank today, at an interest rate of i, to have A at the end of the year. That is, P is the *present value* of A at an interest rate of i.

We can use Equation 4.2 to answer our original question. The value of a promised payment is just its present value. That is,

$$P = \frac{\$10,000}{(1 + 0.10)} = \$9,092$$

You can see from Equations 4.1 and 4.2 that there is an inverse relationship between present value and future value. If the present value of $10,000 at an interest rate of 10% is

---

[1] Notice that in this formula the interest rate is always expressed as a decimal fraction, not as a percentage.

$9,092, then the future value of $9,092 at an interest rate of 10% is $10,000. The present value of $10,000 at an interest rate of 10% is just the amount that would grow into $10,000 (have a future value of $10,000) in one year's time, at this interest rate.

Multiple Periods and Compounding

We can extend the idea of present value to a payment promised after several years. For example, what is the present value at 10% of a $10,000 CD due 2 years from now?

Suppose you leave the amount P in the bank for 2 years at an interest rate of i. At the end of the first year, you will have $P(1 + i)$. At the end of the second year you will have

$$A = P(1 + i)(1 + i) = P(1 + i)^2 \qquad [4.3]$$

The amount A is the future value of P after two periods at an interest rate of i.

Notice that in the second year you earn interest not only on the original amount, but also on the interest you earned in the *first* year. This earning of interest on interest is called **compounding**.

compounding
Calculation of interest on interest already earned.

We can rearrange Equation 4.3 into a present value formula, just as we did with Equation 4.1:

$$P = \frac{A}{(1 + i)^2} \qquad [4.4]$$

Where P is the present value of an amount A due in 2 years if the annual interest rate is i.

Applying this formula to our 2-year CD, its present value is

$$P = \frac{\$10,000}{(1.10)^2} = \$8,264$$

It is easy to extend the future value and present value formulas to any number of periods:

$$A = P(1 + i)(1 + i) \cdots (1 + i) = P(1 + i)^t \qquad [4.5]$$

zero-coupon bond (zero)
Security of long maturity promising a single payment.

and

$$P = \frac{A}{(1 + i)^t} \qquad [4.6]$$

where t *is* the number of periods.

EXAMPLE 4.1

What should you pay for a $1 million, 10-year **zero-coupon bond (zero)**? A zero is a bond that promises a single payment at maturity. This zero promises a payment of $1 million in 10 years time. Suppose that the appropriate interest rate is 9%.

Applying Equation 4.6, we have

$$P = \frac{\$1,000,000}{(1.09)^{10}} = \$1,000,000\,[0.4224] = \$422,400$$

You can do this calculation with a calculator or you can use a present-value table to find the present value factor—the term in brackets.[2]

The present value formula, Equation 4.6, expresses the relationship among three variables—A, P, and i. Given any two, we can calculate the third. Given A and i, we can solve for P, as we have just done. Alternatively, given P and A we can calculate i:

$$i = \left(\frac{A}{P}\right)^{1/t} - 1 \qquad\qquad [4.7]$$

We can use Equation 4.7 to solve problems like the following:

EXAMPLE 4.2

A 2-year zero, with a face value of $10,000 is selling for $8,116.22. That is, its **market price** is $8,116.22. What interest rate would you earn if you held it to maturity? Applying Equation 4.7, we write

$$i = \sqrt{\frac{\$10,000}{\$8,116.22}} - 1 = 0.11$$

That is, you would earn a rate of 11%.

market price
Price at which a security can be bought and sold.

market yield
The interest rate at which the present value of payments promised by a security equals its market price.

The interest rate you would earn by buying a security at its market price and holding it to maturity is called its **market yield**. Note that the market price and the market yield are alternative, but entirely equivalent, ways of describing the value of a promised future payment. Suppose you want to know the value of a particular zero. If you are told its market price, you can easily calculate its market yield. If you are told its market yield, you can easily calculate its market price.

The Compounding Period and the Effective Annual Rate

Interest is often calculated on the basis of some unit of time other than a year. For example, a bank might offer 6-month CDs at an annual percentage rate of 12%, compounded monthly, giving an effective annual rate of 12.68%. What does all this mean?

---

[2] If you do the calculation on a calculator rather than by using a crude table, you will find the answer with greater accuracy: it is $422,410.81.

compounding period
Period over which interest is calculated.

The **compounding period** is the period over which interest is calculated. For this CD, the compounding period is one month. At the end of the first month, the bank calculates how much interest it owes you; at the end of the second month, it calculates again how much interest it owes you, this time including interest on the interest you earned in the first month. That is, the interest is compounded monthly.

periodic interest rate
Rate per compounding period.

The **periodic interest rate** is the interest rate per compounding period. To find the periodic rate, divide the **annual percentage rate (APR)** by the number of compounding periods per year. That is,

$$\text{periodic interest rate} = \text{APR/periods per year} \qquad [4.8]$$

annual percentage rate (APR)
A stated rate of interest from which the periodic interest rate is calculated.

For our CD, the compounding period is one month and the APR is 12%. Since there are 12 months in a year, divide 12% by 12 for a periodic rate of 1%.

If you put $1,000 into such a CD, then after the first month the bank will owe you

$$\$1,000 \times (1.01) = \$1,010$$

after the second month it will owe you

$$\$1,010 \times (1.01) = \$1,000 \times (1.01)^2 = \$1,021$$

and so on.

To know how much you will have after any number of months, just use the future value formula, Equation 4.5. The amount you put into the account is P, the *periodic* interest rate is i, and the number of periods is t.

How does this CD compare to the 1-year CD offered by the bank across the street? That CD offers an APR of 11.9% and weekly compounding. To compare the two CDs, we need to put them on a common basis. The best way to do this by comparing the **effective annual rate (EAR)** on each.

effective annual rate (EAR)
Interest accrued at the end of a year as a percentage of the principal amount.

The EAR is the annual interest rate you would earn if you left your money in either CD for one whole year. Even though the first CD has a maturity of only 6 months, we calculate what it *would* yield over a whole year for the sake of comparison.

At the end of a year, compounding monthly at a monthly rate of 1%, the first CD would give us

$$\$1,000 \times (1.01)^{12} = \$1,126.83$$

The effective annual rate is therefore

$$\frac{\$1,126.83 - \$1,000}{\$1,000} = 0.1268, \text{ or } 12.68\%$$

For the second CD, the periodic rate is

$$\frac{11.9\%}{52} = 0.229\%$$

At the end of a year, therefore, we would have

$$\$1,000 \times (1.00229)^{52} = \$1,126.31$$

The effective annual rate on this second CD is therefore

$$\frac{\$1,126.31 - \$1,000}{\$1,000} = 0.1263, \text{ or } 12.63\%$$

slightly lower than that on the first CD. The more frequent compounding on the second does not quite make up for the lower APR.

Note that the APR alone does not tell us how much we can expect to earn on each CD and that it is not therefore a good basis for comparison. Instead, that we need the effective annual rate. The only economic meaning of the APR is in calculating the periodic rate.

We can summarize the relationship between the periodic rate and the effective annual rate in the following formula:

$$(1 + \text{periodic rate})^{\text{number of periods per year}} = 1 + \text{effective annual rate} \qquad [4.9]$$

Alternatively, we can rearrange Equation 4.9 to calculate the periodic rate from the effective annual rate:

$$1 + \text{periodic rate} = (1 + \text{effective annual rate})^{1/\text{number of periods per year}} \qquad [4.10]$$

EXAMPLE 4.3

Suppose you are offered a $10,000, 3-month T-bill selling for $9,764.54 and a 1-year bill selling for $9,500. Which offers a higher yield? To answer this, we need to calculate the effective annual rates on the two bills.

For the 3-month bill, the interest rate earned is

$$\frac{\$10,000 - \$9,764.54}{\$9,764.54} = \frac{\$235.46}{\$9,764.54} = 0.024, \text{ or } 2.4\%$$

The 2.4% will be earned over a period of 3 months: the 2.4% is a periodic rate. To compare this bill to the other we need to convert the periodic rate into an effective annual rate. To do this, we use Equation 4.9:

$$\text{effective annual rate} = (1 + 0.024)^4 - 1 = 0.0995, \text{ or } 9.95\%$$

The interest rate on the 1-year bill is

$$\frac{\$500}{\$9,500} = 0.053, \text{ or } 5.3\%$$

Since this is earned over a period of a year it is already an effective annual rate.

PRICING SECURITIES PROMISING MULTIPLE PAYMENTS

So far we have looked at securities that promise only a single future payment. It is fairly straightforward to extend what we have learned to securities that promise multiple future payments.

Bonds with Annual Coupons

Consider a 2-year, $1 million Treasury bond with 10% annual coupons. It promises a coupon payment of $100,000 at the end of 1 year, another such payment at the end of 2 years, plus payment of the $1 million principal at the end of 2 years.

We can think of this bond as being equivalent to a combination of two T-bills—the first a $100,000 1-year bill; the second a $1,100,000 2-year bill. The bond is equivalent to the combination of these two bills in that it promises to pay exactly what they would pay.

Suppose the market yield on 1-year T-bills is 7% and on 2-year T-bills, 8%.[3] Then the market price of the payment due at the end of the first year (equivalent to a 1-year bill) is

$$P = \frac{\$100,000}{(1.07)} = \$93,457.94$$

and the market price of the payment due at the end of the second year (equivalent to a two-year bill) is

$$P = \frac{1,100,000}{(1.08)^2} = \$943,072.70$$

Could the market price of the bond differ from the sum of the market prices of its two component parts? That is, could it be other than the following?

$$P = \$93,457.94 + \$943,072.70 = \$1,036,530.64$$

If the market price of the bond were more than this, you could "construct" the 2-year bond more cheaply by buying the two constituent parts. That is, you could buy a 1-year T-bill and a 2-year T-bill that together promised exactly the same payments as the 2-year bond, and pay less for them than you would pay for the bond itself. Since no one would buy the bond in these circumstances, prices would adjust until the price of the bond was no longer higher than the sum of the prices of the two bills.

If the market price of the bond were less than $1,036,530.64, and if you could somehow buy the bond and sell off the two parts separately, you could do so at a profit. The increased supply of 1-year and 2-year bills would drive down their price until the sum of their prices equaled the price of the 1-year bond. At that point it would no longer be

---

[3] There are in fact no T-bills of maturity longer than a year. However, as we shall see, there do exist "synthetic" T-bills, known as "strips" at most maturities.

TREASURY STRIPS

B efore 1984, Treasury zeros were not available at maturities of more than a year. However, for reasons we shall see later in the chapter, many investors prefer zeros to ordinary coupon bonds. The existence of this unsatisfied demand created a profit opportunity that financial innovators were quick to exploit.

In 1982 Merrill Lynch began to offer zeros collateralized by a portfolio of government securities. These Treasury Investment Growth Receipts (TIGRs) worked like this. Merrill would buy $1 billion of 30-year Treasury bonds with an 8% annual coupon. These bonds promised coupon payments of $40 million every 6 months plus a $1 billion principal on maturity. Merrill could sell $40 million of 6-month TIGRs: $40 million of 1-year TIGRs, and so on out to 30 years, plus an extra $1 billion at 30 years. These TIGRs would all be completely backed by the payments due to Merrill from the Treasury. Merrill's innovation was soon imitated by Salomon (CATS) and Lehman (LIONS).

In 1984 the Treasury announced its own program, STRIPS (Separate Trading of Registered Interest and Principal of Securities), which allows separate ownership and trading of the coupon and principal payments that make up a Treasury security. The Treasury hoped that this program would increase the appeal of its securities, allowing it to borrow at a lower interest rate.

stripping
Breaking up a security that promise multiple payments into constituent parts.

Breaking up a security that promises multiple payments into constituent parts is called **stripping** the security. Treasury strips have been enormously popular: some $120 billion of Treasury securities had been stripped by 1991. The success of strips in the United States has led to emulation in other countries. In 1991, the French government authorized a market in stripped government securities.

profitable to break up 1-year bonds. Treasury bonds are indeed broken down in just this way to create longer term bills (see "Treasury Strips").[4]

We can generalize this argument to price any security by breaking it down into its constituent single payments. For example, suppose a bond promises equal annual coupon payments of C. Using our formula for the market price of a single payment, if the market yield on m-year bills is i_m, where m is any number of years, then the market price of the coupon due in m years is

$$\frac{C}{(1 + i_m)^m}$$

This is just the present value of the coupon payment calculated at the appropriate market yield.

---

[4] In practice, the price of the whole does not exactly equal the sum of the prices of the parts. The reasons include differences in liquidity and in trading costs between strips and bonds as well as the stripper's margin. Transactions costs again!

The present value, and hence the market price, of a t-year bond with face value A and coupon C is just the sum of the present values of the various payments, with each present value calculated at the appropriate market yield:

$$P = \frac{C}{1 + i_1} + \frac{C}{(1 + i_2)^2} + \cdots + \frac{(C + A)}{(1 + i_t)^t} \qquad [4.11]$$

EXAMPLE 4.4

If the market yield on bills is the same 8% at all maturities, what is the market price of a $1,000, 3-year bond with 11% annual coupons?

The sum of the present values of the three payments (the total of $1,110 at the end of year 3 counting as a single payment) is

$$P = \frac{\$110}{(1.08)} + \frac{\$110}{(1.08)^2} + \frac{\$1,110}{(1.08)^3} = \$1,077.31$$

Bonds with a Coupon Period of Less than a Year

Bonds generally have coupons due at intervals shorter than a year. How are we to price such securities?

EXAMPLE 4.5

If the market yield on bills is the same 8% at all maturities, how much should you pay for a 20-year $1,000 Treasury bond with an coupon rate of 10% and semiannual coupons?

The value of the bond is the sum of the present values of all the payments due. The coupon payments each year equal the coupon rate, 10%, times the face value of $1,000 or $100. Since coupons are semiannual, the $100 is split into two equal payments of $50. So the bond promises to pay $50 every 6 months for 20 years plus a single payment of $1,000 at the end.

To apply Equation 4.11, we must change our unit of time from a year to a half-year. This gives $t = 40$, $C = \$50$, and $A = \$1,000$.

All that remains is the interest rates. We need to use Equation 4.10 to convert the 8% market yield on bills (an effective annual rate) into a 6-month periodic rate:

$$1 + \text{periodic rate} = (1.08)^{1/2} = 1.039$$

So $i = 0.039$.

Substituting these numbers into Equation 4.11, we get

$$P = \frac{\$50}{(1.039)} + \frac{\$50}{(1.039)^2} + \cdots + \frac{\$50}{(1.039)^{39}} + \frac{\$1,050}{(1.039)^{40}} = \$1,221.00$$

Amortized Loans

amortized loan

Security that promises a series of equal payments.

A bond promises a series of relatively small coupon payments, with a large payment of face value on maturity. Some other securities promise a series of equal payments until maturity. Such securities are called **amortized loans** or, if the payments are annual, **annuities**. Most consumer loans, such as home mortgages and automobile loans, are amortized loans.

The market price of an amortized loan, is just a special case of Equation 4.11, with A set to zero:

annuity

An amortized loan with annual payments.

$$P = \frac{C}{1 + i_1} + \frac{C}{(1 + i)^2} + \cdots + \frac{C}{(1 + i_t)^t} \qquad [4.12]$$

If the interest rates are all the same, the formula simplifies:

$$P = \frac{C}{(1 + i)} + \frac{C}{(1 + i)^2} + \cdots + \frac{C}{(1 + i)^t} = C\left[\frac{1}{i}\left(1 - \frac{1}{(1 + i)^t}\right)\right] \qquad [4.13]$$

The term in brackets is called an *annuity factor*.

EXAMPLE 4.6

An insurance company offers to pay you an annuity of $10,000 a year for 10 years. If the appropriate interest rate is 7%, how much should you be willing to pay for the annuity?

We can use Equation 4.13 directly, using the appropriate annuity factor from a published table. The entry for 10 periods and a rate of 7% is 7.024. So the value of the annuity is

$$\$10,000 \times 7.024 = \$70,240$$

We can also use the annuity formula in reverse to calculate the size of the payment required to pay off a loan in equal installments.

EXAMPLE 4.7

You wish to borrow $100,000 to buy a house and to repay the loan in equal monthly installments over 30 years. If the APR on mortgage loans is 9%, how much must you pay each month?

The relevant period is one month. The periodic interest rate is % or 0.75%. We need to find the value of C that satisfies

$$\$100,000 = C\left[\frac{1}{0.0075}\left(1 - \frac{1}{(1.0075)^{360}}\right)\right]$$

The answer is $C = \$804.62$.

perpetuity

Annuity that is
payable forever.
There is a special type of annuity called a **perpetuity**. This is an annuity that never ends. Alternatively, you could think of it as a bond that pays coupons forever, with payment of the face value deferred indefinitely.

EXAMPLE 4.8

What is the present value of a perpetuity with annual payments of $500 each, beginning a year from now and going on forever, if the annual interest rate is 10%?

With a little ingenuity, we can use the formula for the present value of an annuity, Equation 4.13, to get an answer. Notice that the annuity factor includes the term $1/(1 + i)^t$. As t gets very large, the value of this term approaches zero, so the value of the expression in square brackets approaches $1/i$. Hence, the present value of a perpetuity with payment C, if the interest rate is i, is

$$P = \frac{C}{i} \qquad [4.14]$$

In our case $P = \$500/0.10 = \$5,000$.

Perpetuities do exist in the real world. The best known is the Consol—a security issued by the British government in the early 1800s to consolidate the debt of the Napoleonic wars. The market yield on a perpetuity is particularly easy to calculate: it is simply the annual payment divided by the market price.

Market Yield on a Security Promising Multiple Payments

With securities that promise a single payment, the pricing formula, Equation 4.6, can be used in either direction. Given the market yield, it can be used to calculate the market price. Alternatively, given the market price, it can be used to calculate the market yield.

With the corresponding formula for securities that promise multiple payments, Equation 4.11, it is not that simple. Given the market yields at all maturities, it is straightforward to calculate the market price. However, given the market price, there is no way we can solve for the t different market yields.

**yield to
maturity (YTM)**

Single interest
rate at which the
present value of a
bond's coupon
and principal payments equals its
market price.
What if we replace these many rates with a single interest rate, and then solve for that single rate? That is, solve for the value of i that satisfies[5]

$$P = \frac{C}{(1 + i)} + \frac{C}{(1 + i)^2} + \cdots + \frac{(C + A)}{(1 + i)^t} \qquad [4.15]$$

The periodic rate that satisfies this equation must then be turned into an effective annual rate. That rate is called the **yield to maturity (YTM)**.

---
[5] Equation 4.15 is derived from Equation 4.11 by replacing i_1, i_2, and i_t in the denominators with just plain i.

EXAMPLE 4.9

What is the yield to maturity of a 6%, 10-year bond with semiannual coupons if its market price is $944?

The bond pays $30 semiannual coupons and there are twenty 6-month periods to maturity. The 6-month periodic rate is the value of i that satisfies

$$\$944 = \frac{\$30}{(1 + i)} + \frac{\$30}{(1 + i)^2} + \cdots + \frac{\$1,030}{(1 + i)^{20}}$$

Solving an equation like this is difficult: you generally need a financial calculator or a computer program. In this case the answer is 3.5%.

To turn this into an effective annual rate, solve for i from

$$1 + i = (1.035)^2$$

The answer is 7.12%. This is the yield to maturity.

The market yield on a bond is defined as the yield to maturity calculated from its market price. Although this does give us a number we can call the market yield, we shall see later that there are important differences in interpretation between this number and the market yield on a security promising a single payment.

Because calculating the average annual yield to maturity is difficult, market participants often use an approximation. The **approximate yield to maturity (AYTM)** is

approximate yield to maturity (AYTM)

An approximation to the YTM calculated from a simple formula.

$$i \cong \frac{\dfrac{A - P}{n} + AC}{\dfrac{A + P}{2}} \qquad\qquad [4.16]$$

where n = number of years to maturity
         AC = total annual coupons
              $\cong$ signifies "approximately equal to"

EXAMPLE 4.9 (*continued*)

What is the approximate yield to maturity of the bond in the initial part of this example?

Applying Equation 4.16 to our 10-year bond, we find that n is 10, AC is $60, A is $1,000, and P is $944. So

$$i \cong \frac{\dfrac{\$1,000 - \$944}{10} + \$60}{\dfrac{\$1,000 + \$944}{2}} = 6.75\%$$

Since the exact number is 7.12%, the estimate is not very precise.

selling at a discount
Selling at a price below face value.

In this example, the market price of the bond in question is *below* its face value. The bond is said to be **selling at a discount**. If the bond were selling *above* its face value it would be said to be **selling at a premium**. If the bond were selling at *exactly* its face value it would be said to be **selling at par**.

selling at a premium
Selling at a price above face value.

Generally, if the market yield is above the coupon rate, a bond sells at a discount. If the market yield is below the coupon rate, it sells at a premium. If the market yield equals the coupon rate, it sells at par. We can demonstrate this with the formula for the AYTM.

selling at par
Selling at price equal to face value.

Suppose the bond were selling at a premium, with a price of, say, $1,050. Its market yield would be approximately

$$i \cong \frac{\dfrac{\$1,000 - \$1,050}{10} + \$60}{\dfrac{\$1,000 + \$1,050}{2}} = 5.37\%$$

This is below the coupon rate of 6%.

Suppose the bond were selling at par, with a price of $1,000. Its market yield would be approximately

$$i \cong \frac{\dfrac{\$1,000 - \$1,000}{10} + \$60}{\dfrac{\$1,000 + \$1,000}{2}} = 6\%$$

This equals the coupon rate.

Application: Understanding Treasury Listings

We can apply what we have learned to understand the listings of prices and yields of Treasury securities that appear in the financial press. Exhibit 4.1 shows the listing that appeared in *The Wall Street Journal* on June 1, 2001.

Bonds and notes are coupon securities: the only difference between them is maturity. Notes have an original maturity of 2 to 10 years; bonds, of over 10 years. Notes are indicated by an *n* after the maturity.

bid price
Price that dealers will pay for a security.

The first column gives the annual coupon rate. Coupons are semiannual, so the coupon payment is at half the annual rate. The next column gives the maturity date. Some issues have a range for a maturity date—for example, the bond with a maturity listed as Feb 02–07. Such issues are callable: the Treasury may redeem them at face value, whenever it pleases, beginning with the first date.[6]

asked price
Price at which dealers will sell a security.

The next two columns give the price dealers will pay for this issue (the **bid price**) and the price at which they will sell (the **asked price**). Bid and asked prices are quoted as a

---

[6] The Treasury stopped issuing callable bonds in 1984, after strips became popular: callable bonds cannot be stripped.

EXHIBIT 4.1 Treasuries Listing, Friday June 1, 2001

TREASURY BONDS, NOTES & BILLS

Friday, June 1, 2001

Representative Over-the-Counter quotation based on transactions of $1 million or more.

Treasury bond, note and bill quotes are as of mid-afternoon. Colons in bid-and-asked quotes represent 32nds; 101:01 means 101 1/32. Net changes in 32nds. n-Treasury note. i-Inflation-Indexed issue. Treasury bill quotes in hundredths, quoted on terms of a rate of discount. Days to maturity calculated from settlement date. All yields are to maturity and based on the asked quote. Latest 13-week and 26-week bills are boldfaced. For bonds callable prior to maturity, yields are computed to the earliest call date for issues quoted above par and to the maturity date for issues below par. *-When issued.

Source: Telerate/Cantor Fitzgerald

U.S. Treasury strips as of 3 p.m. Eastern time, also based on transactions of $1 million or more. Colons in bid-and-asked quotes represent 32nds; 99:01 means 99 1/32. Net changes in 32nds. Yields calculated on the asked quotation. ci-stripped coupon interest. bp-Treasury bond, stripped principal. np-Treasury note, stripped principal. For bonds callable prior to maturity, yields are computed to the earliest call date for issues quoted above par and to the maturity date for issues below par.

Source: Bear, Stearns & Co. via Street Software Technology Inc.

GOVT. BOND & NOTES

RATE	MATURITY MO/YR	BID	ASKED	CHG.	ASKED YLD.
5¾	Jun 01n	100:04	100:06	....	3.06
6⅝	Jun 01n	100:06	100:08	....	3.05
5½	Jul 01n	100:09	100:11	....	3.24
6⅝	Jul 01n	100:15	100:17	....	3.16
7⅞	Aug 01n	100:26	100:28	− 1	3.37
13⅜	Aug 01	101:30	102:00	− 1	3.13
5½	Aug 01n	100:13	100:15	+ 1	3.47
6½	Aug 01n	100:20	100:22	....	3.54
5⅝	Sep 01n	100:19	100:21	....	3.53
6⅜	Sep 01n	100:26	100:28	....	3.59
5⅞	Oct 01n	100:26	100:28	− 1	3.66
6¼	Oct 01n	101:00	101:02	....	3.57
7½	Nov 01n	101:20	101:22	− 1	3.64
15¾	Nov 01	105:10	105:12	− 1	3.47
5⅞	Nov 01n	101:00	101:02	− 1	3.66
6⅛	Dec 01n	101:09	101:11	− 1	3.72
6¼	Jan 02n	101:18	101:20	− 1	3.72
6⅜	Jan 02n	101:21	101:23	− 1	3.70
14¼	Feb 02	107:06	107:08	− 1	3.63
6¼	Feb 02n	101:25	101:27	− 1	3.69
6½	Feb 02n	101:31	102:01	− 1	3.68
6½	Mar 02n	102:00	102:02	− 1	3.92
6⅝	Mar 02n	102:04	102:06	....	3.89
6⅜	Apr 02n	102:02	102:04	− 1	3.96
6⅝	Apr 02n	102:09	102:11	− 1	3.96
7½	May 02n	103:06	103:08	− 1	3.96
6½	May 02n	102:12	102:14	− 1	3.96
6⅝	May 02n	102:15	102:17	− 2	3.99
6¼	Jun 02n	102:07	102:09	− 2	4.05
6⅜	Jun 02n	102:11	102:13	− 2	4.05
3⅝	Jul 02i	102:15	102:16	+ 1	1.35
6	Jul 02n	102:02	102:04	− 3	4.10
6¼	Jul 02n	102:11	102:13	− 2	4.09
6⅜	Aug 02n	102:17	102:19	− 2	4.13
6⅛	Aug 02n	102:09	102:11	− 2	4.16
6¼	Aug 02n	102:13	102:15	− 3	4.18
5⅞	Sep 02n	102:02	102:04	− 4	4.20
6	Sep 02n	102:07	102:09	− 4	4.20
5¾	Oct 02n	101:30	102:00	− 5	4.26
11⅝	Nov 02	110:02	110:06	− 6	4.28
5⅝	Nov 02n	101:25	101:27	− 5	4.33
5¾	Nov 02n	101:31	102:01	− 6	4.33
5⅛	Dec 02n	101:02	101:04	− 6	4.37
5⅝	Dec 02n	101:26	101:28	− 8	4.38
4¾	Jan 03n	100:13	100:15	− 9	4.45
5½	Jan 03n	101:19	101:21	− 9	4.45
6¼	Feb 03n	102:25	102:27	− 9	4.49
10¾	Feb 03	109:31	110:03	− 9	4.50
4⅝	Feb 03n	100:04	100:06	− 9	4.51
5½	Feb 03n	101:18	101:20	− 10	4.51
4¼	Mar 03n	99:14	99:16	− 16	4.54
5½	Mar 03n	101:18	101:20	− 11	4.56
8⅛	May 21	125:22	125:28	+ 12	5.90
8⅛	Aug 21	125:26	126:00	+ 12	5.90
8	Nov 21	124:17	124:23	+ 12	5.90
7¼	Aug 22	115:30	116:02	+ 12	5.91
7⅝	Nov 22	120:17	120:23	+ 13	5.91
7⅛	Feb 23	114:19	114:23	+ 13	5.91
6¼	Aug 23	104:04	104:06	+ 12	5.91
7½	Nov 24	120:04	120:08	+ 19	5.89
7⅝	Feb 25	121:24	121:30	+ 18	5.90
6⅞	Aug 25	112:12	112:16	+ 18	5.90
6	Feb 26	101:11	101:13	+ 19	5.89
6¾	Aug 26	111:04	111:08	+ 21	5.89
6½	Nov 26	108:00	108:02	+ 21	5.88
6⅝	Feb 27	109:26	109:28	+ 24	5.88
6⅜	Aug 27	106:20	106:22	+ 24	5.87
6⅛	Nov 27	103:12	103:14	+ 24	5.87
3⅝	Apr 28i	103:04	103:05	+ 3	3.44
5½	Aug 28	95:06	95:08	+ 25	5.85
5¼	Nov 28	91:26	91:28	+ 25	5.85
5¼	Feb 29	91:31	92:01	+ 25	5.83
3⅞	Apr 29i	107:26	107:27	+ 2	3.44
6⅛	Aug 29	104:05	104:07	+ 31	5.82
6¼	May 30	106:15	106:16	+ 29	5.78
5⅜	Feb 31	95:09	95:10	+ 28	5.70

U.S. TREASURY STRIPS

MATURITY		TYPE	BID	ASKED	CHG.	ASKED YLD.
Aug	01	ci	99:09	99:09	+ 1	3.75
Aug	01	np	99:09	99:09	....	3.72
Nov	01	ci	98:13	98:14	....	3.61
Nov	01	np	98:13	98:13	....	3.67
Feb	02	ci	97:23	97:24	....	3.31
May	02	ci	96:15	96:15	....	3.85
May	02	np	96:16	96:16	....	3.81
Aug	02	ci	95:18	95:19	....	3.82
Aug	02	np	95:12	95:12	....	3.99
Nov	02	ci	95:04	95:05	....	3.48
Feb	03	ci	93:06	93:07	....	4.18
Feb	03	np	93:05	93:06	....	4.20
May	03	ci	92:05	92:07	....	4.21
Jul	03	ci	91:16	91:18	....	4.23
Aug	03	ci	91:03	91:05	....	4.26
Aug	03	np	90:30	91:00	....	4.35
Nov	03	ci	90:13	90:15	+ 1	4.15
Nov	03	np	89:25	89:27	+ 1	4.44
Jan	04	ci	89:02	89:04	+ 1	4.46
Feb	04	ci	88:21	88:23	+ 1	4.49
Feb	04	np	88:20	88:22	....	4.50
May	04	ci	87:14	87:17	....	4.58
May	04	np	87:09	87:11	....	4.65
Jul	04	ci	86:23	86:26	....	4.60
Aug	04	ci	86:10	86:12	....	4.63

MAT.		TYPE	BID	ASKED	CHG.	ASKED YLD.
Feb	17	ci	39:01	39:07	+ 14	6.05
May	17	ci	38:14	38:19	+ 14	6.06
May	17	bp	38:14	38:19	+ 14	6.06
Aug	17	ci	37:25	37:31	+ 14	6.07
Aug	17	bp	37:28	38:02	+ 14	6.05
Nov	17	ci	37:06	37:11	+ 14	6.08
Feb	18	ci	36:17	36:22	+ 14	6.09
May	18	ci	35:31	36:05	+ 14	6.09
May	18	bp	36:00	36:06	+ 14	6.09
Aug	18	ci	35:15	35:21	+ 14	6.09
Nov	18	ci	34:30	35:04	+ 14	6.09
Nov	18	bp	34:29	35:03	+ 14	6.09
Feb	19	ci	34:11	34:16	+ 14	6.10
Feb	19	bp	34:14	34:19	+ 14	6.09
May	19	ci	33:27	34:01	+ 14	6.10
Aug	19	ci	33:11	33:17	+ 14	6.10
Aug	19	bp	33:13	33:19	+ 14	6.09
Nov	19	ci	32:29	33:02	+ 14	6.09
Feb	20	ci	32:09	32:15	+ 13	6.11
Feb	20	bp	32:11	32:17	+ 13	6.10
May	20	ci	31:26	32:00	+ 13	6.11
May	20	bp	31:25	31:30	+ 13	6.11
Aug	20	ci	31:12	31:17	+ 13	6.10
Aug	20	bp	31:12	31:17	+ 13	6.10
Nov	20	ci	30:27	31:01	+ 13	6.11
Feb	21	ci	30:13	30:19	+ 13	6.11
Feb	21	bp	30:14	30:19	+ 13	6.10
May	21	ci	29:31	30:04	+ 13	6.11
May	21	bp	29:27	30:01	+ 13	6.13
Aug	21	ci	29:17	29:23	+ 13	6.10
Aug	21	bp	29:15	29:21	+ 13	6.11
Nov	21	ci	29:04	29:10	+ 13	6.09
Nov	21	bp	29:00	29:05	+ 13	6.12
Feb	22	ci	28:20	28:26	+ 13	6.11
May	22	ci	28:07	28:12	+ 13	6.11
Aug	22	ci	27:25	27:30	+ 13	6.11
Aug	22	bp	27:30	28:03	+ 13	6.08
Nov	22	ci	27:12	27:17	+ 13	6.11
Nov	22	bp	27:11	27:17	+ 13	6.11
Feb	23	ci	27:00	27:06	+ 13	6.09
Feb	23	bp	27:05	27:10	+ 13	6.07
May	23	ci	26:19	26:24	+ 13	6.10
Aug	23	ci	26:07	26:12	+ 13	6.09
Aug	23	bp	26:18	26:24	+ 13	6,03
Nov	23	ci	25:26	25:31	+ 13	6.10
Feb	24	ci	25:16	25:22	+ 13	6.08
May	24	ci	25:05	25:11	+ 13	6.07
Aug	24	ci	24:25	24:30	+ 13	6.07
Nov	24	ci	24:15	24:20	+ 13	6.07
Nov	24	bp	24:17	24:22	+ 13	6.05
Feb	25	ci	24:05	24:11	+ 13	6.05
Feb	25	bp	24:08	24:13	+ 13	6,04
May	25	ci	23:29	24:03	+ 13	6.03
Aug	25	ci	23:19	23:24	+ 13	6.03
Aug	25	bp	23:20	23:25	+ 13	6.02
Nov	25	ci	23:08	23:13	+ 13	6.03
Feb	26	ci	23:03	23:08	+ 14	5.99
Feb	26	bp	23:07	23:12	+ 14	5.97
May	26	ci	22:24	22:30	+ 14	5.99
Aug	26	ci	22:13	22:19	+ 14	5.99
Aug	26	bp	22:15	22:20	+ 14	5.99
Nov	26	ci	22:03	22:08	+ 13	5.99
Nov	26	bp	22:05	22:10	+ 13	5.98
Feb	27	ci	21:28	22:01	+ 13	5.97
Feb	27	bp	22:00	22:05	+ 14	5.95

Source: The Wall Street Journal, *June 1, 2001.*

EXHIBIT 4.1 *(continued)*

4	Apr 03n	99:22	99:23	+ 1	4.15
5¾	Apr 03n	102:02	102:04	− 12	4.57
10¾	May 03	111:06	111:10	− 15	4.60
4¼	May 03n	100:02	100:03	....	4.20
5½	May 03n	101:27	101:29	− 13	4.49
5⅜	Jun 03n	101:21	101:23	− 13	4.49
5¼	Aug 03n	101:13	101:15	− 13	4.54
5¾	Aug 03n	102:13	102:15	− 14	4.55
11⅛	Aug 03	113:15	113:19	− 13	4.55
4¼	Nov 03n	99:02	99:04	− 14	4.63
11⅞	Nov 03	116:12	116:16	− 15	4.66
4¾	Feb 04n	100:02	100:04	− 15	4.70
5⅞	Feb 04n	102:30	103:00	− 14	4.68
5¼	May 04n	101:10	101:12	− 13	4.74
7¼	May 04n	106:24	106:26	− 11	4.74
12⅜	May 04	120:16	120:22	− 12	4.76
6	Aug 04n	103:15	103:17	− 11	4.79
7¼	Aug 04n	107:05	107:07	− 11	4.79
13¾	Aug 04	126:00	126:06	− 13	4.82
5⅞	Nov 04n	103:05	103:07	− 9	4.85
7⅞	Nov 04n	109:13	109:15	− 9	4.86
11⅝	Nov 04	121:00	121:06	− 11	4.87
7½	Feb 05n	108:22	108:24	− 8	4.88
6½	May 05n	105:19	105:21	− 6	4.90
6¾	May 05n	106:13	106:15	− 5	4.92
12	May 05	124:29	125:03	− 8	4.92
6½	Aug 05n	105:25	105:27	− 5	4.94
10¾	Aug 05	121:13	121:19	− 4	4.99
5¾	Nov 05n	103:04	103:05	....	4.95
5⅞	Nov 05n	103:17	103:19	− 3	4.96
5⅝	Feb 06n	102:24	102:26	− 1	4.95
9⅜	Feb 06	118:03	118:07	− 1	4.98
4⅝	May 06n	98:20	98:21	....	4.93
6⅞	May 06n	108:00	108:02	+ 4	5.01
7	Jul 06n	108:13	108:15	+ 4	5.10
6½	Oct 06n	106:12	106:14	+ 5	5.11
3⅜	Jan 07i	102:05	102:06	+ 2	2.95
6¼	Feb 07n	105:11	105:13	+ 5	5.14
7⅝	Feb 02-07	102:10	102:12	+ 1	4,13
6⅝	May 07n	107:08	107:10	+ 4	5.18
6⅛	Aug 07n	104:24	104:26	+ 5	5.21
7⅞	Nov 02-07	104:26	104:28	+ 1	4.36
3⅝	Jan 08i	103:06	103:07	....	3.08
5½	Feb 08n	101:12	101:14	+ 6	5.24
5⅝	May 08n	101:31	102:01	+ 6	5.27
8⅜	Aug 03-08	107:27	107:29	+ 1	4.55
4¾	Nov 08n	96:16	96:18	+ 7	5.31
8¾	Nov 03-08	109:13	109:15	+ 2	4.61
3⅞	Jan 09i	104:19	104:20	+ 3	3.19
5½	May 09n	100:29	100:31	+ 8	5.35
9⅛	May 04-09	111:27	111:31	+ 4	4.72
6	Aug 09n	104:01	104:03	+ 8	5.37
10⅜	Nov 04-09	117:04	117:08	+ 4	4.87
4¼	Jan 10i	107:15	107:16	+ 4	3.24
6½	Feb 10n	107:17	107:19	+ 10	5.39
11¾	Feb 05-10	122:27	123:01	+ 4	4.87
10	May 05-10	117:23	117:27	+ 4	4.96
5¾	Aug 10n	102:16	102:17	+ 10	5.40
12¾	Nov 05-10	130:16	130:22	+ 3	4.97
3½	Jan 11i	101:31	102:00	+ 3	3.26
5	Feb 11n	97:08	97:09	+ 9	5.36
13⅞	May 06-11	138:01	138:07	....	5.04
14	Nov 06-11	141:25	141:31	− 7	5.08
10⅜	Nov 07-12	126:27	127:01	− 1	5.36
12	Aug 08-13	138:27	139:01	− 2	5.39
13¼	May 09-14	149:31	150:05	+ 2	5.40
12½	Aug 09-14	146:06	146:12	+ 3	5.42
11¾	Nov 09-14	142:11	142:17	+ 2	5.41
11¼	Feb 15	151:25	151:31	+ 2	5.73
10⅝	Aug 15	146:19	146:25	+ 4	5.76
9⅞	Nov 15	139:21	139:27	+ 4	5.77
9¼	Feb 16	133:23	133:29	+ 4	5.79
7¼	May 16	114:04	114:08	+ 6	5.81
7½	Nov 16	116:23	116:27	+ 5	5.83
8¾	May 17	129:29	130:03	+ 6	5.83
8⅞	Aug 17	131:11	131:17	+ 7	5.84
9⅛	May 18	134:27	135:01	+ 8	5.84
9	Nov 18	133:29	134:03	+ 8	5.85
8⅞	Feb 19	132:21	132:27	+ 8	5.87
8⅛	Aug 19	124:19	124:25	+ 6	5.89
8½	Feb 20	129:08	129:14	+ 9	5.88
8¾	May 20	132:10	132:16	+ 10	5.88
8¾	Aug 20	132:16	132:22	+ 9	5.89

Aug	04	np	86:05	86:08	....	4.69
Nov	04	ci	84:31	85:02	....	4.76
Nov	04	bp	84:21	84:24	....	4.86
Nov	04	np	84:27	84:30	....	4.80
Jan	05	ci	84:02	84:05	....	4.84
Feb	05	ci	83:21	83:24	....	4.86
Feb	05	np	83:22	83:25	....	4.84
May	05	ci	82:14	82:17	....	4.93
May	05	bp	82:10	82:13	....	4.97
May	05	np	82:17	82:20	....	4.89
May	05	np	82:21	82:24	....	4.86
Jul	05	ci	81:31	82:02	....	4.87
Aug	05	ci	81:17	81:20	....	4.89
Aug	05	bp	81:02	81:06	....	5.03
Aug	05	np	81:15	81:18	....	4.91
Nov	05	ci	80:27	80:30	....	4.82
Nov	05	np	80:08	80:11	....	4.99
Jan	06	ci	79:17	79:21	− 1	5.00
Feb	06	ci	79:04	79:08	− 1	5.02
Feb	06	bp	78:31	79:03	− 1	5.06
Feb	06	np	79:10	79:14	− 1	4.96
May	06	ci	77:30	78:02	− 1	5.07
May	06	np	77:28	78:00	− 1	5.09
Jul	06	ci	77:17	77:21	− 1	5.01
Jul	06	np	77:07	77:11	− 1	5.09
Aug	06	ci	77:04	77:08	− 1	5.03
Nov	06	ci	76:13	76:17	− 1	4.98
Feb	07	ci	74:27	74:30	+ 3	5.13
Feb	07	np	74:25	74:29	+ 3	5.14
May	07	ci	73:21	73:25	+ 3	5.18
May	07	np	73:22	73:26	+ 3	5.18
Aug	07	ci	72:22	72:26	+ 3	5.19
Aug	07	np	72:21	72:25	+ 3	5.19
Nov	07	ci	72:11	72:15	+ 3	5.06
Feb	08	ci	70:10	70:14	+ 4	5.30
Feb	08	np	70:19	70:23	+ 4	5.24
May	08	ci	69:07	69:11	+ 4	5.34
May	08	np	69:14	69:19	+ 4	5.29
Aug	08	ci	68:11	68:15	+ 4	5.33
Nov	08	ci	67:15	67:20	+ 4	5.33
Nov	08	np	67:11	67:16	+ 4	5.35
Feb	09	ci	66:05	66:10	+ 5	5.41
May	09	ci	65:05	65:10	+ 5	5.44
May	09	np	65:11	65:16	+ 5	5.40
Aug	09	ci	64:09	64:14	+ 5	5.43
Aug	09	np	64:09	64:14	+ 5	5.43
Nov	09	ci	63:17	63:22	+ 5	5.42
Nov	09	bp	62:12	62:17	+ 5	5.64
Feb	10	ci	62:04	62:09	+ 5	5.52
Feb	10	np	62:12	62:17	+ 5	5.47
May	10	ci	61:06	61:11	+ 5	5.54
Aug	10	ci	60:11	60:16	+ 5	5.54
Aug	10	np	60:20	60:25	+ 5	5.49
Nov	10	ci	59:27	60:00	+ 5	5.48
Feb	11	ci	58:09	58:14	+ 6	5.62
May	11	ci	57:11	57:16	+ 6	5.64
Aug	11	ci	56:16	56:21	+ 6	5.65
Nov	11	ci	55:26	56:00	+ 6	5.63
Feb	12	ci	54:21	54:26	+ 6	5.70
May	12	ci	53:24	53:29	+ 6	5.73
Aug	12	ci	52:28	53:01	+ 6	5.75
Nov	12	ci	51:31	52:05	+ 6	5.77
Feb	13	ci	51:09	51:14	+ 12	5.76
May	13	ci	50:14	50:20	+ 12	5.78
Aug	13	ci	49:19	49:25	+ 12	5.80
Nov	13	ci	48:25	48:31	+ 12	5.82
Feb	14	ci	48:00	48:05	+ 13	5.84
May	14	ci	47:06	47:12	+ 13	5.86
Aug	14	ci	46:12	46:18	+ 13	5.88
Nov	14	ci	45:21	45:27	+ 14	5.89
Feb	15	ci	44:28	45:02	+ 13	5.91
Feb	15	bp	44:19	44:25	+ 13	5.95
May	15	ci	44:04	44:10	+ 13	5.92
Aug	15	ci	43:13	43:18	+ 13	5.94
Aug	15	bp	43:03	43:08	+ 13	5.99
Nov	15	ci	42:20	42:26	+ 13	5.96
Nov	15	bp	42:10	42:16	+ 13	6.01
Feb	16	ci	41:27	42:01	+ 14	5.99
Feb	16	bp	41:24	41:30	+ 14	6.00
May	16	ci	41:04	41:09	+ 14	6.01
May	16	bp	41:07	41:13	+ 14	5.99
Aug	16	ci	40:14	40:20	+ 14	6.02
Nov	16	ci	39:23	39:29	+ 14	6.04
May	27	ci	21:18	21:24	+ 13	5.97
Aug	27	ci	21:10	21:15	+ 13	5.96
Aug	27	bp	21:12	21:18	+ 13	5.95
Nov	27	ci	21:00	21:05	+ 13	5.96
Nov	27	bp	21:03	21:08	+ 13	5.95
Feb	28	ci	20:26	20:31	+ 13	5.94
May	28	ci	20:18	20:23	+ 13	5.93
Aug	28	ci	20:12	20:17	+ 13	5.91
Aug	28	bp	20:15	20:20	+ 13	5.89
Nov	28	ci	20:03	20:08	+ 13	5.90
Nov	28	bp	20:07	20:12	+ 13	5.88
Feb	29	ci	19:31	20:05	+ 13	5.87
Feb	29	bp	20:03	20:08	+ 13	5.85
May	29	ci	19:27	20:00	+ 13	5.84
Aug	29	ci	19:21	19:26	+ 13	5.82
Aug	29	bp	19:23	19:29	+ 13	5.81
Nov	29	ci	19:18	19:23	+ 13	5.79
Feb	30	ci	19:15	19:20	+ 12	5.76
May	30	ci	19:09	19:14	+ 12	5.74
May	30	bp	19:12	19:18	+ 12	5.72
Aug	30	ci	19:09	19:14	+ 12	5.69
Feb	31	ci	19:21	19:26	+ 13	5.53
Feb	31	bp	19:21	19:26	+ 13	5.53

TREASURY BILLS

MATURITY	DAYS TO MAT.	BID	ASKED	CHG.	ASKED YLD.
Jun 07 '01	3	3.38	3.30	−0.21	3.35
Jun 14 '01	10	3.82	3.74	−0.01	3.80
Jun 21 '01	17	3.26	3.18	....	3.23
Jun 28 '01	24	3.27	3.19	−0.20	3.24
Jul 05 '01	31	3.32	3.28	−0.10	3.33
Jul 12 '01	38	3.33	3.29	−0.08	3.35
Jul 19 '01	45	3.37	3.33	−0.06	3.39
Jul 26 '01	52	3.39	3.35	−0.04	3.41
Aug 02 '01	59	3.41	3.37	−0.05	3.44
Aug 09 '01	66	3.47	3.45	−0.01	3.52
Aug 16 '01	73	3.51	3.49	....	3.56
Aug 23 '01	80	3.52	3.50	−0.03	3.58
Aug 30 '01	87	3.58	3.57	+0.03	3.66
Sep 06 '01	94	3.98	3.96	+0.46	4.06
Sep 06 '01	94	3.56	3.55	+0.02	3.63
Sep 13 '01	101	3.53	3.51	+0.01	3.59
Sep 20 '01	108	3.54	3.52	+0.02	3.61
Sep 27 '01	115	3.51	3.49	+0.01	3.58
Oct 04 '01	122	3.52	3.50	....	3.59
Oct 11 '01	129	3.52	3.50	....	3.59
Oct 18 '01	136	3.52	3.50	....	3.60
Oct 25 '01	143	3.52	3.50	−0.01	3.60
Nov 01 '01	150	3.53	3.51	−0.01	3.61
Nov 08 '01	157	3.53	3.51	−0.02	3.61
Nov 15 '01	164	3.54	3.52	−0.02	3.63
Nov 23 '01	172	3.55	3.53	−0.01	3.64
Nov 29 '01	178	3.48	3.47	....	3.60
Dec 06 '01	185	3.48	3.47	....	3.58
Feb 28 '02	269	3.48	3.47	+0.03	3.59

INFLATION-INDEXED TREASURY SECURITIES

RATE	MAT.	BID/ASKED	CHG.	*YLD.	ACCR. PRIN.
3.625	07/02	102-15/16	+ 1	1.350	1101
3.375	01/07	102-05/06	+ 2	2.950	1112
3.625	01/08	103-06/07	....	3.080	1091
3.875	01/09	104-19/20	+ 3	3.190	1074
4.250	01/10	107-15/16	+ 4	3.240	1047
3.500	01/11	101-31/00	+ 3	3.260	1012
3.625	04/28	103-04/05	+ 3	3.440	1089
3.875	04/29	107-26/27	+ 2	3.440	1072

percentage of the face value. For example, the bid price for the $7\frac{1}{2}$% notes of November 2024 is 120:04. The 04 means $\frac{4}{32}$. That is, for a bond of face value $1 million of this issue, the dealer is willing to pay

$$120\frac{4}{32}\% \text{ of } \$1,000,000 = 1.20125 \times \$1,000,000 = \$1,201,250$$

The dealer will pay this amount plus the interest that has accrued on the bond since the last coupon payment in May (coupons on this security are paid in November and May). As of June 1, one month of the 6-month coupon period has already passed. The current owner is therefore entitled to $\frac{1}{6}$ of the next coupon payment (actually the calculation is done in days rather than in months), and the dealer adds this amount to the bid price when paying for the security.

The "chg." column gives the change in the bid price over the bid price of the previous day. The $7\frac{1}{2}$'s of November '24 rose by $\frac{19}{32}$ point between closing on Thursday, May 31, 2001, and closing on Friday, June 1. The number in the yield column is the approximate yield to maturity calculated from the asked price.

The listing for strips is basically similar to that for notes and bonds. In the "type" column "ci" indicates a stripped coupon; "np," the stripped principal of a note; and "bp," the stripped principal of a bond.

For reasons lost in the mists of time, bid and asked prices of bills are stated as "bank discounts." The bank discount is defined as

$$\text{bank discount} = \frac{\text{face value} - \text{price}}{\text{face value}} \times \frac{360}{\text{days to maturity}}$$

The numbers after the period in the bid and asked prices are decimal fractions, not thirty-seconds. Given the bank discount, and the days to maturity, we can use the foregoing formula to solve for the actual price. For example, for a $1,000,000 bill due on June 21, the bid price is 3.26, and there are 17 days to maturity. The price therefore satisfies

$$0.0326 = \frac{\$1,000,000 - \text{price}}{\$1,000,000} \times \frac{360}{17}$$

Solving this, the price is $998,460.56.

We shall discuss the Inflation Indexed Treasury Securities later in the chapter.

INTEREST RATE RISK

interest rate risk
Risk associated with changes in market interest rates.

We have seen that the market yield on a security and its market price are closely related. It follows that when market yields change, prices of securities will change too. The risk of this happening is called **interest rate risk**, and it is a major concern throughout the financial system.

Interest Rate Risk on Securities Promising a Single Payment

The best way to learn more about interest rate risk is by making an investment yourself. Suppose you have some money to invest and you decide to buy three securities of differing maturities:

- A 1-year bill with a face value of $10,000
- A 5-year zero with a face value of $10,000
- A 30-year zero with a face value of $100,000

The market yields on each of these securities is 6%, so their market prices are, respectively,

$$P = \frac{\$10,000}{1.06} = \$9,434$$

$$P = \frac{\$10,000}{(1.06)^5} = \$7,473$$

and

$$P = \frac{\$100,000}{(1.06)^{30}} = \$17,411$$

Holding–Period Yield and Maturity.   A year after you buy the securities, you need your money and must liquidate your portfolio. How much will you get? Since the 1-year bill matures at that time, you receive its face value, $10,000. However, to turn the other two securities into cash, you must sell them. How much you get for them will depend on their market price at the time.

To calculate the market price, we need to know the market yield. Suppose the market yield at all maturities has risen from 6% to 8%. Because the 5-year zero has, after a year, become a 4-year zero, its market price is now

$$P = \frac{\$10,000}{(1.08)^4} = \$7,350$$

The 30-year zero is now a 29-year zero. So its market price is

$$P = \frac{\$100,000}{(1.08)^{29}} = \$10,733$$

How have your three investments done? To compare them, we need to calculate for each its **holding-period yield**. This is the yield it actually earned over the period you held it. The general formula for the holding period yield is

holding-period yield

The annual rate actually earned on a security over the given period.

$$\text{holding-period yield} = \left(\frac{\text{end value}}{\text{amount invested}} \right)^{1/\text{number of years held}} - 1 \qquad [4.17]$$

Here are the holding period yields for the three securities in question.

For the 1-year bill (held to maturity):

$$\frac{\$10{,}000}{\$9{,}434} - 1 = 0.06$$

For the 5-year zero (sold after one year):

$$\frac{\$7{,}350}{\$7{,}473} - 1 = -0.016$$

For the 30-year zero (sold after one year):

$$\frac{\$10{,}733}{\$17{,}411} - 1 = -0.384$$

What have we learned?

- *Lesson 1.* Only if you hold a bill or zero to maturity can you be sure that its holding-period yield will equal the market yield at the time you buy it.
- *Lesson 2.* For a bill or zero sold before maturity, the holding-period yield depends on the market price and so on the market yield at the time of sale.
- *Lesson 3.* The higher the market yield at the time of sale, the lower the market price.
- *Lesson 4.* The greater the bill or the zero's remaining time to maturity, the greater the sensitivity of its market price to its market yield.

Given the outcome, was your investment a mistake? That all depends. It seems that investing in the 30-year zero, which fell the most in value, was a bad idea. However, if market yields had gone *down* rather than up, the 30-year zero, rather than falling the most, would have risen the most. For example, if market yields at all maturities had fallen to 4% the holding-period yields on the three securities would have been 6, 14.4, and 84.2%, respectively. The numbers for our three investments are summarized in Exhibit 4.2.

The differential sensitivity to changes in market yield cuts both ways. You can lose more on long-term securities if interest rates rise, but you can also gain more if they fall.

EXHIBIT 4.2   Holding-Period Yields

	INITIAL INVESTMENT	RETURN AFTER HOLDING FOR ONE YEAR IF MARKET YIELD HAS BECOME:					
	$i = 6\%$	$i = 6\%$		$i = 8\%$		$i = 4\%$	
	Value	Value	Yield	Value	Yield	Value	Yield
1-year bill	9,434	10,000	6%	10,000	6%	10,000	6%
5-year zero	7,473	7,921	6%	7,350	−1.6%	8,548	14.4%
30-year zero	17,411	18,456	6%	10,733	−38.4%	32,065	84.2%

The Sensitivity of Price to Market Yield.   Suppose you hold a portfolio of bills of different maturities. You would like to know how much their value will change if market yields change. Luckily, you do not have to go through all the foregoing calculations. There is a simple formula that will give you the answer[7]:

$$\frac{\Delta P}{P} = -t \frac{\Delta i}{1 + i}$$

[4.18]

where Δi = change in the market yield
ΔP = change in the market price
$\Delta P/P$ = percentage change in the market price

EXAMPLE 4.10

Suppose a you hold a $1 million, 2-year bill. The market yield is currently 11.5%. How much will the market price of this bill change if the market yield rises to 12%?

If the market yield increases to 12%, the change in yield, Δi, is $0.12 - 0.115 = 0.005$. When we use Equation 4.18, the present value, P, changes by

$$-2 \frac{0.005}{1.115} = -0.009$$

If you want to know by what dollar amount the value of the bill changes, you must calculate its market price. At 11.5%, this is

$$\frac{\$1,000,000}{(1.115)^2} = \$804,359.63$$

Therefore,

$$\frac{\Delta P}{\$804,359.63} = -0.009$$

And $\Delta P = \$7,240$.

Equation 4.18 confirms what we have learned about the sensitivity of the price of bills to changes in market yields. Notice the minus sign: an increase in the interest rate

---

[7] Equation 4.6 may be written $P = A(1 + i)^{-t}$. Taking a derivative with respect to i, we obtain

$$\frac{dP}{di} = -t\,A(1 + i)^{-t-1} = -t \frac{P}{1 + i}$$

Rearranging this, and substituting Δ for d, we obtain Equation 4.18.

lowers the market price. Notice too the effect of maturity, t: the longer the maturity, the greater the sensitivity to a change in price. For example, in percentage terms, a 20-year bill will change in value by 10 times as much as a 2-year bill.

Reinvestment Risk.   Since interest rate risk increases with maturity, if you want to play it safe, should you invest only in short-term securities? Not necessarily.

To see why not, suppose you do not need your money after a year, but rather wish to leave it invested for 30 years until you retire. What will your holding-period yield be then on the three different investments of our example?

In this case, it is the 30-year zero that provides the sure return. It matures after 30 years, and you receive the face value, $100,000. We use Equation 4.17 to find the holding-period yield,

$$\left(\frac{\$100,000}{\$17,411} \right)^{1/30} - 1 = 0.06$$

The holding-period yield equals the market yield at the time you bought the bond.

How much will you make from your two other investments? That depends on what you did with the money when each one matured. Suppose when the 1-year bill matured, you used the money to buy another 1-year bill, and so on, for 30 years. Then your holding-period yield will depend on the sequence of 1-year market yields over the 30 years: it will be some sort of average. If interest rates are generally lower, your holding-period yield will turn out to be less than 6%. If they are generally higher, it will turn out to be more than 6%. Similarly for the 5-year zero: its holding-period yield will also depend on how you reinvest.

The holding-period yields over 30 years on these shorter term bills will therefore be subject to the risk associated with reinvestment at uncertain interest rates. This risk is called **reinvestment risk**.

reinvestment risk
Risk associated with reinvestment at uncertain interest rates.

Whether you should invest in long-maturity or short-maturity securities depends, therefore, on a number of considerations:

- What is your time horizon?
- Are you putting the money away for a long time or do you expect to need it soon?
- Do you want to play it safe or gamble?
- If you want to gamble, do you think interest rates will rise or fall?

Interest Rate Risk on Securities Promising Multiple Payments

Equation 4.18 allows us to calculate the sensitivity of market price to market yield for securities that promise a single payment. We need to be able to do the same for securities that promise multiple payments.

Duration.   To do this we will use a principle that we established earlier: the value of a security promising multiple payments is just the sum of the present values of the various payments.

Let us take a security that promises A_1 due in 1 year, A_2 due in 2 years, and so on, up to A_t due in t years. If we know the market yields, we can use Equation 4.6 to calculate the present value of each payment. Call these present values P_1, P_2, and so on, up to P_t. Then, the market price of the security, P, is just

$$P = P_1 + P_2 + \cdots + P_t$$

Now suppose market yields change by Δi. The change in the market price of the security, ΔP, will just equal the sum of the changes in the present values of the various payments:

$$\Delta P = \Delta P_1 + \Delta P_2 + \cdots + \Delta P_t$$

Dividing and multiplying ΔP_1 by P_1 and doing the same for ΔP_2, and so on, we can rewrite this

$$\Delta P = \frac{\Delta P_1}{P_1} P_1 + \frac{\Delta P_2}{P_2} P_2 + \cdots + \frac{\Delta P_t}{P_t} P_t$$

We can now use Equation 4.18 to substitute for $\Delta P_1/P_1$, and so on, to obtain

$$\Delta P = \left[-1 \frac{\Delta i}{(1 + i)}\right] P_1 + \left[-2 \frac{\Delta i}{(1 + i)}\right] P_2 + \cdots + \left[-t \frac{\Delta i}{(1 + i)}\right] P_t$$

or $$\Delta P = -[1\,P_1 + 2\,P_2 + \cdots + t\,P_t] \frac{\Delta i}{(1 + i)}$$

If we divide both sides of this equation by P, we obtain

$$\frac{\Delta P}{P} = -\left[1 \frac{P_1}{P} + 2 \frac{P_2}{P} + \cdots + t \frac{P_t}{P}\right] \frac{\Delta i}{(1 + i)}$$

or $$\frac{\Delta P}{P} = -\,d \frac{\Delta i}{(1 + i)} \qquad [4.19]$$

where $$d = \left[1 \frac{P_1}{P} + 2 \frac{P_2}{P} + \cdots + t \frac{P_t}{P}\right] \qquad [4.20]$$

duration
Measure of the sensitivity of the value of security to changes in market interest rates.

The quantity d is called the **duration** of the security. Notice that the duration plays exactly the same role in Equation 4.19 as the maturity of a single payment does in Equation 4.18. In a sense, the duration is the "average maturity" of the payments that make up the security. Indeed, you can see from Equation 4.20 that the duration is the weighted average of the maturities of the payments, weighting each payment's maturity by the share of the payment's present value in the total value of the security.

EXAMPLE 4.11

You are holding the following three securities, each worth $10,000 at the market yield of 10%:

- A 4-year bond with face value $10,000 and $1,000 annual coupons
- A 4-year annuity with annual payments of $3,155
- A 4-year zero-coupon bond with a face value of $14,641

How will the market prices of these three securities change if market yields increase to 11%?

We need to calculate the duration for each of these securities. This is done in Exhibits 4.3, 4.4, and 4.5. The duration of the bond is 3.487; the duration of the annuity is 2.381; the duration of the zero is 4.0.

If the market yield increases to 11%, $\Delta i = 1\%$. Using Equation 4.19, we find that the change in price of the bond is

$$\frac{\Delta P}{P} = -3.487 \, \frac{1\%}{1.1} = -3.17\%$$

Similarly, the change in price of the annuity is -2.16%, and the change in the price of the zero is -3.6%.

You can see from this example how duration is affected by the timing of the payments on a given security:

- With the zero, the payments are as late as possible—all in the final period. Its duration is longest.
- With the annuity, because it pays equal payments, you receive your money, on average, earlier than with either of the bonds. Its duration is the shortest.
- With the coupon bond, you receive your money earlier than with the zero (because of the coupons), but not as early as with the annuity. Its duration is in between.

Were we to include other coupon bonds in the portfolio, those with larger coupons—higher coupon rates—would have shorter durations.

EXHIBIT 4.3   Duration of a Coupon Bond

	Maturity, i	A_i	P_i	P_i/P	$i(P_i/P)$
	1	1,000	909	0.0909	0.0909
	2	1,000	826	0.0826	0.1652
	3	1,000	751	0.9751	0.2253
	4	11,000	7,514	0.7514	3.0056
P			10,000		
d					3.4870

EXHIBIT 4.4   Duration of an Annuity

Maturity, i	A_i	P_i	P_i/P	$i(P_i/P)$
1	3,155	2,868	0.2868	0.2868
2	3,155	2,607	0.2607	0.5214
3	3,155	2,370	0.2370	0.7110
4	3,155	2,155	0.2155	0.8620
P		10,000		
d				2.3812

We shall see in Chapter 18 that duration is extremely useful in measuring the exposure of financial intermediaries to interest rate risk. A financial intermediary borrows (makes promises of future payment) in order to relend (accept promises of future payment). When market interest rates change, the value of its liabilities (the promises it has made) may change relative to the value of its assets (the promises it has accepted), leaving it with a gain or loss. Its exposure to interest rate risk may be measured by comparing the duration of it liabilities and the duration of its assets.

Reinvestment Risk Again.   With securities promising a single payment, you could avoid the risk of having to reinvest at lower interest rates by buying securities with a long maturity. With securities promising multiple payments, there is no way to avoid reinvestment risk.

For example, with a coupon bond, you receive a coupon payment every 6 months. What you do with this money has nothing to do with the issuer of the bond. You could put it into a savings account, or you could buy more bonds. Your holding-period yield on the original bond will depend on how much you earn when you reinvest the coupon payments.

EXAMPLE 4.12

You buy a $1,000, 20-year bond with 6% annual coupons at a market price of $803.64. Its market yield (average annual yield to maturity) is 8%. If you hold this bond to maturity, what will be its market yield?

EXHIBIT 4.5   Duration of a Zero-Coupon Bond

Maturity, i	A_i	P_i	P_i/P	$i(P_i/P)$
1	0	0	0	0
2	0	0	0	0
3	0	0	0	0
4	14,641	10,000	1.0	4.0
P		10,000		
d				4.0

Suppose that soon after you buy the bond, market yields fall to 6%. Consequently, when you receive the first coupon of $60, you reinvest it at 6%. After 19 years, when the bond matures, the reinvested first coupon will yield $60(1.06)^{19} = $182.

If we repeat this calculation for all of the coupons, assuming they are all reinvested at 6%, we find that the amount you have at the end of 20 years is

$$\$60(1.06)^{19} + \$60(1.06)^{18} + \cdots + \$60(1.06) + \$1,060 = \$3,207$$

By using Equation 4.7, you find that your holding-period yield is

$$i = \left(\frac{\$3,207}{\$804} \right)^{1/20} - 1 = 7.2\%$$

The formula for the yield to maturity assumes implicitly that you will be able to reinvest the coupons at the yield-to-maturity rate. To see this, multiply both sides of Equation 4.15 by $(1 + i)^t$:

$$P(1 + i)^t = C(1 + i)^{t-1} + C(1 + i)^{t-2} + \cdots + C(1 + i) + C + A \qquad [4.21]$$

The investment P will earn a return of i *only* if the coupons can be reinvested at the same rate of i.

When you buy a coupon bond, you do not know in advance at what rate you will be able to reinvest the coupons. Consequently the holding-period yield on a coupon bond is uncertain—subject to reinvestment risk—even if you hold the bond to maturity.

The absence of reinvestment risk is what makes zeros more attractive than coupon bonds to some investors. If you hold a zero to maturity, you know exactly what you will have when the security matures. The desire to avoid reinvestment risk accounts for the popularity of Treasury strips.

EXCHANGE RATE RISK

We have looked so far at securities that promise payment in U.S. dollars. However, financial institutions and markets are becoming increasingly international. To understand them, we need to be able to evaluate securities that promise payment in foreign currencies. It is best to begin with an example.

EXAMPLE 4.13

You have $1 million to invest. Interest rates in Germany are much higher in the United States, so you decide to invest in a 1-year German T-bill with a market yield of 9%. What is your holding-period yield for the year?

To buy the German T-bill you must pay in German marks (deutsche marks). To acquire the marks you need, you must sell your dollars in exchange for marks. The price you receive for your dollars in marks is called the mark–dollar *exchange rate*.

Suppose the exchange rate is 1.60 DM/$. You therefore receive DM1.6 million for your $1 million. If you invest it in German T-bills, at the end of the year you will have

$$DM1,600,000 \times (1.09) = DM1,744,000$$

How much is this in dollars? That depends on what the exchange rate is *then*. Suppose it is 2.00 DM/$. Then you marks will be worth

$$\frac{DM1,744,000}{2.00 \text{ DM/\$}} = \$872,000$$

The return on your original $1 million is not the 9% you might have thought, but -12.8%. Welcome to the world of international finance!

exchange rate risk
Risk associated with fluctuations in the exchange rate.

You have just seen an example of **exchange rate risk**—the risk that the value in dollars of a promise of payment in a foreign currency will change as a result of a change in the exchange rate.

We can summarize the lessons of this example in some useful formulas. For a foreign currency security, the holding-period yield (HPY) in dollars depends on three things:

- The HPY in the foreign currency
- The original exchange rate when you buy the security
- The exchange rate at which you convert back into dollars

If the holding period is t years, the dollar HPY is given by

$$(1 + \$ \text{ HPY})^t = \frac{\text{original exchange rate}}{\text{exchange rate at } t} \times (1 + \text{foreign currency HPY})^t \quad [4.22]$$

For our example,

$$(1 + \$ \text{ HPY}) = \frac{1.60 \text{ DM/\$}}{2.00 \text{ DM/\$}} \times (1.09) = 0.872$$

We can define the rate of change of the exchange rate over the holding period as

$$(1 + \text{rate of ochange of exchange rate})^t = \frac{\text{exchange rate at } t}{\text{original exchange rate}} \quad [4.23]$$

For our example,

$$(1 + \text{rate of change of exchange rate})^1 = \frac{2.00 \text{ DM/\$}}{1.60 \text{ DM/\$}} = 1.25$$

The number of marks per dollar has increased by 25%. This means, equivalently, that (a) the dollar is 25% more valuable in terms of marks, and (b) the mark is 25% less valuable in terms of the dollar. For you, this is bad news. You are *owed* marks. If the mark is less valuable in terms of dollars, you are owed less in terms of dollars.

Using Equation 4.23, we can rewrite Equation 4.22 as

$$(1 + \$ \text{HPY})^t = \frac{(1 + \text{foreign currency HPY})^t}{(1 + \text{rate of change of exchange rate})^t}$$

Taking the *t*th root of each side, we obtain

$$1 + \$ \text{HPY} = \frac{1 + \text{foreign currency HPY}}{1 + \text{rate of change of exchange rate}} \qquad [4.24]$$

A useful approximation to Equation 4.24 is

$$\$ \text{HPY} \cong \text{foreign currency HPY} - \frac{\text{rate of change of exchange rate}}{(\text{foreign currency}/\$)} \qquad [4.25]$$

For a real-world example of how Equation 4.25 can be used to determine the total yield on a foreign currency security, see "Exchange Rate Risk: The Hazard of Investing Abroad."

We have seen that there is exchange rate risk when you are owed payment in foreign currency. But there is also exchange rate risk when you *owe* payment in foreign currency. We saw an example in Chapter 2, when Valley Motors owed payment in Japanese yen.

As we saw in Chapter 2, you can protect yourself against exchange rate risk by trading foreign currency forward. In our simple example here, you could have sold forward to your bank the DM1,744,000 you expected to receive at the end of the year. This would have guaranteed your holding-period yield.

MONETARY EXPANSION AND PRICES

We have looked at the values of promises of future payment on the assumption that the value of a dollar, in terms of what it can buy, remains the same over time. Unfortunately, this is not generally the case in practice. In most countries today, the United States included, the purchasing power of money declines from year to year.

The purchasing power declines because the amount of money that is being spent increases faster than the amount of goods and services being produced. The usual reason for this is that the quantity of money in the economy is growing "too fast."[8] Generally speaking, the faster the quantity of money is increasing, the faster the rise in prices—that

---

[8] "Too fast" is in quotes because there is some disagreement among economists about whether a constant level of prices is better for the economy than a slowly rising level.

EXCHANGE RATE RISK:
THE HAZARD OF INVESTING ABROAD

Throughout 1992, short-term interest rates in Germany were significantly higher than those in the United States; however, an American choosing between a dollar-denominated and a deutsche mark–denominated certificate of deposit (CD) with similar liquidities and default risks would not necessarily have earned a higher return on the German CD. On May 27, 1992, an American saver with $10,000 to invest could choose between a 3-month CD with an annual interest rate of 3.85% from an American bank and a 3-month CD with an annual interest rate of 9.65% from a German bank. After 3 months, the U.S. CD was worth $10,096 and the German CD was worth $11,900 after exchanging the deutsche marks for dollars. As the accompanying table shows, the substantially larger value of the German CD was due primarily to a 16.6% appreciation of the deutsche mark against the dollar from May 27 to August 26.

Now consider the same choice facing our investor on September 30, 1992. A 3-month U.S. CD offered an annual interest rate of 3.09%, and a comparable German investment offered an annual interest rate of 9.1%. Thus the U.S. CD was worth $10,077 after 3 months. If the investor purchased the German CD, however, she would have had only $8,964 at the end of the 3 months, $1,036 less than the purchase price. This loss resulted from the 12.5% appreciation of the dollar against the mark between September and December 1992. With hindsight, the American saver would have preferred the U.S. CD to the German CD even though the German interest rate was higher.

These examples provide a clear message. Even though interest rates play a key role in determining the relative attractiveness of assets denominated in domestic and foreign currencies, the effects of exchange rate changes can swamp the effects of interest rate differentials. Such large differences in returns illustrate why many investors choose to hedge against exchange rate changes.

RETURN ON A 3-MONTH GERMAN INVESTMENT, MAY 27–AUGUST 26

Deutsche Mark Return (for 3 Months)	Percent Change in DM/$ Exchange Rates	Dollar Return
2.4%	−16.6%	19.0%

SEPTEMBER 30–DECEMBER 30

Deutsche Mark Return (for 3 Months)	Percent Change in DM/$ Exchange Rates	Dollar Return
2.3%	12.5%	−10.0%

Source: Patricia S. Pollard, "Exchange Rate Risk: The Hazard of Investing Abroad." *International Economic Conditions.* Federal Reserve Bank of St. Louis, February 1993.

monetary expansion

A net increase in the quantity of money as a result of money creation.

is, the higher the rate of *inflation*. This is particularly easy to see when the rate of monetary expansion is really fast. Exhibit 4.6 shows the connection between monetary expansion and inflation for a number of countries that experienced very rapid **monetary expansion** in the 1970s and 1980s.

REAL AND NOMINAL VALUES

Inflation affects interest rates because it affects the value of money promised in the future. This is best understood from an example.

Suppose you plan to retire in 30 years. You expect to put away $10,000 each year at an interest rate of 7%. When you retire, you should have about $945,000.[9] This looks like a lot of money, but is it? That depends on what it will buy. If prices rise over the next 30 years, it may buy much less than you think.

A Measure of Prices

consumer price index (CPI)

An index of prices faced by an average urban family.

To say anything more definite, we need a measure of the level of prices. The best known measure is the **consumer price index (CPI)**. This estimates what a typical urban family pays for the goods and services it consumes. A rise in the CPI of 10% means that such a family must pay 10% more for its typical basket of goods and services.

The CPI is calculated by the Bureau of Labor Statistics (BLS). Every 10 years or so, the BLS conducts a survey of the buying habits of American families. It uses this survey to construct a typical basket of goods and services, including everything from housing to medical care to entertainment. Each month the BLS sends out surveyors to price this basket of goods and services. It calculates the CPI by comparing the cost of the basket in any month to the cost in the base period, which is usually the period of the most recent survey of spending. For example,

$$\text{CPI for April 2001} = \frac{\text{cost of basket in April 2001}}{\text{cost of same basket in } 1982 - 4} \times 100 \qquad [4.26]$$

By definition, the CPI for the base period is 100. The CPI for April 2001 was 176.9, which means that the reference basket costs 76.9% more then than it did in 1982–1984.

---

[9] Your savings are an annuity. We can calculate the present value of this annuity using a table of annuity factors. The annuity factor for 7% and 30 years is 12.41. So the present value of your savings is

$$\$10,000 \times 12.41 = \$124,100$$

When you retire you will have the future value of this amount. The future value factor for 7% and 30 years, also available from published tables, is 7.612. So you will have

$$\$124,100 \times 7.612 = \$944,649.20$$

EXHIBIT 4.6   Monetary Growth and Inflation in High-Inflation Countries

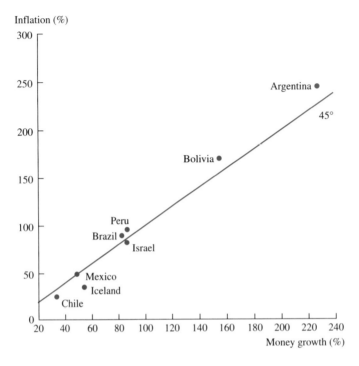

Averages for Bolivia are for 1977–1988.
Averages for Brazil and Chile are for 1977–1985.

Source: **International Monetary Fund,** International Financial Statistics.

rate of inflation
The rate of
change of the
level of prices.

    The **rate of inflation** is the rate of change of prices. Since the CPI measures the level of prices, its *rate of change* measures the rate of inflation. For example, the CPI for April 2000 was 171.2, so that between April 2000 and April 2001, the CPI increased by

$$\frac{176.9 - 171.2}{171.2} \times 100 = 3.3\%$$

The rate of inflation for that 1-year period was 3.3%.

Measuring in Constant Dollars

Suppose the CPI in 2031 turns out to be 300. How much will the $945,000 of retirement savings that you will have then be worth in terms of today's dollars? Since the CPI today is 176.9, $945,000 in 2031 dollars is equivalent to

$$\$945,000 \times \frac{176.9}{300} = \$557,235$$

in 2001 dollars.

measuring in constant dollars
Measuring amounts of money in terms of their equivalent purchasing power in some base period.

Measuring amounts of money in terms of their equivalent purchasing power in some base period is called **measuring in constant dollars**. The general rule is:

$$\text{amount in time } t \text{ \$} \times \frac{\text{CPI at time } s}{\text{CPI at time } t} = \text{amount in time } s \text{ \$} \qquad [4.27]$$

where dollars at time t are being measured in terms of their equivalent purchasing power in the base period, time s.

Since prices do change over time, measuring in constant dollars is essential for making meaningful comparisons. For an example, look at Exhibit 4.7. The lower curve shows average weekly earnings of U.S. production workers in *current* dollars between 1959 and 2000. From this plot, it looks as though earnings rose steadily over time. The upper curve shows average weekly earnings in *constant* (2000) dollars. As you can see, in terms of purchasing power, weekly earnings peaked in the early 1970s and then declined.

All the charts in this book that compare dollar amounts over time measure the amounts in constant dollars.

Real and Nominal Interest Rates

nominal interest rate
Relates the dollar amount of interest to the dollar amount of money lent.

Just as we correct dollar amounts for inflation, so can we correct interest rates. Interest rates *not* corrected for inflation are called nominal interest rates. The **nominal interest rate** on a loan relates the amount of interest on the loan to the amount of money lent. For example, if you lend $1,000 for one year and are repaid the $1,000 plus $100 in interest, the nominal interest rate is 10%.

real interest rate
Interest measured in terms of purchasing power.

What we would like to know is the yield on the loan, not in terms of money, but in terms of *purchasing power*. This is called the **real interest rate**. Suppose, for example, that over the life of the $1000 loan above, the CPI doubles from 100 to 200. Using

EXHIBIT 4.7   Average Weekly Earnings in Current and Constant Dollars

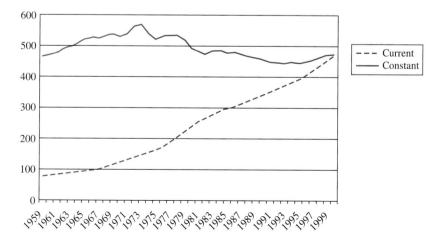

Source: Economic Report of the President.

Equation 4.27, in beginning-of-year dollars, the $1,100 you receive at the end of the year is worth

$$\$1,100 \times \frac{100}{200} = \$550$$

Rather than gaining 10% (the nominal interest rate), you have lost 45% (the real interest rate).

We can state the relationship between the nominal interest rate and the real interest rate in terms of the rate of inflation:

$$(1 + \text{real interest rate}) = \frac{(1 + \text{nominal interest rate})}{(1 + \text{inflation rate})} \qquad [4.28]$$

In our example, the rate of inflation is 100%. Hence

$$(1 + \text{real interest rate}) = \frac{(1 + 0.10)}{(1 + 1.0)} = 0.55 = 1 + (-0.45)$$

A useful approximation to Equation 4.28 is

$$\text{real interest rate} \cong \text{nominal interest rate} - \text{inflation rate} \qquad [4.29]$$

You can see from Equation 4.28 that for a given nominal interest rate, the higher the rate of inflation the lower the real rate of interest.

Historically, inflation has had a significant effect on real interest rates in the United States. Exhibit 4.8 shows how real and nominal interest rates on T-bills have varied over time.

Adjusting to Inflation

Most financial contracts are based on the assumption that "a dollar is a dollar." However, when because of inflation a dollar in one period is no longer equal in purchasing power to a dollar in another, problems occur.

Mortgages and Inflation.   To see how inflation can distort financial contracts, consider a mortgage. A mortgage is an annuity: it is paid off in equal monthly installments to ease the burden of repayment. To see the effect of inflation, let us look at an example.

Consider a $100,000, 30-year mortgage at a real rate of interest of 3% under two scenarios. In the first, there is no inflation; in the second, inflation is 10%.

- *No inflation*: The nominal interest rate is the same as the real rate—3%. The monthly payment, at 3%, is $422. This payment stays the same for the life of the mortgage, both in dollar terms and in real terms.
- *Inflation is 10%*: For the real interest rate on the mortgage to be 3%, the nominal interest rate must be 13%. At 13%, the monthly payment is $1,162. This payment

EXHIBIT 4.8   Real and Nominal Interest Rates 1960–2000

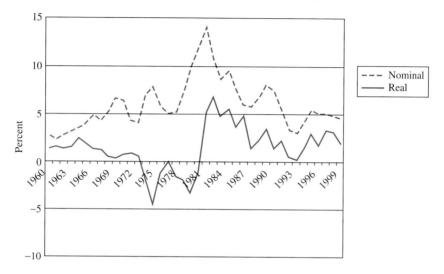

Interest rate is yield on new issues of 3-month T-bills.

Source: Economic Report of the President.

stays the same in dollar terms over the life of the mortgage. But, in real terms it declines. The real value of the final payment in first-year dollars is only

$$\frac{\$1,162}{(1.10)^{30}} = \$67$$

The mortgages in the two scenarios are equivalent in terms of cost: the real interest rate is the same in both. So the borrower is not really paying more in the second scenario than in the first. However, the patterns of repayment in the two scenarios are very different. In the second scenario, the first month's payment is nearly three times as large as in the first scenario and the last month's payment, in terms of purchasing power, is one-sixth. This pattern of repayment is hard for the typical borrower to manage. Payments are high when the borrower is young and income is relatively low. Payments then fall in real terms as income increases.

There have been various financial innovations designed to deal with this problem. The most appealing is called a **price-level-adjusted mortgage (PLAM)**. This is designed to keep the monthly payment constant in terms of purchasing power rather than in terms of dollars.

In our example, with a real rate of 3%, the monthly payment is fixed at $422 in first-year dollars. If inflation is 10% over the life of the mortgage, the monthly payment in dollars increases at a rate of 10% per year. This means a final payment of

$$\$422 \times (1.10)^{30} = \$7,364$$

price-level-adjusted mortgage (PLAM)

A mortgage with payments that are constant in terms of purchasing power.

This may seem like a lot, but by the time final payment is made, the price level will be some 17 times higher than it was originally. Presumably, the borrower's earnings in dollars will also be 17 times higher. As a result, the burden of the $7,364 final payment will be no greater than the burden of the $422 first payment.[10]

PLAMs are popular in many traditionally high inflation countries such as Israel, Turkey, Mexico, and Argentina. Their introduction in the United States has been hampered by regulatory obstacles. It is unclear how the host of regulations surrounding mortgage lending—such as disclosure rules, interest rate ceilings, and tax regulations—would apply to PLAMs. When U.S. inflation was high in the early 1980s, there was some interest in introducing these instruments. With inflation rates down, interest has waned.

indexation
Linking of an amount due to a price index.

Indexation.   The price-level-adjusted mortgage is an example of a more general idea—**indexation**. A financial or other contract is indexed if it stipulates dollar payments linked to some published price index.

Indexation is common in high-inflation countries such as Brazil, Argentina, and Israel, and in medium-inflation countries such as the United Kingdom. In these countries, it is indexation that makes inflation "tolerable." Because wages, savings accounts, and so on are all indexed, life can proceed more or less as normal.

Because inflation has been less severe in the United States, indexation is less common here. However, some wage contracts contain "COLAs" (cost-of-living adjustment clauses); parts of the tax code are now indexed to the CPI, and Social Security payments are indexed to the CPI.

Since January 1997, the U.S. Treasury has been selling inflation-indexed bonds. The coupon and the principal of these bonds are linked to an index of inflation. For example, suppose the CPI is 100 when the Treasury issues a 5-year inflation-indexed bond for $100,000 with semiannual coupons of 1.5%. When a particular coupon is due 3 years later, the CPI has risen to 107. The Treasury is therefore required to pay:

$$\$100,000 \times 0.015 \times \left(\frac{107}{100}\right) = \$1,605$$

Prices for inflation-indexed Treasury securities are listed at the end of Exhibit 4.1. The final column shows the accrued principal. This is the value of the principal adjusted for the inflation that has taken place since the bond was issued. For example, for the bond maturing in May 2029, the dollar value of its principal has increased by 7.2% since it was issued. The yield listed for inflation-indexed securities is a *real* yield. For example, the yield to maturity listed for the inflation-indexed bond maturing in April 2029 is 3.44%. The listed yield on the comparable nonindexed bond maturing in May 2029 is 5.84%. This implies that the market expects the rate of inflation over this period to be roughly the difference between these rates:

$$5.84\% - 3.44\% = 2.4\%$$

---

[10] The PLAM also eliminates the risk of a change in the rate of inflation. If inflation turns out to be higher than 10%, the real rate will be less than 3%, the borrower will gain, and the lender lose. Conversely, if inflation turns out to be lower than 10%, the PLAM ensures a real rate of 3%, whatever the actual rate of inflation.

SUMMARY

- You can calculate the market price of a security promising a single payment from its market yield and vice versa.

- For a security promising multiple payments, you can calculate its market price by summing the present values of the constituent payments. The market yield is the single interest rate at which the sum of the present values of the constituent payments equals the market price.

- If the market yield on a security rises, its market price falls. The longer the maturity (for a security promising a single payment) or the duration (for one promising multiple payments) the greater the fall in price.

- For a given holding period, securities with payments due before the end of the holding period involve reinvestment risk because such payments must be reinvested at an uncertain yield.

- Holding securities that promise payment in a foreign currency involves exchange rate risk

- In the long run, monetary expansion tends to raise prices.

- The CPI can be used to convert current dollars into constant dollars of some base period. Such a conversion is essential for meaningful comparison of dollar amounts over time.

- The real interest rate measures yield in terms of purchasing power. It equals the nominal rate less the rate of inflation.

DISCUSSION QUESTIONS

1. You buy a 20-year strip with a face value of $1 million and a market yield of 6%. How much do you pay for it? Later the same day, the market yield falls to 5%. How much do you lose or gain?

2. First National offers a 3% APR on its 1-year CDs, compounded monthly. Second National offers a 2.95% APR, compounded weekly. Which is the better deal?

3. First National offers a 30-year mortgage at an APR of 9%. The mortgage must be repaid in 360 equal monthly payments. What is the amount of the monthly payment on a $100,000 mortgage?

4. In Exhibit 4.1, there is an 11⅝% Treasury bond maturing in November 2002. If you took a such a bond with a $1 million face value and stripped it, what strips would you have (strips of what maturity, how much of each)? Use the listing of strips to find the value of each of your strips. Add together the value of the strips and compare the total with the price of the bond.

5. The market price of a 20-year bond with face value $1 million and a 7% coupon rate is $900,000. What is the approximate yield to maturity?

6. Exhibit 4.1 lists a bill that matures on August 2, 2001. How much would you have to pay for such a bill with a face value of $1 million?

7. You buy a 5-year bond with 8% annual coupons and a face value of $1 million. You pay $1.1 million for it. You hold the bond to maturity and are able to reinvest the coupons at 8%. What is your holding-period yield?

8. Calculate the duration of a 3-year bond with 10% annual coupons, selling at par.

9. The following is a quotation from a government securities dealer for a $100,000 note:

Rate	Maturity	Bid	Ask	Yield
13.75	Jul93n	105:10	105:14	8.21

   a. How much is the dealer willing to pay for the note? How much is the dealer willing to sell it for? What is the semiannual coupon payment?

   b. Suppose the price of this security falls to 100. Does its yield rise or fall? Can you give the approximate value of the new yield? (Do not attempt to calculate it exactly.)

10. A bank has $10 billion in assets and $9 billion in liabilities. The duration of its assets is 2.2 years. The duration of its liabilities is 1.5 years. Market interest rates rise from 5% to 6%. What is the gain or loss to the bank?

11. You buy a 3-year Japanese government bond with annual coupons of 4%. The exchange rate when you buy the bond is 120¥/$. You reinvest the

coupons in Japanese government securities at a yield of 5%. When the bond matures the exchange rate is 130¥/$. What is your holding-period yield?

12. Using the example of retirement savings in the chapter, how much will you have when you retire—in terms of today's dollars—if inflation over the next 30 years is 3, 6, or 9%? What will be the real interest rate on your savings in each case?

13. Using the same retirement savings example, suppose there is no inflation over the next 30 years. When you retire, you convert your savings into a 20-year annuity with annual payments. What will be the amount of the annuity (assume an interest rate of 7%)? How much will the final payment be worth if inflation is 3, 6, or 9%?

14. What is the value 30 years from now of a 30-year $1,000 annuity if the interest rate is 10%?

15. How long will it take an investment of $100 to double when it is invested at (a) 3%, (b) 10%, and (c) 20%?

16. How much should I be willing to pay for a promise of $1,000 in 10 years time if the market yield on such promises is 10%?

17. An security promises cash flows of $700,000 in year 1, $700,000 in year 2, and $900,000 in year 3.

What is the present value of this security if the interest rate is 5%? 10%?

18. A store offers the same TV for either $320 cash or $20 down and 18 monthly payments of $20. If I can borrow at 1% a month, should I pay cash or use the store's payment plan? What monthly interest rate is the store charging me? What is the APR? The effective annual rate?

19. A bank pays $106 million for bonds with a par value of $100 million, 3 years to maturity, and an annual coupon of 14% (a coupon has just been paid, before the bank bought the bonds). The bank expects the market yield on these bonds one year from now to be 12%. If this is correct, for how much will the bank be able to sell the bonds? If it does sell them then at this price, what will be the holding period yield?

20. One year ago you bought a $10,000, 3-year T-bill at the then-current market yield of 7%. Since then market yields have risen to 8% and you find that you must sell the bill.
    a. What is the current price of the bill?
    b. What is your realized yield on this investment?
    c. Would you have done better with a 1-year bill? With a 20-year bill?

KEY TERMS

present value
future value
compounding
zero-coupon bond (zero)
market price
market yield
compounding period
periodic interest rate
annual percentage rate (APR)
effective annual rate (EAR)
amortized loan
annuity

perpetuity
yield to maturity (YTM)
approximate yield to maturity
   (AYTM)
selling at a discount
selling at a premium
selling at par
bid price
asked price
interest rate risk
holding-period yield
reinvestment risk

duration
exchange rate risk
stripping
monetary expansion
consumer price index (CPI)
rate of inflation
measuring in constant dollars
nominal interest rate
real interest rate
price-level-adjusted mortgage
   (PLAM)
indexation

PART II

INTERMEDIARIES

CHAPTER 5

UNDERSTANDING FINANCIAL INTERMEDIARIES

When you finish this chapter you will understand:

- The different ways banks and other financial intermediaries can increase their profits
- The two biggest dangers they face in doing so
- Why banks are always trying to get bigger and to expand into new activities

Having laid the foundations, we are now ready to study how our financial system is organized and why it is changing. We saw in Chapter 2 that the financial system facilitates payments, lending, and trade in risk. We also saw that it does this in two different ways—indirectly, through intermediaries, and directly, through organized markets. We begin here, in Part II, with financial intermediaries. We look at financial markets in Part III.

In studying financial intermediaries we face a dilemma. To make sense of real-world financial intermediaries, we need to know what is involved in their management. But to understand what is involved in their management we need to know a lot about real-world financial intermediaries.

We will resolve this dilemma by tackling the management of financial intermediaries twice. We take a first look here. While this first look is necessarily schematic and incomplete, it will give us the basic tools we need to understand financial intermediaries. When we have completed our review of real-world financial intermediaries and financial markets, we will, in Chapter 18, take a second look at the management of financial intermediaries. This second look will be more detailed and realistic.

We begin this chapter by looking at the factors that affect the profitability of a bank. We then review them one by one to see how profitability can be improved. We look at the issues involved in setting interest rates on loans and on deposits. We look at reserves and at alternative ways of ensuring liquidity. We look at the role of equity in protecting a bank from insolvency. We then examine the effect of size on a bank's profitability and the possibility of improving profitability by engaging in other, related activities. We conclude by drawing some lessons about the management of financial intermediaries in general.

YOU OPEN A BANK

The best way to learn about managing a financial intermediary is to give it a try. To that end, we will help you set up a bank and learn how to manage it. Much of what you learn about managing a bank applies in equal measure to other types of intermediary.

Balance Sheets and T-Accounts

To start a bank you need to put up some of your own money. Depositors will be more willing to trust you with their money if they see you are also risking some of your own. So, mobilizing your resources, and borrowing from friends and family, you raise $5 million. This is the bank's initial equity—the owners' stake in the bank. Next, you rent a building, obtain a charter, and hang up a freshly painted sign saying "NOVA BANK."

balance sheet
Financial statement that lists a firm's assets, liabilities, and net worth.

To manage your bank effectively, you need a system of accounts. This will enable you to see the effects of your decisions on the bank's profitability. The type of account you will use most often is a **balance sheet**. This lists, at a given moment, the bank's **assets** (what the bank owns), its **liabilities** (what it owes others), and its net worth or **equity** (what belongs to the owners). Equity is calculated as a residual:

$$\text{equity} = \text{assets} - \text{liabilities} \qquad [5.1]$$

assets
What a firm owns.

Your balance sheet, as you open for business, is as follows:

liabilities
What a firm owes.

ASSETS		LIABILITIES AND EQUITY	
Cash	$5m	Liabilities	0
		Equity	$5m

equity
The value of a firm to its owner.

Because of the way equity is defined, the left- and right-hand columns always balance (sum to the same amount). Hence the name. Your initial equity is the amount of money you yourself (the owner) have put into the bank.

With each transaction, the balance sheet will change. For example, suppose you take $4 million of your cash and deposit it at the Fed (this deposit will be useful later for clearing checks). After the transaction is completed, your balance sheet will read:

Cash	$1m	Liabilities	0
Deposit at Fed	4m	Equity	$5m

Rather than rewriting the balance sheet after each change, we will usually describe the effect of a transaction on the balance sheet with a **T-account**. A T-account shows only the *changes* to the balance sheet that result from a particular transaction. For example, the T-account for the foregoing change is

T-account
Accounting statement that lists only the changes that occur in balance sheet items as the result of a transaction.

Cash	−$4m	
Deposit at Fed	+4m	

Entries in a T-account, unlike those in the balance sheet, are always preceded by a plus or minus. This is because all the entries in the T-account refer to changes. Balance sheet items that have not changed do not appear on the T-account. Like the balance sheet itself, the T-account must balance. Total changes on the left (to assets) must equal total changes on the right (to liabilities and net worth). In this case, since there is no change on the right, the changes on the left must sum to zero.

Soon after you open the bank, Meg Willis, the owner of a local camera store, comes in to ask for a 6-month loan of $50,000. She plans to use the money to finance an expansion into audio equipment. After checking out the application, you approve the loan.

As we saw in Chapter 2, fractional reserve banks (like Nova) make loans by creating deposits. The *immediate* effect on your balance sheet of your making the loan is

Loans		Checking deposits	
Willis	+$50,000	Willis	+$50,000

However, Willis soon spends the money she has borrowed. She writes a dozen checks to various suppliers for a total of $50,000. When these checks clear, the effect on your balance sheet is

Deposit at Fed	−$50,000	Checking deposits	
		Willis	−$50,000

As you can see, checks clear through your deposit at the Fed. Your deposit there falls by $50,000, and you debit Willis's deposit for the same amount.

In the months that follow, many more new customers come in to borrow and to open checking deposits. Most new deposits are in the form of checks drawn on other banks. As these clear, the Fed credits your deposit. For example, the effect of one $30,000 deposit is

Deposit at Fed	+$30,000	Checking deposits	
		Smith	+$30,000

A year later—after many deposits, withdrawals, loans, and repayments—your balance sheet reads[1] (Reserves are the sum of Cash and Deposit at Fed):

Reserves	$4.0m	Deposits	$20.0m
Loans	21.0m	Equity	5.0m

Profits and Return on Equity

The time has come for you to take stock. How are you doing in terms of the bottom line? To find out, you need to calculate your income and your costs. The difference is profit.

Loan income.   Your income is what you earn on your loans. The first thing we need to know is the yield you earn. The yield that counts is not the interest rate that appears on the loan contracts, but the rate you actually earn—the **realized yield**. The two differ because repayment is uncertain: some of your borrowers will default.

realized yield on loans
The rate that is actually earned, after subtracting losses.

Your realized rate can be calculated from the following formula:

$$\text{realized rate} = \text{contractual rate} \times \text{fraction of good loans} - (1 - \text{recovery rate}) \times \text{fraction of bad loans} \quad [5.2]$$

Suppose the average contractual rate on your loans is 12%. Some 90% of your loans are paid as promised. On the remainder, you lose 15% of the principal and all of the interest, so your recovery rate is 85%. Then your realized rate is

$$0.12 \times 0.90 - (1 - 0.85) \times 0.10 = 0.0930$$

or 9.3%. (Notice that all the percentages are converted into decimal fractions when used in the formula.)

Your total revenue is your realized yield times the amount of your loans:

$$0.093 \times \$21.0m = \$1,953,000$$

explicit interest on a deposit
The contractual interest rate.

Cost of Deposits.   From this revenue we need to subtract your costs. A bank is a financial intermediary: it borrows in order to lend. So a substantial part of your costs is the cost of the funds that you borrow—your deposits.

The cost of your deposits is made up of two parts. The first is the interest you actually pay. The second is the cost of the services you provide to your depositors free of charge. Such services might include free checking, free ATM transactions, and so on. We will call the interest you actually pay **explicit interest**. We will call the value of free services, expressed as a percentage of the amount of deposits, **implicit interest**.

implicit interest on a deposit
The value of services provided to a depositor without charge, expressed as a percentage of the amount of the deposit.

_____

[1] As we shall see later, these are not exactly the categories that banks use on real balance sheets. However, this way of dividing up the balance sheet is the most useful for our purposes.

If explicit interest is 3% and implicit interest 2%, then your total cost per dollar of deposit is 5%. If we multiply this by the amount of your deposits, then the cost of your deposits is

$$0.05 \times \$20.0\text{m} = \$1,000,000$$

variable costs
Costs that vary directly with the amount of deposits or loans.

fixed costs
Costs that do not vary directly with the amount of deposits or loans.

Fixed Costs.   The cost of your deposits is a **variable cost**: it depends on the amount of your deposits. In addition, you also have **fixed costs** that you must pay whatever the amount of your deposits. Whether you have $1 in deposits or $100 million, you need a bank office, a computer, a bank president, and a security guard. All of these are fixed costs.

In addition, many of the costs of being a financial intermediary are fixed. You need a loan department to process loan applications, to write loan contracts, and to monitor borrowers. To some extent, the cost will vary with the number of loans to be processed. But it will not vary much with the amount of those loans. Much the same work will be involved whether your average loan is for $100,000 or $10 million.[2]

Adding together these and other fixed costs, the total comes to $600,000.

Profits.   We can summarize all the factors affecting profits in a formula:

$$\pi = (L \times i_L) - (D \times i_D) - FC \qquad [5.3]$$

where π = profits
L = amount of loans
i_L = realized yield on loans
D = amount of deposits
i_D = cost per dollar of deposit
FC = fixed costs[3]

Applying Equation 5.3 to Nova Bank, your profit is

$$\pi = (\$21.0\text{m} \times 0.093) - (\$20.0\text{m} \times 0.05) - \$0.6\text{m} = \$353,000$$

return on equity (ROE)
Profit as a percentage return on the owners' stake in a firm.

Return on Equity.   Should you be happy with this level of profit? That depends on what sort of return it is on the sum that you and your friends and relatives have invested in the bank (your equity). That is, it depends on the **return on equity (ROE)**—the profit per dollar invested:

$$\text{ROE} = \frac{\pi}{E} \qquad [5.4]$$

where E = equity.

---

[2] Costs that do vary with the amount of loans are variable costs. We should deduct them directly from the realized yield to see how much an extra dollar of loan adds to revenue.

[3] We are abstracting here from various complications, such as taxes.

EXHIBIT 5.1   Ways to Increase Return on Equity

Lower E
Raise π
   Increase revenue
      Raise i_L
      Raise L
         By increasing D
         By decreasing reserves
   Lower variable costs
      Lower i_D
      Lower D (not very attractive—see revenue)
   Lower FC

Nova's ROE is

$$ROE = \frac{353,000}{5,000,000} = 0.071, \text{ or } 7.1\%$$

Whether this is good or bad depends on the alternatives. Could you have done better with the money you invested in the bank? For example, instead of setting up Nova, you could have bought the stock of existing banks of similar risk. Suppose that that would have yielded 25%. Then your investment in Nova does not look very good at all.

Ways to Increase Return on Equity

Exhibit 5.1 lists the ways you could raise your ROE. From Equation 5.3, you see that to raise ROE you must either lower the amount of your equity or increase the amount of your profits. From Equation 5.4, you see that to increase your profits you must either raise revenue, lower variable costs, or lower fixed costs. To raise revenue you must either raise the realized rate on your loans or increase their amount. From your balance sheet, you see that to increase the amount of your loans you must either attract more deposits or reduce your reserves. To reduce variable costs, you must lower the cost of your deposits or reduce their amount. The latter is not very attractive because it means that you will be able to make fewer loans. We will look at all of these options in turn.[4]

SETTING RATES ON DEPOSITS AND LOANS

Let us begin with the cost of your deposits and the realized rate on your loans. Lowering the former or raising the latter will increase your profits and so your ROE. Your ability to do either will depend on how much competition your face. The desirability of raising the

---

[4] For now, we will assume that your fixed costs are as low as you can make them. We will have more to say about fixed costs later in the chapter.

realized rate on your loans will be further constrained by information problems and by your willingness to bear risk.

The Competitive Environment

If Nova is the only bank in the area, you may be able to get away with paying less on your deposits or charging more for your loans. You may lose some business, but the extra revenue and lower costs on the business that is left will more than make up for it. However, if there are many other banks, then paying less on deposits or charging more for loans than your competitors will lose you a lot of business. The extra profit on the little that is left will not make up for the business you lose.

However, if there are only a few banks in your area, you may be able to arrange things to your mutual benefit. Explicit collusion to set rates is illegal, so you cannot simply get together and agree to lower your deposit rates or raise your loan rates. However, nothing rules out *tacit* collusion. For example, you could try to lower your deposit rates and see whether the other banks follow your lead.

Even if yours is the only bank or if there are few banks in the area, competition from nonbank substitutes may be a problem. For example, thrift NOW accounts and money market mutual funds are substitutes for your checking deposits. Savings bonds, bond mutual funds, and many other things are substitutes for your time deposits. Consumer or business loans from finance companies and mortgage loans from mortgage banks are substitutes for your loans.[5] This means that even if you and the other banks lower your deposit rates or raise your loan rates together, you will as a group lose business to these nonbank substitutes.

We saw in Chapter 3 that competitive pricing is good for the economy. Here we see it from a different perspective. From your point of view as a banker, competitive pricing does not seem so appealing. For you, it means lower profits.

Asymmetric Information and Adverse Selection

Raising the interest rates you charge on your loans has problems beyond the possible loss of business. One of those problems is the business you will *not* lose.

The underlying problem is asymmetric information: your customers know more about their own businesses than you do. Of course, you realize that even some of your "best" loans will turn out to be bad, but you do not know which ones. To you, all the loans in a certain risk class look much the same. For example, you have loans outstanding to Meg Willis and to Sly and Sons. To you, they both look like good risks, so you charge them both your best rate of 10%. Willis is in fact a good risk, but, unknown to you, Sly is in serious trouble.

Now suppose you raise your best loan rate from 10% to 12% while the rates your competitors charge remain the same. Willis will find it relatively easy to switch to another lender. Since her business is in good shape she will be happy to show the books to another bank. Sly, on the other hand, will not want the scrutiny that switching lenders would

---

[5] We will learn about all of them in the following chapters.

involve. Sly will stay with you. The higher interest rate doesn't much matter: the bad risks don't expect to pay it anyhow!

So raising your loan rates above competing rates will increase the default risk of your loan portfolio. You will lose your better customers and be left with the lemons. New customers willing to pay the higher rates will probably be lemons too. Because the default rate goes up, the realized yield will increase by less than the increase in the contractual rate and it may even fall.

What we see at work here is the same process of adverse selection we encountered in Chapter 1 in our discussion of insurance. The loss of good borrowers when you raise your loan rates is very much like the loss of good risks when an insurance company raises its premiums. The problem in both case is asymmetric information and the resulting inability to discriminate good risks from bad.

The Risk–Return Trade-off

Competition and adverse selection prevent you from increasing what you earn from a given type of loan. So how about increasing revenue by changing the type of loan you make?

For example, loans to developers of commercial real estate or to Latin American governments carry higher realized yields than loans to the most creditworthy corporations or to the U.S. government. If you increase the share in your loan portfolio of such higher yield loans, you will increase the average return.

But are you really gaining anything by doing this? Loans of these types have a higher realized yield because there is greater uncertainty of payment. Riskier securities pay a risk premium. Hence, you can increase your average revenue in this way only by increasing the risk of your portfolio. You may decide to so anyhow, but you should be aware of the trade-off.

How about investing in long-term U.S. government securities? There is no uncertainty of payment there, and the yields are very attractive. Or how about Italian government securities? No uncertainty of payment, and even higher yields. Unfortunately, here too you can increase your average yield only by increasing your exposure to risk.

The yields on long-term U.S. government securities are higher for good reason. That reason is interest rate risk. The rate on long-term U.S. government securities may be higher than short-term rates because the market expects short-term rates to rise. If they do, you are in trouble. You pay short-term rates on your deposits: if short-term rates rise, your deposits will become more expensive. However, the rate on the long-term securities you have bought will not change. You may wind up paying more for funds than you are earning on your investments. If the market does not actually expect a rise in short-term rates, the long-term rate may be high because of the *possibility* of such a rise. The term premium is compensation for the interest-rate risk.

We also saw that there is a reason Italian government securities carry such a high yield—exchange rate risk. Italian government securities pay in lire. To fund your purchase, you are borrowing in U.S. dollars (your deposits). If the value of the lira falls, the value of your asset goes down, while the value of the corresponding liability stays the same. You take a loss.

In sum, you cannot get something for nothing. There is no way to increase the yield on your assets without increasing your exposure to risk. We will see in Chapter 18 that there are sophisticated ways to manage these risks and to improve the trade-off between risk and return. For the moment, however, as a beginner, you had best set your loan and deposit rates at competitive levels and keep away from risky investments. Let us move on to the various other ways you might increase your return on equity.

DEPOSITS, RESERVES, AND LIQUIDITY

If you cannot increase your revenue by increasing the yield on your assets, how about increasing the *amount* of your assets? Looking at your balance sheet, there are two ways you can do this—increase the amount of your deposits or decrease the amount of your reserves.

Increasing Deposits

Your bank is a financial intermediary. It borrows in order to relend. If it borrows more it can lend more. Your borrowing takes the form of deposits. To increase their amount, you can try to make your deposits more attractive than those of your competitors. You can do this by paying higher explicit interest or by providing better service (higher implicit interest).

There are dangers here, however. If you attract more deposits by making your deposits more attractive, you are also making them more expensive. We have seen that you cannot expect to earn more on your assets than your competitors do. So if your deposits cost more than theirs, your profit margins will be squeezed. You may be obliged to take on more risky assets to cover your higher costs.

We shall see in later chapters that banks do not have to wait passively for depositors to come in the door. There are ways for banks to borrow money actively. Most of these ways, however, are available only to banks much larger than yours. All of them are expensive.

It is probably best, therefore, to follow a conservative policy and content yourself with the deposits that competitive rates bring to you.

Reducing Reserves

If you cannot expand your deposits, then the only way you can increase your lending is to reduce your reserves. You currently have $4 million of reserves earning no interest at all. How about replacing some of them on your balance sheet with additional loans? Loans, unlike reserves, earn interest and contribute to profits.

For example, suppose you make another $1 million in loans at the expense of reserves:

Reserves	−$1m
Loans	+$1m

If the new loans earn the same 9.3% realized rate as your existing loans, they will add $93,000 to your profits, and your ROE will increase to

$$\text{ROE} = \frac{446,000}{5,000,000} = 0.089, \text{ or } 8.9\%$$

How far can you reduce your reserves? Your freedom is limited by legal reserve requirements. Currently, the Fed requires banks to hold 10% against checking deposits and nothing against other types of deposit. Since half your deposits are checking deposits, you must hold at least 10% of $10 million or $1 million.[6] These are called **required reserves**. So regulations allow you to reduce your reserves by $3 million, increasing your loans by the same amount, and substantially increasing your profits.

required reserves
Minimum amount of reserves a financial institution must hold.

Why a Bank Needs Liquidity

The extra profits would be welcome, but can you manage without the extra reserves? To answer this, we must see why you need reserves in the first place.

Reserves provide you with liquidity—a source of ready money. You need liquidity for two reasons. First, your deposits are convertible on demand (or with specified notice) into cash. As we saw in Chapter 2, pooling takes care of the problem most of the time. Demands for conversion (withdrawals, checks drawn) are offset by new deposits. Sometimes, however, there is an excess of demands for conversion. You must be able to meet such demands.

The second reason you need liquidity is to be able to accommodate your customers when they come to you for loans. Sometimes, this is just a matter of good customer relations. For example, if Meg Willis comes to you for another loan and you have to turn her down because you lack the funds, she may take all of her business elsewhere.

Frequently, though, you have no choice about making the loan. Banks often make formal **loan commitments** in advance to lend to their customers: a majority of commercial loans are made this way. For example, you might have given Meg Willis a formal commitment that she can borrow $100,000 from you at any time over the next 6 months. In that case you would be in default of your commitment if you could not provide her with the funds.

loan commitment
A commitment of a bank in advance to provide credit.

Your $1 million of required reserves will not give you the liquidity you need. Required reserves are just that—required. You cannot draw on them as you please. For example, suppose you made a loan under a commitment by running down your required reserves. This would leave with a reserve ratio of about 5%. You would be in violation of reserve requirements and in serious trouble.

Required reserves are not really there to provide banks with liquidity. Their purpose is different. They help the Fed control the banks' creation of new deposits. And they also provide the Fed with an interest-free loan. This is a source of income for the government, currently worth over $3 billion a year.

excess reserves
Reserves held in excess of the required amount.

You could ensure liquidity with reserves in excess of the those required—**excess reserves**. But excess reserves are expensive: their opportunity cost is the interest you could be earning on something else.

Asset Management and Liability Management

There are ways to ensure liquidity other than by holding excess reserves. The two basic approaches are called *asset management* and *liability management*. Although we must leave the details for Chapter 18, the basic ideas are quite simple.

---

[6] Reserve requirements are a little more complicated than this. We will look at them in detail in Chapter 19.

asset management

The use of a financial institution's asset structure to provide liquidity.

secondary reserves

Earning assets that can readily be turned into cash.

overnight loan

A loan made one day to be repaid the next.

liability management

The use of a financial institution's liability structure to provide liquidity.

With **asset management** instead of holding excess reserves you hold earning assets that can readily be turned into cash. Such assets are called **secondary reserves**. Business loans, like the one you made to Meg Willis, are of no use: they are too illiquid. You cannot ask Willis to repay the loan early, and selling the loan to someone else, say another bank, won't work either. The transactions costs are too high, and it will take too long to close the deal. So you need a different type of asset—one that *can* be turned into cash quickly. One candidate is an **overnight loan**—a loan made one day to be repaid the next. We shall see that much lending by one bank to another is in this form. Another type of asset that is suitable as a secondary reserve is a security that can be sold easily—government securities are perfect.

With **liability management**, rather than holding assets that you can turn into cash, you simply borrow cash as you need it. If you need to make a new loan, or if you have an outflow of deposits, you borrow the cash you need. The trick to liability management is always being able to borrow when you need to.

Weighing all these alternatives, you decide to keep $500,000 of excess reserves, and convert the rest into secondary reserves in the form of government securities.[7] The government securities earn 6%, which is substantially less than the 9.3% you make on loans. So liquidity does have its cost.

After you make these changes, your balance sheet becomes

Reserves	$1.5m	Deposits	$20.0m
Securities	2.5m		
Loans	21.0m	Equity	5.0m

Your profits increase to

$$\pi = (\$21.0m \times 0.093) + (\$2.5m \times 0.06) - (\$20.0m \times 0.05) - \$0.6m = \$503,000$$

This boosts your ROE to

$$ROE = \frac{503,000}{5,000,000} = 0.101, \text{ or } 10.1\%$$

EQUITY AND SOLVENCY

You have done all you can to increase your profits. The only remaining way to increase your return on equity is to reduce your equity (see Exhibit 5.1).

Equity and ROE

Of course, you cannot reduce your equity without some other compensating change in the balance sheet. You cannot reduce reserves or securities because you need them for liquidity. So you will have to reduce the amount of your loans. Say you want to reduce your

---

[7] As we shall see in Chapter 18, liability management is not really an option for a small bank like yours.

equity by $2 million. As $2 million in loans are repaid, instead of making new loans, you take the money out of the bank and invest it elsewhere.[8]

Reducing the amount of loans by $2 million reduces your profits by 9.3% of this amount or $186,000, so profits fall to $317,000. However, because the amount of equity has been reduced, your return on equity rises to

$$ROE = \frac{317,000}{3,000,000} = 0.106, \text{ or } 10.6\%$$

Assuming you invested the $2 million you took out of the bank well (say in the stocks of other banks), your total return on the $5 million of original equity will now be higher.

Reducing equity looks like a good idea. Let's take it further, and reduce your equity to $100,000. The balance sheet becomes

Reserves	$1.5m	Deposits	$20.0m
Securities	2.5m		
Loans	16.1m	Equity	0.1m

Profit falls by a further $269,700, to $47,300. However, return on equity rises to a very satisfying

$$ROE = \frac{47,300}{100,000} = 0.473, \text{ or } 47.3\%$$

Equity and Risk

This looks too good to be true, and, of course, it is. While ROE is up, so is the probability the bank will fail.

For example, suppose one of your larger borrowers defaults on a $200,000 loan and nothing can be recovered. Your assets will have to be marked down by $200,000. To maintain balance on the balance sheet, some item on the right-hand side will also have to be reduced by $200,000. It cannot be deposits. Your debt to your depositors is unconditional. No matter how poorly your loans do, you still owe the depositors $20 million. So the reduction will have to be in equity. Subtract $200,000 from $100,000 and your equity is −$100,000. The minus sign means your bank is **insolvent**: its liabilities exceed its assets.

insolvent

An entity is insolvent if its liabilities exceed its assets.

Since your bank is insolvent, it will be closed down and its charter revoked. When the bank's assets are liquidated, assuming all the other assets can be realized at full value, there will be only $19.9 million available to pay off $20 million in deposits. If your deposits are not insured, your depositors will take a loss. If your deposits are insured, then depositors will be paid off to the extent their deposits are covered (there is a maximum per depositor), and the insurance fund will bear part of the loss.[9]

---

[8] You could take the money out by buying back $2 million of the outstanding stock.

[9] We will discuss deposit insurance and the resolution of bank failures in detail in Chapter 19.

Market Value and Book Value

If your bank fails and its charter is revoked, you will obviously lose your $100,000 equity in the bank. But you may lose much more, because the bank may be worth considerably more than the amount you had invested in it.

market value of a bank
The amount for which the bank could be sold.

The true value of a bank is the amount you could sell it for—its **market value**. The market value of your bank might have been, say, $3 million. Why would anyone pay more for the bank than the equity value on the balance sheet (its **book value**)? Perhaps because the bank had good prospects for future profits. The difference between the book value and the market value is called the **value of the charter**.[10]

book value of a bank
The value of a bank's equity calculated from its balance sheet.

If the bank fails, what you really lose is its market value. So you may have considerably more at stake than just the book value of equity.

Equity, Depositor Behavior, and Bank Runs

value of the charter
The excess of the market value of a bank over its book value.

We have assumed that reducing equity has no effect on the behavior of depositors. But depositors understand very well that as equity falls, the risk of insolvency increases. To prevent them from withdrawing their deposits, you will have to pay them a better rate. So, as you reduce equity, your deposits will become more expensive. If you take the increased cost of your deposits into account, then reducing the amount of your equity becomes less attractive.[11]

Depositor behavior may be affected in more drastic ways. As we saw in Chapter 3, when depositors lose confidence they may run on the bank. A run can be disastrous even for a solvent bank. A bank run might force you to sell off some of your assets to accommodate withdrawals. If you had to sell these assets at "fire-sale" prices, the losses could force the bank under, even if it had been solvent before the run. The larger your equity, the less nervous will be your depositors, and the lower will be the probability of a bank run.

Of course, deposit insurance alters depositor behavior. Depositors who are fully insured will not be concerned about the level of the bank's equity: if the bank fails, they will be compensated. Any increased risk is now borne by the insurer. Consequently, it is the insurer who will now take a keen interest in the level of your equity. Massive recent losses of the federal deposit insurance funds have led bank regulators to impose minimum equity requirements on banks and on other financial institutions. These requirements are quite complicated, and we shall discuss them in detail in Chapter 19.[12]

---

[10] If the bank is sold—say to another bank—for more than its book value, then the difference between its market value and its book value will appear as an asset called "goodwill" on the balance sheet of the purchaser.

In situations more complicated than the one we are considering here, market value may diverge from book value for another reason. Accounting conventions may not reflect the true market values of existing assets and liabilities. Consequently, the calculated book value may not give an accurate estimate of the owner's equity.

[11] As we saw in Chapter 2, the value of the bank to you (its market value) can be seen as a *performance bond*. Intermediaries seek ways to make it easier and cheaper for lenders to lend to them rather than to other potential borrowers. One way to do this is to post a bond. If you yourself stand to lose from bad loans, your depositors can be more confident that you will exercise the necessary care. Reducing the size of the bond reduces depositor confidence.

[12] What we see at work here is the *Modigliani–Miller theorem*. Applied to a bank, it states that the market value of all claims on the bank (deposits plus equity) is invariant to changes in the amount of equity. If depositors are compensated fairly for the increased risk to their deposits, the increase in the expected return on equity does no more than compensate you for the increased risk you bear. Of course, if deposits are insured, and if deposit insurance premiums do not increase with risk, then the value of the bank will increase as equity is reduced. The insurer will therefore want to restrict your freedom to reduce the level of equity.

EXHIBIT 5.2   The Effects of Leverage

		Payoff to equity	Return on equity (%)	Expected return (%)	Standard error (%)
All equity	50% chance	$1,500	50		
$1,000 equity				35	15
	50% chance	$1,200	20		
Leveraged	50% chance	$1,500 − $880 = $620	210		
$200 equity $800 debt (at 10%)				135	75
	50% chance	$1,200 − $880 = $320	60		

The Effects of Leverage

Reducing equity, therefore, increases risk as well as return. Equity is a cushion against insolvency. For example, had your equity been $2 million instead of $100,000, the $200,000 loss would have been painful but not fatal. You would have been able to rebuild your equity over time and the bank would have continued to operate.

leverage
The use of bor-
rowed money to
acquire an asset.

The effect of equity on risk and return is an example of **leverage**—the financing of an investment with borrowed money. We can illustrate the principles with the simple example shown in Exhibit 5.2. There is a $1,000 investment project that pays either $1,200 or $1,500 at the end of the year: both outcomes are equally likely. The return is either 20% or 50%, so the expected return is 35%. The standard error of the return, a measure of the risk, is 15%.[13]

If you finance the project entirely with your own money ("all equity"), then your expected return is the expected return of the project; the standard error of your return is the standard error of the project.

If you finance the project with $200 of your own money and $800 of money borrowed at 10% ("leveraged"), then your expected return and your risk are altered. The return to you, after paying off the debt, is now either $1,200 − $880 = $320 or $1,500 − $880 = $620. The return on your original $200 is either 60% or 210%, for an expected return of 135%. The standard error of the return is 75%. Both the expected return and the risk have increased with leverage.

leverage ratio
The value of an
asset divided by
the amount of the
owner's own in-
vestment in it.

We can express the leverage in terms of a **leverage ratio**. This is the value of the investment divided by the amount you yourself invest. In this case the leverage ratio is $1,000/$200 = 5. The greater the leverage ratio, the higher the expected return and the greater the risk.

---

[13] The variance is 0.5 (0.20 − 0.35)² + 0.5(0.50 − 0.35)² = 0.0225. The standard error is the square root of the variance.

In terms of leverage, your bank is exactly like this simple example. The money you yourself have put up is your equity—originally $5 million. The borrowed money is your deposits—$20 million. The investment project is the bank's assets—$25 million. The leverage ratio is $25 million/$5 million = 5. If you reduce your equity to $100,000, then the leverage ratio increases to $20.1 million/$100,000 = 201. By increasing the leverage, you have increased your expected return and your risk.

Since part of a bank's assets, its reserves, has no effect on either risk or return, its equity position is often described, not in terms of its leverage ratio, but in terms of its **equity ratio**. This is defined as

equity ratio (of a bank)

The amount of a bank's equity divided by the amount of its loans and investments.

$$\text{equity ratio} = \frac{\text{equity}}{\text{loans and investments}} \qquad [5.5]$$

where "loans and investments" means all earning assets, including loans and government securities. With $5 million of equity, your bank's equity ratio is $5 million/$23.5 million = 0.213 or 21.3%. With $100,00 in equity, your bank's equity ratio is $0.1 million/$18.6 million = 0.0054 or 0.54%.[14]

Having weighed the pros and cons, your final decision is to reduce your equity to $1.5 million. Your balance sheet becomes

Reserves	$1.5m	Deposits	$20.0m
Securities	2.5m		
Loans	17.5m	Equity	1.5m

This gives an equity ratio of 7.5%.

You have now done everything you can to increase your return on equity. As a result of your efforts, your profits are now

$$\pi = (\$17.5m \times 0.093) + (\$2.5m \times 0.06) - (\$20.0m \times 0.05) - \$0.6m = \$177,500$$

and your return on equity is

$$\text{ROE} = \frac{177,500}{1,500,000} = 0.118, \text{ or } 11.8\%$$

To see how the various ratios we have discussed look in reality, see "A Balance Sheet of U.S. Commercial Banks."

ECONOMIES OF SCALE AND SCOPE

Although your return on equity is now much improved from the 7% you started with, it is still well short of the 25% that other banks seem to be earning. Why are they doing so much better?

---

[14] We shall see in Chapter 19, that there are measures that adjust for differences in risk among assets in a more sophisticated way.

A BALANCE SHEET OF
U.S. COMMERCIAL BANKS

The accompanying table shows the combined balance sheet of all U.S. commercial banks. Each item on the balance sheet is a total for all banks taken together.

You can see that the average ratio of reserves to checking deposits is

$$\frac{\$40 \text{ billion}}{\$597 \text{ billion}} = 0.067, \text{ or } 6.7\%$$

Total assets are $6,086 billion, so the average leverage ratio is

$$\frac{\$6,086 \text{ billion}}{\$424 \text{ billion}} = 14.4$$

The average equity ratio is

$$\frac{\$424 \text{ billion}}{\$5,222 \text{ billion}} = 0.081, \text{ or } 8.1\%$$

BALANCE SHEET OF U.S. COMMERCIAL BANKS

December 31, 2000
(billions of dollars)

Assets			Liabilities and Net Worth	
Reserves		$ 40	Checking deposits	$ 597
Cash in vault	15		Time deposits	3,252
Deposits at Fed	25		Other liabilities	1,813
Loans and securities		5,222		
Other assets		824	Equity	424

Source: Board of Governors of Federal Reserve, various releases.

One reason they may be doing better is because they are larger. Size is an advantage to a bank. The gains from size are called economies of scale. Another reason they may be doing better is because they are doing things other than straightforward banking. Some complementary activities can be added to banking at little extra cost, but with considerable extra profit. The gains from doing this are called economies of scope.

Economies of Scale

Other things equal, large banks should be more profitable than small ones. To understand why, let us merge your bank, Nova, with a bank in the next town, Super Trust. The combined bank, of which you become a 50% owner, is to be called SuperNova. Super Trust's balance sheet is identical to yours, so each item on SuperNova's balance sheet is exactly double the corresponding item on Nova's:

SuperNova

Reserves	$3.0m	Deposits	$40.0m
Securities	5.0m		
Loans	35m	Equity	3.0m

Given that interest rates on loans and deposits are determined by market forces, SuperNova will charge the same rates on its loans and pay the same rates on its deposits as Nova did.[15] However, SuperNova will be able to improve its profitability in other ways:

- It will have lower fixed cost relative to its assets.
- It will have less need for liquidity.
- It will be able to lower its equity ratio without increasing the danger of insolvency.

Lower Fixed Costs.   Many fixed costs are *indivisible*. A bank needs a computer and a vault whether it has $10 million in deposits or $10 billion. It needs loan officers whether the average loan is for $100,000 or for $100 million. Of course, a bank with a thousand times the deposits may need a more expensive computer or vault, but it is unlikely to be a thousand times more expensive. A bank with a thousand times the loans will need more loan officers, but not a thousand times as many. Moreover, many services that a bank provides its customers, like check clearing, investment advice, or international banking, require specialized staff. There is a minimum cost to providing such services whatever the number of customers served.

As a result of these indivisibilities, fixed costs will rise with the size of the bank, but less than proportionately. When banks merge, fixed costs will fall relative to the size of the bank.

When Super and Nova merge, you should be able to reduce their combined fixed costs. The merged bank will have a variety of duplicate facilities—two computers, two branch offices within a block on Main Street, and so on. You can cut costs by eliminating this duplication. In addition, you will find that other parts of the bank—for example, the combined loan department—are larger than you now need. By reducing their size you can further cut costs.

---

[15] Of course, if the merger significantly reduced the number of banks (say these were the only two banks in the area), then you would be able to raise your loan rates and lower your deposit rates after the merger.

Say the fixed costs of your combined bank can be reduced from $1.2 million, the sum of the fixed costs of Super and Nova, to $1.1 million. As a result, the profits of SuperNova increase from $2 \times \$177,500 = \$355,000$ to $455,000, raising the ROE to

$$\text{ROE} = \frac{455,000}{3,000,000} = 0.152, \text{ or } 15.2\%$$

Liquidity.   In addition to these physical economies of scale, there are also *financial economies of scale*. We saw in Chapter 2 that the financial technology used by banks and other financial intermediaries relies heavily on pooling and netting. The larger the pool, the better it works. The greater the number of transactions, the better the netting.

Better netting reduces the cost of liquidity for larger banks. For example, suppose the chance of a $1 million excess of withdrawals (5% of deposits) for Nova or for Super is one in a hundred. If the chances of such an event for each of the two banks are independent, then the chance of a $2 million excess of withdrawals for SuperNova (the same 5% of deposits) is less than one in a thousand. This is because on many occasions when there is an excess of withdrawals from the Super half of the bank, it will be balanced by an excess of new deposits to the Nova half, and vice versa.[16]

With better netting, SuperNova can afford to be less concerned about liquidity. It can reduce the liquidity of its assets relative to those of Super or Nova without increasing its risk of liquidity problems. So SuperNova cuts its reserves by $500,000 and its securities by $1 million, allowing it to increase loans by $1.5 million. The balance sheet becomes

SUPERNOVA

Reserves	$2.5m	Deposits	$40.0m
Securities	4.0m		
Loans	36.5m	Equity	3.0m

Profits are now

$$\pi = (\$36.5m \times 0.093) + (\$4.0m \times 0.06) - (\$40.0m \times 0.05) - \$1.1m = \$534,500$$

and return on equity is

$$\text{ROE} = \frac{534,500}{3,000,000} = 0.178, \text{ or } 17.8\%$$

Equity.   The better pooling enjoyed by the merged bank also reduces the risk of insolvency. This is because a larger bank can have a more diversified portfolio. A more diversified portfolio of loans means there is a smaller chance that a large loss will wipe out the bank's equity.

---

[16] Say withdrawals for each bank have a normal distribution with a mean of zero and a standard error of $430,000. Then the probability that withdrawals exceed $1 million is 1%. The standard error of the sum of withdrawals from the two banks together, assuming withdrawals are independent, is $600,000. Total withdrawals of $2 million is 3.3 standard errors below the mean. The probability of more than $2 million in withdrawals is less than 0.1%.

Super and Nova each have about 200 loans outstanding with an average size of about $90,000. The amount of each loan is about 6% of each bank's equity. When we combine the portfolios, the amount of the average loan falls to about 3% of combined equity. So the damage done by a single default is proportionately smaller. Moreover, if the chances of default on different loans are independent, the risk of total losses wiping out, say, 50% of equity, is lower. The reason is that on many occasions when the Super half of the bank has a bad year for defaults, the Nova half will have a good year. Only when bad years coincide will there be a large loss for the combined bank.

Of course, the key to improved diversification is independence of risks. If Super and Nova both draw their loan customers largely from the same group—say hog farmers or the automobile industry—then there is little gain in diversification from combining their loan portfolios. A bad year for hog farmers or for the automobile industry will result in a large number of defaults for *both* the constituent banks.

Because of better diversification, SuperNova can lower its equity ratio below that of Super or Nova without increasing the risk of insolvency. So SuperNova cuts its equity by $500,000, reducing its loans by the same amount. Its balance sheet becomes

SUPERNOVA

Reserves	$2.5m	Deposits	$40.0m
Securities	4.0m		
Loans	36.0m	Equity	2.5m

Profits are now

$$\pi = (\$36.0\text{m} \times 0.093) + (\$4.0\text{m} \times 0.06) - (\$40.0\text{m} \times 0.05) - \$1.1\text{m} = \$488,000$$

and return on equity is

$$\text{ROE} = \frac{488,000}{2,500,000} = 0.195, \text{ or } 19.5\%$$

Reputation.   We saw in Chapter 2 that delegation and credit substitution are important parts of the technology of financial institutions. The bank is substituting its own credit when it borrows from depositors and then lends the money out to ultimate borrowers.

Delegation and credit substitution depend on reputation. Depositors must feel that it is safer to lend to the bank than to ultimate borrowers. As a result, a bank's reputation is valuable. If the bank has a good reputation, it will be able to attract more deposits or to attract deposits at a lower rate.[17]

Reputation is indivisible in much the same way as many physical fixed costs. It is therefore a source of economies of scale. Because a large bank does more business, it has more to gain from a good reputation, and more to lose from bad behavior. Also, simple

---

[17] There is another way in which reputation is valuable. As we saw in Chapter 2, bonding and reputation are alternative ways of supporting delegation and credit substitution. So a bank with a stronger reputation will be in less need of bonding. That means that it can reduce its equity and so boost its ROE.

name recognition is an important element of reputation, at least for small depositors. A bank you have never heard of just does not seem as safe as one with a familiar name.

The enhanced reputation of the combined banks attracts $2 million more in deposits. The balance sheet is scaled up accordingly[18]:

SUPERNOVA

Reserves	$2.625m	Deposits	$42.0m
Securities	4.2m		
Loans	37.8m	Equity	2.625m

Profits are now

$$\pi = (\$37.8m \times 0.093) + (\$4.2m \times 0.06) - (\$42.0m \times 0.05) - \$1.1m = \$567,400$$

and return on equity is

$$\text{ROE} = \frac{567,400}{2,625,000} = 0.216, \text{ or } 21.6\%$$

To sum up, your return on equity is much improved by the merger. It has risen from 11.8% to 21.6%. This improvement is the result of two types of economy of scale. The first stems from indivisibilities in fixed costs: increasing the size of the bank increases fixed costs less than proportionately. The second stems from improved pooling—financial economies of scale: increasing the size of the bank lowers the cost of protecting it against illiquidity and insolvency and increases the returns to reputation.

The Limits to Economies of Scale.   Your return is still short of the 25% you could have earned from investing in the stocks of other banks of comparable risk. Of course, you have not fully exploited potential economies of scale. SuperNova is still a very small bank. By increasing its size still further you can expect to increase further your return on equity.

However, we shall see in Chapter 7 that in the United States your ability to exploit economies of scale by increasing the size of your bank is limited by laws that restrict geographic expansion. There may be obstacles to merging your bank with another across state lines, and you will generally not be able to open branches in other states.

Even without these restrictions, a point may come when further increases in size will gain you little or may even lower the return on equity. As banks become larger and larger they start to encounter some *dis*economies of scale. These diseconomies largely result from the difficulties of managing large organizations.

For example, at Nova, you can supervise all the bank's loan officers yourself. At SuperNova, you are already forced to delegate some of the responsibility. At a $100 billion bank, several layers of bureaucracy stand between the loan officers and the CEO. The consequence may be poorer control. A serious mistake (or dishonesty) by a single loan officer can cost the bank millions.

---

[18] Since you have already set the various ratios (reserves, secondary reserves, equity) at their desirable levels, you scale everything up to preserve the same ratios.

More bureaucracy also means less flexibility. At Nova, you could respond to changing circumstances, take the appropriate decision, and have it implemented immediately. At a $100 billion bank, information about changing circumstances has to make its way up the chain of command. Decisions are made by people further removed from the action. And implementation can take a long time as instructions work their way back down the chain of command.

At some point the diseconomies of scale begin to outweigh the economies. Banks beyond a certain size may have little advantage over smaller banks. The point at which there are no further significant net economies is called the **minimum efficient scale**. Banks smaller than the minimum efficient scale are at a disadvantage, but those above this size have no significant advantage.

minimum efficient scale
The scale at which there are no further significant net economies.

Economies of Scope

While economies of scale result from doing more of the same thing, economies of scope result from doing different, but related, things. A firm can sometimes benefit from branching out into new lines of business that are closely related to what it is doing already. It may already possess the necessary tools and know-how, making entry into the new line of business less costly than it would be for a firm starting from scratch. A great deal of innovation is the result of such branching out, and it can be an important source of profit.

What lines of business might offer your bank such economies of scope? Well, you have a lot of experience at processing payments. One possibility is to offer to process firms' incoming checks and ensure that they clear as quickly as possible. Such a service is called a cash management system. You will receive a fee for the service, and, since you already have much of the needed technology and trained personnel, providing the service is relatively inexpensive. This new activity is particularly attractive because it makes no demands on the bank's liquidity and does not increase its risk of insolvency. You have no need, therefore, to increase your provision for liquidity or to increase your equity. In principle, there are many other such services your bank could offer. However, as we shall see in Chapter 6, regulations often stand in the way.

Your new cash management department brings in $200,000 of extra revenue and adds $160,000 to your costs.[19] The net addition of $40,000 to your bottom line brings your return on equity up to 23.1%.

BANKS AND OTHER INTERMEDIARIES

We have seen what is involved in managing one type of financial intermediary—a bank. In many ways, managing any other type of intermediary is similar. Like commercial banks, other intermediaries borrow by issuing their own IOUs and use the proceeds to acquire earning assets. In doing so they face the same problems as you encountered in managing Nova.

---

[19] A completely new firm set up to provide the same services would have costs of about $250,000 a year and would therefore be unable to compete with you.

EXHIBIT 5.3   Major U.S. Financial Intermediaries and Their Functions

	Lending (Billions of Dollars)[a]	Payments	TRADE IN RISK	
			Insurance	Forward Transactions
Commercial banks	6,593	✓	✓	✓
Near banks				
Savings institutions[b]	1,274	✓		
Credit unions	476	✓		
Finance companies	1,124			
Insurance companies				
Life insurance	3,224		✓	
Property–liability	866		✓	
Investment intermediaries				
Pension funds	6,652		✓	
Mutual funds	6,421			
Securities firms	1,333			✓
SPVs[c]	2,797			
Government intermediaries				
The Fed	639	✓		
Agencies[d]	4,984			✓
Nonfinancial companies	2,020	✓		✓

[a] Total financial assets for financial companies and trade credit for nonfinancial companies.

[b] Savings and loans, mutual savings banks, and federal savings banks.

[c] Issuers of asset-backed securities (see Chapter 14).

[d] Includes federally sponsored credit agencies (see Exhibit 12.1 for a breakdown) and federally related mortgage pools (see Chapter 13 for more information).

Source: Flow of Funds Accounts, *Third Quarter, 2001. (http://www.federalreserve.gov/releases/Z1/)*

Exhibit 5.3 lists the major types of financial intermediary in the United States.[20] For each type of intermediary, it shows the amount of lending. You can see that commercial banks are the most important in this respect, although pension funds are close. The exhibit also indicates whether each type of institution is involved in the other two functions of the financial system—payments and trade in risk.

All intermediaries must worry about the cost of their liabilities and the return on their assets. Their liabilities and their assets may be quite different. However, they face the same problems you encountered in managing Nova. Competition constrains their ability to set rates on liabilities and assets. Asymmetric information is a problem in pricing liabilities and in selecting assets. In selecting assets, there is in general a trade-off between risk and return.

All intermediaries must worry about liquidity. Some, such as pension funds, have long-term liabilities, so that liquidity is less of a concern. Others, like money market

---

[20] On the whole, other countries have similar types of intermediary. However, we shall see that some other types of intermediary that exist in other countries have no exact counterpart in the United States.

mutual funds and securities firms, have very short-term liabilities and are in much the same position as banks. We shall look at liquidity management in some detail in Chapter 18.

All intermediaries must worry about solvency. Their assets are subject to uncertainty of payment, interest rate risk, and exchange rate risk. Consequently, losses on their assets may render them unable to honor their liabilities. We shall see in Chapter 18 that there are ways to manage these risks. Nonetheless, the ultimate protection against insolvency is equity.

All intermediaries face economies of scale and of scope. Many of the changes in the financial system that we shall discuss in the coming chapters are the result of attempts by various institutions to capture economies of scale and of scope.

We have focused in this chapter on only one of the three functions of the financial system—lending. But financial intermediaries are also involved in payments and in trade in risk (see Exhibit 5.3). Even for a small bank like Nova, the payments function is important (as was shown by your expansion into cash management). Gauging the importance of financial intermediaries solely in terms of the amount of their lending is therefore a mistake. For example, the payments function of banks and the insurance function of insurance companies are enormously important to the economy, quite apart from any lending the institutions may do.

In managing Nova, your choices were often constrained by government regulation. Regulations set minimum values for your reserves and for your equity. Regulations limit your ability to capture economies of scale by opening new branches and your ability to capture economies of scope by expanding into related activities. In addition, the existence of federal deposit insurance affects the trade-off you face in increasing your leverage.

All intermediaries face government regulations and other forms of government intervention. Managing an intermediary means doing the best you can, given the constraints imposed by government intervention. As we shall see, the desire to escape these constraints has been a major force behind financial innovation.

The forces of innovation and change, constrained and also driven by government intervention, have resulted in enormous shifts in the relative importance of different types of intermediary. Over the twentieth century, commercial banks declined steadily in relative importance. Pension funds have grown greatly in relative importance since the 1940s. Other intermediaries, such as thrifts (savings banks and savings and loans), life insurance companies, and securities firms have fluctuated widely in their relative importance over the years. In the coming chapters we shall see why these changes have taken place and what further changes lie ahead.

SUMMARY

- The profits of a bank are its revenues (loans times realized yield) less its variable costs (deposits times cost per dollar of deposit) less its fixed costs. The return on equity is profits divided by equity.

- The return on equity can be increased by reducing equity or by increasing profits. Profits can be increased by earning more on loans, by paying less for deposits, by increasing loans (through an increase in deposits or a decrease in reserves), or by lowering fixed costs.

- The ability of a bank to raise the rates it charges on loans or to lower the rate it pays on deposits is constrained by competition from other banks and from nonbank substitutes. Moreover, raising the contractual rate on loans may be undesirable because of adverse selection. A higher realized yield on assets will generally mean greater risk.

- The ability of a bank to reduce its reserves is limited by reserve requirements and by its need for liquidity. There are two ways to ensure liquidity, other than by holding excess reserves—asset management and liability management.

- Reducing equity raises the return on equity, but it also increase the risk of insolvency. (This is an example of leverage.) Reducing equity also increases the likelihood of a bank run, although this effect is less pronounced because of deposit insurance.

- Because of economies of scale, other things equal, large banks should be more profitable than small ones. Beyond some point, diseconomies of scale begin to reduce profitability.

- Economies of scale in banking are the result of indivisibilities in many fixed costs, financial economies that result from better pooling and netting with larger size, and economies associated with reputation.

- Economies of scope come from engaging in new lines of business at relatively low cost because they are related to existing lines of business.

- The issues involved in managing any financial intermediary are much the same as those involved in managing a bank—setting rates on assets and liabilities, ensuring liquidity and solvency, economies of scale, and economies of scope.

- The choices of managers of financial intermediaries are constrained by government regulation and affected by other forms of government intervention.

DISCUSSION QUESTIONS

1. Draw up T-accounts for the following transactions:
   a. Meg Willis repays the $100,000 loan from Nova Bank with a check drawn on her deposit at the bank.
   b. Meg Willis repays the $100,000 loan from Nova Bank with a check drawn on her deposit at another bank.
   c. A borrower with a $50,000 loan from the bank defaults and the loan is written off.
   d. After market interest rates fall, Nova sells for $2 million some securities for which it paid $1.5 million.

2. Calculate the effect on Nova's profits and on its ROE of each of the following changes. In each case, start from Nova's final balance sheet (before its merger with Super Trust).
   a. A reserve requirements of 5% is imposed on time deposits (half of Nova's deposits are time deposits).
   b. Bank regulators impose a minimum equity ratio of 10% on all banks.
   c. New banking regulations increase the burden of required paperwork. The cost to the bank is $50,000 a year.

   d. The yield curve steepens, so that Nova can pay 1% less in explicit interest on its deposits and earn 1% more on its loans.

3. Banks have received a bad press for the "excessive" interest rates they charge on credit card debt.
   a. Suppose a bank is paying 4% on its deposits and charging 18% on credit card debt. Is it making a profit of 14%? What might account for the difference in rates?
   b. Banks do not usually compete for credit card business by offering lower interest rates. Why not?
   c. At one time Congress was considering legislation to cap credit card interest rates at 14%. As a banker, what would you have done had the legislation gone through?

4. List all the reasons why there are economies of scale and of scope in banking. Which of them do you think would apply to an insurance company (see Chapter 2)? To a an automobile company?

5. The typical bank has a much higher leverage ratio than the typical manufacturing firm. What are the differences between the two kinds of business that account for this?

6. Suppose that servicing the average checking deposit costs a bank $5 a month and that the bank is willing to pay implicit interest of 5% on checking deposits. What average balance would it require for "free checking"? Banks could, in principle, pay higher explicit interest on checking deposits and eliminate implicit interest. That is, they could charge for the "free" services they now provide (checks, teller machine transactions, and so on). Why do you think they do not do so?

7. Consider the following banks:

BANK A

Reserves	$20m	Deposits	$150m
Loans	140m	Equity	10m

BANK B

Reserves	$15m	Deposits	$110.0m
Loans	105m	Equity	10m

Each bank faces a 12.5% realized rate on loans and variable costs of 10¢ per dollar of deposits. Total fixed cost is $750,000 for Bank A and $700,000 for Bank B.

a. Calculate profit and return on equity for each bank. Why might their return on equity differ?

b. Now Banks A and B merge to form Bank C. Assume that the reduction in fixed costs is such that the total fixed costs for the combined bank is $750,000. Find Bank C's profit and return on equity assuming no change in the combined balance sheet.

c. Owing to improved pooling, Bank C can reduce its reserves by $500,000. What, if anything, happens to profit and return on equity?

8. What are the ways that your choices, as the manager of Nova, are restricted by government regulation? Can you justify these restrictions?

<hr>

KEY TERMS

balance sheet	fixed costs	insolvent
assets	return on equity (ROE)	market value of a bank
liabilities	required reserves	book value of a bank
equity	loan commitment	value of the charter
T-account	excess reserves	leverage
realized yield on loans	asset management	leverage ratio
explicit interest on a deposit	secondary reserves	equity ratio of a bank
implicit interest on a deposit	overnight loan	minimum efficient scale
variable costs	liability management	

CHAPTER 6

WHAT IS A BANK?

When you finish this chapter you will understand:

- The types of institution from which banks have evolved in the past and from which future banks are likely to evolve
- How and why bank assets and bank liabilities have changed and are continuing to change
- How and why banks are constantly expanding into new lines of business

Commercial banking is changing rapidly. Both the nature of the business and the structure of the industry have changed dramatically in the last quarter century. While commercial banks remain the single most important intermediary in the United States, their relative importance seems to have declined. In many other countries, commercial banks seem more important and the business they do and the structure of the industry are very different. What accounts for these changes and for these differences? In this chapter, we begin a two-chapter exploration of commercial banking: its purpose is to answer this question and to prepare you for the changes yet to come.

In this chapter we focus on the business of commercial banking. What is a commercial bank, and what does it do? In Chapter 7 we will focus on the banking industry. What is its structure? How well does it perform? Some aspects of commercial banking are so important that they merit separate chapters of their own: we discuss the payment system and foreign exchange in Chapter 8, bank management in Chapter 18, and bank safety and deposit insurance in Chapter 19.

The basic business of banking is a combination of two functions—payments and financial intermediation. However, that business has changed and continues to change along three dimensions:

- The entry of new types of institution into banking
- The evolution of the intermediation function as banks develop new types of lending and new types of borrowing
- The addition of other, related, functions to the basic ones of payments and financial intermediation

To understand these three dimensions of change, we take a look at how banking has evolved. The past is a laboratory where we will see the forces of change at work—the same forces that are at work today. We begin by tracing the evolution of the commercial bank into its modern form. We then look at the evolution of the banking business. First we see how bank intermediation has changed by looking at the evolution of bank assets and liabilities. Then we look at activities other than financial intermediation. In the final section, we see how all these changes are reflected in bank balance sheets and in bank income statements.

THE EVOLUTION OF THE MODERN BANK

Banks combine payment services and lending. They combine the two to achieve economies of scope. An institution that offers one of the two services is soon tempted by complementarities to offer the other. As a result, banks have evolved both from institutions that began with payments and from those that began with lending.

We will look at the evolution of banking more or less chronologically. Exhibit 6.1 provides a time frame to help you keep track of the different types of bank and when and where they developed.

Banking in Europe

Money-Changer Banks.   Modern banking originated in Europe. The earliest known references to banking are found in Genoese notarial records of the twelfth and thirteenth centuries. In Genoa *bancherius* meant money changer—the name referring to the table or bench at which the money changer conducted his business. Money changers weighed, tested, and sorted coins and exchanged foreign coins for more acceptable local ones. By the thirteenth century, Genoese bankers were accepting time and demand deposits, extending credit, and participating in business partnerships.

money-changer banks
Banks that began as money changers.

These **money-changer banks** began as *warehouse banks*.[1] Their customers made payments by transferring ownership of deposits. Warehouse banking in Genoa and elsewhere gradually developed into *fractional reserve banking*. Reserve ratios of about 30% were typical. It was well understood at the time that such fractional reserve banks created money. In fifteenth-century Venice these transferable deposits were called "bank money" to distinguish them from specie (gold or silver coin).

---

[1] They were much like the fictitious Ruthenian banks of Chapter 2.

EXHIBIT 6.1   The Evolution of The Commercial Bank

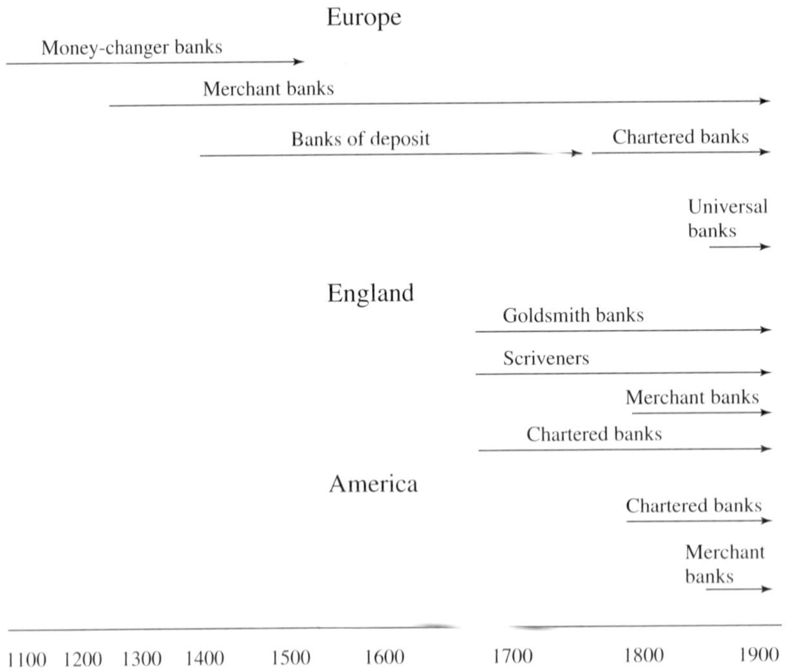

Europe

Money-changer banks

Merchant banks

Banks of deposit   Chartered banks

Universal
banks

England

Goldsmith banks

Scriveners

Merchant banks

Chartered banks

America

Chartered banks

Merchant
banks

| 1100 | 1200 | 1300 | 1400 | 1500 | 1600 | 1700 | 1800 | 1900 |

---

overdraft

A line of credit
that allows a de-
positor to borrow
automatically to
cover uncovered
payments.

Lending was usually in the form of an **overdraft**. For example, Luigi owes Alessandro 2,000 ducats, but he has only 1,000 ducats in his deposit. He nonetheless orders his bank to pay Alessandro the 2,000 ducats, and the bank honors the order. The bank credits Alessandro's deposit with 2,000 ducats, debits Luigi's with 1,000, and accepts an IOU from Luigi for 1,000 to cover the remainder. (In many countries, overdrafts remain the principal form of bank lending to households.)

usury

The charging of
(excessive) inter-
est on a loan.

Some deposits paid a fixed rate of interest; more usually, however, deposits paid a dividend based on the bank's profits. This was a way around the church's ban on **usury**, which then meant the earning of risk-free interest. Since profits were uncertain, the payment of dividends was not considered to be usury.

Widespread failures of money-changer banks in the fifteenth century destroyed public confidence in them and led to increasingly restrictive regulation. As a result, money-changer banks declined in importance, and by the sixteenth century they had largely disappeared.

remittance

The service of
making payment
at a distance.

Merchant Banks.   The disappearance of the money-changer banks left an unfilled demand for payments services. Other types of institution soon stepped in to fill the gap. Money changers had provided the *local* means of payment. However, the making of payments at a distance—**remittance**—had largely been in the hands of merchants. As the money-changer banks declined, **merchant banks** extended their business to provide local

merchant banks

Banks that began
as merchants.

means of payment too. Like the money-changer banks, the merchant banks accepted deposits and made loans.

The typical merchant banker was primarily a merchant. His principal business was international or interregional trade. However, his business connections in other cities allowed him to offer remittance services as a profitable sideline (another example of the economies of scope). For some merchants, this sideline became their main activity; for most, however, their main activity remained trade.

From the thirteenth to the seventeenth century, merchant banking grew to become the predominant form of banking in continental Europe. The Italians, especially the Florentines, dominated the business.

Banks of Deposit.   The increasing problems of the money-changer banks were a major concern for governments. Trade was an important source of revenue in the form of customs and excise taxes. Problems with the payments system were a serious impediment to trade and hence a threat to government revenue.

banks of deposit
Government-
sponsored ware-
house banks.

As a result, cities began to set up **banks of deposit** to perform essentially the same payments function as the money changer banks. The first bank of deposit was the *Taula*, or "table," established in Barcelona in 1401. The most famous was the Bank of Amsterdam, established in 1609. Banks of deposit began as warehouse banks. Just like the money changers, they accepted deposits of coin, which they weighed and sorted, and they allowed depositors to make payments by transferring the ownership of deposits.

**suspension of
convertibility**
A refusal to allow
cash withdrawals,
while continuing
to process check
payments.

Also like the money-changer banks, the banks of deposit soon discovered the attractions of fractional reserve banking. However, rather than lending to merchants, they lent exclusively or primarily to the government. As with the money changers, excessive lending frequently led to problems. However, because they were government institutions, they were able to avoid failure, or at least delay it, by resorting to a **suspension of convertibility**. They refused to allow withdrawals of cash while continuing to process deposit transfers.

Universal Banks.   English and American commercial banks financed the working capital of industrial firms by discounting bills. Generally, however, they did not finance their fixed capital. In England, early industrial development was gradual and the need for fixed capital modest—early machinery was simple and inexpensive. Therefore fixed capital was largely financed out of internal funds. In the United States, industrial development came later—in the late nineteenth century—and it was faster and more capital intensive. It was largely financed by the growing securities market. As we shall see, the banking system provided funds to the securities market in the form of *call loans*.

In continental Europe too, industrial development came later. So European governments, feeling that their countries' industrial development was held back by the shortage of long-term finance, set up special-purpose "industrial banks" to provide it. The prototype for these industrial banks was the Crédit Mobilier, sponsored by the French government, and founded in 1852.[2] The Crédit Mobilier combined traditional commercial banking with long-term lending to finance industrial and urban development. It financed these long-term

---

[2] Actually, the first bank of this type was the Belgian Société Générale, founded in 1822.

loans by issuing long-term bonds and equity shares. In addition to its own long-term lending, it underwrote public issues for its customers. The Crédit Mobilier was initially a spectacular success, but it soon got into difficulties, and it failed in 1867 (it continued in restructured form until 1902). The source of its problems was the illiquidity of its portfolio and poor diversification.

universal bank
A form of bank free to engage in any form of financial activity.

Despite its difficulties, the Crédit Mobilier provided a model for numerous industrial banks in Europe and Asia. Its best known modern descendants are the **universal banks** of Germany and Japan. In Germany, the railroad construction boom of the 1840s and 1850s drew private merchant banks into railroad finance. By the 1890s these banks were playing an active role in financing industrial companies—underwriting issues of securities for their customers as well as providing them with loans. In addition, the banks would often retain a block of stock on their own account and play an active role on the board of the companies that they financed. From the 1920s banks in Japan began to adopt a similar role—combining long-term financing and ownership with short-term financing. In many cases, the Japanese banks were associated with the great family-controlled groups of industrial companies known as *zaibatsu*.

Banking in England

Up to the seventeenth century, banking in England was relatively undeveloped. Only a few foreign merchant banks—Italian, then Dutch—had branches there. Then there came an amazing wave of financial innovation.

The London Goldsmiths.   The money-changer banks that had long since vanished in continental Europe reappeared in late seventeenth century London in the form of goldsmith banks. The London goldsmiths combined money changing with other related activities. They had long accepted jewelry and plate for safekeeping (jewelry and plate being the nobility's main form of liquid asset). They also accepted deposits of coin. Coins of the same nominal value varied greatly in weight because many had been clipped or "sweated" to remove some of the gold. The goldsmiths sorted through the coins deposited with them for the ones nearest full weight. They then melted these down and exported them as gold bullion. Since this activity was quite profitable, they were happy to pay interest on deposits of coin.

banknote
Promissory note issued by a bank and payable to bearer on demand.

By 1660, the receipts that goldsmiths issued for deposits of coin had become transferable, and they began to circulate informally as money. The goldsmiths took advantage of this and started to issue receipts with the express intention that they circulate. These receipts were the origin of the modern **banknote**. Checks also emerged at about this time. The goldsmith bankers soon made the transition from warehouse to fractional reserve banking. They began to issue new receipts through lending rather than against actual deposits of coin.[3]

The Scriveners.   The goldsmiths' principal rivals in accepting deposit were the scriveners. Originally public letter writers and copyists, they evolved into legal practitioners who specialized in drawing up documents, including loan contracts. This work natu-

---

[3] The ban on usury had been abolished in England by Henry VIII, and a 1571 statute allowed interest of up to 10%.

MERRILL LYNCH'S
CASH MANAGEMENT ACCOUNT

Investors usually keep a cash account with their brokers. They use it to pay for securities when they buy and to hold the proceeds when they sell. We saw earlier that generations of securities firms, over the centuries, have made such accounts their stepping-stones into banking. Merrill Lynch followed in this tradition when it began offering its Cash Management Account (CMA) in 1977. Under this arrangement, excess cash is automatically swept out of the cash account each week and into a money market mutual fund. Unlike the cash account, the money fund pays a market rate of interest. Funds needed to pay for a purchase of securities are taken out of the money market mutual fund automatically. The investor may write checks against the CMA. These are debited first against any cash in the cash account and then, if necessary, against the money market mutual fund. If the balance in the latter proves insufficient, credit is automatically extended, up to a limit of 50% of the value of the investor's stock portfolio.* The investor also receives a bank credit card that may be used to access the same line of credit.

Not being a bank, Merrill Lynch may not itself offer either a checking account or a bank credit card. So both are actually provided by BancOne of Columbus, Ohio, which receives a fee from Merrill for this service. Most other brokerage houses now offer their own versions of the CMA.

—————————
*This is the maximum amount of lending allowed against collateral of securities. Such margin lending is regulated by the Fed.

rally led them into brokering loans, especially mortgages. As part of this business, clients would deposit money with them until they found a suitable investment. So the scriveners evolved from brokers into intermediaries who paid interest on their clients' deposits and reinvested the funds at a profit. This evolution from broker into banker been repeated recently by U.S. securities firms (see " Merrill Lynch's Cash Management Account").

The Chartered Bank.   The British government, ever watchful for new ways to finance its frequent wars, followed with great interest the success of the Bank of Amsterdam. In 1694, it decided to set up a bank in London along similar lines—the Bank of England.

chartered bank
A bank established through the granting of a public charter.

The Bank of England was the first of a new breed of banks that we shall call **chartered banks**. The Bank of England, unlike other banks before it, was set up from the very beginning with the explicit purpose of being a fractional reserve bank. It was not operated directly by the government, but rather by private individuals acting under a government charter. The charter granted them certain rights and privileges in exchange for services to the Crown. The rights and privileges included preferential legal treatment and later a monopoly on note issue. The services to the Crown consisted initially of lending to the government—at a preferential rate. Later they came to include acting as a central bank.[4]

Merchant Banks.   Merchant banking developed in England only with the onset of the Industrial Revolution. Trade grew rapidly between London and the provinces, where industry was developing. Provincial merchants who provided remittance to London and collected payments there for their customers evolved into the "country bankers" of the eighteenth and nineteenth centuries. They provided local means of payment in the form of banknotes (sometimes bearing interest).

Banking in America

Banking in America developed relatively late. Economic circumstances were at first unfavorable. Because banking developed late, America had the English and European models to imitate.

The largely agricultural colonial economy provided little potential business for a private bank. Farmers bought on credit from the local store, the local store bought on credit from merchants in Boston or Philadelphia; and they in turn bought on credit from their suppliers in England. At harvest time, the whole chain of credit was paid off by shipping the farmers' crops to England. Because the economy relied so heavily on trade credit originating in England, there was little local demand for banking services, and merchant banking did not develop.

The Colonial Land Banks.   Because of the absence of banks, credit other than trade credit was scarce. In particular, wealthy, but illiquid, landowners found it hard to finance the development of their properties and to pay their taxes. To meet their needs, several of the colonies established land banks. These issued banknotes to make loans against land. Almost immediately, the land banks had problems with overissue and the depreciation of their notes. The few that did not fail were closed in 1741 by the British colonial administration.

The Bank of the United States.   The demand for indigenous banks was given a boost when British credit was cut off during the Revolutionary War. Several states chartered banks to help pay for the war—the first being the Bank of North America, founded in Philadelphia in 1781.

In 1791, at the urging of Alexander Hamilton, the federal government chartered a bank modeled on the Bank of England. The **Bank of the United States** was to serve the Treasury's needs for short-term credit and to provide it with payments services. It was not intended to finance the national debt, and its charter expressly prohibited it from doing so. The Bank of the United States eventually fell victim to politics and its charter lapsed in 1811. A Second Bank of the United States was established in 1816, but it too fell a victim to politics and the renewal of its charter was vetoed by President Jackson in 1836.[5]

---

[4] See Chapter 3 for an explanation of the functions of a central bank.

[5] We shall hear more about the Bank of the United States in Chapters 7 and 19.

State-Chartered Banks.

From 1836 to the Civil War, banking was largely in the hands of state-chartered banks. These were given the right to issue banknotes. Typically, they were expected in exchange to lend to state governments or to state-sponsored projects such as canals or railroads.

Towards the end of this period, there was a movement towards "**free banking**." Under this arrangement, bank charters were no longer a special favor of the state, each one requiring a special act of legislation. Instead, anyone meeting minimum requirements of honesty and capital could receive a charter from the state banking commissioner.

free banking
Granting of bank charter to any qualified applicant, without individual legislation.

National Banking.

The difficulties of financing the Civil War prompted passage of the National Bank Acts of 1863 and 1864, which reinstated the federal government's power to charter banks. National banks were effectively given the exclusive right to issue banknotes. Such banknotes were to be issued to purchase federal debt.

Deprived of the right of note issue, state banks initially declined. However, after they turned to deposits as their principal form of liability, they soon recovered.

Private Banks.

The merchant bank also emerged as an important institution in the United States in this period—just as it was dying out in Europe. Merchant banks—called **private banks** in the United States—developed in much the same way they had in Europe. Merchants with commercial connections in distant cities, at home and abroad, offered remittance services to others. Other banking functions, such as accepting deposits and making loans, naturally followed. As long as they did not issue banknotes, private banks did not require a charter.

private bank
An American merchant bank.

The most famous American private bankers were the Morgans. Junius Morgan, a successful New England merchant, moved to London in 1854. There he conducted a mixed business in trade and finance. Morgan financed American exports of cotton and wheat and American imports of iron for the booming railroad industry. He also traded in commodities on his own account. Morgan accepted deposits, made payments, bought securities in London for his American clients, and arranged for the sale there of his clients' securities.

Near Banks

Banks originally evolved to serve the needs of commerce. Their customers were primarily merchants. Until well into the twentieth century, banks showed little interest in the business of ordinary households. Small deposits and small loans seemed to them to be more trouble than they were worth. This attitude left open a market niche for other institutions to fill, and a variety of institutions grew up to serve the needs of small savers and borrowers. They included savings banks, savings and loans (S&Ls), and credit unions—institutions known collectively as thrifts—as well as finance companies and pawnshops. In terms of financial intermediation, these institutions worked quite a lot like banks; they generally were not involved, however, in payments. We shall therefore call these institutions collectively **near banks**.

near bank
Financial institution with similar intermediation function to bank, but usually without the payment function.

Savings Banks.

Savings banks had their origins in the welfare problems of the late eighteenth and early nineteenth centuries. "Poor relief" was then the responsibility of local governments and of charities. Its increasing cost made the idea of self-help attractive to local taxpayers.

Promoters of savings banks believed that the poor should be encouraged to save, so that in times of need they would be better able to help themselves. Municipalities (in Germany) and private philanthropists (in Scotland and England) set up special savings institutions with this purpose in mind. The idea soon spread to other countries, including the United States. The early savings banks were essentially charitable institutions, intended to provide a safe repository for the savings of the poor. They were therefore very conservative with their funds, placing them with commercial banks, or investing in government securities; they did not make loans. Subsidies from the city or from private philanthropists often allowed savings banks to pay interest rates on their deposits that were above market level. To prevent the more well-to-do from taking advantage of this subsidy, there was typically a maximum on the amount that could be deposited.

In the United Kingdom and in Canada, tight regulation froze savings banks in their original form until quite recently. Consequently, they remained small relative to other intermediaries.[6] In Germany and in the United States, however, regulatory constraints were soon eased and the savings banks rapidly evolved into a much broader type of institution. In both countries, they came to rival commercial banks in importance. In Germany, by the end of the nineteenth century, savings banks had become the main savings vehicle of the middle class and an important source of mortgage and municipal finance. In the United States, savings banks rapidly lost their association with the poor and became simply a safe place for the savings of all classes. In the period before the Civil War, they were the fastest-growing financial institution. At their peak, they accounted for 40% of all long-term lending. Their assets included mortgages, government and corporate securities, and business loans, as well as deposits at commercial banks. However, despite their growth in size, they never really spread much beyond the cities of the Northeast.

Savings and Loans.   While savings banks began purely as safe repositories for household savings, not lending to households at all, S&Ls were created from the very outset to provide households with credit.

The nineteenth and early twentieth centuries saw rapid urbanization, both in Europe and in America. The growth of cities created a tremendous need for mortgage finance. To fill this need, various private groups began to organize building and loan associations (called building societies in England and Canada).

A building and loan association might work as follows. A group of families, say 50, would each commit to buying a $100,000 "share" in the association. Each family pays for its share with 100 consecutive monthly contributions of $1,000, paid into a common fund. Once the fund has accumulated $100,000, it makes its first loan. The recipient is chosen by lot from among the members.[7] As more money accumulates, more loans are made in the same fashion. Loan recipients continue to pay in their $1,000 a month and, in addition,

---

[6] In the United Kingdom, most restrictions on trustee savings banks were removed in the 1970s, and in 1986 the remaining institutions were combined and floated as a single joint-stock bank, the Trustee Savings Bank. In Canada too, regulations were eased in the 1980s.

[7] Sometimes the recipient of the loan was chosen by predetermined order; sometimes, by auction—the loan going to whoever offered to pay the highest rate of interest. The loan was called an "advance" on the share.

pay interest on the loan. The interest on outstanding loans is paid out as dividends to all members. Once all the shares have been paid in (after 100 months), the association is terminated. Each member receives the value of a share—$100,000. Those who have received loans, receive the $100,000 in the form of forgiveness of the loan. Those who have not yet received loans are paid the $100,000 in cash.

There is an obvious incentive problem with this arrangement. Those who receive loans—especially those who receive them early—can gain by quitting the arrangement while they are ahead. In fact, this rarely happened. Good behavior was assured by social pressure. Members of an association typically knew each other well, often being members of the same church or of some other affinity group.[8]

This form of organization—the "terminating building and loan"—was quite successful, but it had its limitations. First, because of the incentive problems, such associations had to remain small. Second, shares were highly illiquid: there were substantial penalties for failure to make the monthly contribution or for early withdrawal. Third, those wishing to continue to save beyond the life of the association had to find somewhere else to invest their money.

In the United States, a new form of association which remedied these disadvantages— the "permanent plan association"—became increasingly popular from the 1880s. Under the permanent plan, members could add to their savings and withdraw them as they wished. And loans could be made to nonmembers. These permanent associations came to be known as "savings and loans."

Credit Unions. **Credit unions** have their origins in the credit cooperatives of mid-nineteenth-century Germany. Groups of artisans, peasants, and small businessmen, finding it impossible to borrow from banks as individuals, set up credit cooperatives. The cooperative would borrow from a bank on the joint credit of all the members, each with unlimited liability. The cooperative used the funds to lend to individual members. Because the members knew each other well, they could judge who was and who was not a good credit risk. Initially, these cooperatives did not accept deposits.

Credit cooperatives came to North America in 1900 when Alphonse Desjardins founded the *caisse populaire* movement in Québec. Unlike the German cooperatives, the *caisses populaires* were intended to be self-sufficient, relying on members' savings for funds rather than on outside borrowing. They also specialized in consumer rather than producer loans. In most cases, the community on which the *caisse populaire* was based was the church parish. In 1909, Desjardins helped to establish the first credit union in the United States, in St. Marie Parish, Manchester, New Hampshire. In the same year he helped Massachusetts lawmakers formulate the first credit union legislation in the United States.

The Massachusetts, and subsequent, legislation required that members of a credit union share a "common bond." The common bond may be one of employment (the most common form), religion, or community. The requirement of a common bond generally

---

[8] The terminating building and loan is an example of *rotating credit*, a common arrangement in many countries. Members of a group pay fixed contributions into a pool each month. The monthly pool is paid out to each of the members in turn. The arrangement ends, or a new round begins, when everyone has had his turn.

keeps credit unions small.[9] The small size makes it easier for members to control management. As a result, credit unions seem to be less inefficient than other types of nonprofit financial institution.

Finance Companies.   The near banks we have looked at so far, thrifts, are similar to banks in that they accept deposits. Our next subject, the **finance company**, does not accept deposits. Its similarity to banks lies on the other side of the balance sheet, in its lending.

finance company
An institution set up to provide credit to households or firms, usually to finance the purchase of appliances or equipment.

Firms that sell durable goods to consumers (cars, appliances, furniture) or to businesses (trucks, airplanes, machinery, computers) have a particular interest in the availability of credit. It is much easier to sell a car or a computer if the customer can finance the purchase at a reasonable cost. Because banks originally had little interest in providing this sort of finance, retailers and manufacturers began to provide it themselves.

The first known example in the United States of a retailer providing installment credit to its customers was the New York furniture company of Cowperwait & Sons, which began this practice in 1807. The practice soon spread throughout the furniture business. It was later taken up by the manufacturers of the major household appliances of the nineteenth century—sewing machines and pianos (Singer began offering installment credit in 1850).

However, installment credit really took off only with the beginning of the mass marketing of automobiles from about 1915. Automobile companies set up specialized subsidiaries called finance companies to provide installment credit to car buyers and to finance the inventories of dealers ("floor-plan financing") and suppliers. The automobile companies were soon followed by retailers and manufacturers of consumer and producer durables.[10] The idea spread from the United States to many other countries.

The funds for installment credit initially came largely from banks. Finance companies borrowed from banks to relend to their customers. Or they discounted their installment loan contracts with banks. When bank lending proved insufficient—as it did for the automobile industry—finance companies began to issue commercial paper in the money market. So, in a reversal of the practice of most intermediaries, finance companies borrowed in large amounts, which they broke down into much smaller loans.[11]

Pawnshops.   Pawnbroking developed in the Middle Ages at about the same time as money-changer and merchant banking. Pawnbrokers in Northern Europe were mostly Italians; in Italy, they were mostly Jews. In the fifteenth century, cities began to sponsor charitable pawnshops, known as *monts-de-piété*, to provide credit to artisans and tradesmen. Through the eighteenth century, pawnshops proved an important source of credit to small retailers and craftsmen who could not borrow from banks.

pawnshop
A financial institution that makes small loans to consumers against a pledge.

Pawnshops continue to operate today. In Europe and Latin America, they are generally nonprofit institutions, sponsored by local governments and charities. In Britain and the United States, they are private and operated for profit. Today, pawnshops in the United States generally serve poor, high-risk borrowers who have no other source of credit. Their

---

[9] Some, however, are quite large. The largest is Navy Federal. The common bond in this case is employment by the U.S. Navy. In 1989, Navy Federal had a million members and some $4 billion in assets.

[10] Sears, Roebuck & Company had already begun to offer installment credit in 1911.

[11] See Chapter 14 for a discussion of the important role of finance companies in the money market.

clientele is perhaps 10% of the adult population. The industry has grown since the beginning of the century, spreading from the Northeast to the South and to the Mountain states.

In 1988, there were some 6,900 pawnshops in the United States, with about $700 million in loans outstanding (about 0.1% of total consumer credit). The average loan was for $50 and took less than 10 minutes to execute. There is no credit check: the lender relies entirely on the value of the pledge. Typical pledges include jewelry, electronic and photographic equipment, musical instruments, and firearms. Default rates are high. Pawnshops are typically financed with the owners' equity and bank credit.

Near Banks in Other Countries.

The development of near banks in other countries parallels their development in the United States. In other countries too, near banks much like our own have developed for much the same reason—to fill market niches left open by commercial banks.

Many countries have near banks that are owned or sponsored by the government. Some are much like private intermediaries: German savings banks (discussed earlier) are an example. However, the most common form of government savings institution is the **post office savings bank**, usually run out of regular post office branches as part of normal service.

post office savings bank
A government owned savings intermediary operated out of post office branches.

The United States set up a post office savings bank in 1911. It grew rapidly during the Depression, being more secure than private institutions. It continued to grow during World War II, when it offered better interest rates than its private competitors. At its peak in 1947, its deposits were about one-third those of the S&Ls. It then began a decline that ended with its closing in 1967. With bank deposits insured, and with banks offering equivalent or better rates, there was no longer much demand for its services. Canada closed its post office savings bank in 1968 for similar reasons.

In many other countries, however, post office savings banks continue to thrive. The most successful is Japan's postal savings system. The single largest savings institution in the world, it had $2.2 trillion of deposits in 2000, 34% of total household deposits in Japan. Because of the banking crisis in Japan, depositors have moved large amounts of deposits out of the banks and into the postal savings system. The Japanese postal savings system channels its funds to the Ministry of Finance, which uses them to fund government borrowing and government-sponsored development projects.

Near Banks and Commercial Banks Converge.

In the early twentieth century, the success of near banks showed commercial banks that doing business with ordinary households—**retail banking**—could be profitable. As a result, commercial banks themselves began to compete for that business.[12] Faced with this competition, near banks have expanded the range of their own activities—to capture economies of scale and scope—and became more like commercial banks themselves. Today most near banks in the United States offer transactions deposits and payments services, lend to businesses, or do both. In

retail banking
Provision of banking services (payments and lending) to households.

---

[12] A pioneer in retail banking was the Bank of Italy, founded in San Francisco in 1904 by Amadeo Giannini and others. Giannini sought out the business of small retailers and artisans, particularly among immigrant and minority groups, accepting their deposits and making them business and installment loans. To extend its customer base, it built up a substantial branch network across the state. In 1930, the name of the bank was changed to Bank of America.

other countries too, near banks have evolved into forms that today closely resemble that of a commercial bank.

In 1908, German savings banks were allowed to offer payments services and were instrumental in setting up the German giro system of payments (equivalent to checking).[13] They soon began to accept transactions deposits and to make short-term loans. By the 1930s, except for their ownership, which was still municipal, they were indistinguishable from commercial banks.

The British building society began in much the same way as S&Ls in the United States, but its history has been much less turbulent. Building societies have grown steadily, and today their total assets are about equal to those of Britain's commercial banks. In the 1980s, they were given permission to offer checking deposits, and they now offer a range of services almost indistinguishable from those of commercial banks.[14]

The process of convergence has sometimes been delayed by regulations that restricted the activities of different types of financial institution and kept them distinct. An example of a regulation that hindered convergence was the one that prohibited U.S. thrifts from offering checking deposits. The story of how they overcame this obstacle is interesting because it illustrates how financial institutions are sometimes able to circumvent obstructive regulation through innovation.

Thrifts and Checking Deposits.   As we saw in Chapter 3, part of the regulatory package enacted during the Great Depression was a section of the Glass–Steagall Act that prohibited banks from paying interest on checking deposits. For many years, however, this regulation was irrelevant. As long as market interest rates remained low, the sacrifice involved in leaving money in a zero-interest checking deposit was small, and the restriction did not matter. However, by the late 1960s inflation had driven up interest rates to the point where the sacrifice had become substantial.[15] Depositors responded by taking their money out of bank checking accounts to earn more elsewhere.

This created a tremendous opportunity for nonbank financial institutions to take business away from commercial banks if they could find a way to offer interest-bearing checking deposits. The problem was that regulation prohibited thrifts from offering checking deposits at all. However, in 1970, the Consumer Savings Bank of Worcester, Massachusetts, found a way around this regulation by inventing the **negotiated order of withdrawal (NOW) account**.

negotiated order of withdrawal (NOW) account
A time deposit on which checks may be written.

The idea is simple. Suppose you need to pay Acme Furniture $100. Before the NOW account, if you had a deposit at a savings bank you had to fill out a withdrawal slip for $100, take it to the savings bank, and then take the cash to Acme. The NOW account allows you instead to simply sign over the withdrawal slip to Acme. Acme can then go to your savings bank to withdraw the cash, or, even easier, it can sign over the slip to its own bank for collection.

---

[13] We shall discuss giro payments, and how they differ from checks, in Chapter 8.

[14] The British equivalent of our mutual savings banks, consolidated in the 1980s into a single institution, the Trustee Savings Bank (TSB), was converted into corporate form. The TSB was chartered as a commercial bank and merged with Lloyds Bank to form Lloyds TSB.

[15] See Chapter 4 for an explanation of the connection between inflation and nominal interest rates.

Although, the negotiated order of withdrawal looks like a check and works like a check, the courts decided that legally it was not a check. Consequently, savings banks were not offering a checking deposit and they were therefore not breaking the law. The NOW account was soon authorized for other savings banks in Massachusetts and then throughout New England.

Credit unions followed much the same path. Their version of the checking deposit that wasn't was the *share draft*, which first appeared in 1974. A credit union customer who writes a share draft on his "checking deposit" is actually writing a check on a deposit held by the credit union at a correspondent commercial bank. The share draft clears through the regular clearing system and details of the transaction are conveyed electronically to the credit union (the check is not returned to the payer).[16] Section 11 of the Glass–Steagall Act does not specifically mention credit unions, and the credit unions have exploited this loophole to offer interest-bearing checking deposits to businesses.

NOW accounts and share drafts provided thrifts with a competitive advantage over commercial banks, because they could offer interest on their checking deposits. The banks fought for the right to do the same, and the banking legislation of 1980 allowed them too to offer NOW accounts.

The Pattern of Bank Evolution

The evolution of banking exhibits some fairly clear patterns. Commercial banks, combining payments functions and financial intermediation, have developed from five main types of institution—payments processors, merchant banks, securities firms, near banks, and chartered banks. Examples of each type are listed in Exhibit 6.2.

Payments processors and merchant banks began with payments functions, but economies of scope led into intermediation. Customers naturally held their liquid reserves

---

[16] Credit union also use deposits at commercial bank correspondents to cover member withdrawals from bank ATMs.

EXHIBIT 6.2   Institutions That Became Commercial Banks

Type of Institution	Examples	Origin
Payments processors	Medieval money changers, English goldsmiths, public banks of deposit	Payments
Merchant banks	Florentine banks, English country banks, U.S. private banks	Remittance, securities business
Securities firms	Scriveners, industrial and universal banks	Securities business and intermediation
Chartered banks	Bank of England, U.S. commercial banks	Created as banks
Near banks	Savings banks, savings and loans, credit unions	Intermediation

with their payments processors and merchant banks as deposits. Pooling these deposits and netting demands for payment provided investible funds. Lending was a natural adjunct to providing payments services. The typical customer of a payments processor or commercial bank was a merchant. Merchants need to borrow to finance trade. The payments processor had the funds available to lend.

The second evolutionary path began with intermediation and added payment functions. This was the case with securities firms and near banks. Part of the business of securities firms is to find investments for their customers. Customers keep funds with them waiting to be invested. Offering payments services out of these deposits is a natural extension of their business. Merrill Lynch's CMA is a classic example of this process. Thrifts find themselves in much the same position as securities firms. Customers keep funds with them in nontransaction deposits; it is natural to offer these customers transactions services. Recent deregulation—in the United States and elsewhere—has removed the regulatory obstacles to their doing so.

In contrast to these stories of evolution, chartered bank were set up from the very beginning as full-fledged fractional reserve banks. Governments set them up initially as an instrument of public finance. They used them both to finance direct government expenditure—often on wars—and to finance government-favored development. Commercial banks remain to this day important purchasers of government debt.

THE EVOLUTION OF BANK ASSETS

We have seen how the commercial bank evolved as an institution. Our next task is to see how its business has evolved. We divide the discussion into three parts—assets, liabilities, and activities other than intermediation.

Commercial Lending

Commercial Bills and the Commercial Bills Doctrine.   Early banks lent mainly to two classes of borrower—merchants and governments. Lending to merchants usually took the form of **discounting** commercial bills. The commercial bill was the standard IOU used by merchants (see "The Commercial Bill: An Early Financial Innovation"). For example, suppose a merchant held an IOU from another merchant for £100, due in 3 months. The first merchant could turn this bill into immediate cash by selling it to his banker. The banker would buy the bill for the present value of the promised payment, say, £95. That is, the banker would buy the bill at a discount or "discount" it.

In addition to lending to merchants, early banks frequently lent to governments. Governments were always in need of credit. They induced early merchant banks to lend to them by offering them in exchange trading rights. Or they made such lending a condition for opening a branch. Later, governments themselves chartered banks as sources of credit. Lending to the government or to causes supported by the government was generally made a condition of the charter.

Lending to governments was the most common source of banking problems. Lending to governments was unsafe: defaulting governments brought down many a bank. Government

discounting
The making of a loan through the purchase of an IOU at the present value of its face value.

THE COMMERCIAL BILL:
AN EARLY FINANCIAL INNOVATION

The standard medieval security was the bond. This was a legal document that publicly recognized a debt. It carried the debtor's personal seal and was sworn before a court or a public notary. Collecting the debt in court was easy. The only possible defense would have been that the bond was not genuine. However, since the bond had already been recognized in public, that defense was ruled out.

The disadvantage of the bond was its high transactions cost. A bond had to be drawn up by a legal professional—a scrivener—who often kept a record of the bond himself as additional evidence. It then had to be sworn in public. The process took time, and all those involved expected to be paid.

Merchants found this instrument too cumbersome and expensive for the debts that routinely arose in trade. Before A would ship goods to B, he would require B's promise of payment. Since shipment took time, often many months, the date of payment was deferred until the goods arrived.

The commercial bill developed as a less expensive way of dealing with such promises of payment. The bill was a private and informal document, written by the parties themselves. It constituted a private, rather than a public, acknowledgment of debt. While the use of a bill greatly reduced transactions costs, it did have a major disadvantage. Because the proper legal procedures were not followed, a bill was not enforceable in court.

This disadvantage was not a big problem for commercial debts. The debts were usually short term and relatively small. Moreover, debtors had a strong incentive to pay. The merchant community was small and merchants dealt repeatedly with one another. A reputation for honesty was essential: the merchant's motto was "My word is my bond." A merchant who reneged on a bill would soon find no one willing to trade with him.

Moreover, lacking the status of a legal document did give the bill some advantages. Because the legal system was not involved, a bill was more readily *assignable* than a bond. The debt of A to B is assignable if B can endorse it—sign it over—to a third party, C. The debt then becomes a debt of A to C. With a bond, assignment had to be registered with the court and it required A's consent (mainly to protect C). Neither registration nor consent was required with a bill.

Ready assignability was useful. If, having shipped goods to A, B did not want to wait months to be paid, he could obtain cash immediately by assigning A's bill to C (typically a banker).

The usefulness of bills was further enhanced when, beginning in the sixteenth century, they became *negotiable*. If B has assigned A's debt to C, then A's failure to pay is C's problem alone. However, if the debt is negotiable, and A fails to pay, then C can collect from B. If the debt has been endorsed more than once, then all

Continued . . .

the endorsers are liable, in order of their signatures, for the debt. A negotiable bill is easier to sell because it is essentially guaranteed by all who have endorsed it.

At the turn of the eighteenth century, England passed a series of laws that gave the bill full legal status. These laws gave England an important advantage in financial development over its economic competitors who did not give legal recognition to the commercial bill. The bill became the principal vehicle of commercial and industrial credit and the key instrument in the development of the banking system.

loans were also illiquid. Unlike commercial loans, they were not tied to an economic transaction that would provide the funds to pay off the loan.

commercial bills doctrine
An eighteenth-century doctrine of banking that held that bank should lend only by discounting commercial bills.

Based on this experience, economists in the eighteenth century developed a doctrine of banking that came to be known as the **commercial bills doctrine**. This doctrine asserted that bank lending should be limited to the discounting of short-term bills based on *bona fide* commercial transactions. Such lending was safe and liquid. It was backed by the goods involved in the transaction, the imminent sale of which would provide the funds to pay the bank. The commercial bills doctrine was specifically intended to preclude lending to governments.[17] By the nineteenth century the commercial bills doctrine was widely accepted as the basis of sound banking. However, in the face of new profit opportunities, it was honored more in the breach than in the observance.

The commercial bills doctrine never really worked in America. Since most American merchants relied on credit from England, the supply of commercial bills to American banks was limited. On the other hand, there was a strong demand for loans to finance development. So commercial lending in the United States took the form of "advances"—direct loans from banks to their customers. During the twentieth century this form of commercial lending came to predominate in all countries.

commercial paper
Unsecured short-term commercial security.

The Revival of the Commercial Paper Market.   Since the 1970s, however, the commercial bill—in the slightly modified modern form of **commercial paper**—has seen a considerable revival.[18] The driving force initially was the combination of rising market interest rates and Depression era limits on the rates that banks could pay on their deposits

---

[17] It was believed, too, that limiting bank lending in this way would prevent the inflationary overexpansion of bank lending. The demand for commercial credit was supposedly limited by the "needs of trade." Government demand for credit, on the other hand was insatiable. Satisfying that demand could only lead to inflation. Economists today do not generally accept the "needs of trade" argument. Commercial lending to satisfy the "needs of trade" can lead to overissue just as easily as lending to a government.

[18] Commercial paper differs from the traditional commercial bill in that it is "single-name paper" backed by the credit of the issuer only. A commercial bill was an IOU generated in trade, used by a purchaser of goods to acknowledge his debt to pay for them at an agreed time in the future. The creditor who received the bill commonly endorsed it and sold it, for a discount, to a bank or to someone else. If the original debtor defaulted, the creditor who had endorsed and resold the bill was then liable. Such a bill was "two-name paper."

(the same combination that we have seen brought thrifts into banking).[19] The increasing gap between bank lending rates and bank borrowing rates created an incentive to bring borrowers and lenders together in ways that did *not* involve banks. For example, suppose banks pay 5% on deposits and charge 20% on loans. If you can find a different way of getting borrowers and lenders together, you can offer lenders 10%, charge borrowers 15%, and still be left with a healthy profit; and you should get plenty of business.

The commercial paper market, dormant since the 1930s, took on new life as various borrowers turned to it as a cheaper alternative to borrowing from banks. Finance companies had borrowed mainly from banks but had sold some commercial paper. From the 1960s on, they began to reverse these proportions. New types of issuer, including nonfinancial corporations, also began to sell commercial paper. The lenders who purchased the commercial paper could earn a much better return than that offered by regulated bank deposits.

The Continuing Cost Advantage of Commercial Paper.   While the limits on bank deposit rates were the reason for the revival of the commercial paper market, when those limits were phased out in the 1980s, the market did not disappear. This was because commercial paper provides a way to avoid a number of **regulatory costs** that regulation continues to impose on banks:

regulatory costs
Costs that a bank incurs in complying with regulations.

- Banks must hold reserves against their deposits.
- Banks must pay deposit insurance premiums.
- Banks must maintain a required equity-to-loan ratio.

These requirements add to the cost of making a loan. To see why, let us look at an example.

United Computer needs to raise $1 million in working capital, so it approaches its bank, Valley National, for a loan. The way the loan is funded is shown in Exhibit 6.3.

Suppose Valley National must maintain an equity-to-loan ratio of 7%. This means that if it adds $1 million to its loans, it must add $70,000 to its equity. So $70,000 of the $1 million needed to fund the loan must come from additional equity.

The remaining $930,000 will come from additional deposits—say negotiable certificates of deposit (NCDs: see later in this chapter). Suppose Valley National must maintain a reserve ratio of 10% on these NCDs. Then 10% of the funds it raises from additional deposits must go into reserves (must be deposited at the Fed). Therefore, to obtain net the $930,000 it needs, it must take in a larger amount of deposits. The amount of additional deposits it requires is

$$\frac{\$930,000}{0.90} = \$1,033,333$$

---

[19] Section 11 of the Glass–Steagall Act of 1933 prohibited payment of interest on checking deposits. In addition the act granted the Fed the authority to regulate interest rates on time deposits. The Fed did this under its Regulation Q, which set a ceiling on permitted rates.

EXHIBIT 6.3   Funding a Bank Loan

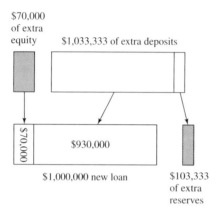

Of this amount, 10%, or $103,333, will be added to reserves. The remaining 90%, $930,000, will go to fund the loan. Although the bank can lend only $930,000, it must pay interest on the whole $1,033,333 of additional deposits.

Suppose Valley National's target rate of return on equity is 20%[20]; the interest rate on additional deposits is 5%; and Valley National must pay a 0.23% premium for deposit insurance. Then the cost of funding the loan is

Equity	$70,000 × 0.20	=	$14,000
Deposits			
Interest	$1,033,333 × 0.05	=	51,666
Deposit insurance	$1,033,333 × 0.0023	=	2,377
Total			$68,043

Therefore, for the loan to be worthwhile, Valley National will require an expected return of at least 6.8% on the loan.[21] In this example, regulation imposes a margin of at least 180 basis points over the bank's borrowing rate.

Of course, even without regulation, there would still be a margin. Valley National would still maintain a certain equity-to-loan ratio and it would still hold reserves. However, in the absence of regulation, its equity-to-loan ratio and its reserve ratio would be much lower. While the deposit insurance premium adds to the cost, deposit insurance lowers the risk of a bank's deposits and so the interest rate it must pay on them. This is a good deal for a small bank, which, being less safe, might have to pay a large risk premium on its deposits. For a sound large bank, the deal is much less favorable, and deposit insurance therefore adds to the cost of funding a loan.

---

[20] If Valley National earns less than this on the equity in the new loan, it will lower the average return on its equity.

[21] In reality, the whole calculation is more complicated than this because of tax considerations and because of other costs. Moreover, this is just the required *realized* rate. If there is a risk of default, the rate charged United Computer (the contractual rate) must be higher to take this into account (see Chapter 5, Equation 5.2, on the relationship between the realized and contractual rates).

The relative importance of the different regulatory costs has fluctuated over time. Between 1983 and 1990, the 3% reserve requirement on NCDs was a significant cost. When the reserve requirement was lifted, this cost disappeared. However, in 1989 required equity-to-loan ratios were raised dramatically and became a major problem. Deposit insurance premiums rose with the banking crisis of the early 1990s, but later fell.

Lending through the money market avoids all the regulatory costs. There are no required reserves, no required equity-to-asset ratio, and no deposit insurance premiums. Consequently, the costs of bringing borrower and lender together through the money market are often lower than they are for bank intermediation.

However, since commercial paper is unsecured, the market is open only to the largest and most creditworthy borrowers. Moreover, as with any public issue, selling commercial paper involves substantial fixed costs. It is therefore only the banks' largest and most creditworthy commercial borrowers that find the commercial paper market attractive.

Banks have lost a lot of commercial loan business to the commercial paper market. However, the business they have lost is not particularly profitable: the margin on loans to such borrowers is small. Moreover, banks have been able to replace some of the loan income they have lost with income from services they provide to the issuers of commercial paper. Banks earn fee income from underwriting commercial paper—from helping their customers place commercial paper with lenders. And, as we shall see, they also earn fee income from guaranteeing commercial paper.

Syndications and Participations.   Some loans to very large business borrowers cannot be shifted to the commercial paper market because they are too risky.[22] Moreover, a bank will be reluctant to make a very large risky loan itself out of considerations of diversification. A way to solve this problem is for a group of banks to get together to make the loan through a syndication or participation.

syndication

A bank loan that is broken up among a number of banks with each lending independently.

In a **syndication**, there is a joint loan agreement between the borrower and a number of banks, but each of the banks lends separately to the borrower. In a **participation**, a lead bank enters into a loan agreement with the borrower and into separate participation agreement with each of a group of other banks. The other banks provide funds and obtain in exchange a claim on a part of the loan *through* the lead bank.

participation

A number of banks lending to a single borrower through a lead bank.

Small-Business Lending and IT.   As we saw in Chapter 2, there is a large fixed element in the cost of making a loan. The lender must assess the credit of the borrower and write a contract whether the loan is for $1,000 dollars or $1 billion. This makes small loans relatively expensive for borrowers and unprofitable for lenders. Information technology (IT), however, has helped to bring down the cost of making small loans and therefore improved the access to credit of small businesses.

credit scoring

Scoring a potential borrower based on characteristics to assess probability of default.

Rather than having a human loan officer decide whether to make a small loan, the bank relies on a computerized system of **credit scoring**. The potential borrower is asked a series of questions about his or her financial situation and credit history. The answers are fed into a statistical model, based on the bank's experience with other borrowers, that pre-

---

[22] A principal example is loans used to finance leveraged buyouts (LBOs) and other corporate restructurings. We shall discuss these in Chapter 15.

dicts the likelihood of repayment. Based on the answer, the bank grants or denies the loan. Because the bank makes many such loans, diversification ensures that the performance of the loan portfolio matches reasonably closely the predictions of the statistical model.[23] Credit scoring was originally pioneered in credit card lending to consumers, but since the early 1990s it has increasingly been applied to small-business loans of up to $100,000

The whole procedure is easy to computerize, greatly lowering the cost of the transaction and the speed with which it can be executed. In addition, IT makes credit histories readily available, so that the bank can check the accuracy of the borrower's information almost instantaneously. There are now online lenders that promise to give small business borrowers an answer in less than 5 minutes. Moreover, the lower cost of making such loans enables banks to offer business credit lines as small as $5,000. The overall result has been a significant increase in small-business lending: loans of under $100,000 were the fastest-growing category of business loans in the late 1990s. Owners of small businesses have been able to rely more on bank financing and less on family and friends.

Lending to Noncommercial Borrowers

The menu of bank assets has grown steadily over the years. The list of borrowers has expanded from merchants and governments to include landowners, other banks, industrial firms, and consumers. This expansion has followed a clear pattern. As the economy has developed, banks have faced demands for credit from new classes of borrower. Satisfying these new demands has generally promised banks higher yields than their traditional assets. However, the new types of asset have typically increased risk and reduced liquidity. Consequently, they have frequently gotten the banks into difficulties.

mortgage lending
Lending against real estate collateral.

Mortgage Lending.   Under the commercial bills doctrine, **mortgage lending**—lending against real estate collateral—is considered inappropriate for commercial banks. Mortgage loans are long term and illiquid. Real estate prices are notoriously volatile.

Nonetheless, country banks were always under pressure from local landowners to lend against real estate. For many American banks, real estate was the only form of collateral their customers had. City banks, too, were drawn into real estate lending. The move from the country to the cities in the nineteenth and early twentieth centuries led to booming urban real estate markets. The demand for mortgages was initially satisfied by near banks such as the S&Ls. However, the high yields to be earned on mortgage loans proved a temptation the banks could not resist, and by the 1920s they were heavily involved in mortgage lending.

Mortgage lending has been a perennial source of banking problems in just about every country in the world. However, it is usually the financing of commercial rather than residential real estate that is the source of the problem. For example, losses on real estate loans were a primary cause of the bank problems in the United States in the 1980s and early 1990s. They have played a major role in the problems of the Japanese banking system. And they were an important source of bank losses in the Asian financial crisis that began in 1997.

---

[23] The standardization of such loans has made it easier for banks to "securitize" them (bundle them and sell them to investors). We shall have more to say about securitization in later chapters.

Consumer Lending. Lending to consumers is a comparatively new activity for banks. It began in the United States in the 1920s, but became important only after World War II. As we have seen, banks did not pioneer in this area, but rather followed the lead of near banks—especially credit unions and finance companies—when it became clear that consumer lending was profitable.

Consumer lending by banks initially took the form mainly of installment credit on consumer durables. Recently in the United States it has developed into credit card lending, now an important source of bank profits. Credit scoring and IT have greatly reduced the cost of this form of lending. By 1996, two thirds of U.S. households possessed bank credit cards.[24]

In other countries, credit cards are less popular and overdraft lending remains the predominant form of consumer loan. With an overdraft, the bank provides a line of credit that is drawn upon automatically if there are insufficient funds to cover a check. Interest rates on such lines of credit are typically similar to those on credit cards. Overdrafts are offered by some U.S. banks, but are much more common overseas. In some countries—Germany, for example—overdrafts are the principal form of consumer debt and consumers "live on their overdraft" in much the same way that some Americans "live on their credit cards."

Securitization. While banks find it profitable to make mortgage and consumer loans, for reasons that we shall explore in later chapters, they often do not wish to carry these loans on their balance sheets. To get them off their balance sheets, they need to sell the loans to someone else. Syndications and participations are a way of doing this: in a sense, the lead bank "sells" a part of the loan to other banks. This solution is, however, unsuitable for mortgage and consumer loans, mainly because they are too small. The transactions costs of selling individual loans would simply be too great.

securitization
The sale of loans to a pool that issues tradable securities to finance the purchase.

For these types of loans, banks have found a different solution—securitization. In a **securitization**, a bank puts together a package of many small loans and sells it or parts of it to other banks or investors. We shall look at the securitization of mortgage loans in Chapter 13 and at the securitization of consumer loans in Chapter 14.

THE EVOLUTION OF BANK LIABILITIES

Two forces have driven the evolution of commercial bank liabilities. First, as banks have expanded the scope of their lending, their need for funds has increased. New types of liability offered new sources of funds. Second, banking regulation frequently placed restrictions on the nature or terms of existing liabilities, so banks came up with alternatives to provide them with the funds they needed. New types of liability, like new types of asset, have often been a source of trouble. The most common problem has been instability: new liabilities have often been "hot money"—money liable to be withdrawn on short notice. The maturity of new liabilities has also sometimes been a problem, potentially increasing banks' exposure to interest rate risk.

---

[24] We shall have more to say about credit cards in Chapter 8.

Checking Deposits, Banknotes, and Time Deposits

Although the classic bank liability is the checking deposit, in the eighteenth and nineteenth centuries, banknotes were a major competitor. Banknotes were particularly attractive to banks in rural and provincial areas. In such areas, transactions were mostly made in hand-to-hand currency, and the use of deposits was limited. In major cities, and for large transactions among merchants and industrialists, deposits generally remained the principal bank liability. In major U.S. cities, the amount of deposits had already exceeded the amount of banknotes by 1830.

By the end of the nineteenth century, governments in most countries had taken over the right of note issue for themselves, forcing banks to look to other types of liability. In the United States, the National Banking Acts effectively deprived state-chartered country banks of the right to issue banknotes. State banks therefore turned increasingly to deposits.

Time deposits were initially of little significance for commercial banks in the United States. Until late in the nineteenth century it was rather the near banks—savings banks, credit unions, and S&Ls—that took in most long-term household deposits. However, following their loss of the right of note issue, country banks expanded their time deposits rapidly, so that by the end of the century over half their deposits were time deposits. City banks began to offer time deposits only in 1913, when national banks were first allowed to operate savings departments. Time deposits became an important source of funds for city banks in the 1920s.

Interbank Deposits

In many countries in the nineteenth century, the deposits of country banks were a major source of funds for city banks. For country banks with more funds than good loan opportunities, a deposit at a city bank was an attractive way to dispose of surplus funds. Competition among city banks ensured that these **interbank deposits** earned attractive returns. Moreover, because they were so liquid, they made an excellent secondary reserve.

interbank deposits
The deposit of one bank at another.

By the end of the century, as technology progressed, city banks in most countries developed extensive branch systems that displaced or absorbed the small country banks (we shall discuss this in Chapter 7). Consequently, interbank balances declined in importance, replaced by interbranch transfers of funds within a given bank. In the United States, however, interstate and intrastate branching restrictions long hindered this process, and interbank balances continued to be an important source of funds for city banks.

call loan
A loan repayable on demand of the lender.

Country banks deposited their surplus funds with city banks. These in turn deposited the funds with banks in the great financial centers—initially Philadelphia and Boston, later New York. The banks in the financial centers used these funds to make **call loans** (loans repayable on demand) to securities dealers and traders. The availability of call loans was an important factor in the spectacular growth of the New York securities market from the 1890s on. By 1900, securities loans accounted for over 40% of all lending by nationally chartered banks.[25]

The Federal Reserve Act of 1913 brought a new type of interbank lending. Members of the new Federal Reserve System (including all national banks) were required to main-

---

[25] We shall have more to say about interbank lending and the money market in Chapter 7.

tain reserves in the form of balances held at the newly established Federal Reserve Banks. To meet this requirement, some banks had to borrow from the Fed through the "discount window." At the same time, other banks found themselves with surplus funds in their deposits.

Beginning in 1921, a market developed in which banks with surplus reserve deposits would lend them to those with reserve deficiencies. This market came to be known as the **Fed funds market**. A Fed funds loan was not only cheaper than a discount loan, but it also relieved the borrower of the need to assemble collateral. Loans were arranged over the telephone. The loan was executed through the exchange of checks drawn on the Fed. As the market expanded, government securities dealers began to take part—first as participants, then as market makers. Brokers in call loans began to broker Fed funds too.

This system of interbank deposits was a significant source of instability. From the Civil War to the Great Depression, a series of banking crises shook the economy. Interbank deposits played a major role in most of them. Typically, a rash of bank runs would cause country banks to withdraw their interbank deposits, spreading the crises throughout the banking system. The Glass–Steagall prohibition of interest on checking deposits was intended to reduce interbank deposits by making them unattractive.[26]

The Fed funds market continues to be important today, but it is not the only interbank market, or even the most important one. It must share the stage with a vast international market for interbank loans—the **Eurodollar interbank market**. Eurodollar banks are banks located outside the United States that accept time deposits in U.S. dollars and make loans in U.S. dollars.[27]

Since banks have the choice of lending to one another in either the Feds funds market or the Eurodollar interbank markets, the interest rates in the two markets are closely related. The rate in the Fed funds market is known as the **Fed funds rate**. The rate in the Eurodollar interbank market is known as the **London interbank offered rate (LIBOR)**.

Interest Rate Restrictions and the Revolution in Bank Liabilities

We have seen how the Glass–Steagall restrictions on interest rates placed banks at a competitive disadvantage when interest rates began to rise in the 1960s. Large depositors, such as corporations and institutions, were the first to react, and they began to withdraw their cash from zero-interest checking deposits in commercial banks, to invest instead in liquid money market securities. Bank deposits, two-thirds of all financial assets in 1947, had fallen to one-third by 1980. To stem the decline, banks had to be able to compete for depositors' funds. This meant they had to find ways around the interest rate restrictions.[28]

Banks found several ingenious ways to pay interest on the checking deposits of their larger customers. These included the bank repo, the overnight Eurodollar, and the interbank Fed funds purchase.

---

[26] We shall discuss the destabilizing role of interbank deposits in Chapter 19.

[27] We shall learn more about the origins of Eurodollar banking in Chapter 7 and about the reasons for the vast interbank market in Chapter 18.

[28] We have already seen how thrifts invented the NOW account as a way of paying interest on the checking accounts of small depositors and that banks soon adopted this innovation.

Margin glossary:

Fed funds market Market for loans of deposits at the Fed.

Eurodollar interbank market Market for loans between Eurodollar banks.

Fed funds rate The rate at which banks lend to one another on the Fed funds market.

London interbank offered rate (LIBOR) The rate at which banks lend to one another on the Eurodollar interbank market.

bank repo

A bank liability secured by government securities.

The Bank Repo.   One way corporate treasurers had found to earn interest on their liquid reserves was to make very short-term secured loans, called repos, to government securities dealers.[29] Banks invented the **bank repo** as a way of luring back these corporate deposits. Here is how it works.

General Computer (GC) has a deposit at Gotham Bank. At the end of each day, the balance of GC's deposit is automatically converted into an overnight loan to Gotham, secured by government securities. In the morning, the loan is repaid automatically into GC's deposit so that it has the use of the funds during the day.

For example, suppose that at 3:30 P.M., GC has $2 million in its checking deposit. The bank automatically converts this into a secured loan. The form of the loan is a sale of T-bills by the bank to GC and a simultaneous commitment by the bank to buy them back again the next morning at a set price.[30] The bank sells the T-bills to GC for $2 million and agrees to buy them back at 9:00 A.M. the next day for $2,000,370. The extra $370 is equivalent to an interest rate of 0.0185% overnight on the $2 million (an effective annual rate of 7%).

The next morning, as agreed, the bank credits GC's deposit for $2,000,370, and GC regains the use of its money. During the day money flows in and out of the deposit. At 3:30 P.M. of the second day, the balance is down to $1 million. Again, the bank automatically sells to GC T-bills for this amount, with an agreement to repurchase the following morning.

For GC this arrangement is entirely equivalent to an interest-bearing checking deposit. Losing the use of its funds overnight is no sacrifice, since the bank is closed then anyhow. The arrangement also has advantages for the bank.

To understand the advantages to Gotham, consider the effect of the repo on its balance sheet:

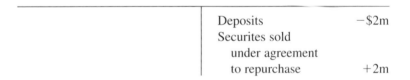

	Deposits	−$2m
	Securites sold	
	under agreement	
	to repurchase	+2m

Gotham's required reserves are determined by the amount of its deposits at 4:00 P.M. each day. Since deposits converted into repos vanish from the balance sheet at 3:30, the bank can hold fewer reserves. If the reserve requirement is 10%, Gotham can reduce its reserves by $200,000, enabling it to earn interest on that amount. Because "securities sold under agreement to repurchase" are considered a "borrowing" rather that a deposit, they are not subject to reserve requirements.[31] Borrowings are not covered by deposit insurance, so Gotham also saves the deposit insurance premium.[32] GC is unconcerned by the lack of insurance, because it is protected from any loss by its ownership of the T-bills.

---

[29] We shall discuss repos in Chapter 12.

[30] This combines a spot sale with a forward repurchase.

[31] For a repo to be exempt from reserve requirements, the securities repoed must be Treasuries or agencies.

[32] Premiums range between 23¢ and 31¢ per $100 of deposits. We shall discuss deposit insurance in Chapter 19.

Overnight Eurodollars.   Another way corporate treasurers had found to earn interest on their liquid reserves was to deposit the money in a bank outside the United States—a Eurodollar bank. Such banks were not subject to any restrictions on the rate they could pay on deposits. Just as banks found a way to mimic the security dealer repo with a bank repo, so did they find a way to mimic the Eurodollar deposit with **overnight Eurodollars**. Let us see how Gotham does this.

Each day, instead of sweeping GC's checking deposit into a bank repo, the balance is formally turned into an overnight loan to Gotham's London subsidiary. The funds lent to London are then lent back again to Gotham in the United States. If the original deposit is for $1 million, then the net effects on Gotham's balance sheet and on the balance sheet of its London subsidiary are

overnight Eurodollars

An overnight interbank loan involving a Eurodollar bank.

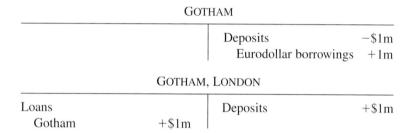

GOTHAM

	Deposits	−$1m
	Eurodollar borrowings	+1m

GOTHAM, LONDON

Loans		Deposits	+$1m
Gotham	+$1m		

Each morning the overnight loans are repaid, and GC regains access to its funds for the day.

The net effect on Gotham's balance sheet is much like that of the repo. All that really happens is that Gotham shifts an amount of $1 million from one category of liability, deposits, to another, Eurodollar borrowings. This allows the bank to pay interest on it. Also, because Eurodollar borrowings are a borrowing and not a deposit, there are no required reserves and no deposit insurance premiums.[33]

Overnight Eurodollars are not insured, and—unlike a bank repo—they are not secured. GC therefore bears some default risk: if Gotham were to fail overnight, GC might take a loss. To compensate for the risk, the interest rate on overnight Eurodollars is a little higher than it is on a bank repo.

There is an advantage for Gotham to the overnight Eurodollar over the bank repo. The funds it raises in the form of overnight Eurodollars are available for any use it chooses. Specifically, it can use them to fund loans. Funds raised in the form of repos are necessarily tied up in government securities and are therefore not available to fund loans.

Correspondent Fed Funds.   Banks found a third device that enabled them to pay interest on deposits. This one was targeted specifically at interbank deposits. The device exploits the existence of the Fed funds market. It works as follows.

Smalltown State Bank has an interbank deposit with Gotham. Suppose the two banks conduct the following two-step transaction:

Step 1. Smalltown withdraws $5 million from its interbank balance at Gotham in the form of Fed funds.

Step 2. Smalltown then lends the $5 million in Fed funds to Gotham.

---

[33] Until 1990, when the requirement was abolished, Eurodollar deposits did have a 3% reserve requirement.

The combined effect of the two steps on the balance sheets of the two banks is

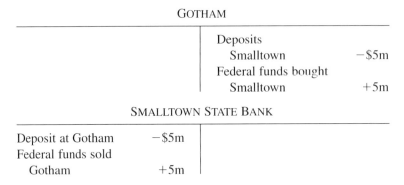

GOTHAM

	Deposits	
	Smalltown	−$5m
	Federal funds bought	
	Smalltown	+5m

SMALLTOWN STATE BANK

Deposit at Gotham	−$5m	
Federal funds sold		
Gotham	+5m	

In reality, the two stages are combined into one. Gotham simply transfers an amount of $5 million from one category of liability, deposits, to another, Fed funds bought. No fed funds are actually withdrawn or lent. To distinguish this type of "Fed funds" transaction from the real borrowing and lending of fed funds, the former is called **correspondent Fed funds**.[34]

correspondent Fed funds

A loan to a correspondent bank that is formally a loan of Fed funds.

The borrowing and lending of Fed funds is called "Federal funds bought" by the borrower and as "Federal funds sold" by the lender. The terminology dates from the days of the commercial bills doctrine, when interbank loans were frowned upon. It is simply a weak attempt to conceal the true nature of the transaction.

The purpose of correspondent Fed funds, like the purpose of bank repos or overnight Eurodollars, is to allow Gotham to pay interest on a deposit. As with the other two devices, Gotham benefits from the Fed funds bought being a borrowing rather than a deposit: there are no required reserves and no deposit insurance premiums. Like overnight Eurodollars, Fed funds bought are uninsured and unsecured, so their yield must be higher to compensate for the risk.

The conversion of deposits into Fed funds bought is possible only if the depositor can, at least in principle, have a deposit at the Federal Reserve. It is limited, therefore, to banks, thrifts, U.S. agencies, government securities dealers, and domestic offices of foreign banks.

NCDs and Other Wholesale Deposits.   As we have seen, the rapidly growing money market of the 1970s competed for the funds of bank depositors. It offered them higher market rates at a time when rates on deposits were limited by government regulation. Banks were quick to realize, however, that the money market was not just a problem: it was also an opportunity. It could provide them with an important new source of funds.

Banks cannot themselves issue commercial paper: commercial paper is intended to finance trade, and banks may not engage in trade. However, bank holding companies can and do issue commercial paper. They then make the funds available to the daughter bank either through deposits or by using the funds to purchase assets from the daughter bank.[35]

---

[34] Gotham is Smalltown's correspondent bank. We shall learn about the correspondent relationship in Chapter 7.

[35] Banks once used this as a way of avoiding reserve requirements. However, in 1970 the Fed imposed a 5% reserve requirement on commercial paper that was issued by bank holding companies to fund the purchase of assets from banking subsidiaries.

This arrangement is less than perfect from the bank's point of view because it fails to exploit the bank's deposit insurance: liabilities of the holding company are not insured. This means that the bank must pay a higher rate of interest on holding company liabilities than it pays on its own.

negotiable certificate of deposit (NCD)
A negotiable bank CD.

Citibank solved this problem in 1961 when it invented the **negotiable certificate of deposit (NCD)**. This was, essentially, commercial paper in the form of a certificate of deposit. The NCD modified the ordinary certificate of deposit (CD) in several ways to make it more attractive to the money market. A regular CD is a time deposit with a fixed maturity. Since it may be withdrawn before maturity only with a penalty, it is relatively illiquid. This makes it unattractive to the typical money market investor—a corporate treasurer managing a firm's cash reserves. The NCD overcame this handicap by being negotiable. Although it could not be redeemed early, unlike a regular CD it could be sold to someone else. Negotiability made the NCD a tradable security competitive with commercial paper or T-bills.

deposit note
A long-term, insured, bank liability.

Banks have created variations on the NCD. When regulators for a time imposed a 3% reserve requirement on NCDs with maturity less than 18 months, banks quickly switched to a longer term substitute, the **deposit note**, with a maturity of up to 5 years.

These new types of time deposit are all issued in amounts of $100,000 or more. They are known collectively as **wholesale time deposits**.[36]

wholesale time deposits
Bank time deposits issued in original amounts of $100,000 or more and sold on the money market.

Wholesale time deposits have changed the way large banks do business. With regular deposits banks must wait passively for funds to come in. If a bank is "loaned up," it will simply be unable to make an additional loan. To prevent this from happening, it must carry secondary reserves such as government securities that can be liquidated as needed to accommodate new lending. With wholesale time deposits, and other money market borrowings, banks no longer have to wait passively for new deposits to come in. If a bank wants to make an additional loan, it can raise the funds whenever it pleases by selling wholesale time deposits in the money market.

Innovations in Consumer Deposits

Heavy reliance by large banks on funding from the money market led to serious problems in the early 1980s. Such funds were "hot money." They were easy to get, but they were also easy to lose.[37] As a result of these problems, banks rediscovered the importance of "core deposits"—checking deposits and small time deposits—that are less likely to evaporate if a bank runs into difficulties.

One way that banks have attempted to increase their core deposits is by marketing retail CDs through securities firms. Securities brokerage firms earn a commission from selling investments to their customers—mainly stocks, bonds, and mutual funds.[38] They are glad to be able to round out their array of products by offering insured CDs as well.

---

[36] Banks also offer wholesale notes called *bank notes*, which are like deposit notes except that they are not formally deposits and so are not insured. Bank holding companies sell *medium-term notes* with maturities up to 7 years. These are mainly used to finance nonbank subsidiaries of the holding company, rather than bank lending.

[37] We shall discuss the resulting problems in Chapter 19.

[38] We shall discuss securities firms in Chapter 11.

brokered
retail deposits
Bank CDs mar-
keted through se-
curities brokers.

Because these **brokered retail deposits** typically have a maturity of several years, they are not inherently very liquid. However, the security brokers marketing them are often willing to create a secondary market.

By the end of 2000, there was some $219 billion of brokered retail deposits outstanding. Almost the entire amount was at the larger banks. Banks have benefited from the additional, stable source of funds. Consumers have benefited from better rates as banks have competed for their business.

THE EVOLUTION OF BANK ACTIVITIES

The evolution of bank assets and liabilities shows us how the intermediation side of a bank's business has developed. But banks are more than just intermediaries. As we have seen, banking evolved as a combination of financial intermediation and payments. It did so because there were economies of scope between these two activities. Economies of scope have also led banks into various other related lines of business.

Economies of Scope Related to Payments

Banks provide payments services, not only to households and businesses, but also to the financial markets. As we shall see in Chapter 17, an efficient and reliable system of settling financial transactions is essential to the proper functioning of securities markets. In addition to payments proper, banks provide a variety of related services. As we saw in Chapter 5, they offer cash management services that enable corporations to speed the payments they receive and delay the payments they make. Banks also provide their customers with foreign exchange to enable them to make payments in other countries. And they provide credit cards and process credit card accounts for small-bank and nonbank issuers. The payments and payments-related activities of banks are so important that we shall devote an entire chapter to them—Chapter 8.

Economies of Scope Related to Intermediation

In the process of intermediation, banks assess the creditworthiness of borrowers and back their judgment by guaranteeing a return to lenders. Banks can engage in these two activities—assessing creditworthiness and providing guarantees—without actually intermediating the loan. That is, they can broker and guarantee, explicitly or implicitly, direct lending from lender to borrower. Unlike actual intermediation, such activity leaves the balance sheet of the bank unchanged.

The Securities Business.   As we saw earlier in the chapter, some types of firm engaged in the securities business (scriveners and trust companies) evolved into banks. They did so because, holding balances for their customers, it was only natural for them to offer transactions services based on those balances. We also saw that there has been movement in the other direction too—from banking into the securities business (universal banks).

The reason why the securities business is attractive to banks is again economies of scope. There is a great deal of similarity and complementarity between the work involved in financial intermediation and work involved in underwriting and trading publicly traded securities. In particular, both intermediation and the securities business require the gathering and processing of information on the creditworthiness of borrowers and monitoring their behavior after credit has been extended. Moreover, if a firm is already borrowing from a bank, the bank will be familiar with its creditworthiness and will be in a good position to help the firm issue securities or to make a market in its securities.

The securities activities of banks therefore include the underwriting of new issues, market making in existing issues, advice to firms in putting together mergers and acquisitions, and monitoring and supervising corporate management on behalf of investors.[39] In addition, many banks provide trust and custodial services. They manage portfolios of securities for corporations, institutions, and individuals, and they manage mutual funds.[40] They hold securities for their clients. They execute the payment of interest and dividends for issuers of stocks and bonds, and they execute purchases and issuance of securities in mergers and acquisitions. They monitor compliance with covenants associated with bond issues.[41]

Loan Origination.   In underwriting securities, banks assess creditworthiness but do not provide the funding themselves. There are additional ways in which banks can originate a loan but not fund it. The lead bank in a syndication or participation does this, and so does a bank that pools its loans and sells them in a securitization. In all of these cases, a bank receives fees for originating the loan, for servicing it, and perhaps for guaranteeing it. However, it does not earn an interest rate margin as it would if it were funding the loan itself.

Guarantees.   When it underwrites securities, a bank does not provide those investing in the securities with any guarantee.[42] In syndications and securitizations, guarantees are possible but unusual. In some circumstances, however, banks do provide guarantees. Such guarantees are important, for example, in the market for commercial paper.

Commercial paper has a very short maturity, typically 30 days or less. Issuers commonly **roll over** their commercial paper: that is, they issue new commercial paper to pay off the old as it matures. Lenders are concerned that the issuer, for whatever reason, may be *unable* to roll over its commercial paper and will therefore default. To protect lenders from this danger, a bank can provide the issuer with a **line of credit**. The bank promises, if necessary, to lend the issuer the funds to pay off the old paper (in effect converting the commercial paper into a bank loan). A variation on this arrangement is the **standby letter of credit (SLC)**. An SLC is a commitment by a bank to pay if the customer fails to repay a loan or defaults on some other contractual obligation. Attaching an SLC to an issue of commercial paper essentially makes it an obligation of the guaranteeing bank. Naturally,

roll over
To pay off existing debt by issuing new debt.

line of credit
A bank commitment to lend to a customer up to a prespecified limit.

standby letter of credit
A bank guarantee used to back some types of security issued in the money market.

---

[39] We shall discuss the activities of securities firms, and of banks engaged in securities activities, in Chapter 11.

[40] We shall discuss portfolio management in more detail in Chapter 10.

[41] We shall have more to say about these functions of commercial banks in Chapter 14.

[42] Nonetheless, as with any underwriter, considerations of reputation ensure that banks are conscientious in their work.

banks charge a fee for backing commercial paper with a line of credit or with a standby letter of credit.

Banker's Acceptances.   There is a variation on commercial paper—the **banker's acceptance**—that involves the bank even more closely in guaranteeing the credit of a customer. The banker's acceptance is essentially a guaranteed postdated check. To see how it works, consider an example.

An American company, United Computers (UC), imports $1 million of computer chips from Kim Electronics in Korea. Normally, when one company purchases from another, the seller extends the buyer trade credit—time to pay. However, Kim knows nothing about the American company's creditworthiness, and it is unwilling to extend it credit. At the same time, UC does not have the funds to pay for the chips in advance. The acceptance provides a way for the deal to go through by substituting the credit of UC's bank.

Along with its order to Kim, UC sends a "letter of credit" from its bank, Chase Manhattan. This states that Chase will be willing to issue an acceptance. When the chips arrive, UC sends Kim a "time draft" drawn on Chase for $1 million, together with documents acknowledging receipt of the goods. The time draft is an order from United to Chase to pay Kim $1 million in 90 days time—in essence a check that cannot be cashed until the future date it carries.

Since, of course, a check may bounce, Kim sends the time draft (with the documents) back to Chase to be acknowledged. Chase does this by stamping on it the word "accepted" to indicate that it will guarantee payment. The acceptance is then returned to Kim.

Kim can hold the acceptance to maturity. However, as is typical, the firm prefers to get the cash immediately. So it sells the acceptance (discounts it) to its own bank. Kim's bank also has the option of holding the acceptance as an investment, but it too prefers to sell it. So it sells the acceptance in the New York acceptance market through its correspondent there.

When the acceptance matures, whoever is holding it at the time presents it for payment to Chase (just like a check). At the same time, UC pays Chase the $1 million to cover the payment.

The acceptance seems a rather roundabout way of doing things. It would seem to be much simpler for UC to raise the money it needs to pay Kim by selling commercial paper. However, this may be impossible if UC is a small firm without the credit required to issue commercial paper. You could think of this banker's acceptance as a way for Chase to substitute its credit for UC's to enable UC to borrow in the money market.

Off-Balance-Sheet Banking.   Banks earn fee income from guaranteeing commercial paper and from providing bankers' acceptances—that is, from credit substitution. Banks are able to substitute their credit in this way because evaluating the credit risk of their customers and monitoring their loan performance are precisely the activities banks are good at. Indeed, helping a customer issue money market paper allows a bank to perform much of its traditional lending function without actually putting the loan on its own books. Such **off-balance-sheet banking** has a number of advantages for a bank.

As we have seen, it avoids the regulatory costs of a regular loan. For the example we considered on pages 145–6, with a bank line of credit, United Computer might be able to sell commercial paper at 5.5%. (This is a little higher than the 5% Valley National must pay on its deposits because the commercial paper is not covered by deposit insurance.) If Valley National charges UC a fee of 80 basis points, UC still borrows more cheaply, and the bank makes a nice profit.

Off-balance-sheet banking effectively increases a bank's leverage. The bank increases its exposure to credit risk, but because the loan does not appear on its balance sheet, its formal equity-to-loan ratio is unaffected. We shall see in Chapter 19 that regulators have caught onto this and now require banks to hold capital against their off-balance-sheet risks. We shall also see that banks have an answer for this too.

Off-balance-sheet banking also relieves a bank of the liquidity risk involved in funding the loan itself. Typically, the deposits used to fund the loan are of shorter maturity than the loan itself. If the depositors wish to withdraw their funds before the loan is repaid, the bank must somehow find the necessary funds. With off-balance-sheet banking, the bank is no longer responsible for the liquidity of the loan, and it no longer bears the associated costs.[43]

Forward Transactions.   As we saw in Chapter 2, there is a great deal of similarity between lending and forward transactions. Forward transactions, like loans, involve promises, and they consequently suffer from the same difficulties. Since banks specialize in dealing with such difficulties by assessing creditworthiness and providing guarantees, it is only natural for them to expand their activities into forward transactions.

Banks offer forward transactions in foreign exchange. Buying and selling forward foreign exchange is a natural outgrowth of their foreign exchange business. Banks also offer forward transactions related to interest rates. The most important is the *swap*. This is an arrangement that allows borrowers to exchange fixed interest payments for payments that fluctuate with current market rates. Banks combine forward transactions in interest rates with lending when they make **loan commitments**—commitments to lend to their customers in the future at a prearranged rate.[44]

loan commitment
A bank's commitment to lend to a customers in the future at a pre-arranged rate.

Economies of Scope in Marketing

The relationship between a bank and its customers, both depositors and borrowers, provides it with an opportunity to sell them other products. Moreover, a bank's branch network and the tellers who provide service to its customers are largely a fixed cost. If they can be used to sell additional products, income will increase with relatively little increase in cost.

This is an important part of the economies of scope between banking and the securities business. New issues have to be sold to investors: the bank's branches provide a distribution network and its depositors provide a natural clientele. This was an important reason for the success of the German universal banks when they entered the securities business. When depositor-investors hold securities, a bank can help its customers to trade them.

There are opportunities for marketing other products. One that seems a natural for marketing to a bank's customers is insurance. There are no obvious economies of scope

---

[43] We shall discuss liquidity risk in Chapter 18.

[44] We shall discuss banks' role as a forward intermediary in Chapter 16.

between banking and insuring. But a bank does not have to be an insurer in order to sell insurance. It is well placed to sell to its customers insurance policies provided by insurance companies.

Banks also sell their customers other financial products that they do not themselves create. For example, when deposit rates fell in the United States during and after the recession of 1990–91, banks lost large amounts of time deposits as consumers switched to higher yielding, long-term investments—especially mutual funds. Banks responded by themselves offering to sell mutual funds to their customers. While some banks sold mutual funds that they themselves managed, others sold mutual funds managed by unrelated companies. The commissions earned on these sales helped to offset the loss of intermediation income from the banks' declining time deposits.

REGULATORY OBSTACLES TO THE EXPANSION OF BANK ACTIVITIES

The ability of banks to exploit economies of scale by expanding into related activities has sometimes been limited by regulatory restrictions. The history of banking in the United States provides a striking example.

The United States

Universal Banking in the United States.   In the 1880s, private banks in the United States became closely involved in the financing of railroads and then, from the 1890s, in the financing of the new industrial companies. As their business boomed, private bankers like Morgan, Brown Brothers, and Kuhn Loeb found themselves in need of ever-increasing amounts of short-term financing. Many therefore acquired control of chartered commercial banks. Commercial banks in turn, seeing the enormous profits being made in underwriting, expanded into the securities business by setting up securities subsidiaries.[45] By 1929, private banks and chartered commercial banks were well on their way to fusing into a new type of institution that combined commercial banking with the securities business.

The Separation of Commercial and Investment Banking.   All this came to an end with the Great Crash of 1929 and the Depression that followed. As we saw in Chapter 3, the collapse of the financial system and of the economy prompted a wave of financial legislation that transformed the structure of the financial system and froze it in place for many years. The new laws rigidly segmented the financial structure in order to keep banks out of danger. The **Glass–Steagall Act of 1933** required that commercial banks restrict their activities to payments and intermediation; the securities business was to be limited to specialized *investment banks*. Commercial banks were required to divest them-

---

[45] Chartered banks had to set up subsidiaries to underwrite securities because they were not themselves allowed to own corporate equities. By 1929, nearly all large chartered banks had securities subsidiaries. These accounted for about half of all underwriting and distribution of corporate securities.

selves of existing securities operations. Private banks wishing to engage in securities business (to be investment banks) were to divest themselves of their commercial banking affiliates. The Morgan bank, for example, split into a commercial bank, J. P. Morgan, and an investment bank, Morgan Stanley. This segmentation was reinforced by later legislation, such as the **Bank Holding Company Act of 1956**, which restricted the affiliation of banking and nonfinancial corporations ("the separation of banking and commerce").

The separation of commercial banking from the securities business was never complete, however. The Glass–Steagall restrictions applied only to corporate securities: subsidiaries of bank holding companies were always allowed to deal in Treasury securities and to underwrite general obligation municipal bonds. Moreover, Glass–Steagall related only to publicly traded securities: banks were quite active in the growing market in privately placed debt.[46] Finally, the Glass–Steagall Act applied only to activities *within* the United States: U.S. commercial banks also engaged in the securities business overseas, and U.S. securities firms (investment banks) had overseas subsidiaries engaged in banking.[47]

Pressure for Deregulation.   Pressure to remove the Glass–Steagall restrictions began to grow in the 1980s. As we have seen, restrictions on commercial banks made it attractive for other financial institutions to try to enter banking and to lure away their business. Like thrifts, securities firms found ways into banking. A favorite method was the **nonbank bank**. The Bank Holding Company Act defined a bank as an institution that accepts checking deposits and makes commercial loans. Consequently, an institution that performed only one of these functions was not, legally speaking, a bank. Merrill Lynch, for example, set up Merrill Lynch Bank and Trust Company in New Jersey. This "nonbank" did not accept checking deposits but it did accept insured time deposits and make commercial loans. The further expansion of nonbank banks was blocked by legislation in 1987.

Commercial banks did not stand idly by while securities firms and others were invading their territory. They responded by trying themselves to expand into activities that had been barred to them by Glass–Steagall. Regulators were sympathetic and used their discretion to interpret the law as much as possible in the banks' favor. In 1983, regulators allowed banks to engage in discount brokerage (executing trades without offering investment advice); by 1990, some 2,000 banks were offering this service. In 1989, the Fed allowed bank securities affiliates to engage in limited underwriting of corporate bonds.[48] Bankers Trust, Chase, Citi, and J. P. Morgan immediately applied for permission. In 1990 the Fed extended the authorization to include corporate stocks. J. P. Morgan was the first bank to receive permission to underwrite equities.

A second source of pressure for deregulation was the increasing globalization of the world financial system. More and more, U.S. banks and securities firms were finding themselves in competition for business, both at home and abroad, with Japanese and European rivals. If there were economies of scope between banking and other financial activities, then prohibiting American financial institutions from combining these activities placed them at a competitive disadvantage in the world marketplace.

nonbank bank
A financial institution that is like a bank except that it either does not accept checking deposits or it does not make commercial loans.

---

[46] We shall discuss Treasury securities in Chapter 12; municipal securities, the Eurobond market, and private placements in Chapter 14.

[47] These were generally Eurodollar banks. We shall have more to say about Eurodollar banking in Chapter 7.

[48] Such underwriting was to constitute no more than 10% of their business.

Repeal of Glass–Steagall.   After many unsuccessful attempts, blocked by this interest group or that, Congress finally dismantled the Depression era segmentation of the financial system with passage of the **Gramm–Leach–Bliley Act of 1999**. This legislation did three things.

- It effectively repealed the Glass–Steagall separation of commercial banking from the securities business.
- It eased the restrictions imposed by the Bank Holding Company Act on the ownership of banks by nonbank financial companies.
- It allowed bank subsidiaries to engage in a broad range of financial activities still not permitted to banks themselves.

The act created two new frameworks under which banks can engage in new types of financial activity or integrate with other types of financial company. A "financial holding company" (FHC) can conduct new activities through a holding company affiliate of the bank regulated by the Federal Reserve Board. A "financial subsidiary" permits new activities to be conducted through a subsidiary of the bank regulated by that bank's normal regulator. For example, to engage in the securities business or in insurance, a bank can set up, or purchase, a securities firm or an insurance company. The new, or newly acquired, company can be a subsidiary of the financial holding company that also owns the bank (making the new company an affiliate of the bank). Or, it can be a subsidiary of the bank itself. These two possibilities are illustrated in Exhibit 6.4.

A financial holding company may engage in any type of financial activity and even, in some circumstances, in nonfinancial activities. Explicitly permitted are securities activities, insurance, and equity investment in financial and nonfinancial companies. The FHC does not need to ask permission to do any of these things: it merely has to inform its regulator, the Fed, after the fact. Financial subsidiaries of banks are more restricted: they may not, for example, engage in underwriting insurance, in real estate development, or in equity investment. With passage of Gramm–Leach–Bliley, the way is now clear for U.S. financial institutions to pursue economies of scope more or less without restriction.

EXHIBIT 6.4   Alternative Structures under Gramm–Leach–Bliley: Financial Holding Company (left) and Subsidiary (right).

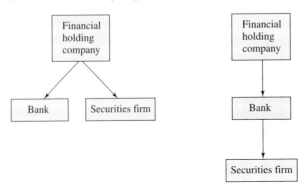

Other Countries

Let us look briefly at the situation in some other countries to see how they compare with our own in terms of the freedom of financial institutions to expand their activities.

Canada. Banking in Canada has historically been much less regulated than banking in the United States. However, until 1987, securities markets were regulated quite tightly and banks were excluded from them. In 1987 Canada deregulated its securities markets and allowed any firm, including banks and insurance companies, to open securities subsidiaries. This effectively removed the distinctions between securities firms, commercial banks, and trust companies.[49] Canadian and U.S. banks have moved into the Canadian securities market, mostly by buying up existing Canadian investment banks.

A 1991 law, which took effect in 1992, removed many of the remaining barriers between different types of financial institution. Banks are now allowed to own insurance companies and trust companies, and to provide various investment banking and trust services previously denied them (however, they are still not allowed to market insurance through their branches or to offer auto leasing). Restrictions on the lending of trust and insurance companies were removed, making it easier for these firms to compete directly with banks; Canadian banks are also allowed to own insurance companies.

The United Kingdom. The financial system in the United Kingdom has largely been free of formal regulatory constraints since the 1870s. Nonetheless it developed along fairly specialized lines until the 1980s. Commercial banks (descendants of country banks, goldsmiths, and scriveners that had incorporated in the late nineteenth century) accepted checking deposits and made loans. Merchant banks specialized in the securities business. Building societies (the equivalent of our savings and loans) accepted time deposits and made mortgage loans.

In the 1980s this segmentation began to break down. Commercial banks expanded into the securities business, insurance brokerage, and other activities, mainly through acquisitions. Building societies and other types of savings institution have begun to offer checking deposits.

Europe

The European Union is in the process of removing all internal barriers to trade in goods and services; as part of this program, a fully integrated European Financial Area is being planned.

The EU's Second Banking Directive, which came into effect in 1993, allows banks from any member country to expand into any other. Any activity allowed the bank in its home country will be allowed it in the host country, regardless of whether such activities are allowed to domestic institutions there (unless the activity is specifically excluded by the Second Banking Directive). A proposed Investment Services Directive would allow the same freedom to securities firms, which may or may not also be banks.

---

[49] Trust companies still existed as distinct institutions in Canada. Before deregulation, they had, in addition to their trust business, accepted time deposits and specialized in mortgage lending.

Banking under the new regime is modeled on the universal banks of Germany, which are free to engage in more or less any activity they please: they provide their customers with long-term loans and equity as well as short-term credit, and they underwrite and market public issues (acting as securities firms).

German universal banks have long been allowed links with insurance companies, as have banks in the United Kingdom and France. The Germans call the combination of banking and insurance *Allfinanz*; the French call it *bancassurance*. Other European countries have traditionally restricted or prohibited such links, and insurance is one of the activities excluded by the Second Banking Directive. Nonetheless, bancassurance has been spreading to other countries. There have recently been major mergers and acquisitions between banks and insurance companies in Spain, the Netherlands, Italy, Sweden, and Switzerland (which is not a member of the EU).

Japan

Postwar regulation in Japan set up a financial system based on the U.S. model. It created a number of distinct types of bank—long-term credit banks, commercial banks, and trust banks—and separate securities firms. Japan's Article 65 is its equivalent of the Glass–Steagall Act. However, Japanese banks, although they could not underwrite securities, were allowed to own equity in other corporations. Indeed, banks and their affiliates came to own some 30% of all equity in Japan. Cross-shareholding is widespread among banks, insurance companies, securities firms, and nonfinancial corporations in so-called *keiretsu* groups (the descendants of the prewar *zaibatsu* groups). This arrangement allows significant integration in practice, despite the regulations prohibiting it.

There has been a gradual deregulation of banking in Japan spurred by the financial crisis that has been going on there since 1990. Ceilings on deposit interest rates were gradually removed. As in the United States, this put pressure on bank profits and caused banks to seek income from off-balance-sheet activities. Banks and securities firms have gradually been allowed to enter one another's lines of business through subsidiaries. In 1992, banks were allowed to underwrite new issues of corporate securities but not to participate in the secondary market; in 1999, bank securities subsidiaries were given full securities powers. Regulation still separates banking and insurance.

THE DECLINE OF THE BANK?

Commercial banks in the United States appear to have been declining in importance for some time. We saw in Chapter 5 that the banks' share of total assets of all financial intermediaries has been declining since the beginning of the century. Exhibit 6.5 shows that even in an area that is classically the province of banks—short-term lending to business—the market share of commercial banks has been declining since World War II and especially sharply since the 1970s. The United States is not alone in this; the relative importance of banks seems to have been declining too in France and in Japan.

Appearances, however, are often deceiving. Looking at bank assets and lending alone does not give a complete picture. For example, as we have seen, banks have voluntarily given up much of their lending to large creditworthy business borrowers because this

EXHIBIT 6.5   Banks' Share of Business Short-Term Credit

Source: Flow of Funds Accounts.

EXHIBIT 6.6   Noninterest Income as a Percentage of Total Gross Income for Banks in Various Countries

	1981	1985	1990	1995	2000
Canada	—	24	31	35	52
France	16	14	20	55	67
Germany	29	30	27	21	29
Italy	26	32	27	20	38
Japan	18	21	24	2	12
Switzerland	53	48	50	57	62
United Kingdom	36	38	40	43	40
United States	24	27	33	35	43

Source: OECD (1991).

lending is unprofitable. Instead, banks today help such customers find direct financing in the money market and earn fee income for doing so.

More generally, as the banks' traditional business of accepting deposits and making loans has become less profitable, activities other than intermediation have become increasingly important as a source of revenue. A measure of this shift is the proportion of noninterest income in banks' total gross income. Exhibit 6.6 shows how this proportion has changed over time in a number of countries.

You can see that the proportion of noninterest income has risen steadily for U.S. banks since 1981 and that banks in other countries have experienced similar trends. The percentage of noninterest income has been highest in those countries with the fewest restrictions on bank activities, such as Germany, Switzerland, and the United Kingdom. It has risen steadily in the United States as restrictions on bank activities eroded and, finally, were removed.

The size of bank assets is a poor indicator of the importance of commercial banking. First, it captures only one of a bank's two basic functions—financial intermediation. The other—payments—is an important source of revenue. In 1996, revenue from payments-related activities accounted for 30 to 40% of the total operating revenue of the 25 largest U.S. banks.[50] Second, as we have seen, the importance of off-balance-sheet activities has been growing rapidly.

Recent research has taken these factors into account and also has looked at alternative measures of the importance of banks such as value added and employment. This research has found that there has, in fact, been no decline in the importance of banks in the United States.[51] It turns out that it is not that banks have been growing less important, but that the answer to the question "What is a bank?" has been changing.

SUMMARY

- Banks have developed from five main types of institution—payments processors, merchant banks, securities firms, chartered banks, and near banks.

- Payments processors (money-changer banks, banks of deposit, goldsmith banks) began by providing local payments services and expanded into lending.

- Merchant banks began with trade and expanded into remittance, the securities business, local payments, and lending.

- Securities firms (scriveners, trust companies, investment banks) began with securities business and lending and expanded into payments.

- Chartered banks were set up from the beginning as banks. Their purpose was to harness fractional reserve banking to the service of public finance. The Bank of England was the first, and it was the model for American chartered banks.

- Near banks began with forms of financial intermediation that were not of interest to banks. They sometimes added payment functions to become banks or were absorbed by banks.

- Banks have evolved in three dimensions: in the type of lending they do (their assets), in the type of borrowing they do (their liabilities), and in the additional activities in which they engage. This evolution has been stimulated by the search for profits, and it has been constrained by government regulation.

---

[50] See Radecki (1999).

[51] See Boyd and Gertler (1994).

- Bank lending began with the discounting of commercial bills and with the purchase of government securities. It expanded into other areas, such as mortgage lending, interbank lending, lending to industrial firms, and lending to consumers, as these types of loan became profitable.

- Bank borrowing began with checking deposits and banknotes. New types of liability were added to satisfy banks' growing need for funds. Interbank deposits became an important source of funds for the New York banks that provided finance to the developing securities markets.

- Restrictions on the interest rate that banks could pay on deposits, together with rising market interest rates, allowed nonbank financial institutions to lure away bank customers with instruments such as NOW accounts and money market mutual funds.

- Banks responded by developing bank repos, overnight Eurodollars, and correspondent Fed funds, and by adopting the NOW account, all as ways to pay interest on checking deposits. They also developed NCDs and other wholesale deposits to tap the money market for funds themselves.

- Banks have pursued economies of scope to steadily expand their activities in payment-related services and in services related to intermediation. The latter include the securities business, loan origination, guarantees, and forward transactions. Banks derive an increasing fraction of their income from such "off-balance-sheet" banking.

- Banks in the United States were long constrained in their expansion into the securities business and into insurance by various regulations. Many of the restrictions were removed with passage of the Gramm–Leach–Bliley Act of 1999.

- In other countries, such as the United Kingdom and Germany, banks have always enjoyed much greater freedom in the allowable range of activities.

- Some measures suggest that the importance of banks is declining. However, this is largely an illusion created by the changing nature of bank activities.

DISCUSSION QUESTIONS

1. Give five examples of types of company that might possibly develop into banks if regulations permitted. In each case explain the potential economies of scope.

2. How did the evolution of banks in America differ from the pattern seen in England and Europe? Do we still see traces of these differences?

3. Why do you think that banks were not originally interested in serving the needs of ordinary households? Why did this business nonetheless appeal to the various types of near bank? How did their motives differ? How did their structure better suit them to this type of business? Why did banks eventually change their minds?

4. Why do you think that governments took the right to issue banknotes away from banks and reserved it for themselves?

5. What changes in American banking can be attributed to government regulations that limited the interest rate that banks could pay on deposits? Were these changes for the better?

6. Show T-accounts for the following changes to the balance sheet of First National Bank:
   a. First National purchases $2 million in Federal funds from a respondent bank.
   b. A customer decides not to roll over a $1 million overnight repo.

7. What were the consequences of interest rate restrictions on bank liabilities? What new liabilities did banks come up with? Explain each.

8. What is off-balance-sheet banking? Give examples. Explain why banks have an advantage in these activities. Why do banks engage in off-balance-sheet banking? Why has the bank share in total financial intermediary assets been shrinking? Does this mean that banks have become less important? Why or why not?

BIBLIOGRAPHY

Alton, Gilbert R. "Requiem for Regulation Q: What It Did and Why It Passed Away." *Economic Review of the Federal Reserve Bank of St. Louis*, February 1986, 22–37.

Born, Karl Erich, *International Banking in the 19th and 20th Centuries.* New York: St. Martin's Press, 1983.

Boyd, J. H., and M. Gertler. "Are Banks Dead? Or Are the Reports Greatly Exaggerated?" *Federal Reserve Bank of Minneapolis Quarterly Review*, summer 1994, 2–23.

Cameron, Rondo. *Banking in the Early Stages of Industrialization.* New York: Oxford University Press, 1967.

Caskey, John P., and Brian J. Zikmund. "Pawnshops: The Consumer's Lender of Last Resort." *Federal Reserve Bank of Kansas City Economic Review*, March–April 1991, 5–18.

Collins, Michael. *Money and Banking in the U.K.: A History.* London: Croom Helm, 1988.

Frankel, Allen B., and John D. Montgomery. "Financial Structure: An International Perspective." *Brookings Papers on Economic Activity* I (1991):257–310.

Hammond, Bray. *Banks and Politics in America.* Princeton, NJ: Princeton University Press, 1957.

James, John A. *Money and Capital Markets in Postbellum America.* Princeton, NJ: Princeton University Press, 1978.

Kindleberger, Charles P. *A Financial History of Western Europe.* London: George Allen & Unwin, 1984.

Krooss, Herman E., and Martin R. Blyn. *A History of Financial Intermediation.* New York: Random House, 1971.

Organization for Economic Cooperation and Development. *Bank Profitability, Statistical Supplement.* Paris: OECD, 1991.

Radecki, Lawrence J. "Banks' Payment-Driven Revenues." *Federal Reserve Bank of New York Economic Policy Review*, July 1999, 53–66.

Roover, Raymond de. *Business, Banking, and Economic Thought.* Chicago: University of Chicago Press, 1974.

KEY TERMS

money-changer banks
overdraft
usury
remittance
merchant banks
banks of deposit
suspension of convertibility
universal banks
banknote
chartered bank
Bank of the United States
free banking
private bank
near bank
savings bank
savings and loan
credit union
finance company
pawnshop
post office savings bank

retail banking
negotiated order of withdrawal (NOW) account
discounting
commercial bills doctrine
commercial paper
regulatory costs
syndication
participation
credit scoring
securitization
mortgage lending
interbank deposits
call loans
Fed funds market
Eurodollar interbank market
Fed funds rate
London interbank offered rate (LIBOR)
bank repo

overnight Eurodollars
correspondent Fed funds
negotiable certificate of deposit (NCD)
deposit note
wholesale time deposits
brokered retail deposits
roll over
line of credit
standby letters of credit
banker's acceptance
off-balance-sheet banking
loan commitment
Glass–Steagall Act of 1933
Bank Holding Company Act of 1956
nonbank bank
Gramm–Leach–Bliley Act of 1999

CHAPTER 7

THE BANKING INDUSTRY

When you finish this chapter you will understand:

- Why there are so many bank mergers and takeovers
- Why banking is becoming globalized
- How banks get around regulations that restrict their growth
- What a Eurodollar is

The number of banks in many countries is shrinking rapidly as larger banks absorb smaller banks and as large banks merge with one another. In the major industrialized economies during the 1990s there were over 4,000 mergers and acquisitions of banks: the value of these deals was some $1.2 trillion. Most of these deals involved banks within a single country, but a significant number involved banks in different countries. Banking is becoming globalized. European and Japanese banks have established a presence in the United States, and American banks are expanding abroad.

Our goal in this chapter is to understand these trends and to explore their implications for the future of banking. We begin by reviewing the history of the banking industry to see how economics has shaped its evolution. We shall see that three factors have dominated the industry's development—economies of scale, the technology of communications, and government regulation. We shall then go on to see how these forces are continuing to shape banking industries today and how the same forces are driving the globalization of the banking industry. Finally, we shall examine the implications of banking consolidation for the industry itself and for its customers.

THE HISTORY OF THE BANKING INDUSTRY

Three Key Factors in the Evolution of the Banking Industry

Economies of Scale.   In Chapter 5, we saw that banks and other financial intermediaries tend to become more profitable as they become larger.

Financial, Operational, and Reputational Economies.   First, there are the financial economies of scale that result from better pooling as the pool becomes larger. We saw that the liquidity costs of a large bank are lower because the larger volume of transactions allows for more netting of deposits and withdrawals. Because larger banks can be more diversified, they can either make loans that are riskier, and so higher yielding, or they can reduce the ratio of capital to assets. In either case, the bank is more profitable.

Many studies of the banking industry have failed to find significant economies of scale because they have ignored these financial economies. Recent research has shown that when the financial economies are taken into account, bigger is always better.[1]

Second, there are the operational economies of scale that result from the element of indivisibility in fixed costs. Because fixed costs increase less than proportionally with the size of a bank, the burden is lower for larger banks. The increasing importance of informational technology has increased the operational economies of scale. Recent studies find that the minimum efficient scale of a bank in terms of operational economies is in the range of $10 billion to $25 billion in assets.[2]

Third, there are reputational economies of scale: people tend to trust large banks more. Larger banks are indeed inherently safer because of the financial economies and the operational economies. But they are also more trustworthy, since they have more to lose if they harm their reputations by taking advantage of their customers.

The Competitive Advantage of Large Banks.   Because of these three types of economy of scale, large banks should be able to outcompete small ones. They should be able to operate at lower cost and to offer their customers better terms—lower lending rates and higher deposit rates. Small banks, unable to compete, should disappear—either closing down or being taken over by the larger banks. The implications of economies of scale were clear as early as 1826, when Lord Liverpool observed, "The solid and more extensive banks will not fail, in time, to expel the smaller and weaker."

Of course, there may be limits to this process. At some point, the economies of scale will be balanced by diseconomies. Large banks become more difficult to control, and the cost of management begins to rise. It is the existence of such diseconomies of scale that guarantees that the whole banking industry will not be taken over by a single, gigantic bank.

Moreover, to capture the potential economies of scale, banks have to grow. To grow, a bank must reach customers over an ever wider geographic area. Historically, this has meant branching. There have, however, been two principal obstacles to geographic expan-

---

[1] See Hughes (2000).

[2] See Mishkin and Strahan (1999).

sion and so to growth. The first is the technology of communications, which has limited the ability of banks to reach their customers and to control their branches. The second is government regulation, which has put obstacles in the way of geographic expansion.

The Technology of Communications.   Early banks did have branches in foreign cities. However, managing these branches was a perennial problem. Poor communications made control and coordination difficult, and the absence of systematic accounting procedures made it hard to monitor performance. Because they could not consult head office on important decisions, branch managers generally had a great deal of independence. To protect their own reputations, banks felt obliged to stand behind the actions of their branch managers. So, a lazy or dishonest branch manager could, and often did, ruin the whole firm.

Poor communications remained a barrier to branching until well into the second half of the nineteenth century. In England, in the 1840s, Manchester was still a 25-hour journey from London by stagecoach. In the United States, the greater distances merely made matters worse.

The advent of the railroads and the organization of regular postal services improved things. But it was not until the spread of the telegraph in the 1860s that branching really became feasible. The telephone was even better. And, as we shall see, the Internet may have profound implications for the structure of the banking industry.

Regulatory Barriers.   The technology of communications was not, however, the only barrier. In many countries, legal obstacles made it difficult for banks to expand geographically. Let us look at England and at the United States as examples.

Barriers in Early Nineteenth-Century England.   To protect the Bank of England's monopoly, an act of Parliament prohibited the creation of any other joint-stock (chartered) bank. The law further limited banking partnerships to no more than six members. Limited in this way, private banks were unable to raise the capital they needed to expand and they generally remained small. Most were **unit banks** without branches. Because most English banks were small and undercapitalized, with each new economic crisis dozens of them failed.

The law imposed to protect the Bank of England did not apply in Scotland, which enjoyed a separate legal system. Scottish banks were therefore organized as extensive partnerships and were consequently well capitalized. The typical Scottish bank was considerably larger than its English counterpart and generally had many branches.[3] The economic crises that did so much damage to the English system left the Scottish banks largely unscathed.[4] The lesson did not go unnoticed in England. The Banking Act of 1826

unit bank
A bank limited to a single office.

---

[3] In the days when banks issued banknotes, there was an additional advantage to size. People generally did not wish to hold notes of distant banks: the soundess of such institutions was unknown and redemption of their notes difficult. So notes that found their way out of the locality of the bank tended to be returned for redemption. A bank with many branches would find its notes accepted more widely, and fewer would be returned. It was largely these economices of scale of reputation that drove the Scottish banks to open branches.

[4] The Scottish system was superior to the English in other respects, too. Vigorous competition promoted good service and rapid technological change. The Scottish banks pioneered the acceptance of small deposits (retail banking), the payment of interest on deposits, and the development of different types of deposit.

began a process of deregulation that would eventually allow English banks to develop branch systems.

The Rise and Fall of the Bank of the United States.   We saw in Chapter 6 that the early banks in the United States were almost exclusively chartered banks, incorporated by either state or federal charter. The federal chartering of banks—"national banking" as it was called—was controversial from the beginning, and the debate over its constitutionality continued for almost a century.

The first federally chartered banks, the First and Second Banks of the United States, were allowed to branch nationwide. Alexander Hamilton, the first Secretary of the Treasury, strongly opposed nationwide branching because he believed that the effective management of an extensive branch system was impossible. The first Bank set up branches in eight major cities. The second, at its peak, had twenty-five branches. Hamilton's misgivings proved well-founded. Branch managers were frequently incompetent or dishonest. They often served local interests rather than those of the bank, causing the bank significant losses.

The Bank's branch network did, however, give it a substantial advantage in executing payments between different parts of the country. This, together with its position as banker to the federal government, contributed to its growing dominance. At its peak, the bank accounted for about a third of all bank assets in the United States.

There was considerable political opposition to the Bank of the United States. Agrarians opposed it for serving urban commercial interests—believing it to be a complicated fraud designed to enrich the city slicker at the expense of the honest farmer. State-chartered banks resented competition from the Bank and the discipline that it imposed on them by insisting they redeem their bank notes in specie. The Jacksonians, who favored private enterprise, opposed the kind of government intervention that a chartered bank represented.

The Bank's enemies succeeded in blocking the renewal of its charter in 1811. The needs of government finance after the War of 1812 led to the establishment of the Second Bank in 1816. But when the Second Bank's charter came up for renewal in 1836, President Jackson vetoed it. The popularity of this move contributed to his reelection the same year. With the demise of the Second Bank, banking was left entirely in the domain of the states.

Obstacles to Interstate Banking.   The expansion of state banks was limited by the terms of their charters. The standard corporate charter of the time, used for banks and nonbanks alike, strictly limited the scope of the corporation's activities. It typically prohibited the corporation from conducting business outside the incorporating state.[5] This made branching across state lines impossible.

In addition to these legal handicaps, state banks too were the victims of antibank sentiment. In many western states, they were banned altogether. In these states, there were no chartered banks at all, although some private banks did operate. In states in which bank-

---

[5] Legal doctrine also permitted states to exclude corporations chartered in other states from doing business within their borders. Although corporations were considered legal persons, they did not in this respect receive the constitutional protections of natural citizens of other states.

ing was permitted, branching was often restricted. Some states allowed no branching at all, limiting banks to a single office under a single roof (a *unit bank*); others allowed branching within a city, within a county, or even statewide. Before the Civil War, branching was most common in the South, and southern banks were therefore among the soundest and most modern.

The Civil War changed the face of American banking. Desperate for funds, the federal government resumed its chartering of banks to help finance the war. The enabling legislation, the **National Banking Act of 1863**, said nothing specific about branching. However, to avoid bringing up any unpleasant memories of the Bank of the United States, the Treasury limited national banks to a single office.

Economies of Scale between Banks: Correspondents and Money Markets

Faced with technological and regulatory barriers to expansion and consolidation, banks developed alternative arrangements to capture economies of scale. These arrangements enabled them to capture such economies *between* banks rather than *within* banks.

correspondent bank
A bank with which another bank in another city has a regular business relationship.

Correspondent Banking.   From the earliest of times, a bank in one city would have regular business relationships with banks in other cities. To make or collect payments in another city, a bank would rely on its **correspondent** there. It might also authorize its correspondent to act for it in trading or in the extension of credit.

In some ways a correspondent bank was better than a branch. The desire to continue a profitable relationship gave both parties an incentive for good behavior. However, since the relationship was arm's length, with carefully defined credit limits and a clear division of responsibilities, a correspondent offered fewer risks than an uncontrollable branch. And, in case of trouble, a correspondent could be disowned in a way that a branch could not.

A country bank's customers typically did a lot of business with the national commercial and financial center—London, New York, or Paris. It was therefore, particularly important for a country bank to have a correspondent there. To facilitate payments, the country bank would normally keep a clearing deposit with its correspondent in the financial center.

Because correspondent banks paid a good return on these deposits, country banks came to keep much of their extra funds in such correspondent balances. Financial center correspondents also provided other services. If a country bank needed additional credit to accommodate its customers, it could turn to its correspondent for help. The correspondent would also clear payments to and from country banks in other regions. In addition, it would provide valuable financial and other information.

respondent bank
A small bank with a business relationship with a city correspondent.

Both in England and in the United States, there grew up a system of financial center correspondents and country bank **respondents**. These systems captured many of the benefits that would have been obtained from branching, had branching been technologically and legally feasible.

money market
Market for short-term debt securities.

The Rise of a National Money Market in England.   In both countries, large amounts of correspondent balances supported the development of a national **money market**. Rapidly developing regions and growing industries, with large appetites for credit, would go to the financial center to borrow. There, the institutions of the money market would satisfy their needs, relying on the funds deposited with them by the country banks.

The Industrial Revolution strained the capacity of England's fragmented banking system. In regions where expansion was taking place, small country banks were unable to satisfy the demand for credit. They therefore sent their customers' bills to their London correspondents to be discounted.[6] At the same time, in regions with little industrial development, banks found they had more funds than loan opportunities. So they bought bills through their London correspondents.

By the turn of the nineteenth century, London had developed a thriving market in commercial bills. Initially, it was organized by bill brokers who brought buyers and sellers together but did not themselves take a position. By 1810, however, these brokers had evolved into dealers who purchased the bills themselves for resale to others. These dealers borrowed from the London banks to finance their inventories.

By 1827 the dealers had further evolved into "discount houses." In addition to being dealers, discount houses invested in bills on their own account. They financed their portfolios with call loans from country banks.[7] For the country banks, these call loans came to replace the outright purchase of bills as an outlet for excess funds.

The Rise of a National Money Market in the United States.   In the United States, too, there developed a market for call loans and a market for commercial bills. In the United States, however, these two markets did not coalesce. Instead, each developed separately. Through the correspondent system, the surplus funds of small local banks found their way to city banks in the major financial centers—particularly New York. The New York banks found an outlet for these "bankers balances" in the form of call loans—but call loans to the stock exchange not to the money market.[8]

Call loans in the United States went into the capital market rather than into the money market because the money market could not absorb them. Before the Civil War, the supply of commercial bills was small. Initially, most of the nation's trade was international, and it was financed in London. As domestic trade developed, the banks were generally able to provide the necessary finance. Industrialization did not come until the Civil War.

A modest money market did exist. Bill brokers gathered commercial bills from firms and took them from bank to bank until they found a buyer. Initially, the business was limited to New York, but it slowly spread. Brokers sent representatives out of town to solicit bills for sale and to sell bills to local banks. For many years, the business was on a commission basis. But, in 1857, one broker became a dealer, buying his customers' paper outright for resale. The practice proved so popular with customers that the other brokers were forced to do the same.

The banking legislation of the Civil War significantly worsened the fragmentation of the American banking system. State-chartered banks were forced to cut back their lending. The lending of the new national banks was restricted too. Lending to any single borrower was limited to no more than 10% of a bank's capital—a serious obstacle because capital

---

[6] Usually, the originating country bank would guarantee such bills against default.

[7] The loans were collateralized with bills deposited with the lending banks' London correspondents.

[8] Because call loans to the stock exchange fluctuated widely in amount, New York banks were reluctant to use them to fund loans.

was often in short supply. Moreover, with little local competition, banks often found themselves with considerable market power. They exploited this by raising their loan rates and limiting their lending.

At the same time that local loan markets were deteriorating, industrialization was increasing the demand for credit. Local borrowers had no choice but to turn to the money market. The market for *commercial paper* grew steadily, both geographically and in volume. By 1900 its reach was nationwide.

The principal buyers of commercial paper were the banks themselves. Commercial paper provided an attractive outlet for their surplus funds. It was relatively liquid, and holding paper from outside a bank's local market improved the diversification of its assets. Any surplus funds not invested in commercial paper still found their way to city correspondents where they fueled an expansion of the call loan market. This expansion played a vital role in the rapid growth of the New York capital market after the Civil War.

Integration through Correspondent Banking and Money Markets. Exhibit 7.1 illustrates how a system of correspondent banks and money market works. Panel A shows how the correspondent system allows lenders in one area to lend to borrowers in another. The lender makes a deposit at his bank. The depositor's bank deposits its excess funds with its correspondent in the financial center. The correspondent lends the funds in the money market. At the same time, the borrower borrows from his bank by discounting a bill, the borrower's bank rediscounts the bill with its correspondent, and the correspondent sells the bill in the money market. Panel B shows how payments clear. The payer sends a check to the recipient, who deposits it with his bank. The recipient's bank sends it to its correspondent, who sends it to the clearinghouse. It then finds its way back to the payer's bank through the payer's bank's correspondent.

Consolidation in England and the Advantages of Branch Banking

Although similar banking structures developed in England and in the United States, their fate was quite different in the two countries. In England, the regulatory barriers were removed in a series of acts between 1826 and 1862 that liberalized joint-stock banking. At the same time, communications and control improved steadily. By the 1840s, joint-stock banks were being formed in growing numbers and were beginning to develop branch systems. As the joint-stock branch banks expanded, they slowly but steadily displaced the correspondent system of country bank, city correspondent, and money market.

Most of what the correspondent system could do, the new branch banks could do better. They could offer payments services at lower cost. Clearing payments within a bank is quicker and cheaper than clearing them between banks. The branch banks could move funds from lending regions to borrowing regions more cheaply. Moving funds among branches is less costly than interbank borrowing and lending.[9]

---

[9] Some joint-stock banks expanded into London to gain direct access to the London Bankers' Clearing House, rather than paying a correspondent for the service. Because of the 1826 act, they were obliged to give up the right of note issue to do this. Since checking deposits were anyhow more important than notes by this time, the joint-stock banks generally found this a small price to pay for direct access to the London payments system.

EXHIBIT 7.1   (A) Lending and (B) Payment through a Correspondent System

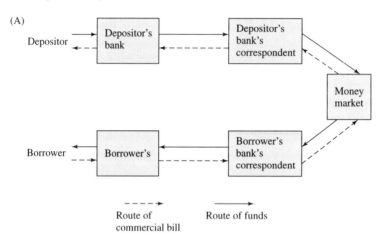

(A)

Route of
commercial bill   Route of funds

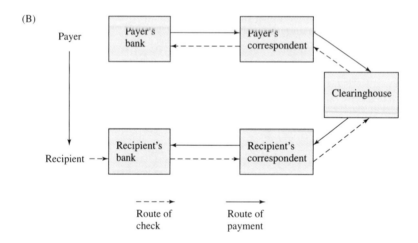

(B)

Route of
check   Route of
payment

By comparing Exhibit 7.2 to Exhibit 7.1 you can see the advantages of a branching system. Lending now involves a single intermediary rather than a series of intermediaries. Since each loan in the series of loans involves all the transactions costs and incentive problems that we discussed in Chapter 1, having a single intermediary is much more efficient. Payments are much simpler, too, again reducing transactions costs.

The large branch systems had other advantages too. In times of crisis the larger, better diversified, joint-stock banks proved safer than the smaller unit banks. Depositors were quick to notice the difference, and they switched their funds to the larger and safer banks. They were encouraged to do so, too, by the higher interest rates the branch banks could offer because of their lower costs.

EXHIBIT 7.2   (A) Lending and (B) Payment through a Branching System

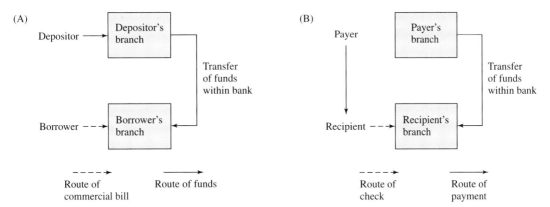

The branch banks also offered advantages to borrowers. Greater safety matters to borrowers too. They need to know that their credit will not dry up in times of general financial crisis, when their need is greatest. Moreover, branch banks were able to satisfy all their customers' needs for credit themselves, rather than having to pass on their securities to the London money market. As we saw in Chapter 2, a borrower in trouble can renegotiate with his bank, while he might be forced into bankruptcy by the anonymous holders of his securities.

Under the pressure of competition, many small private banks failed. Most of the others were bought up and integrated into the expanding branch networks. There was a process of steady consolidation among the branch banks themselves. In 1884, there were 118; by 1913, there were 43; and by 1918, the "Big Five" accounted for two-thirds of all deposits in the country. The branch banks transferred funds internally from region to region and had no need for the services of a money market.

In the same period, the banking systems of other countries, most notably Germany and France, underwent similar consolidations. The reasons were the same—improved communications, the removal of legal barriers, and the pursuit of economies of scale.

CONSOLIDATION IN THE UNITED STATES

The United States was the big exception. Although communications improved, the legal barriers remained. Repeated financial crises brought about the failure of large numbers of unit banks, and this created tremendous pressure for consolidation. The comparative stability of banking structures in other countries with consolidated banking systems made nationwide branching seem very appealing. However, the barriers to interstate banking have only slowly eroded and certain barriers remain in effect even today. The political resistance to the removal of these barriers has been enormous. Small banks have organized politically and exploited populist fears to block consolidation.[10]

---

[10] The American Bankers Association was set up to campaign for the existing structure.

Living with Branching Restrictions

In the face of the legal barriers to interstate banking, U.S. banks have continued to rely on correspondent relationships and money markets much more than banks in other countries. Larger correspondent banks provide smaller respondents with an array of services such as check processing as well as access to securities markets, foreign exchange, and international banking. By offering these services, the correspondent spreads the fixed costs over a much larger volume of business.

The balances small banks keep with their correspondents are useful for both parties. For the respondents, they are an important source of liquidity that can easily be drawn down if, for example, there is a net outflow of customer deposits. For the correspondent, its many respondents are an important source of funds.

There also developed in the United States an interbank market in which the larger banks could borrow from one another to meet liquidity needs. This market had its origins in the Federal Reserve Act of 1913, which required banks to maintain reserves in the form of balances held at the newly established Federal Reserve. To meet this requirement, some banks had to borrow from the Fed through the "discount window." At the same time, other banks found themselves with surplus funds in their deposits.

Beginning in 1921, a market developed in which banks with surplus reserve deposits would lend them to those with reserve deficiencies. This market came to be known as the Fed funds market. A Fed funds loan was not only cheaper than a discount loan, but it also relieved the borrower of the need to assemble collateral. Loans were arranged over the telephone. The loan was executed through the exchange of checks drawn on the Fed.

The correspondent relationship, together with the Fed funds market, provided a way for U.S. banks to replicate the liquidity benefits of pooling deposits that could be done internally by branches of a branch bank. Banks in the United States also found ways to replicate the diversification benefits of a large branch bank through *loan sharing*—a sort of interbank market in loans to parallel the interbank market in funds.

If a correspondent faces a loan request that is too large for it to take on alone, it will farm out parts of the loan to its many respondent banks. As we saw in Chapter 6, this arrangement is called a loan *participation*. Respondents are frequently the buyers. Respondents are also potential buyers when the correspondent securitizes some of its loans.[11] On the other hand, if the customer of a respondent wants a loan too large for the bank to handle, the respondent will turn to its correspondent to take on part of the loan. This arrangement is called an **overline**. In all of these cases, dividing loans among banks improves the diversification of each. This again replicates what is done internally by a large branch bank.[12]

overline
A correspondent's participation in a loan originated by a respondent.

Getting around Branching Restrictions

Banks in the United States have also responded to the legal barriers to interstate banking by finding ways to circumvent these barriers.

---

[11] We encountered securitization in Chapter 6 and we shall discuss it in detail in Chapters 13 and 14.

[12] The movement toward interstate banking (see later) has placed strains on the correspondent relationship. A small local bank now sees its regional or money center correspondent as a potential competitor, since the correspondent may well end up buying the bank across the street. One response to this problem, particularly in the Midwest, has been for groups of small banks to set up regional service centers under joint ownership—so-called *banker's banks*. These provide many of the same services traditionally provided by a correspondent.

holding company
A corporation set up purely to own other corporations.

Multibank Holding Companies.   One popular method was the **holding company**. A holding company is a corporation that does not conduct business itself: all it does is own other corporations. Banks used this structure to get around branching restrictions.

To see how this can be done, consider the two banks, Bank One and Bank Two, in Exhibit 7.3. Bank One would like to buy Bank Two, but it cannot because Bank Two is in another state. So, instead, Bank One sets up a holding company—OneCorp—that becomes the legal owner of Bank One. Because OneCorp is not itself a bank, it *is* able to purchase Bank Two without breaking the law.

multibank holding company
A holding company set up to own several banks, often to circumvent branching restrictions.

A holding company that owns more than a single bank is called a **multibank holding company**. Multibank holding companies have existed since the turn of the century, and they have been particularly popular in states that restricted branching within the state. The most famous example was A. P. Giannini's Transamerica Corporation. Transamerica owned Bank of America and many other banks in several western states. In 1947 it had 43% of all deposits in California, 45% in Oregon, and 79% in Nevada. Transamerica also owned many nonbanking enterprises. The growth of bank holding companies, in particular the growth of Transamerica, aroused populist fears of concentrated financial power. As a result of increasing political opposition, the Bank Holding Company Act, which was largely motivated by a desire to restrain Transamerica, was passed in 1956. The **Douglas Amendment** to the act prohibited this method of expansion across state lines unless explicitly permitted by the states involved.

Recent changes in the law—about which we shall learn presently—have allowed the number of interstate bank holding companies to grow dramatically. In 1990 there were 160 such companies, operating among them some 465 bank subsidiaries in various states.

one-bank holding company
A holding company that owns a single bank plus nonbank subsidiaries.

In contrast to multibank holding companies, **one-bank holding companies** own only a single bank. A one-bank holding company may set up subsidiaries (corporations owned

EXHIBIT 7.3   Direct Ownership vs Holding Company Structure

Direct ownership

Multibank holding company structure

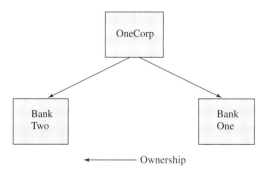

◄——— Ownership

by the holding company) that are not themselves banks and are not owned by a bank and can therefore engage in activities prohibited a bank—for example, the securities business. Most large banks are organized as either multibank or one-bank holding companies and have securities and other nonbank subsidiaries.

Nonbank Banks and Offices.   A bank cannot open branches across state lines. But what is a branch? According to the Bank Holding Company Act, a bank is an institution that "accepts demand [checking] deposits and makes commercial loans." So, if a bank sets up an office that takes checking deposits *or* makes commercial loans—but not both—it is not legally speaking a bank branch.

If the office accepts checking deposits but does not make commercial loans (channeling the funds back to the parent bank), it is called a *nonbank bank*, or *consumer bank*. If the office makes loans (with funds provided by the parent bank) but does not accept checking deposits, it is called a "nonbank office." Nonbank banks, because they accept deposits, require a bank charter; nonbank offices do not. Nonbank banks and offices can be created by buying a bank and stripping it of either its deposits or its loans. They can also be created by opening a new office that is originally a nonbank.

Of course, if a nonbank bank is not legally a bank, there is no obstacle to it being owned by a nonbank financial institution or a nonfinancial corporations, which are barred from owning banks. The nonbank bank proved a popular route into banking—or should we say "nonbanking"—for companies such as Merrill Lynch, Prudential, and Ford. The nonbank loophole was closed by the **Competitive Equality Banking Act of 1987**, which prohibited the opening of any new nonbank banks and limited the expansion of existing nonbank banks.

The Movement towards Interstate Banking

money-center bank
A large bank headquartered in one of the major U.S. financial centers—New York, Chicago, or San Francisco.

The largest banks in the United States are called **money-center banks**, because they are headquartered in the major financial centers—mainly in New York, but also in Chicago and San Francisco. They differ from other banks not only in their size, but also in the range of their activities. They are typically far more involved in international banking and in the financial markets. The 10 or so money-center banks led the way in finding ways around the ban on interstate banking.

regional bank
A medium-sized bank headquartered in a regional financial center.

Regional Interstate Banking.   The success of the money center banks in bypassing the ban on interstate banking created competitive pressure on the banks immediately below them in size. These **regional banks**, several hundred in number, were located in regional financial centers, such as Boston, Los Angeles, and Charlotte, North Carolina. In terms of size and range of activity, they were between the money center banks and the thousands of small local banks. Largely at the urging of the regional banks, groups of states began from 1982 to allow mergers and acquisitions among banks within that group of states.

Regional interstate banking gave a major boost to a number of large regional banks. A number of regional banks—such as Nationsbank of North Carolina, BancOne of Ohio,

superregional

A large regional bank with activities in more than one state.

and Fleet of Rhode Island—were so successful that they came to be known as **super-regionals**.[13] Some of these superregionals grew to be as large or larger than the money-center banks themselves. The superregionals were more interested in expanding further than they were in being protected from competition. As a result, they joined the money-center banks in lobbying for full national interstate banking. A major step in that direction came in 1994.

The Riegle–Neal Interstate Banking Law. The Riegle–Neal Interstate Banking and Branching Efficiency Act of 1994 significantly liberalized interstate banking. It allowed nationally chartered bank holding companies to acquire banks anywhere in the nation (invalidating state laws allowing only regional interstate banking). In general, it bars acquisitions that would give a bank more than 30% of deposits in any one state or 10% of deposits nationwide. Since 1997 nationally chartered bank holding companies have been able to convert the banks they owned in different states into branches of a single bank.[14]

Even under the Riegle–Neal Act some barriers remain. Banks are still not allowed to simply open a branch across state lines. To enter a new state, they must purchase an existing bank in that state. However, once in that state, if state banking laws permit, they may open additional branches.

The Extent of Consolidation in the United States. As a result of the easing of regulatory barriers in the United States, beginning with the barriers to branching within states, there has been a considerable consolidation of the banking industry. In the period 1991–1998, there were 5,686 mergers and acquisitions involving banks; the total value of these transactions was $589 billion. Between 1980 and 1999 the number of commercial banks fell by over 40%—from 14,406 to 8,505. Since Riegle–Neal, multibank holding companies have been restructuring, consolidating 90% of their subsidiary banks into single-branch networks.

While the number of banking firms has fallen, the number of bank offices has increased over the same period by 40%, from 50,804 to 71,383. Much of this increase has come from thrifts converting to commercial bank charters and from the establishment of small branches in supermarkets (about which more shortly). The United States still has considerably fewer bank offices relative to population than does Europe: in the United States there are about 12,000 people per bank office; in Europe there are about 2,000 per bank office. Whether this means that the United States is "underbranched" or Europe "overbranched" is not clear.

Employment in the banking industry rose by 10% between 1980 and 1999, to 1,635,000. The quality of jobs has improved. While the number of tellers has fallen, the number of professionals has increased.

Concentration in the banking industry has increased: in 1999 the 10 largest banks accounted for 37% of total bank assets compared to 20% in 1980. Most of this rise has

---

[13] A superregional was defined in the American Banker Yearbook 1988 as a "non-money-center bank, ranked among the top 100 banking firms in total assets, and has merged across state lines to establish a banking presence in another state."

[14] States had until June 1997 to opt out of this law or to grant their own banks the same rights as national banks.

been the result of mergers and acquisitions rather than of internal growth. Concentration in the United States is still quite low by international standards. In other major industrial countries, the largest 10 banks account for 50 to 95% of total bank assets.

After the rush of mergers and acquisitions following the Riegle–Neal Act, there were signs in 1999 that the pace of consolidation was slowing.

INTERNATIONAL BANKING

Many of the same factors that have caused banks to expand geographically within a given country have also caused banks to expand internationally. There has been an enormous expansion of international banking since the 1960s.

In 1960, only nine U.S. banks had an office overseas (a branch or a subsidiary). By 1985 almost every large and medium-sized bank in the United States had become involved in international banking: 162 banks had offices overseas. These foreign offices had some $344 billion in assets—about 22% of all assets of U.S. banks. Since then the number of U.S. banks with overseas offices has declined: there were 82 in 1998. This was partly because many medium-sized banks found international banking to be harder than they thought and partly a result of consolidation in the United States.

In 1998, the assets of foreign branches and subsidiaries of U.S. banks amounted to $805 billion.[15] This number, large as it is, understates the importance of international banking, since banks conduct much of their off-balance-sheet activity abroad. U.S. banks book over half their derivatives business in their overseas offices, and their overseas offices are very active in the securities business, in trading, and in syndications and securitization.

Japanese banks, too, rapidly expanded their international activities, beginning a little later than the U.S. banks. In 1980, Japanese banks had 139 offices overseas with $189 billion of assets. By 1989, they had over 300 offices with $1.4 trillion in assets. At that time, Japanese banks accounting for 40% of total international lending. Since 1989, severe problems in the domestic economy have caused Japanese banks to cut back their international activities, and their share of international lending has steadily declined.

European banks have always been active internationally, and their relative importance grew in the 1990s as U.S. and Japanese banks retrenched. The banks of the Asian "tigers"—Hong Kong, Taiwan, Singapore, South Korea—were a growing presence until the Asian crisis of 1998.

While the nationality of the leading international banks has changed from time to time, the overall trend of international banking has been the same—steadily upward. Why has international banking grown in this way?

Reasons for the Expansion of International Banking

The Recovery of World Trade and of International Banking.   From its earliest days, banking has been an international business. Indeed, as we saw in Chapter 6, it was the international trading connections of some merchants that led them into the busi-

---

[15] This number represents "claims on unrelated parties." Foreign offices of U.S. banks have in addition a large volume of claims on other offices of their parent banks (recall the overnight Eurodollars of Chapter 6).

ness of remittance, then into securities trading, and ultimately into banking. To a large extent, banking follows trade.

The Great Depression ushered in a long period of diminished trade and restricted international lending that turned banking inward. There was little point in having a foreign branch if there was no international business for it to do. International trade began to recover after World War II, but by 1960 imports and exports still accounted for only 5% of U.S. economic activity. Since then, trade has expanded rapidly, and imports and exports now account for more than 10% of U.S. economic activity. As more U.S. companies have dealings and operations overseas, their banks must expand their international operations and their presence overseas. Japanese banks went through a similar process, following Japanese manufacturers and trading companies overseas.

Liberalization of Financial Sectors.   The second reason for the expansion of international banking is the liberalization of financial sectors and the increase in international lending. Forty years ago there was relatively little private international lending. Most countries did not even allow their citizens to buy foreign securities (the United States was an exception). Consequently, financial sectors in different countries were relatively isolated from one another. As many countries removed restrictions on international investment, the market became more integrated. Banks and other financial institutions expanded overseas to provide better service to their domestic customers.

Together with the liberalization of domestic financial systems and the removal of barriers to international lending, there has been a movement towards free trade in financial services. The Uruguay round of trade negotiations included, for the first time, trade in services as well as trade in goods. These negotiations resulted in 1997 in the **Financial Services Agreement (FSA)**, which came into force in March of 1999. The 102 countries that signed the FSA agreed, in varying degrees, to open their domestic banking, securities, and insurance industries to foreign entry and competition.

Economies of Scale and Scope.   The third reason for the expansion of international banking is provided by the same economies of scale and scope that drive domestic expansion. International expansion is a way to grow bigger and a way to undertake more related activities. By branching overseas rather than relying on overseas correspondents, banks reduce the cost of their international transactions. By lending in more than one country, they improve the diversification of their assets.

Escaping Government Regulation.   The fourth reason for the growth of international banking is restrictive domestic regulation. Restrictions on geographic expansion limited bank growth within the United States; international growth was a substitute. Both U.S. and Japanese banks were prohibited from engaging in many financial activities, such as underwriting corporate securities, at home. The rules for overseas branches and subsidiaries were more liberal.[16] Both U.S. and Japanese banks faced restrictions on the inter-

---

[16] A 1962 amendment to the Federal Reserve Act allowed foreign branches and subsidiaries of national banks to engage in all activities allowed domestic banks of the country concerned, except for nonfinancial commercial business and the underwriting of corporate securities beyond a stated maximum.

est rates they could pay on domestic deposits; overseas expansion enabled them to raise funds more easily and to circumvent these restrictions. Overseas offices sometimes enable banks to avoid regulatory costs such as reserve requirements and deposit insurance premiums, and they sometimes offer tax advantages.

There are two distinct types of international banking— multinational banking and offshore banking. **Multinational banking** involves a bank operating outside its home country and in the local currency. An example would be a German bank with an office in the United States taking deposits and making loans in U.S. dollars. **Offshore banking** involves a bank operating outside its home country but in its home currency. An example would be a U.S. bank with an office in London taking deposits in U.S. dollars and making loans in U.S. dollars. We shall look at each of these types of international banking in turn.

multinational banking
A bank operating outside its home country and in the local currency.

offshore banking
A bank operating outside its home country but in its home currency.

Multinational Banking

U.S. Banks Overseas.   Most of the activity of U.S. banks overseas is offshore banking in U.S. dollars, which we shall discuss presently. Only a few U.S. banks are engaged in local currency banking outside the United States, and most of this activity is concentrated in Latin America. Of the U.S. banks engaged in multinational banking, the outstanding example is Citibank, which now does more business overseas than it does at home: it has over 2,000 offices in 89 countries. Citi has expanded its retail banking in Europe, in Latin America, and in Asia. It has done so by offering overseas consumers services they could not receive from their domestic banks—services like credit cards, teller machines, banking by phone, and home mortgages. Citi's strategy exploits economies of scale: products developed initially for the U.S. market can be extended to additional markets at relatively low cost. Multinational banking has also brought Citi the benefits of diversification. When the U.S. economy has been in recession, profits from overseas operations have helped to offset Citi's losses at home.

In 1994, the North American Free Trade Agreement (NAFTA) created a free trade area encompassing the United States, Canada, and Mexico. Among its provisions, the agreement liberalized trade in financial services. Since U.S. and Canadian banks were already free to operate in each others' countries, the main consequence was the opening up of the Mexican banking market to U.S. and Canadian banks.[17] U.S. and Canadian banks were allowed to acquire or establish Mexican subsidiaries beginning in 1994.

Foreign Banks in the United States.   The foreign presence in the United States has expanded along with the general expansion of international banking. The U.S. market is attractive to foreign banks both because of its size and because of its language. English is the second language in most countries, and many European bankers find it easier to do business here than to expand into other countries in Europe.

In 1975 the 79 foreign banks with U.S banking offices accounted for less than 5% of total bank assets in the United States. By 1998 there were 243 foreign banks in the United States, and they accounted for 23% of total bank assets. But even this understates the increasing importance of foreign banks. For regulatory and tax reasons, foreign banks book much of their U.S. lending overseas (especially in the Caribbean).

---

[17] Foreign banks were not allowed to open branches in Canada until 1999.

The Japanese are the largest single group, but their importance declined during the 1990s as part of the general retrenchment of their international activity. The Europeans together account for nearly 60% of foreign bank assets in 1998 and Canadian banks are a significant presence. Most foreign banks are located in the major banking markets— New York, California, Illinois, and Florida.

"Interstate" Banking in Europe.   The nations of the European Union are committed to removing all barriers to trade in goods and services among them. The **Second Banking Directive**, adopted in December 1989, granted banks based in any member state a license to operate in any other member state without the need to register or to obtain a charter there.[18] Cross-border banking in Europe was further eased in 1999 when a subset of 11 member countries of the EU adopted a single currency, the Euro. These changes have kicked off a process of consolidation in Europe not unlike that in the United States following the easing of restrictions on interstate banking.

So far most of the consolidation has taken place within European countries rather than between them. Governments have encouraged domestic consolidation to create "national champions" that could hold their own in international competition. Some governments, such as those of Holland, Spain, Italy, and Denmark have used tax incentives and deregulation to actively encourage their banks to merge.

Cross-border mergers have mainly involved the smaller Scandinavian and Benelux countries. However, some banks in the larger countries have been active in cross-border acquisitions. For example, Germany's Deutsche Bank owns or controls banks in Austria, Italy, the Netherlands, Portugal, and Spain; France's Crédit Lyonnais bought banks in Spain, Belgium, the Netherlands, and Italy.

In addition to mergers and acquisitions, there have been a number of joint ventures and strategic alliances. These enable firms to work together without either firm relinquishing control of its own operations and activities. They are also a form of "trial marriage." Firms can get to know one another and form ties. If things work out well, a full merger may result. If not, the ties are relatively easy to dissolve. The largest existing alliance centers on Spain's biggest bank, BSCH, which has cross-shareholdings with Royal Bank of Scotland, Société Générale in France, Commerzbank in Germany, and San Paolo IMI in Italy. Such alliances have seen, however, little or no actual integration of activities to reap economies of scale and scope. Some observers suspect that their main motive may be to block acquisition by other banks.

Considerable obstacles to consolidation remain. In many European countries— especially Germany, Italy, Spain, and France—government ownership of banks is significant. In many, too, there are large "nonprofit" banks (mutuals and cooperatives). Since neither governments nor nonprofits are driven by the bottom line, they are less responsive to the imperatives of economic efficiency. Governments, that of France in particular, have found ways to block foreign banks from taking over their "national champions." Even where cross-border acquisitions have taken place, the diversity of legal and tax environments makes it difficult for banks to offer universal products.

---

[18] The license was also available to banks from countries outside the EC as long as their home governments allowed free entry to EC banks.

Problems of Multinational Banking.   In addition to the legal and regulatory obstacles to foreign entry put up by governments, expanding into a foreign country is inherently more difficult for a bank than expanding within its own country. The difficulties include differences in language and culture, poorer information, and fewer business relationships than home-country banks. As a result of the informational disadvantages, when foreign banks expand their loan portfolios, they often wind up with the lemons that domestic banks have turned down. And of course, there is the classic problem of controlling a distant branch. A new overseas branch or subsidiary is initially given considerable independence, on the assumption that it knows local conditions best. The result is frequently disappointing.

In the United States, for example, many foreign banks have taken substantial losses on their U.S. operations, and some have pulled out. Crocker National, owned by Britain's Midland Bank, lost $324 million in 1984 before it was sold to Wells Fargo; NatWest Bancorp, owned by Britain's National Westminster, lost $352 million in 1990 on its U.S. operations; Barclays lost $397 million in 1991 before selling its retail branch network to Bank of New York (it had previously sold its California retail operations to Wells Fargo).

Multinational banking has run into problems in Europe too. Britain's National Westminster lost money on its branches in France as well as those in the United States. And the European acquisition spree of France's Crédit Lyonnais, mentioned earlier, ended in major losses.

Some banks are sufficiently efficient that the economies of scale of multinational expansion outweigh these disadvantages. However, for many, multinational expansion has been less than a stunning success. Studies have generally found that foreign banks in a country do less well on average than comparable domestic banks.

Offshore Banking: The Eurocurrency Market

We turn now to a different form of international banking—offshore banking. Like multinational banking, offshore banking involves banks operating outside their home countries. However, they operate not in the local currency, but in their home currency or in an international currency. Offshore banking is largely synonymous with the Eurodollar or Eurocurrency market. Eurodollar banking, which emerged in London in the late 1950s, is an interesting example of bank innovation.

The Origins of the Eurodollar Market.   One of the risks of international trade is exchange rate risk. For example, if a Brazilian merchant importing cars from Japan agrees to pay in Japanese yen, he faces the risk that the yen will appreciate before payment is made, causing a capital loss. Setting the price in cruzeiros merely shifts the risk to the Japanese exporter. The risk to both can be minimized by invoicing in a stable international currency. Then each trader can limit his risk to changes in the value of his own currency vis-à-vis the international currency—something he is better able to handle.

Up until World War II, the pound sterling played the role of international currency. Not only was trade with Britain conducted in sterling, but so too was a significant fraction of third-party trade. Invoicing trade in pounds sterling had the additional advantage of making it easier to finance and insure in London. This was desirable because London offered the lowest interest rates and the lowest insurance premiums.

For a century and a half, London was the world's financial center. Its preeminence depended on the position of the British pound sterling as the principal international currency. However, after World War II, the chronic weakness of the British economy led to instability in the value of the pound, undermining its usefulness for international transactions. Increasingly, the pound was displaced as the principal international currency by the dollar. The decline of the pound reduced the demand for sterling finance and threatened London's role as a financial center.

London bankers came up with a simple solution: lend in dollars. However, to lend in dollars the London banks needed dollar deposits. Lending in dollars on the basis of deposits in pounds sterling would have exposed them to too much exchange rate risk. The London banks had long accepted small amounts of deposits in foreign currencies to accommodate their customers, but these were not sufficient to support a major increase in dollar-denominated lending.

As luck would have it, there was at the time a growing demand for dollar deposits located outside the United States. Because the postwar monetary system was based on the dollar, most countries kept their foreign exchange reserves in this form. However, many countries—especially those of the communist bloc—were on less than friendly terms with the United States. While they wanted to hold dollars, they did not want to those dollars to be in the United States. There was too great a danger that, in an international crisis, they would be frozen by the U.S. government. Holding dollar deposits at London banks was an attractive alternative.

The London banking market in dollars came to be known as the Eurodollar market. For British and other non-U.S. banks in London, it provided a way of doing business in U.S. dollars—the dominant international currency—rather than in the declining pound sterling.

What is a Eurodollar?   To understand just how Eurodollar banking works, let us look at some typical Eurodollar transactions.

Suppose that a U.S. corporation, AT&T, deposits $5 million at a British Eurodollar bank, Barclays. AT&T makes the deposit with a check drawn in its New York bank, Chemical. When the check clears, the effects on the balance sheets of the two banks are as follows:

BARCLAYS BANK (LONDON)

Deposits at other banks		Time deposits	
Chemical	$5m	AT&T	$5m

CHEMICAL BANK (NEW YORK)

	Checking deposits	
	AT&T	−$5m
	Barclays	+5m

Notice that no dollars have left the United States as a result of this transaction. All that has happened is that 5 million U.S. dollars—in the form of Chemical Bank checking deposits—have passed in ownership from AT&T to Barclays. Instead of the $5 million in its checking deposit in New York, AT&T now has $5 million in a Eurodollar time deposit in London.

Since it earns no interest, Barclays will not want to keep this balance at Chemical. So it uses the funds to make a loan to Microsoft. It does not make the loan by creating new checking deposits in the way we saw in Chapter 2. It cannot. Eurodollar banks in London are not allowed to offer checking deposits. So Barclays makes the loan by writing Microsoft a check on its deposit at Chemical. Microsoft deposits the check at Chase, its New York bank, and the effects are as follows:

BARCLAYS BANK (LONDON)

Deposits at other banks			
Chemical	−$5m		
Loans			
Microsoft	+5m		

CHEMICAL BANK (NEW YORK)

Deposit at Fed	−$5m	Checking deposits	
		Barclays	−$5m

CHASE (NEW YORK)

Deposit at Fed	+$5m	Deposits	
		Microsoft	+$5m

The total effect on the Barclays balance sheet, of the deposit and of the loan together, is

BARCLAYS BANK (LONDON)

Loans		Time deposits	
Microsoft	$5m	AT&T	$5m

Barclays, which is not a U.S. bank and cannot create U.S. dollars, is thus acting as a financial intermediary in U.S. dollars. In this respect, it is doing much the same as would any nondepository intermediary—for example, a finance company or a pension fund.

Notice that all the dollar payments are executed in New York between New York banks. (In reality, they would be made over an electronic network called CHIPS, rather than by check.[19]) There are no dollars in London and no dollar payments are made there.

These transactions are typical of transactions in the Eurodollar market. Eurodollar banks are financial intermediaries, but they cannot themselves create dollars or execute dollar payments. Eurodollar banks rely on the U.S. banking system—mainly on New York banks—to execute their payments.

U.S. Banks in the Eurodollar Market.   Initially, the London branches of U.S. banks had had very little to do with the Eurodollar market. However, in the late 1960s, as

---

[19] We shall discuss CHIPS in Chapter 8.

market interest rates rose, the treasurers of American companies began to switch their business from banks in the United States to Eurodollar banks in London.

Eurodollar banking in London was relatively unregulated. There was no Regulation Q, no reserve requirements, no required equity ratios, and no deposit insurance premiums. This meant that Eurodollar banks could offer higher rates on deposits and charge lower rates on loans. U.S. companies that did business overseas found it easy to keep some of their liquid assets on deposit in London to earn the higher deposit rates and to borrow there at the lower loan rates.[20]

Worried about losing business to the British and to other foreign Eurodollar banks, U.S. banks used their branches in London to enter the Eurodollar market. U.S. banks that lacked branches in London began to open them.

The involvement of U.S. banks in the Eurodollar market increased sharply in 1968 and 1969. The Fed, trying to fight inflation by restricting bank lending, had refused to raise the Regulation Q ceiling on NCDs. Faced with a massive loss of deposits, banks responded by channeling the funds through their Eurodollar branches. A bank with maturing NCDs encouraged its customers to redeposit their funds at its London branch; the London branch then lent the funds back to the U.S. bank.[21]

Another regulation that pushed U.S. banks into the Eurodollar market was a limit, imposed in the 1960s, on bank lending to foreigners. Banks could get around this limit by making foreign loans out of their overseas offices and funding them with Eurodollar deposits. These Eurodollar deposits could come from the Eurodollar market, from the banks U.S. customers, or even from the parent bank itself.

The regulations that pushed U.S. banks into the Eurodollar market were eventually dropped—Regulation Q limits on NCDs in 1970, the restrictions on foreign loans in 1974. However, some regulatory costs remained, such as reserve requirements and deposit insurance. These still gave Eurodollar banking an advantage. In any event, by then U.S. banks had learned the ropes, and they had no reason to give up Eurodollar banking.

The attempts of U.S. regulators to regulate U.S. Eurodollar banks have generally been futile. U.S. regulators have the power to regulate overseas branches and subsidiaries because they have authority over the parent bank in the United States. However, the Eurodollar market is highly competitive. Any additional regulation imposed on U.S. participants that is not imposed on other Eurodollar banks puts the American banks at a competitive disadvantage. For example, imposing a reserve requirement on deposits at overseas branches of U.S. banks would force these branches to lower the rates they offer on their deposits. Because the regulation would not apply to non-U.S. banks, the rates of those institutions would remain the same. Depositors would switch banks to earn the higher rates, and this would simply drive the U.S. banks out of the market.

The appeal of Eurodollar banking to U.S. banks was, therefore, quite different from its appeal to British banks. For U.S. banks, it provided a relatively easy way to move certain activities offshore, beyond the reach of U.S. regulators.

---

[20] We saw in Chapter 6 that at this time corporate treasurers were also withdrawing funds from banks and investing them in the U.S. money market.

[21] The idea is very similar to that employed in the overnight Eurodollar device that we saw in Chapter 6. In this case, the funds are of longer maturity, and there is no automatic transfer between Eurodollars and a checking deposit.

shell branch (booking center)
A bank office that does no business directly but books business sent to it from other offices.

Shell Branches.   Many U.S. banks wishing to enter the Eurodollar market found the cost of a London office too high. A less expensive way to enter the market is to open a Caribbean **shell branch** or **booking center**. This is typically a small office, say in Nassau, that does not conduct banking business directly. It may have hundreds of millions of dollars in loans and deposits, but the loans are made and the deposits are taken in the parent bank's home office. The Nassau "branch" is simply a set of books kept by some local people on instructions from the parent bank. Shell branches are also attractive to the larger banks because of the low tax rates of the host countries. The Caribbean region has a particular advantage as a location for shell branches in that it falls in the same time zone as New York, making office hours there the same as those at the home office.[22]

international banking facility (IBF)
An entity authorized to operate within the United States as an offshore bank.

International Banking Facilities.   Today, Eurodollar banking takes place even in the United States itself—"onshore offshore banking." In 1981, partly to stop the loss of jobs to overseas branches, the Fed authorized banks and Edge Act corporations to establish **international banking facilities (IBFs)** in the United States.

An IBF can do most of the things a Eurodollar bank can. It is not subject to reserve requirements, deposit insurance premiums, or interest rate ceilings. However, an IBF is not allowed to offer overnight deposits. It can do business with entities outside the United States without restriction. However, within the United States, it may do business only with other IBFs and with its parent bank. Physically, an IBF is usually simply a department at a regular bank office in the United States.

The popularity of IBFs among U.S. banks has declined since the mid-1980s as regional banks have reduced their international lending. However IBFs remain popular among foreign banks in the United States, which do considerable international business.

The success of IBFs in the United States spurred the Japanese government to initiate a similar program in 1986. IBFs have proven popular in Japan too, particularly with regional and small banks that previously had no direct access to the Eurodollar market.

Eurocurrency banking
Banking anywhere in any currency other than that of the host country.

From Eurodollars to Eurocurrencies.   While the Eurodollar market was originally limited to U.S. dollar deposits and loans in London, its scope today is much wider. The market has grown, both geographically and in terms of the currency denomination of deposits and loans. The term **Eurocurrency** is now used for deposits and loans anywhere in any currency other than that of the host country. For example, deposits of Japanese yen at a bank in Hong Kong are also considered "Eurocurrency" deposits.

Within Europe, the Eurocurrency market has spread to other financial centers such as Luxembourg, Paris, and Rome. It has spread to the Caribbean—for example, the Cayman

---

[22] Income from a foreign branch is subject to taxation both by the United States and by the country in which the branch is located. For example, if Morgan earns $100 million in London, it might owe $30 million in U.S. taxes and $50 million in British taxes. However, U.S. tax law allows banks to credit payment of foreign taxes against their U.S. tax liability. In our example, Morgan could credit the $50 million it pays in Britain against the $30 million it owes the U.S. This still leaves $20 million of taxes "wasted." However, if Morgan shifts half its business from London to Nassau (where there are no taxes), it will pay only $25 million in British taxes. It can credit this against the $30 million it owes in U.S. taxes. Moreover, while income of foreign branches is subject to U.S. federal income tax, it is not subject to state and local taxes. These are a particular burden in New York City. So shifting business from New York to a shell branch is also advantageous even if it does not reduce federal taxes.

Islands, the Bahamas, and Panama—and to the Middle East (Bahrain). In the Far East, Eurocurrency banking is conducted in Singapore, Hong Kong, and Tokyo. Europe now accounts for approximately 50% of the total, and London itself for no more than a third.

The dollar is no longer the predominant currency of the Eurodollar market. Before 1985, it accounted for 75% to 80% of deposits. By 1987 only 58% of Eurocurrency deposits was denominated in dollars. The German mark, the Swiss franc, and the Japanese yen all increased their share.

The Eurocurrency market offers banks from other countries the same advantages of offshore banking as it offers U.S. banks. It is relatively unregulated, allowing banks to operate at lower cost and to carry on activities that are restricted or prohibited at home. As we have seen, domestic regulators are reluctant to extend domestic restrictions to offshore offices because it would place their banks at a competitive disadvantage. On the other hand, regulators in Eurocurrency centers realize that tougher regulation will simply drive the business to some other, less regulated, center.

The Growth of Eurocurrency Banking.   Exhibit 7.4 shows how Eurocurrency banking has grown since 1973. Measuring its true size is a little difficult because of the enormous amount of interbank lending. We take as our measure of size the amount of deposits *less* deposits of other banks. You can see that growth was interrupted by the banking problems of the early 1980s. Exhibit 7.4 also shows the proportion of Eurodollar deposits denominated in U.S. dollars. This has been trending downward.

THE IMPLICATIONS OF BANKING CONSOLIDATION

We see, then, that the banking industry is undergoing a wave of consolidation. This is true both within countries—for example, the movement towards interstate banking in the United States—and between countries—for example, consolidation within the European Union. What are the implication of this wave of consolidation for the banking industry itself and for its customers?

The Implications of Consolidation for the Banking Industry

Consolidation increases the efficiency of the banking industry—it enables banks to produce their "output" at lower cost. Consolidation does this in several ways: it permits banks to capture economies of scale; it weeds out the least efficient banks; it opens protected markets to greater competition; and it reduces the cost of financial integration.

Economies of Scale.   Consolidation creates larger banks, and, as we have seen, larger banks should enjoy economies of scale—financial, operational, and reputational. There have been a large number of empirical studies that have tried to see whether consolidation really does improve bank efficiency. The evidence is mixed, and there are several reasons for this.

Many studies of mergers focus exclusively on operational economies of scale—on the reduction of cost (mainly fixed cost). In this respect, some mergers have been highly suc-

EXHIBIT 7.4   **The Growth of Eurocurrency Banking**

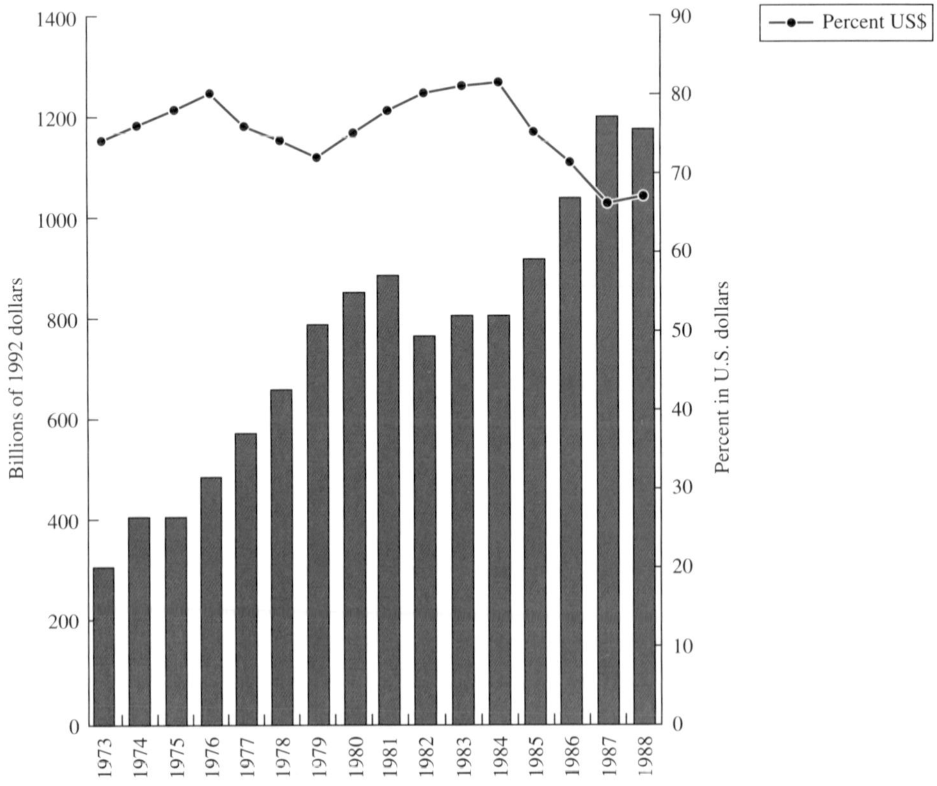

Source: Morgan Guaranty Trust Company (1988).

cessful. For example, the merger of Chemical and Manufacturers Hanover cut the costs of
the combined bank by some $2.5 billion a year, mostly by eliminating overlapping
branches. However, not all mergers have been this good at lowering costs, and, on average,
the gains have been small. However, these studies do not take into account the financial
and reputational economies of scale. Some researchers have attempted to measure these
and have found them to be significant. It seems that the big gains from consolidation come
less from lowering operational cost than from more profitable "production"—higher yielding assets and less expensive funding.

     To some extent, the ability of banks to benefit from the financial and reputational
economies of scale has been limited by government regulation. In principle, because larger
pools work better, large banks should be able to make do with smaller reserves; they
should also be able to manage with less equity; and they should be able, nonetheless, to
offer depositors greater liquidity and safety. Historical studies confirm these theoretical
results. They show that in unregulated banking systems, larger banks had smaller reserves,
lower equity ratios, and were still safer than smaller banks.

     However, there are today few if any unregulated banking systems. Most countries
have legal reserve requirements that impose the same minimum reserve ratios on large

banks as on small.[23] They also have legal capital requirements that impose the same minimum equity ratios on large banks as on small. Many countries have either explicit or implicit deposit insurance that makes deposits at small banks just as safe (for the depositor) as deposits at large banks. In the United States, in particular, small banks have been able to continue to compete with large banks for so long only because the playing field has been 'leveled' by regulation.[24] As we have seen, it is regulations such as these that have driven a great deal of banking into the less regulated offshore market.

The Survival of the Fittest.   Of course, all the theoretical economies of scale merely represent a *potential* for greater efficiency. Whether a given bank achieves this potential depends on the quality of its management. We should not be too shocked to hear that not all banks are managed well. With respect to operational efficiency, for example, studies suggest that the average bank in the United States is at about only 80% of its potential.[25] Since U.S. banks are unlikely to be especially bad in this respect, banks in some other countries may be much further below their potential.

Consolidation improves the overall efficiency of the banking industry by bringing average efficiency closer to potential efficiency.[26] Consolidation does this in several ways. First, common sense suggests, and the evidence confirms, that more efficient banks tend to take over less efficient banks. As the more efficient grow larger and the less efficient disappear, average efficiency increases. Second, the removal of protective barriers that makes consolidation possible also increases competitive pressure. Managers realize that for their banks to survive, they have to do better. So even the banks that are not themselves involved in consolidation tend to improve their efficiency.

Greater Efficiency of the System.   Whatever its effects on the efficiency of individual institutions, consolidation should improve the efficiency of the financial system as a whole. As we saw earlier, banking systems that were prevented from consolidating found ways to capture economies of scale between banks rather than within banks. They did this through correspondent relationships and money markets that helped to integrate the financial system. These solutions, however, were relatively costly: because they involved many more transactions between institutions, they incurred much higher transactions costs.

For example, in a fragmented banking system, a loan made in the West from funds originating in the east passes through a whole series of intermediaries—the eastern depositor's bank, that bank's correspondent, the western borrower's bank, and that bank's correspondent (see Exhibit 7.1). Or if the money market is involved, it passes through the hands of underwriters, dealers, and brokers. At each stage, there are costs. In contrast, with

---

[23] Actually, in the United States, small banks have slightly lower reserve requirements. The general reserve requirement is 10% on checking deposits. However, the first $46.8 million of deposits is subject to only a 3% reserve requirement. There is no economic reason for this break. It is simply evidence of the political power of small banks.

[24] This is not an accident. We shall see in Chapter 19 that preserving small banks from being driven out of business was the major motivation for the enactment of deposit insurance legislation in the 1930s. Small banks have also been helped, as we have seen, by the system of correspondent banks and money markets, which enabled banks to capture some of the financial economies of scale externally rather than internally.

[25] See Berger (2000). These studies compare banks in general to the most efficient banks in the industry.

[26] Jayaratne and Strahan (1996a) find that the consolidation that took place within states after the barriers to statewide branching were removed resulted in both lower operating costs and lower loan losses.

a consolidated banking system, lending is simple. There is a single intermediary, and funds move from east to west within a single bank (see Exhibit 7.2). Because there are fewer transactions, costs are lower.

Consolidation lowers transactions costs, not only in lending, but also in payments (see Exhibits 7.1 and 7.2 again). For example, clearing checks through the relatively fragmented U.S. banking system is considerably more expensive than clearing them through the consolidated Canadian system. For example, when a Miami bank receives a check drawn on one in Seattle, the check must go through a complicated procedure. It is processed and sorted several times by different institutions as it is passes from one to another. The whole process takes several days to complete, while the depositor waits for the funds. In Canada, major banks have branches all over the country. So when a bank in Vancouver receives a check drawn on a bank in Halifax, Nova Scotia, clearing is quick and easy. First, there is a good chance that the two banks are branches of the same institution. In that case, the check clears within the bank almost instantaneously. If not, it is almost certain that the Halifax bank is the branch of an institution that also has branches in Vancouver. That means that the check can be presented for payment at the Vancouver clearinghouse and payment can be received the same day.

The Implications of Consolidation for Bank Customers

Consolidation increases the efficiency of the banking system and lowers the cost of bank "output"—principally intermediation and payment services. In a competitive environment, the lower costs should be passed on to the customer. Evidence suggests that in the United States at least, this has indeed been the case.[27]

Stimulating Economic Growth.   Greater efficiency and lower costs for the customer also have implications for the economy as a whole. As we saw in Chapter 3, a reduction in the cost of borrowing and lending leads to an increase in amount of borrowing and lending and to an improvement in its quality. More funds flow into investment, and they flow into better investment. Once again, the evidence confirms this. A study of the effects of allowing intrastate branching in the United States found that real economic growth increased significantly in the states in question in the period following the change.[28]

Lending to Small Business.   One area of concern is lending to small business. Since small banks typically do more of such lending relative to their overall assets, there were fears that the disappearance of small banks might reduce credit availability for small businesses. However, much of the consolidation in the United States has involved medium-sized banks acquiring smaller banks. The acquiring banks are often themselves specialists in small-business lending, and because they are larger than the banks they acquire, they are able to offer their new customers larger loans without compromising their diversification. At the same time, as we saw in Chapter 6, the really large banks have been using credit scoring to develop automated methods of making small-business loans. In total, recent research suggests that the effect of consolidation on small-business lending has been positive.

---

[27] See Jayaratne and Strahan (1996a).

[28] See Jayaratne and Strahan (1996b).

Better Access to Banking Services. Because of its lower costs, a consolidated banking system of multibranch banks provides better access to banking services, especially for small communities. The overhead costs of setting up a branch are low relative to those of setting up a whole new bank. As a result, branch banks find it worthwhile to set up offices to serve small markets where it would not pay to set up a separate new bank.[29]

Moreover, banking consolidation and the resulting pressure to lower costs, together with modern technology, have led banks to reinvent the bank branch and to find alternative ways of delivering banking services at lower cost. In the past decade, banks have opened thousands of minibranches in supermarkets and other large retail outlets: their number increased from 1,000 in 1990 to 4,500 in 1996.[30] Such minibranches cost only a fifth as much to set up as a traditional branch and only half as much to operate.

Modern technology makes it possible to offer many banking services without actually setting up a branch. Automated teller machines (ATMs) can dispense cash, accept deposits, and conduct various other transactions at locations remote from the bank that owns them. The number of ATMs has risen rapidly—almost doubling between 1994 and 1998 to 190,000. While most of these machines are located at bank branches, many are at remote locations—in shopping malls, gas stations, and airports, for example. Banks are also able to offer many services by telephone and online. Attempts to establish online-only banks on the Internet have not, however, been a success: customers seem to lack confidence in a bank that has no visible physical presence.

In the meantime, banks have been refocusing their traditional branches on providing the kinds of product that require face-to-face contact. These include long-term saving products and insurance.

Competition. We saw in Chapter 3 that there are three conditions for efficiency of a financial system—integration, minimum costs, and competitive pricing. Consolidation certainly helps with the first two, but what about the third?

Consolidation can produce a banking system made up of a few giant banks. A small number of banks can more easily act as a cartel. They find it easier to collude—openly or tacitly—to raise prices and to reduce the level of service. Because customers lack alternatives, the members of the cartel can raise prices without losing much business. If they all agree to close on Saturdays, customers can only grumble. Reduced competition not only leads to monopoly profits and worse service, it may also lead to simple laziness—reduced effort and higher costs. If profits are good, banks may avoid the effort of introducing new technology or the risk of entering or developing a new market.

The experience of banking consolidation in many countries suggests that these concerns are not entirely misplaced. For example, the few big banks in England did for a long time operate as a cartel. They had a gentlemen's agreement not to compete on loan and deposit rates, setting them at common levels. They were also slow to adopt new technology and to enter new markets. The pattern has been similar in other countries.

In the United States, while there has been increasing concentration, the number of banks remains large. The largest single bank still has a market share of well under 10%.

---

[29] Calomiris (1992) quotes a study that found that branching increased the number of bank offices per square mile by about 65%.

[30] This accounts for much of the overall increase in the number of bank branches.

Moreover, concentration at the local level, which is more important, has remained about the same. The geographic restrictions in the United States actually prevented competition at the local level by preventing entry. Removing those restrictions has eroded the market power of local banks and increased the degree of competition.

Moreover, the size of the "local" market has expanded. For example, the average distance between a small firm and the bank it borrows from has increased significantly. As a result of the expansion of the market, banks are less able to exert local market power. Also, as we saw in Chapter 6, financial institutions other than banks now offer many of the same services. For example, small-business borrowers often borrow today from finance companies rather than from banks. As a result of the widening of the market and of the entry of nonbank competitors, local banks have little market power. While it used to be true that banks having few nearby competitors earned unusually high profits, this no longer seems to be the case.

Safety and Stability.   The U.S. banking system has gone from crisis to crisis throughout its history. The instability of the U.S. banking system has much to do with its structure. Many of the banks in trouble were small, inefficient ones. Other, larger, banks got into trouble because of poor geographic diversification. In contrast to the U.S. experience, the Canadian banking system provides an example of stability. The Canadian system was never fragmented: its banks branched and grew with the expansion of the country. Consequently, Canada never experienced anything like the banking turmoil in the United States. Its large, integrated banks, with good diversification and liquidity, have been much better placed to weather economic adversity.

There are good reasons, therefore, to believe that consolidation of banking systems in the United States and in the world will improve bank stability.[31]

SUMMARY

- The banking industry worldwide is undergoing rapid consolidation.

- The evolution of banking structure has been molded by three factors—economies of scale, the technology of communications, and government regulation.

- The historical peculiarities of bank chartering in the United States have resulted in regulations that restrict the ability of banks to branch across state lines. For many years, branching within states was also limited.

- Because of the obstacles to branching, banks in England, the United States, and elsewhere developed alternative methods to capture potential economies of scale. Correspondent system and money markets allowed banks to enjoy many of the advantages of a branch system.

- U.S. banks learned to live with branching restrictions. They also found ways around the restrictions through holding companies and nonbank banks.

- The past 20 years have seen steady progress towards interstate banking in the United States. Initially, the initiative came mainly from the states. But in 1994 the Riegle–Neal Act removed most of the remaining restrictions.

---

[31] We shall discuss the connection between structure and stability more thoroughly in Chapter 19.

- International banking has expanded rapidly since the 1960s. There are four reasons: the recovery of world trade and international lending, the liberalization of financial markets, banks' attempts to capture economies of scale and scope, and banks' attempts to escape government regulation.

- U.S. bank involvement in multinational, as opposed to offshore, banking is small. However, foreign multinational banks have taken a substantial fraction of the U.S. banking market. And the adoption of the Euro has given a stimulus to cross-border banking in Europe.

- Multinational banking is modest, not only because of regulatory obstacles, but also because of inherent difficulties such as language and cultural barriers and information disadvantages.

- Eurodollar banking began in London. When the pound declined as an international currency, British banks began borrowing and lending in U.S. dollars.

- Eurodollar banks take only time deposits. They do not create U.S. dollars. Eurodollar transactions are executed through banks in New York and do not involve any movement of U.S. dollars out of the country.

- The attraction of the Eurodollar market for U.S. banks is that it allows them to escape banking regulations that hamper their operations in the United States. U.S. banks do much of their Eurodollar banking through Caribbean shell branches, and, more recently, through IBFs in the United States.

- The Eurodollar market has grown into a Eurocurrency market, involving many currencies other than the U.S. dollar and operating around the world.

- Consolidation should improve the efficiency of banking through lower costs and greater competition.

- Consolidation should benefit the economy as a whole, stimulating economic growth and improving access to credit and to banking services. There is a risk of market power, but it does not seem great in the United States. Consolidation should improve safety and stability.

DISCUSSION QUESTIONS

1. Why do banks want to expand? What are the advantages a large bank has over a small one? What are the obstacles to expansion?

2. How exactly does correspondent banking allow banks to capture economies of scale? Be specific. How does it help with liquidity, diversification, indivisibilities, and so on?

3. U.S. banks historically have relied heavily on the correspondent relationship. What are the benefits? What are the advantages and disadvantages relative to the branch banking systems that were common in most other countries? Are the relative advantages and disadvantages different today from what they were in 1800?

4. Why do you think that it has proven so difficult to remove the restrictions on interstate banking in the United States? Who stands to gain from their

removal? Who stands to lose? Why do you think that interstate banking laws allow out-of-state acquisition of banks within the state rather than the opening of branches by out-of-state banks? Who benefits from this?

5. Why has international banking grown so rapidly? What do banks stand to gain? Distinguish clearly between multinational and offshore banking.

6. Why do you think foreign banks are more interested in local currency banking in the United States than U.S. banks are in local currency banking overseas? What makes entry into a banking market attractive? What are the obstacles?

7. What are the similarities between multinational banking in the European Community and interstate banking in the United States? What are the differences?

8. Chapter 3 lists three conditions for the efficiency of a financial system. Discuss the benefits and the dangers of banking consolidation in terms of those three conditions.

9. From the point of view of the borrower, the bank, and the banking system, how does lending by a

Eurodollar bank differ from lending by a U.S. bank?

10. For a U.S. bank entering the Eurodollar market, what are the relative attractions of a London branch, a Caribbean shell branch, and an international banking facility?

BIBLIOGRAPHY

Berger, A. "The Integration of the Financial Services Industry: Where Are the Efficiencies?" *North American Actuarial Journal* 4 (2000).

Born, Karl Erich. *International Banking in the 19th and 20th Centuries.* New York: St. Martin's Press, 1983.

Boyd, John H., and Stanley L. Graham. "Investigating the Banking Consolidation Trend." *Federal Reserve Bank of Minneapolis Quarterly Review*, spring 1991, 3–15.

Calomiris, Charles W. "Regulation, Industrial Structure, and Instability in U.S. Banking: An Historical Perspective." In *Structural Change in Banking.* Edited by M. Klausner and L. J. White. Homewood, IL: Business One Irwin, 1992.

Clair, Robert T., and Paula K. Tucker. "Interstate Banking and the Federal Reserve: A Historical Perspective." *Economic Review of the Federal Reserve Bank of Dallas*, November 1989, 1–20.

Group of Ten. *Report on Consolidation in the Financial Sector.* Basel: Bank for International Settlements, 2001.

Hammond, Bray. *Banks and Politics in America.* Princeton, NJ: Princeton University Press, 1957.

Hughes, J. P. "Are Scale Economies in Banking Elusive or Illusive? Evidence obtained by Incorporating Capital Structure and Risk-Taking into Models of Bank Production." working paper no. 00-04, Federal Reserve Bank of Philadelphia, May 2000.

James, John A. *Money and Capital Markets in Postbellum America.* Princeton, NJ: Princeton University Press, 1978.

Jayaratne, J., and P. E. Strahan. "Entry Restrictions, Industry Evolution and Dynamic Efficiency." Working paper, Federal Reserve Bank of New York, December 1996a.

———. "The Finance–Growth Nexus: Evidence from Bank Branch Deregulation." *Quarterly Journal of Economics* 111, no. 3 (August 1996b): 639–670.

Krooss, Herman E., and Martin R. Blyn, *A History of Financial Intermediation.* New York: Random House, 1981.

Mishkin, F. S., and P. E. Strahan. "What Will Technology Do to Financial Structure?" *Brookings–Wharton Papers in Financial Services*, 1999, 249–287.

Morgan Guaranty Trust Company. *World Financial Markets.* New York: Morgan, 1988.

KEY TERMS

unit bank
National Banking Act of 1863
correspondent bank
respondent bank
money market
overline
holding company
multibank holding company

Douglas Amendment
one-bank holding company
Competitive Equality Banking Act of 1987
money-center bank
regional bank
superregional bank
Financial Services Agreement

multinational banking
offshore banking
Second Banking Directive
shell branch (booking center)
international banking facilities (IBFs)
Eurocurrency banking

CHAPTER 8

PAYMENTS AND FOREIGN EXCHANGE

When you finish this chapter you will understand:

- The different methods of making payment and how their use differs across countries
- The difficulties of payment on the Internet
- Why it is harder to make payment to someone in a foreign country

Banks, and many near banks, combine two activities—lending and payments. As we saw in Chapters 2 and 5, the two activities are technologically similar. This similarity generates economies of scope that draw lenders into the provision of payments services and payments processors into lending. In the preceding chapters we focused mainly on lending; in this chapter, we shall look at payments.

The payments system is of great importance to the economy. Payments are an inseparable part of trade in goods and services. The lower the transactions cost of making payments, the more trade there will be and the greater will be the gains from trade. How well the payments system does its job has enormous effects on the overall efficiency of the economy.

For example, consider the mail order business. Before the days of the credit card, mail order involved considerable delays. Payment was by check, and the check would spend several days in the mail. Generally, the merchant would not ship the goods until the check had cleared. This, too, would take several days. The substantial delay made mail order relatively unattractive in comparison to buying from a local merchant.[1]

Today, with payment by credit card, the merchant is guaranteed payment the moment you place the order, and the goods can be shipped immediately. By eliminating the delay, the credit card reduces the trading cost of using mail order. It makes mail order more competitive with buying from local merchants.[2] Because local merchants face this competition, their prices are lower and consumers are better off.

The payments system is also of great importance to financial institutions. For many, the provision of payments services is a substantial source of income. A recent estimate suggests that for the 25 largest bank holding companies between 30% and 40% of their operating revenue came from payments-related services.[3] You cannot understand banking without an understanding of this aspect of the business.

Payments mechanisms are a key element in the structure of financial markets. You cannot make sense of overnight lending or the government securities market, for example, without understanding how payments are executed. Furthermore, the increasing globalization of financial markets has transformed the trading of foreign exchange—one part of the payments system—into a growth industry. Worldwide trading volume in foreign exchange reached $1.5 trillion *a day* in 1999.

We begin our study of the payments system by examining the different types of money in our economy. Next, we look at the different ways of making payments. We then compare the use of different methods of payment in different countries and examine the reasons for the differences. Next, we look at foreign exchange. We conclude by examining the efficiency and stability of the payments system.

THE DIFFERENT TYPES OF MONEY

Payment means the transfer of money. So we begin with money. There are two different types of money—government money and bank money. The branch of government that produces government money is usually the central bank—in the United States, the Federal Reserve. So we will call the two types of money Fed dollars and bank dollars.

Fed Dollars

The most basic type of money in the U.S. economy is the dollar bill. The dollar bill is a Federal Reserve note, created by one of the 12 Federal Reserve Banks (you can see which one by looking at the seal to the left of the picture of George Washington on the front of the bill). In form, Federal Reserve notes resemble the banknotes that commercial banks once issued.[4]

---

[1] Local merchants are more willing to accept checks because it is easier for them to pursue payment if the check bounces.

[2] Of course, the mail order business has also been helped by 800 numbers and overnight delivery.

[3] Radecki (1999).

[4] The first banknote was issued in Europe by the Bank of Stockholm (later the Bank of Sweden) in 1661. We discussed the issue of banknotes by commercial banks in Chapter 6.

In addition to Federal Reserve notes the Fed also creates money in the form of deposits. The Fed is a bank. It accepts deposits from ordinary banks, from the federal government, and from some other institutions (it does not accept deposits from ordinary firms and households). The Fed's depositors can make withdrawals and deposits in the form of Federal Reserve notes, and they can transfer ownership of their deposits by check or electronically. We shall call money that is created by the Fed—Federal Reserve notes and deposits at the Fed—**Fed dollars**.

Fed dollars

Money created by the Fed—Federal Reserve notes and deposits at the Fed.

Fed dollars were once convertible into gold. Today, that is no longer true. You cannot take your dollar bill to the Fed and demand payment in "real money." All you will receive in exchange for your dollar bill is another dollar bill, perhaps less tattered and worn.[5]

definitive money

Money that is not convertible into any other form of money.

Money that is not convertible into anything else—that therefore defines what we mean by "real money"—is called **definitive money**. This role was once played by gold. Today, it is played by Fed dollars. You can think of Fed dollars as a sort of "artificial gold," created by the government. The provision of definitive money is today a normal function of most central banks. Money of this type, which exists by government order or fiat alone, is called **fiat money**.[6]

fiat money

Money that exists by government order or fiat.

In addition to Fed dollars, our definitive money includes some currency issued by the U.S. Treasury, mostly in the form of coins. These coins are token money: their value as metal is well below their face value (the last silver coin was minted for general circulation in 1971). There have been two recent attempts to replace the one-dollar bill with a coin. The Susan B. Anthony dollar was introduced in 1979, and the gold-colored Sacagawea dollar in 1999. However, neither new coin has been a success with the public, which seems to prefer paper.[7]

In May 2001, Federal Reserve notes issued amounted to $565 billion. Deposits at the Federal Reserve Banks amounted to $39 billion. Treasury currency amounted to $27 billion. The total amount of definitive money was the total of these three amounts—$631 billion.

legal tender

Money that must be accepted in payment of a debt.

If our definitive money, unlike gold, has no intrinsic value and is not convertible, then why do people accept it in payment? The main reason is that they know they can pass it on to others in payment. Their ability to do this is reinforced by the status of definitive money as **legal tender**. This means that if you pay a debt in Fed dollars, the debt is legally settled. Your creditor cannot demand payment in some other form—say in gold. The general acceptability of definitive money is also reinforced by the federal government's willingness to accept it in payment of taxes.

Without the constraint of convertibility, what stops a government from creating as much fiat money as it wishes? Nothing at all. This unrestricted power to create money can be both a blessing and a curse. On the one hand, it allows the government to ensure that the quantity of money grows to meet the needs of a growing economy: this could be a

---

[5] Convertibility of Fed dollars into gold coin for private individuals ended in 1933. From then until 1971 foreign governments could convert dollars into gold bullion. Today the dollar is no longer convertible into gold, or into anything else.

[6] We discussed central banks in Chapter 3 and we shall learn more about their functions in Chapters 19 and 20.

[7] The reason for the attempt was a desire to save some of the approximately $400 million a year spent on maintaining notes in circulation. Dollar bills wear out and must be replaced after a year or two; coins last for decades.

problem in the days when definitive money was gold or silver. On the other hand, there is nothing to prevent a government from creating money to pay its own bills. The unrestrained creation of money for this reason is the main cause of inflation around the world.

Bank Dollars

bank dollars

Money created by various depository institutions—transactions deposits at these institutions.

The second type of money in our economy is **bank dollars**—transactions deposits at various types of financial institution. These deposits are convertible on demand into definitive money. They may also be used directly in payment, with ownership being transferred by check or by other means. Bank dollars did once exist in the form of banknotes, but today the issue of banknotes is in most countries a monopoly of the state. We shall discuss the desirability of this monopoly later in the chapter.

In the United States, transactions deposits are offered by commercial banks, by thrifts, and by credit unions. In many other countries, they are also offered by the post office. The total amount of transactions deposits in the United States in April 2001 was $806 billion.

As we saw in Chapter 2, a bank dollar is simply a bank's IOU: it is a bank's promise to pay one dollar of definitive money on demand. Payment in bank dollars developed as an alternative to payment in definitive money on the one hand and to private promises of payment on the other. Payment in bank dollars often involves lower transactions costs than payment in definitive money. And promises of payment by banks are often more credible than promises of payment by individuals or firms.

Payment with dollar bills (with hand-to-hand currency) is straightforward: you just hand them over. Payment with deposits is more complicated. You need some way to transfer ownership of the deposit to the recipient. There are a number of ways to do this.

CHECKS

The most familiar way to transfer ownership of deposits is by check. For example, suppose you have a deposit with First National, and you wish to pay Videomax $700 for a new TV. That is, you need to transfer ownership of 700 of your bank dollars to Videomax. You do this by writing Videomax a check for $700. Note that the check itself is not money: it is merely an order to pay money. It is an order from you to First National to transfer $700 of your deposit at the bank to Videomax.

If Videomax has a deposit at First National, it can present your check to the bank, and $700 dollars will be transferred from your deposit to Videomax's. First National will now owe you $700 less and Videomax $700 more. Payment has been completed. You have made payment in bank dollars of First National Bank and Videomax has received payment in the same.

Suppose, though, that Videomax has its deposit at a different bank, Metrobank. Videomax will then have no use for the bank dollars of First National Bank. It will need to convert the $700 into bank dollars of Metrobank.

One way Videomax can do this is to send a messenger to First National to present your check for immediate payment in cash. The cash can then be taken to Metrobank for deposit (conversion into Metrobank dollars). This method is quick and simple but inconvenient, and it is worthwhile only for large sums of money.[8]

The more usual procedure is for Videomax to delegate collection of the check to its own bank. Videomax signs over the check (endorses it) to Metrobank, converting it into an order to pay Metrobank. Metrobank collects payment from First National and credits Videomax's deposit with $700. In this way, Videomax gets the Metrobank dollars it wants. In exchange Metrobank gets $700 in First National dollars. If Metrobank finds it useful to maintain a deposit at First National, it may keep the $700 in this form. Or Metrobank may demand conversion of the First National dollars into definitive money.

The Check–Clearing System

Metrobank will present your check to First National for payment through the check-clearing system. We saw the basic principles of check clearing in Chapter 2. Actual practice in the United States is somewhat more complicated.

Most small banks do not process checks themselves. Instead, they send them either to a correspondent bank, with which they have an arrangement, or to the Fed, which also provides this service. The checks are sorted and those drawn on local banks are cleared through the local clearinghouse.[9]

At each meeting of the clearing house, representatives of each bank present checks to the banks on which they are drawn and receive in exchange the checks drawn on their own banks. During this process the banks keep track of how much they owe each other bank and how much they are owed by them. At the end of the meeting, the claims of the banks on each other are netted. Banks with a net credit receive payment and those with a net debit make payment of the appropriate amount in "clearing-house funds" (a claim on the clearing house). These are settled in Fed funds (deposits at the Fed) on the following day.

If a check is drawn on a bank outside the area of the local clearinghouse, the procedure is more involved. For example, if First National is in Los Angeles and Metrobank is in New York, Metrobank will deposit your check at the New York Fed. The New York Fed will credit Metrobank's deposit with it for $700. The New York Fed will then send the check to the San Francisco Fed. The San Francisco Fed will send it on to its Los Angeles branch, which will take it to the local clearinghouse to present it to First National. Once the check has cleared, First National's deposit with the San Francisco Fed will be debited $700.[10]

The physical transportation of paper checks is costly, both in the process of present-ment and in the return of canceled checks to the depositor (banks in many countries do not

---

[8] With large sums, the Fed dollars are not usually transferred physically in the form of Federal Reserve notes. Rather Fed dollars in the form of deposits at the Fed are transferred by one bank to the other over Fedwire, which we discuss later in the chapter.

[9] Before 1980 banks that were not members of the Federal Reserve System did not generally have direct access to the Fed's check-clearing services or to Fedwire, but had to go through another bank that was a member. With the passage of the DIDMCA of 1980, as partial compensation for the imposition of reserve requirements, the Fed's services became available to all depository institutions—some 44,000 vs the 5,500 member banks. Although the Fed was now required to charge explicitly for its services, it found itself in direct competition for check-clearing business with the large banks. The latter were not pleased.

[10] Generally, Metrobank will have to wait some time before it is credited.

do this). Attempts have been made, therefore, to use an image of the check, which can be transmitted electronically, rather the physical check itself. The Fed has introduced an experimental program and a group of large banks has set up its own system, Small Value Payments Corporation, to create an electronic check exchange network.

Check Enhancements

Before it accepts your check, Videomax will want to see some form of identification and perhaps some evidence of creditworthiness, like a credit card. The reason for its caution is that it has no way of knowing whether the check is good. If, when the check finally arrives at First National, it turns out that you have less than $700 in your deposit, the check will "bounce." It will be returned unpaid to Videomax, reversing all the steps of the clearing process. Videomax will then have to do the best it can to collect the money from you in some other way. The possibility that a check may bounce reduces the acceptability of checks as a method of payment.

check guarantee card
A card that, if presented when a check is written, obliges the bank to honor the check.

Various ways have been devised to deal with this problem. One is the **check guarantee card**. A bank issues its customers a special card that must be presented whenever a check is written. The bank guarantees to honor checks written in this way up to some limit—say $200. If the check bounces, the bank takes the loss. Check guarantee cards are relatively rare in the United States, but they are quite popular in Europe. In France, banks must honor checks for amounts of 100 francs or less: no check card is required. Presumably this makes French banks more careful about handing out checkbooks.

Another way to reduce the problem of bad checks is the *overdraft*. This is a line of credit that is automatically drawn upon if there are insufficient funds in the customer's deposit to cover a check. Overdraft facilities, too, are more common overseas than they are in the United States. As an alternative to an overdraft, many U.S. banks offer the following arrangement: if there are insufficient funds to cover a check, the bank automatically transfers money from another account, say a savings account, charging the customer a transfer fee.

In some countries, the problem of bounced checks is addressed through criminal penalties. In Japan, for example, if you bounce two checks in a 6-month period you are liable to 2 years of probation. In Taiwan, the penalties are sufficiently severe that postdated checks are used as loan contracts. There is, in Taiwan, an informal or "curb" market for loans outside the highly regulated official financial system. In this curb market, a lender will hand over a sum of money in exchange for a check that is dated on the day the loan comes due (say a year later). The amount of the check includes principal plus interest.

Special Checks

certified check
A check written by a bank on itself.

money order
An order of payment from a nonbank issuer.

Because of the bad check problem, personal checks may be unacceptable in some transactions. For example, if you buy a car the dealer may insist on a **certified check**. This is a promise to pay from the bank itself. The U.S. Postal Service and some private issuers offer similar instruments in the form of **money orders**.[11]

---

[11] There seem to be no restrictions on who may offer money orders.

traveler's check
A form of guaranteed check or insured private banknote.

The **traveler's check** is a related form of payment. Like a certified check, a traveler's check is a promise to pay on the part of the issuer, not the payer. Traveler's checks are issued in small denominations and insured against loss or theft. (They can be seen as a kind of insured private banknote.) Traveler's checks are issued by banks and by other financial institutions. The largest issuer is American Express, which is not a bank.

To obtain a certified check, money order, or traveler's check, it is usually necessary to pay the issuer in advance. Since such payment may be made in cash, these payment instruments are available to those who do not own bank deposits. Certified checks, money orders, and traveler's checks clear through the check-clearing system much like ordinary checks.

Giro Payments

giro payment
An order to pay, presented to the payer's bank by the payer.

The problem of bad checks can be avoided entirely by using a completely different method of transferring ownership of bank deposits—the **giro payment**. The difference between a giro payment and a check is illustrated in Exhibit 8.1.

Like a check, a giro payment is an order from the payer to his bank to pay the recipient. There is, however, an important difference. With a check, the payer gives the payment order to the recipient. The recipient then presents it to the payer's bank, or has it presented by his own bank. With a giro payment, on the other hand, the payer hands the payment order *directly* to his own bank. The payer's bank then makes payment to the recipient's bank, for the account of the recipient. The recipient then receives notification that payment has been made.

EXHIBIT 8.1   Comparison of Payment by (A) Check and (B) Giro.

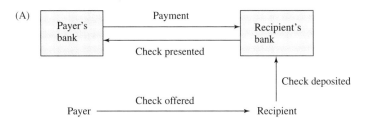

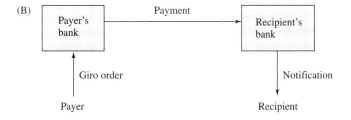

A giro payment cannot bounce. The payer's bank will simply not accept the order to pay unless there are sufficient funds—in a deposit or in cash—to cover it. Because of the way it works, however, the giro payment is not a useful way to pay for unplanned purchases in a store or restaurant. Its principal use is for regular periodic payments like tax or utility bills (or tuition).

Giro payments may be made using a paper form much like a check or they may be made electronically. Paper giro payments are very popular in many countries, often more popular than checks, but they are unknown in the United States.

Electronic giro payments are common in the United States and are executed via *automated clearinghouses* (about which more later). Many U.S. banks also offer telephone bill-paying and home-banking services. With telephone bill paying, customers can instruct their banks over the telephone to make payments on their behalf. The bank does so either with a bank check or electronically. Home banking offers essentially the same service, but using a proprietary terminal or personal computer connected to the bank by telephone.

CREDIT CARDS

The bank credit or debit card is a relatively recent method of payment that offers an alternative to the check or giro payment. The credit card has its origins in store credit.

The Store Credit Card

Historically, it was a common practice for retailers to extend credit to their better customers, allowing them to charge their purchases and to settle up at the end of the month with a single payment. This arrangement made it easier for such customers to spend on impulse; they were not constrained by the amount of cash they were carrying or even by the need to carry a checkbook. Of course the retailer accepted the risk of default, but store credit generated enough extra business to make the risk worthwhile.

store credit card
A credit card that activates a line of credit from a retailer.

As the number of people buying on credit increased, retailers began to issue cards so that sales clerks could identify these creditworthy customers. The identity cards evolved into "charga-plates" and eventually into the modern **store credit card**. With these, stores began to offer cardholders a revolving line of credit, giving them the option of paying over time rather than settling at the end of each month.

In providing these services, large retailers had a considerable advantage. The scale of their business could support a specialized credit department to check credit and to process payments. The extension of credit to a large enough population also gave the big retailers the benefits of pooling. Small retailers, without the benefits of scale, found the extension of credit too expensive.

The Third-Party Card

third-party credit card
A credit card that activates a line of credit from a third-party lender.

The financial system offered small retailers a solution—the **third-party credit card**. The first such cards were travel and entertainment (T&E) cards.[12] They worked as follows.

---

[12] The oil companies were also early issuers of third-party credit cards that could be used at any affiliated gas station.

The issuer, for example, Diners Club or American Express, would check the credit of potential customers and issues them charge cards. Cardholders could use the card at any retailer that had agreed to accept the cards of the issuer, with the issuer guaranteeing payment. When a purchase was made, the retailer would receive immediate payment from the issuer. Such payment would be at a discount of the amount of the purchase (initially 7%). For example, if the amount was $100, the retailer would receive $93. The cardholder would be sent a bill at the end of the month by the issuer of the card for all his or her purchases. Third-party cards did not initially offer customers the option of paying over time.

Banks, such as BankAmerica and Citi, were quick to enter this business, offering third-party cards of their own. However, the acceptability of these early bank credit cards was limited geographically because of the restrictions on interstate banking. Consequently, because these bank credit cards were not widely acceptable, there was little demand for them.

The Four-Party Card

four-party card
A bank credit card, the use of which in payments involves both the issuing bank and the bank of the recipient.

The banks came up with a solution to the problem of acceptability—the **four-party card**. This type of card involves *two* banks in each transaction—the cardholder's bank (the issuer of the card) and the retailer's bank.

The retailer hands over the credit card slips to its own bank for payment (at a discount of 2–5%). The retailer's bank then passes the slips on to a clearing system. The clearing system presents each slip for payment to the bank that issued the card on which it was written. The issuing bank collects from the cardholder.

interchange
A clearing system for four-party credit cards.

The credit card clearing system, called an **interchange**, is very much like the clearing system for checks. In particular, it nets the claims of one bank on another to minimize the need for actual settlement. A large number of regional interchanges were set up along these lines. Most of these have since been consolidated into one of the two international systems of interchanges—Visa and MasterCard.

switch
An online computer system used to monitor and authorize the use of credit cards.

Credit cards proved so profitable that banks sought frantically to sign up more customers. Cards were mailed, unsolicited, to millions of Americans. Not surprisingly, default losses skyrocketed. In response, the credit card industry developed an online computer system, called a **switch**, to monitor and authorize credit card use. Retailers now generally connect to the switch by phone to receive authorization for each purchase. The issuing bank receives instant notification of the purchase, facilitating billing.

secured credit card
A credit card that activates a line of credit secured by collateral provided by the borrower.

Some transactions—renting a car, checking into a hotel, or making a mail order purchase—are today quite difficult without a credit card. Yet many people are unable to obtain a credit card because they are bad risks. However, people who do not qualify for a normal credit card can often obtain a **secured credit card**. With this type of card, the cardholder provides collateral for the line of credit, usually in the form of a time deposit equal in amount to the credit limit on the card.

In 1999, U.S. consumers were holding some 511 million bank credit cards and, in addition, some 595 retailer credit cards.

Delayed Debit Cards

delayed debit card
A card used to make debit payments.

The credit card interchange and switch are the basis of a new method of payment very similar in nature to payment by check or giro—the **delayed debit card**. (The qualifier "delayed" distinguishes this type of debit card from the electronic debit card, to be discussed shortly.)

Unlike the credit card it physically resembles, the delayed debit card involves no credit. Rather than extending the purchaser credit to the end of the month, the issuing bank debits the amount of the purchase from the purchaser's checking deposit as soon as the slip clears through the interchange.[13] Since the bank extends no credit, the discount charged the retailer is correspondingly lower.

Notice that the delayed debit card overcomes many of the problems of payment by check or giro. There is no bad-check problem—the transaction is not authorized unless the purchaser has sufficient funds—and the retailer is guaranteed payment. However, unlike the giro transfer, the delayed debit card can be used for unplanned purchases. While in the United States delayed debit cards are much less popular than credit cards, in Europe the opposite is the case. We will explore the reasons in a later section of this chapter.[14]

ELECTRONIC PAYMENTS

The methods of payment we have looked at so far have all involved the physical transfer of cash or paper. Modern technology has produced electronic methods of payment that involve no physical transfer at all.

Online Electronic Payments: Fedwire and CHIPS

The U.S. payments system includes two online systems of electronic payment—Fedwire and CHIPS—that handle an enormous volume of large payments.

Fedwire

The communications system that allows banks to transfer Fed deposits and government securities.

Fedwire.   **Fedwire** is a communications network that links the computers of some 7,000 banks to the computers of the Fed. Banks use Fedwire to transfer to one another Fed dollars in the form of deposits at the Fed. For example, if Citibank wishes to pay BankAmerica $50 million, an operator at Citi simply types an instruction into a computer terminal. Within minutes, the Fed computer replies, confirming the transfer of $50 million from Citi's deposit to BankAmerica's; BankAmerica is simultaneously notified that it has received payment. In 1999, Fedwire carried about 400,000 payments each day, with an average daily value of some $1.4 trillion.[15]

Payment by Fedwire is final: Citi cannot cancel its payment to BankAmerica once it has been executed. It is completely equivalent to payment in physical Fed dollars. In our example, the Fedwire payment is essentially the same as a magical transfer of $50 million

---

[13] Obviously, banks can issue debit cards only to depositors. In contrast, banks often issue credit cards to people who are not depositors.

[14] By 1992, Visa had some 10.5 million of its debit card outstanding; MasterCard had 1.9 million. There are several hundred million bank credit cards outstanding.

[15] Fedwire is also used to transfer ownership of U.S. government securities. In 1999, there were about 54,000 such transfer each day, involving securities worth some $720 billion. We shall discuss government securities in Chapter 12.

in dollar bills from Citi's vault in New York City to BankAmerica's in San Francisco. Because of its speed and security, virtually all large payments in definitive money are made by Fedwire.

Using Fedwire is more expensive than using a check. The cost is about $10 a message, plus the cost of the hookup (a monthly fee and the cost of the dedicated telephone line). Consequently Fedwire is not used for small payments: the average size of a payment is $3.5 million, versus $1,200 for a check and $10 for a cash payment. Most small banks, because they make few large payments, do not find it worthwhile to be connected to Fedwire. If they require this service, they can always get it from their correspondent banks.

CHIPS.   If Fedwire is the electronic equivalent of payment in cash, then the electronic equivalent of payment by check is **CHIPS** (the Clearing House Interbank Payment System). This system, operated by the New York Clearing House, links some 130 banks with branches in New York City to a central computer.

Most payments over CHIPS are related to the foreign exchange and Eurodollar markets. For example, suppose a British bank needs to pay a French bank $100 million in U.S. dollars. The British bank executes the payment through its branch in New York—if it has one—or through a New York bank with which it has a deposit. The payment is made to the New York branch of the French bank, if it has one, or to a New York bank at which the Paris bank has a deposit. The London bank sends its instructions to New York via **SWIFT** (Society for Worldwide Interbank Financial Telecommunications)—a private electronic message transfer system. The payment is made over CHIPS.[16]

Throughout the day, thousands of payments like this pass from bank to bank. As with the check-clearing process, these payments are netted to minimize the need for final settlement in cash. The CHIPS computer and the computers of the individual banks keep track continuously of each bank's net position relative to every other bank. For example, if Chemical has made a total of $11 billion in payments to Bankers Trust, and Bankers Trust has made a total of $13 billion to Chemical, then the net position of Bankers Trust is that it owes Chemical $2 billion.

At 4:30 P.M., the CHIPS computer sends each participant a summary of its payments for the day and of its final net positions. The summary also indicates the participant's *net net position*—its net position relative to all other participants. For, example, suppose that in addition to the $2 billion it owes to Chemical, Bankers Trust owes a further $2 billion to Dresdner and is owed $5 billion by Barclays. Then the net net position of Bankers Trust is

$$-\$2 \text{ billion} - \$2 \text{ billion} + \$5 \text{ billion} = +\$1 \text{ billion}$$

That is, Bankers Trust is owed $1 billion.

On receiving its summary from CHIPS, each bank checks the information against its own records for accuracy. If it has a net net debt, it must transfer funds over Fedwire to a special account at the Fed by 5:30 P.M. "Settling banks" (some 20 in number) do this them-

SWIFT

A private electronic message transfer system.

---

[16] Before 1978, no foreign bank had access to Fedwire. Since passage of the International Banking Act in that year, non-U.S. banks with branches in this country have had access. Nonetheless, foreign banks continue to prefer CHIPS, generally finding it less expensive.

selves; others have arrangements with settling banks to do this for them. By 6:00 P.M., banks that are owed money receive payment out of the same special account.[17]

In 1999, CHIPS handled some 230,000 payments a day, averaging a total of $1.2 trillion. Because of the economies of netting, these payments resulted in only a few billion a day in settlements.

A payment over CHIPS differs in its basic nature from a payment over Fedwire. While payment over Fedwire (like payment in cash) is final, payment over CHIPS (like payment by check) is merely a promise to pay. As with a check, there is a danger that the promise will "bounce": a bank may be unable to settle at the end of the day. If this happens, all the banks to which it owes money will remain unpaid.

Naturally, there are safeguards. First, the CHIPS system has stringent admission standards. Second, participants set bilateral credit limits on net positions. Third, each bank also has a debit cap on its net net position set by CHIPS, based on these bilateral limits. Fourth, in case a participant does fail during the day, CHIPS has a loss-sharing arrangement to protect the failed bank's creditors on CHIPS. Under this arrangement the other participants must cover the failed bank's debt; each participant's liability is proportional to its bilateral credit limit to the failed bank. To secure the loss-sharing agreement, all CHIPS participants are required to post collateral.

Online Electronic Payments Systems in Other Countries. All major economies have online, large-value electronic payments systems similar to Fedwire and CHIPS. Many have online systems for clearing smaller, mainly giro, payments. For example, in Japan, the Bank of Japan Financial Network System (BOJ-Net) performs the same function as Fedwire. The Zengin system, operated by the Bankers' Association of Tokyo and NTT, and organized much like CHIPS, is mainly used to clear giro payments among banks electronically. In the United Kingdom, CHAPS (Clearing House Automated Payment System) performs essentially the same function as CHIPS in the United States, clearing large payments among the major banks.

Automated Clearinghouses (ACHs)

Fedwire and CHIPS are online systems on which payments can be executed immediately. There is a slower, but less expensive, method of electronic payment that involves the exchange of magnetic tapes rather than of pieces of paper.

For example, "direct deposit" of payroll payments is usually executed in this way. The employer's bank prepares a magnetic tape detailing all the payments to be made. The tape is sent to an **automated clearinghouse (ACH)** where, together with other tapes from other banks, the information is read into a computer. Payment instructions are passed on, and payments to and from the various banks are netted. Settlement of net positions is made over Fedwire.

ACHs handle both credit transfers and debit transfers. Credit transfers are similar in nature to a giro payment (direct deposit is an example). Debit transfers are similar in nature

automated clearinghouse (ACH)
Clearinghouse for off-line electronic payments, involving the exchange of magnetic tapes.

---

[17] Before 1970, settlement was made with bank checks drawn on the Fed. These cleared through the clearinghouse. Settlement was in next-day rather than same-day funds (so-called clearinghouse funds).

to checks. For example, suppose you have authorized your insurance agent to take monthly payments from your bank deposit. The agent will do this by having its bank send a request for the funds each month via magnetic tape to the local ACH. ACHs are particularly well suited to repeated periodic payments—for example, payroll and Social Security payments.

In the United States, most automated clearinghouses are operated by the Fed. However, there are also private operations: for example, NYACH which is operated by the New York Clearing House and a system operated by Visa. In 1999, Fed clearinghouses handled some 17 million payments a day, worth about $52 billion in total. Private clearinghouses handled some 2 million payments, worth $9 billion.

Electronic Debit Cards: ATMs and EFTPOS

electronic debit card (cash card)
A card that can be inserted into a terminal to effect payments, cash withdrawals, and other transactions.

The most ubiquitous medium of electronic payment is the **electronic debit card** or **cash card**. The user inserts the card into a machine, punches in a personal identification number (PIN), and gains access to an electronic payments system. There are two principal types of machine into which the card can be inserted—the automated teller machine (ATM) and the electronic funds transfer at point of sale (EFTPOS) terminal.

ATMs. ATMs allow bank customers easy access to their deposits. A customer can use an ATM to make deposits and withdraw cash, pay bills, and transfer amounts between deposits. The ATM was developed in Britain and spread from there to Europe before it made its first appearance in the United States. The first ATM in the United States was installed by Philadelphia National Bank in 1969. By 1999, there were 227,000 ATMs in the United States, and consumers held some 252 million ATM cards. ATMs are typically located outside banks and at other convenient locations such as shopping malls and airports.[18] About 70% of the 11 billion transactions a year on the machines are cash withdrawals.

network externality
Benefit to existing users of a network from the addition of a new member.

The usefulness of ATMs has been enhanced enormously by connecting them to interbank networks that allow cardholders of one bank to use their cards at the ATMs of other banks. There is an important externality here: when a new bank joins the network it increases not only the value of its own cards but also the value of cards of other banks already in the network (telephone systems and languages exhibit similar **network externalities**). Associated with this externality are significant economies of scale: the larger the membership, the more valuable the network. Consequently, most of the original regional networks have been consolidated into one of the two national networks Cirrus (owned by MasterCard) and Plus (owned by Visa).[19] In 1990, Cirrus and Plus agreed to allow access to each other's customers.

What happens when you use your cash card at the ATM of another bank? Suppose Lucinda, a customer of Golden State Bank, uses her cash card at an ATM of Empire State Bank on the other side of the country. Empire State's ATM is connected to a regional net-

---

[18] A 1984 court ruling that an ATM is not a bank branch ensured that the placement of distant ATMs would not be hampered by interstate banking laws.

[19] Interstate banking mergers and acquisitions have also stimulated consolidation. The acquiring bank finds the acquired bank on a different network, requiring duplicate membership and fees and possibly different protocols for transactions.

work switch (communication system). This is connected in turn to a national network switch. Empire State's ATM communicates via these switches with the computer at Golden State to authorize and record Lucinda's transaction. Golden State pays a switch fee to the network (2–25¢ per transaction) and an interchange fee to Empire State ($0.40–$1). Golden State may pass on these fees to Lucinda. In addition, Empire State may charge her directly as much as $1 for using its ATM.

Plus and Cirrus have extended their networks overseas. They have reached agreements with networks in other countries that allow American cardholders to make cash withdrawals in the local currency. You can use your cash card not only in Seattle and Miami, but also in London, Moscow, and Tokyo.

EFTPOS.   In addition to using your cash card at an ATM, you can use it to pay for purchases at retail outlets. Instead of writing a check, you can insert your cash card into an **EFTPOS terminal** (Electronic Funds Transfer at Point Of Sale terminal) connected to the store's cash register. The terminal connects through the ATM or credit card switching systems to your own bank's computer. After you have punched in your PIN, the amount of the purchase is deducted immediately from your checking deposit and credited to the deposit of the store.

The electronic debit card, in both its ATM and EFTPOS uses, is sometimes described as an electronic check. In reality, it is much closer to a giro payment. The payment order goes directly to the payer's bank and is not executed unless the funds are there: there is no bad-check problem. The electronic debit card (like the delayed debit card discussed earlier) allows much greater flexibility than a paper giro, being well suited to unplanned purchases.

Prepaid Cards.   We saw that "special checks" (traveler's checks, etc.) provide the convenience of a check to those without deposits. The electronic equivalent of the special check is the **prepaid card**, commonly used on many campuses to operate copying machines. You buy the card, often from a vending machine, for cash, say $10. You insert the card into the copying machine to make copies, and the cost of the copies is debited from the balance on the card until the $10 is used up. There are other uses of prepaid cards—for example, paying for tickets on the Washington, DC subway system. Prepaid cards are popular in Europe and extremely popular in Japan.

A more sophisticated version is the **smart card** or "electronic purse or wallet," which embodies a microchip and can be used as a general rather than a specific means of payment. Users "download" cash from their bank deposits via an ATM machine or a specially adapted phone. Smart cards can be used for payment wherever merchants have the equipment to read them. Unlike credit or debit cards, no verification is necessary. This saves on telecommunications costs which can be 8¢ to 15¢ for a credit/debit card transaction. Consequently smart cards are viable for much smaller transactions—purchase of a newspaper, for example.

Smart cards have been slow to catch on. One reason is again network externalities. Merchants do not find it worthwhile to install readers because few consumers have the card. Consumers do not find it worthwhile to acquire the card because few merchants accept it. Moreover, although the cost to the economy of using cash is substantial, the cost to a consumer of an individual transaction is small. There is therefore little incentive to go to a lot of trouble to avoid it.

EFTPOS terminal

A terminal at the point of sale, into which an electronic debit card can be inserted to effect a payment.

prepaid card

A card with a magnetic strip used to make payments up to a total amount registered on the card and paid in advance.

smart card

A more sophisticated prepaid card that includes a microchip.

Payment on the Internet

An increasing fraction of all transactions now take place on the Internet. There are predictions that business-to-consumer transactions (B2C) on the Internet will soon be in the hundreds of millions of dollars and that business-to-business transactions (B2B) in the trillions.

Currently, the overwhelming majority of B2C purchases on the Internet are paid for by credit card. This works reasonably well, but there are some problems. The first is security. Hackers can acquire credit card information, either by intercepting communication between consumer and merchant or by gaining access to merchant computers.[20] Once they have the information, they can use it by faking e-mail from the owner of the credit card. Credit card fraud is 12 times more common for Internet transactions, and the credit card companies consequently charge a larger discount on such transactions. The principal defenses against fraud are encryption of credit card information and better security of merchant computers.

A second problem is that payment by credit card is not available for transactions between consumers (P2P)—for example, to settle purchases in online auctions. Various technologies are being developed to bridge this gap with some form of "online check." One, called eCheck, is a relatively straightforward electronic version of the paper check. Another, called PayPal, provides consumers with the capability of linking up with the existing credit card and ACH networks to make payments. Yet another technology is planned to link up with the existing ATM network.

A third problem with payment by credit card is that it is expensive. There is the potential on the Internet for a large volume of quite small transactions involving the sale of information, such as a single song, photograph, news item, or piece of data. The payments involved are likely to be small—from $10 down to 1¢ or even less. For such transactions, various technologies are being developed to provide some form of "digital cash."

For the time being, however, the credit card continues to dominate Internet commerce. None of the new digital check or cash technologies have yet caught on. Of course the same network externalities that stand in the way of the smart card are part of the problem here. Consumers do not use the new technologies, because not enough merchants accept them. Merchants do not accept them because not enough consumers use them.

THE USE OF DIFFERENT METHODS OF PAYMENT

Different Payments Methods for Different Transactions

Different methods of payment are suited to different types of transaction. The major categories of transaction are

- Payments at point of sale (POS)
- Bill payments

---

[20] The Internet is less secure than the telephone because of the way that information is transmitted. Over the telephone, each connection uses a dedicated circuit, so that eavesdropping is difficult. Over the Internet, information is broken into packets that travel over a common network of lines and relaying computers, so that interception is much easier.

- Disbursements (mainly income payments)
- Financial market transactions

Cash and cards are suited mainly to POS transactions, although bills are sometimes paid by credit card and disbursements sometimes made in cash. Check, giro, and ACH are well suited to bill payments and disbursements. However, checks are very flexible and are often used too at POS and for financial market transactions. Wire transfers are limited mainly to financial market transactions.

What is the relative importance of the different methods of payment? Cash is used in far more transactions than any other method of payment—in most countries for 80 to 90% of all transactions. However, the typical transaction is small, and the total value of cash transactions is therefore modest—less than 5% in most countries. Wire transfers, on the other hand, are used for relatively few payments, but each is large, and the total volume far exceeds that of all other methods of payment combined. Other methods of payment lie somewhere in between.

An International Comparison of Payments Patterns

All developed countries use all of the different methods of payment to some extent. However, the pattern of use differs widely across countries. Americans rely mainly on checks and credit cards. Europeans prefers giro payments and debit cards. The Japanese (and other Asians) rely far more on cash.

Exhibit 8.2 gives a breakdown of the composition of cashless payments in the United States, Europe, and Japan. The breakdown is for the number of transactions per person. This differs radically from the breakdown by value. For example, in the United States, wire transfers account for a negligible percentage of the *total number* of transactions, but they account for 85% of the *total value* (in Exhibit 8.2, wire transfers are included in the category "giro" for the United States).

The total number of noncash payments is highest in the United States because cash is used less than elsewhere (less than 1% of the total value of all transactions). It is intermediate in Europe and lowest by far in Japan. The Japanese rely on cash for most POS transactions. You can see that the United States is the biggest user of checks and that the second largest category is credit cards. Europe relies on giro payments more than on checks and on debit cards more than on credit cards. Japan uses giro more than any other method, but its use of cashless methods of payment is much lower than other countries'.

Why Payment Patterns Differ

Payments patterns differ across countries for a variety of reasons—legal, historical, and economic.

Some Legal and Historical Reasons.   Some countries use checks and others use giro payments for reasons that lie mainly in their legal histories. The check evolved in the English-speaking countries. English courts viewed it as a variety of commercial bill of exchange.[21] The early recognition by English courts of the negotiability of commercial

---

[21] See Chapter 6.

EXHIBIT 8.2   Noncash Transactions, Number per Person in 1993

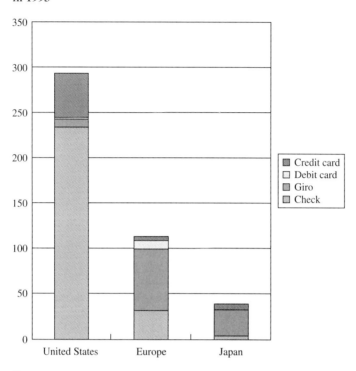

Source: Humphrey et al. (1996).

bills, and so of checks, made their use much easier. If a check is negotiable, you can sign it over to your bank, and your bank can collect payment through the clearing system. If a check is not negotiable, clearing becomes impossible and you yourself must present each check for payment at the payer's bank.

European courts did not regard the check as a variety of commercial bill, but rather as a variety of personal order of payment. The personal order of payment goes back to the medieval money-changer banks that we learned about in Chapter 6. These banks allowed their customers to make payments by transferring ownership of deposits. Initially, orders to transfer deposits were made orally, and they required the physical presence of all the parties involved—the payer, the payee, and the banker. The courts recognized transfers performed in this way as constituting a final discharge of a debt. The money changers had a rudimentary clearing system: transfers were cleared between banks by means of reciprocal clearing accounts that the banks held with one another.

Because European courts regarded the check as a personal order of payment, they did not recognize its negotiability. As a result, the giro proved a much more convenient method of payment—first the paper giro and then, more recently, the electronic giro. Most countries do now recognize the negotiability of checks, but the giro has become entrenched. The French government launched a major campaign in the 1960s and 1970s to encourage the use of checks. The European preference for giro payments over checks has carried over to a preference for debit cards over credit cards.

There are other historical and legal factors that have determined payments patterns. Some examples:

- Until quite recently, in many countries—Germany and the United Kingdom, for example—the law required firms to pay their hourly workers in cash. As a result, such workers generally did not have checking deposits and so did not use checks.
- Low rates of street crime in Japan and high rates in the United States make cash a much more attractive means of payment in the former than in the latter.
- One reason credit cards are less attractive in Japan is the cost of telecommunications there, which makes authorization via switch too expensive. The result is a higher rate of fraud, making credit cards more expensive.
- One reason Europeans are willing to allow routine bills to be directly debited from their deposits is that European banks commonly offer overdraft credit. U.S. banks do not, and Americans therefore feel uncomfortable with automatic payments debited from their deposits.

Economic Incentives and the Use of Methods of Payment.   The different patterns of use of various methods of payment also reflect different relative costs. For example, the cost structure in the United States strongly favors the use of checks and credit cards.

Although your bank provides you with "free checking," checks are in fact far from free. The average checks costs 76¢ to process. Total processing costs for all checks add up to some $45 billion a year. Your credit card transactions are also "free" to you. But processing costs average 44¢ per payment and merchants pay a substantial discount (as much as 5%) to receive payment.

Why is it that you do not pay the true cost of these transactions? One reason for "free checking" is taxes. The receipt of explicit interest on deposits is taxable, while the receipt of implicit interest, in the form of free services, is not. Another reason is the nature of competition among banks. Typically, when there are few firms in a market—as is the case in most local banking markets—they avoid competing on price because of the danger of a price war. Instead, they compete in the services they provide. Free checking is one of these services.

Why don't retailers pass on to you the extra cost to them of a credit card purchase? Credit card customers tend to be wealthier and to spend more. Retailers may be willing to offer them a lower price—which is what they do when they accept a credit card—because on the whole cardholders are better customers.

Float.   The main thing that makes a credit card purchase so attractive to you, and so costly to the merchant, is delay. You receive the merchandise immediately, but you do not have to pay until the end of the billing period. In the meantime you earn interest on the amount of the payment. The merchant avoids having to wait for payment only by discounting the debt with a bank. Essentially the bank lends the merchant the amount of the payment until you pay it. The benefit of delay to you from such a transaction is called **float**.

float
The interest earned as a result of delays in the payments system.

When you pay by check, you also benefit from float. If you send it by mail, the legal date of payment is the date of the postmark. You earn *mail float* on the time it takes the check to be delivered to the recipient. It also takes time for the check to go through the clearing process. You earn *bank float* until your deposit is debited. If the total delay is a week, you earn an extra week's interest on the amount of the payment after it has legally been made.

Methods of payment that do not involve float seem less attractive. The transaction cost of electronic payment (EFTPOS, for example) is much lower than that of payment by check or credit card. It is also much faster. But this speed is a *dis*advantage to you because it reduces float.

The loss of float is one reason debit cards have been slow to catch on in the United States. Checks and credit cards offer greater float. In Europe, payments by cash and giro predominate. Since neither method offers float, the greater convenience of the debit card is not offset by any loss of float, and debit cards have proven very popular.

The Use of Cash. Immediate payment in cash by definition involves no float. Why is it, then, that there are so many cash payments? There are, in fact, good reasons why immediate payment in cash is the preferred method both for very small payments and for very large ones.

Cash is the preferred method for small payments because it is the only method that involves no credit (no promises). Methods of payment that involve credit involve substantial fixed costs. For example, the costs of credit verification and of clearing a check do not depend on the amount of the check. Consequently, a check is relatively more expensive for small transactions. Therefore, when you buy a newspaper at the corner newsstand, a check or credit card will not be accepted. You have to pay in cash.

For quite different reasons, immediate payment in cash is also preferred for very large payments. For large payments, the recipient may not be willing to accept the loss due to float. At an interest rate of 5% per annum, a day's delay on a payment of $100 million costs about $13,000 in forgone interest. Moreover, many large payments are related to very-short-term lending—perhaps for as little as a day. Lending money for a day and sending the money by check would not make much sense. Large payments in "cash" are made by Fedwire.

FOREIGN EXCHANGE

We have looked at payments within a country. Payments between countries involve additional complications.

The Problem of Different Clearing Systems

Most payments are made with bank dollars. To use bank dollars in payment there must be a way to convert the payer's bank dollars (dollars in the payer's bank deposit) into bank dollars the recipient is willing to accept (dollars in the recipient's bank deposit). This is easy if both payer and recipient share the same bank. It is almost as easy, if a little more expensive, if they have different banks but the two banks are part of the same clearing system.

However, if the two banks are not part of the same clearing system, payment is much more difficult. The payer must find a way to *trade* his bank dollars for bank dollars at the recipient's bank or bank dollars that are convertible into the same through a common clearing system. Trade in bank dollars of banks in different clearing systems is called **foreign exchange**.

foreign exchange
Trade in bank dollars of banks in different clearing systems.

A Foreign Exchange Transaction

To see how foreign exchange works, let us look at an example. Henriette Gourmet Foods in the United States imports tea from Chelsea Tea in England. In payment for a recent shipment, Henriette needs to pay Chelsea in pounds sterling the sum of £100,000 (about $140,000). To do this, Henriette cannot simply write Chelsea a check. She does not have a deposit in pounds sterling, and her bank and Chelsea's do not belong to the same clearing system.

Henriette must go to the foreign exchange department of her bank, First National. There she buys £100,000 in British bank money—that is, £100,000 in a bank deposit in the United Kingdom. A check drawn on that deposit is sent to Chelsea. It clears in the normal fashion through the British clearing system, and Chelsea ultimately receives payment in bank money at its own bank.

Where does First National get the British bank money to sell to Henriette? If it is large enough and does enough business in foreign exchange, it may maintain a deposit of its own at a British bank for just such a purpose. If not, it can buy the pounds in the interbank market in foreign exchange where deposits in different countries are traded.

"Domestic Exchange"

As in this example, most foreign exchange transactions today are international and involve bank deposits denominated in different currencies. This was not always the case. Historically, distance and poor communications were more important barriers than differences in currency. In the nineteenth century, a merchant in New Orleans would have found it just as difficult to pay a supplier in New York as to pay one in London. There was then no way to clear checks between different parts of the United States. Banks in New Orleans offered "domestic exchange"—claims on New York deposits—as well as foreign exchange—claims on London deposits.

The introduction of the Euro, a common currency for 11 of the 15 member states of the European Union in 1999 has created a situation in "Euroland" not unlike that in the early United States. The member countries all use the same currency, but they have retained their individual clearing systems and these are only partially connected. The European Central Bank operates a system called TARGET that links the large-value online payment systems of EU member countries. This enables large-value, cross-border payments to be made relatively easily. However, there is no link yet for smaller payments. As a result, the cost of making payments in Euros between, say, Rome and Paris has remained quite high (much like the cost of making a dollar payment between New Orleans and New York 200 years ago). A survey in 2000 found that the average cost of a 100 Euro cross-border transaction was over 17 Euros, with enormous variations from country to country.

The Foreign Exchange Market

The interbank market in foreign exchange is an international market, active around the clock. Its major centers are London, New York, and Tokyo. The prices in the foreign exchange market are the exchange rates we studied in Chapter 4. For example, the exchange rate between the U.S. dollar and the pound sterling might be $1.40 to the pound. This means, in our example, that Henriette would have to give up $1.40 of her bank money (deposits at her bank) in order to obtain a claim on £1 of British bank money (deposits at a British bank). Trade in the foreign exchange market includes forward transactions as well as spot transactions like Henriette's.[22]

Growth of the Market

The foreign exchange market expanded rapidly with the breakdown of the Bretton Woods system of fixed exchange rates in 1971 and exploded with the large increase in exchange rate volatility that began in the late 1970s. In 1977 trading volume in New York amounted to less than $5 billion a day (about $15 billion in 1998 dollars). By 1998 it had increased to $351 billion a day. Trading volume in London, the center of the world market for foreign exchange, was $637 billion a day in 1998, and the worldwide total was about $1.5 trillion a day. By 2001, total trading volume had fallen to $1.1 trillion. One reason for this was the creation of the Euro, which replaced 11 national currencies. Another reason has been the consolidation of the banking industry, which has reduced the number of participants in the market.

Trading volume in foreign exchange is nonetheless many times greater than the volume of international trade. In fact, most foreign exchange transactions are related not to trade but to finance. For example, if a Japanese pension fund wants to buy U.S. government securities, it must change its yen into dollars. Indeed, as the volume of international financial transactions has grown, securities firms have increasingly become dealers in foreign exchange, offering this service to their customers themselves, rather than referring them to a commercial bank.

How the Market Works

Market Organization.   A foreign exchange transaction is a trade. Like trading in securities, trading in foreign exchange is conducted in an organized market. The market is organized by brokers. A bank wishing to buy or sell foreign exchange contacts a broker who will match it with a possible trading partner. Traditionally, transactions were conducted by telephone, but in 1992 the brokers introduced electronic systems that have increasingly taken over the market, accounting for 95% of total volume by 2000.[23] Some 20 major banks worldwide act as dealers, quoting prices at which they are willing to buy or sell a broad range of currencies.

---

[22] In Chapter 2, we saw how Valley Motors bought yen forward to cover its debt to Kamikaze. We shall discuss forward markets in more detail in Chapter 16.

[23] We shall discuss electronic trading systems and their merits and problems in Chapter 17.

Vehicle Currencies.   Trading generally involves one or a few "vehicle" currencies. That is, most of the trading involves trades of the vehicle currency for other currencies. The principal vehicle currency is the U.S. dollar. To see what this means, consider an exchange of Canadian dollars for Italian lire. This typically involves two trades: the first is a trade of Canadian dollars for U.S. dollars; the second is a trade of the U.S. dollars so acquired for Italian lire.[24]

Settlement and Its Problems.   The settlement of foreign exchange trades is much like the settlement of securities trades. Both involve the delivery of one thing in exchange for the delivery of another. We shall discuss settlement and its associated problems in Chapter 17. However, foreign exchange settlement is subject to some special problems because the two items to be delivered must be delivered in different countries and often in different time zones. To see why this is a problem, let us consider an example.

Bank of Tokyo buys dollars in exchange for yen in the Tokyo market from Bankers Trust. There are two "legs" to this transaction: Bank of Tokyo must transfer yen to Bankers Trust; Bankers Trust must transfer dollars to Bank of Tokyo. The yen leg is easy: it is executed immediately by Bank of Tokyo making payment to the Bankers Trust branch in Tokyo through the local clearing system.

The dollar leg, in principle, needs to be executed in New York (that is where the dollars are). But it cannot be executed immediately, because of the 14-hour time difference. This is a problem because it would require Bank of Tokyo to extend credit to Bankers Trust until the dollar payment can be made. If Bankers Trust were to fail in the meantime, Bank of Tokyo would take a loss. This risk is known as **Herstatt risk** in honor of a notorious German bank of that name that failed in the middle of the business day in 1974, causing chaos in the foreign exchange market and significant losses to other banks.

To reduce the delay and the consequent exposure to risk, dollar payments in the Asian interbank market are cleared through the books of the Tokyo branch of Chase Manhattan. During the Tokyo business day, customer payment orders result in debits and credits on Chase's books. Payments are final, guaranteed by Chase, and backed by a loss-sharing agreement among participants. Only net positions need be cleared over CHIPS when New York opens for business.

This sort of clearing arrangement is one solution. Another is some sort of multicurrency netting. Multicurrency netting can potentially reduce the need for final settlement by as much as 75%. There are several competing systems, including ECHO in London and in Chicago, but the banks with the largest foreign exchange operations have yet to sign up with any of them.

The most recent development is the creation of the Continuous Linked Settlement Bank, which began operation in September 2002. The CLSB was established by the 60 major banks and securities firms from 14 countries that dominate the foreign exchange market. Members have multicurrency accounts at the bank with balances in each currency that they use to settle.[25] CLSB completes a transaction only when it can simultaneously

Herstatt risk
The risk a counterparty will fail in the middle of an exchange of currencies.

---

[24] Each foreign exchange transaction generates two payments—one in each currency. So the $1.5 trillion of transactions each day generates about $3 trillion in payments. About 40% of these, or $1.2 trillion, are in U.S. dollars, and this is roughly the daily volume of payments on CHIPS.

[25] Members can overdraw their account in a particular currency as long as their overall balance remains positive.

execute both legs. In our example, it would simultaneously transfer yen from the Bank of Tokyo to Bankers Trust and dollars from Bankers Trust to Bank of Tokyo. CLSB has correspondent accounts at the central bank in each country to which members can make payment and from which they can receive payment via the local payments system. This arrangement can work because the major central banks have extended the hours of their electronic payments system, and there is now a short daily overlap across the major countries.[26]

THE PAYMENTS SYSTEM AND PUBLIC POLICY

The payments system is part of our economic infrastructure. Problems with the payments system can damage trade and slow economic activity. Therefore, both the efficiency of the payments system and its stability have always been objects of public concern.

Efficiency of the Payments System

As we saw in Chapter 3 there are three conditions for efficiency—minimum transactions costs, competitive pricing, and integration. Will a payments system provided by the free market satisfy these conditions?

Minimum Costs. One would expect financial institutions to compete for payments business by developing and offering lower cost methods of payment. The question is, though, whether they will try hard enough. The reason there is a question is that the benefits of a better method of payment to the economy as a whole may greatly exceed the benefits to the developer. That is, there may be significant *externalities*. If so, government action to improve the payments system may be justified. For example, we have seen that the French government waged a campaign in the 1960s and 1970s to encourage a switch from cash to checks.

As in the case of the smart card and various methods of payment on the Internet, network externalities stand in the way of adoption of lower cost technology. Government intervention could help to overcome this barrier. However, there is a danger that the government will "pick losers." Despite the externalities, free competition may be more likely to promote the best technology in the end.

We saw in Chapter 7 that the cost of payments is greatly reduced by integration of the banking system. For example, check-clearing costs are much lower in Canada than they are in the United States. In Canada, because there are relatively few banks, most with branches all over the country, checks can clear rapidly. Many clear within the same bank; most of the others can be presented for payment the same day at the local branch of the bank on which they are drawn. In the United States, as we have seen, checks must go through a long and complicated clearing process.

---

[26] Since 1997, Fedwire has opened at 12:30 A.M. each day and closed at 6:30 P.M. CHIPS, the main function of which is to serve the global market in foreign exchange, has long operated more or less around the clock. But CHIPS relies on Fedwire for settlement.

The availability of low-cost methods of payment is not however enough. For the payment system to be efficient, people actually have to use the lowest cost method. We have seen that there are reasons why they may not. People will choose the method of payment of least cost to them. We have seen that the cost to the payer of using a check or credit card is much lower than the true cost. Consequently, people will use checks and credit cards for payments that could be made more cheaply, in terms of their true cost, in other ways.

We saw that float is an element in the discrepancy between payer cost and true cost. Reducing float will therefore encourage people to use more economical methods of payment. Congress passed a law in 1987 aimed at reducing float. The Canadian government also waged a campaign to reduce float. Banks in Canada now credit depositors the same day for most checks. Of course, the speed with which checks can be cleared in Canada's integrated banking system is a great help in reducing float.

Competitive Pricing.   Will there be sufficient competition in the provision of payments services? Economies of scale and natural monopoly are both potential problems. For example, check processing involves indivisible fixed costs and so economies of scale. Payment networks, such as those associated with credit cards and ATMs, are arguably natural monopolies: costs would be minimized if there were only a single network.

While market power is a concern, the ability to exploit it is limited. Although technology may be conducive to market power in the provision of a particular method of payment, there are many alternative methods of payment. Any attempt to raise the price of one method above its competitive level will result in a loss of business to other methods. Nonetheless, some antitrust vigilance seems justified.

There is one part of the payments system where monopoly is enforced rather than discouraged. Almost universally, central banks have a monopoly on the issue of hand-to-hand currency. Is there any justification for this in terms of efficiency?

There are some arguments for allowing a natural monopoly in note issue. In the nineteenth-century United States, any bank could issue banknotes. There were so many different types of banknote in circulation that merchants had to rely on weekly publications known as "currency detectors" to tell the good from the bad. The resulting confusion added considerably to the transactions costs of payment in currency. A single uniform source of banknotes eliminates the problem and reduces transactions costs.

However, the real reason for the government monopoly of note issue is not efficiency but revenue. The government takes a little paper and some ink, costing very little, and transforms them into a $20 Federal Reserve note that is worth $20. The difference between the production cost and the value is called **seigniorage**. Total seigniorage is substantial. The amount of Federal Reserve notes outstanding in December 1999 was about $601 billion. The annual cost of maintaining the currency—the costs of printing new notes and of replacing worn and damaged old notes—was well under $1 billion. The present value of these maintenance costs (continued indefinitely and discounted at 4%) is under $25 billion. So the seigniorage that results from the monopoly on note issue is worth about $575 billion to the U.S. government.[27] Not an amount to be sneezed at!

seigniorage
The difference between the value of money and the cost of producing it.

---

[27] The government also earns seigniorage on the other form of Federal Reserve dollars—deposits at the Fed.

Integration. Integration of the payments system is a necessary condition for economic efficiency. A major reason for lack of integration is the use of different currencies. For example, suppose a British firm produces spark plugs at lower cost than any other firm in Europe. A German automobile manufacturer might nonetheless prefer to buy from a higher cost German producer because the payments costs of dealing with the British company are so high.

Lack of integration can also be a problem within a country. Domestic payments, too, involve the conversion of one type of money into another. As we have seen, payment in bank money involves the conversion of bank money of the payer's bank into bank money of the recipient's bank. We take it for granted today that the "exchange rate" for this transaction is one for one. However, before the Fed established a nationwide check-clearing system, this was not the case. Banks generally honored checks drawn on banks outside their local clearinghouse at a discount: this was called "nonpar" checking. An important motivations for setting up the Fed in 1913 was a desire to eliminate nonpar checking and so to remove an obstacle to trade within the United States.[28]

The Importance of Stability in the Value of Money

In addition to the three general conditions for efficiency, there is a fourth that is special to the payments system—stability in the value of money. We have seen that delays in payment are costly. Changes in the value of money can increase the costs of delay dramatically, degrading the efficiency of the payments system. There are two reasons for changes in the value of money—inflation and fluctuations in exchange rates.

Inflation. As the price level rises, the value of money in terms of purchasing power falls. The extreme example is a hyperinflation. In a hyperinflation the value of money can fall by a half in a single day. In these circumstances, the delays involved in noncash payment become unacceptable. If a check for $100 takes 2 days to clear, the recipient receives the equivalent of only $25.

In a hyperinflation, even cash payment is a problem, because holding the cash involves a loss. For example, there are stories of people in hyperinflations paying for restaurant meals as soon as they've ordered because the money in their pockets will be worth significantly less by the time the meal is over. Moreover, as money loses value, larger and larger volumes of notes are needed. It may take half an hour to count out the notes required for even a small payment. As all method of payment become prohibitively costly, trade stops, and the economy grinds to a halt.

While the effects of a hyperinflation are dramatic, even moderate inflation is a problem. Inflation raises the nominal interest rate. The higher the nominal interest rate, the greater the costs of delay in payment, and so the greater the benefits—to the individual—of float. As a result, firms and individuals invest substantial resources in zero-sum attempts to capture float and to prevent losses due to float.

---

[28] Another problem of the payments system the Fed was supposed to solve was the proliferation of different types of paper currency. In addition to several types that had been issued by the federal government—greenbacks, silver certificates, and Treasury notes—national banks issued banknotes of their own. Federal Reserve notes were supposed to replace all of these eventually, as the only form of paper currency.

Fluctuation in Exchange Rates.   A second reason the value of money can change is fluctuations in exchange rates. As we have seen, international payments require the conversion of one currency into another. Fluctuations in the rate of conversion—the exchange rate—raise the cost of international payment by making it more risky.[29]

The responsibility for preventing inflation and for ensuring the stability of exchange rates rests with central banks—in the United States, with the Fed.

Stability of the Payments System

While efficiency of the payments system is important, its stability is a matter of life and death. A breakdown of the payments system could completely disrupt the normal functioning of the economy. Here the externalities are obvious and substantial. In the United States, the Federal Reserve Act charges the Fed with ensuring the stability of the U.S. payments system.

Safety of Bank Deposits.   The payments system relies heavily on the banks. Banks provide the most important medium of payment—bank money. As we have seen, they also provide a variety of methods for making payment in this medium. Hence, a major reason for the Fed's concern for the safety of the banks is its responsibility for the integrity of the payment system.

Fedwire and Daylight Overdraft.   The Fed's greatest concern today in the area of stability relates to the safety of the large-value online payment systems—Fedwire and CHIPS. The fundamental problems of the two systems are different because of the different way that they process payments. On Fedwire each payment is settled as it is made. This is called a **real-time gross settlement (RTGS)**. On CHIPS all the payments made during each day are netted, and only the balances are settled.

The way that Fedwire works creates a potential problem. For example, suppose Chase transfers $100 million to Citi over Fedwire. If Chase has $100 million in its account, there is no problem and it is simply debited for the amount. But Chase is making and receiving a large number of payments, and it is quite possible that when it makes this payment to Citi it will have less than $100 million in its deposit at the Fed. In such a case, the Fed automatically allows Chase an overdraft loan to cover the payment. Consequently, regardless of whether Chase has the funds to cover the transfer, Citi is credited immediately. If Chase receives an overdraft loan, it must repay the amount by the end of the business day—hence, **daylight overdraft**. Because daylight overdraft is free—the Fed charges no interest on it—banks have relied on it heavily. Daylight overdraft hit a peak of over $140 billion in 1993, and average per-minute overdraft was about $80 billion.

real-time gross settlement system (RTGS) A system in which each payment is settled immediately and individually, with no netting.

daylight overdraft Overdraft that must be repaid by the end of the day.

---

[29] The same argument can be applied to the conversion of the bank money of one bank into that of another. If bank deposits are unsafe (the bank may fail), this may be an impediment to check clearing at par. This potential problem is sometimes used as a justification for government insurance of bank deposits. Deposit insurance makes the bank money of all banks equally safe.

The extension of daylight overdraft credit exposes the Fed to credit risk. A good illustration of the dangers is provided by the case of Bank of New York. Bank of New York is a major clearing bank in the government securities market, paying and receiving tens of billions of dollars in funds and securities daily. On November 21, 1985, its computers failed, leaving it with an uncleared daylight overdraft at the Fed of $30 billion. Since the Fed had already, in effect, lent Bank of New York the money, it had no choice but to convert the overdraft loan into a discount loan to carry it over to the next day. Had Bank of New York failed that night, the Fed would have taken the loss. Several years earlier Continental Bank of Illinois had failed with a significant daylight overdraft loan outstanding.

In 1994, the Fed tried to address this problem. It took measures to reduce daylight overdraft by setting limits for each bank and by charging borrowing banks for overdraft loans (at four percentage points above the Fed funds rate). The result of these changes was to halve both peak and average per-minute overdraft to about $70 billion and $40 billion, respectively, after 1994.

What more could be done? Daylight overdraft could be abolished altogether. There is none in Japan: an interbank market for intraday loans takes its place. Daylight overdraft was abolished in Switzerland in 1987. There, wire payments are managed by a computer system that executes payment only if the deposit is sufficient. If not, payments go into a queue and are executed in order as funds come in.

CHIPS and Systemic Risk.   Because CHIPS relies on netting, it has a different problem—**systemic risk**. If one participant were to fail during the day, it would be unable to settle its balance at the end of the day. This could have a domino effect, causing the failure to settle of many others to whom it owed payments. The problem is compounded because many of the participants on CHIPS are foreign banks. While the Fed would probably stand behind a major U.S. bank that failed to settle, would it do the same for a foreign bank?

systemic risk
The danger that failure of one participant in a payments system could cause the failure of others.

At the Fed's urging, CHIPS has changed its procedure to improve safety. Whereas payments used to be provisional—a bank could cancel a payment before the end of the day—they are now final. And a loss-sharing arrangement has been set up to cover losses caused by failure of a participant.

SUMMARY

- We have two types of money in our economy. Fed dollars, which exist as Federal Reserve Notes and as deposits at the Fed, are our definitive money. Bank dollars in the form of transactions deposits at various types of depository institution are convertible into Fed money.

- A check is an order to transfer ownership of deposits. Check clearing converts a claim on deposits at the payer's bank into a claim on deposits at the recipient's bank.

- The problem with checks is that they may bounce. There are enhancements and special checks that address the problem.

- A giro is an order of payment, but it differs from a check in that the payer gives the order directly to his own bank. The order, therefore, cannot bounce.

- Credit cards have evolved from store credit via third-party cards into the four-party bank card. Credit card payments clear through an interchange and are monitored and authorized through an online switch. The delayed debit card takes advantage of this system to make giro-like payments.

- Online wire transfer systems handle most financial and interbank transactions. Fedwire allows the transfer of deposits at the Fed (equivalent to payment in cash). CHIPS payments are more like checks, and they clear through a netting arrangement.

- Other electronic methods of payments include ACHs, for the transfer of payment orders on magnetic tape, and electronic debit cards. By inserting an electronic debit card into a terminal (ATM or EFTPOS) the cardholder can make online payments and transfers.

- The dominant means of payment on the Internet is the credit card. This has its limitations. Alternatives are being developed, but none has yet gained widespread acceptance.

- In the United States, most cashless payments are made by check. However, the total value of payments executed by wire transfer is much greater.

- Payment patterns in some other countries are very different. The Germans and the Japanese rely much more on giro and direct debit. These differences in payments pattern have legal and historical reasons, but they also have economic reasons.

- The main advantage of checks and credit cards to the payer is float. Check float is particularly large in the United States because of its fragmented banking system and slow check clearing.

- International payments involve foreign exchange: the exchange of bank dollars in one clearing system for bank dollars in another. The foreign exchange market has mushroomed since the 1970s as exchange rates have become more volatile and as the volume of international financial transactions has grown.

- Efficiency of the payments system requires that transactions costs be minimized and that payers use the least-cost method available. Float is an obstacle to efficiency. Efficiency also requires competitive pricing—which may be a problem because economies of scale and natural monopolies—and integration of the payments system.

- Another necessary condition for payments efficiency is stability of the value of money. This is threatened by inflation and by exchange rate volatility.

- Safety and stability of the payments system are essential to the continued functioning of the economy. Current concerns in this area focus on the safety of the wire transfer systems.

DISCUSSION QUESTIONS

1. What are Fed dollars and bank dollars? How do they differ? What are the different ways of making payment with each?

2. Is a traveler's check money? How is it like a bank deposit? How does it differ?

3. How does a giro payment differ from a check? Why are giro payments more popular in Europe and checks more popular in the United States?

4. Giro payments seem to be more popular in Canada than they are in the United States. Why is this so?

5. How does a Fedwire payment differ from one over CHIPS? What are the dangers associated with the two systems?

6. What is float? How does it affect the efficiency of the payments system? How does it affect the efficiency of the economy? How does it affect the profits of banks? What could be done to eliminate or to reduce it?

7. What are the special problems involved in making international payments? How are these problems addressed?

8. Is a prepaid card like a credit card? How does it differ? Does it resemble any other method of payment discussed in the chapter?

BIBLIOGRAPHY

Baxter, William F. "Bank Interchange of Transactional Paper: Legal and Economic Perspectives." *Journal of Law and Economics* 26 (October 1983):541–588.

Berger, Allen N., and David B. Humphrey. "Market Failure and Resource Use: Economic Incentives to Use Different Payment Instruments." Finance and Economics Discussion Series, no. 34, Division of Research and Statistics, Board of Governors of the Federal Reserve, July 1988.

Committee on Payment and Settlement Systems. *Statistics on Payment Systems in the Group of Ten Countries*. Basel: Bank for International Settlements, March 2001.

Emmons, W. R. "Recent Developments in Wholesale Payments Systems." *Federal Reserve Bank of St. Louis Review*, November–December 1997, 23–43.

Humphrey, D. B., S. Sato, et al. "The Evolution of Payments in Europe, Japan, and the United States: Lessons for Emerging Markets." Policy research working paper no. 1676, World Bank, October 1996.

Radecki, L. J. "Banks' Payment-Driven Revenues." *Federal Reserve Bank of New York Economic Policy Review*, July 1999, 53–66.

KEY TERMS

Fed dollars
definitive money
fiat money
legal tender
bank dollars
check guarantee card
certified check
money order
traveler's check
giro payment
store credit card
third-party credit card

four-party card
interchange
switch
secured credit card
delayed debit card
Fedwire
CHIPS
SWIFT
automated clearinghouse (ACH)
electronic debit card (cash card)
network externality
EFTPOS terminal

prepaid card
smart card
float
foreign exchange
Herstatt risk
seigniorage
real-time gross settlement system
   (RTGS)
daylight overdraft
systemic risk

CHAPTER 9

INSURANCE

When you finish this chapter you will understand:

- The nature of the insurance business
- Why life insurance companies are more involved in pensions than they are in life insurance
- Why property–liability insurance goes through boom–bust cycles
- How and why the government intervenes in insurance markets

In previous chapters, we have seen how the financial system facilitates lending and payments. In this chapter, we shall see how it facilitates one type of trade in risk—insurance.

A knowledge of insurance is important for a complete understanding of the financial system. We saw in Chapter 2 that the three functions of the financial system—the facilitation of lending, payments, and trade in risk—are closely related. All three address similar problems; all three involve similar technology. Moreover, the institutional boundaries that had separated insurance from banking in the United States have been breaking down since the repeal of Glass–Steagall in 1999. In many countries, there are no such boundaries: banks sell insurance and insurance companies engage in banking.

Insurance is of great importance to the economy. First of all, insurance increases individual welfare directly. It does this by increasing security. Without coverage against health costs, automobile accidents, loss of a home, or the death of a breadwinner, we would have to find other ways of protecting ourselves against these risks. These other methods would be more expensive and less effective. Our lives and livelihoods would be far less secure and far more anxious.

Insurance also increases the productive efficiency of the economy. To see why, consider the example of a drug company that is considering developing a vaccine. The project is a risky one. The process of development carries a high risk of technical and commercial failure. Moreover, if it succeeds, there is the additional risk of legal liability: even if the vaccine is highly effective, in a few cases it may cause sickness or even death. The resulting lawsuits could be very costly. If investors have to bear all these risks, they may find the project unattractive and the vaccine may never be developed. However, commercial insurance can help by relieving investors of the liability risk. This leaves them with only the technical and commercial risks that are properly theirs to evaluate and to bear. In this way, insurance can promote innovations that otherwise would not be made.

A measure of the importance of the insurance industry is its sheer size. In 1995, worldwide insurance premiums exceeded $2 trillion for the first time. In the developed countries total insurance premiums run between 5 and 12% of gross domestic product. The Swiss are the biggest purchasers of insurance at over $4,000 per head.[1] The United States is the next biggest spender at over $3,000 per head. In 1997, the insurance industry in the United States employed some 2.3 million people.

We begin the chapter with the basic economics of insurance—how insurance companies set premiums; how premiums generate investible funds; how policies are sold; the special risks and incentive problems involved in insurance. We then examine each of the three main categories of insurance—life insurance, property–liability insurance, and reinsurance; we also take a look at Lloyd's of London, a unique insurance exchange in a category of its own. For each category of insurance, we look at history and development, products offered, and current problems. We conclude the chapter with a look at public policy and regulation, with special attention to the problem of insuring against natural catastrophes.

THE ECONOMICS OF INSURANCE

In Chapter 2, we took a first look at the principles of insurance. We saw that a purchaser of insurance pays a fixed premium in exchange for a promise of compensation in the event of some specified economic loss—for example, a fire or theft. By pooling many such risks, insurance intermediaries convert the uncertainty of an individual loss into a predictable expense. We saw too that insurance suffers from incentive problems—specifically, moral hazard and adverse selection.

To understand the insurance industry, we need to deepen our understanding of these principles. We shall look at the determination of insurance premiums, the marketing of insurance, and at the special incentive problems.

Pricing of Premiums

For an insurance company, the proper pricing of premiums is a necessary condition for profitability. Set them too low, and you will make a loss. Set them too high, and no one will buy your policies.

---

[1] These numbers, from the Organization for Economic Cooperation and Development (OECD), are for 1997.

pure premium
The present value of the expected cost of a claim.

loss adjustment
The process of determining the amount of the loss.

Let us begin with the **pure premium**. This is the present value of the expected cost of a claim. The cost of the claim should include the amount of the loss plus the expected cost of processing the claim. When a claim is made, the insurer must determine the extent of the loss (this is called **loss adjustment**). If the circumstances are suspicious, an investigation may be necessary to verify the merit of the claim. If there is a dispute over the merit of the claim or over the extent of the loss, there may be legal expenses.

For example, suppose the loss is $95,000 and the related costs are $5,000, for a total cost of $100,000. Suppose the probability of loss of 1/1000. Then the expected cost is

$$0.001 \times \$100,000 = \$100$$

Since the loss will be incurred at some time after the premium is paid, we should take the present value of the expected loss. The interest rate we should use, the marginal value of funds to the insurer, should reflect the expected return on investment and a fair return on the insurer's capital (all adjusted for taxes). Suppose the appropriate interest rate is 10%. Then, if the average delay between receipt of premium and payment of claim is 6 months, the present value of the expected cost of the claim is

$$\frac{\$100}{(1.10)^{0.5}} = \$95.36$$

This is the pure premium.[2]

To price premiums accurately, the insurer needs to know the probability of a loss and the size of the claim. This is much easier for some types of insurance than it is for others. For example, with life insurance, the probability of a claim is actuarial. It is known with some reliability, and it is readily available. The amount of the loss is known too, because the policy pays a stipulated amount in the event of death.

Pricing premiums for liability insurance is much more difficult. With liability insurance, the insurer agrees to pay the cost of awards of legal liability against the insured. For example, a manufacturer will carry product liability insurance. This protects it in case it is sued by a purchaser of one of its products for damage caused by a defective product. In this case, the amount of the loss is uncertain: it depends on the generosity of a jury. The probability of loss is also much harder to calculate, because past experience provides little guide.

The *actual* premium charged is the pure premium plus administrative expenses. For reasons we shall see shortly, administrative expenses are much higher for insurance than they are for most other financial products. Total administrative expenses may amount to 25 to 35% of the actual premium—that is, they may add as much as 50% to the pure premium.

insurance reserves
Policyholders' funds that insurance companies are holding in anticipation of paying claims (insurance company liabilities).

Reserves and Premium Smoothing.   Since insurers pay claims after they receive the premiums, they have in the meantime an amount of investible funds. For example, if claims are paid on average 6 months after premiums are received, the insurer will have on average a fund equal in value to 6 months' premiums. This fund is known as **insurance reserves**.

---

[2] This method of calculating the pure premium is only an approximation. The precise calculation is considerably more complicated.

EXHIBIT 9.1   The Effects of Premium Smoothing

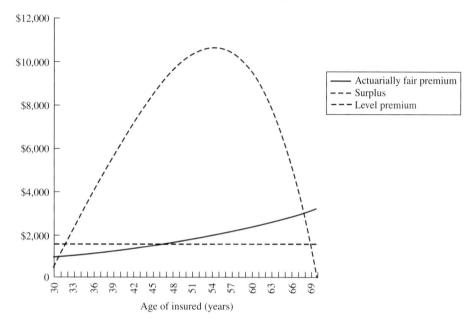

**premium
smoothing**

Charging a fixed
premium over
time when the
pure premium is
changing.

A practice known as **premium smoothing** can increase the size of reserves considerably. The pure premium for life insurance rises with age as the probability of death increases. Rather than paying rising premiums over time—an uncomfortable reminder of mortality—insurance companies offer the option of paying a level premium over a period of years. The amount of the level premium is higher than the actuarially fair premium initially but lower than the actuarially fair premium later on. The surplus at the beginning accumulates, with interest, and is used to cover the deficit at the end. A policy that smoothes premiums in this way obviously generates much larger reserves.

Exhibit 9.1 shows how premium smoothing works. The actuarially fair premium rises from $1,000 a year at age 30 to $3,262 at age 70. A level premium of $1,577 over the life of the policy has the same present value. The surplus rises to a maximum of $10,652 at age 55, then declines steadily to zero.[3]

Marketing

A large part of the administrative costs associated with insurance is the cost of marketing. Marketing involves selling the insurance, screening risks, and writing policies. Marketing costs alone may account for 15 to 20% of premiums.

---

[3] The numbers are fictitious. It is assumed that the actuarially fair premium rises at 3% a year. An interest rate of 5% is used to calculate the level premium and surplus.

Why are marketing costs so high? Insurance companies spend a lot on selling insurance because the effort really pays off. A bank need do no more than publicize its rates; it is hard to talk someone into making a larger deposit. But people tend to underinsure: they typically prefer not to think about unpleasant possibilities. A good salesman can persuade them to buy more coverage, and he will often be doing them a service. This means that it is worthwhile for an insurance company, but not for a bank, to hire lots of salesmen.

Writing an insurance policy is much more complicated than selling a security. The reason is that while selling a security does not expose the *seller* to risk, selling an insurance policy does. The risk (the probability of a claim) differs across potential purchasers. Therefore, to price premiums properly, the insurer must gather and process information about potential purchasers. In addition, it must be careful to weed out uneconomical risks: adverse selection is an ever-present problem.

In addition to these concerns, different customers need different coverage. While every CD or bond is the same, each insurance policy must be tailored to suit the needs of the customer.

Insurance is marketed in a number of ways.

independent agents
Insurance agents that represent several companies.

Independent agents each represent several insurance companies (six on average). There were some 44,000 independent agents in the United States in 1997; most were very small operations.

exclusive agents
Insurance agents that represent a single company

Exclusive agents represent only a single insurance company.

direct writing
The marketing of insurance directly by the insurance company over the telephone or by mail.

Direct writing is marketing insurance companies sometimes do for themselves, through the mail, over the telephone, or via the Internet. Direct writing is particularly important in automobile insurance.

Insurance brokers represent customers rather than insurance companies and find the best coverage for their clients. Insurance brokers are important in certain types of commercial insurance and in reinsurance (which we discuss later in the chapter).

Incentive Problems

insurance broker
Someone who represents the purchaser of insurance, rather than the seller (as does an agent).

There are three parties involved in insurance—the owners of insurance companies, their managers, and policyholders. Owners provide capital and bear risk in exchange for a residual claim on income. Managers set rates and are responsible for marketing, administration, and the investment of reserves. Policyholders pay a premium in exchange for coverage. Each party has its own interests, and its pursuit of those interests may adversely affect the others.

Owners may want managers to invest in risky assets. This would raise the expected return to the owners, but it would also reduce the security of policyholders and risk the jobs of managers. Managers may be lazy in performing their duties; to protect their jobs, they may be excessively cautious in investing reserves; and they may be overly generous in providing themselves with expensive perks.[4] As a result premiums will be higher and profits

---

[4] These problems are not specific to insurance, but rather to all manager-run large businesses. We shall discuss the situation more extensively in the general context in Chapter 15.

will be lower than they might have been. Moral hazard and adverse selection on the part of policyholders may impose losses on owners and threaten the jobs of managers.

There are two mechanisms that can create incentives that align the interests of the different parties in a reasonably efficient way. One is the insurance contract and the other is the organizational form adopted by the insurer.

The Insurance Contract.   As we saw in Chapter 2, the insurance contract may include deductibles or coinsurance to give the policyholder an incentive to exercise due care. It may also require specific actions on the part of the insured, like installing a smoke detector, that reduce the likelihood of a claim.

The Organizational Form of the Insurer.   Insurance companies may be organized either as corporations or as **mutual associations**. While most are corporations, a few large mutuals account for much of the business, particularly in life insurance.[5] A corporate insurance company is owned by its shareholders, who provider it with equity financing. The management is subject to the control of the shareholders, and it is expected to act in their interest. In contrast, a mutual insurance company is owned by its policyholders. Management is formally subject to their control, and it is expected to operate the company in their best interest.

mutual association

A financial institution that is owned by its customers rather than by providers of equity capital.

In practice, exercising control over management is a problem both for corporations and for mutual associations. While in the case of a corporation, there are ways to align the interests of managers with those of the owners, these are generally not available to a mutual association.[6] It should come as no surprise, then, that mutual associations are generally less efficient than corporations.

Mutuals, however, have certain advantages. Because policyholders are also owners, conflicts between owners and policyholders are minimized.[7] Because the managers of a mutual stand to lose much more if it does badly than they stand to gain if it does well, they tend to be conservative. As a result, the company is less likely to get into trouble and policies are therefore more secure. Policyholders need to be confident that if and when they make a claim, the company will be around to pay it. This is especially important for long-term policies, such as those in life insurance, where the exposure of the policyholder to risk is greatest.

Incentive Problems in Marketing.   The marketing structure of insurance is an additional source of incentive problems. Insurance companies that rely on independent agents compete for their business by paying them generous commissions. Commissions do

---

[5] There are two other forms of insurance organization in the United States. There are a few small *Lloyd's associations*, loosely modeled on Lloyd's of London (about which see more presently), and there are some 50 *reciprocals*, which account for some 7% of all premiums. These reciprocals lie somewhere between mutuals and the simple mutual-aid reciprocal insurance we encountered in Chapter 1.

[6] We shall discuss the problem of corporate control in Chapter 15.

[7] They are not eliminated entirely however. A policyholder–owner making an exaggerated claim stands to gain more as a policyholder than he loses as an owner. While the gain is all his, the loss is shared with the other owners.

not generally depend on the claim experience of an agent's customers, so the agent has every incentive to sign as much business as possible, however bad. And the agent has little incentive to vary premiums by risk if it means losing business. In addition to the incentive problem, independent agents usually have high costs. The reason is the typically small size of the business, which precludes economies of scale. Because of high commissions and high costs, premiums too tend to be high.

Why then is insurance marketed this way? Why are customers willing to pay the higher premiums? The advantage of independent agents is their independence. The agent "owns renewals": the client list belongs to the agent, not to the insurance company. If the service provided by one company is unsatisfactory, the agent can easily switch the client to another. Because they have this leverage, independent agents can assure policyholders of better service, especially the prompt payment of claims. This advantage seems to be particularly important for commercial insurance.

Exclusive agents receive a smaller commission than independents (there is no need to compete for their business), so their premiums are lower. There is less of an incentive problem: an agency that signs too much bad business stands to lose its franchise. However, the insurance company owns the client list, so the agent cannot monitor on behalf of the policyholder.

Direct writing has even lower cost, since it is done by salaried employees of the insurance company who receive no commission. Direct writing eliminates any conflict of interest in setting premiums. the one who sets the premium bears the risk. It therefore has a particular advantage where rate setting is important, as in automobile insurance.

With a grasp of the basic economics of the insurance business, we are now ready to look at the different types of insurance. We begin with life insurance.

LIFE INSURANCE

To understand the need for life insurance, think of yourself as an economic enterprise. You can anticipate a certain flow of earnings in the future. You can also anticipate a certain flow of expenditures. The length of these flows is uncertain because you do not know when you will die. This presents you with two types of risk: dying too soon and living too long.

If you die too soon, the flow of earnings will be cut off. While this will not be a concern for you personally, it will matter to others who depend on your earnings. These may include members of your family or business associates, who depend on your continued economic activity, and creditors—for example, the bank that has made you a mortgage loan.

Living too long can also be a problem. On retirement, your flow of earnings will end, while your flow of expenditures will continue. Naturally, you will prepare for your retirement by saving part of your earlier earnings. The problem is that you may outlive those savings.

Life insurance companies offer protection against these risks. Their basic products are life insurance proper, disability insurance, annuities, and health insurance. Life insurance pays off if you die, protecting those who depend on the continuation of your earnings. Disability insurance replaces part of your income if you are unable to work as a result of accident or illness. An annuity addresses the problem of living too long. In exchange for a fixed sum—all or part of your retirement savings—an annuity pays a stream of income for as long as you live. Health insurance covers the costs of medical expenses.

What these various types of insurance all have in common is that they rely on the statistics of mortality (death) and morbidity (illness). While it is hard to predict the death or illness of a specific individual, death rates and illness rates for large populations are fairly stable and predictable. By gathering mortality and morbidity statistics, insurance companies can calculate the probabilities they require in order to price premiums. By pooling a large number of independent risks, they can reduce the chance that claims will significantly exceed premiums.

In addition to insurance, the life insurance industry also offers a variety of savings products geared to life-cycle saving. This is a natural extension of their activity. To buy an annuity, you must accumulate savings. Why not package the two together? While short-term life insurance does not involve saving, long-term insurance with premium equalization does. As we have seen, early payments include an element of saving that is used to pay higher premiums later on.

The Evolution of Life Insurance in the United States

By the early nineteenth century, life insurance had become quite popular in Europe, but it remained insignificant in the United States. In 1841 there were only 1,211 policies in force in the whole country. Life insurance remained a minor part of trust business, mainly written to secure personal loans.[8]

The Mutuals.   Life insurance took off in the 1840s, with the establishment of the first mutual companies. The new mutuals, led by some outstanding entrepreneurs, were aggressive and innovative. They introduced mass marketing, established agent systems, and sent salesmen door to door. They also introduced a variety of new and attractive insurance products. These included whole life insurance in the 1840s (explained shortly), the endowment policy in the 1850s, and the tontine policy in the 1860s (see "Tontines and Related Products"). They copied from England, with great success, the "industrial policy." This was life insurance that was sold door to door with a policy face value of as little as $25. By the end of the century, Americans had more life insurance than all the people in the rest of the world put together.

Life insurance assets grew from $10 million in 1850 to $770 million in 1890. Initially, life insurance companies ("lifes") were tightly constrained in their investments. State regulations typically limited them to securities of specific types and only those issued within the state. In the 1870s and 1880s, these restrictions were gradually lifted, and the lifes became important lenders in the national market.[9]

Initially, lifes were particularly active in mortgage lending in the developing West, buying farm mortgages from brokers there. Towards the end of the century, as the market

---

[8] At this time, repayment of a personal loan often took the form of an annuity. The borrower promised to make a fixed payment yearly for the rest of his life. Life insurance protected the lender from the early death of the borrower and the ending of the stream of payments.

[9] British insurance companies, less restricted in their investments, were by this time already a major factor in British and world capital markets.

TONTINES AND
RELATED PRODUCTS

Louis XIV of France, desperate for a new method to raise money, accepted a suggestion from an Italian financier, Lorenzo Tonti, for a new type of government debt. Each member of a "tontine" would pay a fixed sum. The interest on all the payments would go into a pool that was divided equally among all members still alive. As members died, the payments to survivors increased. The story is told of a French woman who invested 300 livres in a tontine in her youth. By the time she reached the age of 96, all the other members of the tontine had died, and she received an annual payment of 73,500,000 livres.

The tontine proved popular and other governments took it up, including state and local governments in the United States. A tontine was used to fund the construction of the New York Stock Exchange in 1792.

Insurance companies adopted the idea in a variety of products. With the *pure endowment* (or *reverse annuity*), each person in a group made fixed payments into a pool for a set number of years. Those who survived split up the accumulated value; those who did not forfeited their share. With *endowment insurance* the pure endowment was combined with life insurance: if you survived, say to age 65, you were paid the face value of the policy (the endowment part). If you died before then, your beneficiaries were paid the face value (the insurance part).

Insurance companies also sold tontines. They were very popular in the late nineteenth century. A series of scandals related to the marketing and management of the tontines contributed to public pressure for an investigation of the insurance industry. This took place in 1905. One of the investigators' recommendations was that tontines be made illegal, which was done in 1906.

for corporate securities developed, they switched from mortgages to stocks and bonds. Industrials, however, were still considered too speculative. Insurance companies favored investment in railroads and, to a lesser extent, utilities.

Lifes and the Early Securities Market.   By 1900, the major lifes had become important players in the securities markets. They had close connections with the different alliances of securities firms and banks—such as those associated with J. P. Morgan and Kuhn, Loeb—that dominated the financial system at the time. These connections were mutually beneficial. The securities firms gained access to the substantial funds of the insurance companies; the insurance companies earned an excellent return.

This all came to an end with the Armstrong hearings of 1905. A struggle for control of Equitable, one of the largest New York lifes, generated considerable adverse publicity. This, and widespread abuses in the marketing of insurance led to demands for an investigation. A committee of New York State legislators was set up under state senator William

W. Armstrong. The committee recommended, among other things, that insurance companies be barred from underwriting securities. The recommendations became law in 1906. The close ties with Wall Street were severed.

As a result, the growth of the lifes slowed for a few years, but it soon resumed. The firms' investments became more conservative—more mortgages and municipals, fewer bonds, and very few stocks. By 1929, their assets had grown to $17.5 billion.

Lifes Since the Depression.   While they did have their share of troubles, lifes as a whole fared much better during the Depression than banks or S&Ls. Some small companies failed (for reasons we shall see presently). Mortgages proved a headache: life insurance companies became managers of farms and of real estate as a result of widespread foreclosures. Nonetheless, their assets continued to grow, reaching $29.2 billion by 1940.

Low interest rates during and after the Depression were a problem. As we have seen, lower interest rates mean higher premiums. And higher premiums mean lower sales. The lifes looked for higher yielding assets, investing more in industrial securities, which no longer looked much riskier than their traditional investments. They also began to invest in privately placed securities.[10]

The relative importance of lifes as financial intermediaries peaked in the early 1950s and has declined steadily since. Their share of all intermediary assets fell from a peak of over 21% in the early 1950s to less than 12% by the late 1980s. The lifes have declined in relative importance, because pension plans have displaced life insurance as the principal vehicle for life-cycle savings.[11] The lifes have made the best they can of this trend by expanding their offerings of pension-related products. Indeed, in recent years the lifes have derived a much larger fraction of their funds from annuities and other pension-related products than they have from life insurance itself.

Life Insurance Policies

term insurance
Pure life insurance that pays a fixed sum in the event of death.

Term and Whole Life Policies.   The simplest form of life insurance is **term insurance**. This is short-term coverage, typically for one year, that pays a fixed sum in the event of the insured's death.

Term insurance has some serious problems from the point of view of marketing. First, you would rather not think about and discuss your own mortality, so it is hard for a salesman to get in the door. Second, premiums are low when you are young and little concerned about dying and rise steeply as you grow older, when you are more likely to be interested in life insurance. Third, if you fail to die during the life of the policy, you receive nothing: the premium "is wasted."

whole life insurance
A policy with level premiums that combines saving with term insurance.

Lifes came up with a new type of policy that addressed all three of these problems—**whole life insurance**. This combines life insurance with a saving plan. The policy lasts for your "whole life," so it always pays off. You do not have the feeling of wasting your money by paying for something you do not get. The premium is fixed for the duration of the policy, and it is set so that the expected present value of the premiums equals the expected

---

[10] We shall have more to say about the role of lifes in the private placement market in Chapter 14.

[11] We shall look at the reasons for the growth of pension plans in Chapter 10.

present value of the death benefit. Because of premium smoothing, the policy accumulates a cash value in its early years, usually at a fixed rate of interest.[12]

As savings vehicles, whole life policies were initially highly illiquid. If you failed to keep up your payments and the policy lapsed, you forfeited the accumulated cash value. Competition and regulation soon changed this, so that if you terminated the policy, you were guaranteed a surrender value reasonably close to the accumulated cash value. While this was an improvement, you could still not get at your savings without giving up your insurance. The insurance companies came up with a solution—the **policy loan**, which allowed you to borrow an amount, up to the current cash value of the policy, at a pre-determined interest rate. The rate was set substantially above the accumulation rate of the policy to discourage frequent borrowing.

policy loan

A loan from a life insurance company secured by the cash value of a policy.

The Dangers of Policy Loans.   Of course, by providing their policyholders with increased liquidity, the insurance companies were creating a liquidity problem for themselves. As long as life insurance reserves are illiquid, they can be invested for the long term at a known return. This allows the insurance company to promise a fixed rate of return for the duration of the policy. If policyholders take out policy loans or surrender their policies only as a result of personal emergencies, and if such emergencies are uncorrelated across policyholders, then there is no particular problem. The amount of policy loans outstanding will be fairly stable over time because repayments will roughly balance new loans being taken out. The surrender rate, too, will be fairly stable and predictable. If, however, there is a surge in policy loans and surrenders, the insurance company will be forced to sell off some of its long-term assets. If the timing is bad, there is the potential for a serious capital loss.

There are two eventualities that might cause a surge in policy loans and surrenders. The first is a general "personal emergency" that affects many policyholders at once. The Great Depression was just such an emergency. As millions of Americans lost their jobs or found their businesses failing, they drew on the savings they had accumulated in their life insurance policies. Policy loans grew from a normal 3 to 4% of assets to 18%. Surrenders of policies were widespread. As a result, many small insurance companies failed and most took losses. In some states, regulators declared moratoria on policy loans and surrenders to protect the insurance companies.

The second eventuality that might cause a surge in policy loans and surrenders is a rise in market interest rates above the cost of policy loans. Suppose your whole life policy offers you a return of 3% and the rate on policy loans is 5%. Market rates climb to 20%. The savings element of your whole life policy now looks terrible. Why not cash it in, investing the surrender value at market rates, and replace it with a term policy? The idea was captured by the slogan "Buy term and invest the rest!" If you do not want to have to reapply for life insurance, you can take out a policy loan and invest it at market rates.

With each new peak in interest rates began in the 1960s, lifes experienced the same sort of "disintermediation" as afflicted banks and thrifts.[13] Like the thrifts, the lifes were

---

[12] We shall see presently that while whole life addressed successfully the marketing problems of term insurance, as a vehicle for savings, it did not provide policyholders with a very good return.

[13] See Chapter 6.

unable to counter by raising their own interest rates. The rates on policy loans had been guaranteed for the duration of the policy. In addition, most states set a ceiling of 5 or 6%. The steep rise in rates from 1979 to 1982 was the worst. Policy loans peaked at over 9% of life assets. However, while losses were substantial, they were nowhere near as bad as those of the thrifts.

New Life Insurance Products.   The lifes responded to the problems they were having with their traditional fixed-rate policies by offering a variety of new products that were "interest sensitive" or "investment oriented."

universal life insurance

A policy that pays if you die or, if not, at age 65. It allows flexible premiums and pays a market-sensitive return.

The most popular of these is **universal life**. This policy pays if you die or at a specified age, say 65, if you survive until then. The timing and the amount of the premiums are at your discretion.[14] Premiums are divided between a fixed part that covers the pure insurance and a flexible investment part that accumulates at a market rate of interest. Withdrawal of the cash value is relatively easy. Another new type of policy is **variable life**. With this policy, premiums are fixed and a minimum payoff is guaranteed. However, if investment experience is favorable, the payoff is increased. A third type, *variable universal*, combines the ideas of variable and universal: it offers a variable payoff and flexible premiums.

variable life

A policy with fixed premiums and a payoff that depends on the return of invested funds.

The Declining Importance of Life Insurance.   Despite these new products, life insurance has declined in importance as a vehicle of long-term savings. The main reason is the relatively low return that life insurance policies can offer. Because investment in stocks was limited by regulation, life insurance reserves were mostly invested in bonds. When the stock market revived in the 1950s, other savings vehicles that could invest in stocks—mutual funds and pension funds—seemed more attractive, and sales of whole life suffered.

In many other countries, life insurance has held its own much better than it has in the United States. In some countries—for example, in Germany and Japan—life assets are just as tightly regulated, but the absence of good alternatives has protected lifes from any loss of business. In Britain, on the other hand, there is plenty of competition, but lifes have much greater freedom to choose their assets. They have therefore held their own against other intermediaries.

Given the manifest problems of bundling life insurance and savings, why do consumers in the United States still continue to buy these combined products? Today's consumer presumably has the sophistication to see through the marketing "advantages" of whole life. The best explanation for the continued survival of these products is their tax advantage. If you invest in a mutual fund, you must pay tax on the income it earns; if you invest in a life insurance policy, taxes are deferred. This means that your savings accumulate at a higher rate of interest. Pension funds offer even greater tax advantages, but there are limits on the maximum amount that can be accumulated in a pension fund.[15]

---

[14] The IRS limits the accumulated cash value to an amount no greater than the value of the death benefit.

[15] We will discuss the relative tax advantages of different savings vehicles in greater detail in Chapter 10.

Retirement-Related Products

Alternative Savings Vehicles.   As we have seen, lifes responded to declining sales of life insurance by offering new types of policy with more attractive yields. They also responded by offering alternative savings products. They trained and licensed their salesmen to sell mutual funds. To begin with, these were funds managed by investment companies, but later the lifes set up their own mutual funds.

Savings Vehicles for Pension Funds.   As life insurance declined, pension funds grew. For reasons we shall examine in Chapter 10, employer-sponsored pension plans grew rapidly after World War II. Originally, most pension plans were administered by the sponsoring employer or by the trust department of a large bank. Lifes did compete for pension business by offering pension products of their own. However, they were at a severe disadvantage because of their inability to invest in stocks.

separate account
Life insurance assets dedicated to specific liabilities.

In 1959, this handicap was removed: lifes were allowed to offer plans backed by a **separate account**. The idea of a separate account is to dedicate specific assets to specific liabilities. This differs from the usual practice in which holders of all liabilities have essentially equal claim to all assets (the insurance company's "general account"). With the device of the separate account, lifes have been able to offer pension products invested in stocks, while continuing to offer life insurance policies invested mainly in bonds. This has allowed them to compete vigorously and successfully for their share of pension business.

single-premium deferred annuity (SPDA)
Savings vehicle offered by lifes that accumulates at a fixed rate of interest for a specified period.

Two retirement-related savings vehicles that have done particularly well are the SPDA and the GIC. The purchaser of a **single-premium deferred annuity (SPDA)** pays a single premium that accumulates at a fixed rate of interest for a specified period, usually 5 or 10 years. At maturity it may be cashed or converted into an annuity. SPDAs are sold to individuals, commonly as IRAs.

guaranteed investment contract (GIC)
Savings vehicle offered by lifes that allows flexible contributions over a period of years and guarantees a fixed rate of interest.

The **guaranteed investment contract (GIC)** guarantees savers a fixed rate of interest on any amount deposited over a given period of time (usually 10 years). GICs are sold to pension plans with flexible contributions, such as profit-sharing plans and voluntary contribution 401(k) plans. The failure of a number of major companies with large amounts of GICs outstanding has shaken public confidence in these instruments. In response, lifes have begun to offer "participating" or "separate account" GICs backed by specific assets, usually Treasuries or corporate bonds.[16]

life annuity
Standard annuity that pays a fixed payment for the life of the annuitant.

Annuities.   Life-cycle saving creates a need for two types of product. The first is a vehicle for accumulating long-term saving; the second is a way of converting the accumulated savings into a secure income after retirement. In addition to life insurance, which serves the first need, life insurance companies have long offered a product that serves the second need—the annuity.

The forces that moved life insurance away from a fixed rate of return have done the same for annuities. The traditional **life annuity** pays a fixed payment, based on a fixed rate

---

[16] We shall discuss IRAs and 401(k) plans in Chapter 10.

of return, for the life of the annuitant (beneficiary). Lifes have come up with a number of variations:

- The *variable annuity* pays a benefit whose amount depends on the performance of an investment portfolio.
- The *period-certain annuity* guarantees a minimum period of payment even if the annuitant dies.
- The *joint annuity* continues to make payments after the annuitant's death as long as the spouse survives.

Annuities are particularly susceptible to the problem of adverse selection. The rate of return on an annuity is based on average life expectancy. If you are in good health, with better than average life expectancy, the annuity looks like a great deal. You expect to collect the payments for a long time and the expected return will be high. However, if you are in poor health, with worse than average life expectancy, the reverse is the case, and the annuity looks like a poor deal. Consequently, people in good health will buy the annuity in larger than expected numbers and the insurance company will lose money. Examining the health of potential customers and adjusting the price of the annuity will not solve the problem entirely, because customers will always know more about their own health than the examination can reveal.[17]

A variation on the annuity that reduces the adverse selection problem is the *group annuity*. Group annuities are sold automatically to all members of a group— typically the group of all employees covered by a particular employer pension plan. Many pension plans, particularly those of relatively small companies, distribute benefits to retiring participants by purchasing an annuity from an insurance company. Since the purchase of the annuity is not voluntary, there is no problem of adverse selection.

Health Insurance

Blue Cross/ Blue Shield organizations Nonprofit institutions, sponsored by groups of hospitals, that provide medical insurance.

Medicare and Medicaid Government-sponsored medical insurance for the elderly and the poor, respectively.

Most large life insurance companies offer health insurance. Health insurance accounts for about a quarter of total premium income. However, because the lag between the receipt of premiums and the payment of claims is short, it accounts for only a few percent of reserves. Health insurance includes *medical*, which covers medical expenses, and *disability*, which covers loss of income due to disability.

In the provision of medical insurance, lifes compete with **Blue Cross/Blue Shield organizations**. These are nonprofit institutions sponsored by groups of hospitals. Most health insurance provided by insurance companies and by Blue Cross/Blue Shield is group insurance sold to companies that provide health care benefits to their employees. In addition to this private insurance, the government provides health insurance for the elderly and for those on welfare through **Medicare** and **Medicaid**, respectively.

In the 1980s, spiraling health care costs made medical insurance a losing proposition: premiums always seemed to lag behind costs. In response, the insurance companies changed the way that they paid for medical expenses in order to control costs. One method

---

[17] Recent research suggests that individual annuities may not be such a bad deal. See Mitchell et al. (1997).

managed care

Medical insurance that requires the insured to receive approval for non-emergency care.

health maintenance organization (HMO)

Medical insurance under which an insurer makes a fixed payment to a healthcare provider to provide care.

is **managed care**. This requires the insured to receive specific approval for nonemergency care. Another is the **health maintenance organization (HMO)**. In an HMO, the insurance company makes a fixed payment to the health provider to provide care. The risk is borne by the provider: if costs exceed the fixed payment, the provider takes the loss. If they are less, the provider pockets the difference. Obviously, this arrangement provides a strong incentive to keep costs down.

Life Insurance Assets and Liabilities

Exhibit 9.2 shows the financial assets and liabilities of the U.S. life insurance industry. On the liability side, there has been a radical change in the relative importance of life insurance and retirement-related products (these include annuities and supplemental contracts and separate account liabilities). In 1948, reserves against life insurance were over 10 times those against retirement-related products. By 1992, reserves against retirement-related products were more than double those against life insurance. In addition to competition for life-cycle savings, the nature of the life insurance reserves had changed. The lifes did not promise fixed rates for long periods of time, but instead offered market rates.

Changes on the asset side, naturally, have followed those on the liability side (we shall have more to say about how life insurance companies manage liquidity and risk in Chapter 18). There has been an increase in corporate stocks (including mutual fund shares) both in general accounts and as separate account assets. The share of mortgages grew through the 1960s, but it has since declined. Within the mortgage portfolio there have been changes too. There has been a shift from residential mortgages to higher yielding commercial mortgages (the ratio was 3 to 1 in favor of the latter by 1990, about the reverse of the situation in the 1960s). There has also been a shift to more liquid mortgage-backed securities (agency issues).

EXHIBIT 9.2   Financial Assets and Liabilities of Life Insurance Companies at Year End, 2000 (Billions of Dollars)

Financial Assets		Liabilities	
Cash	5	Life insurance reserves	783
Money market mutual fund shares	142	Pension fund reserves	1,374
Corporate equities	941	Miscellaneous liabilities	780
Mutual fund shares	51		
Treasury and municipal securities	80		
Government mortgage-backed security programs	235		
Corporate and foreign bonds	1,222		
Mortgages	236		
Policy loans	102		
Open market paper	71		
Other assets	120		
Total	3,204	Total	2,937

Source: Flow of Funds Accounts.

The large amount of long-term funds that life insurance companies have at their disposal has allowed them to play an important role in the capital market. We shall have more to say about this in Chapter 14.

PROPERTY–LIABILITY INSURANCE

The various types of insurance other than life and health are called collectively property–casualty or property–liability insurance.

The Evolution of Property–Liability Insurance

Property–liability insurance began with marine and fire insurance.

The Origins of Marine and Fire Insurance.   In the early days of international commerce, a merchant would set sail for some distant port with a cargo of goods to be traded there for foreign goods. The latter then had to be brought back and sold. This sort of trade involved business risks: the merchant might be inept or unlucky in his trading; prices might be unfavorable. It also involved nonbusiness risks: the ship might founder, or it might be lost to pirates. Typically, all the risks would be shared by financing the voyage through a partnership. Partners could diversify by investing in many different ships.[18]

The sharing of risk was improved by the introduction of marine insurance. The advantage of insurance is that it separates the nonbusiness risk and allows it to be borne more broadly and at lower cost. The nonbusiness risk of a voyage can be evaluated with little specific information about the particular enterprise: knowing the route and the type of ship is generally enough. Since less specific information is required, it is easier to broaden the circle of those willing to share the risk. The more the risk can be broken down and shared, the less it costs to bear it.[19]

From the mid-seventeenth century, insurance began to be traded in the major commercial centers of northern Europe—Amsterdam, London, Hamburg. Wealthy individuals would underwrite losses—that is, accept a premium in exchange for a promise to pay a specified sum if a ship were lost. Buyers and sellers of insurance would get together regularly at a particular coffeehouse. In London, Lloyd's coffeehouse soon emerged as the center of the market, and by the middle of the eighteenth century, London had eclipsed other centers to become the dominant international market for insurance.

Other forms of insurance also began to emerge at this time. The Great Fire of London of 1666 in which "London town was burnt to sticks," did much to advance the cause of fire insurance. The first fire insurance company was founded in 1680.

---

[18] Important cargo, such as precious metals, would be split among several ships. In terms of risk, there was a preference for small ships. When technology made larger ships possible, they became economically attractive only when better methods of risk sharing had been developed.

[19] The bearing of business risk was also improved at this time as partnerships were replaced by large joint-stock companies such as the Dutch and English East India Companies. These companies permitted a far broader ownership (meaning a smaller stake per investor) and improved liquidity (shares could be traded).

Property–Liability Insurance in the United States.   In the colonies, it was hard to satisfy the need for marine insurance from London because communications were so slow. So local merchants would share the risks of a voyage. Brokers organized the market, writing policies, setting premiums, and selling shares in the policy to a large circle of merchants. In 1757, a group of merchant underwriters formed a formal association—the first marine insurance company. In 1752 a group led by Benjamin Franklin formed the first fire insurance company. A mutual association, it offered a single-payment 7-year policy, and invested the premiums.

At the beginning of the nineteenth century, property insurance companies were the most important type of financial intermediary in the United States, their assets exceeding those of commercial banks. Although they grew steadily throughout the century they were soon eclipsed by the banks. By the 1860s, they were passed too by the exploding life insurance industry.

Periodic disasters have led to waves of insolvencies in the industry. A major fire in New York in 1835 wiped out most of the local fire insurers. The Chicago fire of 1871 was an insurance catastrophe. Of 202 companies with exposure, 68 failed, 83 settled only in part, and only 51 settled in full. Hartford, Connecticut, emerged as a major insurance center at this time because its companies had performed better than those of New York in meeting claims. The San Francisco earthquake and fire of 1906 wiped out many companies.

The technological innovations of the late nineteenth and early twentieth centuries gave property insurance a significant boost. The introduction of electricity was especially good for business: defective wiring caused many fires, stimulating the demand for fire coverage. The introduction of the automobile and of the motor truck created a new and rapidly growing market for casualty and liability insurance. Fire and marine companies quickly expanded into this area.

Property–liability companies suffered along with everyone else during the Depression. Losses on their investments sank many companies, and others were kept afloat only by creative accounting and government bailouts. With the slumping economy, premiums were down. Customers, hard pressed for cash, found it worthwhile to make claims they would not otherwise have bothered to file. For example, one person filed a claim for 50¢ with the Insurance Company of America to patch a pair of overalls damaged by a cigarette burn. The claim cost the company $12 to process.

The Property–Liability Business

The Nature of the Product.   Property–liability insurance today includes a wide range of products. Property–liability insurance is usually sold in a package to provide broad coverage to a given category of customer—for example, homeowner, car owner, or business. The types of policy are described in Exhibit 9.3. Each type of policy typically provides coverage against different types of risk—property damage, casualty loss, and liability. These too are described in Exhibit 9.3. Each type of policy represents some combination of the different types of coverage. For example, your automobile insurance, if it is a comprehensive policy, will compensate you if your car is stolen or destroyed; it will pay losses caused to you by an accident; and it will pay for any damage you may cause to others.

The Nature of the Business.   The property–liability business differs from life insurance in two important respects. The first is that investment issues are much less

EXHIBIT 9.3 Property–Liability Products

Type of Policy

Marine insurance	Covers all sorts of transportation risks.
Ocean marine	Covers ships and their cargoes.
Inland marine	Covers air, rail, truck, armored car, and mail shipment. Also property that is portable, such as construction equipment, personal jewelry, and furs, and "instrumentalities of transportation and commerce," such as bridges, tunnels, pipelines, and radio and TV communications equipment.
Homeowners	Covers the risks associated with home ownership.
Commercial property	Covers the risks associated with ownership of commercial property.
Family and commercial automobile	Covers the risks associated with owning and operating motor vehicles.
Workers' compensation	Covers accidents in the workplace and work-related illness.
Surety bonds	Guarantee against noncompletion of a contract. One party (called the surety) guarantees the obligation of another (the principal) to a third party (the obligee). A surety bond is normally required of anyone bidding on a construction or other contract: the bond protects against nonexecution by the maker of an accepted bid.
Fidelity bonds	Protect employers against embezzlement, forgery, and other theft by employees. Commonly purchased by financial institutions to cover employees who handle cash and marketable securities.
Mortgage insurance	Covers the loss to the lender if the sale of a foreclosed property does not cover the debt.
Deposit insurance	Before federal deposit insurance, insurance companies used to offer private deposit insurance; many took major losses during the great banking collapse of the early 1930s. More recently, some money market mutual funds have been insured by private insurers to help the funds compete with federally insured money market deposit accounts offered by banks.

Type of Coverage

Property	Covers damage or destruction due to specified causes such as fire, theft, negligence. Property coverage usually pays the cost of repair or replacement and may also cover indirect or consequential loss.
Casualty	Covers damage or destruction due to accidents (used to be distinct from property).
Liability	Covers legal liability for damages caused by the policyholder to a third party.
"All risk"	Covers all risks except those explicitly excluded.

important. This is because the life of the typical policy is far shorter—usually one year or less. Therefore, property–liability companies accumulate much smaller insurance reserves than lifes. Consequently they have much less to invest. In recent years, reserves have increased somewhat as the balance of the business has shifted more towards liability insurance, which has longer lags between premiums and claims.[20]

---

[20] There are two types of liability coverage. An "occurrence policy" covers all future claims relating to the period the policy is in force (say a year), even if the policy is not renewed. A "claims-made policy" covers only claims made while the policy is actually in force. For example, suppose an asbestos company bought liability coverage during 1975, and then only, from Gibraltar Insurance. In 1985, an employee who worked for the asbestos company in 1975 sues for health damage. Under an occurrence policy, Gibraltar will pay the claim; under a claims-made policy it will not. The lag between premium and claim on an occurrence policy can be quite long.

The second way that property–liability differs is that the risks involved in writing this type of insurance are much greater. One reason, as we saw earlier, is that the pricing of premiums is more difficult. Probabilities of loss are often not actuarial, and the size of the claim is often uncertain.

Another reason the risks are greater is that pooling is less effective. With life insurance, the risks associated with each policy are independent: pooling works well. With property–liability, there can be significant correlation among risks. A hurricane, an earthquake, a major fire—all of these can trigger thousands or even millions of simultaneous claims. As a result of the greater risk, earnings in property–liability are far more volatile than those in life insurance.

Underwriting Cycles.   In addition to the volatility due to imperfectly poolable risks, and perhaps related to it, industry earnings have historically gone though a regular cycle, known as the **underwriting cycle**.

underwriting cycle
Cycle in market conditions and profitability in the property–liability business.

The cycle typically begins with a period of high profits. These attract new capacity into the industry. As a result, competition pushes down premiums and coverage is readily available. This situation is called a "soft market." In a soft market, profits are low.

At some point, perhaps triggered by unusual losses caused by some natural disaster, there are widespread losses and insolvencies. As a result, the market becomes "hard": premiums rise and coverage is harder to find. In the hard market, profitability is restored. We are then ready to begin a new cycle.

The 1990s saw a soft market that seemed to go on and on, becoming progressively softer, as more and more capital entered the business. There was even some talk of the end of the underwriting cycle. However, there have recently been signs of a hardening of the market.

The Alternative Market.   Each successive "hard market" gave added impetus towards self-insurance, especially in the commercial market. Corporations, doctors, hospitals, and nonprofit institutions have increasingly insured themselves or entered into reciprocal insurance agreements through private insurance groups.[21]

captive insurers
Insurance subsidiary created to provide insurance services to the parent company.

Some large companies have created **captive insurers** (insurance subsidiaries), with their own reserves and assets, to provide them with coverage. There were over 4,000 such entities worldwide in 1998. There are advantages to setting up a captive rather than simply bearing the risk (self-insurance). A captive provides a tax benefit, since the premiums are a deductible expense. It also promotes better internal planning, since units of the company are required to "pay" for the risks they incur.

alternative market
The coverage of property–liability risk through private arrangements that do not involve insurance companies.

In 1994 this **alternative market** accounted for about a third of the $177 billion that U.S. companies spent on insurance. The alternative market doubled in size between 1986 and 1992, while the amount of conventional insurance increased by only 20%. Since then, growth has slowed considerably. The reason is the prolonged soft market and the consequently low rates on conventional insurance.

---

[21] Often they will bear the initial risk themselves; reinsuring against large losses. We saw earlier that this is increasingly the practice, too, with health insurance. See discussion on reinsurance.

Property–Liability Insurance Today

Exhibit 9.4 shows the financial assets of the property–liability insurance companies. Like those of the lifes, the assets of the property–liability companies consist mainly of long-term securities. There are some differences however. Because there are no regulatory obstacles, property–liability companies hold more stocks (although the share of stocks has been shrinking). Because their investment income is subject to federal income tax—lifes' is not—property–liability companies hold a high proportion of municipal and other tax-free bonds; the proportion has varied over the years in response to changes in the tax laws. Because their earnings are so volatile, they require their portfolio to be more liquid. Hence, they prefer marketable securities and avoid private placements, commercial mortgages, and real estate—all categories favored by the lifes.

Another result of the volatile earnings of property–liability companies is a much higher capital ratio. In 1992, theirs was 26%, as opposed to about 8% for lifes. We shall have more to say about how property–liability companies manage liquidity and risk in Chapter 18.

REINSURANCE

The Function of Reinsurance

Despite pooling, insurance companies are left with some residual risk from the policies they write. Total losses fluctuate, and in a bad year they may exceed premiums. In that case, it is the equity capital of the insurance company that must bear the loss. For life insurance, this residual risk is small; for property–liability insurance, it is substantial. The main sources of this risk are liability insurance and natural catastrophes. In both cases, insurance companies can be faced with enormous losses.

EXHIBIT 9.4   Financial Assets and Liabilities of Property–Liability Insurance Companies at Year End, 2000 (Billions of Dollars)

Financial Assets		Liabilities	
Cash	4	Total liabilities	566
Repos	38		
Corporate equities	194		
Treasury securities	52		
Municipal securities	184		
Government mortgage-backed security programs	84		
Corporate and foreign bonds	188		
Commercial mortgages	2		
Trade credit	65		
Other assets	61		
Total	872		

Source: Flow of Funds Accounts.

reinsurance
Insurance purchased by an insurance company to cover part of its exposure on policies it has written.

Rather than bearing all the residual risk themselves, insurance companies can protect themselves by themselves buying insurance. This insurance for insurance companies is called **reinsurance**. Reinsurance, like normal insurance, is based on pooling. A reinsurer diversifies by writing many unrelated policies. Ideally, the potential loss from each is small relative to the reinsurer's capital. And reinsurers sometimes purchase reinsurance themselves (this is called *retrocession*) or have reciprocal loss-sharing agreements with other reinsurers.

About 10% of all insurance worldwide is reinsured—less in the United States and Japan, more in Europe. Naturally, small insurance companies reinsure more than large ones. As we would expect, because of the greater risks, property–liability insurance accounts for a majority of the business—nearly 90%. Worldwide premiums in 1998 came to $115 billion. Some 35% of the demand came from western Europe, 40% from North America, and only 5% from Japan.

The reinsurance market—a wholesale insurance market for insurance companies—has many parallels with the interbank market—a wholesale market in which banks borrow and lend to one another. Interbank interest rates represent the marginal cost of funds for banks and so have a strong influence on the interest rates banks charge on loans. Similarly, reinsurance rates represent the marginal cost of risk for insurance companies and so have a strong influence on the premiums insurance companies charge. The interbank market increases the vulnerability of the banking system to a "chain reaction," in which the failure of one bank could bring down others. Similarly, the failure of a reinsurer could threaten the solvency of many insurance companies.

The Reinsurance Treaty

In exchange for a premium, the reinsurer shares the loss with the primary insurer.[22] There are two basic forms of loss-sharing agreement or *treaty*. Under a *pro rata* treaty, insurer and reinsurer share premiums and losses for a particular line of insurance according to an agreed percentage. Under an *excess-of-loss* treaty, the insurer bears the loss up to an agreed ceiling and the reinsurer bears losses beyond that level. In this case, the reinsurance premium is not proportional but is based on the risk of large losses.

In both types of treaty, the insurer remains exposed to part of the loss. (The arrangement involves copayment in the first case and a deductible in the second.) Consequently, the reinsurer does not face a major moral hazard problem. This means that the reinsurer does not need a great deal of specific information about the insurer and its policies and does not need to monitor the insurer's behavior.

The Reinsurance Industry

Since little specific information or monitoring is necessary, reinsurance is something of a standard commodity. Anyone with the capital can hire an experienced underwriter and enter the business. As a result, reinsurance is highly competitive and very international.

---

[22] There are two types of contract. Under a "quota share," the reinsurer receives a proportion of the premiums, net of expenses, and pays the same proportion of the claims. Under "excess of loss," the reinsurer sets a premium, in exchange for which it covers all claims above a certain amount.

Reinsurance is provided by companies and organizations of various types. Some large insurance companies that do ordinary insurance business also engage in reinsurance. The world's two largest reinsurers are European insurance companies—Munich Re and Swiss Re. There are many specialized reinsurers: the largest reinsurer in the United States is such a company—Berkshire Hathaway Re. There are also pools or syndicates formed by groups of insurers to provide reinsurance on a reciprocal basis—for example, the Workers' Compensation Reinsurance Bureau and the Mutual Atomic Energy Liability Underwriters. In some countries, government-owned companies reinsure catastrophe risk. And there is Lloyd's of London, about which we shall have more to say presently.

While, in principle, entry into the reinsurance market is easy, there is one obstacle: the credibility of the coverage. Reinsurance is generally based on "good faith"—that is, on the reputation of the reinsurer. The contract is typically short and simple, and disputes are normally settled by industry arbitration panels rather than through litigation. There is relatively little regulation.[23] Defaults by reinsurers are not uncommon. For example, in 1990, U.S. insurance companies were owed some $20 billion in unrecoverable reinsurance. Because of the importance of credibility, large reinsurers with reputations to protect have an advantage. As a result, the 4 largest firms control about a third of the market and the 20 largest perhaps two-thirds.

There was a big increase in the capacity of the industry during the 1990s. Major catastrophe losses, especially in 1992, both increased demand and temporarily reduced supply driving up rates. Higher rates and profits attracted entry. In 1998, the total capital of the industry was about $200 billion.

London used to be the center of the reinsurance industry, with almost half the business in the 1980s. However its share had declined to 22% by 1998 as Bermuda became a major center with some 29% of the market. Continental Europe accounted for 19%, the United States for 30%.

LLOYD'S OF LONDON

An interesting part of the reinsurance market is *Lloyd's of London*. Lloyd's is not an insurance company, but an exchange. Risks are traded there much as stocks are traded on the London or New York stock exchanges.

The History of Lloyd's

Lloyd's is the direct descendant of Lloyd's Coffeehouse, the center of the London insurance business in its early days. In its heyday in the nineteenth century, Lloyd's accounted for half the world's nonlife insurance. It had two big advantages. The first was rapid access to information: London was the center of the world. The second was its flexibility in using this information. Lloyd's dealt in types of insurance for which the proper pricing of premiums was both difficult and essential. Its organization allowed it to adjust premiums rap-

---

[23] Reinsurers located in the United States must meet state requirements just like any other insurance company. However, much of the business is international.

idly to reflect new information on the probability of loss. Modern communications and technology have eroded these advantages, and Lloyd's share of the business has correspondingly shrunk.

Today its annual premium income is about $9 billion, comparable to that of a large insurance company. In addition to its importance in reinsurance, the source of half its income, it still handles about 25% of the world's marine insurance (its traditional specialty). Lloyd's is also unique in covering large one-of-a-kind risks—for example, the loss of a communications satellite on launch.[24]

How Lloyd's Works

Risks are brought to the floor of the exchange by independent brokers. On the floor, the risks are accepted by one or more underwriters. The premium is determined by negotiation and by competition.[25]

names
Individuals who offer to provide insurance through Lloyd's of London.

Underwriters are employed by agencies that represent the 120 or so active syndicates. Traditionally, each syndicate, which is formed for one year at a time, was made up of dozens of wealthy individuals. These individuals, known as **names**, were the ones who ultimately bore the risk. Their liability was unlimited: that is, the whole of their personal wealth stood behind their promise to pay a loss. If the loss was large enough, they could be ruined. A name's declared net worth determined the amount of premium income that could be accepted on his behalf.

Members of a syndicate are required to deposit with the exchange collateral equal to 30% of the premiums they plan to accept. Any claim that a member cannot or will not pay is paid out of a central fund managed by the exchange.

Lloyd's Current Problems

Lloyd's enjoyed something of a boom in the 1980s, stimulated by a run of good years and by tax advantages.[26] The number of names peaked in 1988 at some 33,000. Losses for 1989–1992 totaled over $13 billion, ruining some 1,500 names.[27]

The losses were partly the result of a string of disasters. They were also partly the result of the liability explosion in the United States, the source of over a third of Lloyd's business. The losses also reflected the normal underwriting cycle: good years attract new names; competition bids down premiums; losses ensue; names leave; rates and profits revive.

In addition to some spectacular losses, Lloyd's was plagued by a series of scandals. Underlying these scandals were some serious incentive problems in its structure.

---

[24] As we saw in Chapter 2, this type of *external* insurance rests on different principles from the standard one of pooling of risks.

[25] Because Lloyd's has no need to market its services, its administrative costs are much lower than those of insurance companies. Costs used to be as little as 4% of premiums (as opposed to 30–35% for insurance companies), but they have risen recently to 14%.

[26] Marginal tax rates were as high as 98%. This meant that most of the risk was borne by the government. Since any loss is deductible, a £1 million loss would have cost the name only £20,000 after tax.

[27] Because claims take time to come in and to be processed, the book on a given year's business is not closed until 3 years later. Rather than waiting to find out the final result, a name can end his liability by buying "reinsurance to close"—paying someone else to take on his future liabilities arising from that year's business.

Underwriters are paid a commission on the premiums they write, but they do not themselves bear the risk. Consequently they have an incentive to set premiums low and to sign as much business as possible.

Monitoring underwriters was also a problem. Underwriters are in a position to discriminate in favor of syndicates of "insiders." They can send the best risks their way, leaving the worst risks for the anonymous mass. There were also some cases of outright fraud by underwriters and by policyholders. As a result, many names chose to sue rather than to pay.

As a result of these problems, membership declined and there was increasing pressure for reform, which came eventually in 1996. For the first time in its history, corporations (with limited liability) as well as individuals were allowed to become members of syndicates. Individual names too have been allowed to opt for limited liability. By 2000, corporations were providing three-quarters of the capital. U.S. companies, including Berkshire Hathaway, are prominent among them.

The companies that have entered Lloyd's have addressed the incentive problems by taking over the underwriters. The typical structure now is an integrated holding company that combines the provision of capital (traditionally done by the names) with the underwriting of risks, all under one management.

Things seemed to be going well in the late 1990s, with a series of profitable years, but losses have returned since 1998. With the losses has come a wave of new lawsuits from disgruntled names.

THE INSURANCE INDUSTRY

The insurance industry throughout the world has recently seen a large number of mergers and acquisitions. As in banking, this process of consolidation has been driven both by the underlying economics and by increasing competitive pressure.

The Economics of the Insurance Business

Economies of Scale.   In insurance, as in banking, there are significant economies of scale.[28] The financial economies of scale in property–liability insurance and reinsurance derive mainly from the pooling of risks—the larger and the better diversified a pool, the better it works. In terms of diversification, the more extensive the market from which risks are drawn, the better. Since property risks are often correlated geographically, geographical restrictions on insurance are harmful: for example, most fire insurance companies on the West Coast were wiped out by the San Francisco earthquake and fire of 1906.

For life insurance, the financial economies come on the asset side rather than on the liability side as in property–liability. The larger the portfolio of assets, the better diversified a life can be and the larger the individual investments.

Because of these financial economies of scale, a large insurance company doing business over a wide geographic area will be inherently safer than a small, local company. That means that the larger firm will require a lower equity ratio and therefore, that its return on equity will be higher.

---

[28] See Chapters 5 and 7 on economies of scale in banking.

In insurance, as in banking, many of the fixed costs are indivisible. This is true both of specialized personnel, such as actuaries, underwriters and investment managers, and of information technology (of growing importance, as it is in banking). A large insurance company will need to spend proportionally less on these budget items than a small company, giving the former a competitive advantage.

Reputational economies of scale are particularly important in insurance. An insurance policy represents a promise. The value of the policy to the insured therefore depends on his or her confidence that the promise will be kept. A large, long-established, and well-known insurer is more likely to inspire such confidence than a new, small company that no one has ever heard of.

Barriers to Entry.   Apart from reputational economies, there are other barriers facing a new company entering the market for insurance. Information is one. As we have seen, the key to making a profit is pricing premiums correctly. To do this, one needs to know the probability of loss. The ready availability of actuarial information eases entry into life insurance. The *Insurance Service Office (ISO)* was set up by property–liability companies in the United States to pool risk information. The availability of this information makes entry by new companies easier.

Although new entrants have access to the same information, they still face a barrier that is known as the "aging effect." New policyholders are on average worse risks than long-standing ones. The reason is that the worst risks are weeded out over time. For a new company, all its policyholders are new, so it will face worse-than-average claims experience until its customer base matures. New entrants must have the capital to survive these initial losses.

Marketing is also a potential barrier to entry. We have seen that marketing is extremely important in insurance. If any new entrant had to set up its own marketing network, the cost would be prohibitive. Independent agents are a help here, providing access to the market for new entrants. Entry is also easier in the reinsurance market where marketing is not a factor.

Economies of Scope.   Economies of scope draw insurance companies into related activities and draw other financial institutions into insurance.

Life Insurance and Property–Liability.   One obvious economy of scope is between the two types of insurance—life and property–liability. Although the two businesses are different in important respects, there are many similarities. Most major life insurance companies do some property–liability business and vice versa. Generally, a separate subsidiary or affiliate is set up to handle the other type of business, often under the umbrella of a holding company. Some large lifes actually started out as the life insurance subsidiaries of property–liability companies. While there are no barriers in the United States to combining the two types of insurance, in some countries the two types of business are separated by law and companies may not engage in both.

Insurance and Other Financial Services.   As we have seen, life insurance companies are already deeply involved in financial intermediation and in the financial markets. They have tried to build on their knowledge and expertise in these areas in a number of ways. Many large lifes have securities subsidiaries that offer full-service brokerage; some half-dozen even underwrite new securities. Having a securities subsidiary helps an insurance company handle products such as variable annuities and mutual funds that require registration with the SEC.[29]

In addition to investment banking, lifes are engaged in a wide variety of financial activities. These include investment management for others (especially for pension funds), pension plan management, mortgage banking, leasing, advice to real estate investment trusts,[30] writing and trading options, financial data processing, and credit cards. Typically, these operations build on services the company has already developed to meet its own needs.

Insurance and Banking. The economies of scope between banking and insurance seem to lie principally in marketing. As we have seen, marketing costs are a significant part of the cost of insurance. A bank's branch network is well suited to the distribution of insurance, and its list of depositors is a valuable source of potential customers. Conversely, an insurance salesman benefits from being able to offer CDs and money market accounts in addition to insurance products.

Despite the economies of scope, some countries restrict or prohibit links between banks and insurance companies. Britain, France, and Germany have long allowed close links between banks and insurance companies: the French call this **bancassurance**; the Germans call it **Allfinanz**. As the European insurance market has become more integrated, bancassurance has spread to other European countries. In the United States, as we saw in Chapter 6, the Gramm–Leach–Bliley Act of 1999 removed the long-standing barriers between banking and insurance.

bancassurance (Allfinanz)

The combination of banking and insurance.

The Structure of the Insurance Industry

The structure of the insurance industry is fairly similar across countries, as you can see from Exhibit 9.5. Although each country has many insurance companies, both in life and in property–liability, each industry is highly concentrated. The largest 5 companies of each type account for from a quarter to over half of the business, and the largest 15 from nearly a half to over nine-tenths. Reinsurance, too, is quite concentrated: in 1998, the 10 largest reinsurers accounted for over half the premiums.

The structure of insurance in the United States is more like that in other countries than is the structure of banking. Unlike banking, insurance in the United States faced no barriers to interstate expansion. The market is consequently well integrated, and its size has enabled many insurance companies to grow quite large.

The Pressure of Increasing Competition. Concentration in the insurance industry has steadily increased in recent years as the industry has undergone substantial consolidation—both within national markets and internationally. The largest companies in Europe have acquired insurance companies in other European countries and in the United States. U.S. and European companies have acquired insurance companies in Japan. All have shown considerable interest, too, in expanding into developing and transition economies.

---

[29] Many lifes that do not have securities subsidiaries still manage mutual funds.

[30] We shall discuss REITs in Chapter 10.

EXHIBIT 9.5   Insurance Industry Structure in Some Major Economies, 1998

	U.S.	Japan	Germany	U.K.	France
Life insurance					
Number of companies	1,109	46	318	176	135
Share of largest 5	25%	54%	30%	39%	56%
Share of largest 15	52%	83%	56%	73%	90%
Property–liability					
Number of companies	2,499	65	328	599	307
Share of largest 5	30%	54%	23%	68%	56%
Share of largest 15	52%	92%	41%	83%	85%

Source: Bank for International Settlements.

The driving force of this process of consolidation is a significant increase in competitive pressure. Of course, the underlying economies of scale and scope imply that larger, more integrated insurers will have an advantage in terms of costs and profits. However, unless competition actually threatens their profitability, insurance companies—like companies in any other industry—may prefer to take it easy rather than to make the effort necessary to achieve these economies. Under the pressure of competition, efficient companies grow larger and inefficient ones become unprofitable. As their losses mount and as their equity shrinks, they have little choice but to merge or to be taken over by their more successful competitors.

The Liberalization of Insurance Markets.   The increasing competitive pressure has largely been the result of the opening of insurance markets to foreign companies and of domestic deregulation. Various international agreements have opened national insurance markets. The European Union, under its "single market" policy, has since 1994 allowed the insurance companies of member countries to sell insurance anywhere in the EU. The section of the General Agreement on Trade in Services (GATS) which deals with financial services was completed in December 1997, and it requires countries to open their insurance markets. As a result, and under pressure from the United States, Japan has slowly opened what had been one of the most protected markets for insurance. In North America, NAFTA has removed barriers to trade in insurance.

The various international agreements generally require governments to end rate regulation and to allow rates to be determined in the market. There is little point to allowing foreign companies in to compete if they are prevented from offering better rates to attract business.

Demutualization.   Increasing competition and the frenzy of mergers and acquisitions has pushed many mutual insurers to become corporations (to **demutualize**). As corporations, they can issue new shares to replenish depleted equity capital, something that mutuals cannot do. And it is much easier for corporations to participate in mergers and acquisitions.

The advantages of mutual organization—mainly greater safety—seem to be less important today than they were in the past. This is partly because insurance companies today

demutualization
The conversion of a mutual financial institution into a joint-stock corporation.

are inherently more stable than they were in the nineteenth and early twentieth centuries. And it is partly because guarantee schemes protect policyholders if their insurance company fails (more on this presently).

Pressure to Reduce Marketing Costs.   As we have seen, marketing costs are high in insurance. For example, over half the first year's premiums on a new life insurance policy goes to commissions and other administrative costs. Increasing competition in the industry has caused insurers to seek ways to cut these costs. One consequence has been pressure on the agent system.[31] Another consequence has been increasing interest in the Internet as a channel of direct marketing.

PUBLIC POLICY AND REGULATION

Because of its importance to the economy and to individual welfare, society has a particularly strong interest in insurance.

The Regulatory Framework

In the United States, insurance is regulated at the state level: the federal government has no role. The **McCarran–Ferguson Act of 1945** explicitly exempted insurance from federal regulation, including federal antitrust regulation.

An insurance company is regulated primarily by the state in which it is chartered, but it must also comply with the regulations of other states in which it wishes to sell insurance. For example, New York State requires that out-of-state companies "comply in substance" with its investment standards for New York insurance companies. Since New York is such an important market, this means that the New York investment standards are effectively national standards.

Insurance agents and brokers, too, must obtain a state license. Most states have an insurance commissioner responsible for regulating and policing insurance.

National Association of Insurance Commissioners (NAIC) Organization of state insurance commissioners that coordinates regulation and pools information.

Regulation differs considerably from state to state. The **National Association of Insurance Commissioners (NAIC)** was founded in 1871 to coordinate regulation and to make it more uniform. NAIC also conducts research and lobbies in Washington. The *Insurance Regulatory Information System (IRIS)* was developed by a group of state insurance commissioners to provide support for regulators. It gathers and evaluates financial statements of insurance companies and draws up model legislation.

Consumer Protection

The problem of asymmetric information is particularly acute with insurance. Even more than with other financial products, there is a feeling that purchasers of insurance need protection:

---

[31] This parallels in many ways the pressure on other agent marketing systems. For example, retail brokers have been losing business to discount brokers, and travel agents have been under pressure from airlines to reduce their commissions.

"The regulatory system must anticipate and deal effectively with the activities of the pirates and dolts who inevitably will plague an attractive industry such as insurance, where customers hand over large sums of cash in return for a promise of future benefits."[32]

An insurance policy represents a promise. It is sometimes hard for purchasers to understand the exact nature of the promise. What exactly does the policy cover? Regulation can easily help by requiring disclosure and by encouraging the standardization and simplification of language.

Moreover, the promise may not be kept. The reliability of the promise depends on the financial strength of the insurer. Financial strength has several aspects. The first is how the insurer invests premiums. The safer the investments, the less likely it is that financial losses will impair its ability to meet claims. The second is the nature of the insurance pool. The larger and better diversified it is, the less likely are claims to exceed premiums. The third aspect is capital. If claims do exceed premiums, the insurer will bear the loss to the extent of its capital. The greater its capital, the less likely a default.

It is difficult for an individual purchaser of insurance to assess the financial strength of the insurer. Understanding the balance sheet of an insurance company requires specialized knowledge. "Bargain" premiums are sometimes offered by insurers with little capacity to meet claims and, in some cases, little intention of doing so. Such bargain premiums may tempt people into buying worthless insurance.

Because reliability is so important, we would expect the market to provide purchasers with the relevant information. And indeed it does. In the United States, A. M. Best, Moody's, and Standard & Poor's all publish ratings that evaluate the performance and financial strength of insurance companies. These ratings are widely used by insurance agents and by policyholders.

Rate Regulation and Availability

Compared to the prices of other financial services, there is an unusual amount of government intervention in the setting of insurance premiums. Property–liability premiums are often regulated directly. Life insurance premiums are regulated indirectly through the setting of standards for reserves, investments, and surplus (capital). These standards establish a minimum cost for life insurance.

Political Pressure to Lower Premiums.   There has been rising public dissatisfaction with the cost of property–liability insurance. In California, in particular, insurance has become a major political issue. Proposition 103, passed in California in 1989, required a 20% rollback in premiums (and a refund for previous years).

Most of the evidence suggests that insurance is a fairly competitive industry and that rising premiums have been the result of rising costs rather than of monopolistic behavior.[33] If prices are already competitive, then laws like Proposition 103 that lower premiums

---

[32] Representative John. D. Dingell, quoted in Kopcke and Randall, eds. (1991).

[33] Some existing regulations restrict competition. For example, many states prohibit agents from rebating part of their commission to customers. Presumably, the purpose is to protect agents' profits: insurance agents are generous campaign contributors.

below cost can only drive insurers out of business or, at least, out of the state. Some companies indeed withdrew from the California market in the wake of Proposition 103.[34]

The Role of Legal Costs.   Much of the recent increase in rates has been the result of increased legal costs. In some cases, these costs have been so high and so unpredictable that insurance markets have broken down completely. In the mid-1980s, rising court awards led to a crisis in liability insurance. Coverage became unavailable, first for medical malpractice, then for pollution risks, day-care centers, asbestos removal, commercial fishing boats, municipalities, and commercial trucking.

no-fault insurance

An arrangement under which each insurance company pay the losses of its own policyholders irrespective of who is at fault.

Government can help by lowering these legal costs. In many states, tort reform has helped to reestablish markets for some types of liability insurance. **No-fault insurance**, particularly for automobile insurance, eliminates legal costs entirely. Under no-fault, each insurance company pay the losses of its own policyholders irrespective of who is at fault. On average, each insurance company still pays the same number of claims, but litigation costs are avoided and transactions costs are reduced. No-fault insurance is not popular with lawyers.

Availability.   More than most other financial institutions, insurance companies are seen as having a social obligation to make their products available to those who need them. Some types of insurance—health, automobile, homeowners—are so essential to normal living that they are sometimes seen as a "right."

This is particularly true in the United States, since insurance bears a particularly large burden as part of the social "safety net." In many other countries, the government provides most health and retirement insurance directly. In the United States, private insurance provides a large part of these services. So there is an argument that the government should intervene to assure that the "safety net" is available to all.

"Discrimination" in the Setting of Premiums.   To deal with the problems of adverse selection and moral hazard, insurers are sometimes obliged to refuse insurance to certain categories of customer or to limit the types of loss covered. Such practices are often regarded by the public as unfair discrimination, violating the "right" to insurance.

Most states have arrangements for "residual market mechanisms" to provide coverage for those otherwise unable to obtain it (especially for automobile, homeowner's, workers' compensation, and medical malpractice). These arrangements involve reinsurance facilities and assigned-risk plans, usually administered and partially financed by insurers.

In some cases governments have intervened to require insurers to provide insurance. One example is the prohibition of "redlining"—the refusal of insurers to write homeowners' insurance in certain areas. Also, there are regulations requiring health insurers to cover certain categories of medical treatment—cosmetic surgery, some types of psychiatric care—that they would otherwise have excluded. Such regulations have often been the result of successful lobbying by the providers of these categories of treatment.

---

[34] The California Supreme Court took much of the sting out of Proposition 103 when it ruled that insurers were entitled to a "reasonable profit"—interpreted as an ROE of 10 to 15%.

Safety Regulation

The safety of insurance companies is of even greater concern than the safety of other financial institutions. The consequences of default by an insurance company can be particularly severe. For example, if you buy a $10,000 bond and the issuer fails, you stand to lose $10,000 plus the interest. If you insure your $200,000 house, paying a $1,000 premium, and the insurer fails, the *expected value* of your loss is just the amount of the premium—$1,000. However, if your house has just burned down, you stand to lose the $200,000 value of your house. The justification for some public action to promote safety is, therefore, particularly strong in the case of insurance.

Financial Standards.   States set minimum financial standards for granting and continuing a license, and they conduct periodic audits to assure compliance. An insurance company that fails to meet the required standards may be closed down.[35]

The financial standards covers both sides of the balance sheet. They specify the assumptions and procedures that must be used in calculating liabilities to policyholders (insurance reserves). They restricts how the assets covering those liabilities may be invested. Restrictions include limits on

- *Type of assets.* For many years common stock was out of bounds for life insurance companies.
- *Proportions of different types of asset in the portfolio.* There have been limits on stocks, real estate, and foreign bonds, and limits on the amount of lending to any one borrower.
- *Quality of a given type of asset.* Some states have recently prohibited investment in junk bonds.

There are also minimum requirements for the level of capital.[36]

Guaranty Funds.   To protect policyholders in the event that an insurance company does

insurance guaranty funds

Funds established by the states, and financed by insurance companies, to guarantee insurance policies.

fail, most states have **insurance guaranty funds**. The funds date back to the 1960s, when a series of failures of automobile insurers led to demands for federal intervention. The industry established the guaranty funds in the hope of forestalling this. By the late 1970s, most states had guaranty funds for property insurance; funds for life insurance were established later. Today, every state has guaranty funds; only the District of Columbia does not.

The guaranty fund covers each policy up to a maximum, typically $100,000 to $300,000. Some states cover out-of-state policyholders, some do not. In the latter case, the policyholder's own state may provide coverage. Claims on the funds are paid with ex-post assessments on surviving insurance companies. Effectively, the guaranty fund distributes the liabilities of the failed insurance company among surviving companies.[37]

---

[35] As with other financial institutions, an insolvent insurance company is not subject to the provisions of the National Bankruptcy Act. Instead, it is shut down and liquidated by its insurance commissioner.

[36] There are also regulations governing agents and brokers. In particular, New York State has a cap on agents' commissions. Since insurance companies normally compete for the business of independent agents by offering higher commissions, they have exercised considerable ingenuity in getting around this restriction.

[37] There are caps on the amount of annual assessments, so a series of major failures could exhaust the capacity of the safety funds. Nationwide, safety funds for life insurance and property–liability could raise about $3 billion a year each. Should these limits be reached, policyholders would have to wait for compensation.

Promoting Competition

While consolidation of the insurance industry has lowered costs, it has also made it easier to monopolize the market and to raise prices above competitive levels. In practice, this does not seem to have been a problem with insurance, since entry is relatively easy.

The McCarran–Ferguson Act exempts insurance companies from federal antitrust law. The intention was to allow them to share risk information without fear of prosecution for collusion. In fact, however, the exemption does allow them to collude to fix prices. The ISO used to publish "advisory rates," set high enough to ensure a profit for even the weakest companies. Price discipline eventually broke down under the force of competition, and in 1990 publication of advisory rates ceased.

There have been suggestions that McCarran–Ferguson be repealed to stimulate competition. However, the effect would probably be to *reduce* competition. If the ISO could no longer make risk information available to new entrants, entry would be more difficult, and monopoly prices would be easier to sustain.

Market Failure in the Provision of Insurance

There are some particular arguments for government intervention in insurance in addition to the usual ones of consumer protection and the promotion of efficiency and stability that we have already considered.

The market is good at giving people what they want. However, if people do not want what is best for them, then the free-market outcome may not be socially desirable. There is reason to think that this may be the case with insurance. For example, surprisingly few households in disaster-prone areas purchase catastrophe insurance. Only a very few people in Kobe, Japan, had coverage when a major earthquake struck the city in 1995. Remarkably few Californians carry earthquake insurance.

There are two psychological weaknesses that lead people to buy less insurance than they should. First, they prefer not to think about unpleasant events such as death, accidents, or natural disasters. To purchase insurance is to recognize that bad things can happen.

Second, people are not very good at assessing the very small probability that a catastrophe could happen to them. They tend to round down the probability to zero. It is notable that the purchase of earthquake insurance increases notably after a large earthquake. Perhaps the news worries people enough so that the cost of thinking about insurance is no longer an obstacle. Perhaps it causes them to assign the event a larger probability.

In any event, as a result of these failures of rational decision making, people tend to underestimate their need for insurance—"underestimate" in the sense that they regret their decision after the event. There may consequently be an argument for "paternalism"—for the government to improve people's welfare by encouraging them or even forcing them to increase their insurance coverage. This can be done with tax subsidies (life insurance). It can be done by requiring insurance (automobile insurance).[38] And it can be done by the government itself providing universal coverage (Social Security).

---

[38] Usually only liability insurance is required. This can be seen as dealing with an externality. Your use of an automobile endangers others. You may lack the means to compensate them for any damage you may do. Liability insurance protects them against your inability to pay.

CATASTROPHE INSURANCE AND ITS PROBLEMS

Insurance against natural disasters—catastrophe insurance—suffers not only from problems of demand but also from problems of supply. The market may not provide enough insurance or may charge "too high" a price for it.

The Limitations of Conventional Insurance

Are Catastrophe Losses Insurable?   Is the insurance market capable of providing adequate protection against catastrophe risks? Are catastrophe risks *insurable*? A risk is **insurable** if the insurance market is able to cover potential losses reliably—and profitably—at a premium that customers are willing to pay. Whether a risk is insurable will largely depend on whether the financial technology available to the insurance industry is capable of handling it.

insurable risk
A risk that can be insured profitably at a premium consumers will pay.

The basic technology of insurance—pooling and risk sharing—is good at handling risks that are relatively small and independent of one another: automobile insurance is a good example. Such risks are *locally insurable*. The risks of loss due to natural disasters such as storms, earthquakes, and floods are, however, neither small nor independent. A single event can cause billions of dollars in total damage, and many policyholders will experience losses at the same time. While such risks are not locally insurable, they can be *globally insurable*. Up to a point, they can be handled by spreading the risk more broadly, largely through reinsurance. This works reasonably well for small or medium-sized natural disasters, say up to $20 billion in total losses.

The potential losses from some natural disasters, however, are significantly greater than this. Continuing growth and development in disaster-prone areas makes the occurrence of a $50 billion event just a matter of time. The costliest natural disaster in recent times, at least in terms of insured losses, was Hurricane Andrew, which passed just south of Miami in 1992 and cost some $16 billion. A few miles further north and the cost could have quadrupled. The second costliest disaster was the Northridge earthquake of 1994, which struck in the northern suburbs of Los Angeles and cost some $11 billion. Had it hit downtown Los Angeles, the losses would have been much greater.

The Problem of Liquidity.   With even a $50 billion event, the problem is not really the amount. There are, for example, some 10 million households in California. Suppose that a $50 billion earthquake happened there on average every 20 years. Then an annual premium of roughly $250 a year per household would cover it.[39] The problem with a loss of this kind is its "lumpiness." For most of the time there are no claims. Then, suddenly, we need to come up with $50 billion. The problem is essentially one of liquidity.

With the types of risk that are locally insurable, like automobile insurance, there is a steady flow both of losses and of premiums: as a result, current losses can largely be funded out of current premiums. Insurance companies need only relatively modest reserves of capital to cover the occasional shortfall.[40]

---

[39] This is just a rough calculation and ignores the time value of money.

[40] It is also relatively easy if there is a change in loss experience to adjust premiums so as to maintain profitability.

Catastrophe risks are lumpier, and losses in a bad year can be much greater than current premiums. It is reinsurers who make such risks (globally) insurable by covering the shortfall, if necessary out of their own capital. They provide the necessary liquidity by placing their own capital at risk. It takes a lot of capital to do this.

The Limits of Reinsurance.   The capacity of the reinsurance market, however, is limited. Total premiums worldwide in 1998 were $115 billion and the capital of reinsurers was about $200 billion. So, in principle, the reinsurance market could have paid total claims of $315 billion. However, reinsurers, quite naturally, wish to diversify, and they therefore limit their exposure to a single event. So it is difficult to find coverage in this market for even a $10 billion loss, let alone $50 billion.

Reinsurance is also expensive. The level of actual premiums is roughly four to five times the "pure premium" calculated on the basis of expected loss. Reinsurance is so expensive because of its reliance on all that equity capital (the capital of reinsurers) to bridge the gap between premiums and claims. As we shall see in Chapter 15, equity financing is inherently expensive. The expense of catastrophe coverage is another reason why many people do not insure.

Alternative Approaches to Catastrophe Risk

The limitations of the technology of reinsurance as a way of dealing with catastrophe risk have stimulated a search for alternatives.

Catastrophe Derivatives.   One alternative is to place catastrophe risk in the derivatives market—the market for futures, options, and swaps. This is a huge market for other kinds of risk, especially the risk associated with fluctuations in interest rates and exchange rates. Attempts to tap this market for catastrophe risk go back to the early 1990s. However, for reasons that we shall explore in Chapter 16, they have not been particularly successful.

catastrophe ("cat") bonds
Bonds with a return that depends on the incidence of natural catastrophes.

Catastrophe Bonds.   Another alternative is to place catastrophe risk in the bond market. The size of the U.S. bond market alone is over $5 trillion: a $50 billion loss would represent a mere 1% of this—a modest day-to-day fluctuation. To tap this market, there have been a number of issues of **catastrophe ("cat") bonds** (also known as "act-of-God" bonds).

Here is how a cat bond issue might work. Insurers pay $1 billion of premiums for coverage of $20 billion of potential catastrophe losses. The organizers of the issue sell $19 billion of cat bonds. They then invest the proceeds of the bond sale, together with the premiums they have collected, in Treasuries. The Treasuries provide collateral for the insurance, so that the payers of the premiums know that their claims will be met. Because the premiums are invested too, the cat bonds are able to pay substantially more than the Treasury rate, say 10% more. However, in the event of a loss, the Treasuries will be sold to pay the claim, and the debt to the bondholders will be partially or wholly canceled.[41] The volume of cat bonds is still small, but the potential competition is having an effect in bringing down reinsurance rates.

---

[41] The structure that is used for this arrangement is called a "special-purpose vehicle" or SPV. It was developed for the securitization of debt. We shall learn more about securitization and SPVs in Chapter 14.

Government Programs.   A third alternative in dealing with catastrophe risk is some sort of government program. Governments commonly offer disaster relief following a natural disaster in the form of subsidized loans or grants for rebuilding. One can think of this as a sort of national risk pooling via the tax system. A serious problem with disaster relief is moral hazard. Because they know that the government will come to their assistance after the event, people buy less insurance and invest less in measures that would reduce the scale of the damage. Moreover, unlike insurance, disaster relief is "free": there are no premiums to pay. Because they do not themselves bear the full cost of the risk they incur, people are encouraged to build in disaster-prone areas.

In some countries, such as France, the Netherlands, and Japan, government agencies sell catastrophe reinsurance to private primary insurers. The government has an enormous advantage over private reinsurers in dealing with the liquidity problem created by large catastrophe losses. The government does not need to set aside expensive equity capital to cover a potential loss. Instead, it can simply borrow as needed, paying off the debt out of future tax revenue.

SUMMARY

- The pure premium is the present value of the expected cost of a claim. The actual premium adds to this administrative (mainly marketing) costs. Pricing premiums is much more difficult for property–liability than for life insurance.

- Because there is a lag between payment of premiums and payment of claims, insurance reserves generate investible funds. Because the lag is longer with life insurance, and because of premium smoothing, lifes have larger reserves.

- Incentive problems explain the nature of the insurance contract, the preference for the mutual form of organization among lifes, and the survival of cost-inefficient independent insurance agents.

- Lifes offer basic life insurance (term), long-term saving products (whole life, universal, GICs), annuities, and health insurance.

- Lifes played a major role in the early days of the U.S. capital market, but this was ended by regulation. The resulting restriction on permitted assets have put the lifes at a disadvantage in relation to other long-term intermediaries such as pension funds and mutual funds.

- As life insurance has declined as a vehicle for long-term savings, insurance companies have expanded their retirement-related products (including separate account products, SPDAs, and GICs) and their services to pension plans.

- Policy loans were introduced to improve the liquidity of whole life policies, but have occasionally resulted in serious disintermediation.

- Property–liability insurance has its origins in marine and fire insurance. Today its products include commercial property, homeowners, and automobile. Each covers against loss of property and liability.

- Property–liability insurance suffers from underwriting cycles—wide swings in premiums, availability, and profitability. It is also suffering from an increase in self-insurance (the alternative market).

- Insurance companies limit their risks by themselves purchasing insurance in the reinsurance market.

- Lloyd's of London is an insurance exchange in which syndicates of names accept risks in exchange for premiums.

- The insurance industry is undergoing consolidation and globalization as a result of economies of scale, liberalization of insurance markets, and increasing competition.

- Economies of scope have drawn insurance companies into other activities and have drawn other financial institutions, especially banks, into insurance.

- Insurance is the object of considerable government intervention. Reasons include asymmetries of information and the importance of insurance as a part of the social safety net. Many mutual insurers are becoming joint-stock corporations.

- In the United States, insurance is regulated by the states. The main concern of regulators is consumer protection. However, rising premiums have led to increasing political pressure for government intervention to contain them.

- Some recent failures have increased concern about safety. Insurance guaranty funds have been bolstered, and new restrictions placed on permitted assets.

- There is a case for market failure in insurance: people underinsure as a result of failures of perception and decision making. This may justify intervention to encourage or even force people to insure.

- Catastrophe insurance suffers from problems of supply. There are questions of insurability, especially for large disasters, and of liquidity. Reinsurance coverage is expensive. Alternative approaches include catastrophe bonds and derivatives and government provision.

DISCUSSION QUESTIONS

1. The probability of (total) loss is 5 in a thousand. The average lag between premium and claim is 3 months.
   a. What is the pure premium per $1,000 coverage if the interest rate is 10%? 5%?
   b. If $1 billion of insurance has been written, what is the amount of investible reserves?

2. What is the difference between the nature of the reinsurance business and of the property–liability business that makes the former a much more competitive industry?

3. Explain the difference between the principles of risk trading (see discussion in Chapter 2) underlying (a) automobile insurance offered by an insurance company and (b) insurance against a terrorist attack on the Channel Tunnel offered by Lloyd's.

4. Compare and contrast the structure of the insurance industry with that of the banking industry. Discuss economies of scale and scope and how they are realized; integration, concentration, and competition; and regulation. Why do the structures of the two industries differ?

5. What are the differences between life insurance and property–liability insurance? Discuss the nature of these businesses. What would be your main concerns if you were running a life insurance company? If you were running a property–liability company? How do the balance sheets of the two

types of company differ? How do these differences reflect differences in the respective business?

6. How has regulation affected the evolution of life insurance companies? How do you think they would differ today, had there been no regulation?

7. Why did the demand for whole life insurance decline? How did the life insurance companies respond?

8. What are the incentive problems involved in insurance? Discuss the problems among policyholders, owners, and managers; between insurance companies and agents; between insurance companies and reinsurers; between names and underwriters at Lloyd's.

9. Use the arguments of Chapter 3 to discuss whether government intervention in insurance is justified. Are there any additional justifications? What are the forms of government intervention? Have the effects of intervention been beneficial?

10. Why does catastrophe insurance present a challenge for the insurance market?
    a. Is catastrophe risk insurable?
    b. Why does catastrophe risk present problems of liquidity? Why can't private insurers or reinsurers solve this by borrowing?
    c. What are the alternative methods of handling the risk? Discuss their advantages and disadvantages.
    d. Should catastrophe insurance be compulsory? Is there a moral hazard problem?

BIBLIOGRAPHY

American Council of Life Insurance. *Life Insurance Fact Book*. Washington, DC: ACLI (annual).

Borden, S., and A. Sarkar. "Securitizing Property Catastrophe Risk." *Federal Reserve Bank of New York, Current Issues in Economics and Finance* 2, no. 9 (August 1996).

Cummins, J. D., and M. A. Weiss. "The Global Market for Reinsurance: Consolidation, Capacity and Efficiency." *Brookings–Wharton Papers in Financial Services*, 2000, 159–222.

Froot, K. A. "The Market for Catastrophe Risk: A Clinical Examination." Working paper no. w7286, National Bureau of Economic Research, August 1999.

Gastel, R., ed. *Reinsurance: Fundamentals and New Challenges*. New York: Insurance Information Institute Press, 1995.

Harrington, Scott E. "Policyholder Runs, Life Insurance, Company Failures, and Insurance Solvency Regula-

tion." *Cato Review of Business and Government*, spring 1992, 27–37.

Jaffee, D. M., and T. Russel. "Catastrophe Insurance, Capital Markets, and Uninsurable Risks." Department of Economics, Santa Clara University, 1996.

Kopcke, Richard W. "The Capitalization and Portfolio Risk of Insurance Companies." *New England Economic Review,* July–August 1992, 43–57.

Kopcke, Richard W., and Richard E. Randall, eds., *The Financial Condition and Regulation of Insurance Companies*. Boston: Federal Reserve Bank of Boston, 1991.

Mitchell, O. S., et al. "New Evidence on the Money's Worth of Individual Annuities." Working paper no. w6002, Natioanl Bureau of Economic Research, 1997.

KEY TERMS

pure premium
loss adjustment
insurance reserves
premium smoothing
independent agents
exclusive agents
direct writing
insurance broker
mutual associations
term insurance
whole life insurance
policy loan
universal life insurance
variable life

separate account
single-premium deferred annuity (SPDA)
guaranteed investment contract (GIC)
life annuity
Blue Cross/Blue Shield organizations
Medicare and Medicaid
managed care
health maintenance organization (HMO)
underwriting cycle
captive insurers

alternative market
reinsurance
names
bancassurance (Allfinanz)
demutualization
McCarran–Ferguson Act of 1945
National Association of Insurance Commissioners (NAIC)
no-fault insurance
insurance guaranty funds
insurable
catastrophe ("cat") bonds

PENSION PLANS AND MUTUAL FUNDS

When you finish this chapter you will understand:

- Why pension funds and mutual funds have grown so rapidly
- How the different types of pension plan and mutual fund work
- How the growth of pension funds and mutual funds has transformed the financial system

Over the past century, people have felt a growing need to provide for their retirement. Rising life expectancies and earlier retirement have certainly played a role, but the basic reason is a profound social change. Urbanization has undermined the traditional role of the family in providing for the elderly. Because people no longer expect their children to support them in their old age, they have sought other solutions. These solutions generally fall into one of two categories—social security programs and savings.

We begin with a brief look at social security, at how it works, and at its problems. We then review the considerations involved in saving for one's retirement. We shall see that there are good reasons why financial intermediaries play a dominant role in saving for retirement. The financial intermediaries most closely involved in retirement savings are life insurance companies, pension plans, and mutual funds.[1] We looked at life insurance

---

[1] Mutual funds also play a more general role in long-term saving for other reasons. We shall have more to say about this later in the chapter.

companies in Chapter 9. In this chapter we examine pension plans and mutual funds—how each has evolved, how such arrangements work, and how they are regulated.

SOCIAL SECURITY

The Nature of Social Security Programs

The majority of retirement income in most countries comes from a government program of social security or national insurance. Typically, such a program provides welfare benefits and medical insurance as well. The first national insurance program was established in Germany under Otto von Bismarck in 1889. In the United States, the **Old-Age, Survivors, and Disability Insurance Act of 1935** set up the Social Security Administration to provide a minimum income for retired workers and various other benefits.

Social Security Contributions.   National insurance programs are usually funded from a tax on labor. In the United States, Social Security contributions (taxes) are divided equally between employers and employees: each pays a tax of 7.65% on earnings up to a limit that is indexed to the price level.[2] At about 15% of total compensation, the social security tax rate is relatively modest in the United States. It is much higher in continental Europe: for example, in Italy it is about 35% of total compensation.

Of course, the idea that the employer pays a part of the contribution is really an illusion. To the employer, the social security tax is a cost of hiring labor just like the wage. For the employer there is no difference between (a) paying a wage of $100 plus a contribution of $7.65 and (b) paying a wage of $107.65. What matters to the employer is the *total* cost of hiring labor. Consequently, it is the employee who ultimately bears the burden of the tax: if the employer did not have to pay it, the employee's wage would be that much higher.

Social Security Benefits.   In the United States, Social Security benefits are based on a retiree's earnings history. The higher his or her lifetime earnings, the greater the benefits, up to a maximum. There is an element of redistribution: low-income workers receive a relatively better deal than high-income workers. The lowest paid workers today can expect a real return of 4 to 5% on their contributions, while high-income workers will receive a return of less than 1%. Social Security benefits are indexed for inflation.

The adequacy of retirement income is usually measured in terms of a *replacement ratio*—benefits as a fraction of preretirement income. In 1992, the replacement ratio provided by Social Security in the United States ranged from 49% for someone earning $15,000 per year to 24% for someone earning the maximum subject to tax of $53,400. In many countries, the benefits are more generous—commensurate with the higher levels of social security tax in those countries. In Germany the average replacement ratio is roughly 60%, in Japan 50%, and in France 50% to 100%, depending on the age of retirement.

---

[2] Of this, 5.35% goes towards pension benefits, the rest towards other benefits.

How Social Security Programs Work

pay-as-you-go plan

A pension plan that relies on one generation paying the pensions of another.

Despite the talk of rates of return, social security programs are not saving schemes. Your contributions are not invested by the government to provide you with an income when you retire. Rather your contributions today go to pay the pensions of current retirees. In return, when you retire your pension will be paid out of the contributions of those working then. This is called a **pay-as-you-go** scheme.

In a sense, the financial "technology" on which social security relies is the same as that of traditional family-based arrangements. Children support their elderly parents and, in exchange, they are supported by their own children when they grow old. No one "defaults" on this implicit contract because of social pressures to conform. With social security schemes, it is the coercive power of the government that ensures that future generations will keep their part of the bargain.

The Problems of Social Security Programs

The main problem is that the viability of the pay-as-you-go technology depends on the demographics, and the demographics are becoming less and less favorable.

Worsening Demographics.   Life expectancy has risen steadily, so that pensioners collect their pensions for a longer period on average. In Bismarck's time, life expectancy was 45 years, so paying a pension to those over 65 was not very expensive. Today, average life expectancy in the developed countries is 76, but the retirement age generally remains at 65. In addition, as life expectancy has risen and as people have had fewer children, the ratio of young to old has fallen. In 1950, there were 16 people contributing to Social Security in the United States for each person receiving a pension. By 2030, that ratio is expected to fall to less than 2.

As a result of these trends, if nothing changes, Social Security in the United States is expected to be unable to meet its obligations after about 2034. In many other countries, the situation is even worse.

Poor Incentive Effects.   Security programs have another problem—their bad incentive effects. A tax on any activity generally results in less of that activity. So a tax on labor reduces employment: this is especially a problem in continental Europe where the social security tax is very high. High taxes also encourage evasion. There is a great deal of "underground" employment that pays no social security (or any other) tax, further eroding the financial viability of the program. For example, in Italy over 25% of the economy is "underground" as opposed to less than 10% in the United States. And pension programs in many countries encourage early retirement. This too, of course, is harmful to their financial health.

Steps Towards Reform.   Governments are caught between politics on the one hand and the increasingly gloomy arithmetic on the other. In the past, the political pressure has been to make the programs ever more generous: future generations don't have a vote on such measures. This generosity is now coming home to roost. Governments are faced with the choice of reducing benefits (for example, by raising the retirement age) or of increasing contributions. Neither alternative is politically appealing.

Because of the problems of social security, governments are increasingly looking towards the alternative technology for providing retirement income—savings. In some countries, such as Japan and the United Kingdom, participants in savings-based private pension plans may opt out of at least part of social security. Other countries, including the United States, are considering "privatizing" their social security programs—replacing them at least in part with programs based on savings. This has already happened in some Latin American countries such as Chile and Argentina. The Canadian government began investing part of social security contributions in the stock market in 1998. Sweden partially privatized its social security program in 2000, allowing its citizens to invest a part of their contributions in a variety of approved investment vehicles.

In some countries, the private provision of retirement income through savings is already quite important. On the whole, the less generous the social security benefits in any country, the more important are the private arrangements. Consequently, private arrangements are much more important in the United States and Britain than they are in Japan and continental Europe.

Before we examine the nature of these private arrangements, we need to understand the fundamentals of saving for one's retirement.

ISSUES IN SAVING FOR RETIREMENT

The provision of retirement income out of saving involves two separate stages. In the first stage—in the years before you retire—you accumulate assets. In the second stage—after you retire—you convert the assets you have accumulated into income.

Risk and Return

In deciding which assets to accumulate, the considerations are the usual ones—return, risk, and liquidity. In the accumulation stage, since you do not plan to call on these assets for a long time, liquidity is secondary. Your main concerns are return and risk.

The Importance of the Rate of Return

Since saving for retirement is long-term saving, the rate of return matters a great deal. To illustrate, suppose you save $1,000 a year (in constant dollars) for 40 years. Let us see how much you would accumulate, investing in different types of asset.

Exhibit 10.1 shows the average annual rates of return on different types of asset. As you can see, the returns on long-term assets like stocks and bonds are much higher than those on short-term assets like T-bills.

Suppose you invested your $1,000 a year in T-bills. The average annual real return on these is 0.7%. You would therefore expect to have about $46,000 (in constant dollars) after 40 years. If you invested instead in common stocks, with an average annual real return of 9.2%, you would expect to have $357,000.

EXHIBIT 10.1   Annual Returns, 1926–1991

Asset	Average Annual Nominal Return (%)	Average Annual Real Return (%)	Standard Deviation of Annual Nominal Return (%)
Common stocks	12.4	9.2	20.8
Long-term corporate bonds	5.7	2.5	8.5
Long-term government bonds	5.1	1.9	8.6
U.S. Treasury bills	3.9	0.7	3.4

Source: Stocks, Bonds, Bills, and Inflation Yearbook *(1992).*

In general, long-term assets offer a higher rate of return. The normal yield curve slopes upwards. This makes long-term assets a more attractive vehicle for long-term saving.

Investment Risk

investment risk
The risk to retirement income from an uncertain return on retirement savings.

inflation risk
The risk to retirement income from inflation.

longevity risk
The risk that a retiree will outlive his retirement savings.

Before you put all your savings into stocks, however, take another look at Exhibit 10.1. The asset with the highest average return is not necessarily the best. As you can see, the higher the average return, the greater the risk (represented by the standard deviation).

The risk that the return on your savings will be less than you had hoped and that your retirement income will consequently be lower is called **investment risk**. You will have to decide on how much investment risk you are willing to bear.

One type of investment risk that is particularly important to the long-term saver is **inflation risk**. Rates of inflation can change drastically over the long periods involved in retirement saving. A serious bout of inflation can substantially reduce the value of your accumulated assets. It can also reduce substantially the real value of the income you derive from those assets.

Longevity Risk

Suppose that your retirement saving has been successful and that you retire with a substantial nest egg. Your worries are far from over. Since you expect to live from your assets for some time to come, you must once again worry about return and investment risk. You must also worry about another type of risk—**longevity risk**. This is the risk that you will live "too long"—that your savings will expire before you do.

HOW THE FINANCIAL SYSTEM CAN HELP

You can, in principle, save for your retirement by purchasing long-term securities yourself. However, there are good reasons to rely instead on financial intermediaries.

The private provision of retirement income involves a variety of financial institutions. In the United States, the most important ones are employer-sponsored pension plans, mutual funds, and life insurance companies.

Economies of Scale, Pooling, and Risk Bearing

Long-term intermediaries have all the standard advantages of intermediaries in general. As we saw in Chapter 2, delegation of investment to financial intermediaries captures the economies of scale in investing. The gathering and processing of information involved in investing $1 billion is not so much greater than that involved in investing $100,000. Financial intermediaries also offer the benefits of pooling—better diversification and greater liquidity.

In addition, some intermediaries bear all or part of the investment risk that remains after diversification. They guarantee savers a rate of return, and if the return on their investments falls short, they make up the difference out of their own capital. This arrangement reduces investment risk for the saver. It does, however, introduce an additional risk—the risk that the intermediary will default.

The technology of financial intermediation allows intermediaries to offer individual savers a better trade-off between expected return and risk than they could achieve on their own.

Investment Management

Delegation of investment to financial intermediaries can be even more advantageous if intermediaries are more successful than the average individual investor at managing their investments.

Investment management can take the form of active trading of publicly traded securities in an attempt to "pick winners." Academic opinion is generally skeptical about the value of doing this. It is difficult to beat the market by relying only on publicly available information. Statistical studies generally fail to find any improvement in return, after adjusting for increased risk, as a result of active trading. Once management fees are subtracted, the return to active management generally comes out negative. The best strategy with publicly traded securities seems to be a passive one: buy the market portfolio (for diversification) and hold onto it.

Investment management can also mean more than simply trading public securities. It can mean active intervention in the management of publicly traded companies to improve the return on their securities. Or it can mean investment in assets other than publicly traded securities that are not readily available to the individual investor—for example, investments in companies that are not publicly traded or in real estate. There is no reason to think that these other kinds of investment management cannot be fruitful. We shall have more to say about them in Chapters 14 and 15.

Dealing with Longevity Risk

Intermediaries are able to address longevity risk in a way that the individual alone cannot. As we saw in Chapter 9, the basic vehicle for dealing with longevity risk is the annuity. This relies on a form of pooling. The savings of many individuals are placed in a pool, and each member of the pool is guaranteed an income for life. While the time of death of each individual is uncertain, the rate at which members of a large pool die off is fairly predictable. This enables the intermediary to guarantee each annuitant an income for life, with very little risk to itself. While some annuitants may live for many years, others will die early.

However, as we also saw in Chapter 9, there is a problem with annuities—adverse selection. Annuities are most attractive to those who are in good health and who expect to live the longest. Since only healthy people buy annuities, the promised return tends to be low.

The solution to this problem is to make the annuity mandatory. Many life insurance retirement products convert automatically into an annuity. Since you buy the product when you are relatively young and have little information about how healthy you will be when you retire, there is less room for adverse selection. Most pension plans are mandatory for all employees of the company in question, and many provide benefits only in the form of an annuity. Since there is no choice, there is no adverse selection. Social security programs are the most successful at avoiding adverse selection: all employees in the country are required to join, and the benefits are paid only as an annuity.

Tax Advantages

Taxes can change the relative attractiveness of different types of investment: the rate of return that counts is the one you actually receive—the rate of return after tax.

To see how tax treatment affects relative returns, let us look at an example based on the U.S. tax code. Suppose you have $1,000 of pretax income that you wish to save for 40 years until your retirement. Your marginal tax rate is 30%. Upon weighing the risk and returns, you would like the money to be invested in long-term bonds, which currently yield 8%.

From the point of view of the tax implications, there are three different ways you could proceed: (1) invest directly yourself; (2) invest in a life insurance policy and have the insurance company invested in bonds; (3) invest in a pension fund that invests in bonds.

Investing Directly Yourself.   When you receive the $1,000 in pretax income, you must pay 30% of it, or $300, in tax. This leaves you with $700. You invest this in bonds or in a bond mutual fund.[3] Each year, you must pay tax on the 8% the bonds earn. Therefore, after tax, you will earn a yield of

$$(1 - 0.30) \times 8\% = 5.6\%$$

on your investment. After 40 years, assuming you reinvest the accumulated interest at the same rate, you will have

$$\$700 \times (1.056)^{40} = \$6,190$$

Since you have paid tax on all income as it was earned, you will owe no tax on the final amount.

Life Insurance.   Instead of investing your after-tax $700 yourself, you could have put it into a life insurance policy. Even if the life insurance company invests the money in the same portfolio of 8% bonds, your return will differ.

---

[3] We ignore here the differences in yield due to differences in the transactions costs for these two alternatives.

deferred tax

Tax on investment income that is deferred until the investment is realized.

The reason is that the tax on the interest your $700 earns is **deferred**. You are not obliged to pay tax on it until it is actually paid out to you. This makes quite a difference. Because you do not pay tax on the interest as it is earned, your savings accumulate at a rate of 8% rather than 5.6%. After 40 years, you will therefore have

$$\$700 \times (1.08)^{40} = \$15,207$$

When this is paid out to you, you will have to pay tax on the accumulated interest, but not on the principal (you already paid tax on that). Assuming your marginal tax rate is still 30%, you will have after tax

$$(\$15,207 - 700) \times 0.70 + 700 = \$10,855$$

If your marginal tax rate is lower when you retire, because your income is lower, the advantage of deferring the tax will be correspondingly greater.

A Pension Fund.   Suppose that instead of paying you the $1,000 as income your employer contributes it directly to a pension fund. The tax on such contributions is deferred, so the entire $1,000 is invested. As with the life insurance policy, the tax on the interest earned on the investment is also deferred. Consequently, you will earn the full 8% on the full $1,000. Therefore, after 40 years, you will have

$$\$1000 \times (1.08)^{40} = \$21,725$$

Since you have paid no tax either on the principal or on the interest, the whole amount is subject to tax when you receive it. After tax, you will have

$$\$21,725 \times 0.70 = \$15,207$$

Once again, if your marginal tax rate is lower, the advantage of deferring the tax will be correspondingly greater.[4]

Given these numbers, why would anyone invest in anything but a pension fund? There are two reasons. The first is that the tax code limits how much you can shelter in a pension fund. If you wish to save more, you must do it some other way. The second reason is that tax-deferred savings are relatively illiquid. If you withdraw your savings before you reach a specified age, you must pay a tax penalty of 10%, in addition to regular income tax.[5]

Having reviewed the considerations involved in retirement saving, we are now ready to take a closer look at pension plans and mutual funds.

---

[4] Notice that the after-tax amount here is the same as the pretax amount in the case of life insurance. Tax deferral in this case is equivalent to having to pay tax immediately on the $1,000, but then earning a tax-free 8% on what is left.

[5] In some other countries, life insurance premiums are tax deductible, making it easier for life insurance to compete with pension funds.

PENSION PLANS

Pension funds have grown rapidly to become the primary vehicle of retirement saving. Before we look at how and why this has happened, we need to establish some basic terminology.

pension plan

An agreement by a sponsor to provide income to participants upon their retirement.

A **pension plan** is an agreement to provide income to participants upon their retirement. Pension plans are generally sponsored by employers, although some are sponsored by labor unions.

A pension plan may be no more than a promise to the participants by the sponsor, its fulfillment depending on the general credit of the sponsor. In this case, the plan is said to be **unfunded**. On the other hand, the benefits promised by the plan may be secured by assets specifically dedicated to that purpose. If this is so, the plan is said to be **funded**. The sponsor establishes a fund and contributes to it year by year as benefits accrue. The financial intermediary that manages the assets and pays the benefits is called a **pension fund**.

unfunded pension plan

A plan that is not funded and depends entirely on the general credit of the sponsor.

The Evolution of Pension Plans

In the United States, the first pension plans were established towards the end of the nineteenth century by the railroads, the nation's first large employers.[6] The earliest was set up in 1875 by the American Express Company, which was then closely associated with railroading. The number of plans grew slowly until about 1900, then sped up. By 1929, there were 397 plans sponsored by employers and another 13 sponsored by labor unions that covered in all nearly 4 million workers.

funded pension plan

A pension plan secured by assets specifically dedicated to fulfilling its liabilities to participants.

Early employer plans were often quite informal. The granting of a pension and its size were largely at the discretion of the employer. Employers used pension benefits quite openly as a disciplinary device: behave and we will give you a good pension. As a result, unions vigorously opposed employer-sponsored plans. Instead, they sponsored plans of their own and lobbied for plans sponsored by the government.

pension fund

A financial intermediary that manages the assets and pays the benefits of a pension plan.

Both employer-sponsored and union-sponsored pension plans were generally unfunded. In 1929, the few funded plans had assets of only $500 million. Where reserves did exist, they were not set aside from the general assets of the sponsor. Often, pension fund reserves were invested in the stocks or bonds of the sponsor.

The Failure of Pension Plans during the Depression. It is not surprising, therefore, that many pension plans failed during the Depression. In some cases, sponsors were unable to make the required payments and terminated the plans. In others, the sponsors themselves failed.

The widespread collapse of pension plans led to increased regulation, which we shall discuss presently. It was also a major factor in the establishment of a government-sponsored pension plan—Social Security.

insured pension plan

A plan that buys from a life insurance company a group annuity that pays participants' retirement benefits.

A few private plans were **insured**. That is, the sponsor paid premiums to a life insurance company in exchange for a group annuity that would pay participants' retirement

---

[6] Pension plans go back much further than this. Roman legionnaires were granted freehold land on retirement. The Romans even made rough attempts to calculate the value of a life annuity.

benefits.[7] Such insured plans suffered far fewer failures and consequently gained rapidly in popularity through the 1930s.

Expansion during World War II.   World War II brought a major expansion of pension plans. While labor was scarce, government-imposed wage controls made it impossible for firms to compete for workers by offering higher wages. The controls did not extend to nonwage benefits, so firms competed by offering better benefits, particularly pensions.

At the same time, a heavy corporate excess-profits tax made the funding of pension liabilities more attractive. A firm can pay for pension benefits it has promised either immediately, by funding them, or later, when they come due; in both cases the cost is deductible. The temporary tax of 80% on profits made immediate funding the more attractive alternative, because it made the tax saving of immediate funding greater than that of future funding.

These incentives combined to produced an enormous increase in self-administered, funded pension plans. By 1945, private pension plans covered 6.4 million workers, a 50% increase over 1940.[8]

In 1949, the U.S. Supreme Court let stand a decision of the National Labor Relations Board that pensions were a legitimate part of collective bargaining. As a result of this decision, pension benefits became an important part of labor contract negotiations. In 1950, General Motors and the United Automobile Workers agreed on a plan that would be funded with a diversified portfolio of stocks. This plan became a model for other agreements, and within a year some 8,000 similar plans were established.[9]

Growth since World War II.   The growth of pension plans has continued at a rapid pace since World War II. The proportion of private employees covered by pension plans rose steadily to just over half by 1975, and it has stabilized at that level (see later: Exhibit 10.5). In addition, almost all government employees are covered by pension plans.[10] Although coverage has not increased since the mid-1970s, the assets of pension funds have nonetheless continued to grow rapidly (see Exhibit 10.2). Growth has come from increasing contributions and asset appreciation rather than from increasing coverage.

Why Do Employers Sponsor Pension Plans?

Before we look at the different types of pension plan and how they work, we need to address a prior question: Why do workers and firms find it beneficial to enter into this sort of arrangement?

---

[7] The first group annuity was written by Metropolitan in 1921.

[8] The Korean War, during which wage controls and the excess profits tax were reimposed, gave pension funds a similar boost.

[9] Previously pension funds had largely invested either in the stock of the sponsoring company or in government or corporate bonds.

[10] State and local plans cover public employees such as teachers and policemen. Various federal plans cover federal civil servants and the military. There are separate federal plans for the foreign service, employees of the Federal Reserve banks, railway employees, and so on.

EXHIBIT 10.2   Growth of Pension Funds

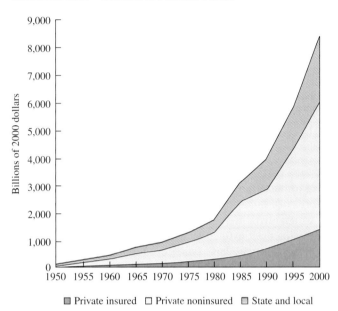

■ Private insured   □ Private noninsured   ▨ State and local

Source: Trends in Pensions.

We have seen that pension plans serve the needs of workers by providing them with a vehicle for retirement saving. But how do pension plans serve the needs of the firms that sponsor them? If they do not, it is hard to see why pension plans would have come into existence. Of course, pension plans today have substantial tax advantages. But pension plans came into existence long before these tax advantages existed.

Alternative Ways to Organize Retirement Saving.   Let us begin by considering three alternative ways of organizing retirement saving[11]:

- Firm A pays its workers $40,000 a year and deducts a 10% pension contribution from their wages.
- Firm B pays its workers $36,000 and promises pension benefits that have a present value of $4,000.
- Firm C pays its workers $40,000 and lets them take care of their own retirement saving.

Firms A and B have pension plans; firm C does not. Workers at firm A pay explicit contributions to their pension plan. Workers at firm B pay *implicit* contributions. From the

[11] We ignore tax differences in the following in order to focus on the nontax reasons for the existence of pension plans.

point of view both of workers and of firms, the arrangements at firms A and B are essentially equivalent. In both cases, workers receive compensation worth $40,000 a year; in both cases, workers cost the firm $40,000 a year.

What advantages, if any, are there to the arrangements of firms A and B over that of firm C? Why should employers act as financial intermediaries, rather than leaving this role to specialized institutions?

Pension Plans as a Performance Bond.   As we have seen, a pension plan can be used by the firm as an incentive device. Because the compensation embodied in pension benefits is deferred, the pension acts as a performance bond posted by the worker. The potential loss of benefits encourages workers to perform well, and it discourages them from quitting the firm.

Workers agree to this arrangement because it increases their compensation. The existence of the performance bond increases the productivity of workers, and employers are therefore willing to pay them more. For example, suppose the productivity of workers in the absence of a pension plan justifies annual compensation of $37,000. Suppose, too, that incentive effects of the pension plan—better discipline, harder work, and less turnover—increase productivity to the point that it justifies annual compensation of $40,000. Then either of the arrangements of firm A or of firm B would work. However, the arrangement of firm C would not: worker productivity without the pension plan would be too low to justify this level of compensation.

Pension plans can have other incentive effects that are valuable to sponsors. They can be designed to provide an incentive for workers to retire at an age that is beneficial to the employer.[12] In addition, a firm with a reputation for taking care of its employees will find it easier to recruit good workers and to motivate them.

Our next task is to understand the different types of pension plan and how they differ. There are two basic types—*defined benefit* plans and *defined contribution* plans.

Defined Benefit Plans

defined pension benefit plan

A plan that promises participants a certain level of benefits when they retire.

Under a **defined benefit plan**, the sponsor promises participants a certain level of benefits when they retire. That level typically depends on the number of years a worker has spent on the job and on the person's pay in the final years of employment. Integrated plans also take into account the retiree's Social Security benefits.

benefits formula

Formula used by a defined benefit plan to determine a participant's pension annuity.

The Benefits Formula.   Benefits are typically determined by a **benefits formula**. The following is typical:

$$\text{pension annuity} = (2\% \text{ of final year's pay} \times \text{years of service}) \\ - (0.5 \times \text{Social Security benefit}) \qquad [10.1]$$

For example, suppose you retired from this company after 40 years service with annual pay of $50,000 and that you are entitled to $12,000 a year in Social Security. Your pension would be

$$0.02 \times \$50,000 \times 40 - (0.5 \times \$12,000) = \$34,000$$

---

[12] This has become especially important since mandatory retirement was made illegal.

With a defined benefit plan, you face no investment risk. The sponsor guarantees a specific level of benefits. Meeting this obligation is entirely the responsibility of the sponsor. However, you do face other risks. You may lose your pension if you leave the job (voluntarily or otherwise). And the sponsor may default on its promise, leaving you with no retirement income. Let is look at these risks more closely.

Protection against Inflation Risk.   Benefits formulas used to be based on a participant's average pay over the whole employment period. In times of inflation, the use of average pay in the formula had the effect of reducing the real value of the annuity.

To see why, suppose that in the preceding example, inflation over the 40 years has averaged 4% and that real annual pay has stayed the same. Then your pay when you started must have been about $11,000 (this is equivalent to $50,000 in today's dollars). Your average pay over the whole period of employment comes out to about $26,000. The higher the rate of inflation over the 40 years, the lower the average will come out to be, and the lower the amount of your pension annuity.

In the inflationary 1970s, most plans changed their benefits formulas to base the pension annuity on pay during the final year or years. This has the effect of protecting participants against the risk of inflation that occurs up to their retirement. As long as pay rises with inflation (real pay does not fall), then whatever the rate of inflation, the value of the pension annuity in real terms will remain the same.

Since the size of the annuity is fixed at the time of retirement, there is no explicit protection against inflation *after* retirement. There is, however, some implicit protection. Sponsors have in the past voluntarily increased annuities to compensate, at least partially, for rapid inflation.

In some countries, such as the United Kingdom, private pensions are explicitly indexed. In others, such as Canada, Germany, and Japan, there is little indexation, explicit or implicit.[13]

vesting rules
Rules that determine a participant's rights to a pension on separation from the employer.

Vesting and Portability.   Pension plans have **vesting rules** that determine your right to a pension if you leave the job. The rules vary from plan to plan. A common arrangement is called "cliff vesting." For example, if you leave the job within less than 5 years, you lose all your pension rights. If you leave after more than 5 years, you are entitled to receive, on retirement, the full benefits as calculated from the benefits formula (see Equation 10.1).

Note that "final year's pay" now means the final year before leaving the job rather than the final year before retirement. Consequently, early vesting in no way eliminates the value of a pension plan as a performance bond. This is particularly true if there is inflation.

For example, suppose you quit after 20 years of service, but 20 years before retirement age, with annual pay of $30,000. If inflation is 4% a year, the "final year's pay" used in the calculation of your benefits will in real terms be only

$$\frac{\$30,000}{(1.04)^{20}} = \$13,690$$

In industries where people move frequently from employer to employer, it is important that they be able to do so without losing their pension rights. One way to arrange this

---

[13] The Canadian government has recently been encouraging increased indexation.

is to have the pension sponsored not by the employer but by the trade union. This arrange-ment is common in industries like trucking, with many small firms and substantial job mobility. If pension rights can be transferred easily from job to job, they are described as being **portable**.

portable pension
One that can be transferred from job to job.

Funding.   The default risk of a defined benefit plan depends on the degree of funding and on external guarantees. If the value of the fund equals the entire present value of ben-efits due to participants, the plan is said to be *fully funded*. If the value of the fund is less than this, the plan is said to be *underfunded*; if it is more, the plan is *overfunded*.

To the extent the plan is underfunded, employees are making an implicit loan to the sponsor. They are lending the sponsor that part of their compensation that would have been contributed to a pension fund. This implicit lending is made explicit in Germany. There, employers are required to "book" their pension liabilities on their balance sheets next to other corporate debt such as bank loans and bond issues.[14]

The degree of funding of a defined benefit plan does not affect the sponsor's obliga-tion to provide the promised benefits. If the fund's investments do poorly, and prove insuf-ficient to cover pension liabilities, the sponsor must make up the difference. If the investments do well, and there is an excess, the excess belongs to the sponsor.[15]

In the absence of external guarantees, the fund provides some assurance that the prom-ised benefits will indeed be paid, even if the sponsor is in difficulties. The advantage of funding for plan participants is essentially diversification: it reduces their exposure to the specific credit risk of the sponsor. When there are external guarantees—as there are in the United States for defined benefit plans—funding limits losses to the guarantor.

Public pension plans are generally unfunded. Consequently, increasing promised bene-fits has no immediate impact on government budgets. This makes an increase in pension ben-efits for public employees much more attractive to legislators than an increase in salaries. As a result, public pension plans tend to be quite generous compared to private plans.

Defined Contribution Plans

defined contribution plan
A pension plan in which the sponsor makes specified contributions to the account of the participant.

Under a **defined contribution plan**, each participant has an account into which the spon-sor contributes a certain amount each year (the participant sometimes contributes too). The contribution is usually proportional to earnings—for example, 10%. On retirement, the amount accumulated in the account is paid out to the participant either in cash or as an annuity.

How Do They Compare with Defined Benefit Plans?   The risks of a defined contribution plan clearly differ from those of a defined benefit plan. With a defined contri-bution plan, your level of retirement income is unknown. It will depend on how well con-tributions have been invested. This investment risk is borne entirely by you, the participant. So is the inflation risk. The sponsor's only obligation to you is to make the contributions as promised.

---

[14] These plans are nonetheless unfunded, since no specific assets are set aside to cover these liabilities.

[15] This is not entirely true. There is usually an implicit commitment to share the excess with participants by paying more than the promised benefits.

On the other hand, you need not worry about the sponsor defaulting. Your pension is guaranteed by the assets that have accumulated in your name over the years. Of course, depending on the form of those assets, default may still be a concern. For example, if your contributions have been invested in GICs with a particular life insurance company, failure of the insurance company may leave you without a pension.[16]

You do not have to worry either about losing your pension rights if you leave your job. With a defined contribution plan, vesting is automatic and immediate. The accumulated fund in your account belong to you and is payable to you on separation from the job.[17] A defined contribution plan is therefore fully portable.

Since the defined contribution plan cannot function as a performance bond in the same way as the defined benefit plan, it is purely a creation of the tax laws. If pension plans did not enjoy tax advantages, it is hard to see why defined contribution plans would continue to exist.

In addition to the basic defined contribution plan, there are some important variations.

401(k) plan
A defined contribution pension plan that allows voluntary, tax-deferred contributions on the part of the participant.

401(k) Plans.   An increasingly popular form of defined contribution plan is the **401(k) plan**, named after the section of the Internal Revenue Code that authorizes and regulates it.[18] These plans allow voluntary, tax-deferred contributions on the part of the participant.

The details of 401(k) plans vary widely. In some cases, employers make contributions independently of the voluntary contributions of participants; in others, employer contributions match or are linked to voluntary contributions; in yet others, the employer makes no contribution. In some cases, the 401(k) plan is the only pension plan offered by the employer; in others, it may supplement a regular defined contribution or defined benefit plan.

profit-sharing plan
A defined contribution pension plan in which the size of the contribution is a function of the sponsor's profits.

Profit-Sharing Plans and ESOPs.   In **profit-sharing plans**, instead of contributing a set amount to the account of each participant, the sponsoring firm will contribute a portion of its profits. The contribution may be in cash or in the form of distribution of stock in the firm. In the latter case, the plan is known as an **Employee Stock Ownership Plan (ESOP)**.

Employee Stock Ownership Plan (ESOP)
A profit-sharing plan in which the contribution takes the form of a distribution of shares of the sponsor's stock.

Cash Balance Plans

A new type of pension plan is the **cash balance plan**. It looks like a defined contribution plan. Each employee receives an "account" to which the employer makes "contributions" each year. The account accumulates interest at a set rate, and the final amount is converted into an annuity on retirement.

However, there are no actual separate accounts as with a defined contribution plan. The "account" is really just an IOU of the employer, and the accumulated balance merely states the value of the benefits that have accrued to the employee. The cash balance plan is in fact just a variation on the defined benefit plan. The only difference from the classic defined benefit plan is that the benefits formula is no longer based on final salary, but rather on "contributions" made over the participant's whole employment history.

cash balance plan
A type of defined benefit plan in which benefits are based on "contributions" over the life of the plan.

---

[16] See Chapter 9. Coverage of GICs by insurance guarantee funds has been problematic.

[17] To avoid paying a tax penalty, you must roll over your account into some other approved vehicle of pension saving like an Individual Retirement Account (see later) or a pension fund of another employer.

[18] Section 401(k) applies to plans for employees of corporations. Section 403(b) provides for similar plans for employees of nonprofit organizations and of public school systems.

The cash balance plan, because it is less "back-loaded" than the classic defined bene-fit plan, is more attractive to workers who switch from job to job.

The Management of Pension Funds

Some sponsors of pension plans manage their pension funds themselves, but most appoint a trustee to do it for them. The trustee is usually the trust department of a commercial bank, an insurance company, or a mutual fund management firm.[19] The trustee–manager invests contributions provided by the sponsor and pays benefits to retired participants.

With defined benefit plans, the assets of the fund remain the property of the sponsor. The sponsor sets general investment policy—such things as portfolio composition, target return, and quality of securities. However, the manager makes the day-to-day decisions on buying and selling specific assets. Some large sponsors divide the management of their pension funds among several managers.

There are advantages to having the plan managed by an outside trustee. First, trans-actions costs are lower. The trustee generally has greater expertise in financial transactions and possesses all the necessary personnel and equipment. The trustee also has greater expertise in dealing with the extensive regulatory requirements imposed on pension plans.[20]

A second advantage of outside management is that it enhances the credibility of the plan. The trustee of a pension plan has a legal responsibility to manage the fund in the interests of its participants. Presumably an outside manager is more trustworthy in this respect than the plan sponsor. Enhanced credibility makes the plan more attractive to par-ticipants, raising its value to the sponsor as a part of the compensation package.[21]

Since participants in a defined contribution plan bear the investment risk, it is only just that they have some control over how contributions are invested. Typically, defined contri-bution plans allow the participant to decide how to split current contributions between, say, a bond fund, a stock fund, and a money fund. They may also allow accumulated contribu-tions to be shifted from one type of asset to another. The recent growth in defined contri-bution plans has led to an increasing demand on the part of plan participants for advice on financial planning.[22]

---

[19] A pension fund managed by an insurance company is not the same thing as an insured pension fund. The former is a distinct entity with its own balance sheet that hires management services from an insurance company: the insurance company is not responsible for the liabilities of the fund. With an insured pension fund, on the other hand, the liabilities of the fund *are* liabilities of the insurance company.

[20] Major pension legislation in 1974 (ERISA: see later) increased enormously the amount of paperwork required to manage a pension fund. As a result, many small self-administered plans were either discontinued or converted into insured plans.

[21] In Canada, the advantage of trustee management is increased by allowing trustees to pool the assets of different plans. This improves diversification and reduces administrative costs.

[22] Regulators have recently made such investor control a requirement for defined contribution plans.

EXHIBIT 10.3   The Employee Retirement Income Security Act (ERISA) of 1974

- Sponsors must fully vest pension rights within 10 years.
- Plans must meet requirements for reporting and disclosure.
- Sponsors must meet standards for funding.
- No more than 10% of the fund portfolio may be invested in the securities of the sponsor.[a]
- Trustees of pension funds must meet certain fiduciary standards. In particular, choice of investments must be guided solely by the interests of the plan participants.
- All plans must purchase federal insurance.
- The Pension Benefit Guarantee Corporation is established to provide this insurance.

[a] This is to prevent firms from getting around the funding requirement. A plan funded by investing in the securities of the sponsor is essentially the same as an unfunded plan. Both rely solely on the general credit of the sponsor.

The Regulation of Pension Plans

A pension plan is a promise. Instead of paying an employee cash now, the firm promises payment many years in the future. The promise is complex. Substantial information and training are required to understand its details and to assess its value. Part or all of the promise may be implicit, making it unenforceable in court. The promise is a very long-term one, and the employer can renege in various ways: it can terminate the plan, fire workers prior to vesting, or simply default.

All these factors suggest a need for some consumer protection. Nonetheless, before 1974, regulation of pension plans was minimal, and abuses correspondingly common.

ERISA.   To address pension plan abuses, Congress passed the **Employee Retirement Income Security Act (ERISA) of 1974**, and it became law on Labor Day of that year. Its major provisions are listed in Exhibit 10.3. They have been modified slightly by a number of acts since, the most important being the Tax Reform Act of 1986.

The pension laws are directed primarily at private defined benefit plans. Public pension plans are exempt. Defined contribution plans are subject to only minimal regulation. Compliance is monitored by the Department of Labor.[23]

Pension Benefit Guarantee Corporation (PBGC)
Agency established by ERISA to insure defined benefit pension plans.

Pension Insurance.   ERISA established the **Pension Benefit Guarantee Corporation (PBGC** or "Penny Benny") to insure defined benefit pension plans. If a plan defaults or is terminated, PBGC guarantees pension benefits up to an annual maximum—$36,614 in 1999. Pension insurance covers about one third of the labor force—some 40 million Americans.

PBGC is financed from the annual premiums levied on participating plans. There are incentives for adequate funding. First, the level of the premium depends on the degree of

[23] The Department of Labor has about 400 investigators to police some 900,000 pension plans and some 4.5 million health and worker compensation plans.

funding. Second, the insurance maximum leaves a substantial part of the benefits of senior management uncovered.

PBGC monitors the plans it insures. If the agency considers funding to be inadequate, it terminates the plan and takes it over. PBGC may seize up to 30% of a sponsor's net worth to support an underfunded plan. In 1996, some 80% of the liabilities of defined benefit plans were in plans that were fully funded or overfunded (up from 45% in 1981).

Like deposit insurance, which we shall discuss in Chapter 19, pension insurance creates a moral hazard problem. A sponsor in financial difficulty will be tempted to underfund the plan and to make risky investments. If the investments pay off, the gain is the sponsor's. If not, the losses are covered by the insurance. Knowing the plan is insured, participants will have no reason to worry or to monitor the sponsor.

The Effect of Regulation on Funding.   The degree of funding of pension liabilities is strongly influenced by the tax code. Before ERISA, many firms found it advantageous to overfund. Contributions to a pension fund are deductible as an expense, and the earnings are tax free. Consequently, firms used overfunded defined benefit plans as a kind of tax-sheltered financial reserve. A firm that found itself short of funds could draw on the excess of pension fund assets over liabilities or even terminate the plan, in which case any excess funds automatically reverted to the sponsor.[24]

ERISA greatly reduced the attraction of overfunding. Sponsors remained liable for shortfalls in pension funds, but it became much harder to benefit if pension fund assets exceeded the accumulated liabilities of the plan. Overfunding was explicitly limited by the Tax Reform Act of 1986, which set a ceiling for deductible funding at 150% of current liabilities.

In some other countries, tax considerations promote underfunding rather than overfunding. In Germany, for example, employer contributions to a pension fund are deductible to the employer but taxable to the employee. Say BMW contributes DM4,000 to its pension fund to cover benefits accruing to Ulriche. BMW can deduct the DM4,000 as an expense, but Ulriche must pay tax on this amount just as if she had been received it in cash. If instead BMW does not fund the liability, just owes Ulriche the extra DM4,000, it can still deduct the whole amount as an expense, and Ulriche does not have to pay any tax. This creates a very strong incentive for unfunded plans.

Several other countries that used to have similar tax codes, most notably Japan, have changed their rules to encourage rather than discourage funding. Since the change, Japanese pension funds have grown rapidly.

Regulation of Fund Management.   Other than the limits ERISA placed on investing in the securities of the sponsor, U.S. pension funds are largely free to invest as they please. Public pension funds, which are exempt from ERISA, are under constant pressure

---

[24] Overfunding also happened accidentally, as a result of an appreciation in the market value of fund assets. The rising stock market left many sponsors with overfunded plans. They could, and did, realize the excess value by terminating plans.

to invest in their sponsors' securities—the securities of the state and local governments that set them up. Recently, some local governments have found a less blatant way to finance themselves with their own pension funds: public pension funds have begun to guarantee issues of municipal bonds for a fee.

Trustees are often under pressure to violate their fiduciary responsibility by using their investments to further goals other than sound investment. Public pension funds are pressed to invest in local businesses, in housing projects and so on—in short, to do some of the things the cash-strapped governments that sponsor them cannot do themselves. Private funds are often pressed to show "social responsibility" in their investment—for example, by divesting their interests in companies that traded with South Africa during the apartheid years.[25]

In other countries, there are often restrictions on the assets allowed to pension fund. In Japan, for example, pension funds may have no more than 30% of their assets in equities and no more than 30% in foreign securities. At least 50% must be in yen-denominated fixed-income securities.[26]

Individual Retirement Plans

As we have seen, employer-sponsored pension plans offer substantial tax advantages as a vehicle for retirement saving. For many years, the self-employed and those employed by firms that did not offer pension plans were unable to enjoy these advantages.

The self-employed were taken care of by the Self-Employed Individuals' Tax Retirement Act of 1962 (the Keogh Act). This provides for tax-deferred plans (**Keogh plans**) for the self-employed. In 1990, such plans amounted to about $50 billion.

Those working for firms than did not offer pension plans were taken care of by the Pension Reform Act of 1978. This authorized **Individual Retirement Accounts (IRAs)** for such employees. Legislation in 1981 and 1982 expanded eligibility, essentially making them available to anyone as a form of supplementary retirement saving.

The enormous popularity of IRAs led to a substantial loss of tax revenue. As a result, Tax Reform Act of 1986 sharply curtailed eligibility. Since then only individuals with no employer-sponsored plan, or those with incomes below a certain limit, have been allowed a full IRA deduction of $2,000. A new type of IRA, the **Roth IRA**, was introduced in 1997. In a Roth IRA, contributions of post tax income are allowed to accumulate tax deferred. The limits on both types of IRA are due to increase gradually to $5,000 in 2008. Contributions to IRAs have nonetheless been small. The large amount that has accumulated in IRAs ($2.6 trillion in 2000) is mainly money that has been rolled over into IRA accounts by beneficiaries who have left pension plans or whose plans have been terminated.

Keogh plan
A tax-deferred retirement saving plan for the self-employed.

individual retirement account (IRA)
A tax-deferred retirement saving plan for low-income employees or those without an employer-sponsored plan.

Roth IRA
An IRA into which contributions are made from after-tax income.

---

[25] Defined contribution plans, such as TIAA-CREF, often offer participants a "social investment fund" as one of their choices.

[26] Despite these restrictions, many Japanese pension funds have experienced massive losses from the collapse of Japanese share prices.

EXHIBIT 10.4   Benefits Paid by Retirement Programs, 1999

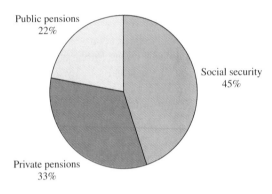

Public pensions
22%

Social security
45%

Private pensions
33%

Source: The 2000 Annual Report of the Social Security Administration.

Pension Plans Today

The Continuing Importance of Social Security.   Before we look at pension plans, we should remember that Social Security continues to provide a very significant part of retirement income in the United States. Some 55 million households are covered by some sort of pension plan (see Exhibit 10.5), while 150 million workers are covered by Social Security (the average number of workers per household is greater than one). Exhibit 10.4 breaks down the $765 billion of retirement income paid to Americans in 1999 by source—Social Security, private pension plans, and public pension plans (federal civilian and military and state and local). In most other countries, the relative importance of social security is even greater, often much greater.

The Decline of Defined Benefit Plans.   The number of households covered by some sort of pension plan remained stable during the 1990s, but the relative importance of different types of plan has changed (see Exhibit 10.5). The share of households covered only by defined benefit plans has been declining steadily, while the share covered by defined contribution plans only or by both defined contribution and defined benefit plans has been growing. Those covered by both types of plan are usually participating in supplementary defined contribution plans. These are voluntary plans that firms offer their workers in addition to the primary pension plan. They allow participants to increase the amount of their tax-deferred retirement saving beyond the share fixed by the primary plan. Supplemental plans are particularly favored by older employees and by those with higher incomes, for whom the tax advantages are most appealing. In recent years, supplementary plans have accounted for as much as half of all pension contributions.

There are a number of reasons for the shift towards defined contribution plans. One is the declining importance in the economy of the large unionized firms that tend to favor defined benefit plans. Another reason is the restrictions that the Tax Reform Act of 1986 placed on overfunding. These restrictions make defined benefit plans less attractive to

EXHIBIT 10.5   **Participation in Private Pension Plans by Type**

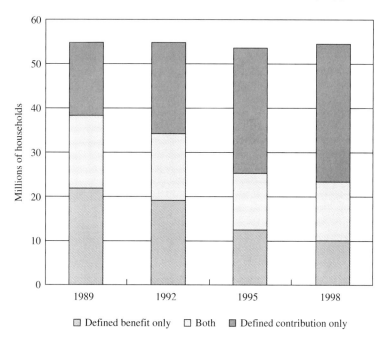

Source: U.S. Department of Labor.

employers. New plans tend overwhelmingly to be defined contribution plans. Small nonunionized firms tend to favor defined contribution and profit-sharing plans, particularly 401(k) plans. When given the choice, employees usually prefer the flexibility offered by 401(k) plans. Younger employees, in particular, often prefer to take their compensation in cash rather than as pension contributions, even if this means sacrificing the tax benefits. The share of defined contribution plans that are 401(k) plans grew from 55% to 78% between 1989 and 1998.

Rising stock prices in the 1990s led to the significant overfunding of many defined benefit plans. Since 1990, plan sponsors have been faced with an excise tax of as much as 50% on any surplus that they withdraw. However, the excise tax falls to 20% if the plan is terminated and replaced with a defined contribution plan. Many sponsors have been making this switch.[27]

Trends in Pension Fund Assets.   Exhibit 10.6 shows how the total amount of pension assets has steadily grown. The assets of defined benefit plans have declined in relative importance as those of defined contribution plans and IRAs have grown.

---

[27] Even if they do not cash out the surplus, sponsors are able to report part of the surplus as a credit on their income statements boosting their reported earnings. Their ability to do this is an unintended consequence of a change in accounting rules that was meant to force companies to recognize unfunded pension liabilities in their reported earnings.

EXHIBIT 10.6   **Amounts of Different Pension Assets by Type of Plan**

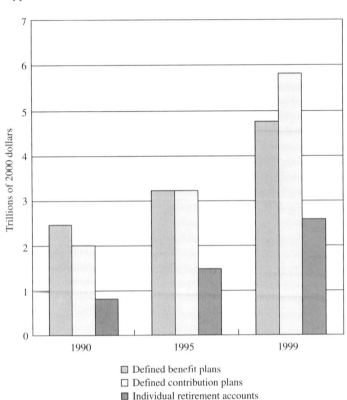

☐ Defined benefit plans
☐ Defined contribution plans
■ Individual retirement accounts

Source: Flow of Funds Accounts, Investment Company Institute.

The nature of pension fund assets reflects the nature of their liabilities. Pension fund liabilities are relatively illiquid. With defined benefit plans, there is no payment before retirement, even if the employee leaves the job. On retirement, participants receive an annuity, the amount of which is quite predictable. With defined contribution plans, separated workers do receive payment of their accumulated account. And on retirement, participants in defined contribution plans usually have the option of taking their benefits as a lump-sum payment. However, both the rate of separations and the amount of lump-sum payments are relatively easy to predict.

Flows out of pension funds are therefore steady and predictable. Flows into pension funds are also steady and predictable. With the exception of plans that allow employees to decide on the amount of the contribution, the amount of contributions is known well in advance. In these circumstances, liquidity is not a major concern.[28]

Return and risk are the dominant considerations. Consequently, pension funds invest

---

[28] Initially, as the fund matures, inflows exceed outflows, so there is no need to liquidate assets.

in longer term, higher yield assets—both equities and fixed-income securities. Generally, defined benefit plans, with a fixed element in their liabilities, have a greater interest in fixed-income securities (corporate bonds and government securities). Defined contribution plans, without this constraint, have a greater interest in equities.

After World War II, pension funds held mainly government securities they had acquired during the war and corporate bonds. With the strong performance of the stock market in the 1950s and 1960s, stocks offered much higher returns, and there was a big switch towards equities. This trend came to an end with ERISA. The new funding requirements gave pension plans a strong incentive to match their assets more closely to their liabilities. As a result, the share of equities has declined and the share of assets whose maturities match those of defined benefit liabilities has increased. These assets include government securities (in the form of strips), corporate and foreign bonds (zero-coupons), and agency securities (strips of mortgage-backed securities).

In recent years, participants in defined contribution plans have had a greater say in how funds are invested. They tend to be quite conservative, favoring fixed-income and short-term assets far more than do the managers of defined benefit plans. This has contributed to the overall shift in pension assets towards securities of these types.

Pension Funds in Other Countries. Pension fund assets in other countries are much smaller than they are in the United States. In 1999, Japan had about $1.5 trillion in pension assets and the United Kingdom about $1.4 trillion. Most continental European countries had very little in the way of pension assets (the Netherlands and Switzerland were the only exceptions). However, in the future, pension assets abroad are expected to grow even faster than those in the United States.

Several European countries, worried about the burden on their social security systems, have recently taken steps to encourage funded private pension plans. In 2002, Germany introduced a program modeled on the U.S. 401(k) that will eventually allow workers to invest up to 4% of gross wages in private defined contribution plans, generating as much as $250 billion a year in contributions. British and American financial firms that manage pension funds are keeping their eyes on such developments, hoping to capture a share of the business.

There are some significant differences among countries in the assets in which pension funds invest. Pension funds in Japan and Germany invest much less in marketable securities than do those in the United States and Britain and rely more on private lending to corporations. In Britain, government regulation requires employers to provide a pension plan and requires that the benefits be indexed. Consequently British pension funds invest heavily in real assets (including index-linked government securities).[29] In Germany, there is no indexation of pensions. Since their liabilities are fixed in nominal terms, German pension funds invest mostly in fixed-income securities.

The Effect of the Growth of Pension Funds on Financial Intermediaries and Markets. The rapid growth of pension funds in the United States and overseas has had an enormous impact on the development of financial intermediaries and securities markets.

---

[29] So stringent are the requirements for defined benefit plans in the United Kingdom that many sponsors have shifted to defined contribution plans.

Exhibit 10.7 shows how the importance of the financial intermediaries most involved with pensions has grown in the last 40 years and how much their relative importance has changed. In 1952, insured pensions offered by insurance companies predominated. Over the years these have declined in relative importance as the assets of pension funds and mutual funds have ballooned.

Competition to manage the enormous amount of assets of pension funds has been intense. In 2001, worldwide pension assets totaled some $13 trillion (80% of this in the United States, the United Kingdom, and Japan). Insurance companies, mutual funds, and bank trust departments have competed furiously for the management fees. The largest asset managers today each manage over $1 trillion in assets.

The sheer size of pension funds makes them an important factor in the market for long-term securities. While U.S. pension funds held only 1% of outstanding U.S. equities in 1952, by 1991 they held 25%. As we shall see in Chapter 17, the way securities are traded has been transformed to serve their needs.

The demand of pension funds for a specific type of asset has prompted a great deal of innovation. Defined benefit plans promise a fixed dollar annuity on retirement: sponsors bear the investment risk. The risk can be minimized by investing in assets that will yield

EXHIBIT 10.7   The Changing Importance of Long-Term Intermediaries

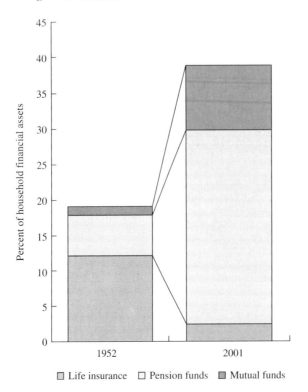

Source: Flow of Funds Accounts.

known dollar amounts when the liability comes due. Example of such assets include zero-coupon bonds, Treasury strips, SPDAs, and mortgage strips.[30]

Their desire to reap the higher return promised by equities, but without the consequent risk has created a strong demand for hedging products (see Chapter 16). It has also led pension funds to diversify internationally. Pension funds have been at the forefront of globalization (for example, U.S. pension funds invested $31 billion in foreign stocks in 1992).

MUTUAL FUNDS

As pension funds have grown, an institution that has grown with them is the mutual fund. Mutual funds serve the needs of pension plans, selling them investment products and managing their assets. They also cater independently to the market for retirement savings, providing investment products for tax-deferred individual retirement plans and for individual savers.

In addition, mutual funds play a more general role. Retirement is not the only reason for long-term saving: people save to pay for their children's' education or to accumulate a down payment for the purchase of a home. In many countries, mortgage and installment credit is less readily available than it is in the United States, and the "down payment" may be a large fraction of the price. In these countries, the need for long-term saving is correspondingly greater. The higher rate of return on long-term securities like stocks and bonds makes them particularly attractive vehicles for long-term saving. Mutual funds reduce the costs of investing in such securities.

Mutual funds have also adapted the technology they developed in the long-term market to create an important vehicle for short-term saving—the money market mutual fund. This has been enormously successful, and it now accounts for a significant fraction of the mutual fund business.

Before we look at how mutual funds have developed, we need to establish some basic terminology.

Investment Companies and Mutual Funds

investment company
A financial intermediary that raises funds entirely by issuing equity claims or shares.

An **investment company** is a financial intermediary that raises funds entirely by issuing equity claims or shares. It passes through to the holders of these claims all the earnings on its assets, less a fee. All of the risk is borne by the holders of the claims. This is very different from the practice of intermediaries such as banks that raise funds by issuing debt claims. A debt intermediary like a bank, promises a set return on the claims it issues. That return does not depend on the return it earns on its assets. The debt intermediary bears the residual risk and takes the residual return.

closed-end investment company
One that issues a fixed number of shares and invests the proceeds in a portfolio of assets.

There are two types of investment company. A **closed-end investment company** issues a fixed number of shares and invests the proceeds in a portfolio of assets. The shares are transferable: you can liquidate your holding by selling your shares to someone else. To

---

[30] On zero-coupon bonds and strips, see Chapter 4. On SPDAs, see Chapter 9. On mortgage strips, see Chapter 13.

make this easy, the shares are usually traded on an exchange. The price of a share is determined by supply and demand.[31]

open-end investment company (mutual fund)
One that issues new shares and redeems old ones according to demand.

An **open-end investment company** does not issue a fixed number of shares. It accommodates investors at any time by issuing new shares or redeeming outstanding ones. The price at which new shares are sold and outstanding shares redeemed is the **net asset value** of the portfolio—essentially its market value—plus or minus a fee. As new shares are sold or old ones redeemed, the investment company expands or contracts its portfolio of assets accordingly.

Open-end investment companies are more commonly known as mutual funds. Although the terminology is not strictly correct, closed-end investment companies are often called "closed-end mutual funds." In the United Kingdom, open-end investment companies are called *unit trusts*, and closed-end investment companies are called *investment trusts*.

net asset value
The price at which new shares of a mutual fund are sold and outstanding shares redeemed.

The Evolution of Mutual Funds

Origins.   Investment companies first appeared in the nineteenth century as a way for small investors to invest in corporate equities. Equities were then considered highly speculative and exotic, requiring a great deal of specialized knowledge and market savvy. Investment companies promised the small investor relatively safe and inexpensive access to the stock market.

Not surprisingly, interest in the stock market was most intense when returns were highest. The first modern investment company, the Scottish-American Investment Company, was founded in London in 1860 at the beginning of a stock market boom that lasted until 1875. By then, there were over 50 investment companies. Many of them failed in the stock market crisis of 1890, and public interest in the stock market waned until it was renewed by the boom of the 1920s.

Boom and Bust.   It was during the same boom of the 1920s that investment companies first became important in the United States. They had existed since the 1890s, but by 1923 there were only 15, with total assets of no more than $15 million. However, as stock prices soared in the late 1920s, and small investors rushed to get in on the action, investment companies mushroomed. By 1929 there were some 400, with $3 billion in assets. Most of these early investment companies were closed-end companies. Some offered "families" of trusts with differing investment objectives, much like the mutual funds of today.

The stock market collapse between 1929 and 1933 was, of course, a catastrophe for the investment companies. Poor management and risky investment practices that had gone unnoticed in the boom became painfully apparent in the collapse. For example, many of the funds were highly leveraged, with as much as 40% of their assets funded with debt or preferred stock. As long as the market rose, their common stock paid spectacular returns. When the market crashed, the value of the common stock was wiped out. A dollar invested

---

[31] For reasons that are imperfectly understood, shares of closed-end investment companies usually trade below the net asset value of the company's portfolio.

in the stock of a typical leveraged investment company in July 1929 was worth 5¢ by 1937 (while a dollar invested in a typical nonleveraged investment company was worth 48¢). The shares of one investment company, Goldman Sachs Trading Corporation, sank from 104 to 1¾.

After the Great Crash.   The 1930s saw relatively rapid growth of open-end companies (mutual funds), partly because of the disrepute into which the closed-end companies had fallen. In particular, open-end companies are not allowed to issue debt. The first mutual fund, the Massachusetts Investors Trust, had been formed in Boston in 1924. It promised to redeem its shares at net asset value less $2.00 per share.

Interest in mutual funds picked up again after World War II, when the stock market revived. Between 1945 and 1965, mutual funds grew at an average rate of 18% a year. The number of shareholders grew from 3 million to over 50 million. Assets grew from $2 billion to $50 billion. When the stock market began to decline in the 1970s, interest in mutual funds declined too (mutual funds at that time were almost 90% invested in stocks).

Money Market Mutual Funds.   Fund managers looking desperately for new products noticed that much of the money fleeing the stock market was going into the money market. So to capture this money, they set up mutual funds that invested in money market securities rather than in stocks. These **money market mutual funds** succeeded beyond their wildest dreams.

The reason for the success of the money market mutual funds was that investors found them a good alternative not only to stocks but also to bank and thrift deposits. In the 1970s, interest rates in the money market rose well above deposit rates that were then capped by Regulation Q. However, the money market is a wholesale market. Repos, commercial paper, Eurodollar deposits, and other money market instruments all have large minimum denominations. They usually start at $100,000 ($10,000 for T-bills), and the typical transaction is in the millions of dollars. This put high money market rates well out of reach of the ordinary household.

Money market mutual funds offered a solution. They sold shares to investors, mostly in small amounts, pooled the money, and invested in a diversified portfolio of money market assets. Moreover, as pools, they offered investors greater liquidity and better diversification than could be had from owning money market instruments directly. As a result, they proved attractive even to large investors who already had direct access to the money market. Because of their great liquidity, money market mutual funds could offer shareholders limited check-writing privileges.[32]

To be competitive with bank deposits, money market mutual funds need to be stable in value. The value of deposits is unaffected by changes in the value of bank assets to which they are an indirect claim; bank capital and deposit insurance absorb the risk. Mutual funds are not insured, and their sponsors are not obliged to absorb changes in the value of the underlying assets. However, in many cases, mutual fund managers have

**money market
mutual fund**
A mutual fund
that invests in
money market
instruments.

---

[32] Of course, not being banks, they cannot do this directly. So they set up a joint account for their shareholders at a commercial bank on which checks can be drawn. There is usually a minimum amount for each check (say $500) and a maximum number of checks per month (say three or four).

absorbed losses rather than "breaking the buck" (paying out less than a dollar for a dollar invested in the fund).

Money market funds were a tremendous success. Their success encouraged fund managers to develop other types of fixed-income fund, including tax-exempts in the late 1970s and junk bonds in the 1980s (there were already funds invested in ordinary corporate bonds).

Investment Objectives

Typology of Investment Strategies.   Mutual funds differ widely in their stated investment objectives. *Growth funds* invest in stock, but with an eye to capital gains rather than current income. *Income funds* aim to produce current income; there are both equity and bond varieties. *Balanced funds* have more general investment goals and invest in both stocks and bonds. *International* funds invest in foreign securities. *Global* funds invest in both foreign and U.S. securities.

There are funds that invest in corporate bonds, high-yield bonds, Treasury securities, municipal securities, or mortgage-backed securities. There are specialized funds that invest in particular industries or sectors, in options and futures, or in potential takeover targets. There are even funds, called *multifunds*, that invest in a portfolio of other mutual funds.

One type of closed-end fund extends the idea of an investment company to real estate. It is called a **real-estate investment trust (REIT)**. REITs invest either in actual real estate or in mortgages and construction loans. REITs were an enormous success in the late 1960s and expanded rapidly. After many REITs collapsed in the recession of 1973–1974, the public lost interest. But business picked up again in the real estate boom of the 1980s.

real estate investment trust (REIT)
An investment company that invests in real estate.

Managed Funds and Index Funds.   There is an important distinction between *managed funds* and *index funds*. **Managed funds** engage in active trading, trying to pick individual securities that best fulfill their investment objectives. Management is costly: it requires considerable investment in acquiring and processing market information and incurs substantial trading costs. **Index funds**, on the other hand, are passive investors. They purchase the securities that make up some market index—for example, the S&P 500—and hold them without any further trading. Passive investment is inexpensive: there is no need to employ analysts, and trading costs are minimized.

managed fund
A fund whose assets are actively managed to fulfill its investment objectives.

index fund
A fund that invests passively in a basket of securities.

The question, of course, is whether the extra cost of a managed fund is worthwhile. That is, do managed funds do any better than index funds—net of costs and allowing for differences in risk? Most academic opinion and most empirical evidence suggests that they do not. As this view has gained increasing acceptance with the public, the share of index funds has steadily increased.

Organization and Management

Organizational Form.   Formally, a mutual fund is a joint-stock company owned by its shareholders.[33] The shareholders elect a board of directors responsible for carrying out the fund's investment policies and objectives. The board is authorized to appoint managers

---

[33] In the United Kingdom, mutual funds (called unit trusts there) are organized as trusts rather than companies. The investors are the beneficial owners, receiving beneficiary receipts rather than shares, and the managers are trustees.

or to delegate that function to a management company. The shareholders pay the management company a fee, the size of which does not generally depend directly on the success of the fund's investments.

Management Companies.   While this is formally what happens, the reality is different. In fact, it is the management company that takes the initiative in setting up the mutual fund. Typically, a management company will organize and manage many different funds.

The type of company that organizes mutual funds differs from country to country. In the United Kingdom, most mutual funds are organized by life insurance companies. In Europe, most are organized by banks. In the United States, some are organized by life insurance companies, and some by securities firms. Before the 1930s, when legislation in the United States separated banking and securities markets, many of the largest mutual funds had been managed by banks. Bank trust companies continue to offer their customers investment funds that are functionally identical to mutual funds.[34] Most of the largest managers of mutual funds in the United States, such as Fidelity, Vanguard, and Putnam, are specialized companies that do nothing else.

Managing Risk and Liquidity.   Because their liabilities are equity shares, risk considerations for mutual funds differ from those for most other intermediaries. The risk is passed on directly to the shareholders rather than being borne by the intermediary as it is, for example, with banks and insurance companies. Mutual funds provide investors with a menu of choices in terms of risk and return, and investors take their pick. Since they are required to redeem their shares on demand, liquidity is a concern. Mutual funds generally invest only in marketable securities. We shall have more to say on how mutual funds manage risk and liquidity in Chapter 18.

Other Functions.   In addition to a manager, a fund typically contracts separately with a custodian, a transfer agent, and a principal underwriter. The custodian, usually the trust department of a bank, is responsible for executing portfolio transactions and holding the portfolio securities. The transfer agent is responsible for handling transactions with the shareholders—purchase and redemption of shares, distribution of dividends, and so on. The underwriter is responsible for marketing and distributing new issues.

Types of Mutual Fund

Open-End and Closed-End Funds.   We have seen that there are two basic forms of mutual fund: closed end and open end. In the United States, open-end funds predominate. One reason is that closed-end funds, like other publicly quoted companies, are not permitted to advertise their shares except at the time of issue. Open-end funds, on the other hand, can and do advertise extensively.

Both open-end and closed-end forms have some limitations. Because an open-end fund is obliged to redeem its shares at any time, it must ensure its liquidity. If redemptions

---

[34] Some 100 banks operate 850 of these funds with total asset of about $160 billion (compared to a total of $1.1 trillion for regular mutual funds). Citibank, for example, offers its customers its Landmark family of funds. Customers can buy, sell, or transfer these funds through Citibank teller machines.

exceed new purchases, it must be able to sell off its assets. That means its assets are limited to highly marketable securities.

The closed-end fund, because it achieves liquidity through transferability rather than through redemption, is able to invest in less marketable assets. For example, most funds that invest in stocks in developing countries are closed-end funds.

However, closed-end funds suffer from a different disadvantage: their shares typically trade at a discount below net asset value. In some cases, especially in the United Kingdom, the discount is large enough to make it worthwhile for someone to buy up the outstanding shares and sell off the assets at a profit. A number of theories have been advanced for the closed-end fund discount, but its cause remains controversial.

exchange-traded fund (ETF)
An basket of stocks that trades as a single security on an exchange.

Exchange-Traded Funds (ETFs). A new type of investment company was invented in the early 1990s—the **exchange-traded fund (ETF)**. This is an index fund that trades on an exchange. The organization is somewhat different from that of an investment company. Rather than issuing shares, the organizers of an ETF sell to the public "warehouse receipts" for a basket of shares that they have deposited with a custodian. The basket is designed to replicate a particular share index like the Dow Jones, the S&P 500, or perhaps an index of biotech or Russian stocks.

The structure was invented by the American Exchange in 1993 in the hopes of reversing the steady decline in its trading volume. Its first ETF, the SPDR (S&P Depository Receipt) was a tremendous success and was followed by others linked to other indexes. By 2000, trading in ETFs accounted for two-thirds of trading volume on the American Exchange. There were over $70 billion of ETFs outstanding in May 2001. This was only about 1% of the total amount of mutual funds outstanding.

ETFs have some advantages over open-end index funds. Because ETFs trade continuously throughout the day, their prices are continuously available rather than only at the end of the day. Similarly, investors can move in and out at any time rather than only at the end of the day as with a mutual fund. Because the structure is so simple, management fees are very low, even compared to most index funds. However, trading in ETFs, like any trading on an exchange, incurs brokerage fees while the purchase and redemption of most index mutual funds does not involve fees. ETFs also have some tax advantages.

Although ETFs trade on an exchange like closed-end funds, they generally do not suffer from the same problem of trading at a chronic discount. The reason is that they are less "closed." The sponsors of an ETF stand ready to exchange receipts for shares and vice versa.[35] Consequently, if SPDRs start trading at a discount relative to the S&P 500 index, arbitrageurs will buy them up and redeem them for the underlying shares. Their buying will drive the price of the SPDRs up and eliminate the discount.

The Importance of Distribution

The economics of the mutual fund industry is driven above all by distribution. Managing people's money is pretty easy. The trick is to get them to give it to you to manage. There are basically two ways to do this—two methods of distribution.

---

[35] There is a minimum size of transaction.

Load and No-Load Funds.   One way for a management company to sell mutual funds is through a network of agents. Mutual funds sell their shares through securities brokers employed by brokerage firms, through financial planners, and through insurance agents. Funds sold in this way carry a **load** or sales charge of 3 to 8.5% of the amount invested, which the seller receives as a commission.

load (no-load) fund

A fund with (without) a sales charge set at a percentage of the amount invested.

Alternatively, a management company can sell its mutual funds directly itself, relying on media advertising, direct mail, 800 numbers, and the fund's own sales staff. Funds sold in this way are called **no-load** funds because they have no sales charge. The cost of marketing is recovered as part of the annual management fee. Index funds tend to be sold directly; managed funds are more commonly sold through agents.

Mutual Fund "Supermarkets."   A recent innovation in distribution is the mutual fund supermarket. An investor with an account at such a supermarket can choose among hundreds of funds offered by a variety of different management companies. It is easy, too, to transfer money from one fund to another. There is no sales charge to the investor: the supermarket is compensated by the manager of the purchased funds.

The concept was pioneered by Schwab, the discount broker, but was soon taken up by others—including some of the larger mutual fund management companies such as Fidelity. Through its supermarket, Fidelity now markets funds of other management companies as well as its own. Supermarkets account for an increasing share of sales (21% of the total in 1997), largely at the expense of direct sales.

Online Distribution.   Management companies have been relatively slow to adopt the Internet as a channel of distribution. One problem is payment. Another, for load funds, is the danger of alienating existing distributors by competing with them for business (this is an obstacle, too, to the sale of insurance over the Internet). However, most management companies use the Internet to provide information to their customers and to allow them to switch money from one fund to another. Fund supermarkets have been quicker to make use of the Internet: in 1999, Schwab was conducting 40% of its transactions online and Fidelity over 30%.

The Importance of Service.   A factor of major importance in attracting and keeping investors is the quality of service that a management company can offer. Investors expect to be able to conduct transactions quickly and reliably over the telephone or online. The quality of service is especially critical in periods of stock market turbulence. Then, the volume of transactions rises sharply, and worried investors are particularly sensitive to delays and failures. The key to good service is information technology, and this does not come cheap. Fidelity, for example, invests some $500 million a year in improving its computers and systems.

The Importance of a Track Record.   The managed funds that attract most money from investors, not surprisingly, are the ones that earn the highest returns. A rating agency, Morningstar, rates funds for their performance, and the funds in the top third of the ratings attract some 80% of the new cash. Of course, much of this comes from other funds as investors shift from one to another in search of higher returns. In the 1960s, investors sold 7% of their stock funds each year. In 1999, they sold some 40%.

Responding to the competitive pressure, managers trade furiously in search of higher returns. In the 1960s, they traded about 15% of their portfolios each year. By 1999, the proportion had risen to over 90%. Of course, more trading means higher trading costs and higher taxes. Not surprisingly, expense ratios have steadily been rising.

Economies of Scale

Like other financial institutions, mutual fund management companies enjoy considerable economies of scale. There are, first of all, financial economies. Larger portfolios can more easily be diversified, and the information and skill needed to manage a portfolio of $1 billion differ little from those needed to manage a portfolio of $1 million. Also, management companies that offer investors a larger choice of different mutual funds are more likely to keep their money. On the other hand, there are also financial diseconomies. The largest mutual funds find it harder to outperform the market. In addition, their purchases and sales of securities tend to have a greater impact on the market: when they buy the price rises, and when they sell the price falls. For these reasons, some of the larger funds have recently been closed to new investors.

Because of the importance of distribution and information technology, there are enormous operational economies for management companies. The overhead costs of computers and personnel increase much less than proportionately with the amount of assets managed by a given management company. So the larger the total amount under management, the lower the average costs; and the lower the costs, the higher the profits of the management company.

Supermarkets have to some extent mitigated the operational economies of scale by taking care of distribution and transactions processing for smaller mutual fund management companies. However, this leaves the latter very much at the mercy of the former. The customer "belongs" to the supermarket rather than to the fund, and the fund does not even know the customer's name.

Finally, there are reputational economies of scale. As we have seen, a good track record attracts business. However, a good track record is as much a matter of luck as of skill. A management company with many different funds is more likely to see at least one of them near the top of the ratings in a given quarter. The success of such a fund will catch the attention of investors and draw them to other funds managed by the company.

Consolidation

Because of the economies of scale, there is a strong incentive to expand. One way to do this is organically through growth. There is, therefore, particularly vigorous competition among management companies to attract new accounts. Another way to increase in size is through mergers and acquisitions. There was a wave of consolidation in the early 1990s, with many of the smaller management companies merging or being taken over.

Some mutual fund management companies have been taken over by other financial institutions, especially life insurance companies. The reason is economies of scope in distribution, operations, and investment management. Economies of scope have also drawn mutual fund management companies into related activities such as brokerage. And the money market mutual funds have expanded their banking services to provide ATM/debit cards and automatic payment of bills.

The Regulation of Mutual Funds

In the United States, mutual funds are far less closely regulated than pension funds. Federal and state regulation focuses primarily on reporting and disclosure. The intention is to ensure that the investor has a clear understanding of the risks and the fees.

Mutual funds are subject to the same general regulations as those of other publicly traded companies. Under the Securities Acts of 1933 and 1934, all new issues must be registered with the SEC, and any solicitation of purchase must be accompanied by a prospectus detailing the nature of the security. Since open-end funds are constantly offering new issues, they are permanently in registration.

The **Investment Company Act of 1940** was addressed specifically to mutual funds. Its main provision are listed in Exhibit 10.8.

Under the "conduit" theory of taxation, a mutual fund is exempt from federal corporate income tax if it distributes at least 90% of its taxable income to shareholders (most funds distribute 100%). Of course, the shareholders themselves are in general liable for tax on this income.

To qualify for this tax exemption a mutual fund must be "diversified." The interpretation given to diversification is a little strange: a fund is considered diversified if it holds no more than 10% of the stock of any one company. This is strange because it relates to how big a stake the fund has in the company rather than in how big a part of the fund's portfolio that stake represents. The law is clearly intended to limit the power of mutual funds over corporate managements, rather than to ensure diversification. We shall have more to say about this in Chapter 15.

Hedge Funds

The result of these regulations is to limit quite narrowly the investment strategies open to mutual funds. To escape these limits, there are two options. The first is to set up an investment company that is not legally an investment company and is therefore not subject to regulation. The other is to set up an investment company offshore, outside the jurisdiction

---

EXHIBIT 10.8   The Investment Company Act of 1940

- Regulates the composition of boards of directors and the nature of the contract with the management company.
- Requires that the intended investment policy be filed with the SEC. That policy may be changed only by a vote of the shareholders.
- Prohibits mutual funds from issuing debt, selling securities short, or purchasing on margin.

hedge funds
Unregulated invest-
ment companies.

of U.S. regulators. Both types of fund exist and are known jointly as **hedge funds**. They acquired this name because, unlike regulated mutual funds, they are able to take positions in derivatives.

How to set up an investment company that isn't? Up to 1997, any fund with fewer than 100 investors was considered not to be selling securities to "the public" and was therefore exempted from the Investment Company Act and from regulation by the SEC. In 1997, the exemption was extended to an unlimited number of investors as long as these were "qualified." This means institutions with over $25 million in assets and individuals with over $5 million.

Without the protection of regulation, how can investors in hedge funds know that their interests will be safeguarded? The answer is incentives. The typical hedge fund is set up as a limited partnership, with the fund managers investing a substantial amount of their own capital in the fund. Their reward depends strongly on the return the fund earns for investors (the fees of managers of regulated mutual funds depend little, if at all, on the funds' performance[36]). As with ordinary mutual funds, there are reputational incentives too: hedge fund managers can attract investors to their new funds only by providing a good return on existing funds.

One disadvantage of hedge funds for investors is their poor liquidity. Because their positions are often less liquid than those of ordinary mutual funds, hedge funds usually require investors to commit funds for a period of years, with limited possibility of withdrawal.[37]

The investment record of hedge funds has been mixed. In some periods they made spectacular gains. Funds poured in, and the number of hedge funds and their size grew rapidly. In other periods they sustained spectacular losses, and investors withdrew their funds and called for tighter regulation. Although hedge funds have existed since the late 1940s, they really took off after some spectacular successes in the early 1990s. However, a much more uneven record in the mid-1990s resulted in something of a decline. The extension of the exemption in 1997 made the hedge fund structure attractive to companies that manage regulated mutual funds, and many have added hedge funds to their range of offerings.

Because hedge funds are unregulated, the data on them is sketchy. At the end of 2000, there were thought to be between 2,500 and 5,000 hedge funds worldwide. About half were in the United States and most of the rest in offshore financial centers such as Bermuda and the Caribbean. Total assets were between $200 billion and $300 billion. Most of the funds were small, with half having less than $25 million in assets and only 32 with over $1 billion each.

Unlike ordinary mutual funds, hedge funds are allowed to borrow. Consequently the amount of assets they hold can be much larger than the amount invested in them. The typical hedge fund borrows one dollar for every dollar invested. Some have a much higher leverage ratio. One fund that became notorious when it collapsed in September 1998,

---

[36] Only 1% of mutual funds make their management fees contingent on fund success, although this 1% does include some of the larger funds such as Magellan. Even so, the sensitivity of manager rewards to performance is much less than with hedge funds.

[37] For more on limited partnerships, see Chapter 15.

Long-Term Capital Management, had a leverage ratio of 25. Its positions in various instruments were so large that it threatened to wreak havoc on the corresponding financial markets when it failed.[38]

Mutual Funds Today

The Recent Surge in Mutual Fund Growth in the United States.   Booming stock markets are good for the mutual fund industry. It is not surprising, therefore, that mutual funds saw rapid growth during the 1990s. However, there was more to that period of growth than the bull market alone. Changes in the nature of retirement saving provided a long-run stimulus. Defined contribution pension plans, 401(k), and IRAs grew in importance, and much of the money in these programs went into mutual funds.

Exhibit 10.9 shows the distribution of assets among the different types of mutual fund as of year end 2000.

Mutual Funds in Other Countries.   In 2000, there was $4.8 trillion of assets in mutual funds in countries other than the United States (compared to the over $7 trillion in U.S. mutual funds). Until World War II, mutual funds were primarily an Anglo-American

EXHIBIT 10.9   Assets of Mutual Funds by Type (Year End 2000)

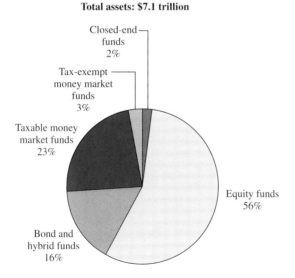

Source: Investment Company Institute, Mutual Fund Fact Book 2001.

---

[38] We shall discuss this episode in Chapter 18.

institution, largely because stock markets were much less important in other countries. In continental Europe and in Japan, long-term finance was handled primarily by industrial or universal banks.[39] Debt and equity issued by these institutions were important instruments of long-term saving for individuals. While a few mutual funds were established in France, Switzerland, and Japan in the 1930s, serious growth did not take place until the 1950s.

The 1990s saw a major expansion of mutual funds in Europe: between 1991 and 2000, total assets in mutual funds grew fivefold to about $3 trillion. This expansion was partly driven both by worries about social security programs and by partial privatization in some countries. And it was partly driven by increasing enthusiasm for investment in stocks as a result of booming stock markets. Money market funds have proven exceptionally popular in several countries, most notably in France. Because they were not allowed in Germany until 1994, German investors poured money into "offshore" money market funds in Luxembourg.

Growth in Europe has been helped by the determination of the European Union to create a "single market" in financial products. A series of directives has made it easier to sell mutual funds across national borders. A fund registered in one member country of the EU may be sold in any other member country. The adoption by several member countries of a single currency, the Euro, has also been a help. However, there is still one big obstacle—distribution. In most continental European countries, distribution is firmly in the hand of the banks, which sell only their own funds. It is therefore hard for outsiders to break in. However, Deutsche Bank, Crédit Suisse, and Barclays (as well as Fidelity and Citi) have begun to offer online fund supermarkets in Europe.

SUMMARY

- Provision for retirement in the advanced economies relies either on social security programs or on savings.
- Social security programs are usually funded from a tax on labor. They do not rely on saving but rather on one generation paying for the retirement of another.
- Social security programs in most countries are in trouble because of deteriorating demographics and bad incentive effects. Consequently, governments are increasingly looking to supplement or partially replace them with programs based on saving.
- For retirement saving, return and risk are more important than liquidity. Return is generally higher on long-term assets like stocks and bonds. The important risks are investment risk, especially inflation risk, and longevity risk.
- The financial system (pension plans, mutual funds, lifes) can help to improve the efficiency of saving through economies of scale, pooling, and trade in risk.
- The tax code gives life insurance an advantage over individual saving and a pension plan an advantage over both.

---

[39] See Chapter 6. The Société Générale de Belgique, founded in 1822, was the first industrial bank. It is often cited as the first investment company. However, it does not fit our definition of an investment company because the claims it issued were deposits, promising a fixed return, much like those of a commercial bank.

- Employer-sponsored pension plans began as a performance bond for employees. They received a big boost during World War II when wage controls left benefits, including pension, as the only way firms could compete for scarce workers. They have grown steadily since, largely because of the tax advantages.

- Under a defined benefit plan, the size of the pension annuity depends on pay in the final years of work (this provides some protection against inflation).

- A pension plan is funded if the employer sets aside specific assets to cover its liabilities under the plan. The degree of funding does not affect its obligation to provide the promised benefits.

- Under a defined contribution plan, sponsors make specified payments into each participant's account. Participants sometimes also make voluntary contributions. The share of defined contribution plans has been rising; especially popular are 401(k) plans.

- The recently introduced cash balance plan, although it looks like a defined contribution plan, is really a defined benefit plan with a different kind of benefits formula.

- The principal legislation regulating (private defined benefit) pension plans is ERISA. This set standards for vesting, funding, and management and established PBGC to guarantee pensions.

- IRAs provide tax-deferred retirement saving for employees of firms without pension plans. Keogh plans do the same for the self-employed.

- As a result of ERISA, sponsors have tried to match assets to liabilities. This has created a demand for securities such as Treasury or mortgage strips that have a known nominal payoff and little or no reinvestment risk.

- Mutual funds serve the needs of pension plans and of individuals saving for their retirement. They also provide an attractive vehicle for long-term saving for other reasons. An adaptation of the original mutual fund, the money market mutual fund, competes with banks as a vehicle for short-term saving.

- There are a great variety of types of fund: closed-end, open-end, and exchange-traded; managed and index; load and no-load. Index funds differ in the index they mimic; managed funds differ in their investment objectives.

- Mutual funds are managed by securities firms, insurance companies, and firms that specialize in this function. Banks manage investment funds that are functionally quite similar.

- The economics of the mutual fund industry is driven by distribution. Operational and reputational economies of scale have led to consolidation, and economies of scope in distribution have led to acquisition of mutual fund management companies by other financial institutions. The mutual fund "supermarket" has somewhat offset these trends.

- Mutual funds are subject to the general securities laws but otherwise are relatively lightly regulated.

- Hedge funds are essentially unregulated mutual funds. In the absence of regulation, they are structured to safeguard investors' interests.

- The growth of mutual funds as accelerated in the last few years. Because of low short-term interest rates, investors have shifted into long-term assets via purchases of mutual fund shares. The enormous popularity of 401(k) plans has also given mutual funds a boost. Mutual funds have also been growing in other countries.

DISCUSSION QUESTIONS

1. Why are employers involved in the retirement saving of their employees? What are the advantages to each of the parties? What part of your answer applies to cash balance plans? Explain.

2. a. A potential employer offers you an unfunded, defined benefit pension plan with cliff vesting after 3 years; the plan is not portable. What does all this mean?

   b. You are offered shares in a no-load, open-end, global index mutual fund. What exactly is that?

3. For each of closed-end funds, open-end funds, exchange-traded funds, and hedge funds,

a. How is liquidity provided?

b. How is price determined?

c. Could you take a leveraged position? If so, how?

d. Could you take a short position? If so, how?

4. What is the difference between an exchange-traded fund and a closed-end fund? Why doesn't the former suffer from the problems of the latter?

5. From the point of view of a saver, compare the different vehicles for retirement saving—life insurance, defined benefit pension plans, defined benefit pension plans, mutual fund, direct investment in securities. How do they differ with respect to risk of various kinds, return, and liquidity?

6. Is government intervention in retirement saving justified? (Use the framework of Chapter 3 and the discussion of government intervention in insurance in Chapter 9.) What are the forms of government intervention in this area? How has government intervention shaped the nature of retirement saving? Have the effects of this intervention been beneficial?

7. What are the interactions between pension funds, life insurance companies, and mutual funds?

8. Is the shift from defined benefit to employee-directed defined contributions plans desirable from the point of view of participants? What are the pros and cons? What are the implications for the financial system?

9. How do mutual funds and banks differ? What are the similarities? Use the frameworks provided by Chapters 2 and 5.

10. If mutual fund management companies were free to expand their activities, where do you think that economies of scope would lead them?

BIBLIOGRAPHY

American Council of Life Insurance. *Pension Facts.* Washington, DC (annual).

Bodie, Zvi. "Pensions as Retirement Income Insurance." *Journal of Economic Literature* 28 (March 1990): 28–49.

———. "Managing Pensions and Retirement Assets: An International Perspective." American Enterprise Institute for Public Policy Research, May 1990.

Born, Karl Erich. *International Banking in the 19th and 20th Centuries.* New York: St. Martin's Press, 1983.

Davis, E. P. "Financial Market Activity of Life Insurance Companies and Pension Funds." Economics Paper, No. 21, Bank for International Settlements, Basle, January 1988.

Edwards, George W. *The Evolution of Finance Capitalism.* London: Longmans, 1938.

Investment Company Institute. *Mutual Fund Fact Book.* Washington, DC (annual).

Ippolito, Richard A. "A Study of the Regulatory Effect of the Employee Retirement Income Security Act." *Journal of Law & Economics* 31 (April 1988): 85–125.

Krooss, Herman E., and Martin R. Blyn. *A History of Financial Intermediation.* New York: Random House, 1971.

Lavington, Frederick. *The English Capital Market.* London: Methuen, 1921.

Neufeld, E. P. *The Financial System of Canada: Its Growth and Development.* New York: St. Martin's Press, 1972.

Sellon, Gordon H., Jr. "Changes in Financial Intermediation: The Role of Pension and Mutual Funds," *Federal Reserve Bank of Kansas City Economic Review*, third quarter 1992, 53–70.

Stocks, Bonds, Bills, and Inflation Yearbook.™ Chicago: Ibbotson Associates, 1992. Annual updates by Roger G. Ibbotson and Rex A. Sinquefield.

Warshawsky, Mark J. "Pension Plans: Funding, Assets, and Regulatory Environment." *Federal Reserve Bulletin*, November 1988, 717–730.

KEY TERMS

Old-Age, Survivors, and Disability
    Insurance Act of 1935
pay-as-you-go
investment risk
inflation risk
longevity risk
deferred tax
pension plan
unfunded pension plan
funded pension plan
pension fund
insured pension plan
defined pension benefit plan
benefits formula

vesting rules
portable pension
defined contribution plan
401(k) plan
profit-sharing plan
Employee Stock Ownership Plan
    (ESOP)
cash balance plan
Employee Retirement Income
    Security Act (ERISA) of 1974
Pension Benefit Guarantee
    Corporation (PBGC)
Keogh plan
individual retirement account (IRA)

Roth IRA
investment company
closed-end investment company
open-end investment company
    (mutual fund)
net asset value
money market mutual fund
real estate investment trust (REIT)
managed fund
index fund
exchange-traded fund (ETF)
load (no-load) fund
Investment Company Act of 1940
hedge funds

PART III

FINANCIAL MARKETS

CHAPTER 11

UNDERSTANDING
FINANCIAL MARKETS

When you finish this chapter you will understand:

- Why financial markets are important
- How financial markets work
- Who makes them work
- How innovation, globalization, and other forces are transforming them

The financial system facilitates lending, payments, and trade in risk. We saw in Chapter 2 that it does so in two distinct ways—through financial intermediaries and through organized financial markets. In Part II, we discussed financial intermediaries. Here, in Part III, we discuss financial markets.

Financial markets facilitate the sale and resale of *transferable securities*. There is a close connection between financial markets and *direct lending*. Most transferable securities arise out of direct lending; most securities that arise out of direct lending are transferable. However, as we shall see, some transferable securities arise out of indirect lending—for example, mortgage-backed securities and syndicated loans—and these too are traded in financial markets. And some securities traded in financial markets do not represent lending at all—for example, futures and options contracts.

The principal financial markets that we shall study are:

- *The market for government securities* (Chapter 12). This is the single largest securities market, and it plays a central role in the financial system.
- *The mortgage market* (Chapter 13). Residential mortgages are bundled together and sold in large packages. This process, known as securitization, enables mortgages to trade in financial markets.
- *The debt market* (Chapter 14). This is the market for the debt of corporations and municipalities.
- *The equity market* (Chapter 15). This is the market for ownership shares in corporations.
- *The market for derivatives* (Chapter 16). The market for derivatives is a market for risk contracts. Its major instruments are futures, options, and swaps.[1]

Each of these markets provide arrangements for the trading of securities—exchanges, trading systems, and mechanisms for clearing and settlement. In Chapter 17 we shall study the nature of these arrangements.

Before we look at the individual markets, we need to understand in general what a financial market is, what it does, and how it does it. That is the purpose of the current chapter. While different markets involve different securities, they all perform the same basic functions and face the same fundamental problems. We begin by examining the nature of those functions and problems.[2] We then take a look at *primary markets*—the markets for new securities—and *secondary markets*—the markets where existing securities are traded. Finally, we look at the securities firms whose activities make financial markets work.

WHAT DO FINANCIAL MARKETS DO?

The standard depiction of the role of financial markets goes something like this: "Financial markets channel household savings into corporate investment." This statement is quite misleading—especially for the most visible financial market, the stock market (the market for equities). Let us begin by looking at the numbers.

A Picture of Financial Markets

The Numbers.   Exhibit 11.1 charts new issues of bonds and equities in the United States. You can see that in most years new issues of bonds exceed new issues of equities by a factor of 4 or 5.

Exhibit 11.2 shows the net amounts of funds raised through these issues. You can see that these amounts are far smaller than the gross value of new issues. For bonds, this is because the proceeds of many of the new issues are used to pay off existing issues, either

---

[1] Swaps are not market-traded securities. They are risk contracts offered by financial intermediaries. We shall discuss their relationship with market-traded risk contracts in Chapter 16.

[2] Our focus will be on financial markets that are involved in lending (the subject of Chapters 12 through 15). We shall discuss the specific functions and problems of markets for risk in Chapter 16.

EXHIBIT 11.1   New Issues

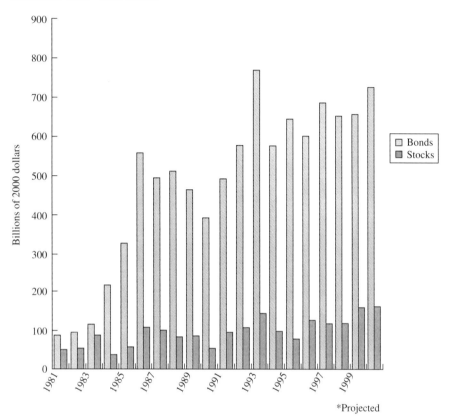

Source: The Federal Reserve Bulletin.

because the latter are maturing or because lower current interest rates make refinancing attractive. In addition, in the aggregate, a good part of the remaining new issues is offset by bonds that mature and have to be repaid. While equities never need to be repaid, large amounts are nonetheless removed from the market as a result either of mergers and acquisitions or of companies buying back a portion of their outstanding stock. Moreover, since some new issues of bonds are used to repurchase equities (and sometimes vice versa), the net amounts raised through new issues of bonds and equities *combined* is even smaller than Exhibit 11.2 suggests.

If new issues of bonds and equities provide corporations with so little in the way of additional funds, how do they finance their investment? Exhibit 11.3 provides an answer. Most corporate investment is financed out of internal funds—preponderantly out of their own past profits.

These numbers are for the United States. However, as you can see from Exhibit 11.4, the pattern is very similar in all the major economies. In all of them, investment is financed

EXHIBIT 11.2   Net Funds Raised through New Issues

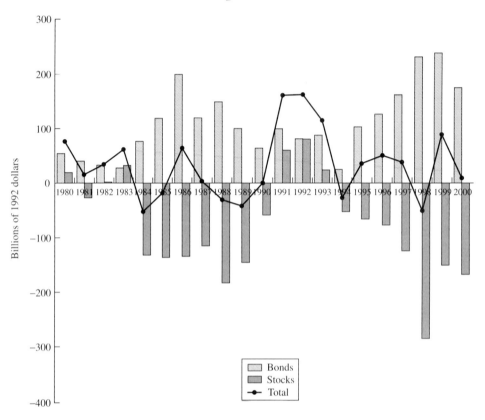

Source: Flow of Funds Accounts.

predominantly out of internal funds. In all of them, external financing is mostly in the form of debt rather than equity. In most of them, most debt is indirect (loans from financial intermediaries) rather than direct (issues of debt securities). The United States and Canada are exceptional in their reliance on the bond market.

The Importance of External Financing.   Why do we observe this pattern of financing? The reason is that external financing is fraught with difficulty and therefore expensive (we shall look at the details presently). As a result, corporations rely on internal funds whenever they can and on external financing only when they have to. It is the difficulties of external financing that explain the relatively small amount of external financing and, as we shall see, the different forms that it takes. The preference for internal finance is one reason bond issues exceed stock issues by such a large margin. Internal funds are a source of equity rather than of debt finance: they are a substitute for the issue of stock. Firms are forced to go to the bond market if they wish to increase their debt, but they can increase their equity finance by retaining internal funds.

EXHIBIT 11.3   Fixed Investment of Corporations and Its Financing

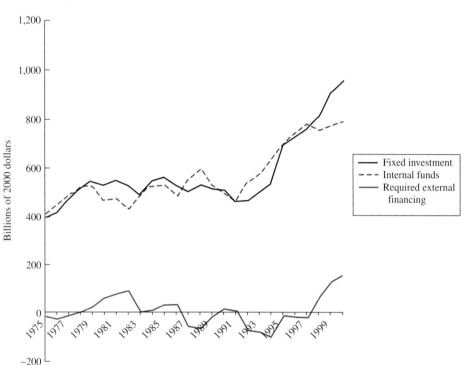

Source: Flow of Funds Accounts.

Given the limited role of financial markets in financing corporate investment, what exactly do they do? First of all, "limited" does not mean unimportant. External financing in general, and financial markets in particular, are the *marginal* source of funds for investment. And economics teaches us that the margin is crucial.

While external financing is small on average, it can be very important for industries that are expanding rapidly or investing heavily in new technology. For such industries (information technology and telecoms are recent examples), internal funds are not nearly enough. In addition, new firms and new industries have to rely heavily on external financing for their investment because they do not yet have internal funds. Recent examples include the overnight delivery industry and the "dot-coms."

The rather modest role of the equity market as a source of external financing belies its true importance. It is above all a market for ownership. It makes possible the restructuring of the economy through mergers and acquisitions and privatization. And it helps to impose market discipline on managers: if a company performs below its potential, it becomes an attractive target for takeover and reorganization.

In these ways financial markets have a much greater effect on the *quality* of investment than on its quantity. Some countries that lack developed financial markets undertake

EXHIBIT 11.4   Net Financing of Nonfinancial Enterprises, Average 1970–1985

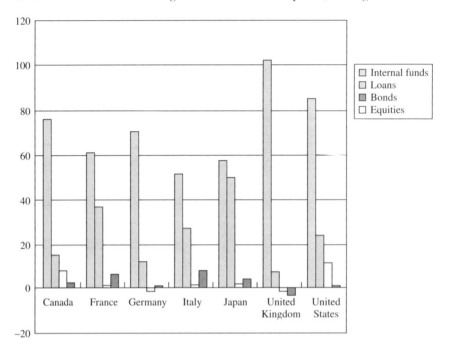

Source: *Mayer (1990).*

a great deal of investment. But typically that investment is much less efficient—earns a much lower return—than investment in countries with well-developed financial markets. Financial markets ensure that investible funds flow to the best uses. They make an economy more adaptable by facilitating the growth of new industries and the closing down of declining industries.[3]

We have talked so far only about the role of financial markets in corporate finance. But financial markets also provide funds to other sectors of the economy. You can see from Exhibit 11.5 that both households and governments are major borrowers in U.S. financial markets. Indeed, historically, financial markets served the need of governments long before they started to finance corporations in the late nineteenth century.

The Difficulties of External Financing

Before we see how financial markets work, let us review the difficulties involved in external financing. It is through an understanding of these difficulties that we will be able to see why financial markets are organized the way they are.

---

[3] A recent study by Jeffrey Wurgler (2000) presents empirical evidence that financial markets improve the quality of investment. He shows in particular that countries with more developed financial markets see more investment in growing industries and less in declining industries.

**EXHIBIT 11.5   Amounts Outstanding of
Long-Term Financial Instruments**

Total debt: $13.9 trillion

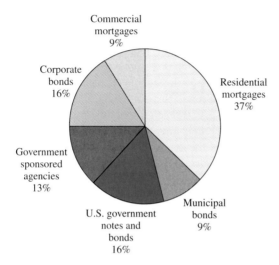

Source: Flow of Funds Accounts.

As we saw in Chapter 1, the fundamental problem of financing is this: the providers of financing hand over money today in exchange for promises of money in the future, and promises are not always kept. Once the recipients of financing have the money, they may decide not to keep their promises, or they may be unable to keep them. Financing in financial markets is mostly long term, and this magnifies the problem: the longer the period of financing, the greater the opportunity for the recipient to misbehave and the more time there is for things to go wrong.

The nature and the degree of the problem depend on the form of financing. There are two basic forms—debt and equity. With debt financing, borrowers promise to make specified payments of interest and principal irrespective of how the enterprise fares. If the enterprise does well, the profits are theirs; if it does badly, they bear the losses. In principle, the provider of debt financing is unaffected. With equity financing, on the other hand, the recipients do not promise the providers payments that are specified in advance. Rather, they promise them a share of the profits. The providers of financing get to share in the profits, but they get to share in the losses too.

Let us look at the relative merits of the two types of financing from the points of view, respectively, of the providers of the financing and of the recipients.

Debt vs Equity from the Point of View of the Providers of Financing.

With debt financing, while it is true in principle that all the risk is borne by the borrower, it is not true in practice. The borrower may default on his obligations, failing to pay interest or to repay principal as promised. Default faces the lender with a dilemma. The lender can force the borrower into *bankruptcy*—a legal process that provides for a liquidation of the borrower's assets to pay off, to the extent possible, his debts. Bankruptcy, however, is not always in the lender's best interest: it all depends.

If the borrower's problems are temporary, especially if they are not of his own making, the lender may ultimately recover more of what is due to him if he allows the borrower some slack. Circumstances may well improve and the borrower will then resume repaying his debt. In this case, forcing bankruptcy would be unproductive. Unless there are sufficient assets that could be sold to cover the debt, bankruptcy would just destroy the borrower's capacity to repay. On the other hand, if the problems are permanent or if they are the result of incompetence on the part of the borrower, bankruptcy is the best option. Allowing the borrower slack in this case will just compound the losses. Rapid liquidation of the enterprise is most likely to salvage as much as possible for the lender. The dilemma of what to do in case of default is a serious one, and resolving it requires good judgment and a great deal of work on the part of the lender.

In reality, problems begin even before actual default has taken place. Once default becomes a real possibility, the incentives of the borrower become distorted. In these circumstances, as we saw in Chapter 1, the borrower has an incentive to "go for broke" (see Exhibit 1.2). It is to his advantage to take on high-risk projects. In the unlikely event that they succeed, he has salvaged his situation and will receive most of the gains. If, as is more likely, they do not succeed, the loss is borne by his creditors. The borrower has little to lose. What this means for the lender is that he needs to know if there is a substantial increase in the probability of default. As a result, he has to monitor the borrower constantly to ensure that the borrower does not misbehave in this way.

In all, there is a huge difference between debt that is safe—where the probability of default is essentially zero—and debt that is risky. Safe debt is "low maintenance": it involves no effort on the part of the lender. Moreover, pricing safe debt is easy. Usually, there is a **benchmark rate** of interest for safe debt, typically that on government securities, and this can be applied directly to price the debt in question.

Risky debt, on the other hand is "high maintenance." Constant monitoring and the exercise of judgment are required of the lender. The risk is all downside: at best the lender receives what is due to him; at worst he loses everything. To control the risk, the lender will demand some sort of security in case of default (we shall see in Chapter 14 the various ways this is done). Where the risk remains large, the lender may require some sort of equity component—a possible upside if things go well to compensate for the downside. For example, **convertible debt** can be converted into equity at the discretion of the lender if the enterprise does well. Because default is a real possibility with risky debt, the arrangements to deal with it—bankruptcy laws, the laws relating to collateral, and so on—are very important and will affect lenders' willingness to provide financing. Unlike safe debt, risky debt is difficult to price. To do so, lenders must assess and quantify the risks involved.

Equity financing avoids some of the problems of risky debt, but it brings others instead. Because the recipient does not promise specific fixed payments, but rather a share in the enterprise's profits, default is impossible. This avoids the problem of what to do in case of default, with all its attendant costs of decision and negotiation. However, this arrangement leaves the recipient of equity financing with a great deal of discretion over the size and timing of payments to the provider. The big problem for the provider, therefore, is to ensure that the recipient does not abuse this discretion. As protection, equity financing gives the provider a right of control over the management of the enterprise—something

benchmark rate
The rate on safe debt that serves as reference for pricing other debt.

convertible debt
Debt that can be converted into equity at a prespecified price at the discretion of the investor.

corporate governance

Control over a corporation to ensure providers of equity financing with an appropriate return.

the provider of debt financing does not have. However, exercise of this right of control—**corporate governance**—is fraught with problems, and it involves considerable effort and cost. In addition, equity is even harder to price than risky debt. Not only are there risks to assess, but even the amounts of future payments are unknown. A kind of equity that addresses this problem, and is therefore easier to price, is **preferred equity**. Like debt, this promises specific payments.[4]

preferred equity

Equity that pays a fixed income, like a bond.

Debt vs Equity from the Point of View of Recipients of Financing.   To understand the relative attractiveness of different forms of financing for the recipient, it is important to keep firmly in mind one crucial fact: the costs of dealing with any problems associated with the financing have to be borne by the recipient. The reason for this is that the provider of financing always has the alternative of safe lending, say to the government. To be persuaded to provide financing to anyone else, the provider has to be compensated for any additional risk and any additional effort or cost.

Safe debt, because it involves hardly any additional risk, effort, or cost, is a relatively cheap source of financing for the recipient. Enterprises that have excellent credit or can find ways to make their debt safe (we shall see how in Chapter 14) are therefore able to find external financing at relatively low cost.

Risky debt and equity are more expensive sources of external financing for the recipient. The average yield has to be higher to compensate the provider of financing for the additional risk, effort and cost. Moreover, there is an additional disadvantage. To protect their interests, providers of financing through risky debt and equity require some degree of control over the enterprise. Such external interference in the management of the enterprise is potentially costly because it limits the freedom of decision of the recipient and consequently the ability to take advantage of profitable opportunities.

THE PRIMARY MARKET AND THE UNDERWRITING OF NEW ISSUES

Having reviewed the problems involved in debt and equity financing, we are now ready to see how financial markets address them. We will divide our discussion into two parts. In the first, we will discuss the market for new issues—the primary market. In the second, we will discuss the market in which outstanding issues of securities are traded—the secondary market.

The primary market has to address all the standard problems of financing that we reviewed in Chapter 2. Financing involves risk. To manage this risk, providers of financing need to acquire and process information, to draw up a contract with the recipient, and to monitor compliance. As we saw in Chapter 2, various institutions have evolved to address these needs.

At different times and in different countries, different methods have been used to sell new issues of securities to investors. The issuer may sell directly to investors, it may pay a broker a commission to distribute the new issue, or it may sell the whole issue to an

---

[4] As long as the payments are made, the provider of financing has no right of control over the enterprise. If, however, the payments are not made as promised, the provider of financing obtains control rights and has first claim on future profits until the payments have been made up.

CORPORATE SECURITIES

The basic instruments of the capital market are shares of stock (equity) and bonds. The following are the most important varieties:

secured bonds: bonds with a lien on specific assets of the borrower (collateral)

mortgage bonds: secured bonds with a lien on real property (land or buildings)

unsecured bonds (debentures): bonds that are a claim on the general credit of the borrower

subordinated debentures: bonds that, in the event of bankruptcy, have a lower priority claim in the borrowers assets than ordinary debentures

put bonds: bonds that allow the investor to demand redemption at a predetermined price

callable bonds: bonds that allow the issuer to redeem the bonds before maturity (but usually after a fixed period) at a predetermined price

variable-rate bonds (floaters): bonds that pay a variable coupon rate linked to a designated short-term market rate

common stock: stock that provides the purchaser with ownership rights and a claim on a share of the income and assets of a corporation

class A stock: stock that pays dividends but is nonvoting

class B stock: voting stock that pays no dividends

preferred stock: technically equity but pays a fixed income like a bond; in the event of bankruptcy, preferred stock has priority over common

convertible bond: a bond that can be converted into stock at a prespecified price at the discretion of the investor

underwriter who resells it to the public.[5] Distribution to individual investors may take place through networks of retail brokers, through financial institutions (primarily banks), through public advertising, or even by salesmen going door to door.

Today, in the United States and Japan, most new issues of corporate and municipal securities are sold through underwriters and distributed through networks of brokers. Underwriters provide investors with some assurance of the quality of the securities they sell. Underwriters are obliged to exercise **due diligence** in uncovering the facts and in making them known to the purchasers of securities. Investors can, and do, sue to recover losses if they believe the underwriter has been negligent or dishonest.

due diligence
A conscientious effort to uncover the facts relating to an issue of securities.

---

[5] Sale for a commission is often called *best-effort underwriting* to distinguish it from *firm-commitment underwriting*, where the underwriter purchases the whole issue for resale. With *standby underwriting*, the underwriter promises to buy securities that could not be sold at a prespecified price.

The main incentive for due diligence, however, is not legal liability but reputation. An underwriter that acquires a reputation for selling lemons will find it hard to sell future issues. Because of its poor reputation, its clients will have to pay a high yield on their securities (sell them at a low price). This means that good issuers will avoid such an underwriter.

Underwriters provide issuers with a variety of services. They advise the issuer on the type of security to issue (see "Corporate Securities"), on the timing of the issue, and on its pricing. They also handle the extensive paperwork required by securities regulation.[6] Each new issue must be registered with the SEC: this requires the collection and disclosure of a great deal of financial information. Bond issues must receive a rating from a rating agency such as Standard & Poor's or Moody's.

The underwriter negotiates a price with the issuer and then buys the whole issue at that price with the intention of reselling it, at a higher price, to the public. This arrangement has two advantages for the issuer. It removes the uncertainty about the amount of funds the issue will raise, and it relieves the issues of the considerable transactions costs of marketing the issue. For large issues, underwriters typically form **underwriting syndicates** to provide the necessary finance and to spread the risk.

underwriting syndicate

A group of underwriters who combine to float a particular issue.

Having purchased the issue, the underwriters sell it off to investors. This process takes time and, as we shall see, involves risks. Underwriters often commit themselves to repurchasing from investors the securities they underwrite (at the market price) in order to enhance the securities liquidity. This makes the securities more attractive and easier to sell.

Who are the underwriters? Mostly they are securities firms. However, as we saw in Chapter 6, banks have started to reenter the business. The top underwriters in 2000 are shown in Exhibit 11.6. Notice that underwriting is a highly concentrated industry, with the

EXHIBIT 11.6   The Top 10 Underwriters

	Disclosed Fees ($ billions)	Market Share (%)
Goldman Sachs	2,382	19
Crédit Suisse First Boston[a]	1,895	15
Morgan Stanley Dean Witter	1,784	14
Merrill Lynch	1,436	11
Salomon Smith Barney	1,169	9
J. P. Morgan Chase	756	6
Lehman Brothers	635	5
Deutsche Bank	392	3
FleetBoston Financial	391	3
Bank of America Securities	281	2
Top 10	11,121	89
Industry total	12,500	100

[a] Includes Donaldson, Lufkin & Jenrette.

Source: The Wall Street Journal, *January 2, 2001.*

---

[6] See Chapter 20.

top 10 underwriters accounting for nearly 90% of the business; the top 5 account for nearly 70%. This concentration is largely a result of reputational economies of scale.

The Risks and Rewards of Underwriting

Underwriting is a risky business. An underwriter that misprices an issue stands to make a loss. For example, in April 1988, First Boston, a major investment bank, underwrote a $125 million issue of Connecticut Light and Power at a yield spread of 70 basis points (that is, it paid a price that implied a yield of 70 basis points over the Treasury rate). However, investors were willing to buy the bonds only at a spread of 85 basis points. The loss to First Boston was about $1.4 million.[7]

With an IPO, the underwriter often stabilizes the price of the issue in the secondary market until it is sold off.[8] This can sometimes leave the underwriter with large amounts of unsold shares.

Even if the underwriter prices the issue correctly, there is a risk that market interest rates will rise between the time the underwriter buys the issue and the time it can be resold. For example, in October 1979, IBM floated a $1 billion bond issue. A syndicate led by Salomon and Merrill Lynch won out over IBM's usual underwriter, Morgan Stanley, in underwriting the issue. On October 3, the syndicate agreed on a yield of 9.5%, a spread of only 10 basis points above the Treasury rate. Later the same day, anticipation of a major tightening of monetary policy caused the yield on Treasuries to jump to 9.8%. When the tightening was announced several days later, the yield on Treasuries rose above 10%. Naturally, as the price of Treasuries fell, so did the price of the IBM bonds. Wall Street estimates of the loss to Salomon and Merrill Lynch ran as high as $20 million (presumably to the joy of Morgan Stanley).

As compensation for the risks they take and for the services they provide, underwriters earn a spread and often also an explicit fee. In Exhibit 11.6, which shows how much the leading underwriters earned in 2000, the whole fee is credited to the lead underwriter of the syndicate, which typically keeps only 50%. Some 40% of the fee covers the direct costs of the issue (administrative, legal, sales expenses, etc.).

Although the risks of underwriting have increased in recent decades, spreads and fees have shrunk. The greater risk is the result of the increased volatility in interest rates. The lower spreads and fees are the result of increased competition.

Increasing Competition in Underwriting

One reason for the increased competition is SEC **Rule 415**, which came into force in 1982. Rule 415 allows a corporation to register a new issue with the SEC and then wait up to 2 years to sell it: this is called **shelf registration**. Rule 415 has several advantages for issuers. It gives them greater flexibility in timing, allowing them to sell when they think

Rule 415
The SEC regulation that allows shelf registration of securities.

shelf registration
Registration with the SEC of intention to issue securities over a period of time without specifying a particular time of issue.

---

[7] Assume the duration of the bonds was about 8 years and the Treasury rate about 10%. First Boston's loss would be about $125 million $\times$ 8 $\times$ 0.0015/(1.1) = $1.4 million. This calculation uses Equation 4.19 in Chapter 4, which you should see for further explanation.

[8] This is legal for up to 30 days after a new issue, as long as the intention to support the price is declared in advance.

market conditions are most favorable. It also gives them much greater bargaining power in negotiating a deal with an underwriter. Under Rule 415, they do not have to name an underwriter when they register a new issue. When they are ready to float the issue, they can simply shop around for the best bid.

Another reason for increased competition in underwriting is the development of alternative markets, such as the market for private placements, the Euro market, and the market for syndicated loans, all of which we will discuss in Chapter 14. Borrowers with good alternatives are in a strong position when bargaining with their underwriter over the fees for a new issue. These alternatives are more relevant for debt than they are for equity: all of the above-mentioned markets are predominantly markets for debt. This is one reason why the fees on equity issues are much higher than they are on bond issues (up to 10 times higher). Another reason is the greater difficulty in pricing new issues of equity and the consequent dependence on the reputation of the underwriter.

The Secondary Market

When you provide financing by purchasing securities in the primary market, you give up money now in exchange for a promise of money in the future. Sometimes you may wish to "undo" this transaction—to convert the promise of money in the future back into money now.

When you lend your money to a bank or to a mutual fund, the institution stands ready to redeem your loan on demand: such a loan is said to be *redeemable*. However, if you have provided financing to a corporation by purchasing its bonds, the corporation has no obligation to redeem them before maturity. If you have provided financing by purchasing its stocks, it has no obligation to redeem them at all. Consequently, the only way you can convert these securities into money now is to sell them to someone else who is willing to hold them: securities that permit you to do this are said to be *transferable*.

It is the secondary market that allows you to "undo" the provision of financing by selling the resulting securities to someone else. As we saw in Chapter 2, secondary markets are made by brokers and dealers. *Brokers* bring buyers and sellers together without themselves actually buying or selling; *dealers* set prices at which they themselves are ready to buy and sell (*bid price* and *asked price*, respectively). Brokers and dealers come together in organized markets like the New York Stock Exchange and NASDAQ.

A good secondary market is less important for short-term securities. They mature quickly, so normal repayment turns them into cash soon enough. Over its short lifetime, a money market security is unlikely to vary very much in value. There is little time for drastic changes in the circumstances of the issuer, and because of its short duration, the price of the security is not very sensitive to changes in interest rates.

With long-term securities, the situation is very different. Repayment is far in the future (for bonds) or nonexistent (for stocks): the secondary market is the only way to turn them into cash. There is plenty of time for the circumstances of the issuer to change, so it is important to be able to unload or acquire them rapidly, to benefit from new information. Changes in market interest rates have a large effect on their price. If you can anticipate such changes and adjust your position accordingly, you stand to profit substantially. Given these reasons to trade long-term securities, especially stocks, it is not surprising that they have a particularly well-developed secondary market.

The Economic Role of Secondary Markets

There are two things any secondary market must do:

- Determine a fair price for the securities it trades (*price discovery*)
- Enable transactions to be made at this price quickly and easily (the *provision of liquidity*)

Let us look at each of these in turn.

fair asked price
The lowest price at which any well-informed trader is willing to sell a security to you.

Price Discovery.   A security represents a promise of future payment or payments. Its value depends on expectations of the amount of those payments and an evaluation of the risks involved. Expectations and evaluations reflect both the information available and the conclusions people draw from that information. With the same information, different people may reach different conclusions on the value of the same security.

A **fair asked price** for a security is the lowest price at which any well-informed trader is willing to sell it to you. A **fair bid price** is the highest price any well-informed trader is willing to pay you for it.

fair bid price
The highest price any well-informed trader is willing to pay you for a security.

In an **ideal market**, all trades take place at fair prices. In an ideal market, prices change immediately to reflect any new information, so that no one ever buys or sells a security for more or less than its fair price. The ideal market is, of course, just that—an ideal. No actual market achieves it. The ideal market is, however, a useful benchmark against which we can measure the performance of actual markets.

Price discovery is the process of arriving at fair prices for securities. We shall see that different markets do this in different ways. We shall see too that the different ways of organizing a market affect how closely the market approaches the ideal of fair prices.

ideal market
A market in which all trades take place at fair prices.

price discovery
The process of arriving at fair prices for securities.

The Provision of Liquidity.   A securities market provides **liquidity** if you can buy or sell in it quickly without loss. For example, take your 100 shares of IBM. If you can sell them immediately for a fair price, the market provides you with good liquidity. If it takes a long time to sell them, or if you can sell them immediately only at a sacrifice, it does not.

As another example, suppose that you are managing a large pension fund and you have $100 million of new contributions to invest. If you can buy this amount of securities immediately with little effect on the price you must pay, the market provides good liquidity. If, on the other hand, buying the securities immediately drives their price up, while buying them gradually over a few days or weeks does not, then the market does not provide good liquidity.[9]

liquidity
The ability to turn an asset into cash quickly without loss.

As we saw when we looked at financial intermediaries, the basic source of liquidity is pooling. For example, some people wish to make withdrawals from their bank deposits and others wish to make new deposits. To a large extent, the bank can satisfy the former with the funds provided by the latter. Sometimes, however, there will be an excess of withdrawals over new deposits. The bank must be ready to deal with this, whether by holding reserves or by other means.

---

[9] The ability of the market to absorb large trades of this type with no effect on prices is called *resiliency*.

In terms of liquidity a securities market is much like an intermediary. Some people wish to turn their securities into cash; others wish to turn their cash into securities. Pooling works here too. To a large extent the two groups can accommodate one another. However, there may be a **liquidity imbalance**—more of one group than of the other. Just like a bank, a securities market must be able to deal with such a situation. We shall see that different markets do this in different ways.

liquidity imbalance
A situation in which the desire to cash an asset does not balance the desire to exchange cash for the asset.

In a securities market that provides good liquidity, the market price should not fluctuate in response to a liquidity imbalance. As we have seen, the fair price of a security depends on a well-informed assessment of the value of promised future payments. A temporary liquidity imbalance should not affect this assessment. It should not therefore affect the market price. If the market price does fluctuate in response to a liquidity imbalance, then the market price is not "fair" and the market is not ideal.

The Organization of Secondary Markets

Dealer Markets and Auction Markets.   There are two alternative ways to conduct trading—the dealer market and the auction market.

If you want to buy or sell a T-bill, you go to your bank. The bank calls up a government securities dealer and asks for a price. The dealer quotes bid and asked prices for the T-bill in question. The government securities market is a **dealer market**. Dealers are "market makers" who quote prices at which they are willing to trade and stand ready to accommodate traders at these prices.

dealer market
A market made by dealers, who quote prices at which they are willing to buy and sell.

If you want to buy or sell a futures contract, you tell your broker how many contracts you want to trade and perhaps the price at which you are willing to buy or sell. Your broker passes on your order to the trading pit. At the same time, other traders are submitting their orders. The trading pit takes all the orders and matches them against one another. The futures market is an **auction market**. While dealer markets are quote driven, auction markets are order driven.

auction market
A market in which the orders of traders are matched directly.

How Dealer Markets Work.   In a dealer market, the responsibility of setting the price rests with the dealers. For a market to function like an ideal market, dealers should change the prices they quote as new information becomes available, but they should *not* change their prices when there is an imbalance of liquidity. They should absorb such an imbalance by buying for their own inventory or by selling out of their own inventory.

In practice, this is far from easy. If all information were immediately available to everyone and its implications were generally understood, being a dealer would be relatively simple. In reality, however, some traders have better information than others, and some are better at interpreting it.

Information Traders and Liquidity Traders.   For example, suppose a computer company called Prometheus is quoted at 100. Leah has been studying the computer industry and realizes that a new chip announced by another company will make the machines produced by Prometheus less competitive. She reckons that future earnings will drop enough to lower the fair price for its stock to 95. Leah can profit from her superior understanding of the computer industry by **selling short**. She can borrow Prometheus stock and sell it

sell short
To borrow a security and sell it.

immediately at 100. After the market as a whole realizes the implications of the new chip, Prometheus will fall to 95. She can then buy back the stock at 95 and return it to whomever she borrowed it from.

We will call traders like Leah, who trade to profit from better information or from better interpretation of generally available information, **information traders**. Information traders trade only when the market price differs from the fair price. We will call traders who buy and sell for reasons other than a belief that the market price is wrong, **liquidity traders**.[10]

The dealers' problem is that they often cannot distinguish liquidity traders from information traders. Information traders are a menace to them. In our example, Leah's profit is the loss of the dealer who bought the stock from her at 100.

The threat from information traders gives dealers a strong incentive to set prices accurately. As a result, prices tend to respond to new information quickly in a dealer market. Prices can change drastically with little or no actual trading.

The threat from information traders also gives dealers an incentive to hoard information. The only special information they have is about the trading process itself. They can see the volume of buy and sell orders coming in and they know at what prices transactions are actually taking place. Dealers often guard this information and make it available to the public only with a delay. This gives them a temporary advantage over the information traders they fear.

The Role of the Bid–Asked Spread.   However hard dealers try to price accurately, they are sure to be wrong some of the time. Their best defense against the consequent losses to information traders is their bid–asked spread. For example, suppose the dealer thought the fair price for Prometheus was 100, but set his bid price at 95 and his asked price at 105. Then, in this case, Leah could not profit at his expense. In general, the greater the uncertainty about the fair price, and the greater the threat from information traders, the greater will be the bid–asked spread.

Whatever the bid–asked spread, a dealer will occasionally take losses from trading with information traders. However, the larger the bid–asked spread, the greater will be the dealer's profits from trading with liquidity traders. The larger profit he makes on liquidity trades will compensate him for the occasional losses to information traders.

Liquidity traders are willing to pay a bid–asked spread because the dealer provides them with liquidity. They know they can buy the security from the dealer, or sell it to him, at any time they wish at a fair price—plus or minus the bid or asked differential. Of course, the greater the bid–asked spread, the worse the liquidity. So the greater the uncertainty about a fair price, and the greater the threat from information traders, the less well will a dealer market provide liquidity.

Interdealer Markets.   In dealer markets there are usually multiple dealers buying and selling the same securities. Since they set bid and asked prices independently, there is nothing to guarantee that their prices are the same. This would seem to suggest a profit opportu-

information traders
Traders who trade to profit from discrepancies between the market prices and the fair price.

liquidity traders
Traders who trade for reasons unrelated to the price of a security.

---

[10] In an ideal market, in which the market price always equals the fair price, there are no information traders. All traders are liquidity traders.

nity: buy from a dealer with the lowest asked price and sell to the dealer with highest bid price. Such an opportunity is hard to find for two reasons. The first, of course, is the bid–asked spread. The second is that most dealer markets have an "inside" market in which dealers trade with one another, and trading on this interdealer market tends to bring the prices of the different dealers into line with one another.

Dealers use the interdealer market primarily to adjust their inventories—to top up if they are running short or to dispose of an excess if they have too much. Usually they can get the best price from another dealer. In addition, because this is where dealers themselves trade, the interdealer market serves a pivotal informational function. If a dealer acquires new information, he immediately checks his fellow dealers' quoted prices on the interdealer market. If these do not reflect the new information, he can profit by trading against them—buying if their prices are too low or selling if they are too high. In this market, it is the other dealers who are the information traders. It is precisely this information trading by the dealers that brings prices into line. Moreover, because new information typically affects the interdealer market first, this is where price discovery takes place for the market as a whole.

How Auction Markets Work.   In an auction market there is no dealer to set the price. Instead, buy and sell orders are brought together and the price is set to clear the market.[11] If there are relatively many buy orders, the price will rise. If there are relatively many sell orders the price will fall.

An auction market does not differentiate between information trading and liquidity trading: supply is supply and demand is demand. The price of the security rises or falls equally in response to new information or to liquidity imbalances.

Of course, information traders are watching the market. If the price of the security is forced far enough away from its fair price by a liquidity imbalance, they will come in to take advantage of it. For example, if the price is forced down, traders will buy and hold, expecting the price to return to normal when the liquidity imbalance passes.

In an auction market, therefore, it is the information traders who provide liquidity. Far from being a menace, their presence is essential to the proper working of the market. For example, as we shall see in Chapter 16, there are in the futures markets professional information traders known as "locals." It is the locals who provide the futures markets with liquidity. Prices on a futures market without locals would fluctuate widely as a result of liquidity imbalances, and prices would therefore rarely be fair. Such a market would attract little business from liquidity traders.

In an auction market, prices generally change more slowly in response to new information than they do in a dealer market. Prices are not set by a market maker: they cannot change until they are moved by trading. The price will therefore rise or fall more gradually as trading takes place.

The way auction markets treat trading information differs from the way dealer markets treat it. Far from hoarding trading information, auction markets usually make it available as quickly as possible. The better the information, the easier it is for information traders to come in and smooth out liquidity imbalances.

---

[11] We shall see how in Chapter 17.

SECURITIES FIRMS

We have seen that the functioning of financial markets depends on the activities of numerous specialized professionals—underwriters, dealers, brokers, and information traders. We have talked about them as though they were independent entities. While some are indeed independent, most work for large, multifunction securities firms. As we shall see, securities firms are large because of significant economies of scale, and they are multifunctional because of significant economies of scope.

The Nature of the Business

investment banking
Activities related to the issuing of new securities and the arrangement of financial transactions.

The traditional business of securities firms may be divided into two broad categories—investment banking and brokerage.[12] **Investment banking** comprises those activities related to the *primary market*, the market in which new issues are sold for the first time. **Brokerage** comprises those activities related to the *secondary market*, the market where existing securities are traded. In addition, securities firms have recently been drawn into a third major line of business—risk management.

Investment Banking

brokerage
Activities related to the trading of securities.

Underwriting.   Investment banking, of course, involves the underwriting of new issues. As we have seen, this includes advising the client on the type of security and its pricing, gathering and processing information and completing the necessary paperwork, and marketing the issue to investors.

Advising on Restructuring.   Since many new issues are brought to market as a consequence of some sort of corporate restructuring—mergers and acquisitions, spinoffs, or privatizations—investment bankers have accumulated a great deal of expertise in this area. Consequently, they are often closely involved in advising clients in restructuring transactions, even when no new issue is involved. The fees they earn from this are substantial. For example, the securities firms involved in advising RJR and Nabisco in their merger earned some $600 million in fees.

The volume of mergers and acquisitions has grown rapidly in the last 20 years. In 2000, according to *The Wall Street Journal*, there were nearly 11,000 deals in the United States totaling some $1.8 trillion. Worldwide there were nearly 30,000 deals totaling some $3.5 trillion. Because of the experience they have acquired in the United States, U.S. securities firms are frequently called in to advise on restructuring transactions overseas.

merchant banking
Investment banking activities that involve taking an equity stake in corporations.

Merchant Banking.   Because of their close involvement in new issues and restructuring, investment banks encounter many good investment opportunities. They have increasingly exploited these opportunities by taking positions themselves in the companies in question—an activity known as **merchant banking**.[13]

---

[12] This terminology is not, by any means, followed consistently in the market.

[13] Not to be confused with the historical meaning of merchant banking that we encountered in Chapter 6. The connection is that merchant bankers in England evolved into investment bankers, but the name "merchant bank" stuck.

Brokerage

Brokerage consists of three distinct activities: wholesale and retail brokerage, market making and trading, and money management.

Wholesale and Retail Brokerage.   Wholesale and retail brokers help institutional investors and small investors respectively, in buying and selling securities. Mostly, the securities in question are existing securities traded in the secondary markets, but brokers also market new issues to their customers. Selling securities has expanded into selling other financial assets—for example, mutual funds and bank certificates of deposit.

Market Making and Trading.   Securities firms are also active in making markets as dealers and brokers. To be able to advise their customers on the purchase of securities and to function as market makers, securities firms need to acquire information and undertake research. This puts them in a good position to trade on their own account as information traders.

Money Management.   Wholesale and retail brokerage has naturally led to money management. Securities firms manage asset portfolios for a variety of customers. One important category of customer is pension plans. Securities firms compete with banks, insurance companies, and mutual fund management firms to manage pension funds.[14] Securities firms also set up and manage mutual funds, which they offer to their customers.

Another important clientele for money management is wealthy individuals. Managing portfolios for the wealthy is known as **private banking**. The worldwide market is huge—estimated at $17 trillion. In 1999 there were estimated to be over 500 billionaires in the world, of these 276 were in North America. There were estimated to be some 7 million "high net worth" individuals in the world (those with over $1 million in liquid assets); of these some 2.5 million were in North America.[15] The number of the "mass affluent" ($100,000 to $1 million in liquid assets) is much, much larger. Until recently this last group has been ignored by private bankers because providing them with money management services was unprofitable (there are, of course, economies of scale). However, the Internet has greatly lowered costs, and private bankers have been rushing to offer services online to the merely affluent.

private banking
Money management for wealthy individuals.

Risk Management and Derivatives

Securities firms have always been financial intermediaries. In order to function as underwriters and dealers, they have to hold positions in securities. They largely finance such positions with funds that they borrow in their own name. However, the extent of their financial intermediation has grown rapidly in recent years as merchant banking and trading have become increasingly important parts of their business.

Their growing balance sheets have exposed them to considerable risk, and they have consequently become increasingly involved in **risk management**.[16] This has led to two

risk management
Techniques used to protect the balance sheet from risk.

---

[14] See Chapter 10.

[15] Numbers from *The Financial Times* (2000a).

[16] We shall discuss the details in Chapter 18.

new lines of business. Having developed methods of risk management for themselves, they have been able to offer this service to their clients. And their involvement in risk management has led them into the derivatives market, where they now rank among the largest intermediaries for swaps and options.[17]

THE ORGANIZATION OF A SECURITIES FIRM

The Importance of People

More than most businesses, securities firms depend on the skill and talent of their personnel. This is especially true in those lines of business that involve trading and deal making. The organization of securities firms reflects this dependence on talent, and it has to address two important consequences—the need to retain good people and the importance of providing them with incentives that align their interests with the interests of the firm.

Internally, a securities firm is typically organized as a collection of separate departments. Each department acts independently in a particular line of business or in a particular securities market. The firm provides each department with capital, and the department is expected to earn a target return on that capital. Organization within departments is similar, with individuals being allocated capital by their respective departments. To ensure that each individual gives the maximum, he or she is rewarded according to personal results. To ensure cooperation, each has a significant stake in the overall profits of the department and the firm.

The Form of the Securities Firm

Because of the need to give the individual members of a firm a strong stake in its success, securities firms have typically been organized as partnerships. Historically, securities firms evolved from general auctioneers and merchants that were organized as individual proprietorships or small partnerships. Auctioneers sold securities along with lottery tickets and commodities. Merchants traded in securities as part of their general business of buying and selling. Until late in the nineteenth century, most American securities were sold abroad. Consequently, most American securities firms developed from merchants and merchant bankers involved in international trade. For example, the Morgans bought iron rails in England for American railroads and sold their bonds in the London market. Like law and accounting firms, which also depend heavily on the talent of their members, but unlike most other businesses, securities firms retained the partnership structure as they grew.

Recently, however, there has been a trend towards incorporation. Converting a partnership into a corporation has several advantages. By being able to sell shares to outsiders, rather than relying only on retained profits, the firm is able to increase its capital more quickly when the need arises. The enhanced ability to raise capital, together with the ability to buy and sell ownership in the firm, makes mergers and acquisitions easier (we shall see presently that the industry is experiencing a wave of consolidation). For members of

---

[17] We shall discuss derivatives and derivative markets in Chapter 16.

the firm, their ownership stake is now much more liquid: they can cash it out more easily, borrow against it, and diversify their wealth. Moreover, as shareholders, their liability is now limited to their stake in the firm. As partners, their liability had been unlimited.

Incorporation, of course, has its disadvantages too. Relative to a partnership, the incentives of the members are diluted: unlimited liability and the inability to cash out or diversify certainly focus the attention. In addition, as we shall see in Chapter 15, bringing in external investors as shareholders creates conflicts of interest between these outsiders and insiders that can be harmful to the efficiency of the enterprise. Neither of these disadvantages is as serious as it might be, since the members of the firm retain a significant stake in it as major shareholders.

Employee Risk

Because they are so dependent on the talent of their people, securities firms are especially vulnerable to employee risk. To make the most of their skills, individuals have to be given the freedom to act. As long as the interests of the individual and of the firm are aligned, this should work well. There will be losses as well as gains, of course, but that is the nature of the business. However, when interests diverge, the individual can make decisions that are disastrous for the firm.

A notorious example is the case of Nick Leeson a 28-year-old trader for Barings in Singapore. He had earned large profits for the firm trading in derivatives but suffered a series of major setbacks in early 1995 that put him deeply in the red. He hid the losses and went for broke, engaging in some desperate transactions in an attempt to salvage his position. The losses on these transactions were so large that they completely wiped out the firm's capital.

The incentive problem here is that once he had suffered the initial reverses, Leeson no longer had anything to lose. If his subsequent trades went well, he would be saved; if they did not, Barings, not he, would bear the cost.[18] Soon after the Barings collapse, Salomon, another securities firm, introduced a new system of incentives intended to address this issue. It required its traders to bank their bonuses so that they could repay the firm, at least in part, for any subsequent losses. Not surprisingly, this plan was highly unpopular and led some star traders to move to other firms. Salomon soon abandoned its new system.[19] Salomon's experience illustrates the inherent conflict between aligning incentives and providing conditions that are attractive to traders.

Since incentives cannot be perfectly aligned, securities firms have no choice but to monitor their personnel very carefully. It is not only traders who expose the firms to risk. There have been a number of lawsuits against securities firms by customers who incurred losses on securities or risk instruments that were sold or recommended to them by the firms' brokers. And the losses are not always financial. Misbehavior by a single individual working for a securities firm can seriously damage the reputation of the whole firm, which together with its people, is its most valuable asset.

---

[18] This is very much like the problem, discussed earlier in the chapter, of a debtor in serious danger of default.

[19] *Euromoney* (1995).

THE SECURITIES INDUSTRY

To understand what is happening in the securities industry, we need to understand the profound changes that have been taking place in its environment. We can divide these changes into four interrelated categories:

- Globalization
- Deregulation
- Innovation
- The growing importance of institutional investors

These changes have greatly increased the competitive pressure on securities firms, and this has led to a restructuring of the industry. Before we look at this restructuring, let us review the causes of change.

Globalization

globalization
The integration of securities markets across national borders.

The first major source of change in financial markets has been **globalization**—the increasing integration of financial markets across national borders. Growth in international financial transactions exploded in the 1980s and 1990s.

Of course, international lending is nothing new. Since the earliest days of financial markets, international lending has been the rule rather than the exception. Typically, as an economy matures and its financial system develops, the supply of funds increases relative to the demand, and domestic interest rates fall. As a result, lending outside the domestic market becomes increasingly attractive, and the economy in question becomes an international lender. This pattern has been repeated over and over again—the role of lender being played, successively, by Florence, the Netherlands, England, and France. The pattern was interrupted by the collapse of international trade during and after the Great Depression. However, since World War II, international lending has steadily recovered.

The recent explosion in international securities has, however, brought something new. It has gone beyond the traditional pattern of lender countries lending to borrower countries—for example, the European countries lending and the United States borrowing. It has been characterized by reciprocal trade in securities: countries selling their securities and, at the same time, buying the securities of other countries. For example, the United States buys European securities at the same time that the European countries buy U.S. securities in amounts much larger than any net lending.

Deregulation

deregulation
The process of repealing or liberalizing existing regulations.

Globalization has been both the consequence and the cause of **deregulation**. While there is a tendency to increase regulation aimed at protecting investors, other forms of regulation are on the decline worldwide. There has been a loosening of regulations restricting entry into financial markets by institutions such as banks and by foreign securities firms. There has been a movement away from regulations that fix the price of financial services (beginning with the United States in 1975). There has been a removal of restrictions on international lending. New markets have been authorized—particularly money markets and markets for derivative securities

Deregulation has been driven by powerful market forces. Countries with restrictive regulations have found themselves at a disadvantage in the world securities market relative to countries with less restrictions. Business has gravitated to the freest markets. Deregulation in one country has increased the pressure for deregulation in others.

Innovation

Financial Engineering.   Throughout their history, the growth of financial markets has been associated with the emergence of new types of securities. In the nineteenth century, the big innovation was railroad bonds. At the turn of the century, it was the highly speculative "industrials" (bonds and then stocks of industrial companies). In recent years, we have seen an explosion of new instruments in the money market, and the development of a market for junk bonds. In all of these cases, what was new was the issuer. The nature of the securities themselves did not change. The basic instruments—bonds, bills, and equities—have existed for centuries.

Recently, however, we have also seen an outpouring of completely new *types* of security. Of the five major securities markets listed at the beginning of the chapter, two simply did not exist 30 years ago: the mortgage market and the market for derivatives. Rather than evolving gradually through trial and error, these new types of security were created deliberately to fill a specific need. This process is called **financial engineering**.

financial engineering
The design of new types of security to fill needs not satisfied by existing securities.

Financial engineering was made possible by advances in the theory of finance. These improved our understanding of the valuation of securities and of the relationship between different types of security. Improved understanding suggests new types of security that do not currently exist but could be created.

Information Technology and the Internet.   A second important contributor to the creation of these new securities has been the rapid advance in information technology. This has made possible complex calculations and has facilitated the quick and inexpensive execution of complicated trades. The "rocket scientists" identified a security that did not actually exist, but for which there might be a demand. Then practitioners used computer technology to create such a security.

The related technology of the Internet has also had a significant impact on financial markets—much larger so far than its impact on banking. The attraction of the Internet is its potential to reduce transactions costs. Its greatest impact so far has been on brokerage.[20] In the United States, E*Trade, an online broker founded in 1996, had 2.6 million accounts by 1999. Schwab, an existing "bricks and mortar" broker, had over half of its 7 million customers trading online by then. In 1999, some 16% of all equity trades were undertaken online. Other U.S. securities firms have been trying to catch up. Online brokerage is growing even faster in Europe, but from a smaller base, since fewer Europeans owns shares (12% of adults vs 50% in the United States). However, it is in Asia where online broker-

---

[20] The following information is from *The Economist* (2000).

age has had the greatest impact: in South Korea, for example, online trading accounts for 30% of stockmarket turnover.

There has been a push to create online trading systems, and we shall learn more about this in Chapter 17. And there have been some attempts at online underwriting. The first major bond issue to be sold, marketed, and traded solely on the Internet was a $3 billion offering by the World Bank in January 1999, arranged by Goldman Sachs and Lehman Brothers.[21]

The Growing Importance of Institutional Investors

The popular idea of the typical investor is Jack Smith buying some shares in General Motors. In reality, however, the typical Jack Smith does not buy General Motors shares directly; he does so indirectly when he buys shares in a mutual fund or, without even knowing it, when his employer contributes to his pension fund. Households have steadily shifted from owning transferable securities themselves directly to owning them indirectly through their claims on financial intermediaries such as pension funds, mutual funds, and life insurance companies. (We explored some of the reasons for this shift in Chapter 10.) These **institutional investors** have replaced households as the principal holders of transferable securities.

institutional investors
Financial intermediaries that invest in transferable securities.

In the United States, households owned directly some 92% of outstanding stocks in 1952. Today, that proportion is around 50%. In other large developed countries, households hold directly an even smaller proportion of total stocks—typically less than 25%. In the United Kingdom, ownership has been shifting much as it has in the United States, and institutional investors have attained an even greater share of the market. In other developed countries such as Germany and Japan, institutional investors have always been the predominant holders of transferable securities. The amount of financial assets held by institutions has grown enormously: in the countries of the OECD (a club of developed economies), total institutional assets rose from $3.2 trillion in 1981 (38% of GDP) to $24.3 trillion in 1995 (107% of GDP).

The growing importance of institutional investors has had an enormous impact on financial markets. As we saw in Chapter 10, competition to manage institutional portfolios has been fierce. The way to attract more money to manage is to show high returns on the money you manage already. The consequent pressure to show success has driven money managers to engage in a tremendous amount of trading. Although institutions own only half of all outstanding equities in the United States, they account for 70% of trading volume.

Because they trade so much, institutional investors are very sensitive to trading costs. They have put enormous pressure on the markets to lower costs. As we shall see, this pressure has led to profound changes in the major stock markets and to the proliferation of alternative trading systems offering lower costs. The desire of institutions to lower trading costs has been an important driving force behind deregulation.

Much of the innovation in financial markets has been motivated by the needs of institutional investors. Securities firms and financial markets have developed new products designed to serve the needs of institutional clients. Such products include strips, mortgage-

---

[21] *The Financial Times* (2000a).

backed securities, and financial futures and options. Institutional investors have enthusiastically adopted the Internet: by 2000, they were expected to be doing a majority of their equity trading online.[22]

It is also institutional investors that have provided the impetus for globalization. A number of countries, most notably the United Kingdom and Japan, removed restrictions that used to prevent their residents from buying foreign securities. Institutions in those countries, particularly pension funds and life insurance companies, seized the opportunity and bought large amounts of foreign stocks to diversify their portfolios. Japanese pension funds increased the share of overseas investments in their portfolios from 1% in 1980 to 16% in 1990; British pension funds increased it from 7% to 18%. In the same period, U.S. pension funds increased the share of overseas investments in their portfolios from 1% to 4%. Remaining restrictions on the overseas investments of continental European pension funds were lifted in 1992, giving a further boost to cross-border trading.

Increasing Competition

The principal result of these changes in the environment of the securities industry has been a significant increase in competitive pressure. Deregulation has spurred competition among securities firms in each country, and globalization has brought the securities firms of different countries into competition with one another. Innovation has opened up new markets that securities firms struggle to dominate, and the Internet has opened new avenues of competition. The growing importance of institutional investors, too, has stimulated competition: the greater bargaining power of institutional investors has enabled them to demand cheaper and better service.

For example, there used to be little competition in brokerage. The business was divided between a small number of wholesale firms and a much larger number of retail firms. In addition to their activities in the secondary market, the wholesale firms usually also underwrote new issues and the retail firms distributed them to the public through their extensive branch networks. Competition between the two groups and within each group was minimal. Commissions were generally fixed.

This structure was undermined by the rise of institutional investors and by the corresponding decline in direct household ownership. Institutions wanted volume discounts and did not want to pay for research and advice. It was largely pressure from institutional investors that led the SEC to deregulate NYSE commissions in 1975.

discount brokers
Stockbrokers that offer low-cost execution of orders without investment advice or safekeeping services.

The ending of fixed commissions opened the way for competition, which soon arrived in the form of **discount brokers**, firms that offer execution of orders without the investment advice and safekeeping services offered by **full-service brokers**. Discount brokers now account for a large part of the market.

full-service brokers
Traditional stockbrokers that offer a full range of services.

The fierce competition for a diminishing volume of retail business, at lower commissions, led to the failure of many small retail firms and the consolidation of others. The larger firms were hurt less and reoriented their business to serves institutional investors—offering them investment advice, trading expertise, and risk management services. They also expanded into wholesale brokerage and the management of mutual funds.

[22] *The Financial Times* (2000a).

Global Consolidation

As a result of the increasing competitive pressure, the securities industry is undergoing a major restructuring. It is rapidly consolidating to reap economies of scale and economies of scope. Some truly enormous firms have emerged, known as the "bulge bracket" firms, that operate worldwide and offer a complete range of services.

Exhibit 11.7 lists the largest securities firms in the world. As you can see, U.S. firms are particularly prominent. One reason is that financial markets have historically been more important in the United States than in other countries. Another reason is that deregulation and intense competition came to the United States earlier than it did to other countries, and this created a group of efficient and aggressive securities firms. When globalization opened other markets to them, they had a significant advantage over the local firms, which had been operating in a much less competitive environment.

Economies of Scale.   The economies of scale in the securities business are of three types that are already familiar to us from our discussion of banks and other financial intermediaries—financial economies, indivisibility of fixed costs, and reputational economies.

In the securities business, the most important financial economies of scale arise from diversification. As we have seen, securities firms deliberately take on risks in their underwriting, merchant banking, and trading activities. Although they have been pioneers in risk

EXHIBIT 11.7   Largest Securities Firms

Name	Market Capitalization (billions of dollars)[a]	Share of Worldwide Underwriting (%)[b]	Share of World Advising on Mergers and Acquisitions (%)[a]
Citigroup	280	12	19
J. P. Morgan Chase	103	8	18
Morgan Stanley Dean Witter	99	8	32
UBS Warburg (Switzerland)	75	5	11
Crédit Suisse First Boston (Switzerland)	62	9	27
Merrill Lynch	59	13	22
Deutsche Bank (Germany)	55	5	4
Goldman Sachs	49	6	36
Barque Nationale de Paris (France)	42	—	—
Dresdner Bank (Germany)	24	—	4
U.S. firms above		47	127[c]

[a] 2000.

[b] First quarter, 2001.

[c] More than one firm may advise a given deal.

Sources: The Wall Street Journal; The Financial Times.

management, diversification is still a big help, and the larger the firm, the greater the potential for diversification.

The indivisibility in fixed costs has always been an important source of economies of scale in the securities business—for example, in information acquisition and in trading infrastructure and back-office support.[23] However, innovation has increased the importance of indivisible fixed costs enormously. This is true for supporting the teams of "rocket scientists" who develop knew financial products, and it is equally true for information technology. Securities firms have invested billions in computer hardware and software over the last decade.

Reputational economies are especially important in investment banking. Consequently, this part of the business has always been highly concentrated. In the United States, the top 10 underwriters have long accounted for nearly 90% of the total, and the picture is no different elsewhere. Even worldwide, the top 10 underwriters account for roughly 70% of the total. Reputation is important too in brokerage (especially in money management), in raising funds to finance a firm's positions, and in intermediating derivatives.

Globalization itself has been a direct source of important economies of scale. To provide cross-border services, and to be able to arbitrage across markets, securities firms have to establish a presence in every important market. With traders in different time zones trading the same securities, some markets are active around the clock. Many firms have therefore taken to "**passing the book**" from one office to another. That is, control of the firm's trading in a given security is passed from traders in London to traders in New York to traders in Tokyo. Round-the-clock trading in securities has created a demand for round-the-clock trading in derivatives.

passing the book
The practice, in an around-the-clock market, of passing trading from one office to another in a different time zone.

To defray the (fixed) cost of their presence is so many markets, securities firms try to expand their local activities. Activities that are relatively easy to expand, and in which large international firms have an advantage over local competitors, include advising on mergers and acquisitions and privatizations and private banking.

A firm that has a substantial presence and is able to compete in every market is necessarily very large. Midsized firms have consequently found themselves unable to compete in the global market, and increasingly they have merged or been snapped up by bigger international firms. Some of the larger deals in 2000 included the purchase of PaineWebber by United Bank of Switzerland (UBS), of Donaldson, Lufkin & Jenrette by Crédit Suisse, and of J. P. Morgan by Chase Manhattan.[24]

Economies of Scope.   The multifunction securities firm is a relatively recent phenomenon. Even 10 or 15 years ago, most firms were specialized. Some specialized in investment banking, others in wholesale brokerage, and yet others in retail brokerage. Many market makers were small and independent. Securities firms specialized too by type of security—for example, corporate, government, or municipal; by industry—for example, oil and gas or utilities; or by the geographic region in which they operated. Only a very few firms provided a complete range of services over a wide geographic area.

---

[23] We shall learn more about this in Chapter 17.

[24] *The Financial Times* (2001).

Over the last decade, however, through mergers and acquisitions, specialized securities firms have largely been combined to form large multifunction firms. The reasons for this change are economies of scope and diversification.

There are several sources of economies of scope in the securities business. Information or expertise acquired in one market or activity may be useful in another. For example, a securities firm acquires information about a company in underwriting it and distributing its securities or in advising it on mergers and acquisitions. Possessing that information will lower the costs of making a market in those securities or of making a direct investment in the company (merchant banking). Moreover, companies will be more likely to pick an underwriter that is able to make a market in their securities after they have been issued: this makes the securities more attractive and raises the price of the issue.

Customers for one type of service are potential customers for others. This is true both in investment banking and in brokerage. In investment banking, it is ultimately the customer that must bear the cost of providing information. Consequently, it is cheaper for a company to continue to deal with a securities firm that is already familiar with its operations. In brokerage, customers for one type of security are potential purchasers of others; they are also potential customers for mutual funds, money management, and risk management.

static economies of scope
Reduction of costs on one activity as a result of engaging in another.

These are example of **static economies of scope**: engaging in one activity or line of business lowers the cost of engaging in another. However, there are also **dynamic economies of scope**: these might best be described as "one thing leading to another." We have already seen how underwriting drew securities firms into advising on mergers and acquisitions and into merchant banking. And we have seen how brokerage drew securities firms into money management and how internal risk management evolved into the sale of risk management services and derivatives. In each of these cases, the new activity was less a matter of static economies of scope than of exploiting new profit opportunities as they occurred.

dynamic economies of scope
Reduction in the cost of entry to a new activity as a result of already engaging in another.

The economies of scope reach beyond the securities business itself. We have seen in previous chapters that economies of scope have drawn securities firms into other areas of finance too. We saw in Chapter 6 that especially since the repeal of Glass–Steagall, securities firms have been combining with commercial banks through mergers and acquisitions. We saw in Chapter 9 that they have been combining, too, with insurance companies.

The expansion into new lines of business that results from dynamic economies of scope provides diversification. Of course, it promotes diversification in the risk management sense that profits in one risky activity tend to offset losses in another, leaving overall profits more stable. But it also provides diversification in a different sense—a diversification of business risks. Because the securities business is changing so rapidly, a line of business that is profitable today may be quite unprofitable tomorrow. So having a finger in many pies makes it easier to replace declining lines of business with growing ones.

We have seen, for example, that retail and wholesale brokerage have increasingly become standardized, highly competitive businesses with low margins. While commissions accounted for over 50% of the income of securities firms before 1975, they accounted for only 14% in 2000. Brokerage income has consequently come increasingly from trading (19% in 2000). In underwriting, the effect of increasing competition has been similar. In the early 1980s, underwriting fees amounted to about 1.5% of the value of securities underwritten; by 1993 that number had fallen to 0.7%. In recent years, declining profitability has partly been offset by increasing volume, but underwriting fees accounted for only 7% of securities firms' income in 2000. In compensation, investment bankers have found a veritable gold mine in advising on mergers and acquisitions and other restructuring. The worldwide volume of mergers and acquisitions announced in 2000 alone was some $3.5 trillion. Nearly half of securities firm income in 2000 came from advising and from merchant banking (long-term investments).[25]

Now that we have a basic understanding of what financial markets do, how they work, and who makes them work, we are ready to examine individual financial markets in greater detail in the coming chapters.

SUMMARY

- New issues of bonds exceed new issues of stock by about a factor of five. Net funds raised through issues of stocks and bonds are far less than the amounts of new issues. Corporations finance most of their investment from internal funds.

- The reason for this pattern is that external financing is highly problematic, and this makes it expensive.

- External financing is nonetheless important as the marginal source of funds, particularly for expanding and new industries. Moreover, financial markets have a much greater effect on the *quality* of investment than on its quantity.

- Financial markets serve not only business, but also consumers and governments.

- From the point of view of the lender, the main concern is avoiding loss. Default presents a dilemma—to enforce or to accommodate. The prospect of default encourages risk taking by the borrower.

- There is a preference for safe debt. It is "low maintenance," and pricing it is easy. Risky debt is "high maintenance," and lenders may require an equity component to compensate for the downside risk.

- Equity financing avoids the problems of default, but has the problem of ensuring a fair return—the problem of corporate governance.

- The cost of financing is borne by the recipient. So financing with safe debt is relatively cheap, but financing with risky debt or equity is expensive.

- In the United States, public issues of securities are generally sold through underwriters. An underwriter purchases an issue from an issuer and sells it to the public. There are two risks: the risk of overpaying for the issue and the risk of a rise in interest rates before the issue can be sold. For large issues, underwriters typically form syndicates to spread the risk.

- There has been increasing competition in underwriting as a result of shelf registration and the growth of alternative markets—the market for private placements, the Euro market, and the market for syndicated loans.

- The two primary functions of a secondary market are price discovery and the provision of liquidity. A good secondary market is particularly important for long-term securities because the need for liquidity is greater.

- In an ideal market, trades take place at a fair price, and the price should not fluctuate as a result of a liquidity imbalance.

- Dealer markets are quote driven: dealers quote bid and asked prices at which they are willing to trade. Dealers provide the market with liquidity. Information traders are a threat to them.

---

[25] These numbers are for member firms of the New York Stock Exchange, which is pretty much all securities firms.

- Auction markets are order driven: orders of traders are matched directly. In an auction market, it is the information traders who provide the market with liquidity.

- Because of economies of scale and scope, professional traders and market makers are organized in large, multifunction securities firms.

- Securities firms engage in investment banking, which mainly involves the primary market, and brokerage, which mainly involves the secondary market. They have recently grown in importance as financial intermediaries, and this has led them into risk management and the derivatives market.

- Securities firms rely more than most on the talent of individuals. To retain good people, they need to provide incentives that align the interests of those who perform well with the interests of the firm.

- Change in the securities industry has been driven by four interrelated trends: globalization, deregulation, innovation, and the growing importance of institutional investors.

- These changes have increased competitive pressure and this has led to consolidation to exploit economies of scale and scope.

DISCUSSION QUESTIONS

1. Why is the amount of funds raised through the sale of stocks and bonds so much smaller than the amount of new issues?

2. Why do corporations rely so little on the capital market to finance investment? Explain why both debt and equity finance are difficult. How *do* firms finance investment?

3. "Since financial markets finance only a small part of business investment, they are not really very important." Is this true? Explain.

4. What is an "ideal" financial market? Explain how a market's liquidity and trading costs affect whether it is or is not "ideal."

5. Obviously dealers organize a dealer market. Who organizes an auction market? How exactly do the organizers of each type of market make a living? Which would you expect to earn more from a given volume of trading?

6. What effect do information traders have on dealer markets? On auction markets?

7. Some securities markets are dealer markets, others are auction markets. What are the factors that might explain which type of market exists for a given security?

8. Why are financial market professionals organized in large, multifunction securities firms? Why is the internal organization of these securities firms different from that of banks? What are the resulting problems?

9. Compare and contrast the ways that securities markets and financial intermediaries provide liquidity. What are their relative advantages and disadvantages? What can go wrong in each case?

10. Compare and contrast price discovery in dealer and in auction markets. In each case, who decides on what the price should be? What incentives do they have to set the price correctly?

11. What are the economies of scale and scope in securities firms? Are there economies of scope between investment banking and brokerage?

12. Many economists regard secondary markets with disdain. They often see them as more of a gambling casino than as a source of financing. For example, Joseph Stiglitz, when he was the chief economist for the World Bank, wrote: "Improvements in secondary markets do not necessarily enhance the ability of the economy either to mobilize savings or to allocate capital."

    a. What is the economic function of secondary markets?

    b. Do good secondary markets enhance the ability of the economy to mobilize savings and allocate capital?

    c. Suppose the answer to part b were negative. Would secondary markets then be of no value? In particular, consider the stock market.

BIBLIOGRAPHY

Abken, Peter A. "Globalization of Stock, Futures, and Options Markets." *Federal Reserve Bank of Atlanta Economic Review*, July–August 1991, 1–22.

The Economist. "The Virtual Threat: A Survey of Online Finance," May 20, 2000.

Euromoney, September 1995.

The Financial Times, "Global Investment Banking Survey," February 28, 2000a.

———. "Private Banking Survey," July 7, 2001b.

———. "Global Investment Banking Survey," February 26, 2001.

Mayer, C. "Financial Systems, Corporate Finance, and Economic Development." In *Asymmetric Information, Corporate Finance, and Investment*. Edited by R. G. Hubbard, Chicago: University of Chicago Press, 1990, 307–332.

Smith, Clifford W., Jr. "Globalization of Financial Markets." *Carnegie–Rochester Conference Series on Public Policy* 34 (1991): 77–96.

Wurgler, Jeffrey. "Financial Markets and the Allocation of Capital." *Journal of Financial Economics* 58, no. 1–2 (October–November 2000), 187–214.

KEY TERMS

benchmark
convertible debt
corporate governance
preferred equity
due diligence
underwriting syndicates
Rule 415
shelf registration
fair asked price
fair bid price
ideal market

price discovery
liquidity
liquidity imbalance
dealer market
auction market
selling short
information traders
liquidity traders
Investment banking
brokerage
merchant banking

private banking
risk management
globalization
deregulation
financial engineering
institutional investors
discount brokers
full-service brokers
passing the book
static economies of scope
dynamic economies of scope

CHAPTER 12

THE MARKET FOR GOVERNMENT SECURITIES

When you finish this chapter you will understand:

- How government securities are sold and traded
- How to make a profit as a securities dealer
- Why scandals in the market led to new regulations and procedures
- Why the market may disappear and what will replace it

Historically, the earliest securities markets were markets for government securities. In most countries even today, the market for government securities remains the largest securities market. Worldwide, there was some $9 trillion of government securities outstanding at the end of 1996, about 40% of all outstanding securities.

The market for U.S. government securities is by far the largest and most active securities market in the world. Trading volume in this market dwarfs that in any other. Major dealers alone traded an average of $190 billion a day in 1999, with as much as $600 billion more in related financing transactions. In comparison, trading on the New York Stock Exchange, with a daily volume in the tens of billions of dollars a day, appears quite modest.

Exhibit 12.1 shows the amount of government debt outstanding for the largest issuers. The U.S. government was long the largest borrower in the world, but no more. Since 1999 that honor has passed to the government of Japan. Large government budget surpluses in

EXHIBIT 12.1   Amount of Government Debt Outstanding in Several Major Issuing Countries

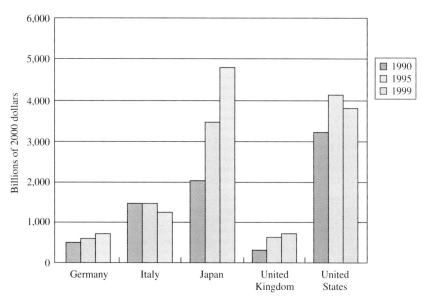

Source: Organization for Economic Cooperation and Development.

the United States and large deficits in Japan have changed the rankings. The introduction of the Euro in 1999 has created the third major market. The combined debt of the countries that have adopted the Euro is comparable in size to that of Japan and that of the United States.[1]

Markets for government securities are important not only because of their size. Government securities play a special role in the economy. The interest rate on government securities is the "risk-free rate"—the benchmark against which all other interest rates are measured. In many countries, the central bank regulates the quantity of money by buying and selling government securities. The market for government securities in the United States is among the least regulated financial markets, and it has therefore been at the forefront of innovation. Participants in this market have played a major role in creating some of the other financial markets we shall study in later chapters—the market for mortgage-backed securities (Chapter 13), the money market (Chapter 14), and the market for financial futures (Chapter 16).

We shall study the government securities market in particular detail as an example of how a real securities market works. We shall focus in particular on the market for U.S. government securities, since it is the most developed in the world and the model for govern-

---

[1] In 1999, the debt of Japan accounted for 33% of all OECD government debt. That of the United States for 27%, and that of the European Union (not all of whose members have adopted the Euro) for 34%.

ment securities markets in other countries. Once you understand how this market works, you will find it easier to understand others.

We begin with a brief review of the history of government securities markets. We then examine how new issues of government securities are sold (the primary market) and how outstanding issues are traded (the secondary market). We then see what it is like to be a dealer in government securities. We conclude with a discussion of regulation and of the implications of globalization and government surpluses.

THE HISTORY OF THE GOVERNMENT SECURITIES MARKET

When governments spend more than they currently raise in taxes, they must borrow. Historically, the main cause of government borrowing has been wars. Ever since the late Middle Ages, wars have frequently been won less by military skill than by financial strength. Moreover, many financial innovations have been responses to an urgent need to finance a war.

Initially, kings borrowed mainly from banks, frequently from foreign banks. The banks often required the king to provide guarantees from private individuals or from cities. The reason was that the latter could be sued in court for their debts while the king could not.

Birth of the Market in Sixteenth-Century Europe

The first public issue of government securities took place in Holland in 1542. Charles V, the Hapsburg emperor, had imposed a war levy on his provinces in the Netherlands. To raise the necessary funds, the County of Holland issued various securities, the interest to be funded from excise and property taxes levied for the purpose. Some of these securities were transferable and therefore suitable for resale, and there developed a limited secondary market.

If the Dutch invented the market for government securities, the English perfected it. The first English government securities, issued in 1693, were illiquid and for that reason sold poorly. The English government soon found a solution. In 1694, it chartered the Bank of England to buy government securities. As we saw in Chapter 6, some of the bank's lending to the government took the form of issuing banknotes. But it also funded additional purchases of government debt by issuing permanent stock.[2]

Government Securities in the United States

Alexander Hamilton issued the first U.S. government securities in 1790 to fund the debts of the Revolutionary War. The issue was snapped up eagerly by the public: at the time, there was little else available to satisfy the demand for financial assets.

An active secondary market soon developed. At first, merchants and auctioneers traded "government stock," as it was then called, as part of their general business. Soon,

---

[2] The idea was not original. In the thirteenth century, the Italian city-state of Genoa had used a similar structure to fund its debt.

however, specialized brokers emerged in New York, and in 1792 these brokers organized themselves into an exchange. Originally, most of the business of this New York Stock Exchange was in government stock.

Despite the great initial enthusiasm, the market soon found itself in danger of dying out (as we shall see, this is a problem we face again today). After the war, the government steadily paid off its debt, with little in the way of new issues. As the amount of securities outstanding declined, trading volume shrank. The market was saved from extinction by renewed government borrowing to finance the War of 1812. The federal government, cut off from major capital markets in Europe, sold its securities to the American public.

Tragic as it was in other ways, the Civil War proved a boon for the market in government securities. As Jay Cooke put it, "a national debt is a national blessing." He was in a position to know: by the end of the war he had earned some $7 million in commissions (about $75 million in today's dollars) from selling federal debt.

Cooke's success stemmed from his innovative methods. Having observed how French banks underwrote securities, he adapted the same method to the sale of government debt in the United States. He set up an organization of some 2,500 local agents—local bankers, lawyers, clergymen, storekeepers, and postmasters. A smaller number of traveling representatives supervised the local agents. Cooke bought securities from the U.S. government and used his sales force to market them to the American public. Cooke's methods, imitated later by others, were the basis for modern investment banking in the United States.[3]

THE INSTRUMENTS OF GOVERNMENT DEBT

The Evolution of Instruments of Government Debt

The instruments of government debt have evolved over the years. Early Dutch and English government securities were mainly fixed-interest-rate annuities, payable for the life of a named annuitant. They were transferable, but transfer was difficult. Sale required a title search, much like that required today for the sale of a house. To receive interest, the new owner had to furnish proof that the annuitant was still alive—usually a letter from a parish priest.

Using a joint-stock company as an intermediary was attractive because the sale of its shares was much easier. The company kept a register of share ownership in a ledger (literally "book-entry securities"). When shares were sold, the register was changed accordingly. No title search was needed.

To eliminate the need to prove an annuitant was still alive, governments began to issue permanent annuities or perpetuities that could be sold or left in inheritance. The best-known perpetuities are the Consols issued by the British government to *consol*idate the debt of the Napoleonic wars. These securities are still traded today.

In addition to long-term borrowing to finance their deficits, governments sometimes use short-term borrowing for liquidity reasons—to bridge temporary imbalances between

---

[3] Cooke's later attempt to use the same methods to finance the Northern Pacific Railroad ended in disaster. The failure of Cooke's firm in 1873 precipitated a major stock market crash.

tax receipts and spending. The English government first issued such short-term government debt in 1696 in the form of an interest-bearing "exchequer bill."

Governments have often tailored the instruments they issue to exploit successful existing markets for private securities. One example is the issue of lottery loans to exploit the popularity of private lotteries in the late eighteenth and early nineteenth centuries.[4] Another example is the Treasury bill, created by the British Treasury in 1877 at the urging of Walter Bagehot, the editor of *The Economist*. The T-bill is a discount instrument intended to mimic the commercial bill. The idea was to tap the thriving London money market, which traded in commercial bills. The Treasury bill proved enormously successful. Not only did it replace the exchequer bill as a source of short-term liquidity, but governments soon began to roll over Treasury bills to fund their long-term borrowing. A more recent example is the Treasury strip, designed to exploit the popularity of zero-coupon bonds.[5]

Types of U.S. Government Debt

Gross and Net, Nonmarketable and Marketable.   Today, the U.S. government makes use of all the foregoing types of debt and more. In early 2001 the *gross* debt of the U.S. government was $5.7 trillion. A good part this is debt the U.S. government owes itself—securities held by various agencies of the U.S. government. Such debt is, of course, an accounting fiction. Debt you owe yourself is meaningless; only debt you owe to others means something. You are neither richer nor poorer when you write yourself an IOU for $100 million. The principal reason for this accounting fiction is to keep track of how much one part of the government owes another. The debt the U.S. government owes to others is called the *net* debt: in early 2001 this amounted to some $ 3.3 trillion—still a tidy sum.

Of the $3.3 trillion held by the public, some $436 billion was *nonmarketable*. Nonmarketable debt is more like a deposit than a tradable security. The original purchaser cannot sell it to anyone else. It can be redeemed before maturity only from the Treasury itself. The most familiar example of nonmarketable debt is U.S. Savings Bonds, which the Treasury sells to households. Other nonmarketable securities are sold to state and local governments and to foreign governments.

The remaining $2.9 trillion of U.S. government debt is marketable (transferable), and it consists of a variety of securities. These are issued by the Department of the Treasury and are known in the market as *Treasuries* or *governments*.

Bills, Notes, and Bonds.   The shortest maturity Treasuries are 13- and 26-week T-bills.[6] As we saw in Chapter 4, T-bills sell at a discount. In addition, the Treasury offers coupon securities (called *coupons* by the market) with maturities of from 2 to 30 years. Those with maturities of 2 to 10 years are called *notes*; those with longer maturities are called *bonds*. Coupons on these securities are paid semiannually. As we saw in Chapter 4, notes and bonds may sell at par, at a discount, or at a premium, depending on market interest rates.

---

[4] See "Gambling and Lotteries" in Chapter 1.

[5] See Chapter 4 for a discussion of strips. The governments of Japan and the United Kingdom issue zero-coupon bonds directly. France is another country that allows its bonds to be stripped.

[6] The Treasury stopped selling 52-week T-bills in March 2001.

EXHIBIT 12.2   Marketable U.S. Government Debt by Type

Total marketable debt: $2.7 trillion

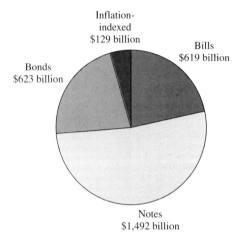

Source: *The Public Debt Online.*
http://publicdebt.treas.gov/opd.htm

Since January 1997, the Treasury has also been selling inflation-indexed securities.[7] Bills, notes, and bonds are all available in denominations of $1,000 to $1 million. Exhibit 12.2 shows the breakdown of marketable U.S. government debt into these categories.

We saw in Chapter 4 that the Treasury's STRIPS program allows the stripping and reconstitution of most coupon Treasuries. In 1999 there was about $200 billion of strips outstanding. Roughly a third of long-term bonds were stripped.

The Government as Financial Intermediary. In addition to borrowing to finance its own budget deficit, the federal government acts as a financial intermediary, borrowing to relend to others. Examples include mortgage loans to veterans, farmers, and low-income families; commercial loans to farmers, exporters, and small businesses; and education loans to students. To make these loans, the federal government must borrow the necessary funds. The amounts involved are considerable: at the end of 2000 the total amount outstanding of such debt was close to $2 trillion.

Federal financial intermediation is conducted through a variety of agencies. Most of the smaller ones do not issue their own securities, but rather borrow from the **Federal Financing Bank (FFB)**.[8] This is funded by the sale of regular Treasury securities.

Federal Financing Bank (FFB)

The federal institution that borrows from the Treasury and lends to various government agencies.

---

[7] See Chapter 4 for a discussion of these bonds and how they are indexed.

[8] Before the FFB was set up, some 20 small government agencies issued securities in their own names. Because these issues were small, their liquidity was not as good as that of Treasuries, and their yield was therefore higher. That is, the agencies had to pay more to borrow. Borrowing through the FFB lowers their borrowing cost.

agencies
Securities issued
by certain agen-
cies of the federal
government.

book-entry
securities
Securities that
exists only as a
computer record.

Treasury/Reserve
Automated Debt-
Entry System
(TRADES)
A book-entry sys-
tem for Treasury
securities oper-
ated by the Fed.

Agencies.   Some of the larger government agency intermediaries issue securities in their own names. These securities are known in the market as **agencies**. Exhibit 12.3 lists the principal agencies and describes briefly what they do.

Book-Entry Securities

All new U.S. government securities are issued in the form of "book entries." These are not literally entries in a book, but rather records on a computer. **Book-entry securities** are much easier to trade than physical certificates. A computer record can be changed instan-taneously to reflect a change in ownership, whereas the physical transfer of a piece of paper may take hours or even days and is far more costly.

The structure of the book-entry system is illustrated in Exhibit 12.4. The system con-sists of two parts. The major part, officially called the **Treasury/Reserve Automated Debt-Entry System (TRADES)**, but more generally known as the commercial book-entry system, is operated by the Federal Reserve Banks. The minor part, Treasury Direct, is operated by the Treasury itself.

In the commercial book-entry system, only depository institutions (banks and thrifts) are eligible to hold a securities account at the Fed. Others—dealers, brokers, and their customers—can access the system indirectly by keeping a securities account at a deposi-tory institution that has an account at the Fed.

EXHIBIT 12.3   Principal Federal and Federally Sponsored Credit Agencies

DEBT OUTSTANDING, SEPTEMBER 2000

(billions of dollars)

Federal agencies	
Tennessee Valley Authority:	26
coordinates resource conservation, development, and land-use programs in the Tennessee River Valley	
Others (including Post Office, Export-Import Bank, etc.)	38
Federally sponsored agencies	
Federal Home Loan Banks:	600
provide credit to thrifts to finance mortgage lending	
Federal Home Loan Mortgage Corporation:	486
"Freddie Mac" makes mortgage funds available by buying conventional and government-insured mortgages in the secondary market[a]	
Federal National Mortgage Association:	612
"Fannie Mae" is a private corporation authorized by Congress to make mortgage funds available by buying mortgages in the secondary market[a]	
Farm Credit Banks:	73
provide credit to farmers	
Student Loan Marketing Association:	42
"Sallie Mae" is a government-sponsored corporation that provides funds for student loans	

[a] See Chapter 13 on the mortgage market.

Sources: Federal Reserve Bulletin *and the* Washington Information Directory.

EXHIBIT 12.4   The Book-Entry System for Government Securities

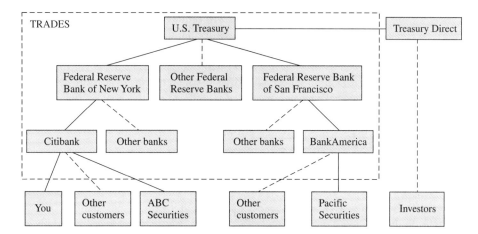

EXAMPLE 12.1

For example, you might hold your securities in a securities account at Citibank. Citi's computer keeps a record of your ownership of the securities. Citi, in turn, has a securities account at the New York Fed. The Fed's computer keeps a record of Citi's ownership of the securities. To see how it works, suppose you buy a new $10,000 Treasury bond. When the Treasury issues the bond, it records on its computer that Security no. 6462648 belongs to the New York Fed; the New York Fed's computer records that Security no. 6462648 belongs to Citi; and Citi's computer records that Security no. 6462648 belongs to you. When coupons payments are due, the Treasury pays the New York Fed, which pays Citi, which pays you.

Suppose you later sell this bond to Pacific Securities, which has a securities account at BankAmerica in San Francisco. This requires the following changes in computer records. Citi debits your account and requests over Fedwire that Security no. 6462648 be transferred from its own account to that of BankAmerica, for Pacific Securities. The New York Fed notifies the San Francisco Fed that Security no. 6462648 is being transferred to it and debits Citi's account. The Treasury transfers Security no. 6462648 from the account of the New York Fed to the account of the San Francisco Fed. The San Francisco Fed credits the account of BankAmerica with Security no. 6462648. Finally, BankAmerica credits the account of Pacific Securities with Security no. 6462648.

Treasury Direct
A book-entry system operated by the Treasury, mainly for small investors.

In addition to the commercial book-entry system, the Treasury maintains a system called **Treasury Direct**. Investors who keep their securities with Treasury Direct have coupon and principal payments credited directly to their bank accounts. However, securities held on Treasury Direct cannot be transferred to others; investors who wish to trade their securities must first transfer them to the commercial book-entry system. Treasury Direct is therefore useful only for investors who intend to hold their securities to maturity. Some 1 million investors hold over $70 billion in Treasury securities on Treasury Direct.

T-bills exist *only* as book entries. But some notes and bonds issued before 1986 are still available in "definitive" form—as handsomely engraved certificates. Ownership of these certificates may be registered with the Treasury, or the certificate may be in bearer form. Possession of **bearer securities** is sole proof of ownership. The advantage of bearer securities is that they are easier to trade because the cost of reregistering ownership is avoided. The disadvantage, of course, is that if they are lost or stolen, there is not much you can do.[9]

bearer securities
Securities for which possession is primary evidence of ownership.

THE PRIMARY MARKET

New issues of Treasury securities are sold at auction. The Treasury sells an average of $7 billion of new issues each week. When the federal budget was in surplus, all of this represented refinancing of old debt: all of the money raised was used to pay off old issues that had matured. The auctions are organized by the Federal Reserve Bank of New York.

There is a regular calendar of new issues, with weekly auctions of bills and periodic, mostly quarterly, auctions of notes and bonds. The amount, maturity, and denomination mix of each new issue are announced at least a week in advance, so the new issue can be absorbed smoothly by the market.

Reopenings

reopening
additional sales of new securities of an existing issues.

Some new issues are **reopenings**, or additional sales of existing issues. For example, suppose that an outstanding 26-week Treasury bill has 13 weeks left to run. Rather than issuing a completely new 13-week T-bill, the Treasury might choose to "reopen" the outstanding 26-week bill by issuing an additional quantity.

In terms of borrowing, the result is the same: the Treasury receives money that it must repay in 13 weeks. However, the reopening offers an advantage for the secondary market. Because there is now a larger amount of this issue outstanding, its liquidity should be improved. The improved liquidity makes the security more desirable and is reflected in a higher price. The higher price means a lower cost of borrowing for the Treasury.

Auction Procedures

Anyone wishing to buy part of a new issue must submit a sealed bid to any one of the Federal Reserve Banks by the stated deadline (most bids are submitted to the New York Fed).[10]

---

[9] A registered certificate, if lost or stolen, will be replaced (the original cannot be cashed by anyone but the registered owner); partial compensation may be available for the loss or theft of a bearer certificate, but none is available for lost or stolen coupons. The movement to book-entry securities was prompted by the refusal of several major insurance companies, in 1970, to insure dealers against the theft of their securities while the instruments were being delivered in settlement of a trade.

[10] Since 1998, investors who have accounts with Treasury Direct have been able to purchase government securities from the Treasury over the Internet, with the cost of the securities being debited to their checking accounts.

competitive bids
Bids for purchase
of new Treasury
issues specifying
a bid price.

**noncompetitive
bids**
Bids for purchase
of new Treasury
issues not specify-
ing a bid price.

There are two types of bid: **competitive bids** specify a price; **noncompetitive bids** do not. The noncompetitive bidders are usually less sophisticated small investors. Competitive bidders are either dealers, who expect to resell the securities at a profit, or institutional investors, who believe they can get the securities more cheaply by bidding themselves than by buying from a dealer. Any bid for more than $5 million of securities must be competitive. No single competitive bidder may purchase more than 35% of a given issue.

Competitive bids are accepted only if they bid at or above the auction price. Noncompetitive bids are all accepted and pay the auction price. To see how this works, consider Example 12.2.

EXAMPLE 12.2

The New York Fed has $1 billion in one-year T-bills to sell. It receives the following bids:

Competitive (8 bids)
      $100 million at 95.54
      $ 70 million at 95.52
      $ 90 million at 95.51
      $350 million at 95.51
      $350 million at 95.50
      $300 million at 95.50
      $200 million at 95.48
Noncompetitive (many bids)
      $325 million in total

A bid of 95.54, for example, means that the bidder is willing to pay 95.54% of the face value of the bill.[11] So a bidder for $10 million of bills at this price would pay $9,554,000 for them if the bid were accepted.

First, the New York Fed accepts all noncompetitive bids. So subtract the $325 million of noncompetitive bids from the $1 billion to be sold, leaving $675 million. This is the amount to be divided among the competitive bidders.

Among the competitive bids, the highest are accepted first. The first four bids, at 95.54, 95.52, and 95.51 (two bids), will be accepted in full; the total amount of these four bids is $610 million. Subtracting this from $675 million leaves $65 million.

The $65 million of remaining securities is divided proportionally among those bidding the next highest price, 95.50. Since there is a total $650 million of bids at this price, and only $65 million available, each bidder at this price will receive 1/10 of the amount bid for.

The auction price is the price of the lowest accepted competitive bid. In this case, the auction price is 95.50. This is the price that all accepted bidders, competitive and noncompetitive, must pay.

---

[11] Actual bids for bills are made on a discount basis. In this example, bids have been converted into prices for clarity. For example, the bid of 95.54 corresponds to a discount of 4.41%, which is how the bid would have actually have been stated. See Chapter 4 on converting discounts into prices.

The When–Issued Market

when-issued (wi) market
A forward market in Treasury issues that have been announced but not yet issued.

How do dealers know what price to bid? The most important source of information is the **when-issued (wi) market**. This is a market for forward delivery of newly announced issues. Trading begins in this market as soon as an issue is announced, and trades are settled several days after the auction, when the securities are issued. Investors buy new securities forward from dealers, and dealers hedge these sales by buying on the wi market. The wi price is generally a little higher than the expected price of the security, reflecting a risk premium. Speculators who believe the price in the wi market is too high take short positions.

Recent Changes in the Primary Market

Following the Salomon Brothers scandal in 1991 (described later in the chapter), the Treasury modernized the auction process and changed the bidding procedure.

Fedline
A communications system that links depository institutions with the Federal Reserve banks.

Electronic Bidding.   In 1992 the Fed began to accept noncompetitive bids electronically over Fedline. **Fedline** is a general communications system that links some 9,000 depository institutions with the Federal Reserve banks. Terminals were also made available to nonbank securities brokers and dealers. In April 1993, the Fed began accepting competitive bids over a new, enhanced communications system called Fast Fedline. Unlike the old system, Fast Fedline is able to handle the last-minute rush of competitive bids. The bids are processed by an automated system called TAAPS.

English auction
An auction in which successful bidders pay the price they have bid.

winner's curse
The association between having a bid accepted and having bid too high.

Dutch auction
An auction in which all successful bidders pay the price of the lowest accepted bid.

From English to Dutch Auctions.   Until the 1990s, the Treasury used a different auction procedure, known as an **English auction**.[12] According to this procedure, accepted competitive bidders paid the price that they had bid. The problem with this procedure was something called the **winner's curse**. Having your bid accepted is not entirely good news: it may mean that you have bid too high and that you will take a loss when you resell the securities. Fear of the winner's curse leads bidders to shade their bids down somewhat. It also creates an incentive for bidders to collude to find out the market consensus and so avoid bidding too high. One way to do this is to pool bids. Rather than entering individual bids a group of investors will pool their orders with a dealer and have the dealer place a single bid; each investor then pays the average price.

As we have seen, in the current procedure, known as a **Dutch auction**, successful bidders pay the price of the lowest accepted bid.[13] While this seems to be worse for the Treasury, this is not necessarily so. No longer fearful of the winner's curse, bidders can enter higher bids. With the incentive for collusion eliminated, more investors are willing to enter bids on their own. With higher bids and more bidders, the price at which the issue sells may well be higher, or at least no lower.

---

[12] The technical name for this kind of auction is a first-price, sealed-bid auction.

[13] Technically, this procedure is a second-price, sealed-bid auction. Calling this a Dutch auction is a misnomer. The true Dutch auction, used in Holland in the wholesale flower market, is quite different. It is a descending-price, open-bid auction. The auctioneer cries out descending prices until a bid is made. The first bidder gets one unit at the price bid. The price continues to fall until all units are sold.

THE SECONDARY MARKET

While the primary market for U.S. government securities may seem large, it is dwarfed by the secondary market. In addition to the $190 billion a day of transactions reported by major dealers, the secondary market also encompasses the transactions of the smaller dealers and transactions overseas.

The secondary market for government securities operates around the clock and is worldwide. The market is very liquid. Bid–asked spreads are small. The market is deep, routinely accommodating trades in the billions of dollars with nary a ripple.

How the Secondary Market Is Organized

The secondary market for U.S. government securities is a decentralized, over-the-counter dealer market. Information is carried on computer terminals, but actual trading takes place mainly over the telephone. The market operates 24 hours a day, worldwide. Although it has no single physical location, it is centered in New York City. The principal participants are *dealers*, *brokers*, and *clearing banks*.

Dealers make the market: they quote bid and asked prices at which they are willing to buy and sell government securities. To back up their quoted prices, they must take a position in securities. If someone wants to buy, dealers must have the securities available to sell; if someone wants to sell, they must be ready to buy and to add the securities to their inventory.

Dealers

primary dealers

Securities dealers recognized by the Fed as potential trading partners.

In 1999, there were some 2,000 dealers registered with the SEC. Dealers large enough and sound enough to be "recognized" by the Fed as potential trading partners are known as **primary dealers**. The rest are known as **secondary dealers**. They are generally smaller and they do not deal directly with the Fed. Secondary dealers buy government securities from the primary dealers and sell them to the public. Almost anyone can set up as a secondary dealer.

secondary dealers

Dealers in government securities who are not primary dealers.

The Benefits and Costs of Being a Primary Dealer.   To carry out its monetary policy, the Fed does an enormous amount of trading in U.S. securities. Only primary dealers get a piece of this action. They also enjoy considerable prestige from their status. Many large institutional investors will trade only with a primary dealer.

There are also important informational benefits to being a primary dealer. You have immediate information on what the Fed is up to. You are connected, via brokers, to other primary dealers. This helps you know what other major players in the market are doing. All this information gives you an edge in predicting interest rate changes. As we shall see presently, being able to do this successfully is the key to making a profit as a dealer.

However, being a primary dealer has its costs. To be recognized as a primary dealer, a dealer must demonstrate to the Fed that it has the capital, the expertise, and the capacity to be a reliable trading partner. Dealers who have applied for recognition but have not yet been approved are called "aspiring" dealers.

The balance between benefits and costs changed in the early 1990s when the Fed deliberately distanced itself from its primary dealers in response to a scandal involving a leading primary dealer, Salomon Brothers. To dispel any notion that it vouched for the soundness—or integrity—of primary dealers, the Fed significantly reduced its requirements for primary dealer status. It stopped monitoring primary dealers, lowered the required capital, and eliminated a market-share requirement. However, by making it easier to become a primary dealer, the Fed also made it less prestigious. As a result, the number of primary dealers has declined from its peak of 46 in 1988 to 30 today.

The Inside Market.   Primary dealers trade with one another on what is called the **inside market**. There are two reasons you, as a primary dealer, might trade in this market. One is to adjust your inventory of securities. For instance, a customer might want more of a particular security than you have in stock. The inside market is where you would buy what you need.

inside market
Market in which primary dealers trade among themselves.

The second reason you might trade in the inside market is to turn a profit at your competitors' expense. You constantly check the bid and asked prices of all the other dealers. If you think another dealer is bidding too high, you "hit the bid" (sell him securities at the bid price). If you think his asked price is too low, you buy the offered securities, expecting to resell them later at a profit. You are not alone in looking for profit opportunities: all the other primary dealers do the same. If you make a mistake in your pricing, they will be quick to pounce.

As a result of this trading, the prices of all the dealers tend to be brought into line with one another quite quickly. The common price that results from this process expresses the market's consensus of the "fair" price for a given security. Essentially, the inside market is where the price of government securities is determined.

The customers of primary dealers include secondary dealers, corporations, financial institutions, and individuals. Competition among primary dealers for this retail business is intense. As a result, customers can expect to buy and sell securities at prices that are close to those of the inside market.

Brokers

Unlike dealers, brokers never take a position in securities. Their role is merely to bring together buyers and sellers. Brokers are particularly important in the inside market.

Anonymity.   Brokers provide anonymity. In general, as a dealer, you would rather other dealers did not know the nature of your trades. First, that information might be useful to them. For example, seeing you unloading long-term bonds, they might think you had new information suggesting that long-term rates were going to rise. As a result, it might be harder for you to sell the bonds. Second, you do not want everyone to know if you make a mistake.

Broker screens do not indicate the source of the prices they display. When transactions clear, both securities and payment go through the broker to preserve anonymity. The broker is paid by the dealer initiating a trade (hitting a bid or taking an offer).

Centralization.   Brokers also provide centralization. Were primary dealers to trade directly with one another, each of the 30 would have to keep in touch simultaneously with 29 others. However, with the market mediated by brokers, each dealer need keep in touch only with one or two brokers. A dealer quotes to the brokers his bid and asked prices and the quantities he is willing to trade. The broker displays this information on computer screens provided to other dealers.

The more centralized a market, the more efficient it is. With, say, 20 different brokers, there would be little centralization. Dealers could do almost as well trading with one another directly. Reducing the number of brokers to five would be a big improvement. Of course, the greatest efficiency would result from having a single broker. Then, all the information could be displayed on a single screen. There are, in fact, only six brokers of government securities, with four accounting for most of the business.

Market Power and Competition.   However, concentration also increases market power. The small number of brokers used to mean that there was little competitive pressure. Despite a tremendous increase in volume and despite costs that were falling steadily because of technological progress, brokers refused to lower their commissions. They made enormous profits on volumes in the tens of billions of dollars a day.

In 1986 Salomon Brothers organized a group of dealers to set up a brokerage house of their own. They called it Liberty. As a result of the competition, commissions immediately dropped by 50% and then continued to drop. For example, before Liberty was set up, the commission on coupon securities was $78 per $1 million face value; by 1991 it had fallen to $18. Liberty did so well and took such a large share of the business that some began to fear that it might itself monopolize the market.

Electronic Trading

cross-matching system
Trading system that allowing buyers and sellers to post desired trades and to trade anonymously with one another.

While most trading still takes place over the telephone, a number of electronic trading systems are beginning to attract business. By the fall of 1999, electronic trading accounted for about 4% of all reported trading.

One type of system, the **cross-matching system**, provides much the same service as a broker, allowing buyers and sellers to post desired trades and to trade anonymously with one another. Most of the interdealer brokers have introduced such systems. In addition, State Street Bank, a major securities custodian, operates BondConnect, and the New York Stock Exchange operates its Automated Bond System.

multidealer system
Trading system that allows institutional investors to trade with a number of different dealers, but not with each other.

A second type of system, the **multidealer system**, allows institutional investors to trade with a number of different dealers, but not with each other. A consortium of primary dealers has set up TradeWeb, the most successful. Bloomberg, a major provider of information, has launched Bondtrader.

Electronic trading of government securities is more significant in some other countries. In Italy, for example, MTS, a cross-matching system, accounts for 90% of trading volume. EuroMTS was set up in the Spring of 1999 to trade the Euro-denominated government securities of Germany, France, and Italy, and plans to expand trading to the securities of other Euro countries were announced.

Information

GovPX
An information system that reports in real time all trades on the inside market.

Because the market for government securities is an over-the-counter market rather than an exchange, it is harder for participants to know what is going on. Consequently, market information on prices and quantities traded is particularly important. Apart from the individual interdealer brokers, the main source of such information is **GovPX**, a system organized by dealers and brokers that reports in real time all trades on the inside market. **Information vendors** provide this information, along with market-relevant news, on screens that they supply to dealers and institutional investors. The leading information vendor to the government securities market is Telerate, with 90,000 terminals worldwide. Bloomberg, with 14,000 screens is of growing importance.

information vendor
Service that provides screen with market information and market-relevant news.

Clearing and Settlement

U.S. government securities are traded under three conventions—same-day, next-day ("regular way"), and forward settlement (which includes wi trades). All same-day trades are settled directly between the counterparties. Other trades may be settled either directly or through a clearinghouse, the **Government Securities Clearing Corporation (GSCC)**.

Government Securities Clearing Corporation (GSCC)
A clearinghouse for trade in government securities.

To see how direct settlement works, let us trace the steps of an actual trade. Meg Chambers, a trader at Pacific Securities in San Francisco, has just sold $10 million of a bond issue maturing in 2010. The buyer is another dealer, ABC Securities, in New York. Meg fills out a "trade ticket" with the details of the trade and passes it on to Chuck in operations. Chuck checks the ticket for errors and calculates the amount of money to be received. He then sends instructions by direct computer link to Pacific's clearing bank to clear the trade.

Pacific Securities keeps its securities in a book-entry account at BankAmerica, its **clearing bank** (refer again to Exhibit 12.4). Pacific also keeps a checking deposit there to be used in executing trades. As we shall see presently, a clearing bank will also lend to a dealer as necessary to facilitate settlement. Most major banks do some clearing, but a few specialized banks handle most of the business. The one that does the most is Chase; other major clearing banks are Bank of New York and HSBC (formerly Marine Midland).

clearing bank
A bank that executes trades for securities traders.

To return to our trade, on receiving Chuck's instructions, BankAmerica transfers the securities against payment by Fedwire to ABC's clearing bank, Citibank (see Exhibit 12.4). That is, securities are transferred from BankAmerica's account to Citibank's and, simultaneously, money is transferred to BankAmerica's deposit at the Fed. If Citi has the funds in its Fed deposit, it is debited. If not, the Fed lends it the money as "daylight overdraft."[14] Similarly, if ABC has the necessary funds in its deposit with Citi, Citi debits it for the purchase and credits its securities account. If not, Citi makes ABC a temporary loan and holds the securities as collateral.

Notice that the trade was never confirmed. Waiting for confirmation would simply take too long. To deal with the possibility of error, the recipient of securities has the right to return them before the closing of the securities wire the same day. Such a return is known as a DK for "don't know."

---

[14] See Chapter 8 on daylight overdraft.

Notice, too, that there is no netting. If both counterparties to a trade use the same clearing bank, which is frequently the case, the trade can be settled internally by the clearing bank. This reduces transactions costs. There is also some bilateral netting between dealers. If ABC had sold Pacific some of the same security earlier, the two firms could have netted the two trades. However most trades are cleared one at a time over Fedwire. Apart from being costly, this practice exposes dealers, clearing banks, and the Fed to considerable settlement risk.[15]

Instead of settling directly, trades that are not same-day transactions can be cleared and settled through GSCC. Formed in 1986 by the primary dealers and brokers, GSCC is a clearing organization registered with and regulated by the SEC. GSCC offers both comparison and multilateral netting. It handles Treasuries, agencies, and strips. Its members are brokers, dealers, clearing banks, and institutional investors.[16] There is no associated depository, since the securities are already in book-entry form. Settlement is over Fedwire.[17]

Settlements of transactions involving U.S. government securities exceed $800 billion a day. Over $500 billion is settled directly over Fedwire and over $150 billion on GSCC. An additional $150 billion is settled within the major clearing banks: this is possible when both parties to a transaction have accounts at the same bank. After the Fed began charging daylight overdraft on Fedwire, making its use more expensive, market participants increased their use of alternative methods of settlement.

The Global Market for U.S. Government Securities

U.S. government securities trade around the clock. The day's trading begins in Tokyo at 7:30 P.M. (New York time) and continues there until 3:00 AM. It then passes to London, where it continues until 7:30 A.M. New York then takes over, and trading there continues until 5:30 P.M.

New York accounts for most of the trading volume—94% in September 1999. Trading in London made up 4% of the total and trading in Tokyo, 2%. Much of the trading in London and Tokyo takes place at the opening when traders for each major dealer "pass the book" to colleagues in another market. Despite the small volume, the overseas markets plays an important role in providing prices and allowing hedging when New York is closed. When important news breaks after New York hours, trading in London or Tokyo picks up markedly.

The markets in London and Tokyo have a structure similar to that in New York. They are dominated by the local offices of five to ten of the major primary dealers in New York, with a larger number of smaller dealers. Four of the New York interdealer brokers coordinate the markets in London and Tokyo. The overseas markets are much less liquid than New York, with wider bid–asked spreads and less depth. Transactions, wherever they originate, are normally settled in New York the next day or later. The 24-hour trading in Treasuries has created a demand for 24-hour trading in related derivatives, which takes place in Chicago, London, and Tokyo.

---

[15] The Fed's recent crackdown on daylight overdraft may force dealers to change the way same-day trades are settled.

[16] Institutional investors may use GSCC for comparison, but they do not take part in the multilateral netting.

[17] In Chapter 17, we shall discuss mechanisms of clearing and settlement and the meaning of terms such as bilateral and multilateral netting, comparison, and depository.

HOW TO BE A SECURITIES DEALER

Let us switch now from a bird's-eye overview of the markets to the view from the trenches. What is it like to be a government securities dealer? The best way to find out is to give it a try yourself. So let us imagine that you have decided to become a dealer in government securities.

You will, of course, need some equity capital. You raise $3 million from your own resources and from friends, relatives, and classmates. You rent office space and set up in business. In contrast to banking, no charter or permission is required. Government regulation is light, and anyone can set up as a dealer. There used to be even less regulation before some major scandals in the early 1980s motivated Congress to impose minimum standards. As a result, you do now need to register with the SEC.

To settle trades you need a clearing bank, so you put your $3 million into a checking deposit at Chase and open a securities account there. You also need market information. So you get a screen from Telerate to receive up-to-date information on bond prices.

Buying and Selling Securities

The bread and butter of your business is buying and selling securities. To have something to sell, you buy $150 million worth of various securities from a primary dealer. How can you buy $150 million worth of securities when you have only $3 million? By getting a **dealer loan** from Chase for the difference.

dealer loan

A loan from a clearing bank to a dealer to finance the purchase of securities.

Chase will lend you the money and hold the securities as collateral. As you sell the securities, Chase will release them against payment, subtracting the money you owe, and crediting you for the rest. The $147 million that Chase is willing to lend you is less than the value of the securities, because their market price might fall. The bank wants to be sure the value of the collateral stays above the amount of the loan.

The Bid–Asked Spread

Why would anyone pay you more for these securities than you paid for them yourself? Your customers are investors who want to buy or sell securities quickly. You provide a service by always being ready to trade with them. For this service you charge a premium— the bid–asked spread. Of course, the larger the premium you charge, the less business you will get. If your prices are unattractive, potential customers will find it worthwhile to shop around for a better deal elsewhere. Why don't they go to a primary dealer, who is sure to offer them a better deal? Because primary dealers will generally not trade in small quantities.

Need you worry about losses to information traders? Probably not. They are interested in much larger trades than you can accommodate and do their trading on the inside market.

Your trading volume grows steadily, and soon you are taking in a small but steady income from your bid–asked spread. As you buy and sell, your inventory fluctuates. However, it stays in the $150 million range.

Carry and the Yield Curve

carry
The difference between the interest received on securities and the interest paid to finance the holding of those securities.

In addition to the bid–asked spread, you have an additional source of profit—**carry**. Your inventory, unlike that of a car dealer or boutique, earns interest. Of course, the interest is not all profit: you have to subtract the interest you pay on the funds you borrowed to finance your inventory. If the interest rate you earn is more than the interest rate you pay, you make a profit—a positive carry. If the interest rate you earn is less than the interest rate you pay, you take a loss—a negative carry.

yield curve
A plot of yields—for example, of government securities—against maturity.

Whether the carry is positive or negative depends on the shape of the **yield curve**. The yield curve is a plot of Treasury rates against maturity. Exhibit 12.5 shows some possible shapes of the yield curve. The most common—that shows yields rising steadily with maturity—is called, not surprisingly, a **normal yield curve**. Another relatively common shape is the *inverted* yield curve, with rates falling steadily with maturity. Sometimes the yield curve is humped or U-shaped.

normal yield curve
A yield curve that rises with maturity.

The rate you pay to finance your inventory is a short-term rate. The amount you borrow varies day by day, and Chase charges you a quarter of a percent above the overnight Fed funds rate. Since the maturity of your securities is longer than overnight, you will earn positive carry as long as the yield curve has a normal shape. The longer the maturity of your securities, the greater the carry will be. If the yield curve is inverted, your carry will be negative: you will lose money on your inventory. However, you may have to take this loss to be able to accommodate your customers. It is a cost of doing business.

EXHIBIT 12.5   Different Yield Curve Shapes

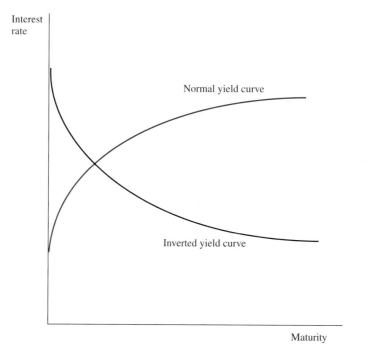

Repurchase Agreements

If you can reduce the cost of financing your inventory, you can increase your profit from carry. To do this, you need to borrow from someone other than your clearing bank. The problem, of course, is trust. How can you persuade strangers, who do not know you as well as your bank does, to lend to you? One solution is a **reciprocal loan**. In exchange for the loan of funds, you can lend the securities that they are financing. In the government securities market this is usually done through a **repurchase agreement** (**repo** or **RP**). Formally, this transaction is a sale together with an agreement to repurchase. However, functionally, it is a loan of money in exchange for a loan of securities.[18]

For example, suppose you do a repo with General Computer. You agree to sell GC a specified amount of securities for $20,000,000 and, at the same time, agree to buy them back (repurchase them) the next day for $20,003,700. Formally this is a sale and a repurchase. However, in reality, GC is making you a $20 million loan for one day. The extra $3,700 in the buyback price is the interest on the loan: it translates into an effective annual rate of about 7%. Like a dealer loan, a repo is usually overcollateralized to protect the lender of the funds from a fall in the market price of the securities.[19]

You execute the first stage of the agreement, the sale, immediately. GC's bank wires the $20 million to your bank, Chase, and most of it goes to repay the dealer loan on those securities. Rather than wiring the securities back in exchange, Chase transfers them from your account to a special custodial account in the name of GC. This is cheaper than actually transferring ownership through the book-entry system.[20]

The next morning you buy back the securities at the agreed price by having your bank wire $20,003,700 to GC's bank, and you regain possession of the securities. You borrow the money you need to buy back the securities from Chase. Banks used to make no charge for such a loan as long as it was repaid before the end of the day, since the banks borrow in turn from the Fed at no cost. After the Fed began to charge for daylight overdraft in 1994, however, banks began to charge too.[21]

How will you repay the bank? By doing another repo, either with GC again or with someone else. Since daylight overdraft is no longer free, you will try to arrange this repo as soon as possible. You finance your inventory by rolling over your repo borrowing day after day, bridging the gap between repos with daylight loans from your clearing bank. Alternatively, you could do a repo for a longer period (such repos are called *term* repos).

---

[18] The repurchase agreement was invented by the Bank of England in the 1820s. The repo has an advantage over a straightforward collateralized loan in case of bankruptcy: the lender of the funds already has legal title to the securities. With a collateralized loan, title would have to be established in court.

[19] Of course, the lender of the securities also faces risk. Suppose the securities are lent for full value. If the market price of the securities rises, and if the borrower of the securities fails to return them, the lender of the securities will have cash that is worth less than the lost securities. The overcollateralization increases the risk of the lender of the securities. Nonetheless, perhaps because the funds are the more liquid asset, overcollateralization rather than undercollateralization is the custom.

[20] A repo in which a clearing bank holds the securities in question in a special account is called a *triparty repo*, in contrast to one in which securities are actually transferred via Fedwire. For a triparty repo to be possible, both the parties need to have custodial accounts at the same bank.

[21] See Chapter 8 on daylight overdraft.

---

reciprocal loan
A loan of funds in exchange for loan of securities.

repurchase agreement (repo or RP)
A simultaneous arrangement to sell securities and to repurchase them later at a specified time and price.

It is worth going to all this trouble because the interest rate on repos is substantially below the rate on dealer loans.

For GC, investing in a repo may be more attractive than simply holding Treasuries for several reasons. First, the transactions costs are generally lower.[22] Second, a repo involves no interest rate risk. Investing in T-bills does involve interest rate risk: a rise in market interest rates will lower their value. With a repo, there is no such risk: the yield on the repo is fixed in advance, and it is unaffected by changes in market interest rates that change the value of the underlying securities. If there is a change in the value of the securities, the loss or gain is not GC's but yours.

Trading Profits

Bid–asked spread and carry may pay your utility bills, but they will not make you rich. The only way to make a lot of money is through "position plays"—capital gains on your position in securities.

There are two reasons why you can make—or lose—a lot on position plays. The first is interest rate volatility. As we learned in Chapter 4, large changes in interest rates mean large changes in security prices. The second reason position plays have such potential for profit or loss is *leverage*. As is customary in the securities business, you are financing most of your inventory with borrowed money. To see why this matters, consider the effect on your net worth of a 2% fall in interest rates.

Before the change your balance sheet is:

Securities	$150m	Borrowing	$147m
		Equity	3m

Suppose the average duration of your inventory of securities is one year. Then the value of your securities will rise by 2% to $153 million.[23] The value of your liabilities is unaffected by this change in market interest rate. For example, if you are financing with repos, the repurchase price is already set and is not affected by changes in the market value of the underlying securities. Hence, the effect of the increase in interest rates on your balance sheet is:

Securities	$153m	Borrowing	$147m
		Equity	6m

Leverage has turned the 2% rise in security prices into a doubling of your equity.

So a fall in interest rates is good news. But what do you do if you think interest rates are going to rise? With this same balance sheet, a 2% rise in interest rates would wipe out your equity.

---

[22] Buying and selling T-bills involves commissions and other transactions costs; moving the securities between the dealer's account and a custodial account at the clearing bank is much cheaper. Since the maturity of a repo can easily be tailored to match the lender's needs—from overnight to several weeks—the number of transactions is smaller too.

[23] See Equation 4.19 in Chapter 4.

Taking a Short Position

short position
The position of
owing, but not
possessing, a
security.

long position
The position of
owning a security.

The way to profit from an expected rise in interest rates (fall in the price of securities) is by taking a **short position** ("going short"). You do this by borrowing securities and selling them. This puts you in the position of *owing* securities. When their price falls, you owe less, and you therefore make a profit. In contrast, when you take a **long position**, you *own* securities. So when their price falls, you take a loss.

Let us look at how you might take a short position. Begin by liquidating your long position by selling off your inventory. If you expect prices to fall, then holding securities is a bad idea (we shall see presently that there are ways you can continue to operate as a dealer, even though you have no inventory). After paying off the money you borrowed to finance your inventory, you are left with $3 million of your own.

Now borrow $150 million in Treasuries for 10 days from Pacific Securities and sell immediately. As a result of these transactions, your balance sheet will now be:

Cash	$153m	Short position in securities	$150m
		Equity	3m

Before, you held securities and owed money; now you hold money and owe securities.[24]

As you expected, interest rates rise and the market price of the securities you borrowed falls by 2%. The effect on your balance sheet is:

Cash	$153m	Short position in securities	$147m
		Equity	6m

Notice that the value of your assets has not changed: you still have $153 million in cash. The value of your liabilities, however, has fallen to $147 million: the securities you borrowed from Pacific Securities are now worth only $147 million. Your equity—the difference between what you have and what you owe—has doubled to $6 million.

To realize your gain, you need to unwind your short position. You go into the market and buy securities equivalent to those you borrowed from Pacific Securities. You do not have to return the very same securities—just equivalent ones. For example, if you borrowed the bonds maturing in March 2010, you must return bonds maturing in March 2010. However, they do not have to have the same serial numbers. It is just like borrowing money. If you borrow $10 from a friend, your friend does not expect you to return the same $10 bill.[25] When you buy the securities you need, because their prices have fallen, you pay only $147 million for them.

Reverse Repos

**reverse
repurchase
agreement (a
reverse)**
Simultaneous
arrangement to
buy securities and
to resell them
later at a specified
time and price.

In reality, the way you would borrow securities would be through a **reverse repurchase agreement** (also called a "reverse repo," "reverse RP," or simply a "**reverse**"). That is,

---

[24] Rather than holding cash, you could lend out the $153 million for a few days. Doing so does not affect the outcome, and you do earn some interest.

[25] Any coupons paid on the securities while you were borrowing them belong to Pacific Securities.

EXHIBIT 12.6   A Repo/Reverse Repo

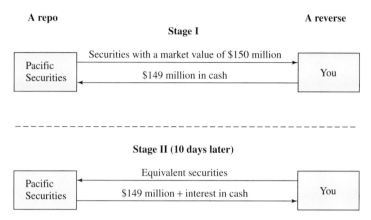

Pacific would repo you the securities, and in exchange you would lend Pacific the money you received when you sold them.

The transaction is illustrated in Exhibit 12.6. Pacific Securities repos you the $150 million in securities. That is, your receive the securities in exchange for $149 million in cash (the difference in value or "haircut" protects you against the credit risk of a change in the value of the securities). Ten days later, you return equivalent securities and receive your cash plus interest. From your point of view, this transaction is a reverse: you are "reversing in" the securities. From Pacific's point of view the transaction is a repo: it is "repoing out" the securities.

Any interest you receive on the securities from the Treasury during the 10 days of the agreement belongs to Pacific Securities. You will be expected to pay it to Pacific at the end of the agreement.

Running a Book in Repos

There has been enormous growth in the market for repos and reverses. In 1999, repo transactions amounted to something like $600 billion a day. Repos are also important in other countries. The Japanese equivalent is called the *gensaki*. The two European clearing organizations, Cedel and Euroclear, facilitated some $500 billion a week in repo transactions.

For dealers, repos provide a cheap way to finance inventory. Banks and other institutions can raise money quickly by repoing the securities they hold. Apart from the lower transactions costs compared to actually selling securities, there is another advantage. Banks carry some securities on their books as long-term investments, valued at face value. If they sell these securities, they must revalue them at the sales price and take a gain or loss. Repoing the securities rather than selling them avoids this revaluation and its consequent effects on reported earnings and tax liability.

Reverses are attractive to dealers, and to anyone else who wants to take a short position in government securities. Reverses also provide dealers with a way of filling customers' orders without holding inventory. For example, if one of your customers wants

$1 million in 6-month T-bills that you do not have, you can reverse the T-bills in to make delivery. You might prefer this to buying securities outright, for example, if you were expecting delivery of some of the same securities quite soon.

Clearly, then, the underlying demand for repos and reverses is there, but there is no market unless somebody makes one. Those wanting to do repos and those wanting to do reverses need to be able to find one another easily. If they cannot, the instrument becomes much less attractive. Buyers and sellers also need to know a price: the "price" in this case is the repo rate.[26]

The market in repos and reverses is made by the same dealers who make the market in securities.[27] Dealers reverse in securities from some clients and repo them out to others. This is called **running a book in repos**. Dealers earn a spread by paying a lower rate on repo loans of money (their bid price) than they charge for such loans (their asked price). The growth of repo intermediation by government securities dealers is shown in Exhibit 12.7.

running a book in repos
The practice of simultaneously entering into off-setting repos and reverses.

Hedging

As a dealer, your overall exposure to interest rate risk depends on your combined position in securities and in repos. For example, you might be running a book in repos, with $400 million in repos and $300 million in reverses. The difference is just enough to finance the $100 million in securities that you are holding. Overall, you are in a long position: you own more securities than you owe. If interest rates fall, you will make a profit; if they rise, a loss. Alternatively you might be in an overall short position. You have $400 million in reverses and only $300 million in repos, having sold the remaining $100 million in securities. If interest rates rise, you will make a profit; if they fall, a loss.

You may well want to take a bet on the direction of interest rates. Given your familiarity with the market and your careful monitoring of events, you are in a good position to profit from a judicious bet. However, you may want to limit your exposure. Moreover, you do not want considerations of risk to interfere with your basic business. You need to be able to accommodate the needs of your customers, buying from them and selling to them as they require and providing them with repos and reverses. You cannot afford to turn away business just because accepting it would expose you to more risk.

Fortunately, as we shall see in Chapter 16, you can hedge interest rate risk with a variety of instruments, including futures, options, and swaps. We will study the details in

---

[26] The repo rate normally follows the Fed funds rate quite closely because for banks, repoing their Treasuries is a close substitute to borrowing Fed funds. Mostly, the repo rate does not depend on the particular government securities involved. However, when a particular security becomes scarce, it is said to "go on special." For repos of that particular security, the rate is lower than the regular rate (the "general-collateral" rate). It is lower because the loan of the securities is more valuable, so that the compensation for the loan of money need not be as high.

The Fed does not like to see securities going too deeply on special because this implies that the market for such securities is illiquid. The central bank therefore stands ready to lend primary dealers scarce securities overnight out of its own enormous portfolio, allowing the dealers to post other securities as collateral. The fee for such loans is set by competitive daily auction, but the minimum is high enough to discourage borrowing except in extreme cases.

[27] There is also a brokered inside market for repos that parallels the inside market for securities.

EXHIBIT 12.7   Reverses and Repos Outstanding of U.S. Government Securities Dealers

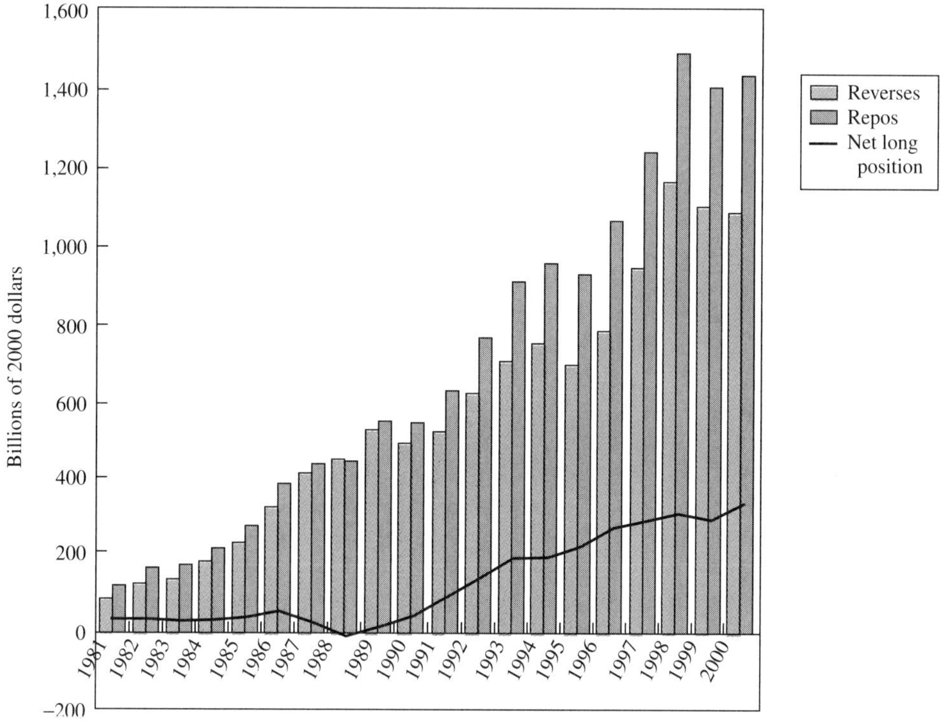

Source: Federal Reserve Bank of New York.

Chapter 16, but the basic idea is simple enough. You take a position in the hedging instrument that offsets your position in securities and repos.

For example, if you are long securities, you can hedge by going short in futures. If interest rates rise, you will take a loss on the securities, but you will make an offsetting gain on your position in futures. On the other hand, if interest rates fall, the loss on the futures will offset the gain on the securities. By hedging in this way you can hold securities you need to serve your customers without exposing yourself to too much interest rate risk. At any time, the total amount of repos entered into by dealers as a whole generally exceeds the total amount of reverses, so that dealers are typically in a long position with respect to securities.

In reality, it is much easier to make your bets on interest rates by adjusting your position in futures than by adjusting your position in securities and repos. If you think interest rates are going to fall, you can just reduce the size of your hedge. Then, if they do fall, the loss on the futures will be less than the gain on the securities and repos. If you think interest rates are going to rise, you can take a short position in futures larger than that required to hedge your long position in securities and repos. Then if interest rates rise, the gain on the futures will be greater than the loss on the securities and repos.

REGULATION OF THE GOVERNMENT SECURITIES MARKET

In the 1970s and 1980s, the rapid growth of the government securities market generated substantial profits and drew all sorts of new firms into the business. Supervision of the market was minimal, so entry was easy. Many of the entering firms were highly respectable—often foreign banks and securities firms. Some new entrants, however, were not so respectable. In the early 1980s, a number of scandals shook the industry.

Drysdale Government Securities

Drysdale Government Securities entered the market in 1982 with only $20 million of its own capital. Within a few months it had managed to build up a position of over $6 billion in government bonds.

There was at the time an inconsistency between conventions in trading repos and securities. When bonds were repoed, the owner retained title to any coupon interest due on them, so the cash loan paid to the owner covered only the securities themselves and not the accrued interest. However, when securities were *sold*, the price *did* include accrued interest.

Drysdale exploited this inconsistency by reversing in securities and selling them. By doing this, it generated an amount of cash equal to the accrued interest on the bonds. It then used this cash to expand its speculative positions. Unfortunately, interest rates zigged when Drysdale expected them to zag, and the firm took some heavy losses.

As a result of its losses, Drysdale was unable to pay the accrued interest it owed on the bonds it had reversed in. In particular, it defaulted on some $160 million of accrued interest it owed Chase on $2 billion in bonds. These bonds, it turned out, had not actually belonged to Chase itself. They were bonds Chase was holding for its customers. Chase was repoing these securities, with its customers' consent, to earn extra income.

Chase's first reaction to the loss was to disown it. It claimed to be an innocent agent in the transaction and therefore not liable for the loss. This had a predictably poor effect on the public's confidence in the market. The Fed, together with the other major dealers, persuaded Chase, for the sake of the general good, to change its mind and to shoulder the loss.

E.S.M. and BBS

As we have seen, dealers run a book in repos, repoing securities that have been reversed to them. In 1985, it transpired that two small dealers—E.S.M. Government Securities and Bevill, Bresler, and Schulman (BBS)—had been repoing the same securities simultaneously to more than one lender at a time. Both dealers were found out only after trading losses caused them to fail. An examination of their books showed that they actually held fewer securities than they had repoed.

How was this possible? As we have seen, with a normal repo, the securities are either delivered to the lender or held in a custodial account at a clearing bank. There is therefore no way to repo the same securities twice. Obviously, this was not the procedure followed by E.S.M. and BBS. Instead, they did what is called a "trust me" repo. Under this arrangement, to save the transactions costs of putting the securities in a custodial account, the dealer retains possession of the securities. The customer receives written notification from the dealer certifying that the securities have been set aside in the customer's name. The two dealers in question simply lied.

Several of E.S.M.'s customers were thrifts that had been repoing securities as a cheap source of short-term finance for mortgages they were going to sell in the secondary market.[28] These thrifts took substantial losses. Some of them, in Ohio and in Maryland, had state-sponsored rather than federal deposit insurance. The losses of these thrifts bankrupted the state deposit insurance funds. As a result, depositors ran on other banks insured by these insurance funds, forcing many to close.

Salomon Brothers

The scandals of the early 1980s involved relatively small dealers and did not really tarnish the reputation of the market. However, a scandal in the early 1990s involved one of the largest and most respected primary dealers.

On August 9, 1991, Salomon Brothers notified the Fed that its traders had violated the rule limiting competitive bids from any one bidder to no more than 35% of a given issue. Salomon's traders had gotten around the limit by submitting phony bids in the names of Salomon customers. In this way, they had been able to purchase as much as 85% of some issues.

to squeeze the market

To accumulate a dominating position in an issue, so that shorts have no alternative but to accept your terms.

With such a large position Salomon was able to **squeeze the market**. As we have seen, once a new issue is announced, trading begins in the "wi" market for future delivery of the issue. Typically, many dealers take short positions in the wi market, anticipating that the price of the issue will fall. They expect to be able to cover their position either by buying at the auction or by borrowing securities from other dealers who have done so.

By submitting a high bid at the auction, Salomon guaranteed itself a large part of the issue, and other dealers came away with their bids unfilled. Dealers that were short in the wi market had no way to settle except by borrowing the bonds from Salomon. Since they had nowhere else to go, Salomon could insist on terms that were highly advantageous to itself. It did this by paying a really low rate of interest on the repo loan. Salomon could then relend the funds at a handsome profit.

When the Fed began to investigate, it turned out that Salomon's transgressions were far from unusual: at various times, dozens of firms had violated the rules in much the same way. Indeed, the main reason the traders at Salomon had engineered the squeeze was to get even. They were trying to recoup losses they themselves had suffered as a result of an earlier squeeze by another dealer. In January 1992, some 105 different banks and securities firms agreed to pay about $5 million in fines to settle charges of improper behavior.

---

[28] We shall learn about the secondary market for mortgages in Chapter 13.

The Regulatory Response

The scandals of the early 1980s—Drysdale, E.S.M., BBS and others— cost customers an estimated at $750 million. Not surprisingly, there was considerable pressure to increase regulation of the government securities market. The response to this pressure was the **Government Securities Act of 1986**, which requires all dealers (except banks, which are regulated by other agencies) to register with the SEC. The act also gives the Secretary of the Treasury the authority, in consultation with the Fed and with the SEC, to formulate rules on matters such as capital requirements for dealers and trading practices for repos and reverses.[29]

The Salomon scandal led to further changes. The rules and penalties for dealers were codified. The requirements for being a primary dealer were eased, to reduce the exclusivity and power of the primary dealers. While before only primary dealers were allowed to submit bids in the names of their customers, now any dealer was able to do so. Steps were taken to automate bidding and to change the auction procedure to a single-price auction, reducing the incentives for collusion.

In 1993 Congress amended the Government Securities Act. One of the new provisions requires anyone holding a large position in a particular security to report this position if a shortage emerges. To make a squeeze less profitable, the Treasury announced that it would reopen an issue (issue more of an outstanding security) if a squeeze seemed to be taking place in that issue. Knowing that the Treasury may intervene in the market, will, of course, make attempting a squeeze much less attractive.

Despite these changes, the government securities market is still relatively lightly regulated compared to other markets. One reason is that the Treasury fears that excessive regulation could harm the working of the market and raise its borrowing costs.

GLOBALIZATION OF THE GOVERNMENT SECURITIES MARKET

The market for government securities has become increasingly globalized. In the countries of the OECD, on average 20% of government securities are held by foreigners. Some 40% of marketable U.S. government debt was held by foreigners in 1999 (up from 20% in 1994). Japanese and British investors held the largest amounts.

This globalization has put competitive pressure on domestic markets for government securities. As investors have found it easier to invest in the securities of foreign governments, domestic markets have had to modernize or face a decline in demand, with a consequent increase in borrowing costs for the government.

In the past, many governments considered the placement of their debt to be too important to leave to the market. It was common to set the price of government securities and to more or less require financial institutions, especially banks, to buy them. Purchasers were expected to hold the securities to maturity: trading them was considered unpatriotic. Consequently, secondary markets were not well developed.

---

[29] The Government Securities Act expired in 1991 but was renewed.

All this has changed in recent years. The governments of many countries, fearing that their ability to borrow might be compromised, have pushed through reforms. The model for these reforms has been the U.S. market. Many countries have switched to auctions in the primary market and to dealer-based, over-the-counter markets in the secondary market. They have introduced new instruments such as strips, repos, and derivatives.

Governments have also had to change their tax rules. Withholding taxes, for example, are very unpopular with international investors. When New Zealand abolished its withholding tax for foreign residents it increased the demand for its securities so much that the fall in its borrowing costs more than compensated for the loss of revenue. Another common obstacle is a tax on financial transactions (often in the form of a "stamp duty") that raises the cost of trading and so undermines the liquidity of the secondary market. This has been a particular problem in Japan.

Reforms have gone furthest in the countries of the European Union. Deregulation stimulated by the "single-market" policy has helped, and the introduction of the Euro has placed governments in direct competition with one another for the money of institutional investors. There is no reason now why an Italian insurance company should prefer its own government's securities to those of, say, Germany.[30] Japan, today with the world's largest government debt, has dragged its feet, and its market remains relatively backward, but there has been some progress.

THE DISAPPEARING GOVERNMENT SECURITY?

After a period of widespread government budget deficits and growing public debt, governments seem to have learned fiscal religion. Governments everywhere have been putting their budgetary houses in order. Increasingly, deficits are giving way to surpluses. *Gross* new issues continue to be positive: governments still issue new securities. However, *net* new issues are frequently negative, with the amount of existing debt being paid off exceeding the amount of new issues.

For example, in 1999 the United States issued about $350 billion in new securities but paid off about $460 billion. Not only is the Treasury paying off maturing debt, but it has begun to buy back outstanding issues before they mature. In 2000, it bought back about $30 billion of 30-year bonds—the first buyback since 1933.[31]

The picture is similar in Europe, where countries aspiring to join the Euro zone were required to balance their budgets first. Other countries, such as Australia, have also brought their government budgets into surplus. The great exception is Japan, which continues to rack up massive budget deficits. In 2001, when the United States is expected to reduce its outstanding debt by $230 billion, Japan is expected to add over $300 billion to its outstanding debt.

---

[30] Under a common currency, the debt of individual governments is no longer risk free. Since they can no longer print the money to repay their debt, default becomes a possibility. Consequently, the debt of some countries using the Euro may be more attractive (and carry a lower yield) than that of others.

[31] The bonds were purchased in a reverse auction. Primary dealers could submit offers for themselves or for their customers.

Shrinking government debt in most countries is having an effect on government securities markets. In the United States, trading volume in Treasuries peaked in 1997 and has been shrinking ever since. The drop has been particularly marked for T-bills, which have experienced the largest decline in the amount outstanding. The market is generally becoming less liquid, with bid–asked spreads steadily increasing.

To preserve liquidity as much as possible, the Treasury has been eliminating maturities to concentrate trading volume in fewer issues. In March 2001, it stopped issuing 52-week T-bills. Since projections suggest that the debt will be paid off completely within a decade, the Treasury is also considering issuing no more new 30-year bonds.

How will the financial markets function without Treasuries? What will take their place as a benchmark and as liquid collateral? The most likely candidate is agencies.[32]

In 1998, the two government-sponsored agencies involved in the mortgage market, Fannie Mae and Freddie Mac, introduced new series of notes and bonds designed to mimic Treasuries. So that no one should be in doubt about their intentions, they called these series "Benchmark" and "Reference," respectively. They consist of noncallable coupon securities issued on a regular schedule and in large amounts.[33] At the end of 1999, with some $150 billion already outstanding at maturities of from 2 to 30 years, the agencies began to auction bills. Futures in these securities were introduced in March 2000, and there is an active market for overnight repos. Trading volume at primary dealers had reached $18 billion a day in early 2000. While this was still only a small fraction of trading in Treasuries, the potential for growth is clearly there.

SUMMARY

- The market for U.S. government securities is the largest and most active securities market in the world by far. Trading volume in this market dwarfs that in any other.

- The Treasury issues bonds, notes, and bills. In addition, various federal agencies issue debt of their own (agencies).

- Most Treasury securities exist only in book-entry form.

- New issues of Treasury securities are auctioned by the New York Fed. Bids may be competitive or noncompetitive. Before they are issued, newly announced issues trade in the wi market.

- The Treasury has recently introduced electronic bidding and switched from English to Dutch auctions.

- The secondary market for government securities is a decentralized, over-the-counter market mediated by dealers.

- There are two types of dealer—primary and secondary. Being a primary dealer is not as attractive as it once was, and their number has fallen.

---

[32] Some larger issuers in the corporate bond market, such as Ford, have also aspired to the role, but their securities are less suitable. Although the corporate bond market is comparable to the Treasury market in size, individual issuers are much smaller. Moreover, default risk is always a concern.

[33] To make these securities more attractive to foreigners, they can be transferred through Cedel and Euroclear as well as through TRADES.

- Primary dealers trade with one another in a broker-mediated inside market, where the market price of government securities is determined.

- Brokers provide centralization and anonymity. Concentration created market power, but new competition has eroded this.

- Electronic trading systems have recently begun to have an impact on the market.

- In an OTC market, market information is particularly critical. It is provided by several information vendors.

- Same-day trades are settled directly between the counterparties through their clearing banks using Fedwire. Other trades may be cleared either directly or though GSCC, a clearinghouse.

- The market for U.S. government securities is a worldwide market and trading goes on around the clock. Nonetheless, the bulk of trading occurs in New York and all trades are settled there.

- Dealers finance a high proportion of their inventory, usually with repos (they also rely on dealer loans).

- Dealer profits come from the bid–asked spread, from carry, and—most of all—from position plays.

- It is possible to profit from an expected rise in interest rates (fall in security prices) by taking a short position. This is usually done by using a reverse repo.

- Major dealers generally run a book (deal) in repos and reverses as well as in the securities themselves.

- Dealers reduce their exposure to interest rate risk by hedging in futures. They can also use futures than taking a position in securities to speculate on interest rate movements.

- Scandals in the government securities market have created pressure for more regulation, but the market remains relatively free of regulation.

- The market for government securities has become increasingly globalized. This has put competitive pressure on domestic markets for government securities. Governments, fearing their ability to borrow might be compromised, have pushed through reforms. The model for these reforms has been the U.S. market.

- Widespread government surpluses have caused government debt to shrink in many countries. Trading in the U.S. market is down, and liquidity has deteriorated. If Treasuries disappear, the agencies are likely to replace them as the market benchmark.

DISCUSSION QUESTIONS

1. What are a government securities dealer's sources of income?

2. In what different ways are government securities dealers involved in repos and reverses?

3. Why do you think government securities dealers make a market in repos and reverses? Why don't their repo customers and reverse customers simply get together and cut out the middleman?

4. Why is the Treasury so worried about regulation of the government securities market? The Treasury doesn't borrow in the secondary market, so why does it care what happens there?

5. Who are the principal participants in the government securities market? How do they interact with one another? Are any of them subject to economies of scale? Is market power a problem?

6. Is a securities dealer a financial intermediary? In what ways is a securities dealer like a bank? In what ways different?

7. "In structuring an issue of government debt, minimum denominations should be small enough for households to be able to invest in such instruments."
   a. What do you think is the rationale for this statement?
   b. Suppose this advice is not followed and the government issues debt only in large denominations. Does this create a profit opportunity? How do you think the financial system will respond?
   c. Is the outcome better or worse for the government than the situation in which it does issue debt in small denominations?

BIBLIOGRAPHY

Blommestein, H. J. "Trends and Recent Structural Changes in OECD Public Debt Markets." *Financial Market Trends* 78 (March 2001): 141.

Bröker, G. *Government Securities and Debt Management in the 1990s.* Paris: OECD, 1993.

Dupont, D., and B. Sack. "The Treasury Securities Market: Overview and Recent Developments." *Federal Reserve Bulletin*, December 1999, 785–806.

Fleming, M. J. "Financial Market Implication of the Federal Debt Paydown." *Brookings Papers on Economic Activity* no. 2 (2000): 221–251.

Kindleberger, Charles P. *A Financial History of Western Europe.* London: George Allen & Unwin, 1984.

Madigan, B., and J. Stehm. "An Overview of the Secondary Market for U.S. Treasury Securities in London and Tokyo." Washington, DC: Federal Reserve Board, 1994.

Neal, Larry. *The Rise of Financial Capitalism: International Capital Markets in the Age of Reason.* Cambridge: Cambridge University Press, 1990.

Parkinson, Patrick, et al. "Clearance and Settlement in U.S. Securities Markets." Special study no. 163, Board of Governors of the Federal Reserve System, March 1992.

Rosengren, Eric S. "Is There a Need for Regulation in the Government Securities Market?" *New England Economic Review*, September–October 1986, 29–40.

Stigum, Marcia. *After the Trade: Dealer and Clearing Bank Operations in Money Market and Government Securities.* Homewood, IL: Dow-Jones Irwin, 1988.

———. *The Money Market.* 3rd ed. Homewood, IL: Dow-Jones Irwin, 1990.

KEY TERMS

Federal Financing Bank
agencies
book-entry securities
Treasury/Reserve Automated Debt-
    Entry System (TRADES)
Treasury Direct
bearer securities
reopening
competitive bids
noncompetitive bids
when-issued (wi) market
Fedline
English auction

winner's curse
Dutch auction
primary dealers
secondary dealers
inside market
cross-matching system
multidealer system
GovPX
information vendor
Government Securities Clearing
    Corporation (GSCC)
clearing bank
dealer loan

carry
yield curve
normal yield curve
reciprocal loan
repurchase agreement (repo or RP)
short position
long position
reverse repurchase agreement (a
    reverse)
running a book in repos
squeeze the market
Government Securities Act of 1986

THE MORTGAGE MARKET

When you finish this chapter you will understand:

- Why the mortgage market is so important
- Why a secondary market for mortgages has developed in the United States and how it works
- What mortgage strips are and how they can cause securities firms to lose hundreds of millions of dollars
- Why mortgage markets are very different in other countries

Securing a loan with collateral reduces the risk to the lender. The reduction in risk reduces the cost to the borrower and makes loans more readily available. The most common form of secured loan is the mortgage—a loan secured by real property such as buildings or land. Of particular importance are residential mortgages—mortgage loans to finance housing. Housing is the single largest component of the capital stock in any country, and the need for financing is correspondingly large. Consequently, in many countries the mortgage market is one of the largest debt markets.

In the United States, at the end of 2000, there was some $7 trillion of mortgage debt outstanding, of this $5.2 trillion was home mortgages. Net residential mortgage borrowing in 2000 was $455 billion, and there was another $137 billion of commercial and farm mortgage borrowing. In comparison, net borrowing in the corporate bond market was $175 billion.

The mortgage market is interesting not only because of its size, but also because of the dramatic changes it has seen, especially in the United States. While 20 years ago there was no secondary market in mortgages, in 2000 about half the home mortgages written were resold on the secondary market. Understanding why this has happened will teach us a great deal about the workings of the financial system.

The changes that have taken place in the U.S. mortgage market have been a response to a number of chronic problems. To understand the nature of these problems, we begin by reviewing the historical background and by examining the special nature of the mortgage instrument. We then look at the problems experienced by the industry and how the development of a secondary market has addressed those problems. We conclude with a look at mortgage markets in other countries, examine the differences, and ask why they have changed much less than the mortgage market in the United States.

THE HISTORICAL BACKGROUND

Origins

Historically, mortgage borrowing has played a variety of roles. It was always the predominant form of borrowing in rural economies, where land was the most important asset. Landowners borrowed against future rents to finance current consumption or the development of their estates (in agriculture, mining, and processing). Farmers borrowed to finance expansion, improvement, and investment in new equipment. With urbanization and industrialization, urban developers used mortgage borrowing to finance construction; industrial firms used it to finance new plant; and households used it to finance the purchase of homes.

The earliest form of mortgage lending, beginning in the Middle Ages, was a direct loan from one individual to another—both of them usually wealthy. The mortgage contract was written by a lawyer, who usually also acted as a broker, matching borrowers with lenders. As economies developed, this traditional arrangement was transformed and supplemented by others.

Early Mortgage Lending in the United States

mortgage broker
A middleman who brings together mortgage borrowers and lenders.

In the United States, the westward expansion created a continuing demand for long-term agricultural credit. Banks were reluctant to satisfy this demand: experiments with long-term lending in colonial times had generally ended badly. Bank reluctance was reinforced in many states by regulations that prohibited them from mortgage lending. The National Banking Act of 1863 copied these state restrictions and barred national banks from mortgage lending (this prohibition endured until 1913).

The growing need for mortgage credit was therefore satisfied by **mortgage brokers**, who developed extensive networks to match mortgage borrowers in the West with investors in the East. The growing savings banks and insurance companies of the period were the principal investors. Some mortgage brokers shared premises and even management with national banks.

mortgage bank
A nonbank institution that originates and sometimes funds mortgages.

Under the pressure of competition, some mortgage brokers began to guarantee the mortgages they sold, and in the 1880s some became intermediaries. These **mortgage banks**, as they were called, issued bonds and used the proceeds to fund portfolios of mortgages. At the height of their popularity, about 1890, there were 167 such companies. An agricultural depression in the 1890s resulted in many defaults and foreclosures and, with land prices falling, many mortgage banks failed.

S&Ls and the First S&L Crisis

As we saw in Chapter 6, savings and loans were writing an increasing number of mortgages by the end of the nineteenth century. However mortgage credit remained tight until World War I. After the war, national banks were allowed to make mortgage loans, and it became easier to borrow. Partly as a result, there was a tremendous real estate boom in the 1920s. All types of mortgage lending expanded rapidly. S&Ls accounted for more than a third of new residential mortgages. By 1929, they held 24% of all nonfarm residential mortgages, more than any other type of institution. Mortgages accounted for 80 to 90% of their assets.

This narrow specialization in mortgage lending proved disastrous during the Depression. Many borrowers were thrown out of work and were unable to make their payments. Foreclosures multiplied. By 1935, foreclosed properties made up one-fifth of S&L assets. Many S&Ls lost the cash reserves they had held with commercial banks when these banks failed. Depositors withdrew their funds from the S&Ls, both because they needed them and because their faith in financial institutions had been badly shaken. By 1935, S&L assets had fallen by a third.[1]

balloon loan

A mortgage loan structured like a bond, with all of the principal due on maturity.

The problem was worsened by the form of mortgage loan then in use—the **balloon loan**. Typically, this was structured like a 3- to 5-year bond. Up to maturity, only interest was due, with no repayment of principal. At maturity, the principal came due. The lender usually renewed the mortgage with another similar loan. In a crisis, however, lenders were unwilling to renew and borrowers were unable to repay.

Government Intervention

The federal government stepped in to restructure both the mortgage market and the savings and loan industry. In keeping with the generally anticompetitive character of Depression era legislation, S&Ls were virtually prohibited from nonmortgage lending. The intention was to prevent S&Ls from competing with commercial banks and to help the housing industry by preventing the funds from going to any other use. Geographic restrictions were tightened by prohibiting lending against property more than 30 miles from the lending institution. The intention here was both to restrict competition and to guarantee that local funds would be made available to local borrowers (as we saw in Chapter 3, this is not exactly a recipe for efficiency in lending).

The federal government also set up a number of institutions to support the struggling S&Ls and to strengthen the mortgage market. One was set up to buy up delinquent mort-

---

[1] Many solvent S&Ls were so illiquid that they were forced to freeze their deposits (suspend convertibility). In some cities, a highly organized market developed in frozen passbook accounts. Quote sheets were published, listing the discounts at which passbooks of different S&Ls were trading (commonly at a discount of 20–30% below their face value).

gages from thrifts (we shall learn about others later in the chapter). This institution allowed borrowers to pay off their mortgages over time in installments. The savings and loans built on this idea to introduce a new type of mortgage contract—the long-term, fixed-rate, amortized mortgage. This allowed borrowers to pay off the loan over time, rather than in a single large payment. The new instrument proved to be extremely popular, and its popularity helped the reconstituted savings and loans seize a large share of the mortgage market when it recovered.

THE MORTGAGE INSTRUMENT

To understand recent developments in the mortgage market, we need to understand the nature of the mortgage instrument. The basic instrument today remains the long-term, fixed-rate mortgage that took over the market after the Great Depression.

The Structure of the Cash Flow

As we saw in Chapter 4, the standard fixed-rate mortgage is an amortized loan. Let us look at an example. Suppose you take out a 30-year mortgage from Federal Savings and Loan for $100,000. The loan has an APR of 12%. With a compounding period of one month, the interest rate for the compounding period is $12\% \div 12 = 1\%$. The effective annual rate is 12.68%:

$$(1.01)^{12} = 1.1268$$

To calculate your monthly payment, we must find the constant amount such that the present value of a stream of monthly payments of that amount for 30 years equals $100,000. That is, we need to find the value of C that satisfies

$$\$100,000 = \frac{C}{(1.01)} + \frac{C}{(1.01)^2} + \cdots + \frac{C}{(1.01)^{360}}$$

We can use Equation 4.13 in Chapter 4 to find that $C = \$1,028.61$.

We can break your monthly payments down into interest and repayment of principal as shown in Exhibit 13.1. At the beginning of the first month, you owe the full $100,000. Interest on this at a monthly rate of 1% is $1,000. The remainder of the $1,028.61 payment, $28.61, is used to repay principal. The principal remaining at the start of the second month is therefore

$$\$100,000 - \$28.61 = \$99,971.39$$

The interest due at the end of the second month is 1% of this amount, or $999.71. The remainder of the payment,

$$\$1,028.61 - \$999.71 = \$28.90$$

EXHIBIT 13.1   Calculation of Mortgage Payments

Month t	Principal Owed at Beginning of Month	Interest Paid (1% of Principal), I_t	Principal Payment, P_t	Total Payment, $C = I_t + P_t$
1	$100,000.00	$1,000.00	$28.61	$1,028.61
2	99,971.39	999.71	28.90	1,028.61
3	99,942.49	999.42	29.19	1,028.61
⋮	⋮	⋮	⋮	⋮
360	1,018.43	10.18	1,018.43	1,028.61

is again applied to repaying principal. The changing breakdown of your payments into interest and principal repayment over the life of the loan is shown in Exhibit 13.2.

Points.   Lenders are often willing to charge a lower interest rate in exchange for **points**—a percentage of the loan amount—up front. For example, Federal might offer you a rate of 11.5% in exchange for 2 points (2% of the loan). This means, in effect, that you will receive only $98,000 of the mortgage (you could compensate for this by taking out a slightly larger mortgage). Your payments will, however, be calculated on the basis of the full $100,000.

points

Percentage of the face value of a mortgage charged by the lender as a fee.

EXHIBIT 13.2   Mortgage Repayment: Principal and Interest

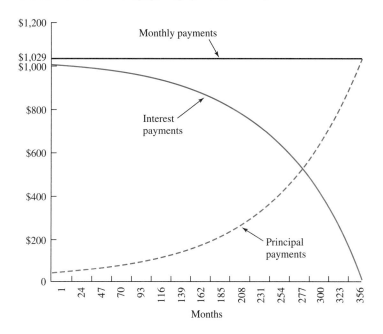

Is this a good deal? Because of the lower rate of interest, your payment will be only $990.29. However, the loan too is, in effect, smaller. To see what kind of deal it is, we need to calculate the effective annual rate. To do that, we need to solve the following equation for i:

$$98,000 = \frac{990.29}{(1 + i)} + \frac{990.29}{(1 + i)^2} + \cdots + \frac{990.29}{(1 + i)^{360}}$$

The answer (found by using a financial calculator) is 0.98%. Converting this into an effective annual rate, we obtain 12.42%:

$$(1.098)^{12} = 1.1242$$

prepay
To pay off a loan before maturity.

So, on the face of it, the mortgage with points is cheaper. However, this assumes you will pay the mortgage for the full 30 years. If you **prepay**—pay it off early—the story is very different. Exhibit 13.3 shows the effective annual rate as a function of the date at which you prepay the mortgage. You can see that the earlier you pay it off, the higher will be your effective annual rate (EAR). This result is not accidental: the points are designed to provide you with an incentive not to prepay. We shall see why presently.

EXHIBIT 13.3   EAR on a Mortgage as a Function of Prepayment

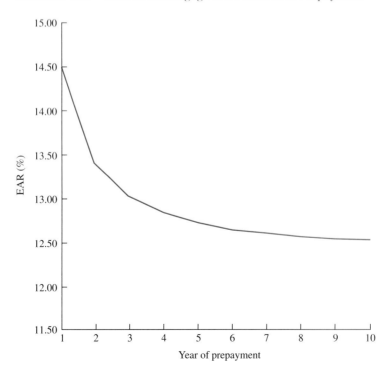

Lending Terms

lien
A clause in a title to real estate that prevents its sale unless the mortgage loan is repaid.

When you take out a mortgage from Federal Savings and Loan to buy a house, the house becomes collateral for the loan. If you default, Federal can foreclose and sell the house to recover what you still owe; anything left over from the sale is yours. There is a **lien** on the property—a clause in the title document that prevents you from selling unless the mortgage loan is repaid.

To cover itself in case of default, Federal insists that the value of the house be *greater* than the amount of the mortgage. For example, if the house is worth $125,000, Federal will lend you only $100,000. The S&L will expect you to make a **down payment** of $25,000 yourself. Now, if you default, Federal can be fairly sure of recovering its money, even if the value of the house has fallen in the meantime or if Federal overestimated its value.

down payment
The part of a home purchase to be paid by the purchaser rather than financed.

Federal may be willing to lend you more—to accept a smaller down payment—if you take out **mortgage insurance**. This is a guarantee from an insurance company to make up, in case of default, any discrepancy between the value of the house and the amount of the loan. For example, if the bank lent you $110,000 and the value of the house, after you defaulted, turned out to be only $105,000, the insurance company would pay Federal the remaining $5,000.

mortgage insurance
Insurance that covers a mortgage lender against any discrepancy between the value of a property and the amount of the loan.

Although the collateral protects Federal in the case of default, the lender would much prefer that you pay the loan as promised. Foreclosure is costly and, in the absence of mortgage insurance, the amount recovered from the sale of the house uncertain. To minimize the chance of default, Federal will lend you no more than it thinks you can repay. Specifically, it will not lend you an amount for which the payments exceed some fraction, say, 25%, of your income.

income test
Ratio of mortgage and other housing expenses to income, used by mortgage lender to determine eligibility for loan.

For example, as we calculated earlier, the monthly payment on your mortgage is $1,028.61. Federal will make the loan only if this is no more than 25% of your income or, equivalently, if your income is at least four times this amount—that is, about $4,100 a month, or $49,200 a year. If you fail this **income test**, you will not qualify for a mortgage of this size. You will have to come up with a larger down payment or find a less expensive house.

Prepayment and Refinancing

refinancing
Repayment of one loan with another.

There are a variety of reasons you might prepay your mortgage. You might sell the house because you want to buy a larger one, or because you are moving out of town.[2] Or you might want to replace your current mortgage with another one at a lower rate of interest. This is called **refinancing**.

Let us consider whether it is worthwhile to refinance. Suppose it is 5 years since you took out your mortgage (12% APR with 0 points) and mortgage rates have fallen to 9.6% (APR with 0 points). Should you refinance? To find out, we first need to see how much you still owe on the original mortgage. The easiest way to do this is to take the present

---

[2] Most mortgages require repayment if the house is sold. This is called a *due-on-sale* provision.

value of the 300 remaining payments, discounted at the monthly rate *of the original mortgage*:

$$\frac{\$1,028.61}{(1.01)} + \frac{\$1,028.61}{(1.01)^2} + \cdots + \frac{\$1,028.61}{(1.01)^{300}} = \$97,662.97$$

Therefore, to pay off the old mortgage, you will need to take out a new one that covers this amount. With the monthly interest rate now $9.6\% \div 12 = 0.8\%$, the monthly payment on the new mortgage is the value of C that satisfies

$$\$97,662.97 = \frac{C}{(1 + 0.008)} + \frac{C}{(1 + 0.008)^2} + \cdots + \frac{C}{(1 + 0.008)^{300}}$$

That value of C is $860.08. Comparing this with your original payment, you can see that refinancing saves you $168.53 a month.

To see whether refinancing is worthwhile you will have to weigh this gain against the transactions costs of refinancing. These are called **closing costs**. In your case, closing costs are $2,000. To make the comparison, you need to calculate the present value of the stream of monthly savings. If you plan to pay the mortgage to maturity, this turns out to be $19,137.19.[3] So refinancing does look attractive.

closing costs
The fees charged by a lender for making a mortgage loan (in addition to interest and points).

Your ability to refinance the mortgage in this way is exactly like the call option on a bond. You can "call" the mortgage at any time. Your gain if you do is the difference between the market value of the mortgage and the call price. The market value of the mortgage is just the present value of future payments calculated at the market rate of 0.8%. This is $116,800.16. The call price is just the outstanding balance, $97,662.97. Your gain is the difference: $116,800.16 − $97,662.97 = $19,137.19. As you can see, this amount is precisely the present value of the payments you save.

Of course, your gain is Federal's loss. The call option on the mortgage is valuable to you and costly to the bank. Federal will do what it can to discourage you from exercising the option. Charging points is one way; charging high closing costs is another. The bank's ability to deter you will, however, be constrained by competition. If it offers you worse terms than other mortgage lenders, you will take your business elsewhere.

THE WEAKNESSES OF POST-DEPRESSION MORTGAGE FINANCE

The method of mortgage finance that emerged after the Great Depression—fixed-rate amortized mortgages, largely made by thrift intermediaries—suffered from two major weaknesses. The first was fragmentation of the mortgage market. The second was a dangerous vulnerability of the lending institutions to interest rate risk.

---

[3] If you expect to pay off the mortgage sooner, because you expect to sell the house, the saving will be correspondingly smaller.

Fragmentation of the Mortgage Market

The concentration of mortgage lending in the hands of thrifts and banks resulted in a highly fragmented mortgage market. Because branching restrictions limited the geographic expansion of individual institutions, funds were mainly raised locally and lent locally. S&Ls did have some access to the national capital market through the **Federal Home Loan Banks**. These issued bonds and lent the proceeds to member institutions. However, most funds for mortgage lending came from local deposits. Lending was localized too: regulations restricted it to a "normal lending territory" within 50 miles of the lending institution (the limit was later increased to 100 miles and finally abolished in 1980).

Federal Home Loan Banks
System of 12 regional banks set up by the federal government to provide liquidity to S&Ls.

As a result of this fragmentation, conditions in the mortgage market could vary enormously from region to region. In the Sun Belt, where the housing market was booming, mortgage money would be scarce and mortgage rates high. In the Rust Belt, where the housing market was in a slump, mortgages would be plentiful and rates low. As we saw in Chapter 3, such fragmentation harms the economy.

In addition to harming the economy, fragmentation of the mortgage market in the United States made lenders more vulnerable to default losses. A lender with thousands of mortgages outstanding might have *looked* diversified but in reality was not. Because all those loans were made in the same area, they were not independent risks. A slump in the local economy would cause many borrowers to default simultaneously.

Interest Rate Risk for Financial Intermediaries

An even more serious threat to intermediaries than default risk was interest rate risk. The mortgage market as it emerged after the Great Depression relied largely on specialized mortgage lenders. Their principal asset was the long-term, fixed-rate mortgage; their principal liability, the short-term time deposit. This balance sheet suffered from a dangerous maturity mismatch.

To understand the danger, consider the following example. Federal Savings and Loan has outstanding $100 million of 30-year mortgages earning an average 9%. It is funding these mortgages with $95 million of time deposits paying an average 5%. Its equity is $5 million. Its interest income is

$$\$100m \times 0.09 - 95m \times 0.05 = \$4.25m$$

Now suppose market interest rates rise and Federal has to pay 12% for its deposits. The rate on the mortgages is fixed, so they continue to earn 9%. Interest income is now

$$\$100m \times 0.09 - 95m \times 0.12 = -\$2.4m$$

Two years of such losses and Federal's equity will be wiped out, and it will fail.

The Second S&L Crisis

The underlying weaknesses of the mortgage market were exposed by the second great S&L crisis that took place in the 1980s.

Regulation Q and Disintermediation.   For many years after World War II, the inherent dangers of the S&Ls' maturity mismatch remained hidden. Market interest rates remained relatively stable, and Regulation Q ceilings on deposit rates kept deposit rates more stable yet.

Because of Regulation Q, when interest rates did rise in this period, rather than taking major losses, S&Ls experienced a loss of deposits. Since Regulation Q prevented S&Ls from raising their deposit rates to match rising market rates, households withdrew their funds and bought T-bills and other money market assets instead. Such a substitution of direct lending for indirect lending is called **disintermediation**.

disintermediation

Loss of deposits by financial intermediary because direct lending becomes more attractive.

The withdrawal of funds from the S&Ls caused a serious liquidity problem for these institutions. Their principal assets, mortgages, were illiquid and could not easily be sold to raise the required cash. The S&Ls were saved from collapse only because they could borrow against these assets from the Federal Home Loan Banks.

Faced with this outflow of funds, S&Ls were unable to write new mortgages. So whenever interest rates went up, mortgages became unavailable, the demand for housing dried up, and the housing industry went into a slump. In this way, disintermediation contributed to a number of postwar recessions.

Although disintermediation was a problem for the economy, it did not generally do much harm to the S&Ls themselves. The real damage began with the demise of Regulation Q. Without its protection, the S&Ls were exposed to the full force of the interest rate risk inherent in their balance sheets.

The Demise of Regulation Q and Its Consequences

Regulation Q limits on interest rates were becoming increasingly ineffective by the late 1970s. Banks and thrifts had found a variety of ways to get around them and to compete for deposits. So when interest rates roses sharply, beginning in 1979, there was little disintermediation. S&Ls kept their deposits, but they had to pay much more to do so.

The S&Ls were in a vice. Although they raised the rates they charged on new mortgages, they could not raise retroactively the rates on the outstanding mortgages that they had written years earlier. They were forced to fund these old, low-interest-rate mortgages at a loss, paying more for the necessary deposits than they were earning on the loans. If they paid less than competitive rates for the deposits, they would lose the funds.

The resulting losses were staggering. The industry lost $6 billion in 1981 and $5 billion in 1982. The small profits for the industry as a whole in 1983 through 1986 masked continuing losses for about one-third of the S&Ls. The number of S&Ls fell from 5,050 in 1980 to 4,100 in 1983, and then to 3,200 by 1986. The S&L bailout of the 1990s had its origins in these losses of the early 1980s.

Attempts in the early 1980s to save the industry turned out to be seriously flawed, and by the end of the 1980s, a costly bailout proved necessary.[4]

---

[4] We shall discuss this in Chapter 19.

ALTERNATIVE APPROACHES TO MORTGAGE FINANCE

Clearly, then, funding long-term, fixed-rate mortgages with short-term deposits is not a good idea. What are the alternatives? One is to change the mortgage instrument. The other is to change the way that mortgage lending is funded.

The Adjustable-Rate Mortgage

adjustable-rate mortgage (ARM) A mortgage with a variable interest rate, pegged to some short-term market rate.

One way for a depository institution, a thrift or a bank, to make mortgage loans safely is to change the nature of the mortgage loan to better suit its source of funds. With an **adjustable-rate mortgage (ARM)**, the interest rate, rather than being fixed for the life of the mortgage, is linked to some short-term market rate.[5]

How It Works.   To see how an ARM works, let us convert your $100,000 fixed-rate mortgage from Federal Savings and Loan into an adjustable-rate mortgage. For reasons we shall see in a moment, the interest rate is lower—say an APR of 9.5% rather than 12%. Your payment is therefore lower too—$840.85 rather than $1,028.61 (assuming no points).

You will continue to pay this amount for one year. At the end of the year, the rate will be adjusted to 2.5% above the 6-month T-bill rate at that time. Suppose the T-bill rate turns out to be 9%. Then the rate on your mortgage will rise to 9% + 2.5% = 11.5%. The principal remaining at the end of the first year is $99,383, so at the new rate your monthly payment will go up to $988.18. You will pay this amount for another year, when the rate will be adjusted again. Of course, if the T-bill rate had been lower than 7%, your payment would have gone down rather than up.

The Relative Popularity of Adjustable-Rate and Fixed-Rate Mortgages. The relative popularity of adjustable-rate and fixed-rate mortgages with borrowers fluctuates both with the spread between adjustable and fixed rates and with the overall level of rates. When the spread increases, the proportion of new mortgages that are ARMs increases with it. Also, when rates on both types of mortgage are relatively high, borrowers may not have much choice but to take an ARM. While they do not meet the income requirement for a mortgage at the higher fixed rate, they do meet it for the lower rate on an ARM. When rates on both types of mortgage are low, borrowers prefer fixed-rate mortgages even when the spread between the two rates is large. Indeed, many borrowers with existing ARMs refinance with fixed-rate mortgages to lock in the low rate. Clearly, many borrowers are willing to pay a premium for a fixed-rate mortgage that relieves them of the need to worry about interest rates. The fixed-rate mortgage eliminates the risk of a rate increase and leaves the borrower with the option of refinancing if interest rates come down.

---

[5] ARMs were first introduced in the United States in California in 1975. Regulators gave federal S&Ls limited permission to offer ARMs in 1979 and lifted all restrictions in 1981. In many other countries, ARMs have been the major, sometimes the only, type of mortgage for many years.

What Happens to the Interest Rate Risk?   An ARM greatly reduces the interest rate risk of the lender. When interest rates go up and it has to pay more for its deposits, it can also raise the rate in charges on its outstanding mortgages. That way its net interest income remains roughly the same.

Of course the interest rate risk has not disappeared. It has been shifted from lender to borrower. That is why the initial rate is lower. Because of the lower initial rate, your payments to Federal will be lower than they would have been for a fixed-rate mortgage even if interest rates rise a little. What happens, though, if interest rates go up a lot? Suppose the T-bill rate jumps to 16.5%, raising your mortgage rate to 16.5% + 2.5% = 19%. Your monthly payment increases to $1,459.82. If you could barely afford the original $840.85 a month, there is no way you can manage $1,459.82. As a result you are forced to default. Federal sells the house to cover the loan but finds that housing prices are depressed—many other houses are being sold for similar reasons—and the sale must be made at a loss.[6]

So shifting the interest rate risk to the borrower has its problems, not only for you, but also for Federal. The reduction in interest rate risk comes at the expense of an increase in credit risk. To reduce this credit risk, many ARMs have a cap on how much the rate may be raised each year and on how much it may be raised over the life of the mortgage.[7] While caps such as these do reduce credit risk, they also reduce the lender's protection against interest rate risk.

Nondeposit Financing

The adjustable-rate mortgage, then, offers only a partial solution to one of the basic problems of the traditional mortgage market—interest rate risk. And it does not help with the other—fragmentation.

A different and more radical approach offers solutions to both problems. Keep the fixed-rate mortgage, but have it funded not by depository intermediaries but, rather, by long-term financial institutions such as pension funds or life insurance companies. Because the liabilities of such lenders are long-term, mortgage lending does not expose them to interest rate risk. In addition, if these institutions can fund mortgage lending nationwide, this will create a national market integrating local mortgage markets and ending their fragmentation. This approach has in fact been taken through the creation of a secondary market in mortgages in the United States, and it has been a great success.

SECURITIZATION AND THE SECONDARY
MARKET FOR MORTGAGES

Before the funding of fixed-rate mortgages could be shifted from depository intermediaries to insurance companies and pension funds, a number of obstacles had to be overcome.

---

[6] This was the scenario in the United Kingdom, on a wide scale, when short-term rates rose sharply in 1992. The result was a record number of mortgage defaults and foreclosures.

[7] Some ARMs have a cap on the monthly payment. If this maximum monthly payment proves insufficient to cover the interest due, then the balance of the loan increases by the difference. When interest rates come down again, principal repayment resumes, but the term of the mortgage may have to be extended.

Obstacles to Long-Term Funding of Mortgages

There are a number of things about a residential mortgage that make it an unappealing investment for a long-term intermediary such as a pension fund:

- The amount of the loan is small relative to the typical commercial loan. That means high transactions costs.
- The information requirements—especially in relation to the sum involved—are large. The lender needs information both about the borrower *and* about the property. How likely is the borrower to default? How much is the property actually worth? To assess the value of the property, the lender must know the local real estate market. A lender in Chicago, for example, will have little direct knowledge of property values in Los Angeles.
- The servicing of a mortgage is costly. Monthly payments must be collected and processed. Sometimes payments are late, and the borrower must be contacted and payment arranged. If the borrower defaults, the property must be foreclosed and sold.
- Mortgages are very heterogeneous. Not only do both borrower and collateral differ in each case, but also the terms may vary. For example, one mortgage may have a prepayment penalty. Another may require the borrower to take out life insurance to pay off the mortgage if the borrower dies. The heterogeneity adds to the burden of investing in mortgages because it adds to the information and processing costs.
- A secondary market for individual mortgages is simply out of the question. Who would want to make such a market, given the small amounts and high information costs? In the absence of a secondary market, mortgages are highly illiquid.
- For investors like lifes and pension funds that want assets to match their long-term liabilities, the possibility of prepayment is a serious drawback. Because they are committed to paying fixed long-term rates on their liabilities, these institutions want to avoid reinvestment risk.

All these qualities make a mortgage an unappealing investment. Compare it, for example, to a corporate bond. Bonds are issued in large amounts. Information costs are low. The terms of different bonds are very similar. The large amount of essentially interchangeable bonds supports a decent secondary market, which makes them fairly liquid. Bonds are usually not callable until close to maturity, so prepayment is a much less serious problem.

The mortgage market has developed ways to overcome the problems of the mortgage instrument. **Securitization** turns illiquid mortgage loans into securities that can be sold in a secondary market. The existence of this secondary market allows the origination and servicing of mortgages to be separated from their funding. Banks and thrifts can still originate mortgages—something they do well. They can then sell the mortgages to a long-term investor better able to bear the interest rate risk. The investor pays the originator a fee to continue servicing the mortgage. The market has also found ways of dealing with prepayment risk. Let us see how this secondary market developed.

securitization
The issue of transferable securities secured by illiquid securities.

The Origins of the Secondary Market

The secondary market for mortgages is largely a creation of the federal government. The government created this market, however, for reasons largely unrelated to the ones we have discussed. It was not really concerned about the bearing of interest rate risk. It was, concerned, rather, about the availability of mortgages in certain geographic areas and to certain classes of borrowers (the poor, farmers, returning veterans).

Government Involvement in the Mortgage Market.   As we have seen, the federal government first became involved in the mortgage market during the Great Depression. Housing finance had been part of the general collapse. There had been innumerable defaults and foreclosures, and a large number of thrifts had failed. As part of its program of reconstruction, the government set up several agencies to help revive the mortgage market.

The **Federal National Mortgage Association (FNMA or "Fannie Mae")** was set up to buy existing mortgages from thrifts. It sold bonds to raise the necessary funds. Being able to sell off existing mortgages for cash provided the thrifts with liquidity. The **Federal Housing Administration (FHA)** was authorized to insure mortgages made to certain categories of borrower. Such insurance made it easier to sell these mortgages on the secondary market because it reduced the information cost to the buyer. Because the mortgages were insured, the buyer had no need to examine the collateral. If the borrower defaulted and the property was worth less than the unpaid principal, the insurer would pick up the difference. After World War, II government insurance was extended through the Veterans Administration (VA) to mortgage loans made to veterans.

Standardization.   Mortgages that were to be insured by the government had to use a standard loan contract. The use of a standard contract overcame two of the obstacles to the resale of mortgages—their heterogeneity and their small size. Because insured mortgages were all alike, it was easy to bundle them into large packages that could be sold to institutional investors.

From the 1940s to the 1960s, veterans and other borrowers took full advantage of these programs, and the proportion of insured mortgages rose to 45% of all new mortgages. The principal buyers of these mortgages were mutual savings banks and life insurance companies.

The Revival of Mortgage Banking

Although many mortgage banks had collapsed during the Depression, some survived and continued to do business. The new market in government-insured mortgages gave them a new lease on life. As the market developed, new mortgage banks sprang up—many of them subsidiaries of other types of financial institution. Among the largest mortgage banks today there are subsidiaries of banks (Citicorp, Chase, Fleet), finance companies (GMAC, Sears, GEO), and insurance companies (Firemans Fund, Prudential), as well as specialized mortgage lenders (Lomas, Countrywide).

How a Mortgage Bank Works.   The way a mortgage bank works is this. It originates mortgages, initially funding them itself. When it has accumulated enough mortgages, it puts them together into a package and sells the package to an investor. The mortgage bank therefore needs to fund the mortgages only for the short period it takes to put the package together—a few months at most.

Federal National Mortgage Association (FNMA, or "Fannie Mae") Federally sponsored private company that buys and securitizes residential mortgages.

Federal Housing Administration (FHA) Federal agency that insures "conforming" mortgages up to a certain limit.

Mortgage banks earn income from origination fees and from servicing fees they receive from the investor for collecting payments and dealing with the borrower. They may also earn a positive carry on their inventory of mortgages. A "normal" (upward-sloping) yield curve means that the long-term rate they earn on their inventory of mortgages is higher than the short-term rate they pay to finance that inventory. If long-term rates fall between the time of origination of a mortgage and the time of its resale, the banks can sell the mortgages at a profit. Of course, if long-term rates rise, they will take a loss. If they want to avoid this risk, they can sell the mortgages forward to an investor or hedge in various ways.[8]

The Parallel Mortgage Market.   This method of mortgage lending—origination by mortgage banks and funding by institutional investors—provides an alternative to the combination of both functions by thrifts and banks. This parallel structure has some major advantages. Obviously, it is better at handling interest rate risk. Also, because mortgage banks take no deposits, they face no geographic restrictions: they may and do operate nationwide. This allows them to grow to a substantial size and to capture economies of scale. Their size also gives them ready access to the securities markets. Nationwide operation allows them to put together packages of mortgages that are well diversified.

These advantages allowed mortgage banks to undercut depository institutions and to capture most of the business of writing insured mortgages. On the whole, the depository institutions were left with the noninsured mortgages. Because investors were reluctant to buy these, fearing possible losses in case of default, they were hard to sell on the secondary market. They were therefore of little interest to mortgage banks.

The parallel mortgage market was generally more efficient than the traditional market. While the traditional market was fragmented, with rates varying across the country, the parallel market was well integrated. Rates were the same for insured mortgages everywhere. Because mortgage banks competed with each other nationwide, pricing was competitive and costs were minimized.

Mortgage-Backed Securities

mortgage-backed securities (MBSs)
Securities secured by portfolios of mortgages.

Despite its success, the parallel market started to shrink in the 1960s as the number of veterans taking out mortgages declined. The share of insured mortgages fell to about 30% in 1970. To keep the market going, the government took steps between 1968 and 1970 to extend the secondary market to noninsured mortgages and to expand its scope.

Government National Mortgage Association (GNMA, or "Ginnie Mae")
Federally owned corporation that guarantees mortgage-backed securities and arranges for their issue.

From Private Placement to Public Issue.   The secondary market had until them been largely a market for "private placements." Mortgage banks had placed most of their mortgages with lifes and mutual savings banks. The government now acted to develop a market for public issues—a market for **mortgage-backed securities (MBSs)**.

The government reorganized Fannie Mae, which had not been particularly active until then, and created two new agencies—the **Government National Mortgage Association**

---

[8] One way mortgage banks address interest rate risk is to issue callable bonds. If there is a lot of prepayment, rather than having to reinvest the money at a lower rate, they can call the bonds and return the money to the purchasers. We shall see the various other ways of addressing interest rate risk in Chapter 18.

Federal Home Loan Mortgage Corporation (FHLMC, or "Freddie Mac") Federally sponsored private company that buys and securitizes residential mortgages.

passthrough An equity share in a pool of mortgages.

(GNMA, or "Ginnie Mae") and the **Federal Home Loan Mortgage Corporation (FHLMC, or "Freddie Mac")**. The three agencies were authorized to issue and to guarantee a variety of mortgage-related securities backed both by insured and, for the first time, by noninsured mortgages.

The Passthrough.   The basic mortgage-backed security is the **passthrough**. This is rather like a share in a closed-end mutual fund invested in a pool of mortgages. The agency puts together a large pool of mortgages and sells shares in the pool. An investor who buys, say, a 1% share in the pool receives 1% of all the payments on all the mortgages in the pool.

The structure is illustrated in Exhibit 13.4. The *borrower* borrows in the ordinary way from the *originator* (say a savings and loan) who finances the loan until the passthrough is organized. The loan is pooled, together with many others, into a *trust*, administered by a *trustee*. After the credit of the pool has been enhanced by purchasing insurance or a letter of credit, securities are issued. The securities are sold, by an *underwriter*, to *investors*. The proceeds from this sale go back to the originator of the mortgage. The borrower makes payment on the mortgage to the originator, who passes them on to the trustee. The trustee "passes through" the payments to investors, after deducting fees for himself, for the originator, and for the credit enhancer.

EXHIBIT 13.4   The Structure and Cash Flow of a Passthrough

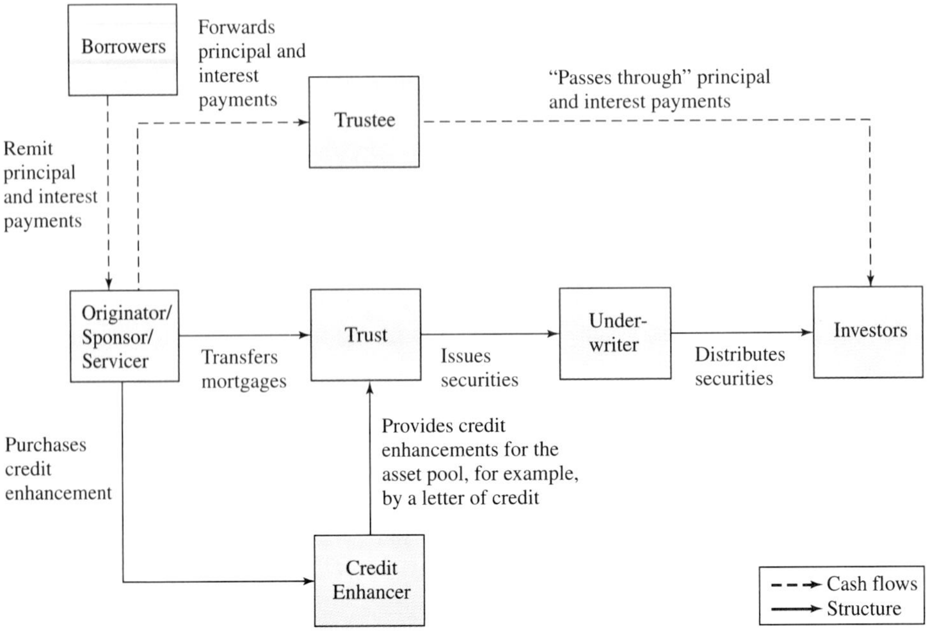

Source: Boemio and Edwards (1989).

The first passthrough was offered by Ginnie Mae in 1970; it was based on a pool of mortgages insured by the FHA and VA. In 1971 Freddie Mac began to issue passthroughs based on conventional mortgages. In 1977, BankAmerica sold the first private passthrough without a government guarantee. Passthroughs were an enormous success. Between 1971 and 1992 the amount outstanding grew at an average rate of more than 30% a year to reach $1.5 trillion. An increasing proportion of all new fixed-rate mortgages have found their way into passthroughs.

The Advantage of the Passthrough for the Agencies.   As we saw earlier, the traditional way the agencies funded mortgages was to issue bonds in their own name and use the proceeds to purchase mortgages from the originators. The problem with doing it this way is interest rate risk—more specifically, reinvestment risk. If interest rates fall and the mortgages they have purchased are prepaid, the agencies will have to reinvest the money in new mortgages at a rate lower than the rate they are paying out on the bonds they issued. With passthroughs, in contrast, the interest rate risk is "passed through," along with the cash flow, to the purchasers.

However, financial intermediation offers not only risks but also profits. The agencies continue to issue bonds (as we saw in Chapter 12), but they now invest the proceeds in mortgage-backed securities rather than in mortgages directly. There are now new methods of addressing the interest rate risk that we shall explore in Chapter 18. At the end of 1999, the agencies owned nearly $500 billion of mortgage-backed securities, and intermediation accounted for nearly 60% of their profits.[9]

The CMO, the REMIC, and the Strip

The enormous amount of passthroughs issued soon made it profitable for government security dealers to organize a secondary market (we shall learn more about it presently). Trading in this market mushroomed rapidly, and by 1985 its volume already exceeded that of the NYSE. The existence of this secondary market greatly enhanced the liquidity of passthroughs and made them more attractive to investors. Passthroughs were immediately a popular investment for thrifts and for commercial banks. Because of the government guarantee, passthroughs are as safe as Treasury securities. Because of the active secondary market, they are almost as liquid.

However, passthroughs were less popular with long-term investors such as lifes and pension funds because of the prepayment risk. Purchasers of passthroughs receive a share of all receipts from the underlying mortgages, including a share of prepayments. Because of the prepayment risk, passthroughs generally carry a higher yield than comparable Treasuries. To expand the market for mortgage-backed securities, issuing agencies and securities firms turned to financial engineering. The idea was to break up the cash flow from a passthrough, so that some "pieces" would be less subject to prepayment risk than others.

---

[9] Intermediation is so profitable for the agencies partly because they can borrow at very advantageous rates since their securities are seen as virtually U.S. government securities. We shall have more to say about this later in the chapter.

collateralized mortgage obligation (CMO)
A security with a partial claim on the cash flow of a portfolio of passthroughs.

The CMO.   In a **collateralized mortgage obligation (CMO)**, Freddie Mac splits the cash flow from a portfolio of passthroughs among several types of securities it issues called **tranches** (slices). For simplicity, suppose there are two tranches, A and B. tranche A might get one-third of the interest payments from the passthroughs and tranche B two-thirds. Thus, if the passthroughs pay 12% interest, tranche A gets 4% and tranche B 8%. The principal repayment and prepayment from the passthroughs, rather than being paid out immediately, go into a redemption fund. Every 6 months, Freddie Mac uses the accumulated redemption fund to call some of the CMOs at par. Those to be called are picked by lot, initially only from tranche A. When all of tranche A has been called, Freddie Mac starts to call tranche B. Tranche A, therefore, has a short duration and carries much of the prepayment risk; tranche B has a longer duration and less prepayment risk. In reality, there are usually a number of tranches, each with progressively longer duration and less prepayment risk.

tranche
One class of several types of CMO based on the same portfolio of passthroughs.

real estate mortgage investment conduit (REMIC)
A vehicle for restructuring the cash flow of mortgage pools.

The REMIC.   Efforts to develop the CMO further ran into difficulties with the tax laws. These difficulties were addressed by the Tax Reform Act of 1986, which established a new vehicle for restructuring the cash flow of mortgage pools—the **real estate mortgage investment conduit (REMIC)**. The REMIC expanded enormously the ways in which the cash flow of a pool of mortgages could be split up without tax complications and made it much easier for various financial institutions to invest in the resulting instruments.

mortgage strip
A REMIC that divides the cash flow of mortgage pools into interest and principal components.

Mortgage Strips.   An example of the type of instrument that the REMIC made possible is the **mortgage strip**. This divides the payments received on a portfolio of passthroughs into interest payments and principal payments (including prepayments). Investors in **interest-only strips (IO strips)** receive all the interest payments; investors in **principal-only strips (PO strips)** receive all the principal payments, including prepayments. Let us see how to calculate the value of a strip and how that value changes with interest rates.

interest-only strip (IO strip)
A claim on the interest component of the cash flow from a mortgage pool.

The Value of a Strip.   Exhibit 13.1 showed how the payments on a mortgage are divided between principal repayment and interest payments. Suppose we split this single mortgage into an IO strip that is a claim to the interest payments on this single mortgage and a PO strip that is a claim to the principal repayment.

If there is no prepayment, the value of the PO strip is

$$V_{PO} = \frac{28.61}{(1.01)} + \frac{28.90}{(1.01)^2} + \cdots + \frac{1,018.43}{(1.01)^{360}} = \$10,197.62$$

principal-only strip (PO strip)
A claim on the principal component of the cash flow from a mortgage pool (including prepayments).

and the value of the IO strip is

$$V_{IO} = \frac{1,000}{(1.01)} + \frac{997.91}{(1.01)^2} + \cdots + \frac{10.18}{(1.01)^{360}} = \$89,802.38$$

Notice that the interest payments are large to begin with and then decline, while the principal payments are small to begin with and then grow. As a result, the value of the IO strip is substantially larger than the value of the PO strip. Of course, the sum of the two values must equal the value of the underlying mortgage—$100,000. As payments are made, and fewer payments remain, the value of each strip declines. The value of each strip is just the present value of the remaining payments.

As a result of the different time patterns of the two streams of payments, the duration of the IO strip is much shorter than that of the PO strip. The former turns out to be a little under 7 years; the latter, 15 years.

How does prepayment affect the values of the two strips? Suppose the mortgage is prepaid after 60 months. The stream of interest payments stops. Consequently, the value of the IO strip, which is the present value of the remaining interest payments—there are now none—drops to zero. The PO strip is a claim to the remaining principal payments *and* to any prepayment. Prepayment does not therefore affect the total amount received by the owner of the PO strip. To pay off the mortgage, the borrower pays the remaining balance. This equals exactly the sum of the remaining principal payments. While the amount is the same, it is now paid *earlier*. Earlier, of course, is more valuable. So the value of the PO strip goes up as a result of prepayment.

Real IO and PO strips are based on passthroughs that include thousands of mortgages. A certain proportion of the mortgages will routinely be prepaid each month as people sell their houses. These routine prepayments over the life of the mortgages will make a real PO strip more valuable than the simple present value of the principal repayments that we calculated earlier, and it will make an IO strip less valuable. In fact, IO strips usually account for about two-thirds of the total value and PO strips, one-third.

The Effect of a Change in Market Interest Rates.   The value of mortgage strips is particularly sensitive to changes in interest rates. PO strips fall sharply in value and IO strips *rise* sharply in value when interest rates rise.

Let us begin by assuming that the rise in interest rates has no effect on the pattern of prepayment and so none on the stream of future payments. The rise in interest rates reduces the present value of all of the expected payments, lowering the value of both types of strip. We shall call this effect the **discounting effect**.

discounting effect
The effect of a change in interest rates on the value of a strip due to changes in present values.

Our assumption that prepayment is unaffected by the rise in interest rates is, of course, unrealistic. As we saw earlier, a rise in market interest rates will cause borrowers to do their best to avoid prepayment. A low-interest-rate mortgage is valuable: Why give it up? Prepayments will therefore decrease.

For a PO strip, that means that principal payments will be received later than expected. This decreases the value of the PO strip. For IO strips, because fewer mortgages are prepaid, future interest payments will be higher than previously expected. This increases the value of the IO strip. Call this effect of a change in prepayment the **prepayment effect** of a change in the interest rate. When the interest rate rises, the prepayment effect *lowers* the value of a PO strip and *raises* the value of an IO strip.

prepayment effect
The effect of a change in interest rates on the value of a strip due to changes in the expected cash flow.

Now take both effects together. For a PO strip, the prepayment effect *reinforces* the discounting effect, and its value falls sharply. A 1% rise in market interest rates can reduce the value of a PO strip by as much as 60%. This makes the sensitivity of the value of a PO strip to interest rates about the same as that of a conventional security with a duration of 60 years.

For an IO strip, the prepayment effect *offsets* the discounting effect. In fact, the offset is so great that the value of the IO strip actually rises when interest rates rise. A 1% rise in market interest rates can *increase* the value of an IO strip by as much as 30%. This makes the sensitivity of the value of an IO strip to interest rates the same as that of a conventional security with a *negative* duration of -30 years, were such a thing possible.

A fall in market interest rates has the reverse effect. The discounting effect raises the value of both types of strip. The prepayment effect raises the value of PO strips and lowers the value of IO strips. In total, the value of PO strips rises and the value of IO strips falls.

Their extreme sensitivity to interest rates makes strips an attractive hedging instrument. Long-term investors, such as pension funds, can hedge the holding of otherwise attractive short-term assets by holding PO strips; short-term investors, such as banks, can take on more long-term assets and hedge them by holding some IO strips.

The extreme sensitivity of strips to changes in interest rates also makes them dangerous to hold unhedged. Merrill Lynch, an active dealer in strips, found this out to its embarrassment. In April 1987, Merrill was caught holding a large amount of unhedged PO strips when long-term rates suddenly rose. Although the firm never admitted the size of its loss, others estimated it at over $300 million. With strips, it is just as easy to lose on a *fall* in interest rates. In March 1993, Salomon announced that it lost $250 million on unhedged IO strips when interest rates rose sharply. Losses of this size are staggering, even by Wall Street standards.

Despite these problems, mortgage strips have been enormously successful. Their success has prompted securities firms to construct similar instruments based on other types of security, as we shall see in Chapter 14.

Organization of the Market for Mortgage-Backed Securities

New issues of mortgage-backed securities are usually sold forward, several months before they are actually delivered. They are sold on a "to-be-announced" basis. While the coupon rate, the type of mortgage-backed security, and the settlement month are specified, technical details such as the number of pools are left blank. These details are filled in later when the information becomes available.

The organization of the secondary market is very similar to that of the secondary market in government securities and is in fact closely related to it. Many of the same dealers and brokers participate in both markets. As in the government securities market, there is an inside market mediated by interdealer brokers. Trading volume is not as great as in the government securities markets, but it is still substantial. In 2000, average daily trading volume was $25 billion in the interdealer market and another $44 billion with others.

There are repos and reverses in passthroughs just as there are in Treasuries. There is a potential problem with repoing passthroughs because, unlike Treasuries, they are very heterogeneous: issues differ in their size, prepayment characteristics, and geographic distribution. To overcome this problem, repos in passthroughs do not, as is usual with repos, require return of the identical security. Rather the agreement—called a *dollar roll*—permits return of "substantially identical" securities—that is, those reasonably close in nature.

Guidelines for trading, clearing, and settlement are set by the Public Securities Association (PSA) a group of some 300 banks, dealers, and brokers involved in the markets for federal, municipal, and mortgage-backed securities. Fannie Mae and Freddie Mac securities are in book-entry form on Fedwire. So settlement is over Fedwire, as with Treasuries.

The Benefits of Securitization

Mortgage securitization clearly has had substantial benefits. The practice of separating the funding of mortgages from their origination and servicing has lessened the vulnerability of the system to interest rate risk.

Securitization has also reduced the inefficiencies caused by the fragmentation of the financial system. The secondary mortgage market integrated mortgage lending in much the same way that the money market integrated commercial lending. Potential mortgage lenders with surplus funds can now buy passthroughs, and those with more mortgages to fund than deposits can sell off the excess in the secondary market. Lenders can also improve the diversification of their mortgage portfolios by selling off some of their own mortgages and replacing them with passthroughs based on mortgages from all over the country. Passthroughs also improve lenders' liquidity. If cash is needed, passthroughs, unlike ordinary mortgages, may be sold or repoed at a moment's notice.

Mortgage securitization has improved integration in another way too. It has given mortgage borrowers access to the national capital market. Before, the mortgage market was separated from the capital market. As a result, mortgage rates could be substantially higher than rates on comparable long-term debt of other issuers. Today, mortgage rates move much more closely with capital market rates.

THE MORTGAGE MARKET TODAY

Securitization has transformed the mortgage market. At the end of 2000, roughly 60% of the $5 trillion of outstanding home mortgages were in mortgage pools, with an even higher proportion for new mortgages. Exhibit 13.5 shows how the pattern of origination of mortgages has changed. The market share of mortgage banks has steadily expanded to replace the declining market share of the thrifts.

Mortgage Brokers and the Internet

As a result of securitization, the organization of the market has changed drastically. Less than half of all new mortgages today are originated by local banks and thrifts. The rest are originated by mortgage banks, finance companies, and banks at a distance. Distant lenders are able to originate mortgages because of the reappearance, since the late 1980s, of mortgage brokers. Today, there are some 30,000 mortgage brokers who match up borrowers and lenders for a fee (usually about 1% of the value of the loan). Many are real estate agents and housing developers; many others are specialized brokers. There are no firm statistics, but brokers probably arrange some 50% of all home loans.

The growth of mortgage broking has been greatly facilitated by the rise of the Internet. From the beginning, brokers made use of computer networks to find the best rate

EXHIBIT 13.5   Share of Originations of Residential Mortgage Loans by Different Financial Institutions

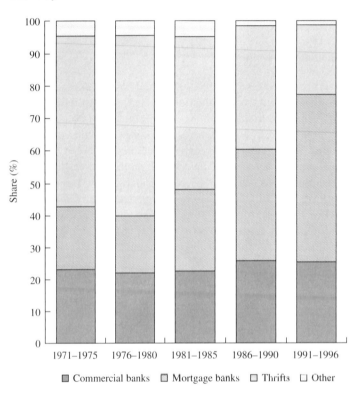

Source: U.S. Housing Market Conditions.

offered by a selection of mortgage originators. Then, in the mid-1990s, Fannie Mae and Freddie Mac made available online their automated underwriting systems. After a broker has entered basic data on the borrower and the property, the system pulls up credit agency information and uses scoring to predict default. Within minutes, it announces whether the mortgage is acceptable for purchase by the mortgage agencies. With the result in hand, the broker is in a strong position to get an originator to fund the mortgage at a competitive rate.

More recently there has been an explosion of online broking. Many existing brokers have gone online to offer their services nationwide. They have been joined by a number of web startups, such as E-Loan and Homeshark, and Microsoft and Quicken have entered the business too. There are now over 100 mortgage websites. Online broking is very competitive: E-Loan and QuickenMortgage charge a broker's fee of 37.5 basis points vs the customary 1% of conventional brokers. In 2000, over 15% of new mortgages were generated online and about 2% ($20 billion total) were actually closed online.

The change in the organization of the market from local to national and the resulting increase in competition has led to a growing concentration of loan origination. In 1999, the top 25 mortgage originators accounted for 57% of all originations, up from 26% a decade earlier. The top 10 accounted for 39% of originations. Some of this increasing concentration is due to consolidation among both commercial banks and mortgage banks as they have sought to capture economies of scale.

The Controversial Role of the Mortgage Agencies

Government-sponsored and government-related agencies, particularly Fannie and Freddie, dominate the secondary market. However, private institutions play an active role too. They create CMOs and strips, "hitching a ride" on the government guarantee of the underlying passthroughs. They also lead the way in securitizing ARMs and home equity loans (second mortgages). Furthermore, the government agencies accept mortgages only up to a certain maximum value—$275,000 in 2001. Private institutions have been active in packaging mortgages above this limit—"jumbo" or "nonconforming" mortgages—into private passthroughs or using them as collateral for private mortgage-backed bonds. They are active too in securitizing commercial and other nonhome mortgages. However, despite all this private activity, the agencies still accounted for 72% of securitizations of all mortgages in 2000 and 82% of securitizations of home mortgages.

The reason for this domination is that the agencies enjoy several powerful competitive advantages. Unlike private institutions, they are exempt from state and local taxes, and they are not required to register their securities with the SEC (thus saving some $1 billion in 1999). They have lower capital ratios than private institutions, and they have the benefit of an $8.5 billion emergency line of credit from the Treasury.

Although their securities are not backed by the "full faith and credit" of the federal government, the market assumes that there is an implicit guarantee. Their borrowing rate is therefore quite close to the Treasury rate. This reduced their borrowing costs by an estimated $6.5 billion in 1995. The agencies pass on to mortgage borrowers about half the benefit of the lower rate, and the rest goes to swell the agencies' bottom line.

As a result of these advantages, the return on equity of the agencies has averaged in recent years a very healthy 24%. Moreover, the benefit goes largely to private individuals. Although Fannie Mae and Freddie Mac were established by the federal government, they are publicly traded companies, and their shares are held by private investors.

There have been repeated calls to fully privatize the agencies, cutting them loose completely from the federal government. The idea is to end their unfair competition with private institutions and to end taxpayer exposure to their potential losses. These calls have so far fallen on deaf ears, not least because of successful lobbying by the agencies themselves.

MORTGAGE MARKETS IN OTHER COUNTRIES

The scale of residential mortgage lending differs widely across countries. In the United States, the value of outstanding residential mortgages equals 53% of GDP (in 1998). In the European Union it equals only 36%. However, there is a great deal of variation within the EU. In Germany and the United Kingdom it is 53%, the same as in the United States; in Denmark it is even higher, at 70%. On the other hand, it is only 20% in France and less than 10% in Italy, Austria, and Greece.

One reason for these differences is differences in the legal environment. In continental Europe, especially in the south, foreclosure is difficult and time-consuming. This makes mortgage lending much less attractive and consequently less available. Lenders, to protect themselves, require down payments of up to 40%. In contrast, in the United Kingdom, where foreclosure is easy, mortgages are readily available and down payments are in the range of 0% to 5%.

The attractiveness of homeownership relative to renting also differs from country to country. In some countries, generous tax benefits make homeownership more attractive. The United States has the most generous tax benefits; Australia and Canada, on the other hand, have none. Taxes on the sale of property can make property a much less liquid investment, making homeownership less attractive relative to renting. In the United States the tax is typically about 1.5%, but it is much higher in continental Europe: Belgium has the highest rate at 17%.

Homeownership rates therefore differ widely across countries. They are 60% to 70% in the United States, Britain, Canada, and Japan, but only 40% to 60% in continental Europe (in Switzerland, only 30%).

In many European countries, the government is a major provider of rental housing. In the Netherlands government housing makes up 40% of the total. Private rental housing is biggest in Germany, but it is substantial too in the United States.

Mortgage Lending by Banks and Thrifts

In most countries, mortgage lending has always been done by banks and thrifts. Generally, this has worked better than it has in the United States because of the absence of geographic restrictions on branching. Because lending institutions in most countries could branch nationwide, they could move funds from low-demand areas to high-demand areas and keep mortgage rates fairly uniform across the country. Moreover, being larger and better diversified, they were much less vulnerable to regional slumps.

Of course, the issue of interest rate risk remains. In Europe, banks generally address this by lending at an adjustable rate. In the EU, adjustable-rate mortgages make up 70% of the total. In general, where lending is at a fixed rate there are stiff prepayment penalties. For example, nearly a million Italian households took out mortgages in the late 1980s at 12 to 14%. But because the prepayment penalty is 20% of the value of the mortgage, they were unable to refinance when interest rates subsequently fell.

In some of continental Europe and in Japan, banks do their mortgage lending through special mortgage subsidiaries that rely on longer term liabilities. These mortgage subsidiaries are particularly important in Germany, Denmark, and Sweden.[10] They finance their portfolios of mortgages by issuing long-term **mortgage-backed bonds**, called *Pfandbriefe* in Germany.

In Japan, a government-subsidized mortgage loan program accounts for 40% of all mortgages. The Government Housing Loan Corporation purchases mortgages that are

mortgage-backed bonds
Bonds secured by portfolios of mortgages.

---

[10] These institutions are known in Europe as mortgage banks. However, they differ substantially from the American institutions of the same name.

originated by bank housing finance companies. It is primarily funded by the Post Office Savings Banks.

Securitization and Secondary Markets

Securitization has been slow to catch on outside the United States. While over half of all residential mortgages are securitized in the United States, only about 1% are securitized in the EU. The only real markets there are in the United Kingdom and the Netherlands, and even in the United Kingdom only 3% of residential mortgages are securitized.

In many countries, the need for securitization is less pressing because traditional mortgage lending by banks and thrifts works better than it used to do in the United States. In other countries, traditional lending works less well, but there are major tax and legal obstacles to securitization. One general obstacle is that the rules of the EU prevent member countries from setting up government-assisted institutions on the model of Fannie Mae and Freddie Mac.

The market for mortgage-backed bonds (*Pfandbriefe*) is in some sense an alternative to securitization. Like securitization, it does provide long-term funds for fixed-rate mortgages, and it does integrate the mortgage market with the capital market. Mortgage-backed bonds finance some 19% of mortgage lending in the EU—with much higher percentages in Germany, Denmark, and Sweden.

SUMMARY

- The basic mortgage instrument in the United States, created in the 1930s, is the long-term, fixed-rate, amortized mortgage. Lenders often charge points on a mortgage, which increase the EAR if the mortgage is prepaid.

- A mortgage is secured by a lien on a property. It is usually overcollateralized: the borrower must finance a part of the purchase with a down payment. The lender is sometimes also protected by mortgage insurance.

- The U.S. mortgage market, dominated by thrifts and banks, suffered from two main problems. It was fragmented because of geographic restrictions on lenders. And thrifts, because of their extreme specialization in mortgage lending and the resulting duration mismatch, were extremely vulnerable to interest rate risk.

- Since the S&L disaster, depository institutions have largely switched to adjustable-rate mortgages. While they still originate fixed-rate mortgages, they now sell these on the secondary market rather than holding them themselves.

- After World War II, the federal government began to insure mortgages and to purchase insured mortgages with funds raised through bond issues. Insured mortgages were also bought by insurance companies and mutual savings banks.

- The market for insured mortgages was soon dominated by mortgage banks, which were generally more efficient and less restricted than depository institutions.

- When this parallel mortgage market showed signs of dying out in the late 1960s, due to declining availability of insured mortgages, the government helped to develop a market for mortgage-backed securities.

- The basic instrument is the passthrough, which is an equity claim on a pool of mortgages. A secondary market for passthroughs soon developed, and this market has become one of the largest securities markets. Its organization parallels that of the market for government securities.

- Financial engineering has created a variety of instruments to split up the cash flow from passthroughs. CMOs are issued in different tranches with different susceptibility to prepayment risk. IO and PO strips split the payment stream into interest and principal components.

- With PO strips, the discounting effect and the prepayment effect of a change in market interest rates combine to give it a very long effective duration. With IO strips the two effects work against one another, but the prepayment effect dominates. The result is that the value of IO strips moves in the same direction as interest rates, rather than inversely as with most securities.

- There has been some talk of privatizing the secondary market, but the federal government remains deeply involved.

- Securitization, by separating funding from origination, has improved the integration of the financial system and reduced vulnerability to interest rate risk. It has also integrated mortgage lending with the bond market.

- Much mortgage lending today is arranged by mortgage brokers, with increasing use of the Internet. This has led to an increasing concentration in origination.

- The extent of mortgage lending differs widely across countries as a result of differences in foreclosure laws, tax codes, and home ownership. In most countries, mortgage lending is done by banks and thrifts, but with fewer problems than in the United States because of less fragmentation; adjustable-rate mortgages are the rule. In some countries, special institutions issue bonds to finance long-term fixed-rate mortgages. Securitization has been slow to catch on outside the United States.

DISCUSSION QUESTIONS

1. You buy a house and, to finance the purchase, you apply for a $50,000, 30-year mortgage at 10.5% APR from your local bank.
    a. What is the effective annual rate? The interest rate for the compounding period? Your monthly payment?
    b. Suppose the bank charges you 2 points on the mortgage. How much will the bank then actually lend you? What will be the effective annual rate? The monthly payment?

      Ten years have passed since you took out the mortgage. The interest rate (APR) on new mortgages has fallen to 8% and you are considering refinancing.
    c. How much do you still owe on the mortgage?
    d. Assume the bank charges 2 points on the new mortgage, and that you can take out a 20-year mortgage. What will be your new payment? What is your gain? Should you refinance?

2. Why is the residential mortgage a difficult loan for the financial system to handle? What are the different ways financial systems have dealt with it?

3. In Chapter 3, we looked at the possible reasons for government intervention in the financial system?

Discuss the U.S. government's role in the mortgage market in terms of those reasons. Has government intervention been beneficial?

4. Why are mortgages prepaid? Why, and for whom, is this a problem? How does the mortgage market deal with this problem?

5. What are the relative advantages and disadvantages of fixed-rate and adjustable-rate mortgages from the point of view of a borrower? From the point of view of a bank? From the point of view of the secondary market?

6. To illustrate IO and PO strips, consider a 4-year, fixed-rate mortgage with annual payments (that is, the mortgage is paid off in four equal annual payments).
    a. For an interest rate of 10% and a loan amount of $100,000, calculate the size of the payments and break them down into interest and principal repayment.
    b. What would be the value of an IO strip and of a PO strip based on this mortgage?
    c. Suppose you have IO strips based on a large pool of such mortgages, and the day after they are issued, market interest rates fall to 9%. Half

the mortgages are prepaid. What is the change in the value of the IO strip?

d. In the circumstances of part c, what is the change in the value of the PO strips?

BIBLIOGRAPHY

Becketti, Sean. "The Prepayment Risk of Mortgage-Backed Securities." *Economic Review of the Federal Reserve Bank of Kansas City*, February 1989, 43–57.

Boemio, Thomas R., and Gerald A. Edwards. "Asset Securitization: A Supervisory Perspective." *Federal Reserve Bulletin*, October 1989.

Hardt, Judith, and David Manning. *European Mortgage Markets: Structure, Funding and Future Development.* Paris: OECD, June 2000.

Marcus, Alan J., and Arnold Kling. "Interest-Only/Principal-Only Mortgage-Backed Strips: A Valuation and Risk Analysis." Working paper no. 2340, National Bureau of Economic Research, August 1987.

Roche, Ellen P. "Loans Around the World." *Secondary Mortgage Markets: A Freddie Mac Quarterly* 14 no. 1 (April 1997).

Sellon, Gordon H., Jr., and Deana Van Nahmen. "The Securitization of Housing Finance," *Economic Review of the Federal Reserve Bank of Kansas City*, July–August 1988, 3–20.

KEY TERMS

mortgage brokers

mortgage bank

balloon loan

points

prepay

lien

down payment

mortgage insurance

income test

refinancing

closing costs

Federal Home Loan Banks

disintermediation

adjustable-rate mortgage (ARM)

securitization

Federal National Mortgage Association (FNMA or "Fannie Mae")

Federal Housing Administration (FHA)

mortgage-backed securities (MBSs)

Government National Mortgage Association (GNMA or "Ginnie Mae")

Federal Home Loan Mortgage Corporation (FHLMC or "Freddie Mac").

passthrough

collateralized mortgage obligation (CMO)

tranche

real estate mortgage investment conduit (REMIC)

mortgage strip

interest-only strip (IO strip)

principal-only strip (PO strip)

discounting effect

prepayment effect

mortgage-backed bonds

CHAPTER 14

DEBT MARKETS

When you finish this chapter you will understand:

- How lenders protect themselves against losses
- The fundamental difference between borrowing from a bank and borrowing in the bond market
- Why some issuers of bonds prefer to sell them privately
- How securitization and financial engineering can turn lead into gold

In Chapter 11, we saw that there were two basic forms of financing—debt and equity. In this chapter and in the next, we shall look at the markets for these two types of financing in greater detail.

The key to understanding debt in all its forms is the need for the lender to control risk. As we saw in Chapter 11, the risk of debt, unlike the risk of equity, is all downside: there are no potential gains to balance potential losses. Consequently, the value of debt depends to a large extent on how successfully risk can be controlled. We shall therefore begin by looking at the various methods lenders use to control risk. We shall then take a tour of the debt markets and see how these methods are put into practice.

WAYS TO CONTROL THE RISK OF DEBT

Credit Information

The first rule in controlling risk is "avoid the lemons"—avoid the loans that are sure to be unprofitable. The key to this, of course, is information. A potential lender needs to know the risks involved before making a particular loan. Once a loan is made, information continues to be important. The lender cannot take steps to control the risk of an ongoing loan without knowing what the borrower is doing.

Information as a Public Good.   Borrowers generally borrow from more than one lender—either at the same time or at different times. Consequently, credit information is something of a public good: it can be used by many lenders at no greater cost than by a single lender. Because of this, it makes sense to gather and assess credit information once and to make it available to all potential lenders. There are various arrangements, public and private, to do this.

due diligence
A conscientious effort to uncover the facts relating to an issue of securities.

In the United States, borrowers who sell their debt to the public at large are required to register with the SEC. Registration involves the disclosure of all information that bears on the borrower's creditworthiness. Borrowers must update this information over the life of the security with periodic filings with the SEC. The process of registration is generally handled by the underwriter of the issue, who is responsible for exercising **due diligence** in obtaining, verifying, and disclosing the relevant information. Underwriters have strong incentives to do this well. They are legally liable if the information is unreliable, and, perhaps more important, their reputation, and so their future business, depends on their credibility with investors.

rating agencies
Independent agencies that collate information on issuers of debt and rate issues for likelihood of repayment.

There are many other sources of public information. There are the financial media—newspapers and periodicals like the *Wall Street Journal* and *Investor's Business Daily*; specialized cable TV channels such as MSNBC and CNNfn; and websites such as Bloomberg. Analysts working for securities firms and banks do their own research on issuers and publish ratings and recommendations. However, the most important source of credit information for debt securities is the **rating agencies**.

rating
A letter grade assigned to publicly issued debt by an agency to indicate likelihood of repayment.

Ratings.   Several independent agencies provide ratings of the credit quality of debt. A **rating** is an assessment of the likelihood of timely payment. The agencies generally assign ratings to individual issues rather than to issuers, since the specific characteristics of an issue affect the likelihood of default. Exhibit 14.1 shows the scale of ratings for bonds used by the two largest agencies, Moody and Standard & Poor. Debt with a rating of at least Baa

EXHIBIT 14.1   A Guide to Bond Ratings

Moody's	S&P/Others	Meaning	
Aaa	AAA	Highest quality	
Aa1, Aa2, Aa3	AA+, AA, AA−	High quality	**Investment grade**
A1, A2, A3	A+, A, A−	Strong payment capacity	
Baa1, Baa2, Baa3	BBB+, BBB, BBB−	Adequate payment capacity	
Ba1, Ba2, Ba3	BB+, BB, BB−	Likely to repay; ongoing uncertainty	**Speculative grade, noninvestment grade**
B1, B2, B3	B+, B, B−	High risk obligations	

Source: Partnoy (1999).

**investment-
grade bonds**
Bonds with a rat-
ing of at least Baa
(Moody) or BBB
(Standard & Poor).

(Moody) or BBB (Standard & Poor) is described as being of **investment grade**. The two
agencies tend to agree on the higher ratings, but they often differ on the lower ratings.

Moody and Standard & Poor, together with the two smaller agencies Fitch and Duff
and Phelps, dominate the business of rating debt in the United States and, increasingly,
worldwide. In 1999, Moody alone rated some 20,000 public and private issuers in the
United States and some 1,200 elsewhere. Ratings are not as widely used outside the United
States, but the practice is spreading, especially in Europe. American rating agencies have
a head start in providing this service.

Originally, there was no charge to the issuer for a rating, with the agencies earning
their living by selling publications that listed their ratings to investors. But this has
changed, and today issuers pay to be rated: almost all the agencies' revenue now comes
from issuer fees. The charge for a rating is typically about 2 to 3 basis points of the principal per year. Issuers are more than happy to pay this, since a good rating can make an
enormous difference to their borrowing costs or even to their ability to borrow at all.

The importance of ratings, and the consequent prosperity of the ratings agencies, is a
bit of a puzzle, because the informational value of ratings is questionable. The agencies
rely almost exclusively on publicly available information from the issuer and the underwriter (most of it from filings with the SEC): the agencies contribute little or no informational value added. The agencies pride themselves on the reliability of their ratings: it is
true that only one company with an investment-grade rating has defaulted on its debt in the
last 20 years. However, this record has largely been achieved by revising ratings downward
after new information becomes public but before default actually takes place. There is no
evidence that ratings provide a better predictor of default than the public information on
which they are based. At best, they are a convenient summary of that information.

The solution to the puzzle of the importance of ratings and the prosperity of the agencies, despite the modest informational value, is the growing significance attached to ratings by financial regulators. Regulators of various types of financial institution limit the
ability of those institutions to invest in debt that is of less than investment grade. Consequently, an issue that does not obtain an investment-grade rating faces a much reduced
potential market and must consequently pay a significantly higher yield. For example, a
ruling in 1991 that severely restricted investment by money market mutual funds in below-
investment-grade commercial paper essentially wiped out overnight the market for such
paper.

Information Sharing.   Borrowers who borrow from individual institutions rather
than selling their debt to the public at large are not required to make credit information
public. However, the lending institutions themselves—banks, finance companies, insurance companies, and so on—require at least as much information. To gather and assess this
information, each lending institution has its own loan department. However, because of the
public-good nature of information, lending institutions find it worthwhile to share information on creditworthiness. Knowing that a borrower has regularly paid other lenders, or
has failed to do so, will help new lenders in deciding whether to make a loan.

credit bureau
An agency that
collates and make
available credit
information on
borrowers.

Borrower information is centralized and distributed through **credit bureaus**. Such
institutions exist in many countries either as independent companies or as ventures set up
by consortia of lenders. In the United States, Dun & Bradstreet provides credit information on businesses, and three agencies (Equifax, Experian, and Trans Union) provide credit

information on households. In some countries, especially in continental Europe and Latin America, there are government agencies, called public credit registers, that perform much the same function as private credit bureaus.

A credit bureau gathers data from lenders and collates this with data from other sources such as courts and tax authorities on bankruptcy and tax delinquency. For business borrowers, it gathers additional information from the businesses themselves. The bureau compiles a file on each borrower and make it available for a fee to potential lenders or extenders of credit. For example, a standard business information report from Dun & Bradstreet contains the payment history of the firm, its financial condition, business history, and management experience, and details on its lines of business, parent company and subsidiaries, as well as public records, and so on. Dun & Bradstreet's global database covers 48 million businesses, of which 10 million are in the United States. Today, much of the information flow to the credit bureaus is electronic, and their reports are available online via the Internet.

If such credit information is readily available at low cost, financial institutions will be more willing to make loans, and they will experience fewer defaults. This is especially important for small loans, where the cost of information is potentially high compared to the revenue from making the loan. In countries with established credit bureaus, therefore, creditworthy small borrowers will find it easier to obtain a loan.

There is an additional, important type of information-sharing with respect to collateral. Lenders making a loan on collateral need to know that the collateral has not been pledged already to secure a loan from another lender. Just about every country has a public register for real estate collateral. Some countries also have public registers for other types of collateral.

The Debt Contract

indenture
A loan contract spelling out the terms of the loan.

The making of a loan requires the writing of an **indenture**—a loan contract between borrower and lender. The terms of the indenture offer the lender a number of ways to limit potential losses and to control risk.

priority
The position of a particular debt in the order in which debts are paid in bankruptcy.

The Terms of the Loan Contract.   The loan contract first of all establishes the **priority** of the loan over other possible debt. In the event of default and liquidation, priority determines the order in which loans are paid off. Loans that are more senior are paid off first; only then and only if something is left are more junior loans paid off. **Subordinated debt** is debt that is paid off only after all other debt has been paid. The contract may also specify security for the loan in the form of collateral or guarantees (we shall have more to say about this presently).

subordinated debt
Debt that, in case of insolvency, is paid off only after other debt has been paid.

The contract specifies the maturity of the loan and the timing of payments. The lender can use maturity as a way of controlling risk. Rather than granting a long-term loan, the lender can lend on a short-term basis and roll the loan over. Having the option not to roll over the loan gives the lender some control over the borrower's actions. A similar effect can be achieved by making the loan long term but writing into the contract an option for the lender to call the loan either at discretion or when certain specified circumstances occur—a downgrading of the borrower's rating or a fall in the borrower's equity-to-debt ratio, for example.

covenant

A condition written into the loan contract.

The option to call is an example of a **covenant**—a condition written into the loan contract. Other common covenants are those that limit the borrower's right to issue additional debt or to pay dividends to shareholders. Because covenants constrain a borrower's actions, they are potentially damaging to the borrower. While they are intended to prevent actions that would be harmful to the lender, they may also prevent actions that are of benefit to the borrower and harmless or even beneficial to the lender. For example, the borrower might be better able to repay if able to issue additional debt to finance a lucrative new investment: a covenant might prevent this. So lenders need to be flexible in administering covenants. Covenants are potentially most damaging to borrowers with a high potential for growth. Consequently, lenders to such borrowers usually prefer to rely on one of the other methods of dealing with risk such as taking an equity stake in the enterprise.

A violation of the terms of the loan contract, either a failure to make required payments of interest or principal or a violation of a covenant, constitutes default on the loan. Default entitles the lender to seek redress through the legal system. This may involve the seizure of collateral or other assets or the activation of guarantees. The resolution of a default often triggers a formal proceeding of bankruptcy.

Bankruptcy. The purpose of bankruptcy is to bring about an orderly resolution of default that protects the interest of all parties involved. There are two potential conflicts of interest. The first is among the different creditors and classes of creditors: each will want to be paid, but there may not be enough for all. The second is between creditors and others with an interest in the debtor enterprise—equity holders, managers, employees, and companies with which it does business.[1]

The creditors and the other interested parties may have different interests in choosing between liquidation of the enterprise and the reorganization of its debts. In a liquidation, the debtor's assets are sold off to satisfy its creditors, essentially putting an end to the enterprise as a going concern. In a reorganization, debts may be deferred or partially forgiven to allow the enterprise to continue in business. Creditors may prefer a liquidation because that minimizes their losses. However, liquidation may destroy a great deal of value. This matters little to the creditors, but it is of great concern to the other parties who would bear the loss.

Bankruptcy codes in different countries differ in the degree to which they favor creditors over other parties to the enterprise. In the United Kingdom, Germany, and Japan the law leans towards liquidation and the rights of creditors.[2] In France and the United States, the law gives greater protection to the rights of noncreditors. In the United States the law aims to be evenhanded, but in practice tends to favor the interests of equity holders. Under Chapter 11 of the bankruptcy code, debtors may seek protection from their creditors for a specified period of time, during which a plan for reorganization is to be submitted by the managers. To take effect, the plan has to be approved by both creditors and equity holders.

---

[1] Our discussion will relate to business rather than personal bankruptcy, but similar considerations will hold in both cases.

[2] In Germany and Japan, liquidation is nonetheless unusual, as major efforts are usually made to find a negotiated solution first. The strong legal position of creditors gives them considerable bargaining power in such negotiations.

Since equity holders have nothing to lose from delay, the proceedings often go on for years, compounding the losses of the creditors. If reorganization fails, as it eventually does in most cases, the enterprise is liquidated under Chapter 7 of the bankruptcy code.

The best form of bankruptcy code is controversial. There is, of course, a trade-off. A law that is more permissive minimizes unnecessary harm to firms in distress and to their equity holders and employees. However, such a law weakens the incentives to repay of the much larger number of debtors that are not in distress. It therefore leaves lenders more hesitant to make loans. On the other hand, a harsh law that causes excessive harm to firms that default may provide strong incentives for repayment and so increase the supply of lending.

Security

An important feature of many loan contracts—one that can minimize losses in case of default and help the lender to control risk—is security for the loan. Security may take the form either of collateral or of guarantees.

collateral

A specific asset earmarked as security for a loan.

Collateral. **Collateral** is a particular, specified asset that may be seized by the lender in case of default and sold off to pay the debt.[3] Collateral can reduce or even eliminate any loss to the lender in case of default. This is its function in secured lending to consumers—mortgage finance of housing, for example, or secured automobile loans. This is also its function in lending against securities—repurchase agreements or margin lending to investors. In these cases, collateral not only protects the lender from loss, but also reduces or eliminates the need to assess the general credit of the borrower. Depending on the costs associated with the use of collateral, this can reduce significantly the overall cost of making the loan.[4]

The Role of Collateral in Commercial Lending. The function of collateral in *commercial* lending is, however, somewhat different. Its main purpose is not so much to compensate the lender in case of default as it is to provide the lender with a way of controlling the borrower's behavior and so reducing the probability that default will occur.

Often, an asset that serves as collateral is vital to the enterprise yet has little or no resale value to the lender—for example, enterprise-specific software. The role of collateral in such a case is to serve as a "hostage" or performance bond. The threat of losing the collateral asset is a strong incentive for the borrower to pay up. At the same time, the borrower has the reassurance of knowing that the lender will gain nothing by foreclosing unjustifiably.

Perhaps the most important way that collateral reduces the risk of default is by preventing the borrower from taking additional loans and so increasing leverage. Once an asset has been pledged as collateral for one loan, it cannot be used to secure another.

From the point of view of the borrower, the control that collateral gives the lender is a nuisance because it constrains the borrower's freedom to pursue new profit opportunities.

---

[3] This may be done either through a separate legal procedure of foreclosure or in the framework of a bankruptcy.

[4] In lending against securities, the securities in question are more like a pawn than collateral in that they are taken out of the possession of the borrower. This, together with the ease of verifying the value of the securities, greatly reduces the cost of making such a loan.

Moreover, a collateralized loan has greater transactions costs, which must, of course, be borne by the borrower. So why do borrowers provide collateral? Because collateral reduces the risk to the lender, loans are more readily available, rates are lower, and maturities are longer. Of course, the extent of these potential benefits depends on how risky the borrower is in the first place. For low-risk borrowers, the potential benefits are negligible and consequently they rarely borrow against collateral. Collateralized lending is largely restricted to high-risk borrowers. For them, the benefits exceed the costs.

leasing

A form of secured lending in which the lender has ownership of the collateral.

Leasing.   An important variation on the use of collateral is **leasing**. With a lease, rather than lending a firm the money to buy a piece of equipment, the lending institution buys the equipment itself and lends the *equipment* to the firm.[5] Leases are used to finance investment in computers, commercial aircraft, construction equipment, machine tools, and medical equipment. For the lender, the lease has some legal advantages over a collateralized loan. It may be easier for a lender to repossess the asset, and in a bankruptcy the rights of a lessor are stronger than those of a secured lender (especially under Chapter 11). Leasing is a particularly attractive form of collateralized lending, therefore, for firms that are relatively likely to default. A lease may also provide some tax advantages.[6]

guarantee

A third-party promise to repay a debt if the borrower defaults.

Guarantees.   Collateral is one form of security, the other is a **guarantee** from some third party having better credit than the borrower. There are government guarantees—of mortgages and student loans for example; companies that guarantee the debt of their subsidiaries and affiliates; insurance companies that guarantee the debt of municipal borrowers; and banks that guarantee commercial paper (we shall learn more about the last two examples presently).

The use of guarantees raises an interesting economic question. Since the guarantor places itself at risk, it presumably assesses the borrower's credit and monitors the borrower's behavior to control risk and ensure repayment. Why is it advantageous for the guarantor to do this rather than the lender? The reason must be that the guarantor can perform these functions at lower cost. If so, then why does the guarantor not do the lending? The guarantor could lend to the borrower out of its own funds, or it could borrow from the lender and relend to the borrower. The three-way relationship of borrower–lender–guarantor is more complicated and involves higher transactions costs. What are the compensating advantages?

One answer is that the three-way arrangement provides better security for the loan, since both the borrower *and* the guarantor are liable. This is especially important if there is a chance that the guarantor itself may fail—for example, when a company guarantees the debt of a subsidiary, or when one individual guarantees the debt of another.

---

[5] While the lender is the legal owner of the asset, it is not always the *economic* owner. Under many leases, the lessee has the option to purchase the asset at the end of the lease at a predetermined price (a call option on the asset). This gives the lessee a claim on the residual value of the asset and an incentive to take good care of it.

[6] The lessor can deduct the depreciation of the asset as an expense and claim investment tax credits if these exist. This is particularly advantageous when the lessor faces a higher tax rate than the lessee. For example, local governments because they are not themselves subject to tax frequently sell and lease back assets. Similarly a growing firm that shows no taxable profits may benefit from leasing equipment.

Another answer is that there are circumstances in which the guarantor is willing to take on the risk exposure but prefers not to have the loan on its balance sheet. For example, for governments there may be a political advantage to helping favored constituencies "off budget" with guarantees, which are less visible than actual loans. And consideration of regulation, accounting, or taxation may make it advantageous for financial institutions, such as banks and insurance companies, to provide guarantees rather than to lend directly. As we saw in Chapter 6, this was the case with bank guarantees of commercial paper.

One can think of a guarantee as a way of separating credit risk from funding. One party bears the credit risk; a different party provides the funds for the loan. Each party is rewarded for its contribution. The separation is worthwhile because each of the parties has an advantage in performing one of the functions and can therefore perform it more cheaply. Separation of the two functions therefore lowers the overall cost of the loan to the borrower.

Financial Engineering

The idea of separating credit risk from funding can be generalized and built upon in many ways. In recent years, a whole science has grown up around this idea—the science of *financial engineering*. Its practitioners use sophisticated mathematical and legal techniques to design new ways of repackaging and trading risk.

One class of methods used by financial engineers involves the separation of risk from funding, as with a guarantee, but embodies the risk in an instrument that can itself be traded. There exists a whole range of derivative securities that do this, and we will learn about them in detail in Chapter 16. Credit derivatives allow the trading of credit risk; interest rate and exchange rate derivatives allow the trading of market risk. We can see insurance, too, as a form of trade in risk. It allows certain "insurable" risks to be separated and carried separately from the risk of lending. For example, a lender against collateral generally requires the borrower to insure the collateral against casualty losses (fire, catastrophe, theft, etc.) rather than bearing these risks as part of the loan.

A second class of methods involves splitting up the cash flow from an asset (a loan or a pool of loans) to create new instruments with different risk characteristics. Rather than separating risk from funding, different classes of funding are created, each with different risk characteristics. The strips we saw in Chapter 4 and the mortgage derivatives we saw in Chapter 13 were examples of this. In a sense, debt and equity securities issued by an enterprise embody the same idea: the debt has first claim on the enterprise's income and is relatively safer; the equity has a residual claim and is riskier. Similarly with senior and junior debt.

Taking an Equity Stake

Providers of debt financing and of equity financing exercise very different degrees of direct control over the recipient. The payments promised under the debt contract are very specific. As long as these payments are made and other terms of the contract are met, debt holders have no way to control the behavior of the borrower. In contrast, the payments promised to the providers of equity financing—a share in future profits—are very uncertain, and equity holders obtain a measure of direct control over the enterprise to ensure that they receive their due.[7]

Avoiding the Costs of Bankruptcy.

In the event of bankruptcy, however, debtors (or their representatives) take over direct control of the enterprise and become, in effect its "owners" until its debts are paid.[8] As we have seen, the process of bankruptcy is costly and problematic. It can be less wasteful, therefore, to avoid the cost of bankruptcy and to build the transfer of control to debt holders into the contract. This is done with an instrument known as **preferred equity**. Like debt, and unlike ordinary equity, preferred equity promises specific payments much like the interest on a loan. As long as these payments are made, the holders of preferred equity have no direct control over the enterprise (specifically, they have no voting rights). However, if the borrower fails to pay, the holders of preferred equity obtain control (they receive full voting rights), and no dividends may be paid to ordinary equity holders until the arrears on the preferred equity are paid. Once that happens, the situation goes back to what it was before the payments were interrupted. In effect, this is a way of going into and out of bankruptcy automatically at much reduced cost.

An Equity Stake as a Way of Protecting Loans.

One way for debt holders to protect their interests is by taking a simultaneous equity stake in the borrowing enterprise. As equity holders, they have a measure of direct control that enables them to prevent the borrower from acting against their interests as lenders. Banks in the United States are limited by regulation in their ability to take an equity stake in their borrowers. However, banks in other countries and finance companies in the United States are not. It is common, therefore, for these institutions to do this.[9]

Equity to Provide an Upside.

Unlike debt, equity has an upside. If the enterprise does well, the equity will increase in value, and this possibility helps to balance the downside risk of the enterprise doing badly. Consequently, debt can be made more attractive by giving it some of the upside associated with equity. This is particularly attractive with rapidly growing borrowers for which other methods of risk control, such as restrictive covenants, are inappropriate.

One way of including an equity element is **convertible debt**. This is debt (or preferred equity) that can be converted into equity at a prespecified price at the discretion of the lender. If the borrower does poorly, the lender will choose not to convert, since debt provides a senior claim on the borrower's assets. However, if the borrower does well and the value of its equity rises, the lender can convert the debt into equity and share in the gains.

Alternatively, the debt or preferred equity may be issued with attached **warrants**, which entitle the holder to purchase new shares at a prespecified price. The recipient may hold the warrants or sell them to others. Thus a warrant is a form of option.

---

preferred equity
Technically equity, but pays a fixed income like a bond.

convertible debt
Debt that can be converted into equity at a prespecified price at the discretion of the investor.

warrants
Options to purchase shares at a preset price, attached to an issue of bonds.

---

[7] We shall discuss the mechanisms of control in Chapter 15. As we shall see, these mechanisms of "corporate governance" are far from perfect.

[8] Risky lending can be seen as a combination of risk-free lending with the sale of a put option on the assets of the enterprise. We shall discuss options in Chapter 16.

[9] Under U.S. bankruptcy law, a lender with an equity stake in the enterprise is at a disadvantage in liquidation. So banks probably would not want to take an equity stake in their borrowers even if they could.

RELATIONSHIP LENDING VS ARM'S-LENGTH LENDING

relationship financing
Financing that involves continued monitoring by the lender.

arm's-length financing
Financing that does not involve continued monitoring by the lender.

In thinking about financing, it is useful to divide it into two categories. In **relationship financing**, the provider of financing is involved with the recipient in a close and continuing relationship of monitoring in order to ensure a fair return. In contrast, in **arm's-length financing** it is a matter of "finance and forget": while there is screening before financing is provided, there is little or no direct monitoring by the provider afterwards. Our focus here is on lending, but the same distinction can be made for equity financing.

On the whole, arm's-length lending corresponds to public issue—direct lending through financial markets. Relationship lending corresponds to private loans—indirect financing through financial intermediaries. We shall see, however, that there are exceptions. For example, the public market for junk bonds involves a considerable element of relationship, and financial intermediaries such as mutual funds and pension funds are primarily arm's-length lenders.

The Nature of Arm's-Length Lending

Direct lending through financial markets tends to be an arm's-length affair because of the nature of the typical lender—historically, a small investor or a foreigner investor.[10] Small investors do not find it worthwhile to devote much effort to screening and monitoring: because each has only a small amount at risk, the benefit does not cover the cost. Moreover, because a small investor's share in the total loan is small, most of the benefit of such an effort would go to others (this is known as a "free-rider problem"). Foreign investors are unlikely to do much direct screening and monitoring because the cost to them of doing so is high. It is harder for them to acquire and interpret information, and it is harder for them to exert control over the borrower from a distance.

Relying on Screening and Monitoring by an Interested Party.   Nonetheless, if lenders are to receive a fair return, someone has to do some screening and monitoring. There are several possible arrangements. One is to have the screening and monitoring done by a party with enough at stake to make the effort worthwhile. As we saw in Chapter 11, underwriters have a legal and reputational interest in screening the issues they underwrite. In some cases there will be a large lender, in addition to the many small ones, who will find it worthwhile to monitor. There is evidence, for example, that an issuer of public debt will be able to borrow more cheaply if it simultaneously has a long-term borrowing relationship with a bank. The purchasers of the public debt rely on the bank to do the monitoring, or at least see the continuing relationship as evidence of good credit.[11]

Relying on the Government.   Another potential protector of the interests of arm's-length lenders is the government—through regulation and through the legal system. Public issues in the United States, for example, are regulated by the SEC. As we have seen,

[10] Recently, of course, institutional investors such as pension funds and mutual funds have played a growing role in financial markets. But these, too, are largely arm's-length investors. Their entry into the financial markets was made possible by the arrangements already in place to protect the interests of small investors and foreign investors.

[11] In compensation, bank debt and other relationship debt almost always enjoy priority over publicly issued debt.

SEC regulations require issuers of public debt to disclose all relevant information both before and during the life of an issue. Effective government protection of investors requires, of course, good laws and regulations and effective regulators and courts: these are not equally available in all countries. Legal protection is particularly important for public equity, and we shall have more to say about it in Chapters 15 and 20.

The Difficulty of Risk Control.   The nature of the mechanisms for screening and monitoring arm's-length debt has implications for the appropriateness of the different methods of risk control that we have discussed. For publicly issued debt, covenants are rare: with no one in charge, it is impossible to ensure the necessary flexibility.[12] Collateral too is unusual. If the collateral is easy to sell (for example, securities), it can cover losses in case of default, but it cannot be used as a means of controlling borrower behavior. If problems do occur with arm's-length debt, it is difficult to show much flexibility in resolving them. Because so many parties are involved, renegotiation of the terms of the debt contract is extremely difficult.[13]

In the end, the methods available to control the risk of arm's-length debt are limited. Consequently, this form of lending is unsuited to risky borrowers. With low-risk borrowers, since there is little risk to begin with, the inability to control risk is much less important.

While high-risk borrowers are unsuitable, their debt can be made suitable by eliminating the risk. Guarantees are one way to do this, financial engineering is another. And risky debt can be made attractive, even in the absence of good risk control, by providing a compensating upside through convertibility or warrants.

In dealing with risk, as with any other problem, there are basically two alternatives—voice and exit.[14] That is, one can try to do something about the problem or one can bail out. As we have seen, voice (risk control) is not a realistic option for arm's-length lenders. Consequently, it is especially desirable that exit be easy. Arm's-length lenders have a strong interest in liquidity, especially with long-term lending. If things start to go wrong, they want to be able to get out.

The Nature of Relationship Lending

With arm's-length lending there are usually many lenders, each with only a small share in the loan. With relationship lending there is only one lender or at most a few. Moreover, the lender is usually a financial intermediary that specializes in lending and in the techniques of controlling risk. This means banks, of course, but also finance companies and, as we shall see, insurance companies.

---

[12] There is also a free-rider problem in monitoring compliance with covenants. For this reason, public issues of bonds designate a paid trustee—usually a bank—to monitor compliance and, if necessary, to represent the debt holders in court.

[13] In the United States, the Trust Indenture Act of 1939 requires unanimity among lenders to alter the interest or principal payments on public debt. Therefore, the only realistic way for a borrower to change the terms of outstanding debt is to buy it back (at less than face value) or to offer to exchange it for new securities with less stringent terms (either debt or equity). There is a free-rider problem for an individual investor faced with such a tender: if other investors accept, he would do better sticking with his original claim.

[14] The terminology is due to A.O. Hirschman, a distinguished development economist.

The Advantages of Relationship Lending.   The change in the number of lenders and in their nature changes the picture completely. With relationship lending, there is no free-rider problem in monitoring: the lender now enjoys the full benefits of any effort to control risk. Also, because authority rests with one or a few lenders rather than with many, it is easy to make decisions. Thus, it is relatively easy to show the flexibility required in using collateral or covenants to control borrower behavior or to negotiate with a borrower in distress. Consequently covenants and collateral are much more common: some 70% of bank loans and over 90% of loans from finance companies are secured with collateral. Most involve restrictive covenants. Guarantees, on the other hand, are much less common. Where the lender holds equity in the borrower, it is primarily for control rather than to capture the upside.

Another advantage of having one or a few lenders is that the borrower is more willing to disclose sensitive information because that information will remain confidential. The "informational capital" that a relationship lender accumulates over time makes it costly for the borrower to switch to another lender. This attachment is important because relationship lending sometimes requires the lender to make a short-term sacrifice for long-term benefits—for example, easing up when the borrower is in difficulty in exchange for higher interest later. If, afterward, the borrower can easily switch to another lender, such a sacrifice will not be worthwhile.

Because "voice" is more effective with relationship loans, "exit" is a less pressing issue. Consequently, liquidity is less important for a relationship lender. Moreover, precisely because relationship loans do involve a relationship, they are harder to transfer to other lenders.

Why Are All Loans not Relationship Loans?   Since relationship lending provides lenders with better protection, why is all lending not relationship lending? One reason is availability. Financial intermediaries, the principal relationship lenders, are limited in the types of loan they can make by the nature of their liabilities. As we have seen, banks prefer to make short-term, liquid loans. However, there are other types of intermediary willing to make other types of loan. In particular, insurance companies have longer term liabilities and they are therefore willing to engage in longer term lending. Moreover, as we shall see in Chapters 16 and 18, financial engineering makes it possible to separate interest rate risk from credit risk, allowing banks to increase the maturity of their loans.

A second factor that limits relationship lending is capacity. A borrower can raise very large sums relatively easily through a public issue because each investor need take only a small part of the total loan. In contrast, a single financial intermediary will be unwilling to take on such a large loan. As we saw in Chapter 6, there is a solution. The lending intermediary can break the loan into smaller pieces and sell those pieces to other intermediaries—a process known as syndication. It is difficult, however, to maintain the same degree of relationship in these circumstances. For example, syndicated loans are generally less encumbered with covenants because it is more difficult to ensure the necessary flexibility.

The main factor, however, that limits relationship lending is cost. The effort that the relationship lender puts into monitoring the borrower and controlling risk is costly. That cost must ultimately be borne by the borrower. For higher risk borrowers, this cost is worthwhile because it lowers the overall cost of borrowing and increases the availability of loans. For low-risk borrowers, the cost is simply not warranted. They have the alternative of borrowing from arm's-length lenders, and they can do so more cheaply. Of course, anything that raises the cost of relationship lending—for example, regulation of financial intermediaries—will tilt the balance away from relationship lending and towards the public issue market (a process known as "disintermediation"). We saw an example of this in Chapter 6, when we discussed how rising regulatory costs for U.S. banks encouraged the development of the commercial paper market.

Now that we understand the different methods of controlling risk, it is time to take a tour of the debt markets and to see how these methods are applied in practice.

THE BOND MARKET

We begin our tour with the market for long-term debt—the bond market. We shall look, in turn, at the market for municipal bonds, the market for corporate bonds, the international bond market, the private placement market, and the market for high-risk or "junk" bonds. We have already studied, in Chapter 12, the market for government bonds.

Municipal Bonds

municipal bonds (munis)
Long-term bonds issued by state and local governments.

Municipal bonds are bonds issued by local and regional governments—levels of government below the national level. "Munis" differ fundamentally from debt of the national government in that they are not risk free. While national governments can always print the money to pay off their debt if they have to, local governments cannot do this. Consequently, they may, and do, default.[15]

The Relative Importance of Muni Markets in Different Countries.   The market for "munis" is quite large in the United States, very small in the United Kingdom, and somewhere in between in other countries such as Japan and Germany. Why the differences? One reason is that there are other ways for local governments to borrow. In the United Kingdom, largely because they lack the credit to borrow in their own name, local governments borrow from the national government. In Germany, local governments mostly borrow from banks, which issue their own bonds to finance their lending.

Another reason why munis are particularly big in the United States is their special tax treatment. The interest they pay is exempt from federal taxes. In many cases, it is also exempt from state and local taxes. For example, residents of New York City who hold New York City bonds receive interest that is exempt from federal, New York State, and New York City income taxes. This tax exemption enables state and local governments to borrow at lower rates, sharing the tax benefit with investors.

In 2000, some $1.2 trillion of municipal bonds was outstanding in the United States, with some $200 billion of new issues during the year.

---

[15] The risk of municipal bonds in the United States is exacerbated by a lack of disclosure. The Tower Amendment of 1975 largely exempts municipal securities from the SEC disclosure requirements to which corporate bonds are subject.

general obligation bonds
Muni bonds backed by the full faith and credit of the issuer.

revenue bonds
Muni bonds payable out of the revenue of a specific project.

bond insurance
Guarantee of a bond issue provided by an insurance company.

Types of Muni.   There are two types of municipal bond. **General obligation bonds** are repayable out of general tax revenue and are backed only by the "full faith and credit" of the issuing authority—by the issuer's ability to levy taxes. **Revenue bonds**, on the other hand, are repayable out of the specific revenue of a particular project—for example, out of the income from a municipal airport. Because many state constitutions restrict the issue of general obligation bonds, most of the recent rapid growth in the market has been in revenue bonds. Defaults on general obligation bonds were relatively rare in the twentieth century; most defaults involved revenue bonds.

Bond Insurance.   A peculiar feature of the municipal bond market is **bond insurance**. When an issue would not otherwise obtain an investment-grade rating, the issuer purchases insurance from an insurance company or consortium of insurance companies. In exchange for a fee from the issuer, the insurer promises to make the scheduled interest and principal payments on the issue in question if the issuer defaults. While bond insurance was rare 30 years ago, today 60% of new issues are insured.

Why are municipal bonds insured while corporate bonds are not? And why has bond insurance become more prevalent recently? The answers to both questions lie in the special tax status of municipal bonds. Because income and capital gains are taxed differently, default on a municipal bond is especially costly to investors. As a result, insurance enhances the value of a municipal bond more than it would that of a corporate bond.

The increasing prevalence of insurance is also partly a result of the tax reform of 1986. This eliminated a tax break for financial intermediaries that had made lending to municipalities especially lucrative. There has since then been a shift from relationship to arm's-length borrowing by municipal borrowers: today about 75% of munis are held by households, either directly or through mutual funds. As a result of this shift, it has become increasingly important to reduce the risk of an issue and to obtain an investment-grade rating. For less than stellar credits, insurance provides a way to do this.

Corporate Bonds

Corporate bonds are long-term debt securities issued by financial and nonfinancial corporations. Nonfinancial borrowers use the proceeds to finance investment; financial borrowers use the proceeds to lend to others to finance investment.

Differences in Corporate Bond Markets across Countries.   Historically, the comparative size of the market for corporate bonds and the split between nonfinancial and financial issuers has differed from country to country. In the United States and in other English-speaking countries, corporate bond markets have been large and nonfinancial issues have predominated. Elsewhere, especially in continental Europe, corporate bond markets have been smaller and have been dominated by financial issuers.

These differences are largely due to historical differences in banking and in regulation. The commercial banks of the English-speaking countries have traditionally limited themselves to short-term loans, forcing corporations to rely on financial markets for long-term financing. In contrast, the universal banks of continental Europe have traditionally provided long-term financing to their customers and have raised the necessary funds by borrowing in their own names in the bond market. This pattern has been reinforced by regulations that made it extremely difficult in some countries for nonfinancial corporations to issue bonds.[16] Where such regulations have been relaxed, as in Japan, issues by nonfinancial corporations have grown rapidly.

Exhibit 14.2 shows the pattern for 1995 and 2000. You can see that although the U.S. market is still dominated by nonfinancial issuers, the share of financial issuers has been growing. On the other hand, in Germany and Japan, the share of nonfinancial issuers has been growing, and in Japan it is rapidly approaching 50%.

Who Are the Issuers?   Corporate bonds issued to the public are arm's-length securities: they need to be low-risk and low-maintenance instruments. In the United States, before the rise of the junk bond market in the 1980s (about which more soon), only issues with an investment-grade rating were brought to market. Loan contracts rarely include restrictive covenants or collateral; guarantees are more common.

The need for an investment-grade rating largely limits access to the regular public issue bond market to certain kinds of company. Issuers need to be large and established,

EXHIBIT 14.2   Financial vs. Nonfinanical Issuers of Bonds in Different Markets

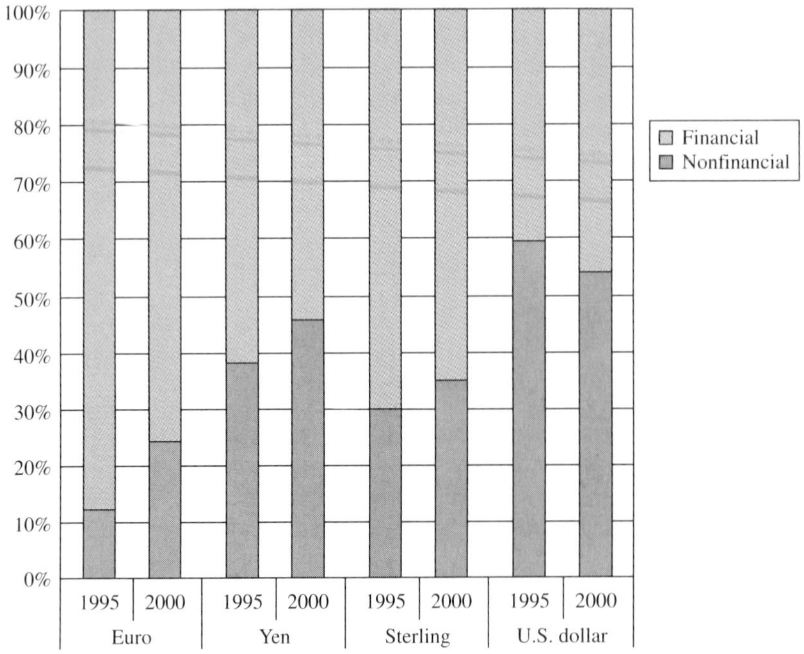

Source: Bank for International Settlements (2001).

---

[16] These regulations, of course, favored the banks.

and have good track records. They also need to be engaged in relatively low-risk businesses that are easy to monitor.

The classic nonfinancial issuers are railroads and utilities. Others types of business that fit the bill include hotels and companies involved in resource extraction. Types of business that rarely issue bonds are those whose activities are hard to evaluate and in which funds are easily diverted to risky projects—for example, trading, resource exploration, and research and development.[17]

In 2000, there was about $2.2 trillion of corporate bonds outstanding in the United States, with over $500 billion of new issues during the year.

The International Bond Market

International lending has always been important in the bond market. Historically, it took the form of foreign borrowers selling their bonds in the domestic market of the financially dominant country of the period. In the eighteenth century, Amsterdam was the great international financial market; in the nineteenth and early twentieth centuries it was London and, to a lesser extent, Paris.

Since World War II, the United States has been the financially dominant country, but the U.S. bond market for many years played a less important international role than one might expect: outstanding bonds of foreign issuers ("Yankee" bonds) accounted for less than 20% of the total. The reason for this was regulation. Since the regulation of U.S. financial markets in the 1930s, the burden of regulation—especially disclosure requirements—discouraged foreign borrowers from issuing bonds in the United States.

As we shall see presently, the recent creation of an important regulatory loophole—Rule 144a—has opened the U.S. market to foreign issuers. However, the long-standing regulatory obstacle to foreign issues in the United States contributed to the rise of a different kind of international bond market. We saw in Chapter 7 how banking regulation stimulated the development of offshore Eurodollar banking. In a similar way, regulation of the bond market has stimulated the growth of an offshore market for bonds—the **Eurobond market**. Like Eurocurrency banking, the Eurobond market began in London in U.S. dollars and has since spread to other countries and to other currencies.

Eurobond market
The offshore market for long-term securities.

Exhibit 14.3 shows the growth of the international bond market since 1994. Notice how the proportion of international bonds issued in the United States has increased dramatically in recent years. Of the over $6 trillion outstanding at the end of 2000, 70% were fixed rate, 26% floating rate, and 4% equity related. Some 49% were denominated in U.S. dollars and 30% in Euros. Some 47% were issued by financial institutions, 20% by governments, and 25% by nonfinancial corporations.

The Origins of the Eurobond Market.   In addition to the regulatory obstacles already present, the United States in 1963 imposed a tax on foreign issuers designed to raise by 1% their effective cost of borrowing in the United States. This effectively killed the Yankee market and led foreign issuers, including the overseas subsidiaries of U.S. multinationals, to seek an alternative.

---

[17] The main financial issuers in the United States are finance companies.

**EXHIBIT 14.3   International Bonds and Notes
Outstanding by Issuing Country**

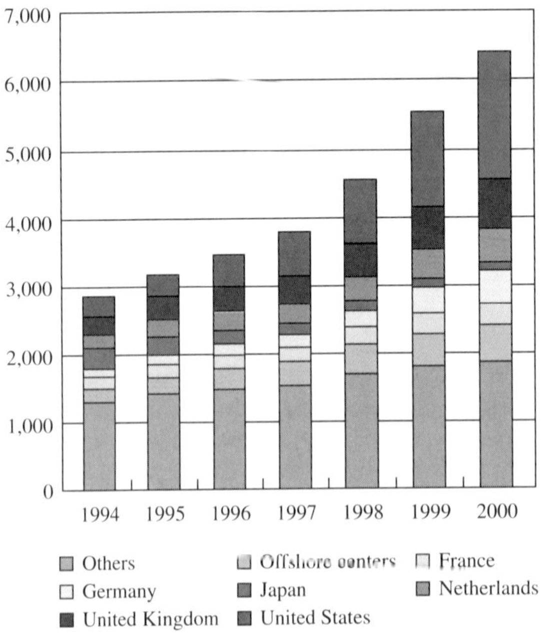

Source: *Bank for International Settlements (2001).*

As it happened, there was a large potential market overseas for high-quality, dollar-denominated bonds. The potential investors were mainly Europeans and others who wished to hold assets outside their home countries or in currencies other than their own. Such investors were driven by two main concerns: to avoid paying taxes and to protect themselves against the falling value of their domestic currencies. Bonds issued in the United States answered the second concern, but not the first. U.S. tax laws then required issuers to register ownership of the bonds and to withhold a 30% tax on interest payments.

Dollar-denominated Eurobonds were designed to tap this market by addressing both tax and exchange-rate concerns. Issued in bearer form, these Eurobonds had no record of ownership, and no tax was withheld. Eurobonds were issued outside the United States by U.S. and foreign corporations and by foreign governments. They proved so popular that U.S. corporations were able to sell Eurobonds at yields *below* those on comparable Treasuries.

Some U.S. corporations exploited what was essentially an arbitrage possibility by issuing Eurobonds and then invested the proceeds in Treasury securities to make a riskless profit.[18] In response, the U.S. Treasury acted to eliminate the advantage of the Eurobond market over the domestic market. In 1984, it ended tax withholding on foreign-owned securities. It also allowed corporations to issue bearer bonds in the United States for sale

---

[18] To eliminate any interest rate risk, they sold zero-coupon bonds and bought zero-coupon strips.

to foreign investors. Although the Treasury itself does not issue bearer bonds, it does allow banks to sell bearer certificates backed by Treasury bonds. As a result of these steps, the yields on Eurobonds and bonds issued in the United States have more or less equalized.

The Eurobond Market Today.   The Eurobond market, however, has continued to thrive. By 1990, the Eurobond market accounted for some 75% of the international bond market.

While the tax penalty on foreign borrowing in the United States was removed, the regulatory obstacles remained. Indeed, the lack of regulation of the Eurobond market makes it attractive to U.S. issuers as well as to foreigners. By avoiding the need to file with the SEC, issuers can raise money more quickly and with less disclosure. The Eurobond market has also been attractive to issuers in other countries that restrict their domestic bond markets: the Germans and the Japanese have been big issuers.

Another attraction is that intense competition among Eurobond underwriters has kept fees and spreads extremely low. As a result, transactions costs for a Eurobond issue are generally lower than they are for a domestic issue. Indeed, competition has been so intense that many underwriters and dealers have lost money and quit the market.

The center of the Eurobond market remains in London, and a majority of bonds are still denominated in U.S. dollars. However, a growing fraction are denominated in other currencies. In particular, since the introduction of the Euro, there has been rapid growth in Euro-denominated bonds.

The Private Placement Market

private placement

An issue of securities that is sold privately to a few large institutions and wealthy individuals.

Rather than being sold to the public at large—a public issue—securities can be sold privately to a few large institutions and wealthy individuals—a **private placement**. There are really two very different categories of private placement—the traditional and the 144a.

Traditional Private Placements.   In early capital markets, most bond issues were private placements. However, as methods of underwriting and distributing public issues steadily improved in the United States from the Civil War through the 1920s, private placements steadily diminished in relative importance.

The private placement market was given a new lease on life by the Securities Acts of the 1930s. These Depression era laws imposed stringent disclosure requirements on public issues but exempted private placements. Many companies balked at the new disclosure requirements and therefore found private placements more attractive. At the same time, life insurance companies, the main investors in corporate bonds, were dissatisfied with the low market interest rates available on public issues. They were willing to accept greater risk for a higher yield.

With a revival in both supply and demand, the share of all new debt going to private placement rose from 14% in 1936 to 73% in 1948. But as market interest rates rose again in the 1950s, the relative importance of the private placement market began to shrink once more.

However, private placements continued to be important for medium-sized companies. Either such companies lack the credit standing for a public issue, or their financing needs

EXHIBIT 14.4   Size and Maturity of Different Types of Debt

	Bank Loans	Private Placements	Public Bonds
Size (80% in range)[a]	$10,000–$1 million	$10 million–$100 million	$100 million–$500 million
Maturity[b]	80% less than year	50% between 7 and 15 years	70% over 10 years

[a] Data for 1993.
[b] Data for 1989.

Source: Prowse (1997).

are too small to justify the large fixed cost of a public issue. For such companies, private placements are relationship loans, much like a bank loan but longer term and at a fixed rate. (Exhibit 14.4 compares the maturity and the size of traditional private placements to bank loans and to publicly issued bonds.)

traditional private placement market
Private relationship market for bonds of medium-sized issuers.

Like bank loans, loans in this **traditional private placement market** involve a continuing lending relationship. There is close monitoring by the lender based on restrictive covenants, with frequent renegotiation as necessary. Security is less common than with bank loans, perhaps because the borrowers are generally more creditworthy.

The principal lenders in this market are life insurance companies. In contrast to banks, the liabilities of the lifes provide a good basis for long-term fixed-rate loans.[19] For many years, lifes accounted for some 90% of private placement lending, with the 10 largest alone accounting for 55 to 65%.

The 144a Market. The exemption of the private placement market from SEC regulation sometimes attracted issuers that did have access to the public bond market. For example, it was common to try out complex or novel types of debt in the public placement market before attempting a public issue.

However, the appeal of the market was severely limited by its lack of liquidity. The reason for this was that the resale of a private placement risked being construed by regulators as a public issue, with all the regulatory burdens that this implied. Consequently, private placements were generally expected to be held to maturity. The disadvantage for the issuer was that this restricted the market to investors, such as lifes, for whom illiquidity was not a problem. The restricted market meant less competition and higher rates.

Rule 144a
The SEC regulation that allows limited resale of private placements.

All this changed when the SEC enacted **Rule 144a** in 1990. The new rule permitted unrestricted trading of privately placed securities among "qualified institutional buyers"—institutional investors with at least $100 million in assets. This created a secondary market in these securities, making them attractive to new categories of lenders, such as mutual funds and pension funds.[20]

The expansion of the market lowered rates and attracted to the private placement market the larger, more creditworthy borrowers that had previously avoided it. For these com-

---

[19] There is typically a heavy penalty for prepayment.

[20] Rule 144a also makes it possible for securities firms and banks to underwrite private placements. In contrast, traditional private placements were distributed by "agents" or brokers because underwriting could have been construed as a public issue.

panies, the attraction of the private placement market is much the same as the attraction of the Eurobond market—the absence of SEC regulation. For foreign issuers, who account for about a third of the volume, the appeal is the lack of disclosure. For U.S. issuers the appeal is the speed with which an issue can be brought to market: almost all U.S. issuers subsequently register with the SEC, converting their bonds into public issues.

144a market
Private arm's-length market for bonds of relatively good credits.

The **144a market** has grown rapidly. By 1992 it was rivaling the traditional market in size. By 1997, with $249 billion in new issues, it was much larger.

Syndicated Loans

Traditionally, in loan syndications and participations, the lead bank sold off the parts of the loan to other banks. However, increasingly, syndications have found a market with mutual funds, pension funds, insurance companies, and other institutional investors. This is not surprising, since there is considerable similarity between a syndication and a private placement.

As a result of this expansion of the market, the volume of syndicated lending has grown enormously—from $137 billion in 1987 to over $1 trillion in 1997. In comparison, private placements in 1997 amounted to about $300 billion and junk bonds to about $125 billion. Syndicated loans have, in fact, become the predominant form of corporate financing, accounting for 51% of new funds raised by corporations in 1997.[21]

The liquidity that Rule 144a has permitted in the private placement market has put competitive pressure on the syndicated loan market to follow suit. As a result, a secondary market has been developing for syndicated loans: some $70 billion traded in 1998. Banks too have started to exploit this market as a way of managing risk. In a syndication, voice is limited. So exit is attractive.

Junk Bonds

Traditionally, only borrowers that were able to obtain an investment-grade rating attempted a public issue. While there were some bonds outstanding with less than an investment grade, these were "fallen angels"—bonds whose ratings had been downgraded. Fewer than 5% of large or medium-sized companies were eligible for an investment-grade rating, and perhaps 800 of these actually had public issues of bonds outstanding in 1980. The vast majority of companies had no access to the public issue bond market, and they had to turn elsewhere for financing—often to the private placement market.

junk (high-yield) bonds
Bonds with less than an investment-grade rating.

The Origins of the Junk Bond Market.   The picture changed in the 1980s, when there developed, quite rapidly, a substantial market for new issues of below investment-grade bonds. These are known as "high-yield bonds" or **junk bonds**. The reason for the rise of the market for junk bonds is twofold. First there was an increase in the supply of potential issuers. Second, an enterprising securities firm managed to overcome some of the problems inherent in arm's-length lending to risky borrowers, and this created a demand for junk bonds.

---

[21] Syndications were also highly profitable for their underwriters, providing some $6 billion in fees in 1998, compared to $4.6 billion for equities and $3.2 billion for bonds.

An Increase in Potential Supply.   The potential supply of junk bonds increased in the early 1980s for several reasons. One was a crunch in the private-placement market: firms unable to borrow there were forced to consider public issues, despite the cost. Another reason was the steady increase in corporate leverage—an increasing reliance on debt rather than equity finance. As leverage increased, firms' debt became riskier and their ratings fell. A third reason was the increasing popularity of the *leveraged buyout (LBO)*— the purchasing of a company largely with borrowed money.[22]

Addressing the Problems of Risky Public Issues.   The growth in potential supply would not by itself have been enough to create a market had there not been a simultaneous growth in demand. The growth in demand was largely the accomplishment of Michael Milken, an investment banker with the firm of Drexel Burnham Lambert.

To create a demand for junk bonds on the part of financial institutions such as lifes, pension funds, and savings and loans, Milken had to address two problems. The first was poor liquidity: as we have seen liquidity ("exit") is especially important for risky securities. For investment-grade bonds, liquidity is generally assured by the underwriter, who implicitly promises to make a market in the bond after it is issued. Drexel took on this role of market maker in the market for junk bonds.

The second problem with junk bonds was the potential for significant losses due to bankruptcy. As we have seen, arm's-length lending is not well designed to deal with borrower distress. For investment-grade bonds, this is not really an issue. The likelihood of default is small, so the expected value of losses due to bankruptcy is insignificant. However, for high-risk borrowers, the likelihood of default is relatively large, so the potential for losses due to bankruptcy is substantial.

To minimize potential losses, Drexel stood ready to help junk bond issuers that got into difficulty, doing everything possible to avoid formal bankruptcy. Milken would, if appropriate, renegotiate the firm's debt or even arrange for additional lending. In essence, Drexel added an element of "relationship" to what was otherwise a purely arm's-length market. Drexel developed relationships not only with borrowers but also with the institutional investors that purchased the bonds. The availability of this support from Drexel reduced potential losses from default. This made junk bonds more attractive both to issuers and to investors.

It was well worth Drexel's while to bear the considerable cost of monitoring and negotiating. Even though it was not itself a lender, it stood to profit from underwriting additional issues if it could solve the problems of the market.

The Evolution of the Junk Bond Market.   Milken was spectacularly successful. Exhibit 14.5 shows how the market grew. Because of the growth of the junk bond market, some 1,800 firms that previously had had no access to the bond market tapped it for funds in the 1980s, helping to fuel the rapid economic growth of the period. In Milken's words: "Junk bonds allowed entrepreneurs outside the system to get capital to realize their dreams."

---

[22] We shall discuss this in Chapter 15.

EXHIBIT 14.5   New Issues of High-Yield Bonds

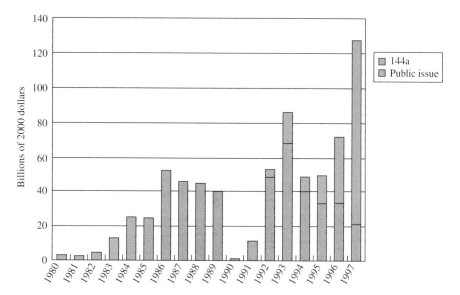

Source: Altman (1998).

Of course, Drexel and Milken did well too. The generous underwriting fees—2% to 3% vs the normal 0.4% to 0.7% on investment-grade issues—transformed Drexel from a minor investment bank in the 1970s into the most profitable firm on Wall Street by 1987. Milken himself earned over $1 billion between 1983 and 1987.

As you can see from Exhibit 14.5, the junk bond market has undergone a number of ups and downs. The heavy dependence of the market on Drexel and in particular on Milken proved to be a weakness. In the late 1980s, at a time that the junk bond market was drawing increasing public and regulatory hostility, both Milken and Drexel were implicated in a growing insider-trading scandal. With Drexel's ability to provide issuers with a "safety net" impaired, several large defaults shook the market. Demand then dried up as institutions either became unwilling to purchase junk bonds (in the case of lifes) or were prevented from doing so by regulators (in the case of S&Ls).

As a result of the collapse of the market, Drexel itself failed in February 1990. The failure of Drexel left the junk bond market "orphaned" without its relationship support, and a wave of defaults followed. Between 1989 and the end of 1991, some 250 companies defaulted on a total of $56 billion of bonds.

After 1991, the market began to recover, as other securities firms took over the role Drexel had played, having recruited members of the team that Milken trained at Drexel. New issues began to increase again, and the market grew until a temporary setback with the international debt crisis of 1998. By mid-2000, there were some 3,700 issuers of junk bond in the United States with some $666 billion of bonds outstanding. In Europe there were 160 issuers with $42 billion in bonds outstanding. The first issues of junk bonds were being offered in Japan.

Two recent developments have again given the market a boost. The first is Rule 144a. Many issuers of high-yield debt are in a hurry—especially those involved in LBOs and other corporate restructurings. As we have seen, Rule 144a enables them to issue the debt first and worry about registration later. As you can see from Exhibit 14.5, by 1997 the great majority of junk bonds were issued in this two-step process. The second development is the securitization of high-yield debt. As we shall see presently, this provides a way to (partially) convert junk bonds into investment-grade debt, improving liquidity and tapping new categories of investor.

THE MONEY MARKET

We move on from the bond market to the money market—the market for short-term publicly issued debt. What is most interesting about the money market is that, in principle, it should not exist at all. Short-term lending is not well suited to a public issue, because it is hard to cover the considerable costs of a public issue over a short period. Relationship lenders—especially banks—should be able to make short-term loans more cheaply.

However, as we saw in Chapter 7, money markets have emerged nonetheless in various countries because of constraints on banks that prevented them from fulfilling their natural function. At various times, such constraints have included geographic restrictions (in England), bank lending limits (in Spain, Portugal, and France), caps on deposit interest rates (in Japan, France, and Austria), and all of the above in the United States. Even in the absence of constraints, the regulatory costs imposed on banks can be high enough to negate their natural advantage in short-term lending. This is the reason for the continuing importance of the money market in the United States.

We shall focus on the U.S. money market, which is by far the largest. Money markets exist today in many other countries. Some have existed for a long time. Others have developed recently or expanded in imitation of the success of the U.S. money market. Exhibit 14.6 shows the amounts of money market instruments outstanding in the United States over the period since 1980.

Commercial Paper

The basic instrument of the money market is commercial paper. This is short-term debt publicly issued by financial and nonfinancial corporations. It promises a single fixed payment on maturity and sells at a discount. At the end of 2000, there was about $960 billion of directly issued commercial paper outstanding in the United States.[23] Of this, some $560 billion (58%) was issued by financial institutions—primarily finance companies, but also securities firms, bank holding companies, and insurance companies. Some $280 billion (29%) was issued by nonfinancial corporations such as manufacturers, retailers, and public utilities. And some $120 billion (13%) was issued by foreign companies.[24]

---

[23] There was also a large amount of asset-backed commercial paper. More on this shortly.

[24] Much of this was swapped into foreign currencies. We shall discuss swaps in Chapter 16.

EXHIBIT 14.6   Money Market Instruments Outstanding

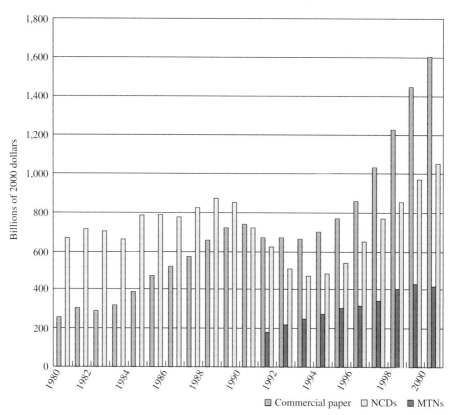

Data on MTNs from 1991 Only.

Source: Federal Reserve System

Issuing Costs.   Since the short maturity of commercial paper makes issuing costs weigh especially heavily, it is essential to keep them as low as possible. The cost of registration with the SEC can be avoided by keeping the maturity below 270 days. However, a rating is essential, and it costs the issuer $5,000 to $25,000 a year. There is also the cost of underwriting.[25] Issuing costs are about the same for large and small issues, making small issues very expensive. Consequently, only large borrowers find it economical to issue commercial paper. In 1992, the average size of an issue was about $330 million, and the largest issuers had several billion dollars of paper outstanding. In that year, of the 2 million or so corporations in the United States, only around 1,700 issued commercial paper. Of these, some 5% accounted for over half the total amount outstanding.

---

[25] Large issuers used to find it less expensive to distribute their own paper (this is called direct placement). However, underwriting costs have fallen to the point that most issuers today rely on dealers (mainly government securities dealers) to place their paper.

Maturity and Liquidity Backup.   The typical maturity of commercial paper is actually much shorter than the 270 days required to avoid the attention of the SEC—usually 2 to 6 weeks. The reason for this very short maturity is liquidity. The secondary market for commercial paper is generally poor. There are many different issues outstanding, and the potential trading volume in many of them is small. The potential business does not justify the significant fixed costs to a dealer of making a market.[26] Investors therefore usually have to hold the paper to maturity. The short maturity makes this less of a problem. Since issuers typically need to borrow for longer than the maturity of their paper, they usually **roll it over**—that is, they issue new paper to pay off the old. This is commonly done in the framework of an announced program with a declared borrowing limit. The borrower's continued presence in the market also helps to defray the issuing costs.

roll over
To pay off one loan by taking out another.

Because commercial paper is rolled over so frequently, issuers—even good credits—need backup liquidity to obtain an investment-grade rating. There is the worry that a disruption to the market could prevent the borrower from issuing new paper and so find itself unable to pay off the old. The reason for default in this case would be a lack of liquidity rather than insolvency: the borrower would be good for the money, but not on time. To protect themselves against such a situation, almost all issuers obtain a line of credit from a bank that they can draw on to pay off their maturing paper if rolling it over proves impossible.[27]

Only Low-Risk Paper Need Apply.   Commercial paper is arm's-length debt. Its short maturity makes any monitoring effort on the part of an investor even less attractive. Consequently, it needs to be low risk. At one time money market mutual funds, the largest investors in commercial paper, did provide a market for below-investment-grade paper, relying on diversification rather than on monitoring to deal with the risk. After some defaults in the early 1990s, however, regulators restricted the funds' investment in such paper, and the market dried up.

Over half the issues, making up some 85% of the total amount, have credit good enough to earn them an investment-grade rating on their own merits, with no credit enhancement. About a third of issuers (often smaller finance companies) rely on guarantees from parent companies to boost their rating to investment grade. Another quarter of issuers rely on third-party guarantees—mainly standby letters of credit from banks. Standby letters are useful not only for issuers whose own credit is weaker or less well established, but also for those that wish to avoid the disclosure necessary to obtain a rating in their own name (foreign issuers, for example).[28]

A way for smaller borrowers to access the market is through the *banker's acceptance*.[29] With an acceptance, a bank not only guarantees payment but also issues the paper in its own name, saving the borrower the issuing costs. Acceptances were once an important part of the money market, but in recent years they have virtually disappeared. At the

---

[26] See Chapter 2 for a discussion of those costs.

[27] Such a line is a liquidity facility, not a credit enhancement. The bank does not guarantee the paper, and the line of credit is dependent on the continuing good financial condition of the borrower.

[28] See Chapter 6 on standby letters of credit

[29] See Chapter 6 for details.

peak of their popularity, around 1980, the amount of acceptances outstanding was about half the amount of commercial paper. In 2000, it was only about 0.5% of that amount (about $8 billion).

One reason for the disappearance of bankers' acceptances is that the money market has developed a new way of dealing with high-risk borrowers—*securitization*. Basically, a pool is set up to purchase the debt of high-risk borrowers. The pool finances the purchase by issuing its own investment-grade paper, backed by the debt that it has purchased. We shall discuss the details of this magical transformation presently. At the end of 2000, there was some $640 billion of such asset-backed commercial paper outstanding.

master note
Privately placed short-term debt, rolled over repeatedly.

Privately Placed Paper. Another alternative for higher risk borrowers is the private placement section of the money market—the market for **master notes**. This is privately placed short-term debt, generally 6 to 9 months in maturity.[30] The continuing relationship with a particular lender avoids the issuing costs of rolling over public paper and allows tailoring of the terms and periodic renegotiation.[31] The lenders were originally the trust departments of banks, but the market has expanded to include other financial and non-financial investors.

Variations on Commercial Paper

There are a number of variations on commercial paper that extend the money market to noncommercial issuers and to longer maturities.

Extending the Market to Different Issuers. The single biggest issuer of short-term paper is the federal government: we discussed the market for T-bills in Chapter 12. Historically, the market for T-bills developed out of the market for commercial paper.

municipal note
Commercial paper issued by state and local governments.

State and local governments, too, issue short-term paper in the form of **municipal notes**. Municipal securities are generally exempt from the requirement to file with the SEC, so municipal notes do not have to have a maturity of under 270 days. Their maturity is nonetheless generally under a year. To avoid tax complications, they are usually interest-bearing rather than discount securities.[32] At the end of 2000, there was about $48 billion in municipal notes outstanding.

negotiable certificate of deposit (NCD)
A transferable bank CD.

Banks are not allowed to issue commercial paper directly, but bank holding companies can and sometimes do. However, banks can issue various types of money market paper that are essentially equivalent to commercial paper (we called them "wholesale deposits" in Chapter 6). The basic instrument is the **negotiable certificate of deposit (NCD)**, with a maturity of one month to a year (the 270-day limit is irrelevant, because

---

[30] Master notes are usually callable by either borrower or lender at short notice, although this right is rarely exercised.

[31] There is another advantage to master notes. To avoid regulation by the SEC, the funds raised from the sale of commercial paper must be used to finance "current transactions"—that is, they must not be used to finance long-term investments. No such restriction applies to funds raised from privately placed paper.

[32] The increase in value of a discount security as it matures is taxed as a capital gain, while interest is taxed as income. Since the rate of capital gains is lower, the benefit of the tax exemption on municipal debt is thus reduced.

bank note

Short-term non-deposit debt of a bank.

banks are not subject to SEC regulation). NCDs have partial credit enhancement: as a form of deposit, they are covered by deposit insurance up to a maximum of $100,000. Banks also issue **bank notes** of similar maturity that are not considered deposits and so are not covered by deposit insurance.

As with commercial issuers, the credit of banks that issue money market paper must be first-rate. The first banks to tap the money market, therefore, were the large money center banks. These institutions have been joined by large regional banks, U.S. branches of foreign banks (their NCDs are called "Yankee" NCDs), and major thrifts. Small banks need not apply.

Bank paper is mostly issued in denominations of $1 million or more. It includes fixed-coupon instruments with fixed interest payments; floating-rate instruments that pay interest that varies with some reference market rate (for example, LIBOR, or the T-bill rate); and zero-coupon instruments that pay no explicit interest and, like T-Bills, are sold at a discount. The total amount of bank-issued paper in the money market at the end of 2000 was some $1,045 billion.

medium-term notes (MTNs)

Unsecured paper intermediate in maturity between commercial paper and corporate bonds.

Extending the Market to Longer Maturities.   **Medium-term notes** (MTNs) were designed to bridge the gap between commercial paper and long-term bonds. Although they are not strictly speaking a money market instrument, they are in many ways similar to commercial paper. Maturities run from 270 days to over 30 years. The most common maturities are 5, 10, and 15 years. The MTN market has grown rapidly since the mid-1980s. Exhibit 14.6 showed the growth in the amount outstanding since 1991.

The first MTN was issued by General Motors Acceptance Corporation in 1972. Its purpose was to match the maturity of its automobile loans. GMAC was soon followed by other finance companies, and then by bank holding companies, industrial corporations, thrifts, foreign governments, and securities firms. Banks and finance companies each account for about a third of the market, the others the rest. The banks' version of the MTN is a longer term bank note or deposit note.

Initially, MTNs were fixed-rate instruments and unsecured, like bonds. However, more recently floating-rate notes (FRNs) have become more common. And there has been increasing reliance on credit enhancement in the form of guarantees, bank credit lines, or collateral (usually for asset-backed issues). MTNs are generally rated by the rating agencies.

Of course, the issuance of any security with a maturity of over 270 days requires filing with the SEC. *Shelf registration* initiated under SEC Rule 415 in 1982 has considerably eased this burden.[33] Rule 415 allows the issuer to file a general financing plan, good for a period of time, rather than having to file with each individual issue. The cost of setting up such a program is substantial; once it is established, however, the incremental cost of another issue is quite small. Most MTNs are now issued under such programs.

The International Money Market

Alongside Eurocurrency banking and the Eurocurrency bond market, there is a Eurocurrency money market. At the end of September 2000, securities outstanding in this market

---

[33] See Chapter 11.

were valued at $286 billion. The market first developed after the debt crisis of the early 1980s when many less developed countries (LDCs) defaulted on their loans from international banks. Many major Eurocurrency banks took large losses on these loans, impairing their creditworthiness. Major borrowers found all of a sudden that their own credit was better than their banks'. As a result, they could borrow more cheaply by issuing paper in their own names rather than by taking a bank loan.

note-issuance facility (NIF) or revolving underwriting facility (RUF)

A multiyear commitment by a bank to lend to a customer or to help it issue paper, whichever is cheaper for the customer.

The banks helped their customers do this through an arrangement called a **note-issuance facility (NIF)** or **revolving underwriting facility (RUF)**. This is a multiyear commitment by a bank to help a customer issue paper or to lend to it, whichever is cheaper for the customer. Effectively a combination of liquidity facility and credit enhancement, this arrangement performs the same function as the line of credit and standby letter of credit in the U.S. commercial paper market. The paper issued under a NIF or RUF, usually 1 to 6 months in maturity, is called a *Euronote*.

Later, borrowers began to issue their paper through dealers rather than through banks. Such paper is called *Euro commercial paper*. This paper is less often rated than U.S. commercial paper, although rating is becoming more common. To compensate for the lack of a rating, issuing dealers disclose to potential buyers extensive information on the issuer.

Banks too borrow in the Euro money market. Because Eurodollar time deposits have fixed maturities, they are illiquid. So banks began to offer—at lower interest rates—NCDs that are transferable. The amount of Euro NCDs outstanding is relatively small—less than 10% of the amount of regular Eurodollar deposits.

Like the U.S. money market, the Euro money market has extended into longer maturities. The instrument is the *Euro MTN (EMTN)*. The EMTN market has grown rapidly, and by 1996 was larger in size than its U.S. counterpart. Because of its speed of issue and low cost (once a program is established) and its flexibility, the EMTN is becoming the dominant instrument of the international debt market.

Much of the paper in the Euro money market is denominated in U.S. dollars (although the Japanese yen is the dominant currency in the EMTN market). Issuers that issue in a currency other than their own, however, generally "convert" the funds they raise into their domestic currencies using currency swaps. Investors generally do the same when they purchase paper denominated in other currencies. We shall see how swaps work in Chapter 16.

SECURITIZATION

receivables

Payments owed by others.

special-purpose vehicle (SPV)

A legal entity created to hold receivables and issue securities backed by them.

Both the money market and the bond market make use of securitization—a technique we first saw in Chapter 13 applied to mortgages. Indeed, the securitization of mortgages has been so enormously successful that investment bankers have been busily applying the same idea to everything they can. The idea has been catching on too outside the United States—in Europe, in Japan, and in the international debt markets.

What exactly *is* the idea? The simplest way to think of it is this. An entity has assets in the form of **receivables**—money owed to it by others. This entity, instead of borrowing directly to finance its receivables, chooses to sell them to a specially created entity called a **special-purpose vehicle (SPV)**. To fund its purchase of the receivables, the SPV issues

asset-backed securities
Securities created by securitization.

securities in its own name, using the receivables as collateral. The securities that the SPV issues are therefore known as **asset-backed securities**.[34]

In a mortgage securitization the "entity" is a bank or thrift; the receivables are mortgages; the SPV is a mortgage pool; and the asset-backed securities are passthroughs, CMOs, and mortgage strips. However, as we shall see, the idea generalizes quite easily to other entities, to other receivables, to other SPVs, and to other types of asset-backed security.

Why would an entity use this complicated arrangement rather than simply borrowing directly itself to finance its receivables? Securitization offers several possible advantages that may be more or less important in any given case.

Asset–Liability Mismatch

As we saw in Chapter 13, the main motivation in the case of mortgage securitization was the mismatch for the lending thrifts and banks between mortgages as an asset and their typical liabilities. Funding long-maturity, fixed-rate mortgages exposes these institutions to a great deal of interest rate risk because the maturity of their liabilities is short. Also, because mortgages are illiquid, they create the potential for a liquidity problem if the lending institution experiences a loss of deposits. Both these problems can be solved by taking the mortgages off the balance sheet of the originating institution through securitization.

Avoiding Regulatory Costs

We have seen that banking regulation has greatly increased the cost of bank-intermediated lending and that the financial system has found "workarounds" to avoid these costs. For example, banks have taken a large part of their commercial lending off their balance sheets by helping their customers issue commercial paper or by selling syndications and participations to nonbanks. The saving in regulatory costs is passed on to the customer in lower borrowing rates, and the bank replaces the interest rate margin that it would have earned with fee income.

Because they involve arm's-length lending, these methods are appropriate only for loans to large and creditworthy borrowers. With lending to consumers, the individual loans are too small to cover the transactions costs and the credit of the borrowers is not good enough. In addition, arm's-length lending does not readily accommodate the element of relationship that is necessary in consumer lending.

However, as mortgage securitization demonstrated, it is possible to solve all of these problems. The size issue is addressed by pooling the loans in an SPV and issuing large-denomination securities backed by the pool. The credit issue can be addressed by enhancing the credit of the pool in some way. The relationship problem can be addressed by having the originator of the loan continue to service it in exchange for a fee.

---

[34] The SPV is set up as a corporation or trust and is legally distinct and separate from the parent entity selling the receivables. This protects the receivables, and so investors in the asset-backed securities, from the creditors of the parent entity in case of its bankruptcy. Since the legal costs of setting up an SPV are considerable, many are set up to purchase receivables from several or many entities at once rather than from just one. Such is the case with mortgage pools, for example.

Banks have increasingly used these methods to securitize loans of various types. Automobile loans (the asset-backed securities are called CARs) and credit card receivables ("plastic bonds") were the first. Since then many other types of consumer loan have been securitized, including home equity loans, loans for manufactured housing, and student loans. Banks have also securitized loans to commercial borrowers. Typically these are borrowers that are too small or lack the credit for an issue of commercial paper. Computer leases were, in fact, the first type of nonmortgage debt to be securitized.

The rapid growth of the amounts outstanding of various types of asset-backed securities can be seen in Exhibit 14.7. In addition, Eurocurrency banks have started to securitize syndicated loans. And the biggest growth area in securitization has been the securitization of higher risk commercial paper. Securitization has begun to catch on in Europe, but it is still a small market there. New issues in Europe were about $34 billion in 2000, compared to over $200 billion in the United States.

The Benefits of Financial Engineering

An essential feature of the securitization of commercial paper and syndicated loans is that it creates an opportunity for financial engineering. The SPV can issue different types of security, each with a different claim on the cash flow of the underlying assets. The different types of security will differ in their risk and in other ways and will consequently appeal to investors of different kinds. We saw an example of this in Chapter 13, with the creation

EXHIBIT 14.7   Asset-Backed Securities Outstanding, 2000

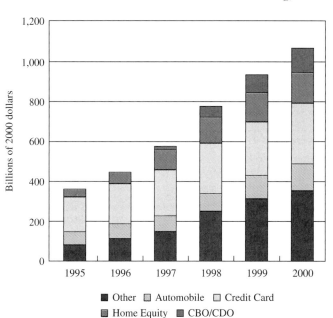

Sources: The Bond Market Association; the Federal Reserve System.

of IO and PO strips based on mortgage passthroughs. By issuing the right mix of securities, the organizers of the securitization can minimize the cost of funding the underlying assets.

An Example.   To see how this works, let us consider a simple example. An SPV purchases a pool of $1 billion of risky loans. It funds the purchase by issuing $900 million of bonds and $100 million of equity.

While the purchased loans are below investment grade, losses even in the worst case are unlikely to exceed $100 million. Since the bonds issued by the SPV have a prior claim on its assets, almost all of the risk is born by the purchasers of the equity. If there are defaults, it is they who will bear the loss.

Consequently, the bonds are virtually risk free, and they can obtain an investment-grade rating. This makes them far more marketable than the underlying loans. The bonds are typically sold to pension funds and mutual funds. The equity can be sold to hedge funds, willing to bear the risk in exchange for a higher expected return.[35]

In reality, more complicated combinations of securities are often used. Typically the SPV issues several tranches of debt with different seniority and so different degrees of risk—rather like the CMOs we saw in Chapter 13. There are also more exotic variations. For example, hoping to appeal to the enormous market for mortgage-backed securities, some SPVs have issued "index amortizers." These are bonds with a cash flow that mimics that of mortgage-backed debt.[36]

asset-backed commercial paper
Commercial paper issued by SPV.

collateralized loan obligations (CLOs)
Asset-backed securities backed by syndicated loans.

collateralized bond obligations (CBOs)
Asset-backed securities backed by junk bonds.

catastrophe-linked or "cat" bonds
Bonds issued by an SPV with level of repayment contingent on the occurrence of catastrophe.

Some Applications.   Financial engineering is being used to "convert" (at least partially) various types of risky debt into investment-grade debt. Risky commercial paper, which would be hard to sell as such, is converted into investment-grade **asset-backed commercial paper**. At the end of 2000, there was some $640 billion outstanding, accounting for some 40% of all commercial paper. Securitized syndicated loans are the basis for **collateralized loan obligations (CLOs)**. Some $36 billion was securitized in 1999 (down from a peak of $78 billion in 1998). And securitized junk bonds are the basis for **collateralized bond obligations (CBOs)**. Some $53 billion of junk bonds was securitized in 1999.[37]

Cat Bonds.   A particularly interesting application is the creation of **catastrophe-linked or "cat" bonds** as an alternative to traditional reinsurance. Here is how these bonds work.

Suppose an insurance company has written catastrophe coverage that could face it with claims of up to $1 billion. It can protect itself by setting up an SPV into which it pays a $30 million "premium." The SPV sells $970 million of "cat bonds." The proceeds of the sale, together with the premium, are invested in Treasury securities.

---

[35] To ensure the desired ratings, the ratings agencies are consulted in structuring the securitization.

[36] Credit enhancements are also used to boost the ratings of asset-backed securities—for example, guarantees from highly rated third parties (we saw in Chapter 13 how mortgage default insurance facilitates the securitization of mortgages). For asset-backed commercial paper, or if the cash flow of the receivables is unpredictable, a liquidity facility is often obtained from a bank.

[37] Most CBOs are sold in the 144a private placement market.

If there are no losses, all of the assets of the SPV go to the purchasers of the cat bonds. That is, the purchasers of the $970 million of bonds receive the interest and principal repayment on the full $1 billion of Treasury securities—quite a good return.

However, if there are losses, the assets of the SPV go first to cover those losses. Then, whatever is left goes to the purchasers of the cat bonds. If losses equaled $300 million, for example, the purchasers of the cat bond would receive back only $700 million.

Avoiding Negative Credit Substitution

A different reason for an entity to securitize its receivables is that this may provide it with cheaper funds than borrowing in its own name. This will be the case when the receivables are more attractive as an asset than the debt of the entity itself.

An Example.   Suppose a Turkish company has sold chemicals to a large industrial corporation in Germany on 3-months' trade credit. The Turkish company might find it hard to borrow in its own name internationally because its credit is not well known and because of the risk that a devaluation of the Turkish currency might make it difficult for the firm to repay. The Turkish company could raise funds instead by selling its receivables from the German company to an SPV, which would then issue securities in the international money market. Directly backed by high-quality receivables and located outside Turkey, the SPV would have excellent credit and also would be free of currency risk.

When the Turkish company borrows to fund trade credit to others, it is acting as a financial intermediary. Usually we expect credit substitution by a financial intermediary to lower the cost of credit. However, in this case, because the Turkish company is a weaker credit risk than its customers, it is raising rather than lowering the cost. This is a case of negative credit substitution. The securitization avoids the negative credit substitution by cutting the Turkish company out of the middle and linking the financing directly to the receivables.[38]

factoring

Purchase of receivables at a discount, the debts to be collected by the purchaser.

Factoring and Forfaiting.   The practice of selling receivables is not a new one. It has traditionally taken the form of **factoring**. Take the example of a clothing manufacturer that has sold a total of $1 million worth of goods to 20 different retailers. Suppose the manufacturer has extended the retailers 60 days' trade credit. However, it needs the cash right away and wishes to avoid the hassle of collecting the receivables. The manufacturer can sell its receivables to a factor for immediate cash, and the factor will take over the work of collection. In the United States, factoring is most common in the apparel and textile industries, and the factor is typically a bank-related finance company. Factoring is a big business. In 1999, worldwide volume was some $575 billion, and it was growing rapidly. Factoring is more important in Europe than it is in the United States, especially in Italy and in the United Kingdom. London is center, too, of the **forfaiting** business, which is essentially the factoring of receivables generated in international trade.

forfaiting

Factoring of receivables created in international trade.

In factoring and forfaiting, receivables are sold to an intermediary, which funds itself by issuing its own liabilities. In a securitization, receivables are sold to an SPV, which then

---

[38] The principle is not so different when the purpose is to avoid regulatory costs. In that case the regulatory costs imposed on the intermediary outweigh the advantages of intermediated lending, so that there too, there is negative value added in intermediation.

issues securities in its own name. The structure is quite similar. The main difference is that factoring and forfaiting involve a greater element of "relationship" and require considerably more work in collecting the receivables. It is not surprising then that factoring is more expensive for the owner of the receivables than securitization.[39] The SPV is a shell corporation—purely a legal entity. It is not a real financial intermediary like a factor or forfaiter, and it is not set up to do any actual work. If there is work to be done, it must be done by the originator of the receivables for a fee, as in the securitization of mortgages and consumer loans.

Securitizing Other Types of Receivable.   Our example of the Turkish company illustrates one class of borrower that can use securitization to avoid negative credit substitution—firms in developing countries that hold receivables from firms in developed countries. Another class of borrower that can benefit is firms with weak credit—smaller firms, firms in distress, or firms in volatile industries—that have receivables owed to them by better credits. There are also classes of noncommercial borrowers that can benefit from securitization. Municipal governments have securitized toll revenues, revenues from parking tickets, and tax liens: all of these revenue sources are more solid than the debt of the municipalities themselves. And individuals—movie stars, rock stars, and authors—have securitized royalties from movies, records, and books.

When it comes to securitization of toll revenues and royalties, however, we are not really talking about *receivables*—actual debts owed by others. However, the assets securitized are similar to debts in that they represent expected future cash flows. Although the cash flows are not promised by anyone, as is the case with true receivables, they are fairly reliable and predictable. This makes them a good basis for securitization. This type of securitization is called a "future flow securitization." The idea has been taken up by commercial borrowers too: for example, mortgage banks have securitized the fees they expect to receive for servicing (securitized) mortgages.

We have completed our tour of the debt markets and we are ready to move on to the other main form of financing—equity.

SUMMARY

- The key to understanding debt in all its forms is the need for the lender to control risk.
- The key to controlling risk is information. Since credit information is something of a public good, there are various arrangements to gather it and assess it and make it available to any potential lender.
- Several independent agencies provide ratings of the credit quality of debt. The importance of ratings, despite their modest informational value, is due to the growing significance attached to ratings by financial regulators.
- The making of a loan requires the writing of a contract between borrower and lender. The terms of the contract offer the lender a number of ways to limit potential losses and to control risk—priority, covenants, and security in the form of collateral or guarantees.

---

[39] Factors purchase the receivables at a discount of 5 to 10% and, in addition, charge a factoring fee of 15 to 20%. Moreover, they do not generally advance all the funds immediately. Securitization, if it is an option, can yield the seller of the receivables 30 to 40% more cash up front.

- The function of collateral in *commercial* lending is less to compensate the lender in case of default than it is to provide the lender with a way of controlling the borrower's behavior, so reducing the likelihood that default will occur.

- One can think of a guarantee as a way of separating credit risk from funding. One party bears the credit risk; a different party provides the funds for the loan.

- Some forms of debt include an equity element—to introduce greater flexibility, to provide greater control, or to compensate for downside risk by providing upside potential.

- In relationship financing (mostly lending by intermediaries), the provider is involved with the recipient in a close and continuing relationship of monitoring. In contrast, in arm's-length financing (mostly public issues), there is screening ex ante, but little or no direct monitoring ex post.

- The methods available to control the risk of arm's-length debt are limited. Consequently, this form of lending is intrinsically unsuited to risky borrowers.

- Relationship lending provides better risk control, but it is more expensive. Consequently, low-risk borrowers are more likely to rely on arm's-length borrowing.

- Municipal bonds, issued by levels of government below the national level differ from debt of the national government in that they are not risk free. Municipal bonds enjoy tax advantages in the United States. Unlike corporate bonds, they are often insured.

- Corporate bonds issued to the public are arm's-length securities: they need to be low-risk and low-maintenance instruments. Issuers tend to be large, established firms with good track records. They also tend to be engaged in relatively low-risk businesses that are easy to monitor.

- Most international lending takes place offshore in the Euro market. This avoids the regulatory costs of domestic issues. Underwriting is extremely competitive.

- The traditional private placement market offers smaller issuers the advantages of a relationship loan. The Rule 144a private placement market offers large issuers a way to avoid the delays of a public issue and the need for public disclosure.

- The junk bond market has opened the bond market to below-investment-grade issuers by providing an element of relationship.

- The money market exists because of regulatory costs imposed on short-term lending through financial intermediaries.

- Commercial paper is issued only by good credits. Because it is rolled over so frequently, issuers generally obtain backup liquidity from a bank. Some issuers gain access to the market by purchasing credit enhancement or through bankers' acceptances.

- A number of variations on commercial paper extend the money market to noncommercial issuers and to longer maturities.

- Securitization allows an entity to fund its receivables directly by setting up an SPV to issue securities backed by those receivables. The motivation is to avoid regulatory costs, to provide an opportunity for financial engineering, or to take advantage of receivables that are more solid than the entity itself.

DISCUSSION QUESTIONS

1. Why is information important to lenders? To borrowers? What type of information do parties engaging in financial transactions need? Why does it make sense to centralize information gathering and provision? How is this done? Is good availability of information beneficial to borrowers? For which borrowers in particular?

2. Why is the importance of ratings agency surprising? What is the explanation?

3. What sorts of condition are typically included in loan contracts? What is the function of each?

4. What sorts of issuer are naturally suited to public issue debt market? Ill suited?

5. How can the public issue debt market be extended to "ill-suited" borrowers? Give examples and explain the techniques.

6. In many developing countries where debt financing is scarce, the deficiency is made up to some extent by the informal sector. A common device is to secure the loan with a postdated check. In countries where this device is used, failure to honor a check is a felony. If the borrower fails to pay, the lender deposits the check. If it bounces, the borrower goes to jail (in Bolivia, for about 4 years).
   a. Is this a good method of dealing with default? How does the answer depend on the riskiness of the loan?
   b. How will reliance on this method affect the amount of lending that takes place?

7. Soporifics Inc. wishes to borrow $2 million from Second National Bank. Second National must maintain an equity-to-loan ratio of 8% and a reserve ratio of 8% on NCDs.
   a. What additional funds must the bank raise (how much and in what form) to fund the loan?
   b. Second National requires a return on equity of 20% and must pay 10% interest on NCDs as well as 25¢ per $100 in deposit insurance premiums. What is the minimum rate of interest it must charge on the loan to make a profit?

8. Why is it surprising that money markets exist? Why do they exist nonetheless? What factors explain the relative size of money markets in different countries?

9. Why is it surprising that the Eurobond market exists? How would you expect international lending to take place? What were the initial reasons for the growth of the Eurobond market? Why does the Eurobond market continue to thrive?

10. How does the function of collateral differ between a mortgage loan and a loan to a business secured by the software written for its website? What are

the benefits to the lender in each case? What are the benefits to the borrower?

11. Guarantees and financial intermediation are both example of credit substitution. What are their relative merits? When is each likely to be used?

12. What are the ways that a lender might take an equity stake in a borrower? Why might it do so?

13. What were the obstacles to the development of a market for junk bonds? How were they overcome?

14. What is an SPV? How does it differ from a mutual fund?

15. What are the reasons for securitizing each of the following?
    a. mortgages
    b. credit card debt, auto loans, leases
    c. asset-backed commercial paper and CBOs
    d. foreign exchange receivable for companies in developing countries
    e. music royalties

16. There are two categories of borrowers that use the private placement market:

    Category 1: medium-sized companies.

    Category 2: large creditworthy companies.
    a. In 1990, the SEC adopted Rule 144ae. Is Rule 144a likely to lead to the development of an active secondary market in "category 1" private placements?
       i. Why is public issue not a realistic option for category 1 companies?
       ii. Are their securities easily transferable? What makes a security easily transferable?
       iii. What is likely to be the attitude of the borrower to transfer of its debt by the initial lender?
    b. Will Rule 144a make the private placement market more attractive for "category 2" issuers?
       i. What types of company are likely to be "category 2" issuers?
       ii. Why did these issuers not use the private placement market before? How does Rule 144a change things?
       iii. How will the introduction of Rule 144A affect the efficiency of the financial system?
       iv. Is Rule 144a consistent with the SEC's mission of protecting investors?

BIBLIOGRAPHY

Altman, E. I. "The Anatomy of the High Yield Bond Market: After Two Decades of Activity—Implications for Europe." New York University Center for Law and Business, 1998.

Alworth, J. S., and C. E. V. Borio. "Commercial Paper Markets: A Survey." *BIS Economic Papers* no. 37, April 1993.

Bank for International Settlements. "The Changing Shape of Fixed Income Markets." Discussion paper 5, BIS, 2001.

Cantor, R., and F. Packer (1994). "The credit rating industry." *Federal Reserve Bank of New York Quarterly Review*, Summer–Fall 1994, 1–26.

Carey, M., S. Prowse, et al. "The Economics of the Private Placement Market." *Financial Markets, Institutions & Instruments* 2 (3): 1–67.

Carey, M., M. Post, et al. "Does Corporate Lending by Banks and Finance Companies Differ? Evidence on Specialization in Private Debt Contracting." *Journal of Finance* 53, no. 3 (June 1998): 845–878.

Fortune, P. "The Municipal Bond Market, I: Politics, Taxes, and Yields." *New England Economic Review*, September–October, 1991, 13–36.

Katz, A. W. "An Economic Analysis of the Guaranty Contract." *The University of Chicago Law Review* 66 no. 1 (winter, 1999): 47–116.

Mann, R. J. "Explaining the Pattern of Secured Credit." *Harvard Law Review* 625 (1997): 639.

Partnoy, F. "The Siskel and Ebert of Financial Markets? Two Thumbs Down for the Credit Rating Agencies." University of San Diego School of Law, June 1999.

Prowse, S. D. "The Economics of Private Placements: Middle Market Corporate Finance, Life Insurance Companies, and a Credit Crunch." *Federal Reserve Bank of Dallas Economic Review*, third quarter, 1997, 12–24.

Rosengren, Eric S. "The Case for Junk Bonds." *New England Economic Review*, May–June 1990, 40–49.

Schwartz, S. L. "The Alchemy of Asset Securitization." *Stanford Journal of Law, Business & Finance* 1 (1994): 133–154.

Sharpe, S. A. N., and H. Hien (1995). "Capital Market Imperfections and the Incentive to Lease." *Journal of Financial Economics* 39, no. 2–3 (1995); 271–294.

KEY TERMS

due diligence
rating agencies
rating
investment-grade bonds
credit bureau
indenture
priority
subordinated debt
covenant
collateral
leasing
guarantee
preferred equity
convertible debt
warrants
relationship financing

arm's-length financing
municipal bonds (munis)
general obligation bonds
revenue bonds
bond insurance
Eurobond market
private placement
traditional private placement market
Rule 144a
144a market
junk (high-yield) bonds
to roll over
master notes
municipal notes
negotiable certificate of deposit (NCD)

bank notes
medium-term notes (MTNs)
note-issuance facility (NIF) or revolving underwriting facility (RUF)
receivables
special purpose vehicle (SPV)
asset-backed securities
asset-backed commercial paper
collateralized loan obligations (CLOs)
collateralized bond obligations (CBOs)
catastrophe-linked or 'cat' bonds
factoring
forfaiting

CHAPTER 15

THE EQUITY MARKET

When you finish this chapter you will understand:

- The real economic function of the stock market
- The advantages of widespread shareholding and its problems
- How venture capital works and why it is important

The equity market is the market for shares in the ownership of corporations. In this market, investors hand over money today in exchange for a promise of part of the distributed profits. We saw in Chapter 11 that equity financing avoids some of the problems of risky debt. Because the promised payment is not specific, there can be no default, with all its attendant dilemmas and costs. However, the very vagueness of the promise creates difficulties of its own.

If the issue with debt financing is controlling risk, the issue with equity financing is ensuring a return to the provider of the financing. Will those in control of the enterprise do their best to make the profit as large possible? Will they distribute it to equity holders as they should? Since the amount of profit is a matter of accounting, will their accounting be honest?

corporate governance mechanisms
Mechanisms to ensure providers of equity financing a fair return.

All these uncertainties make it essential that there be mechanisms to protect the interests of equity holders—**corporate governance mechanisms**. Without such mechanisms, equity financing will not work. Different countries have different mechanisms of corporate governance. Understanding these different mechanisms and their relevant merits is our first goal in this chapter.

In Chapter 14 we learned that there are two basic modes of lending—*relationship* lending and *arm's-length* lending. With relationship lending, the lender remains closely involved and continues to monitor the performance of the borrower. With arm's-length lending there is some screening in advance, but no direct monitoring once the loan has been given. We shall find the same distinction with equity financing. We shall see that there is both public equity and private equity. The former is largely, but not entirely, at arm's length; the latter is very much relationship financing.

We shall look at public equity first. We shall see that its function is not, as is often supposed, the financing of new investment. Rather, its primary functions are liquidity and price discovery. We shall then take a look at the private equity market. Although this market is relatively small, we shall see that it can play a vital role in economic growth.

CORPORATE GOVERNANCE

The Nature of the Problem

The Enterprise as a Web of Relationships. To understand the issues involved in corporate governance, we need to understand the nature of the business enterprise. A business enterprise brings together resources, adds value to them, and sells the resulting product. In doing this, it engages in transactions with a variety of parties. Some provide the necessary inputs—suppliers, employees, managers, and providers of financing—while others purchase the output. We can think of the enterprise itself as constituting a web of relationships among these different parties.

Some of these relationships are *transient*: for example, those involving customers that purchase the product for cash in the open market. However, many of the relationships are ongoing and involve a degree of commitment. Such relationships are normally **contractual**: they are governed by a contract between the party in question and the enterprise that spells out the rights and obligations of each. Examples include employment contracts with employees and managers and debt contracts with those who provide debt financing.

A special type of contractual relationship with the enterprise is one of **ownership**. The essence of ownership is two rights. The first is the right of control: owners have the final say on the management of the enterprise.[1] The second right is the right to receive the residual earnings of the enterprise—what is left after all contractual and cash payments have been made. It is natural that these two rights go together—that those responsible for the decisions bear the consequences or, alternatively, that those who bear the consequences get to control the decisions. In the business corporation, ownership rights reside with those who provide equity financing.[2]

The Shareholder as Bearer of Risk. Because they are the residual claimants, it is the equity holders who bear the risk. If the enterprise does well, they benefit; if the enterprise does badly, they absorb the loss. By bearing the risk, the equity holders provide a

contractual relationship

A relationship with an enterprise involving specific rights and obligations.

ownership relationship

A relationship combining right of control and right to receive residual income.

---

[1] They are, of course, restricted in their decisions by the enterprise's contractual obligations.

[2] In other types of economic enterprise ownership resides with other parties. For example, in the vast majority of business enterprises that are sole proprietorships, it is the proprietor who is the owner. In a partnership it is the suppliers of labor who are the owners: securities firms were traditionally partnerships. In a cooperative, it is the customers who are the owners: we shall see in Chapter 17 that exchanges are consumer cooperatives. Over time, different types of economic enterprise evolve so that ownership resides with the parties who derive the greatest benefit from it [see Hansmann (1996)].

valuable service to those parties that have a contractual relationships with the enterprise. Because equity holders bear the risk, the enterprise can more reliably fulfill its contractual obligations: for example, it can more reliably pay wages and salaries and more reliably repay its debts. This additional security makes it more attractive for the contractual parties to commit to the enterprise. We have seen how this works with debt: the higher the equity ratio, the safer it is to lend. The same principle holds for employees and managers who invest in enterprise-specific skills and for suppliers and customers who make investments that depend on the continued performance of the enterprise.

Dispersed Shareholding

The Advantages and Problems.   As we have often seen, the bearing of risk is easier if the risk is divided. There is therefore a great advantage in dividing the equity shares of an enterprise into many small portions. Then each portion can be held by a well-diversified investor, for whom it is a relatively small part of his or her portfolio.

Unfortunately, the advantages of dispersed shareholding come at a cost. When shareholding is dispersed, small shareholders cannot be expected to exercise direct control over the enterprise themselves: dispersed shareholding is of necessity an arm's length arrangement. A single small shareholder has little power to affect the enterprise's decisions and lacks the incentives to do so (the free-rider problem). If an investor is unhappy with how the enterprise is run, it makes more sense to sell the shares than to lobby for change. Exit is more attractive than voice.[3]

insiders

Those in effective control of an enterprise, as opposed to arm's-length investors.

Insiders and Insider Abuse.   Because dispersed shareholders are neither able to control the enterprise nor interested in doing so, effective control is left in the hands of others. We shall call these others **insiders**. As we shall see, these insiders may be the managers of the enterprise or individual shareholders with a sufficiently large stake in the enterprise to make their control rights effective. Not surprisingly, in exercising control over the enterprise, insiders will tend to put their own interests first.

There are many ways for insiders to further their own interests at the expense of arm's-length shareholders. The most blatant is outright theft. Insiders can simply steal income and assets that rightly belong to outsiders. When it is hard to get away with outright theft, there are many ways to disguise it. For example, insiders can arrange for the enterprise to sell product or assets at give-away prices to entities that they or their friends or relatives control. When there are obstacles to this sort of self-dealing, there are yet other alternatives. For example, managers can boost their own salaries and perks. Or, probably the most damaging of all, they can be lazy and incompetent and get away with it.

Why It Matters.   What is the harm in all this? Does insider abuse really matter? It does, for two reasons. The first is that the economy works best when economic enterprises are run with the objective of maximizing the return to their shareholders. This does not mean that the interests of other parties should be ignored: their interests are protected by contract. However, given this protection, the best use will be made of the economy's resources if

---

[3] We found the same pattern with respect to arm's-length debt in Chapter 14.

those in control of its enterprises pursue single-mindedly the interests of shareholders—that is, if they focus on the bottom line. For example, the managers may not like it, but if they are incompetent, it is best that they be fired. Or if the enterprise is in a declining industry and running at a loss, the employees may not like it, but it is best that the enterprise be shut down.

The second reason why it is not a good idea for insiders to abuse arm's-length shareholders is that it makes arm's-length shareholding unattractive. If insiders routinely cheat arm's-length shareholders, the supply of willing arm's-length shareholders will dry up. Arm's-length equity financing simply will not work in these circumstances. This does not mean that the return to arm's-length shareholders actually has to be maximized. However, it must be good enough to make being an arm's-length shareholder worthwhile. Some theft by insiders may be tolerable, but insiders must not steal too much.

The Two Basic Mechanisms of Corporate Governance.   What we need, then, is some way to constrain the behavior of insiders to ensure arm's-length shareholders a reasonable return on their investment. There are basically two possible mechanisms. One is **legal protection**: laws and regulations, properly enforced, can to some extent protect arm's-length investors from abuse by insiders. The other mechanism is reliance on some party with sufficient power and interest to monitor the enterprise on behalf of arm's-length investors.[4]

We shall see that equity markets in different countries and at different times have relied on some combination of both these two mechanisms. Neither on its own seems to be sufficient.

legal protection of shareholders
Laws and regulations protecting arm's-length investors from abuse by insiders.

Legal Protection

Shareholder Democracy.   Shareholders have certain legal rights. Indeed, formally, it is they who have ultimate control of the enterprise. They are supposed to exercise this control by voting for a board of directors, which in turn appoints the managers and monitors their performance. Legal systems vary in the precise nature of the voting rights of arm's-length shareholders, and this will affect their potential power.

However, "shareholder democracy" is rarely effective. It is usually the insiders who nominate candidates for the board, and individual arm's-length shareholders rarely even bother to vote. Because the members of the board are effectively chosen by insiders, they are generally more interested in pleasing them than in pleasing the multitude of anonymous shareholders they are supposed to represent. Moreover, monitoring is hard work. Acquiring the necessary expertise and information involves effort. Why bother? Why not simply accept insiders' assurances that all is well?

Recourse to the Courts.   There is, however, a second line of defense. If shareholders feel they have been cheated, they can sue. The law in most advanced economies rec-

---

[4] This is very similar to what we found in Chapter 14, when we considered debt. We found that a public market in debt relies on some combination of two mechanisms—legal protection and a party with a large enough interest to be willing to monitor.

ognizes that those in control of the corporation have a "duty of loyalty" to the shareholders. Most forms of self-dealing are seen as a violation of this duty.

Of course, there is a free-rider problem here too. It is not worthwhile for a shareholder with only a small stake in a company to go to the trouble and expense of a lawsuit when most of the benefits will go to others. In the United States, a solution to this problem has evolved in the form of the *contingency fee* (lawyers are paid only if they win) and the *class-action suit* (a suit in the name of all shareholders). Unfortunately, this solution has its own problems. It can lead to a form of "legal predation" in which corporations find it cheaper to settle even frivolous suits than to battle it out in court.

The Need for Transparency.   Of course, legal protection is worthless without good information. Without knowing what is happening inside the corporation, shareholders will be unable to exercise effectively either their voting rights or their right to sue. So adequate disclosure of information is essential. That is, for legal protection to work, the corporation must have sufficient **transparency**.

transparency
The situation in which the workings of a corporation are sufficiently clear to outsiders.

Cross-Country Differences in Legal Protection.   The effectiveness of legal protection—the strength of the law, the vigor of its enforcement, and the stringency of disclosure requirements—varies from country to country. Legal protection is strongest in the English-speaking countries, where legal systems are founded in common law. Legal protection is not as effective in countries such as Germany and Japan with a legal system based on German civil law. And legal protection is weakest in countries such as France, Italy, and Spain with a legal system based on French civil law.[5]

Not surprisingly, there is a strong correlation between the effectiveness of legal protection and the extent of arm's-length shareholding in a given country. In countries with a common-law tradition, the amount of publicly held stock averages about 60% of one year's GDP; in countries with a tradition of German civil law, about 45%; in countries with a tradition of French civil law, about 21%. The number of companies listed on the stock exchange in the United States and the United Kingdom (two common-law countries) is over 30 per million citizens; in France, Germany, and Italy, it is fewer than 10 per million citizens.[6]

Monitoring by Interested Parties

Legal protection is one mechanism of corporate governance. The second mechanism is monitoring on behalf of arm's-length investors by some party with the requisite power and an interest in using it for this purpose. To see the many ways in which this can work—more or less well—we shall look at the very different arrangements that have evolved in Germany and Japan on the one hand and in the United States on the other.

---

[5] This is the finding of research by La Porta et al. (1997).

[6] La Porta, et al. (1997).

Germany and Japan: Banks as Monitors.   In Germany, ever since the 1850s, firms have mostly relied on banks for their long-term financing.[7] Initially, this was in the form of long-term loans. However, when incorporation became easier in the 1870s, banks built on close relationships with their borrowers to underwrite their issues of equity. The banks held some of the shares for their own account and used their branch networks to market the rest. The banks also made a secondary market in the securities that they distributed. Purchasers of shares were generally happy to leave them in the custody of a bank and to grant the bank proxy rights to vote their shares. As a result, much of the ownership rights of German industrial firms became concentrated in the hands of the banks. This system largely persists today.

Japan has developed, since the 1920s, a system of monitoring that, like the German system, relies heavily on banks. Because banking regulation in Japan is much more restrictive than it is in Germany, the Japanese system of monitoring is less direct. In Japan, monitoring is carried out within the framework of the **keiretsu**—a group of financial and nonfinancial firms with ties of reciprocal ownership.[8] Each *keiretsu* is built around a main bank that provides member firms with short-term financing (sometimes rolled over to provide long-term funding). While the main bank generally owns less than 5% of the equity of any individual member firm (the limit set by banking regulation), the group as a whole may own 20% or more. This stake provides the main bank with the power to monitor member firms quite effectively. If a firm gets into trouble, the main bank will intervene rapidly, often replacing key management with its own people. The bank's exposure as a creditor gives it a strong incentive to monitor effectively.

As large shareholders, banks in Japan and Germany certainly have the ability to monitor and to control management. In their role of underwriters, German banks have an incentive to protect the interests of arm's-length investors, so that there will be a willing market for subsequent share issues. Japanese banks, because they are prohibited from securities activities, lack this incentive. However, the fact that banks in both countries are not only shareholders but also substantial lenders to the companies in question also affects their incentives. As lenders, they want the companies they control to play it safe so that they can repay their debts. In many cases such conservatism will not be in the interests of arm's-length shareholders.

keiretsu

A group of financial and nonfinancial firms with ties of reciprocal ownership.

Corporate Governance in the United States

Monitoring by Underwriters.   While Germany and Japan have historically relied on monitoring by banks, the U.S. capital market began by relying on monitoring by underwriters. The underwriting of industrial securities was pioneered in the United States by J. P. Morgan. Up to the 1880s, Morgan was a traditional private banker, specializing in the placement of American securities overseas. However, a series of defaults by his customers shook investor confidence and made it difficult for him to sell new securities. To save

---

[7] See Chapter 6 on Germany's "universal banks."

[8] The *keiretsu* is the modern descendent of the *zaibatsu*, the powerful family-controlled groups of companies that dominated the Japanese economy before World War II.

his business, he became involved in the management of the railroads whose securities he was selling.[9]

Morgan's intervention was highly successful. Investors soon learned that the presence of "Morgan's men" on a railroad's board of directors meant that the company would be managed well and that investors' interests would be protected. They were therefore willing to pay a premium for the securities of such companies. Morgan extended the same methods to financing industrial firms, particularly in the steel industry. Other private bankers—Speyer, J. & W. Seligman, Brown Brothers, and Kuhn, Loeb—extended the method to other industries.

To secure the large sums they needed to underwrite larger and larger issues, securities firms developed connections with commercial banks, trust companies, and life insurance companies. Each securities firm became the hub of a group of financial and industrial companies, rather like the main bank of a keiretsu or a German universal bank.

The reputational economies of scale in this form of monitoring were overwhelming. The larger a firm, the more valuable was its reputation, and the less likely it was to jeopardize its future for the sake of quick profits from a doubtful deal. Economies of scale led to concentration, to market power, and to enormous profits.

Political Opposition to the "Money Trust."   The concentration of power and the enormous profits aroused increasing popular resentment and political opposition. From the turn of the century, Progressive politicians campaigned against the **"money trust"** that they believed monopolized industry and controlled the country. Their first victory came with the Armstrong hearings of 1905. These led to regulation that limited the ability of life insurance companies to hold equity and so to play a role in corporate governance.

"money trust"
A group of powerful financiers alleged to control the U.S. economy.

However, it was the collapse of the stock market in 1929 and the ensuing Depression that gave the opponents of the "money trust" the opportunity they had been waiting for. There was a tidal wave of new regulation that essentially broke up the "money trust" and wiped out existing mechanisms of corporate governance.[10] The Glass–Steagall Act of 1933 excluded banks from the capital market, depriving the securities business of an important source of funds. The Investment Company Act of 1940 prohibited mutual funds from holding more than 10% of the equity of any company, making it difficult for them to play an effective role in corporate governance.

The Separation of Ownership and Control.   The Depression era legislation with the greatest impact on corporate governance, however, was the **Securities and Exchange Act of 1934**, which established laws to protect small investors and set up the Securities and Exchange Commission to enforce those laws. While the act strengthened one mechanism of corporate governance—legal protection—it weakened the other—active intervention by large shareholders.

---

[9] Initially, the securities in question were bonds. Later, they were equities.

[10] The power of the "money trust" had already been eroded by the stock market boom of the 1920s. Firms found it so easy to raise funds in the market that they didn't need the help of Morgan or the others. This greatly reduced the power of the securities firms to monitor. The Japanese system experienced similar erosion during the Japanese stock market boom of the 1980s.

The new regulations made it much less attractive to be a large shareholder. It limited the ability of large shareholders to trade their stock (insider trading) or to do business with the company. The new regulations also exposed large shareholders to potential prosecution by the SEC and to class-action suits if they took an active role in controlling a company.

The destruction of the Morgan-style system of corporate governance and the introduction of the new securities laws resulted in a "separation of ownership and control." Shares came increasingly to be held by arm's-length investors, none of whom had a large enough stake to make controlling management either feasible or worthwhile. Control was largely left in the hands of managers.

Managers Monitoring Managers.   Of course, to some extent, managers can monitor managers. One framework in which they do so is the **multidivisional ("M-form") corporation** that first appeared in the 1920s. In the M-form corporation, divisions largely operate as independent firms and are monitored by corporate headquarters. The M-form corporation acts as a sort of internal capital market with corporate headquarters using surplus profits from one company to finance another.

multidivisional ("M-form") corporation
A corporation organized as a group of semi-independent companies with an internal capital market.

Another example of managers monitoring managers is the takeover. When a firm is doing badly, the managers of another firm who think they can do a better job can purchase the firm in trouble and increase its value through reorganization and better management.

Both the M-form corporation and the takeover are most effective when the divisions and firms in question are in the same industry. Headquarters does a better job of monitoring its divisions because it understands the nature of their business. Managers are best able to identify poor management in another firm when they are in the same business. It is unfortunate, therefore, that these mechanisms of corporate governance were hampered by yet another piece of Progressive era legislation—antitrust. The antitrust laws threatened large specialized M-form corporations with breakup, and they made takeovers within an industry very difficult. The result was the growth of the **conglomerate**—a large firm with divisions in different, often unrelated, industries.

conglomerate
A large firm with divisions in different, often unrelated, industries.

There is of course a more fundamental problem with the idea that managers will monitor managers: who will guard the guards themselves? While the managers at corporate headquarters could monitor those in the divisions or take over other firms that were poorly run, they themselves were largely free of any external control or monitoring. Moreover, large companies that did not get themselves into serious trouble were largely safe from takeovers.

In the absence of monitoring and control, large corporations were run for the benefit of their managers rather than for the benefit of their shareholders. The result was typified by the problem of *free cash flow*.

Free Cash Flow.   As we saw in Chapter 11, because of the high cost of external financing, firms tend to rely as much as they can on internal funds to finance their investment. For example, suppose that Hewlett Packard has profits of $1 billion and is planning a $1.5 billion investment in new technology. It raises $500 million through the sale of new bonds and needs a further $1 billion in new equity. It has two options. It can pay out this year's $1 billion in profits as dividends and simultaneously float a new stock issue of $1 billion. Or it can cancel the dividend payment and use the $1 billion in profits directly to fund the new investment. The first alternative is wasteful. Registration and underwriting costs of a new issue could easily total 5% of the amount raised, $50 million in this case. Hewlett Packard could save the $50 million by using retained earnings.

But doesn't this use of internal funds cheat shareholders of their dividends? Not if the project is worthwhile. If it is, the value of Hewlett Packard's outstanding stock should increase by *more* than $1 billion when it reinvests its retained earnings. The resulting capital gain on their stock compensates stockholders no less than would a payment of dividends.[11]

When managers are free of effective monitoring, however, they can invest internal funds in projects that are not worthwhile from the point of view of shareholders. One study found that a sample of large U.S. firms between 1970 and 1988 increased the value of their stock on average by only 34¢ for each dollar they invested.[12]

Some companies, particularly mature ones, generate large amounts of internal funds. The problem is that they frequently generate more cash than can be invested profitably within the company. The excess is known as **free cash flow**. In principle, the company should pay out free cash flow to the owners—either as dividends or through the repurchase of stock. However, managers gain nothing from doing this. Naturally, they would rather use free cash flow to further their own interests. In the absence of effective monitoring, they are free to do so.

There are various ways managers can misuse free cash flow. Just holding onto the cash is attractive. A large reserve of cash protects them if the company runs into trouble: it enables them to avoid default on debt and even allows them to continue to pay dividends to appease stockholders. A large reserve of cash also allows managers to fund new projects without having to persuade the capital market of their value. Since management compensation is largely a function of the size of the firm, managers have an incentive to expand even when expansion is unprofitable. They will therefore overinvest in their companies and engage in unprofitable takeovers to increase the size of their empires.

Hostile Takeovers and Leveraged Buyouts.   By the 1980s, slack management and the abuse of free cash flow was so extensive that it had created a significant profit opportunity. Many large corporations were sitting on hoards of cash. Many had expanded to become unwieldy and unfocused conglomerates. By stripping them of cash, by divesting unrelated and unprofitable divisions, and by refocusing management on the bottom line, a great deal of value could be created and released. The principal instrument by which this profit opportunity was realized was the hostile takeover through **leveraged buyout (LBO)**.

The problem the LBO addressed was that the larger the corporation, the harder it is to put together a big enough share of ownership to gain control and to make monitoring worthwhile. The solution that the LBO provided was to make the equity of the corporation smaller by replacing much of it with debt. Then ownership and control could be achieved with a much smaller amount of capital. The organizers of the LBO borrowed to buy the outstanding shares of a company. They then had the company issue debt to retire a large

free cash flow
The excess of internal funds over the amount needed to finance worthwhile investments.

leveraged buyout (LBO)
The purchase of a majority of the outstanding equity of a company, funded by the issue of debt.

---

[11] Moreover, if the tax rate on capital gains is less than the tax rate on dividend income, investors will *prefer* an increase in the value of the stock to an equivalent cash dividend.

[12] Mueller and Reardon (1993).

part of the shares that they held.[13] They retained the remainder and used it to control the company. The principal vehicle for leveraged buyouts was a specialized form of financial intermediary—the **LBO partnership**.[14]

Well-known LBO partnerships included Kohlberg Kravis Roberts, Forstmann, Little Co., and Clayton, Dubilier Rice. Some active private investors, such as Carl Icahn, Warren Buffet, and the Pritzker family, employed very similar methods. Similar arrangements also emerged in other countries—for example, the Hanson Group in the United Kingdom and the Bronfmans in Canada.

The most famous LBO was RJR Nabisco. Kohlberg Kravis Roberts put together $18.9 billion to buy up 74% of RJR Nabisco's stock. Most of the $5 billion in short-term notes used in the deal was paid off later with a $4 billion issue of junk bonds—the largest bond issue of any kind to that date. The LBO was extremely successful: recent estimates suggest that it increased the value of RJR Nabisco by some $17 billion.[15]

In all, between 1984 and 1990 nearly half of all major corporations in the United States received takeover offers. Many corporations, not yet targets of LBOs but fearful of being taken over, issued debt themselves to buy back their own stock. By eliminating free cash flow, this maneuver made a hostile takeover much less attractive. Some $500 billion of stock was bought back in this way between 1984 and 1989.

The pace of mergers and acquisitions slowed dramatically in the early 1990s. Financing was hard to come by. Good deals were harder to find. And managers successfully applied political pressure to gain regulatory protection from hostile takeovers. Many states passed antitakeover legislation, and the courts allowed various defensive measures designed to make takeovers unattractive. The volume of LBOs never regained the level it had reached in the late 1980s. Although mergers and acquisitions rebounded in the mid-1990s, they were usually friendly rather than hostile and were driven by considerations other than corporate control. As hostile takeovers have become more difficult and less frequent, other mechanisms of corporate control have come to play a greater role.

Aligning the Incentives of Managers and Shareholders. Perhaps the most important new mechanism is actually a legacy of the LBO. When LBO partnerships took over a company, they often retained the existing managers. This might seem puzzling, since the usual motive for a hostile takeover was to end the mismanagement of the company in question. However, mismanagement was usually less a result of incompetence than of bad incentives. So the LBO partners changed the incentives. Far from firing the managers, they gave them a stake in the success of the company in the form of stock or **stock options**. In this

---

[13] Enabling them to repay the loan they had taken, usually from a bank or group of banks, to purchase the shares initially.

[14] The structure of the LBO partnership is very much like that of the private equity partnership that we discuss presently.

[15] Such results are typical. The average return to buyout investors has been 42% of the purchase price, giving a return of 785%, or 125% per annum. Pre-buyout shareholders have done well too: the buyout price is on average 40% above the previously prevailing market price; there have been some losses to pre-buyout debt holders. There is no empirical evidence of the cuts in R&D or massive layoffs that the media often attribute to restructurings.

LBO partnership

A financial institution that specializes in LBOs.

management stock options

Options that allow managers to buy shares of the company at a prespecified price.

way, the managers' interests became aligned with those of the shareholders. Because their compensation depended on it, managers had an incentive to maximize the value of their companies.

Not surprisingly, managers have found this aspect of the LBO quite attractive, and the practice has been widely imitated. An equity interest in the companies they manage has became an important component of executive compensation in most corporations. By 1998, share options accounted for over 50% of the compensation of top executives, compared to only 2% in the mid-1980s. At end of 1998, shares and share options in such incentive schemes amounted to 13% of total corporate equity in the United States and were worth over $1 trillion.

Institutional Investors as Monitors.   A second recent development has been the increasing assertiveness of institutional investors in matters of corporate governance. In principle, institutional investors would seem to be natural candidates to monitor managers on behalf of arm's-length investors. Together, institutional investors hold almost half of all corporate equity. Some hold huge portfolios. For example, TIAA-CREF, a pension fund for teachers and professors, holds over $100 billion of stocks, as does Calpers, the pension fund of California state employees. Institutional investors are diversified. However, with portfolios of this size, the funds' stakes in individual companies are large enough both to give them some power and to give them an incentive to monitor.

However, monitoring by institutional investors faces a number of obstacles. As we have seen, regulations have made it impossible for mutual funds or insurance companies to play much of a role.[16] Private pension funds are generally sponsored by corporations themselves: corporate managers have not encouraged them to take an active role in the governance of other corporations. So it is the public and nonprofit pension funds such as Calpers and TIAA-CREF that have taken the lead. When a company performs poorly or fails to meet certain standards of corporate governance, the funds make their displeasure known and the company in question generally responds. However, it is uncertain whether actual performance, in terms of returns to investors, is much improved by these interventions.

A Comparison of Corporate Governance Systems

A Diversity of Systems.   As we have seen, the practice of corporate governance varies considerably from country to country. However, where it is effective, it generally contains both our basic elements. There is adequate legal protection, and there is some form of monitoring by a party with sufficient power to exercise control and a sufficient interest in doing so.

In the common-law countries, such as the United States and the United Kingdom, legal protection of arm's-length investors is strong. As a result, shareholding is dispersed, and it is rare for any individual shareholder to have a large enough stake to be an effective monitor. In these countries, mechanisms have evolved, in a continuing battle with man-

---

[16] However, regulations have actually pushed pension funds to play a role. Pension regulators see voting rights as part of a pension plan's assets and consider it to be part of the plan's fiduciary responsibility to vote its shares.

agers, to overcome this weakness. The threat of a hostile takeover enforces some discipline. And the alignment of incentives between managers and shareholders through the use of stock options has helped to reduce the problem.

In the civil-law systems of continental Europe and Japan, legal protection is weak. Consequently, being a shareholder is relatively unattractive unless you have a large enough stake in the company to allow you to protect your interests. As a result, shareholding is much more concentrated than it is in the United States and the United Kingdom. The big shareholders in Germany and Japan are banks. Elsewhere they are typically families. Hostile takeovers are rare in these countries because the large shareholders in control of a company are better able to resist them.

Are the Different Systems Converging?   Why do corporate governance mechanisms differ so much? One would think that there was a "best solution" and that all economies would converge on that solution. The differences are largely the result of different legal and regulatory systems. As we have seen, these differ in the protection they afford arm's-length investors. They also differ in their friendliness to concentrated ownership. The United States in particular has made it relatively unattractive to be a large shareholder. This is partly a consequence of the strong legal protection of arm's-length investors and partly a result of the political influence of managers. In Germany and Japan, regulations have limited the access of companies to the securities markets and forced them into the arms of the banks (which have considerable political influence in these countries). Since legal and regulatory systems are slow to change, so are the corporate governance regimes that they have created.

Another reason why corporate governance regimes have not converged on a "best solution" is that it is not clear that any model is uniformly best. There are, as is so often the case, trade-offs. The Continental model serves arm's-length shareholders less well, but it provides better protection to parties that have contractual relationships with the corporation—workers, managers, lenders, suppliers. The security that this provides can lead to greater commitment and greater efficiency. On the other hand, the Anglo-American model is much more adaptable. Because the interests of shareholders come first, there is little hesitation in making drastic changes even when these harm the interests of other contractual parties.

When the business environment is relatively stable, as it was in the 1970s and 1980s, the Continental system looks good. Americans wrote dozens of books praising the efficiency of Japan and Germany and urging U.S. companies to emulate their practices. When the business environment is changing rapidly, as it has since the 1990s, the Anglo-American system looks good. Europeans and Japanese have written dozens of books praising the adaptability of U.S. and British companies and urging their own companies to adopt U.S. practices.

Apart from their different effects on the efficiency and adaptability of corporations, the different systems of corporate governance differ in the sort of equity market that they create. The Anglo-American system of corporate governance, because it is more friendly to arm's-length investors, produces a market with more widely dispersed shareholding and better liquidity. It is this advantage of the Anglo-American system above all that is driving the Continental economies to seek to emulate it. To understand why they regard a well-functioning public equity market as so important, we need to take a closer look at what it is that a public equity market actually does.

THE PUBLIC EQUITY MARKET

What Does the Public Equity Market Do?

The problems of corporate governance make external equity a very expensive source of financing. Providers of external equity require a high expected return to compensate them for the risks. This high return means a high cost for companies that fund themselves by issuing equity. Moreover, all the mechanisms that have arisen to mitigate the problems of corporate governance are costly, and it is the company that issues the stock that ultimately must bear this cost.[17]

Given how expensive it is, it is not surprising that external equity is not a major source of funds for corporate investment. As we saw in Chapter 11, firms rely primarily on their own internally generated funds to finance investment and secondarily on external debt. External equity is a last resort, and to the extent that it is used at all to finance investment it is usually private equity rather than public equity.[18]

If public equity does not provide much financing for investment, what then is its function? The market for public equity is above all just that—a market. It is a market for *ownership*. Like any market, it offers liquidity and price discovery, and by doing so it makes it easier to transfer the ownership of corporations.

restructuring
Reorganization involving changes in ownership of companies or parts of companies.

Restructuring: Mergers, Acquisitions, and Divestiture.   The transfer of ownership is a vital element in the **restructuring** of industries and of economies. For example, in earlier chapters we saw how economies of scale and scope have stimulated a wave of consolidation in the financial sector—in banking, insurance, mutual fund management, and the securities business. The process of consolidation involves firms merging with one another or firms acquiring one another. Mergers and acquisitions involve changes of ownership. In a merger, shareholders of the two merging companies give up their shares in the individual companies and receive in exchange shares in the merged company. In an acquisition, the acquiring company purchases the stock of the target company from its existing shareholders for cash or with its own stock. In the recent stock market boom, the proportion of acquisitions paid for with stock increased enormously—from 20% or less in the 1980s, to 60% or more by 2000.

The public equity market facilitates such changes in ownership. Because the market is liquid, it is relatively easy for an acquiring company to purchase the shares it needs to take over a target company. Because the market provides price discovery, the parties to a restructuring transaction have a good idea of the value of the companies concerned and therefore of the fair price for the transaction (how many shares of company A to pay for each share of company B, for example). If the market does not consider the price to be fair, shareholders can either vote against the transaction or simply refuse to sell the shares they hold.

The financial sector is not alone in undergoing restructuring. As we saw in Chapter 11 and earlier in this chapter, there has been a wave of restructuring in the U.S. economy in particular and throughout the advanced economies in general. This recent restructuring has

---

[17] Some of the cost of legal protection is borne by the taxpayer.

[18] We shall look at private equity later in the chapter.

been driven by a variety of factors. As in the financial sector, deregulation has removed long-standing barriers to consolidation in many industries. This together with freer trade among countries has also increased competitive pressures, and this in turn has pushed companies to exploit economies of scale and scope. Rapid technological change has been a factor too. Notable examples of industries undergoing restructuring are the airline industry, the oil industry, and telecoms. Exhibit 15.1 shows the rapidly increasing volume of mergers and acquisitions in the late 1990s.

Increasing competitive pressure and rising pressure for shareholder value has led to divestiture as well as to consolidation. Companies have found it best to focus on their "core competence"—the line of business in which they have the greatest expertise and comparative advantage. As a result, companies have been selling off divisions that are not related to their principal line of business. In addition, the greater pressure for shareholder value has led companies to sell off divisions that were insufficiently profitable. Once again the public equity market has facilitated the process. A liquid market has made it relatively easy to sell off divisions, either to other companies or to arm's-length investors. Good price discovery has provided an estimate of the fair price for the sale.

Privatization. A particular kind of restructuring, virtually absent in the United States but very common elsewhere, is privatization. Up to the 1980s, the governments of most countries owned a significant proportion of the companies in their economies. This was the case in western Europe no less than in the developing and communist countries.

EXHIBIT 15.1   Announced U.S. Mergers and Acquisitions

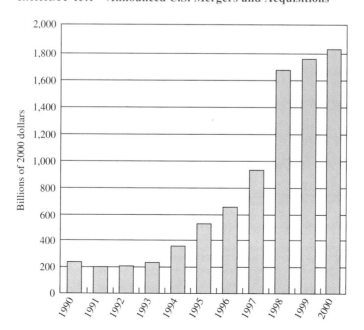

Source: Investment Dealers Digest, *Thomson Financial.*

Governments frequently owned utilities, airlines, and banks and, less frequently, industrial companies. In the communist countries, of course, they owned everything.

Since the 1980s governments everywhere have been selling off the companies they own either partially or completely—a process known as **privatization** (see Exhibit 15.2). Worldwide proceeds from privatization peaked in 1997 and have declined somewhat since as privatization programs in most major countries matured and as equity values have fallen.

By 1999, the total value of companies worldwide that had been privatized had reached $2.5 trillion, up from $50 billion in 1983. In 1999, over 20% of the market value of all publicly traded companies outside the United States was represented by firms that had been privatized. Some privatization has involved the direct sale of a government-owned enterprise to a private company. However, much of it has involved the sale of at least a part of the shares to arm's-length investors. Once again, it is the public equity market that has made this possible.

Privatization has had an enormous impact on the equities markets of the countries concerned. There have been some 750 privatizations involving the issue of shares to the public since 1977. These included the 25 largest common stock issues ever. As a result of these privatizations, shareholding in many countries has become much more widespread. Of the 54 non-U.S. companies with more than half a million shareholders, some two-thirds are privatized companies.

Exit for Existing Owners.   Privatization is one example of how the existing owners of a company can reduce their stake in it by selling shares to the public: in this case, the existing owner is the government. Other examples include family owners taking their com-

privatization

Transfer of state-owned enterprise to private or partial private ownership.

EXHIBIT 15.2   Government Revenues from Privatizations Worldwide

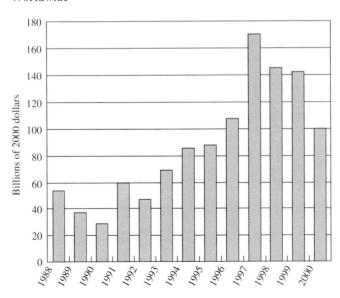

Source: Privatization International.

panies public and LBO and venture capital partnerships selling their stake in companies they control.

exit

Existing owners of a company reducing or ending their stake in a company.

Existing owners may wish to reduce their stake in a company—to **exit**—for a variety of reasons. Privatization is driven by the belief that privately owned companies perform better, and also by the need of governments for cash (privatizations worldwide have raised over $1 trillion for the governments concerned). Family owners may wish to diversify their wealth. And LBO and venture capital partnerships who feel they have done all they can for the company in question may wish to cash out their investment so that they can reinvest in other companies.[19]

In all these cases, the public equity market provides existing owners with liquidity: it enables them to turn their assets into cash. And, by providing price discovery, it establishes a value for the company being sold.

Facilitating the Investment of Internal Funds.   As we have seen, because external financing is so expensive, corporations finance most of their investment out of internally generated funds. Shareholders are willing to let the companies they own reinvest profits rather than pay them out as dividends because successful investment should raise the price of their shares by more than the dividends they have sacrificed. For this to work, however, the price discovery function of the market must assess correctly the value added by the investment. Moreover, shareholders may want to cash out their gains by selling some of their shares. But their ability to do so at a fair price depends on the liquidity of the market.

We have seen that the reinvestment of internal funds faces the "free cash flow" problem. It is the price discovery function of the equity market that reveals the existence of the problem when share prices rise by less than the amount invested. And it is the liquidity of the market, by opening the way for a hostile takeover, that provides an antidote. In this way, the public equity market polices the efficiency of investment of internal funds.

Market Discipline.   In a more general sense, a well-functioning public equity market is a powerful instrument of discipline. The price discovery of the market evaluates not only investments but also business strategies and the competence of management. For example, when a company engages in an ill-considered merger or acquisition, the market value of the combined company will drop to below the sum of the values of the two separate companies. This is what happened when AT&T acquired a computer company and when Daimler acquired Chrysler. Another example: when an incompetent manager is replaced, the market value of a company soars. By providing a clear signal of the consequences of actions and policies for the value of a company, the public equity market provides those in control with guidance. Moreover, if those in control are themselves large shareholders, they have a strong incentive to listen.

We have seen, then, that the primary function of the public equity market is to facilitate changes in ownership of one kind or another. It does this both through the primary market and through the secondary market. In the primary market, shares of a company are offered to investors for the first time. In the secondary market, shares already in the hands of investors change hands.

---

[19] We shall have more to say on this presently.

The Primary Market

The Different Types of Offering.   There are several different types of offering in the primary market. In an **initial public offering (IPO)**, a company that has until then been privately owned sells shares to the public for the first time and so becomes publicly traded. Typically, only part of the total number of shares are sold, with the original owners retaining the rest. In a **secondary offering**, some of the shares that had been retained by the original owners or shares that have been created and given to managers are sold to the public. In a **follow-on offering**, a company that is already publicly traded (has already undergone an IPO) creates additional shares and sells them to the public.[20] That part of the shares that has been sold to the public and is in the hands of investors, as opposed to shares that remain in the hands of the original owners or managers, is called the **float**.

The Various Methods Used in the Primary Market.   In different countries and at different times, various methods have been used to sell shares to the public. In the United States, the favored method is underwriting by a securities firm (we saw the details in Chapter 11). In the United Kingdom, securities laws require that follow-on offerings be offered first to existing shareholders in what is called a "rights issue." In Germany shares are distributed by a bank, acting as a broker, for a commission. In France, the shares are sold to the public through an auction, like government securities in the United States.

The IPO.   Historically, IPOs have accounted for about half the total amount of new share issues in the United States. This proportion rose in the late 1990s with the IPO boom associated with the Internet bubble (see Exhibit 15.3).

A company wishing to "go public" solicits proposals from a number of underwriters. The underwriter that wins this "bake-off" negotiates with the company a tentative price range for the offering. Pricing is particularly important for the success of an IPO and particularly difficult because there is no existing market price to provide guidance. The underwriter then holds a series of "roadshow" meetings with institutional investors that might be interested in purchasing blocks of shares. In this way, the underwriter "builds a book" of tentative orders from these investors. The day before the actual IPO, and based on the success of the roadshow, the underwriter finally sets the issue price.

Typically, the issue is greatly oversubscribed: that is, the underwriter has many more orders at the price that was set than can be filled with the number of shares available. The underwriting firm therefore allocates the issue, usually among its best institutional customers.

IPO Underpricing.   There is considerable evidence that IPOs are underpriced—that they are sold *on average* at a price below their "fair" value. As a result, a considerable part of the value of the issue is "left on the table" by the issuer (given away to investors). **IPO underpricing** seems to be quite general. It has been observed in different countries that use different methods of distribution (not just underwriting), and it has been observed in different time periods going back to the late nineteenth century.

initial public offering (IPO)
An issue of stock by a company selling equity for the first time ("going public").

secondary offering
The sale to the public of shares retained by original owners or created and given to managers.

follow-on offering
The sale to the public of additional newly created shares by a company that is already public.

float
The shares of a company in the hands of the public, as opposed to the original owners or managers.

IPO underpricing
The practice of pricing IPOs below the market price expected to obtain after issue.

---

[20] In practice, there is some confusion in the terminology. Follow-on offering are sometimes called secondary offerings, and the term "IPO" is sometimes used for all share offerings.

EXHIBIT 15.3   The Volume of IPOs

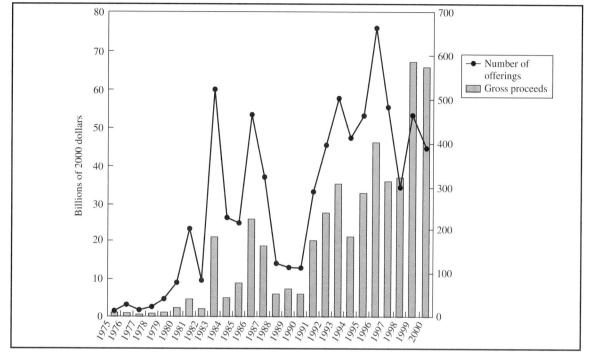

Source: Ritter (2001).

Many explanations have been offered for this phenomenon, and most of them focus on the uncertainty about the ultimate valuation that the market will place on the stock. Some researchers suggest that average underpricing is a premium to investors to induce them to take on the risk. Other researchers argue that underpricing pays off in reputational benefits to both underwriter and issuer. If the stock does well after it is issued, the underwriter will find it easier to sell other IPOs and the issuer will find it easier to sell secondary and follow-on issues.

Whatever the reasons, underpricing constitutes a significant cost to the issuer. Added to the already high explicit costs of underwriting, it can make the total cost of an IPO as much as 30% of the amount raised. Why are issuers willing to pay so much? What are the benefits the public equity market offers them? We have already seen the answer—liquidity and price discovery.

Original owners who sell most of their stake convert an illiquid asset into cash. Those who sell only part of their stake convert an illiquid asset into one that can be realized relatively easily through a secondary offering. Typically, the shares sold in an IPO amount to a third or less of the shares outstanding after the issue.

Going public provides a market valuation of the company's value: it is hard to know how much a privately held company is worth. As we have seen, the market's valuation provides valuable feedback to the company's managers and imposes discipline on the management of the company.

The Secondary Market

The Importance of a Well-Functioning Secondary Market. A well-functioning secondary market is particularly important for public equity. There are a number of reasons for this.

- Unlike debt securities, equities have no maturity date: they are perpetual. The only way for investors to liquidate their investment in equities is by selling them to someone else.
- As we have seen, because of the reinvestment of internal funds, much of the return on equities comes in the form of appreciation rather than in the form of dividends. To realize this return, investors need to be able to sell some of their stock.
- The value of equities is much more uncertain than the value of debt and fluctuates constantly as circumstances change. Because of the uncertainty, investors need to have a panic button: they must be able to sell easily when they feel uncomfortable with continuing to hold a stock.
- We have seen that arm's-length investors prefer exit to voice: if they are unhappy with how a company is being managed, it makes more sense for them to sell than to try to change things. Therefore, they will feel comfortable holding a stock only if they can sell it easily if they want to.

The Conditions for a Well-Functioning Secondary Market.   As we saw in Chapter 11, by a well-functioning secondary market we mean good liquidity and good price discovery. That is, it should be possible to buy or sell quickly without sacrifice. And it should be possible to buy or sell at a fair price. To a large extent, good liquidity and good price discovery are consequences of the actions of market participants themselves.

Liquidity Traders and Information Traders.   We saw in Chapter 11 that there are two types of traders—*information traders* and *liquidity traders*. Information traders trade when, based on their information, they believe that the market price differs from the fair price. If they think the market price is too low (below the fair price), they buy in the expectation that the market price will rise to the fair price, enabling them to sell at a profit. Similarly, if they think the market price is too high (above the fair price) they sell short, expecting that the market price will fall, enabling them to cover at a profit.

Liquidity traders are those traders who trade for reasons other than a belief that the market price is wrong. They buy because they think a company is a good long-term investment, or they sell because they are unhappy with its prospects. They buy because they wish to increase the amount of stocks in their portfolios, or they sell because they need the cash. They buy because they wish to gain control of a company, or they sell because they wish to pull out.

Both liquidity traders and information traders contribute to the liquidity of the market. To a large extent, liquidity traders provide liquidity to one another, because the trades of liquidity traders tend to offset one another. When some want to buy, others want to sell. When the trades of liquidity traders do not offset one another and a liquidity imbalance results, then the market price will be pushed away from the fair price. Information traders will begin trading to profit from this. Trading by information traders will offset the excess

of buying or selling by liquidity traders, so reducing the liquidity imbalance. In doing this, trading by information traders will also drive the price back towards the fair price.

Another reason for information traders to enter the market is new information coming into their hands that suggests that the current market price differs from the fair price. That is, they will enter when the fair price changes but the market price lags. For example, if good news about a stock suggests the price should be higher, they will buy. Their buying will of course push the market price up towards the fair price. In this way, the trading of information traders incorporates new information into prices and ensures liquidity traders that they are buying or selling at a fair price.

For information trading to be profitable, however, there must be an underlying base of liquidity trading. A market consisting purely of information traders would not work. For example, if you were an information trader and I, another information trader, wanted to buy from you at the market price, you would be a fool to sell to me. The only reason I could possibly want to buy is because I had information suggesting that the market price was too low.

So it is the presence in the market of liquidity traders that makes it attractive to information traders, and it is the presence in the market of information traders that improves the quality of the market for liquidity traders. The key to a well-functioning secondary market, therefore, is to create conditions that are friendly both to information traders and to liquidity traders.

Transactions Costs and Market Structure.   Information traders are particularly sensitive to transactions costs. They buy and sell constantly, typically holding a position for only a short time. And many of their plays rely on relatively small discrepancies between market price and fair price. For such trading to be profitable, the cost of the transaction needs to be sufficiently small. For example, say the discrepancy between market price and fair price is 2%, and the cost of a "round-trip" transaction (a purchase and a sale) is 3%. It will not be worth an information trader's while to trade on the 2% discrepancy.

Moreover, if transactions costs are high, information trading will be unprofitable in general. Discrepancies large enough to provide a profit are unlikely to be sufficiently common to make the profession of information trader an attractive one. With information trading unprofitable, there will be few information traders.

With few information traders, price discovery will be poor and liquidity imbalances common. Liquidity traders will suffer from this: they will not be assured of a fair price, and they will find it difficult to buy or sell quickly or in quantity without incurring a loss. The difficulty of liquidity trading will make holding equities less attractive, and their price will therefore be lower. A lower price makes the issuing of equities in the public equity market less attractive to issuers, so that fewer companies will be publicly traded.

Low transactions costs, therefore, are essential for a well-functioning secondary market. The level of transactions costs largely depends on the structure of the market. In Chapter 17 we shall look at the structure of securities markets—at exchanges, trading systems, and systems of clearing and settlement.

Corporate Governance and Market Regulation.   Most liquidity trading comes from arm's-length investors. Relationship investors need to hold onto their shares in order to exert the control they need to protect their investment. They may buy initially to gain a sufficient

stake in the company, and they will sell when they wish to end their involvement. However, in between they will not be doing much trading. Relationship investors rely on voice rather than exit to protect their interests.

Consequently, for there to be a large volume of liquidity trading, a large part of the float must be in the hands of arm's-length investors. This will be the case only in those public equities markets that are friendly to arm's-length investors. As we have seen, the markets that are friendly to arm's-length investors are those that enjoy good corporate governance—some combination of legal protection and effective monitoring by interested parties. Such markets are more liquid, and because liquidity is a necessary condition for information trading, they also enjoy better price discovery.

Arm's-length investors require legal protection not only as investors, but also as traders. Because individually they trade only a little, it is not worth their while to police the market themselves to ensure they are not being cheated. Consequently, they need effective market regulation to assure them that they are getting a fair deal when they trade their stocks.

We shall look in detail at the regulation of securities markets in Chapter 20. We shall learn there of another problem associated with equities markets that is of concern to all investors—their propensity to crash. Here, too, regulation can be helpful in minimizing the damage.

The Importance of Information

Good information is essential both in the primary market and in the secondary market. Assessing the value of equity is much harder than assessing the value of debt because the former does not involve a promise of specific payments. Investors consequently need good information on issuing companies, as well as on their industries and on the economy, to assess the likely future profitability of these companies, and so the return on their stocks. Investors also need information on current market prices, which can change rapidly, in order to manage their portfolios.

As we saw in Chapter 14, information is something of a public good. Rather than each investor separately seeking out his or her own information, it makes economic sense to gather and assess information once and provide it to all. Since the ownership of equities is much more dispersed than the ownership of debt, the argument is even stronger here. As with debt, there are a variety of arrangements, public and private, to provide information to investors.

In the United States, companies that issue equities to the public and whose stocks trade publicly are required to register with the SEC and to provide a considerable amount of information about their finances and plans. Most other countries have similar, although often less stringent, requirements. Disclosure is required when the stock is first issued in an IPO and then periodically thereafter as long as the stock is publicly traded. The exchanges where stocks trade often impose their own disclosure requirements, frequently more rigorous than those required by government regulators. The exchanges also provide current information on market prices for the stocks that they trade.[21] The raw information

---

[21] We shall have more to say about exchanges and price information in Chapters 17 and 20.

provided by issuers and exchanges is processed and made available to the public by a host of media— newspapers and periodicals, radio and TV, and the Internet.

There is a great deal of room for interpretation of this information. That is one reason why equities are traded much more actively than debt securities. Even given the same information, some investors may consider the stock of a particular company overpriced, while others see it as a bargain. Differences of opinion not only make horse races, they also generate trading volume on the stock exchange.

With interpretation and judgement so important, there is a considerable demand for analysis and investment advice. This demand is satisfied, abundantly, by brokers and their in-house analysts, by media analysts and commentators, by the authors of investment newsletters, and by all sorts of investment advisers. Many investors, large and small, decide to leave the decisions to the experts and let others, such as private bankers and mutual fund managers, manage their portfolios for them.[22]

PRIVATE EQUITY

private equity
Equity sold privately (not through a public issue) to relationship investors.

As we have seen, equity financing is problematic, and arm's-length equity financing especially so. To ensure arm's-length investors in the public equity market a reasonable return, we need effective mechanisms of corporate governance. There is, however, another part of the market for equity that addresses the inherent problems of equity financing in a different way. The market for **private equity** is a market for relationship equity financing. Rather than on relying on others to protect their interests, providers of private equity do their own monitoring and control.

Types of Private Equity Financing

private placement equity market
Equity sold mainly to institutional investors in a way that does not constitute a public issue.

In the most general sense, private equity is any equity that does not involve a sale of stock to the general public and therefore is not regulated by the SEC or equivalent agency. Under this general heading there are several different and quite distinct submarkets.

Private Placements.   As with debt, there is a **private placement market for equity** in which firms sell stock directly to institutional investors.[23] Much of this today takes place under Rule 144a. Functionally, this market is much like the public equity market—more arm's length than relationship. The motivation, as with private placement debt, is mainly to avoid the delays and especially the disclosure requirements involved in SEC registration. Many of the issuers are non-U.S. companies, often traded publicly in their own countries. As with debt, we can see the private placement equity market as an alternative to the offshore market—the **Euroequity market**—which fills much the same need.

Euroequity market
Market for equities sold in the issuer's home currency, but outside the issuer's domestic market.

Angel Investing.   There is also an informal private equity market in which agents sell unregistered equity to institutional investors and to wealthy individuals. Direct equity

---

[22] See Chapter 10 on money management and advice.

[23] See Chapter 14 on the private placement market.

angel investing
Direct private purchase of equity in small companies by wealthy individuals.

investment in small private companies by wealthy individuals is known as **angel investing**. One study suggests that there are as many as 250,000 angel investors in the United States investing as much as $20 billion a year in some 30,000 companies. The typical investment is small—about $50,000.[24]

The Organized Private Equity Market.   Finally, there is the **organized private equity market**. In contrast with the informal market, this market is intermediated. Institutional investors and wealthy individuals provide funds to specialized financial intermediaries, and these intermediaries take significant, often controlling, positions in private companies. In some cases, the purpose of the transaction is purely to provide financing, with control by the intermediary only necessary to protect its interests as a provider of funds. Usually, however, control by the intermediary is itself a major benefit of the transaction, with the intermediary bringing management skills to the enterprise that the original owners lack.

organized private equity market
A market in which specialized intermediaries invest in private companies.

There are several categories of organized private equity—the difference being in the type of company in which the intermediary invests:

venture capital
Equity funding of startups by specialized intermediaries.

- **Venture capital** involves investment in startups—very new companies that often consist of little more than an idea and a business plan.
- *Expansions* are investments in midsized companies (between $25 million and $500 million in sales) that are established but require further financing and improved management to reach the next level.
- *Buyouts and buyins* are takeovers of private companies by their managers and by outsiders, respectively, with the intention of reorganization to improve profitability (they are much like the LBOs discussed earlier, except that they involve private rather than publicly traded companies).
- *Vulture capital* involves investment in firms in financial distress by "turnaround partnerships" with the intention of bringing these firms back to health or at least salvaging the maximum possible value from the wreck.

How Private Equity Works

The Intermediaries.   Private equity intermediaries are specialized financial institutions that raise funds from investors and invest in the equity of private companies. Some of these intermediaries are independent; others are subsidiaries ("captives") of nonfinancial corporations or of financial institutions such as banks, securities firms, and insurance companies.[25] In the United States and other English-speaking countries, independent intermediaries predominate, while in Germany and in Japan captives are much more important.

---

[24] The study, by the University of New Hampshire Center for Venture Research was quoted in *The Economist*, November 11, 1997.

[25] In the United States, there is also a group of intermediaries regulated by and receiving funding from the Small Business Administration, a government agency. These Small Business Investment Companies, first established in 1958, accounted for about a third of all private equity in the 1970s, but today they are of negligible importance.

The way private equity intermediaries are organized in a given country depends on regulations and on tax laws. In the United States and other English-speaking countries, the great majority are organized as limited partnerships.

The Limited Partnership.   In a **limited partnership**, there are two classes of partners—**limited partners** and **general partners**. The limited partners are purely investors: they provide most of the funding but exercise no control over the enterprise (they are arm's-length investors).[26] The general partners are the ones who run the show. They select which companies to invest in, and it is they who actively monitor and manage those companies.

Given the lack of control of the limited partners, what ensures that they receive a fair return on their investment? This looks a lot like our old friend, the corporate governance problem. In this case, the solution is to structure the deal in such a way that the "insiders"—the general partners—have the best interests of the arm's-length investors at heart. The structure that has evolved to do this combines a number of elements.

- The general partners are required to provide a part of the financing themselves, so that a significant amount of their own money is at risk alongside that of their investors.
- The lifetime of the partnership is limited—usually to 10 or 12 years. At the end of that time, the assets of the partnership must be liquidated and the proceeds distributed among the partners (the limited partners receive nothing until then). This imposes a deadline for performance, and it avoids the potential problems of trying to calculate the profits of an ongoing enterprise.
- The general partners are paid for performance rather than for effort. They receive modest compensation during the life of the partnership, and most of their reward is in the form of a share of the profits on liquidation—typically 20%.[27]
- The general partners are typically members of a management firm that specializes in setting up limited partnerships.[28] Their ability to find investors for new partnerships depends on their past success and on how well they have treated their investors in the past. That is, the general partners do repeat business, and they consequently have a reputational incentive to do their best for their investors.

Investors and Market Organization.   The largest category of investors, of limited partners, in private equity partnerships in the United States is pension funds. At the end of 1996, pension funds provided 40% of total funding and 50% of new funding. Other large categories, each providing about 10% of funding, are endowments and foundations, bank holding companies, and wealthy individuals. Smaller amounts are provided by life insurance companies, securities firms, and nonfinancial corporations. Typically there are some 10 to 30 limited partners in a partnership, each contributing a minimum of $1 million.[29]

---

[26] Because the limited partners exercise no control, their liability is limited to their investment in the partnership (hence limited partners).

[27] This is much larger than their share in the initial capital.

[28] In venture capital their background is likely to be in industry or technology, in other types of private equity they are more likely to have a background in finance.

[29] Like hedge funds, limited partnership must be restricted either to no more than 99 partners or, since 1997, to no more than 499 partners who are "qualified investors." The latter are either institutions with over $100 million in assets or individuals with liquid assets of $5 million or more.

Margin notes:

limited partnership
A legal form of organization that offers tax and incentive advantages.

limited partners
Partners in a limited partnership that are purely passive investors.

general partners
Partners in a limited partnership that exercise control.

The investment is, in principle, illiquid for the 10- to 12-year life of the partnership. However, private equity intermediaries known as "secondary market funds" specialize in buying out institutional investors that wish to exit a limited partnership, so providing some liquidity to the market.

Advisers, mainly securities firms and banks, help investors find suitable limited partnerships in which to invest. Some of them have recently begun to offer "funds of funds" that accept investments from their institutional and private banking customers and invest in turn in limited partnerships—a second level of intermediation. The advantage of the "fund of funds" is that it provides some diversification and relieves the investor of the problem of choosing limited partnerships. It also requires a smaller minimum investment (typically $0.5 million) and provides better liquidity (typically a 5-year commitment). On the other side of the market, there are placement agents who help new private equity partnerships find investors (limited partners).

The Portfolio Companies.   A typical private equity partnership will invest in 10 to 50 portfolio companies, adding perhaps 2 to 15 to its portfolio in each of its initial years, depending on opportunities. In each company that it adds to its portfolio, it purchases an equity stake that it hopes to be able to resell eventually at a substantial profit. The partnership is therefore looking for companies to which it can add the most value, through financing and management, over the lifetime of its investment.

Companies seeking private capital are represented by placement agents who advise them and help them to find investors. The agents submit proposals to potential investors, who screen them very carefully: some 99% of venture capital proposals, for example, are rejected at this stage. If a proposal passes the initial screening, the private equity partnership begins a thorough and painstaking analysis of the company's prospects. Since there is typically little or no public information on such companies the task is onerous and costly.

For those companies in which it decides to invest, the private equity partnership provides financing and expertise in exchange for a substantial equity interest, with seats on the board. The form of the equity stake is usually convertible preferred stock with voting rights. To align the interests of the managers of the enterprise with those the investing partnership, the managers too receive a significant equity stake in the company, and this accounts for a large part of their compensation.

Private equity is a very expensive form of external financing. The original owners of the company must compensate investors for the substantial costs of screening and monitoring, and they must also give up a large part of their control over the company. Private equity financing is therefore a last resort. A company will seek it only if it needs funds but is unable to borrow (enough) and if it cannot obtain equity financing in the public market.

The typical candidate is too risky for arm's-length debt. It is also unsuitable for relationship debt. Perhaps it lacks collateral or a reliable cash flow. Or perhaps control by a lender would be fatal to the company's growth prospects because it would inhibit risk taking. With debt ruled out, we are left with equity financing. However, the company is not eligible for the public equity market because it is too small and because it lacks a sufficient track record. As we saw earlier, the types of company that fit this description include startups (venture capital), midsize companies seeking to expand (expansions), mid sized companies or divisions of companies being sold off (buyouts and buyins), and companies in financial distress (vulture capital).

Exit Mechanisms.   It is in the nature of private equity investment to be of limited duration. If the investment is made in the framework of a limited partnership, the investment has to be liquidated by the time the partnership is wound up. However, even apart from this, there is good reason to limit the life of the investment. Private equity investors earn a return on their expertise. Once they have done what they can for a particular company, it makes sense for them to move on and apply their expertise elsewhere.

exit mechanisms
Ways for private
equity investors to
sell their stake in
a company.

There are three possible ways for private equity investors to end their involvement in a company—three possible **exit mechanisms**. The first is to take the company public through an IPO. Private relationship investors sell out their stake to public arm's-length investors. The second form of exit is a "trade sale"—a sale of the company to a nonfinancial corporation, usually in the same industry. The purchasing corporation typically has a "strategic" interest in the company in question. The third form of exit is a sale to another private equity investor. In the second and third cases, one private relationship investor is replaced by another.

The most common exit mechanism for successful portfolio companies is the IPO. It is the form of exit that the original owners prefer, since it generally puts them back in control of the company. Sometimes, when a potential trade sale is more lucrative, the process of the IPO is halted before the stock is actually issued. An IPO involving part of the shares, or even an incomplete IPO process, facilitates a trade sale by providing some idea of the value of the company. For less successful portfolio companies, the most common exit is a private sale to another private equity investor.

The Significance of Private Equity

The Numbers.   The organized private equity market, negligible in 1980, has grown rapidly in the past two decades—especially in the United States. Most private equity investment in the United States involves venture capital or expansions, with the majority of the activity concentrated in the technology sector. Total financing provided by private equity investors has often matched and sometimes exceeded that from IPOs or from the junk bond market. For startups and midsized companies in particular, the role of private equity is even more important. Microsoft, Dell, and Genentech are among the major companies that relied heavily on private equity to get a start in life.

By year-end 1996, venture capital investments outstanding in the United States totaled some $200 billion. The impact is larger than this number suggests because of the relatively rapid turnover in venture capital investments. In 1999 and 2000, at the height of the Internet bubble, venture capital investment exploded: see Exhibit 15.4. The bursting of the bubble has resulted in overall losses for venture capitalists and a considerable cooling of enthusiasm.

Private equity in general and venture capital in particular are much bigger in the United States than in most other countries. In 1995 the size of the pool of private equity relative to GDP was nine times higher in the United States than in Asia and eight times higher than in Europe. Venture capital is significant in Britain, France, and Canada. But in other countries, what activity there is occurs mainly in buyouts and buyins: in continental Europe, much of this is in retailing. There is little venture capital in Germany and Japan: much of what is called venture capital there is really long-term bank debt.

EXHIBIT 15.4   Venture Capital Investment

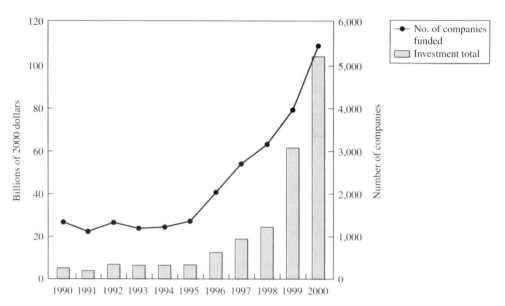

Source: National Venture Capital Association.

Why Is Private Equity so Big in the United States?   Several factors since the 1980s have contributed to the success of private equity in the United States. Changes in regulations and tax laws have increased the supply of potential investors. Most important was a 1979 ruling by the Department of Labor, the regulator of pension funds, that allowed the funds to invest a part of their portfolio in small and new companies.[30] Changes in regulations have also made it easier for banks and wealthy individuals to participate. And since most of the return from private equity investment comes in the form of capital gains, reductions in the tax rate on capital gains have helped too.

The creation of the limited partnership vehicle has been crucial because it avoids the double taxation implicit in the use of the corporate form. If an investment intermediary is set up as a corporation, the intermediary has to pay tax on all its income and its shareholders then have to pay tax again on the income that is distributed to them.[31] In contrast, a partnership pays no taxes itself: only the partners pay taxes.[32] As a result, the return to the investor is significantly greater.

We have seen that ease of exit is very important to the process of private equity investment. Because the *public* equity market is so well developed in the United States, exit through an IPO is relatively easy. In the NASDAQ, the United States has a well-developed

---

[30] This has also been a major stimulus to the IPO market.

[31] If the intermediary received its income from corporations in which it invested, these too would be paying taxes, so that we would have triple taxation.

[32] Similarly, mutual funds and SPVs are considered "conduits" for tax purposes and do not have to pay taxes themselves.

second-tier secondary market for public equity that trades shares of smaller and less mature companies that would not qualify for listing on the New York Stock Exchange. By increasing the liquidity of the stock of such companies and by providing price discovery, this market makes IPOs much easier and more attractive.

Private equity is less developed in most other countries because they lack one or more of the foregoing advantages. In some countries, there is a lack of potential investors in private equity intermediaries. Either pension funds and life insurance companies are not allowed to invest in private equity or, as in Germany and some other continental European countries, there are no pension funds at all.[33]

Some countries lack a suitable legal and tax framework. In Japan, for example, the limited partnership is not a recognized legal form; convertible preferred equity, the favored instrument for investment in portfolio companies does not exist; and, until recently, venture capitalists were not allowed seats on a portfolio company's board.

Many countries lack good exit mechanisms. In some, especially in continental Europe with its relatively underdeveloped public equity markets, exit through an IPO is difficult. Securities regulations can hamper the development of a second-tier secondary market. The Japanese and European attempts to imitate NASDAQ, called JASDAQ and EASDAQ, respectively, have both been failures. Where IPOs are difficult, exit is usually by trade sale, and it generally takes much longer than it does in the United States. For example, average time to exit in the United States is 5 to 7 years; in Japan, it is 29 years.

The public and private equity markets, therefore, offer different solutions to the corporate governance problem and perform different functions. The public equity market is an arm's-length market and relies heavily, but not exclusively, on legal protection for corporate governance. Its main function is to facilitate changes in ownership. The private equity market is a relationship market and relies on close monitoring by specialized intermediaries for corporate governance. It is an important source of funding for new and growing companies that have difficulty finding financing elsewhere.

SUMMARY

- The main issue with equity financing is ensuring a return to the provider of the financing. Without effective mechanisms of corporate governance, equity financing will not work.
- The owners of an enterprise have the final say on its management and the right to receive its residual earnings. By bearing the risk, they enable the enterprise to fulfill its contractual obligations more reliably.
- When shareholding is dispersed, small shareholders cannot be expected to exercise direct control over the enterprise themselves. Effective control is left in the hands of insiders, who tend to put their own interests first.
- The two possible mechanisms of corporate governance are legal protection and reliance on some party with the power and incentive to monitor on behalf of arm's-length investors.
- The effectiveness of legal protection varies from country to country. There is a strong correlation across countries between the effectiveness of legal protection and the extent of arm's-length shareholding.
- Germany and Japan have a tradition of monitoring by banks.

---

[33] Private pension plans are unfunded defined benefit plans. See Chapter 10 on pension funds.

- In the United States, monitoring was first undertaken by underwriters, but this system was destroyed by Depression era legislation.

- The absence of effective monitoring, large corporations were run for the benefit of their managers rather than for the benefit of their shareholders. The result was typified by the problem of free cash flow.

- The resulting inefficiency provided a profit opportunity and led to a wave of hostile takeovers and LBOs in the 1980s and early 1990s.

- Since then, the interests of managers have been aligned with those of shareholders through stock options. Some institutional investors have also become more assertive.

- Mechanisms of corporate governance vary across countries. Partly this is a result of legal and regulatory differences. Partly it is because there is no single best solution.

- The principal function of the market for public equity is to be a market for ownership. It offers liquidity and price discovery, making it easier to transfer the ownership of corporations.

- Ownership transactions include mergers, acquisitions, divestitures, privatizations, and exit.

- The market for public equity also facilitates the reinvestment of internal funds and imposes a sort of discipline on traded companies.

- A stock issue is an expensive source of funds, and the expense is increased considerably by the underpricing of IPOs.

- A well-functioning secondary market is particularly important for public equity. A well-functioning secondary market requires low transactions costs, good corporate governance, and effective market regulation.

- Good information is essential both in the primary market and in the secondary market.

- The market for private equity is a market for relationship equity financing. In the organized private equity market, investors provide funds to specialized financial intermediaries, and these intermediaries take significant, often controlling, positions in private companies.

- The majority of such intermediaries are organized as limited partnerships. In such a partnership, the general partners run the show, while the limited partners are purely investors. The partnership is structured to ensure that the general partners will act in the interests of their investors.

- Private equity is a very expensive form of external financing. It is therefore sought only by companies that are unable to borrow (enough) and lack access to the public equity market.

- Private equity, mostly in the form of venture capital, has been an important source of financing for the companies of the "new economy."

- Private equity is much more important in the United States than elsewhere. Many other countries lack a suitable regulatory environment and good exit mechanisms.

DISCUSSION QUESTIONS

1. How do providers of equity financing benefit debt holders, employees, suppliers, and customers? What are the conflicts of interest between equity holders and these other groups?

2. What are the advantages and disadvantages of dispersed shareholding?

3. Why does it make sense that the right to residual income and control go together? If they are separated, how does this affect the value of a claim to residual income? What are the implication for the equity market?

4. In Chapter 3 we saw why integration of the financial system is important for economic efficiency. How does the problem of free cash flow affect integration? How might its elimination affect the productivity of the economy? In light of your answer, should the government encourage or discourage LBOs?

5. Should institutional investors be "active investors" (intervene in the management of companies whose shares they own) or simply "vote with their feet" (sell companies they don't like)? What are the incentives? How are they affected by regulation? Should the government encourage or discourage active investing?

6. "The whole of the Industrial Revolution in the United Kingdom could have been financed by any one of several existing private fortunes. New industries were unable to find finance, even at rates exceeding 20%, when land-connected industries (agriculture, mining, brewing and milling) were able to command large amounts of capital with rates of return at or below zero."—M. M. Postan

   a. Explain how the foregoing quotation describes an example of the free cash flow problem.

   b. How does the problem of free cash flow affect the efficiency of the economy?

   c. How does the problem of free cash flow affect the adaptability of the economy?

   d. Given the difficulty of financing the new industries, an observer might have argued that the United Kingdom was suffering from too little saving and consequently too little investment. Would you agree?

7. Different types of shareholder may hold a large position in a firm's equity. For each of the following, what are their incentives to exercise effective control? What is their capacity to do so? Are their interests aligned with those of small shareholders?

   a. institutional investors (e.g., pension fund, mutual fund, investment fund)

   b. an LBO partnership

   c. an M-form (multidivisional) corporation

   d. a bank

   e. a family

   f. the government

8. The degree of managerial discretion, and so the possible extent of managerial misbehavior, depends on the economic circumstances of the firm.

   a. How will it depend on the degree of competition in product and input markets?

   b. How will it depend on the financing of the company: debt vs equity (leverage), long-term debt vs short-term debt?

9. In the advanced economies, there are two main systems of corporate governance. In the English-speaking countries, there is strong legal protection and shareholding is dispersed. In most other countries, legal protection is weak and concentrated shareholding is the rule.

   a. Compare the two common systems in terms of the protection they provide to both nonfinancial "stakeholders" (employees, suppliers, etc.) and arm's-length investors.

   b. What are the implications for the willingness of the two groups to commit resources to the enterprise?

   c. What are the implications of your answer to question 2 for the productive efficiency of the corporation?

   d. What are the implications of your answer to question 2 for the adaptability of the corporation in the face of changing economic conditions (for example, shifts in consumer demand that make some lines of business unprofitable)?

   e. How do they differ with respect to the need for information disclosure by companies? Restrictions on insider trading?

   f. How do they differ with respect to the need for a well-functioning secondary market? The importance of good price discovery and liquidity?

BIBLIOGRAPHY

De Long, J. Bradford. "Did J. P. Morgan's Men Add Value? A Historical Perspective on Financial Capitalism." Working paper no. 3426, National Bureau of Economic Research, August 1990.

Fenn, G. W., N. Liang and S.D. Prowse. "The Private Equity Market: An Overview." *Financial Markets, Institutions & Instruments* 6 no. 4 (1997): 1–105.

Garfinkel, Michelle R. "The Causes and Consequences of Leveraged Buyouts." *Economic Review of the Federal Reserve Bank of St. Louis*, September–October 1989, 23–34.

Hansmann, H. *The Ownership of Enterprise*. Cambridge, MA: Belknap Press of Harvard University Press, 1996.

Holmstrom, B., and S. N. Kaplan. "Corporate Governance and Merger Activity in the U.S.: Making Sense of the 1980s and 1990s." Department of Economics, M.I.T., Cambridge, MA, February 2001.

Jensen, Michael C. "Eclipse of the Public Corporation." *Harvard Business Review*, September–October 1989, 61–74.

———. "Corporate Control and the Politics of Finance." *Continental Bank: Journal of Applied Corporate Finance* 4 no. 2 (summer 1991), 13–33.

Kaplan, S. N., and P. Strömberg. "Venture Capitalists as Principals: Contracting, Screening, and Monitoring." Working paper no. W8202, National Bureau of Economic Research, April 2001.

La Porta, R., F. Lopez-de-Silanes, A. Shleifer, and R. W. Vishny. "Legal Determinants of External Finance." *Journal of Finance* 52 (1997): 1131–1150.

Megginson, W. L., and M. K. Boutchkova. "Privatization and the Rise of Global Capital Markets." *Financial Management*, winter 2000.

Mueller, D. C., and E. A. Reardon. "Rates of Return on Corporate Investment." *Southern Economic Journal*, 1993, 430–453.

Ritter, Jay R. "Some Factoids About the 2000 IPO Market." University of Florida, Gainesville, 2001.

Roe, M. J. *Strong Managers, Weak Owners: The Political Roots of American Corporate Finance.* Princeton, NJ: Princeton University Press, 1994.

Shleifer, A. and R. W. Vishny. "A Survey of Corporate Governance." *Journal of Finance* 52 (1997): 737–783.

Wurgler, J. "Financial Markets and the Allocation of Capital." *Journal of Financial Economics* 58, no. 1–2 (October–November 2000): 187–214.

KEY TERMS

corporate governance mechanisms
contractual relationship
ownership relationship
insiders
legal protection of shareholders
transparency
keiretsu
"money trust"
Securities and Exchange Act of 1934
multidivisional ("M-form") corporation

conglomerate
free cash flow
leveraged buyout (LBO)
LBO partnership
stock options
restructuring
privatization
exit
initial public offering (IPO)
secondary offering
follow-on offering
float

IPO underpricing
private equity
private placement equity market
Euroequity market
angel investing
organized private equity market
venture capital
limited partnership
limited partners
general partners
exit mechanisms

CHAPTER 16

THE DERIVATIVES MARKET: FUTURES, OPTIONS, AND SWAPS

When you finish this chapter you will understand:

- What futures, options, and swaps are and how they are traded
- How to use futures, options, and swaps to hedge against risk
- Why there are so many different hedging instruments
- Why the market for financial derivatives grew from nothing to over $100 trillion in only 30 years

forward transaction
A transaction in which two parties agree in advance on the terms of a trade to be executed later.

The financial system facilitates lending, payments, and trade in risk (insurance and forward transactions). We have seen how it facilitates lending. We have studied payments and insurance. In this chapter, we take a look at forward transactions and in particular at derivatives.

A **forward transaction** is one in which two parties agree in advance on the terms of a transaction to be executed later. As we saw in Chapter 1, forward transactions are like lending in that they involve promises, and they are subject to the same kinds of problem. We saw in Chapter 2 that the financial system provides solutions in two ways—through markets (for example, futures contracts in copper) and through intermediaries (for example, forward trading in foreign exchange with a bank).

forward trade

A trade in which the parties agree to trade at a specified time in the future, at a price set now.

There are two basic types of forward transaction—the forward trade and the derivative. In a **forward trade**, the parties agree to trade at a specified time in the future, at a price set now. One example is forward trading in commodities—copper, for example, as in our story in Chapter 1. Another example is forward trading in foreign exchange, which we discussed in Chapter 8.

derivative

A contract in which two parties agree to pay in the future sums that depend on the value then of some market price.

A **derivative** differs from a forward trade in that it involves only payments of money, with no delivery of any commodity or asset. With a derivative contract, the two parties agree that they will pay or receive from each other at a set time in the future certain sums of money. The amounts to be paid or received will depend on the value at that time of some market price. That is, the payments are *derivative* of the market price—hence the name.

In recent decades, the volume of derivative contracts created and traded by the financial system has grown enormously. New instruments have proliferated, and trading volume has exploded. The principal area of growth has been **financial derivatives**—derivatives based on financial prices such as interest rates, exchange rates, and stock prices. Thirty years ago financial derivatives did not even exist; today the amount outstanding is well over $100 trillion.

financial derivatives

Instruments involving forward transactions related to securities.

A major motivation for the creation and trading of derivatives is hedging. If you own a good that you are planning to sell in the future, you are said to be long the good or in a **long position**. If you expect to buy the good in the future, you are said to be short the good or in a **short position**. A rise in price means a gain if you are long and a loss if you are short. A fall in price means a loss if you are long and a gain if you are short. Longs and shorts can reduce the risk of a change in price by entering into forward transactions—either forward trades or derivatives.

long position

The position of owning a good that you plan to sell in the future.

We shall see that there are three main types of derivative—futures, options, and swaps. We shall examine each of these instruments in turn. In each case, our goal is to understand the nature of the instrument, how it is used, and how it is traded. We will then address some of the questions raised by the explosive growth of this market. Why has it grown so rapidly? Why do there exist different types of derivative that seem to do the same job? Why do some new derivative contracts succeed, while others fail? An appendix to the chapter reviews the pricing of futures, options, and swaps.

short position

The position of expecting to purchase the good in the future.

Our interest in this burgeoning market is twofold. First, its development has much to teach us about how financial markets work, about what succeeds, and about how new markets spring up. Second, the use of financial derivatives has transformed the way financial institutions deal with risk. We shall focus in this chapter on the instruments and markets themselves and leave the discussion of how financial institutions use the instruments to Chapter 18.

FUTURES

Let us begin our study of futures by looking at an example of how they can be used to hedge an underlying position.

Hedging with Futures: An Example

Valley Motors receives a shipment of cars from Japan on January 1. It has 3 months' trade credit from the manufacturer: that is, Valley must pay the ¥250 million cost of the cars on

April 1. To do so, it will have to buy yen on or before April 1. Consequently, Valley Motors is in a short position with respect to the Japanese yen. Potential fluctuations in the yen/dollar exchange rate expose Valley Motors to exchange rate risk: the auto dealer stands to gain if the yen falls relative to the dollar and to lose if the yen rises.

The Risk of an Unhedged Position.   To see how possible fluctuations in the exchange rate might affect the company's profits, let us consider three possible scenarios for the value of the yen on April 1. The exchange rate (the **spot** exchange rate) on January 1 is 125¥/$ or 0.80¢/¥.

spot price

The current market price for immediate delivery.

Scenario 1. The yen stays at 0.80¢. Valley will have to pay for the yen it needs

$$¥250 \text{ million} \times 0.80¢/¥ = \$2,000,000$$

Since it expects to sell the cars for $2,200,000, its profit will be

$$\$2,200,000 - \$2,000,000 = \$200,000$$

Scenario 2. The yen rises in value to 0.85¢. Valley will have to pay

$$¥250 \text{ million} \times 0.85¢/¥ = \$2,125,000$$

and its profit will be only $75,000.
Scenario 3. The yen falls in value to 0.75¢. Valley will have to pay

$$¥250 \text{ million} \times 0.75¢/¥ = \$1,875,000$$

and its profit will be $325,000.

futures price

A parameter of a futures contract that together with the market price determines the payoffs to the parties.

Hedging with a Forward Trade.   Valley Motors can hedge the risk of a change in the exchange rate by entering into a forward trade. It can agree with a bank now to purchase ¥250 million on April 1 for 0.81¢/¥, the current forward price for yen delivered on that date. If it does so, it will pay

$$¥250 \text{ million} \times 0.81¢/¥ = \$2,025,000$$

and its profit will be $175,000 regardless of the actual value of the yen on April 1.

notional amount

A parameter of a futures contract that determines the scale of the payoffs.

How a Futures Contract Works.   An alternative way for Valley Motors to hedge its exchange rate risk is by entering into futures contracts. Before we look at the details, let's see how a futures contract works.

There are two parties to a futures contract—the buyer and the seller. The buyer and the seller agree on a **futures price**, on a **notional amount**, and on a **maturity date**. Who pays and how much depends on what the actual price turns out to be on the maturity date. If the actual price turns out to be above the futures price, the seller must pay the buyer

maturity date

The time of final settlement of a futures contract.

$$(\text{actual price on maturity date} - \text{futures price}) \times \text{notional amount}$$

If the actual price turns out to be below the futures price, the buyer must pay the seller

$$(\text{futures price} - \text{actual price on maturity date}) \times \text{notional amount}$$

You can see that the buyer of a futures contract is in a long position with respect to the underlying price: the buyer stands to gain from a rise in the underlying price. Conversely, the seller is in a short position: the seller stands to gain from a fall in the underlying price.

Hedging with Futures.   Since Valley Motors has a short position in yen of ¥250 million, it can hedge by taking a long position of the same size in yen futures—that is, by becoming a buyer of yen futures contracts. The International Monetary Market (IMM) of the Chicago Mercantile Exchange offers such a contract. Each contract has a notional amount of ¥12.5 million, so Valley needs to buy 20 contracts to establish a long position of ¥250 million. The futures price for April 1 is 0.81¢/¥. Let us see the gains or losses from this futures position under our three exchange rate scenarios:

Scenario 1. The yen stays at its current price of 0.80¢. Since this is below the futures price, Valley Motors will have to pay

$$(0.81¢/¥ - 0.80¢/¥) \times ¥250 \text{ million} = \$25,000$$

Scenario 2. The yen rises in value to 0.85¢. Since this is above the futures price, Valley will receive

$$(0.85¢/¥ - 0.81¢/¥) \times ¥250 \text{ million} = \$100,000$$

Scenario 3. The yen falls in value to 0.75¢. Valley will have to pay

$$(0.81¢/¥ - 0.75¢/¥) \times ¥250 \text{ million} = \$150,000$$

To see what this means for the overall profit or loss from the sale by Valley Motors of the shipment of Japanese cars, look at Exhibit 16.1. You can see that the profit or loss on the futures position exactly compensates for the change in the profit on the underlying position. Consequently, the net profit remains the same, $175,000, whatever the actual price turns out to be. Notice that the effect is exactly the same as it would have been, had Valley purchased yen forward.

EXHIBIT 16.1   **The Effect of a Hedge in Futures on the Profits of Valley Motors**

	Actual Price April 1	Cost of ¥250m at Actual Price	Profit from Underlying Position (1)	Profit or Loss on Futures (2)	Net Profit: (1) + (2)
1.	0.80¢	$2.0m	$2.2m − 2.0m = $200,000	−$25,000	$200,000 − $25,000 = $175,000
2.	0.85¢	$2.125m	$2.2m − 2.125m = $75,000	$100,000	$75,000 + $100,000 = $175,000
3.	0.75¢	$1.875m	$2.2m − $1.875m = $325,000	−$150,000	$325,000 − 150,000 = $175,000

The Futures Price

How is the futures price determined? Why, in our example, is it $0.81¢/¥$ rather than some other value?

A futures contract is, in essence, a wager. Valley Motors, the buyer, is betting that the price will go up; the seller, whoever it is, is betting that the price will go down. *The futures price is the price at which the market considers this to be a fair wager.*[1] At this value of the futures price, the market believes the expected gain from a rise in price to be just balanced by the expected gain from a fall in price. The value of the futures price is such that, at the margin, traders are equally willing to take either side of the wager.

Notice that neither party to the futures contract pays or receives anything for entering into this wager.[2] This is because the market value of a futures contract at its initiation is exactly zero. In the market's estimation, the expected gains and losses exactly offset one another. The value of any fair wager is zero. For example, suppose you wagered $1 on the flip of a coin. Neither party would pay or receive anything for entering into this wager precisely because the wager is fair.

The possibility of arbitrage between futures prices, forward prices, and spot prices enforces certain relationships between them. The details are explained in the Appendix to this chapter.

How the Futures Market Works

futures commission merchant (FCM)
A securities firm that acts as a broker in the futures market.

To buy the contracts it needs, Valley places an order with its **futures commission merchant (FCM)**—a securities firm that offers trading services in futures and options. The FCM passes the order on to a **floor broker** on the trading floor of the exchange. The floor broker goes to the yen trading pit and joins in the open-outcry auction to acquire the 20 contracts. He can accept the most current offer price, he can wait for it to come down, or he can call out a price at or above the current bid price in the hope that it will be accepted.

floor broker
A broker on the floor of an exchange who fills orders for customers of the exchange.

In any event, the floor broker will quickly close a deal with one of the other brokers. This may be another floor broker, representing a customer wishing to sell futures contracts, or it may be a **local**. Locals are brokers who trade on the floor of the exchange on their own account rather than filling orders for others, and they play an essential role in the functioning of the exchange.

locals
Brokers who trade on the floor of an exchange on their own accounts.

The Role of the Locals.   It is the locals who provide the market with liquidity. For example, if a temporary excess of buyers drives the futures price above its fair value, locals will step in to sell, expecting the price to fall later, making them a profit. Their selling will drive the price back to its fair value. The danger for the locals is that they may mistake a rush of buying driven by new information for a temporary liquidity imbalance. If they sell in this case, the price will not fall later, as they expect, and they will take a loss.[3]

---

[1] The futures price is a lot like the odds quoted by bookmakers on a horserace or other sporting event.

[2] There are, of course, transactions costs to both parties in the form of commissions and fees. However, they do not pay *each other* anything for entering into the agreement.

[3] The danger is that they may confuse information trading for liquidity trading—the same danger that dealers face in a dealer market (see Chapter 11).

To protect themselves against such mistakes, locals invest heavily in information. They want to be the first to know when something happens to affect the fair price. Having good information, they will themselves be active information traders. For example, news of an increase in the Japanese trade surplus will cause locals to buy yen contracts in the expectation that the futures price will soon rise. Their doing so will *cause* the price to rise. So locals perform a second important function: they ensure that new information is reflected quickly in the futures price.

Replacement Risk and Exchange Guarantees.   The broker representing Valley Motors has purchased 20 contracts from a broker representing Northwest Lumber. In principle, Valley is now protected against a rise in the yen, and Northwest, which is expecting to receive payment in yen in April, is protected against a fall.

This protection, of course, depends on both parties fulfilling their obligations. Suppose, however, that a month after the contracts are written, Northwest goes out of business and is no longer able to fulfill its part of the bargain. Valley must now scramble to replace its contracts with Northwest with contracts with someone else. The futures price might have risen in the meantime, and Valley might have to enter into new contracts on terms less favorable to it.

For example, suppose the futures price for April 1 has risen in the meantime to 0.83¢. Valley's loss is the difference between its payoff under the new contracts and what would have been its payoff under the contracts it had with Northwest. Suppose, for example, that the actual price turns out to be 0.85¢/¥. Valley's payoff will now be

$$(0.85¢/¥ - 0.83¢/¥) \times ¥250 \text{ million} = \$50,000$$

instead of

$$(0.85¢/¥ - 0.81¢/¥) \times ¥250 \text{ million} = \$100,000$$

In fact, whatever the actual price turns out to be, its loss will be

$$(0.83¢/¥ - 0.81¢/¥) \times ¥250 \text{ million} = \$50,000$$

replacement risk
The risk that a counterparty will fail to execute an agreed transaction, leaving you to find another deal.

The risk of such a loss on the original contracts through a default by a counterparty is called **replacement risk**.

To protect both parties against replacement risk, the exchange guarantees fulfillment of all contracts. If Northwest defaults, the exchange will ensure that Valley bears no loss; if Valley defaults, the exchange will ensure that Northwest bears no loss.[4]

Because the exchange guarantees fulfillment, traders do not need to check the credit of their counterparty each time they strike a deal. This greatly reduces the cost of trading, and it makes the exchange a much more attractive place to trade. That means more volume and more commissions. So it pays the exchange to provide the guarantee.

---

[4] In reality, each party's FCM guarantees its fulfillment. The exchange guarantees fulfillment by FCMs.

However, the guarantee exposes the exchange itself to replacement risk. Exchanges have developed procedures to protect themselves against this risk.

Daily Settlement and Marking to Market. The exchange can eliminate replacement risk by requiring traders to pay their losses day by day. This is called **daily settlement**. Exhibit 16.2 shows how this works in the case of our example.

daily settlement

Daily payment of gains or losses on a futures contract.

On January 3, the futures price rises to 0.82¢. If Northwest were to default on its contracts now, the cost of replacing it with a new counterparty would be

$$0.82¢/¥ - 0.81¢/¥ = \$25,000$$

So the exchange requires Northwest to pay Valley the $25,000 immediately. That way, if Northwest defaults, there will be no loss.

marking to market

Daily repricing and rewriting of futures contracts to the current futures price.

Since Northwest has already compensated Valley for the change in the futures price, we need to change the contract between them accordingly. Doing this is called **marking to market**. This means that the original contract is canceled and a new one is written at the current futures price of 0.82¢. Valley is now a buyer on ¥250 million of contracts at a futures price of 0.82¢, and Northwest is a seller at this futures price.

This procedure of daily settlement and marking to market continues day by day. On January 4, the futures price falls back to 0.81¢, so Valley pays Northwest $25,000. (When the price falls, it is Northwest that stands to lose from a default by Valley.) On January 5, the futures price falls another 0.02¢, so Valley must pay another $50,000. On January 6, the futures price rises 0.01¢, so Northwest pays Valley $25,000. Each day, with daily settlement, the exchange marks the contracts to market. This procedure continues day by day until the contracts expires on April 1.

The final column in Exhibit 16.2 shows the accumulated payments from Northwest to Valley up to that day. You can see that this amount depends on the difference between the futures price on that day and the futures price when the contracts were first written. For example, on January 4, the futures price is the same as it was on January 1, so the accumulated payment is zero. On January 6, the futures price is 0.01¢ lower than the price on

EXHIBIT 16.2   Daily Settlement

	Futures Price for April 1	Valley Motors Pays	Northwest Lumber Pays	Accumulated Payment to Valley Motors
Jan. 1	0.81			
Jan. 2	0.81			
Jan. 3	0.82		$25,000	$25,000
Jan. 4	0.81	$25,000		0
Jan. 5	0.79	$50,000		−$50,000
Jan. 6	0.80		$25,000	−$25,000
⋮	⋮			⋮
April 1	0.85			$100,000

January 1, so the accumulated payment is $-\$25,000$ (Valley has paid a net total of $25,000 to Northwest).

At the maturity date, the futures contract is marked to market for the last time at the actual spot price on that day.[5] As it happens, the spot price is 0.85¢, as in our scenario 2. The final futures price, therefore, is set to 0.85¢. Since the final futures price is 0.85¢, the accumulated payment to Valley is $100,000 (see Exhibit 16.2).

You can see that the complicated arrangement of daily settlement and marking to market produces the same payoff in the end as simply settling up when the contracts mature.[6] There is a big difference, however, in replacement risk. Doing nothing until the contracts mature exposes the parties (or the exchange) to replacement risk. Daily settlement and marking to market eliminate that risk.

Marking to market has additional advantages. It makes bookkeeping much easier. The exchange has no need to keep track of many different contracts, each written at a different price. At any given time, all the contracts outstanding will have been marked to the current futures price and will therefore be identical. As we shall see, marking to market also helps liquidity.

Margin Requirements.   Of course daily settlement eliminates replacement risk only if the parties actually pay up. To ensure that they do, the exchange requires that each of them post collateral. In our example, Valley must put up a **margin** of 20% of the face value of the yen contracts it buys, or $400,000. This covers any possible loss to the exchange if Valley fails to settle, as long as the futures price has fallen by no more than 20% (that is, as long as it is no lower than 0.64¢). Northwest must also put up a margin of $400,000. This covers the exchange in the case of a default by Northwest as long as the futures price has risen by no more than 20% (that is, is no higher than 0.96¢).[7]

Each day, the exchange debits the amount of the daily settlement from the loser's **margin account** and credits it to the winner's. For example, on January 3, it credits Valley with $25,000 (raising its margin account to $425,000) and debits Northwest for the same amount (lowering its margin account to $375,000).

If Valley's margin account falls below a critical level (called the **maintenance margin**—usually 75% of the initial margin), it receives a **margin call** from its FCM demanding more collateral. If Valley fails to pay up immediately, its position will be closed out (we will see how in a moment). Proceeding in this way minimizes any risk to the exchange of a default by Valley Motors.

For many contracts, there is an additional safeguard. The exchange sets a limit on how far the contract price may move in any one day. If the price reaches that limit, trading stops

margin
Cash or collateral provided by a customer to a broker to protect the broker from loss on a contract.

margin account
The amount of margin that a customer has with a broker.

maintenance margin
Predetermined level of a margin account that must be maintained by the client.

margin call
A broker's request for more collateral to bring a customer's margin account up to maintenance margin.

---

[5] In reality, currency contracts are settled by delivery rather than by cash settlement. That is, if the contract is allowed to continue to maturity, the seller is actually obliged to deliver currency to the buyer. Arbitrage between the spot market and the futures market ensures that the futures price equals the spot price on the date of maturity.

[6] The payoff is not exactly the same because of interest costs. The timing of the payments over the life of the contract differs between daily settlement and settlement on expiration. So the interest earned or lost on the payments also differs.

[7] Actually each of the parties must put up a margin with its FCM. The FCM in turn must put a margin with the exchange against the net position of all its customers.

and is resumed the next day. This ensures that margin accounts do not get wiped out by large price movements. The halt in trading allows time for margin calls to protect the exchange against default by traders.[8]

Settlement by Offset.   What happens if Valley changes its mind and decides it wants to cancel its hedge? For example, suppose it sells the whole shipment of cars to another dealer and wants to pay the manufacturer right away. It then has no further need for the hedge.

Marking to market makes it very easy for Valley to close out its position at any time. All it need do is sell 20 contracts at the current futures price. Once it has done so, it is simultaneously a buyer and a seller of the same contracts. For example, if it wants to close out its position on January 5, it sells 20 contracts at 0.79¢. Because of marking to market, the original contracts it bought have been transformed into contracts at the same price of 0.79¢.

Since Valley is now both a buyer and a seller of identical contracts, its net position with respect to the market is zero. The exchange simply cancels the offsetting contracts. This is called **settlement by offset**.

settlement by offset
Closing out a futures contract before maturity with an offsetting trade.

cash settlement
Settlement of a maturing futures contract by cash payment.

Settlement by Delivery.   Many types of futures contract, especially financial futures, are settled at maturity in cash, as we have described. Older contracts, mainly contracts for various commodities, were designed to require delivery in the underlying commodity. Although **cash settlement** makes more sense, it was impossible for many years for legal reasons.

Futures trading in its modern form emerged in mid-nineteenth-century America. The futures contract evolved from the "to arrive" contract that required delivery of goods at a previously agreed price on their arrival in port. Such contracts were common in Europe in the eighteenth century and were used in the grain trade of New York, Buffalo, and Chicago before the Civil War. The war brought wide fluctuations in prices and greatly increased trading. The Chicago Board of Trade (CBOT) was created in 1865 to establish rules for trading and to bring some order to the market. A second futures market, subsequently renamed the Chicago Mercantile Exchange (CME), was opened a few years later. The Chicago exchanges had evolved into their present form by the 1920s.

In 1972, the CME set up a subsidiary, the International Monetary Market (IMM), to trade futures contracts in foreign currencies. Until then, futures contracts had been written only in commodities—mainly agricultural commodities and metals. These first financial futures were extremely successful and were soon followed by others. The CBOT began trading futures in Ginnie Mae passthroughs in 1975, and the IMM began trading futures in T-bills in 1976. The T-bill contract was an enormous success, especially with government securities dealers. Trading volume peaked in 1982 at over $30 billion a day, exceeding the trading volume in T-bills themselves. Numerous other contracts have followed.

A futures contract with cash settlement looks to the courts very much like a wager on the price of the underlying asset (which, of course, it is). This is a legal problem because a

---

[8] A system of margin and daily settlement very similar to the one described was used by the Japanese rice futures market in the eighteenth century.

**settlement
by delivery**
Settlement of a
maturing futures
contract by deliv-
ery of the under-
lying commodity.

wager cannot be enforced in court.[9] As a result, the futures contract had to be made to look like a forward trade, and this required that it be settled in the underlying commodity—**settlement by delivery**. The legal obstacle was removed by the Commodity Futures Trading Commission Act of 1974, which specifically authorized cash settlement. Since then, most new types of contract have opted for cash settlement.

Why is settlement by delivery of the underlying asset not the way to go? Locals, and others taking speculative positions, are obviously not interested in delivery: their intention is just to profit from changes in the price of the underlying asset. Even for hedgers, how-ever, the time, place, and conditions of delivery often do not match their exact requirements (for reasons that we shall see presently). They can usually match their needs better by set-tling in cash and then buying or selling the actual commodity in a separate transaction.

Although some types of futures contract require settlement by delivery of the under-lying commodity, very few of these contracts are actually settled in this way. Indeed, it is so unusual that exchanges typically required prior notice of the intent to make or to take actual delivery. Most contracts requiring delivery are settled before maturity by offset. Settlement by offset is a device that allows traders to convert a forward trade into a wager, which better suits their needs.

Basis Risk

Why is it that futures contracts do not meet the exact needs of hedgers? For a contract to be viable, there must be a minimum volume of trading. First, there are substantial fixed costs to setting up a market. To keep transactions costs low, those fixed costs must be spread over a large volume of transactions. Second, locals will not participate in a market that does not provide them with a good return on their investment in information. Without the participation of locals, the market will be illiquid and unattractive to other traders. Third, it is much easier to manipulate a small illiquid market: a large volume of trading helps to keep a market honest and competitive.

To ensure a large trading volume for each contract, contracts are written for relatively few of the most important commodities, securities, and currencies. The contracts are for standard amounts, and for delivery at a few specific dates. This concentrates all the demand on relatively few contracts and so increases the trading volume in each.

basis risk
The risk that de-
rives from an im-
perfect match be-
tween the futures
contract and the
position being
hedged.

However, the relatively small range of available contracts creates a problem—**basis risk**. This is the risk that derives from an imperfect match between the futures contract and the position being hedged. There are several possible sources of basis risk.

Timing. Valley must make its payment in yen on April 1. Contracts mature on the sec-ond business day before the third Wednesday of the month. Say the March and April contracts mature, respectively, on March 15 and April 19. Neither of these dates match Valley's requirements exactly. It can buy March contracts and hold the yen for 2 weeks, losing interest. Or it can buy April contracts and take the chance that on April 1

---

[9] The distinction, in the eyes of the law, is that with a legal contract both parties benefit, while with a wager one party benefits at the expense of the other. A wager is not legally enforceable. In the nineteenth century, Illinois courts had a lot of trouble distinguishing futures contracts from wagers. Settlement by offset was a particularly troublesome feature.

there will be a large discrepancy between the spot price and the current futures price of the April contract.

Contract size. Contracts come in a standard size: in the case of yen, this is ¥12.5 million. Valley was fortunate in that it wished to hedge an amount that was an exact multiple of this. Had it needed to hedge ¥255 million, it would have had to choose between 20 and 21 contracts, neither of which would have matched exactly.

Underlying. Valley was fortunate again in that it needed to hedge a position in yen. Had it needed to hedge a position in Swedish kronor, it would have had a problem: there is no Swedish krona contract. It could have hedged in Euros, for which there is a contract, because the Swedish krona moves relatively closely with the European currency. However, once again the hedge would not have been perfect.

To see how basis risk can cause a loss, suppose that Valley hedges in April contracts at 0.81¢. On April 1, the contract price is still 0.81¢, so Valley closes out its position without loss or gain. However, the spot price of yen on April 1 is 0.83¢, and this is what Valley must pay for its yen. The 0.02¢ gap between the spot price and the futures price causes it a loss of $50,000.

To eliminate basis risk entirely, there would have to be contracts in every currency, in every amount, and for every possible delivery date. The trading volume in many of these contracts would be very small. Consequently, these contracts would not be viable. So some basis risk is unavoidable.

Types of Futures Contract

Exhibit 16.3 gives a partial list of the futures contracts traded on exchanges in the United States as of October 2001. There are contracts in commodities, such as copper, corn, and crude oil. There are contracts in currencies, such as the yen, the Euro, and the British pound. There, are contracts in interest rates, such as U.S. Treasury bonds and bills and Eurodollars. And there are contracts in stock market indexes such as the S&P 500 and the Nikkei 225. Financial futures today make up 75% of total volume on U.S. futures exchanges. To understand how futures are listed in the financial press, see "Reading the Futures Listings."

stock index

A weighted average of the prices of a particular basket of stocks.

Index Futures.   A particularly important type of futures contract is the stock index contract. A **stock index** is a weighted average of the prices of a particular basket of stocks. Typically, the weight of each stock is the value of its shares outstanding divided by the total value of shares outstanding of all the stocks included in the basket. The best-known index is the Standard & Poor's (S&P) 500. This is a broad index based on a basket of the 500 most important U.S. stocks (most are traded on the New York Stock Exchange).

The S&P 500 futures contract is a wager on the value of the S&P 500 Index on the maturity date. The notional amount of each contract is $500. For example, if you buy one S&P 500 contract at a futures price of 1200, and the S&P 500 Index turns out to be 1,210 when the contract matures, your gain will be

$$(1,210 - 1,200) \times \$500 = \$5,000$$

EXHIBIT 16.3   Selected Futures Contracts

Type of Contract	Contract Size	Exchange[a]	Open Interest October 10, 2001 (Thousands of Contracts)
Interest rates			
U.S. Treasury bonds	$100,000	CBT	569
Eurodollars	$1,000,000	CME	4,538
U.S. Treasury notes	$100,000	CBT	1,026
U.S. Treasury bills	$1,000,000	CME	1
Currencies			
Euros	125,000	CME	112
Japanese yen	12,500,000	CME	71
Swiss francs	125,000	CME	48
Pound sterling	62,500	CME	40
Stock indexes			
S&P 500	Index × $5.00	CME	524
Nikkei 100 (Japan)	Index × $5.00	CME	50
CAC-40 (France)	Index × Euro 10.0	MATIF	456
FTSE-100 (U.K.)	Index × £10.00	LIFFE	324
DJ-Euro	Index × Euro 10.0	EUREX	802
Commodities			
Crude oil	1,000 bl	NYM	446
Corn	1,000 bu	CBT	409
Soybeans	5,000 bu	CBT	191
Gold	100 Tr. oz.	CMX	135

[a] CBT, Chicago Board of Trade; CME, Chicago Mercantile Exchange; CMX, Commodity Exchange, New York; LIFFE, London International Financial Futures Exchange; MATIF, Marché à Terme International de France; EUREX, European Exchange; NYM, New York Mercantile Exchange.

Source: The Wall Street Journal, *October 11, 2001.*

index arbitrage
Trading to profit between the price of index futures and the prices of the underlying securities.

The price of index futures tracks the price of the underlying basket of stocks quite closely because of a type of trading known as **index arbitrage**. If the price of the index is too high relative to the price of the underlying stock, traders sell the futures and buy the stock to benefit from the discrepancy. If the price is too low, they buy the futures and sell the stock. As a result of this trading by arbitrageurs, the two prices move closer together.[10]

Index arbitrage requires the simultaneous purchase or sale of a large number of individual stocks that make up an index (500 individual stocks in the case of the S&P 500). This would be impossible without computer technology. Computers identify arbitrage possibilities as soon as they occur and automatically generate the appropriate buy and sell orders for both stocks and futures. This is an example of *program trading*, and we shall have more to say about it in Chapter 17. In Chapter 18, we shall see how index futures can be used to hedge a portfolio of stocks—a strategy known as *portfolio insurance*. We shall

---

[10] For more details see the chapter appendix.

These listings for futures in Eurodollars, taken from *The Wall Street Journal*, describe trading on Wednesday, October 10, 2001:

	OPEN	HIGH	LOW	SETTLE	CHANGE		YIELD	CHANGE	OPEN INT.
Eurodollar (CME)-$1 Million; pts of 100%									
Oct	97.56	97.65	97.55	97.56		....	2.44	....	74,722
Nov	97.69	97.69	97.65	97.68	−	.01	2.32	+.01	13,971
Dec	97.72	97.73	97.68	97.71		....	2.29	....	829,684
Ja02	97.72	97.73	97.70	97.72	−	.02	2.28	+.02	1,527
Mar	97.64	97.65	97.57	97.62	−	.02	2.38	+.02	596,616
June	97.34	97.34	97.26	97.29	−	.04	2.71	+.04	589,600
Sept	96.91	96.93	96.84	96.87	−	.05	3.13	+.05	404,243
Dec	97.42	97.42	96.34	96.37	−	.04	3.63	+.04	360,188
Mr03	96.06	96.06	95.99	96.02	−	.03	3.98	+.03	238,491
June	95.65	95.66	95.62	95.65	−	.02	4.35	+.02	170,059
Sept	95.33	95.35	95.31	95.34	−	.01	4.66	+.01	172,341
Dec	95.01	95.05	95.00	95.05		....	4.95	....	144,743
Mr04	94.89	94.93	94.87	94.93		....	5.07	....	146,915
June	94.74	94.76	94.70	94.76		....	5.24	....	115,830
Sept	94.59	94.63	94.55	94.62	+	.01	5.38	−.01	92,146
Dec	94.40	94.46	94.38	94.45	+	.01	5.55	−.01	81,602
Mr05	94.37	94.44	94.35	94.42	+	.02	5.58	−.02	61,607
June	94.29	94.35	94.26	94.33	+	.02	5.67	−.02	64,833
Sept	94.19	94.26	94.17	94.25	+	.03	5.75	−.03	82,308
Dec	94.03	94.12	94.02	94.10	+	.03	5.90	−.03	58,130
Mr06	94.03	94.11	94.01	94.10	+	.03	5.90	−.03	39,169
June	93.97	94.04	93.94	94.03	+	.03	5.97	−.03	27,924
Sept	93.90	93.98	93.88	93.97	+	.03	6.03	−.03	33,078
Dec	93.76	93.86	93.76	93.83	+	.03	6.17	−.03	25,434
Mr07	93.77	93.87	93.77	93.84	+	.03	6.16	−.03	18,492
June	93.71	93.81	93.71	93.78	+	.03	6.22	−.03	16,623
Dc10	93.00	93.14	93.00	93.11	+	.03	6.89	−.03	2,145
Mr11	93.10	93.17	93.08	93.14	+	.03	6.86	−.03	3,170

Est vol 630,662; vol Tue 399,209; open int 4,538,184, +18,217.

Source: The Wall Street Journal, October 11, 2001.

Eurodollar futures trade on the CME. Each contract is for $1 million notional amount. Eurodollar futures are trading for delivery in each of the next 3 months and for March, June, September, and December of each year, going out 5 years. Prices are quoted as 100 minus a percentage yield. For example, the opening price for the October contract is 97.56. This is equivalent to an interest rate of 100 − 97.56 = 2.44%. The expiration price of the contract will be calculated as 100 − 6-month LIBOR on the expiration date.

For each delivery date, the listing gives the opening price for the day, the high and low prices, and the final (settlement) price. Then comes the change in the settlement price from the previous day. Next come the implied yield calculated from the settlement price; and the change in the yield from the previous day. The final column shows the *open interest*—the number of contracts outstanding.

At the end of each listing there is a summary of the day's trading volume, trading volume on the previous day, open interest, and the change in open interest.

discuss the effect of program trading and portfolio insurance on the stability of the market in Chapter 20.

Single-Stock Futures.   In 2001, preparations were under way in Chicago for the launching in December of single-stock futures. These are futures contracts based on the prices of individual stocks. Several futures markets around the world offer such instruments, but they have generated relatively little interest. LIFFE in London began trading Universal Stock Futures in January 2001. These are single-stock futures based on the prices of some 65 major stocks in the United States, Europe, and the United Kingdom. The response to these has been more enthusiastic. The three major derivatives exchanges in Chicago launched a joint venture to introduce single-stock futures in the United States, to be traded on a separate electronic exchange.

When Congress expanded the definition of "commodity" in 1974 to allow trading in financial derivatives, it created a conflict of jurisdictions between the Commodity Futures Trading Commission (CFTC), which regulates derivatives markets, and the Securities and Exchange Commission (SEC), which regulates securities markets. Is a derivative based on the price of a security in the domain of the CFTC because it is traded in derivative markets, or is it in the domain of the SEC because it is based on the price of a security? Single-stock futures were seen as posing particularly serious problems in this respect, so they were simply banned. That ban was lifted in December 2000 by the Commodities Futures Modernization Act, and the SEC and CFTC were instructed to work out the rules by December 2001.

OPTIONS

Let us return to our Valley Motors example in order to make the acquaintance of another type of derivative—the option. By hedging in futures, Valley protects itself against a loss if the yen rises in value against the dollar. But it also "protects" itself against a gain if the yen falls in value. It can obtain the same protection against a loss without giving up the potential for a gain by hedging instead in options. A futures contract is equivalent to a commitment to purchase or to sell the underlying asset at the contract price. In contrast, an **option contract** is equivalent to a *right* to purchase or to sell the underlying. This right may be exercised or not at the discretion of the buyer of the option.

option contract
A contract that gives the purchaser the right but not the obligation to buy or to sell at an agreed price.

Options on individual stocks have existed for as long as there have been stock markets (for example, the stock market in seventeenth-century Amsterdam offered a wide range of "modern" hedging instruments). Until relatively recently, the market for stock options was an over-the-counter market, with brokers bringing buyers and sellers together. If no counterparty to a trade could be found, brokers were often willing to take on that role themselves— so becoming dealers. Broker–dealers in options organized the Put and Call Brokers and Dealers Association in the early 1900s to formulate rules and procedures.

Options were first traded on an exchange in 1973, when the Chicago Board of Trade set up the Chicago Board Options Exchange. Since then, several stock exchanges and most futures exchanges have offered trading in options.

Hedging with Options

Before we see how Valley can hedge its position with options, we need to understand the different types of option and learn a little terminology.

Types of Options.   There are basically two types of option—the put and the call. Buying a **put option** is equivalent to buying the right to *sell* the underlying at the **exercise or strike price** (the contract price). Buying a **call option** is equivalent to buying the right to *purchase* the underlying at the exercise price. With an **American option**, the buyer may exercise the option at any time through the maturity date. With a **European option**, the buyer may exercise the option only *on* the maturity date.

Let us suppose that Valley hedges its anticipated payment in yen by purchasing European calls on Japanese yen with an expiration date in April (the contract with the date closest to the time it is due to make payment). To cover the ¥250 million it will need to pay, it must buy 40 contracts, each one for ¥6,250,000.

How an Option Contract Works.   Like futures contracts, some options are settled in cash and others by delivery. It is easier to understand how an option contract works by considering cash settlement. We have seen that a futures contract with cash settlement is a fair wager on an underlying price. An option contract with cash settlement is equivalent to a one-sided wager. The payment at maturity depends on what the actual price of the underlying turns out to be.

For a call option, if the actual price turns out to be above the exercise price, the seller must pay the buyer

$$(\text{actual price at maturity} - \text{exercise price}) \times \text{notional amount}$$

If the actual price turns out to be below the exercise price, the buyer does not exercise the option, and there is no payment.

Notice that if the option is **in the money** (the actual price is above the contract price), the payoff to the buyer of the option is exactly the same as it would have been, had the buyer bought a futures contract. However, if the option is **out of the money** (the actual price is below the contract price), the buyer of a call option avoids the loss a futures contract would have imposed. Because the option provides the buyer with a potential gain but no potential loss, it is clearly not a fair wager.

Why then does the seller enter into an option contract? Because the seller is compensated for doing so with an up-front payment—the **premium**. If the option expires in the money, the seller takes a loss. If it expires out of the money, the seller gets to keep the premium without making any payment. For the seller, the prospective gain just balances the prospective loss.

A futures contract is like a wager on the flip of a coin. Because the wager is fair, neither party has to compensate the other for entering into the wager. An option contract is like a lottery ticket. Since the purchaser can only win, the seller must be compensated with an up-front payment for the ticket.

In the case of a futures contract, supply and demand determine the contract price. Its value is such that the market considers the contract a fair wager. In the case of an option, supply and demand determine the *premium*. Its value is such that the market considers it fair payment for the possible gain to the buyer and loss to the seller. Note that the contract price of an option (the exercise price) is not the price of the option, but rather one of the parameters of the wager. At any time, there will be options trading for a range of different exercise prices.

put option
The right to sell at some future time at a price specified now.

exercise or strike price
The purchase or sale price specified on an option contract.

call option
The right to buy at some future time at a price specified now.

American option
An option that may be exercised at any time up to maturity.

European option
An option that may be exercised only at the date of maturity.

in the money
Describing an option whose exercise price makes current exercise profitable.

out of the money
Describing an option whose exercise price makes current exercise unprofitable.

premium
The price of an option.

The size of the premium depends on the likelihood that the option will be in the money and on the likely payment if it is. Anything that increases the likelihood of payment or the size of the likely payment will tend to raise the premium. Consequently, for a call option, the premium will be higher

- When the expiration date is farther away (more time for the price of the underlying to rise)
- When the price of the underlying is more volatile
- When the exercise price is lower[11]

The Payoff from Hedging with Options.   Returning to our example, Valley Motors decides to buy call options with an exercise price of 0.81¢/¥. The premium for calls with this exercise price and this maturity is 0.012¢/¥. Valley must therefore pay a total of

$$0.012¢/¥ \times ¥250 \text{ million} = \$30,000$$

Let us see how Valley's hedge with options might work out under the same three scenarios we considered when we looked at earlier. The numbers are summarized in Exhibit 16.4.

Scenario 1. The yen stays at its current price of 0.80¢. Since this is below the exercise price of the options, Valley Motors does not exercise them and receives no payment. Its net profit, therefore, is its profit from the underlying position less the cost of the hedge. The cost of the hedge is the *future value* of the $30,000 premium at the time the contracts expire. We need to take a future value because the premium is paid 3 months earlier, when the options are written, not when the contracts expire. If we assume an annual interest rate of 10%, the future value after 3 months is $30,723.

Scenario 2. The yen rises in value to 0.85¢. Since this is above the exercise price, Valley exercises the options and its profit on them is

$$(0.85¢/¥ - 0.81¢/¥) \times ¥250 \text{ million} = \$100,000$$

---

[11] See the appendix to this chapter for more on pricing options.

EXHIBIT 16.4   **The Effect of a Hedge in Options on the Profits of Valley Motors**

	Actual Price, April 1	Exercise Price of Options	Profit on Options Position (1)	Profit from Underlying Position (2)[a]	Net Profit: (1) + (2) − Future Value of Premium
1	0.80¢	0.81¢	$0	$200,000	$0 + $200,000 − 30,723 = $169,277
2	0.85¢	0.81¢	$100,000	$75,000	$100,000 + 75,000 − 30,723 = $144,277
3	0.75¢	0.81¢	$0	$325,000	$0 + 325,000 − 30,723 = $294,277

[a] See Exhibit 16.1.

To find the net profit, we add the profit from the options position to the profit of the underlying position and subtract the cost of the hedge.

Scenario 3. The yen falls in value to 0.75¢. This again is below the exercise price of the options. The calculation is as in scenario 1.

Like hedging with futures, hedging with options protects Valley Motors against a rise in the value of the yen. However high the yen may rise, Valley's net profit cannot fall below $144,277. But, unlike hedging with futures, hedging with options allows Valley to gain if the yen falls in value. There is, of course, a price to be paid for the higher net profit if the yen falls—a lower net profit if it rises. The minimum net profit guaranteed by the options hedge, $144,277, is lower than the net profit guaranteed by a futures hedge, $175,000. The reason why it is lower is the premium—the up-front cost of the options. The different payoffs of the two types of hedge are illustrated in Exhibit 16.5, which plots net profit against the actual price of the yen on April 1 for each of the two types of hedge.

market makers

Traders on the floor of an options exchange who trade on their own accounts.

How the Options Market Works

Trading and trading rules for options are a little different from those for futures. The CBOE, the largest options exchange, is closest to a futures exchange in its organization. There are floor brokers, who fill orders, and **market makers**, who trade on their own

EXHIBIT 16.5   Hedging in Futures vs Hedging in Options

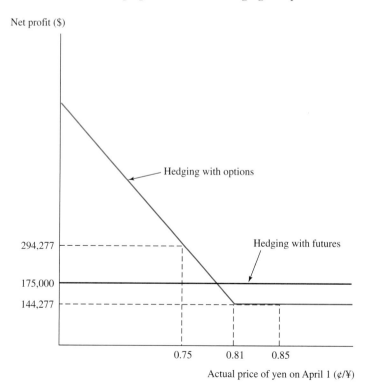

accounts. Market makers play much the same role as locals do in the futures market except that the former are required to quote both bid and asked prices. In addition, the exchange maintains a public limit-order book in which limit orders not immediately fillable are registered. The organization of the Pacific Stock Exchange is similar to that of the CBOE, but American Stock Exchange (AMEX) and the Philadelphia Stock Exchange rely on specialists (a combination of market maker and auctioneer) rather than on competitive market makers.[12]

The exercise of an option usually involves actual delivery, but some options (for example, options on stock indexes) are settled in cash. Buyers of options have no need to put up collateral. They simply pay the premium. Sellers, however, must provide some assurance that they will pay up or deliver if the option is exercised. They must either put up the underlying asset as collateral—a "covered option"—or provide a cash margin.[13]

Options have the same sort of basis risk as futures. The options actually available may not suit precisely the needs of a particular hedger with respect to amount, maturity, or nature of the underlying asset.

Types of Option Contract

Exhibit 16.6 gives a partial list of the options currently traded on exchanges in the United States. As with futures, there are options on commodities as well as financial options.

options on futures

Options to buy and sell futures contracts rather than to buy and sell the underlying asset itself.

In addition to ordinary options, there are also **options on futures**. These are options to purchase and sell futures contracts rather than to purchase and sell the underlying asset itself. For example, on exercising a call option on yen futures, the buyer receives, in exchange for the exercise price, a yen futures contract rather than actual yen. Options on futures have some advantages over regular options in terms of their liquidity and their flexibility in tailoring precisely the size of the hedge. The market for options on futures has grown rapidly in recent years.

To understand how options are listed in the financial press see "Reading the Options Listings."

path-dependent option

An option whose payoff depends on the path of the underlying price over the whole life of the option.

The exchanges are constantly inventing and offering new types of option. One new class of options—the **path-dependent option**—pays off in a way that depends on the path of the price of the underlying asset over the whole life of the option rather than just on the price at expiration. For example, with one variant, the "lookback option," the exercise price is set at expiration at the level most favorable to the buyer. With a lookback call, for instance, it is set at the lowest price over the life of the option.

Another example is the "capped option" on stock indexes launched by the CBOE and AMEX in 1991. A capped call might have a strike price of 390 with a cap of 30 points. This means that if the index reaches 420 during the life of the option, it is automatically exercised: the seller pays out (30 × $100/pt) and the option is terminated. Otherwise, it behaves like a regular option. The capped option is more attractive to sellers because it sets a limit on their possible losses if the price moves against them.

---

[12] See Chapter 17 for more on specialists.

[13] The risk to a seller of an uncovered call is unbounded, and to the writer of an uncovered put, large. Consequently brokers are very cautious about allowing their customers to write uncovered options.

EXHIBIT 16.6   Selected Options Contracts

Type of Contract	Contract Size	Exchange[a]	Open Interest, October 10, 2001 (Thousands of Contracts)[b]
Option on interest rate futures			
U.S. Treasury bonds	$100,000	CBT	511
Eurodollar	$1 million	CME	3,334
U.S. Treasury notes (5- and 2-year)	$100,000	CBT	902
Options on currency futures			
Euro	125,000 Euros	CME	
Japanese yen	¥12,500,000	CME	
Swiss franc	SF125,000	CME	
British pound	£62.500	CME	
Options on commodities futures			
Crude oil	1,000 bbl	NYM	757
Soybeans	5,000 bu	CBT	230
Corn	5,000 bu	CBT	406
Gold	100 troy oz.	CMX	250
Options on stock indexes			
S&P 500	$500 × premium	SPX	1,635
Options on stock index futures			
S&P 500	$500 × premium	CME	231
LEAPS (long-term options)	$500 × premium	CBT	1,249
Options on individual stocks			
Regular options		CBOE, AMEX, PHLX, PSE, INT	299 million shares (total)
LEAPS (long-term options)		CBT, PSE	33 million shares (total)

[a] AMEX, American Stock Exchange; CBOE, Chicago Board Options Exchange; CBT, Chicago Board of Trade; CME, Chicago Mercantile Exchange; CMX, Commodity Exchange Inc.; INT, International Securities Exchange; NYM, New York Mercantile Exchange; PHLX, Philadelphia Exchange; PSE, Pacific Stock Exchange.
[b] Total of put and call contracts.

Source: The Wall Street Journal, *October 11, 2001.*

SWAPS AND OTHER OTC DERIVATIVES

The third major type of derivative security, and the fastest growing, is the swap. Compared to futures and options, swaps are a very recent invention. The first swap, a currency swap, was written in 1981 between IBM and the World Bank. The first interest rate swap, involving Sallie Mae, was written in 1982. Our first task is to understand what a swap is and how it is used.

READING THE OPTIONS LISTINGS

This options listing, taken from *The Wall Street Journal*, describes trading on Wednesday, October 10, 2001.

Eurodollar (CME) $ million; pts of 100%						
STRIKE	CALLS-SETTLE			PUTS-SETTLE		
PRICE	Oct	Nov	Dec	Oct	Nov	Dec
9700	7.15	7.15	7.17	0.00	0.00	0.05
9725	4.65	4.70	4.72	0.00	0.05	0.10
9750	2.15	2.35	2.52	0.00	0.20	0.37
9775	0.20	0.67	0.95	0.55	1.02	1.30
9800	0.00	0.10	0.25	....	....	3.10
9825	....	....	0.10	....	....	....

Est vol 195,431;
Tu vol 107,351 calls 57,793 puts
Op int Tues 3,344,113 calls 3,247,078 puts

Source: *The Wall Street Journal*, October 11, 2001.

The listing is for options on Eurodollar futures (American puts and calls) traded on the Chicago Mercantile Exchange. Each contract is for $1 million.

Actively traded options are listed in rising order of the strike price (exercise price), which appears in the first column. The next three columns show the final (settlement) value of the premium for call options at that strike price for contracts maturing in October, November, and December. The final three columns show the premium for put options at that strike price for the three maturity dates. The premiums are quoted in tenths of a percent of the notional value.

For example, the first strike price listed is 9700, corresponding to a yield of 3%. The premium for a call option maturing in October is 7.15 tenths of 1 percent of $1 million or $7,150. That is, the purchaser of this option pays $7,150 for the right to buy one Eurodollar futures contract of $1 million at a price of 9700 at any time up to the maturity date.

At the end of the listing there is an estimate of the day's trading volume, trading volume the previous day in calls and puts, and the open interest in calls and puts on the previous day.

Using Interest Rate Swaps

**interest
rate swap**
Exchange of one
type of interest
payment for an-
other.

While the details are complicated, the basic idea of an **interest rate swap** is simple enough: two companies take out loans and swap the interest payments. Each company, rather than paying the interest on the loan it itself took out, pays the interest on the loan taken out by the other. To understand why two parties might do such a thing, let us look at an example.

Using a Swap to Lower Borrowing Costs

International Computer (IC) is a well-known multinational corporation. It can borrow at a very good rate both in the direct market and in the indirect market. IC pays 60 b.p. over the Treasury rate on its bonds and 30 b.p. over LIBOR on its bank loans. Biosoft Inc. is smaller and less well known. So it pays more to borrow in both markets. Biosoft pays 300 b.p. over the Treasury rate on its bonds and 100 b.p. over LIBOR on its bank loans. Exhibit 16.7 shows the rates the two firms would pay if LIBOR were 5% and the rate on 20-year Treasury bonds, 9%.

You can see that even though Biosoft pays more than IC both on a bond issue and on a bank loan, the premium is much bigger on the bond issue. This means that, compared to IC, Biosoft has a *comparative advantage* in bank loans: it is at less of a disadvantage compared to IC when it borrows from a bank than when it borrows in the bond market. Correspondingly, compared to Biosoft, IC has a comparative advantage in the bond market. Although it has an *absolute advantage* in both types of borrowing (it can borrow more cheaply than Biosoft in both), its advantage over Biosoft is greater in the bond market.[14]

Given these differences in comparative advantage—in relative borrowing costs—there exist potential gains from trade between the two. A swap enables the two companies to capture these gains, allowing each to borrow more cheaply.

Suppose, for example, that IC needs a floating-rate loan for working capital and Biosoft needs a fixed-rate loan to finance investment in a new factory. The straightforward way for each of them to meet these needs is for IC to borrow from its bank and for Biosoft to float a bond issue. However, they could do better if each took out the type of loan in which it has a comparative advantage and they then used a swap to exchange the interest payments.

EXHIBIT 16.7   Borrowing Rates for IC and Biosoft

	IC	Biosoft
Bank loan	5.30	6.00
Bonds	9.60	12.00

---

[14] We saw in Chapter 14 that borrowers like Biosoft with significant default risk are ill suited to the arm's-length public issue market. They are a better match for the relationship lending of a bank loan.

EXHIBIT 16.8   An Interest Rate Swap in Principle

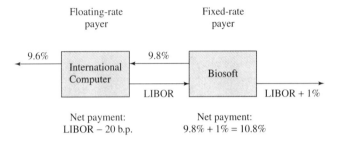

Exhibit 16.8 shows how the swap works. IC borrows $1 million in the bond market, selling fixed-rate, 15-year bonds with annual coupons of 9.6%. Biosoft takes a renewable $1 million floating-rate loan from its bank, with annual interest payments at 100 b.p. over LIBOR. That is, the interest due at the end of each year is 1% over LIBOR at the beginning of the year. For the first year the rate is 6.0%.[15]

Under a 15-year swap, the two companies exchange payments for 15 years. Each year, Biosoft pays IC a fixed payment at a rate of 9.8%; IC pays Biosoft LIBOR (whatever that is at the time). In this arrangement Biosoft is called the **fixed-rate payer** and IC, the **floating-rate payer**. The net interest payments for the two companies at the end of the first year are shown in Exhibit 16.9.

Exhibit 16.9 shows that by entering into the swap, IC has transformed its fixed-rate borrowing into a floating-rate loan at a rate of LIBOR − 20 basis points (4.8% initially). As you can see from Exhibit 16.7, had it instead simply taken a loan from its bank, it would have had to pay LIBOR + 30 b.p. (5.3% initially). Therefore, as a result of the swap, IC reduces its borrowing costs by 50 b.p. Over the life of the swap, LIBOR will fluctuate, but

fixed-rate payer
The party to a swap that makes fixed payments in exchange for floating.

floating-rate payer
The party to a swap that makes floating payments in exchange for fixed.

EXHIBIT 16.9   Net Interest Payments under a Direct Swap

	Interest Payment (%)	
IC		
Pays on the bond	9.6	
Receives from Biosoft	−9.8	
Pays to Biosoft (LIBOR)	5.0	
Net interest payment		4.8%
Biosoft		
Pays on the bank loan	6.0	
Receives from IC (LIBOR)	−5.0	
Pays to IC	9.8	
Net interest payment		10.8%

[15] In reality, the coupon payments on the bonds are usually semiannual, as is the period for adjusting the interest rate on the bank loan. We will use an annual period to keep the calculations simple.

whatever it is, IC will still pay 50 b.p. less than it would have had to pay on a floating-rate bank loan.

Turning now to Biosoft, Exhbiit 16.9 shows that it has transformed its floating-rate bank loan into a fixed-rate loan at a rate of 10.8% (180 b.p. over the 9% Treasury rate). Biosoft will continue to pay 10.8% however much LIBOR fluctuates. If LIBOR goes up, and Biosoft has to pay its bank more, it will be compensated by a higher payment from IC. As you can see from Exhibit 16.7, had Biosoft simply issued fixed-rate bonds, it would have had to pay 12% (300 b.p. over the Treasury rate). By entering into the swap, Biosoft has reduced its borrowing costs by 120 b.p.

notional principal
Amount of the underlying loans in an interest rate swap.

IC and Biosoft each remains responsible for repayment of the principal on its own borrowing. The $1 million principal never actually changes hands between them. However, this amount—the **notional principal** of the swap—does determine the size of the payments each must make to the other. Biosoft must pay

$$\$1 \text{ million} \times 0.098 = \$98,000$$

every year; IC must pay

$$\$1 \text{ million} \times \text{LIBOR at the beginning of the year}$$

For the first year, LIBOR is 5%, so the first floating-rate payment is $50,000.

Why Is It Possible to Lower Borrowing Costs with a Swap?   The ability of the two firms to lower their borrowing costs through the device of a swap is on the face of it rather surprising. It seems like a "free lunch." What is going on here?

The swap gives Biosoft a long-term, fixed-rate loan. There are two types of risk involved in such a loan—credit risk and interest rate risk. Banks and securities markets differ in their ability to handle these two types of risk.

As we saw in Chapter 14, relationship lenders like banks have an advantage in handling credit risk for risky small companies like Biosoft. Banks often have better information; they are better at monitoring loan performance and more flexible in dealing with repayment problems. Because the arms-length bond market performs these functions less well, it demands a higher risk premium from borrowers like Biosoft.

However, the bond market is better able than a bank to bear the interest rate risk of a fixed-rate loan. Typical bond investors, such as pension funds and life insurance companies, have long-term liabilities at fixed rates of interest. For them, long-term, fixed-rate assets match their liabilities and so minimize their interest rate risk. Banks, on the other hand, typically have short-term liabilities on which they pay a variable rate of interest. So long-term, fixed-rate assets involve substantial interest rate risk.

The swap allows the credit risk of the loan to Biosoft to be separated from the interest rate risk. The bank bears the credit risk: if Biosoft defaults, the bank takes the loss. However, the bank does not bear the interest rate risk. That is borne by the investors who buy the bonds from IC. Through the swap, Biosoft is paying the fixed-rate interest payments to them.

Similarly, the credit risk on the loan to IC is borne by the bond market. If IC defaults, the purchasers of its bonds take the loss. It is less expensive to handle the credit risk this way: IC is a good risk, and the bond market handles good risks relatively inexpensively. The interest rate risk on the loan to IC is borne by the bank. IC is, through the swap, paying its floating-rate interest payments to the bank.

The swap allows the interest rate risk and the credit risk on each of the two loans to be borne where it can be borne most cheaply. That is why the swap reduces the cost of borrowing for each of the two borrowers.

By "unbundling" loans in this way, swaps allow borrowers to separate the decision on *where* to borrow from the decision on *what form* the borrowing should take. For example, the swap allows Biosoft to borrow from a bank (where) and at a fixed rate (the form).

The Swap as a Wager

To understand the pricing of swaps and the various ways they can be used, it is useful to think of them as wagers. In fact, as we shall see, a swap is closely related to another form of wager—the futures contract.

In a swap contract, the two parties agree on a *swap rate*, on a *notional principal*, and on a *series of maturity dates*. In explaining the function of a swap, it has been useful to describe it in terms of one party paying a fixed rate (the swap rate) and the other party paying a floating rate (LIBOR). In reality, at each maturity date, it is only the difference between the two rates that changes hands. Which party pays at each maturity date and how much depends on what LIBOR turns out to be on that date. If LIBOR turns out to be above the swap rate, the floating-rate payer must pay the fixed-rate payer.

$$(\text{LIBOR} - \text{swap rate}) \times \text{notional principal}$$

If LIBOR turns out to be below the swap rate, the fixed-rate payer must pay the floating-rate payer

$$(\text{swap rate} - \text{LIBOR}) \times \text{notional principal}$$

This looks, of course, very much like the payoff from a futures contract. A futures contract involves a single wager on a market price at one maturity date. A swap differs only in that it involves a series of wagers on a market price at a series of maturity dates.

As with a futures contract, there is no up-front payment for a swap, because, like a futures contract, a swap is a fair wager. Of course, it is a fair wager only at the right level of the swap rate. If the swap rate is too high, the wager favors the floating-rate payer. If it is too low, it favors the fixed-rate payer. Supply and demand in the market for swaps will establish the swap rate at a level that the market considers to be fair.[16]

Because a swap contract is a fair wager at the time it is written, its market value at that time is zero: the expected gains just balance the expected losses for each party. However, over time, if interest rates change, the value of the swap to each of the two parties will change too. For example, if market interest rates rise, the present value of the stream of fixed payments will fall. However, the floating-rate payments will rise with the rise in interest rates, preserving the present value of the stream of floating-rate payments. So a rise

---

[16] See the appendix to the chapter on the determinants of the swap rate.

in interest rates means a capital gain for the fixed-rate payer and a capital loss for the floating-rate payer. A fall in interest rates means a capital loss for the fixed-rate payer and a capital gain for the floating-rate payer.

Using a Swap to Hedge or to Speculate.   Since the value of an outstanding swap changes with changes in market interest rates, it can be used as a hedge against interest rate movements. For example, suppose you are holding a portfolio of long-term bonds and you are worried that an imminent rise in interest rates might cause you a capital loss. Becoming a fixed-rate payer on a swap agreement is a way of hedging the risk. The capital gain on the swap will balance the capital loss on your bond portfolio. Another way to think about it: by becoming a fixed-rate payer, you are, in effect, converting your fixed-rate bonds into floating-rate assets. The value of the latter is immune to a change in interest rates.

Another example. Suppose you have long-term, fixed-rate liabilities (like a life insurance company), and you are worried that a fall in interest rates might increase the value of those liabilities. You could hedge the risk by becoming a floating-rate payer on a swap agreement. The capital gain on the swap will offset the capital loss on your liabilities. Alternatively, you can think of the swap as, in effect, converting your fixed-rate liabilities into floating-rate liabilities that are insensitive to changes in interest rates.

Of course, any instrument that can be used to hedge can also be used to speculate. Suppose that, contrary to the view of the market, you think interest rates are going to fall. In your view, the current swap rate is therefore too high. One way to profit from this "mistake" is to take a **naked position** as a floating-rate payer. That is, you enter into a swap agreement with no underlying position—with no future interest rate payments to swap. If you are right and interest rates do fall, you will make a capital gain on the swap that is not balanced by any capital loss on an underlying position.

naked position
A position in a derivative contract not matched by an offsetting position in the underlying.

How the Swap Market Works

A swap is a forward transaction. Like all forward transactions, it involves an exchange of promises. For example, when Biosoft and IC write a swap, Biosoft promises to pay IC $98,000 on a sequence of 15 future dates, and IC promises to pay LIBOR on $1 million on those dates. As we know, transactions that involve promises are difficult for the parties to arrange directly. It should come as no surprise, then, that the financial system has developed ways to facilitate swap transactions.

Unlike the markets for futures and options, however, the swap market is not an auction market organized through an exchange. Rather, it is a dealer or **over-the-counter (OTC) market**. The dealers who make the market are mostly large banks and securities firms, although some large nonfinancial firms, such as British Petroleum, also deal in swaps.

over-the-counter (OTC) market
A dealer market.

To understand the role of a dealer, let us make the IC–Biosoft example a little more realistic. The flow of payments is shown in Exhibit 16.10.

Rather than trading directly with each other, both IC and Biosoft sign a swap agreement with Metrobank, a swap dealer. Metrobank offers a standard 15-year swap, quoting a bid of 70 and an asked of 90. The swap rate is quoted as a spread in basis points over the Treasury rate for this maturity. So a bid of 90 means the 15-year Treasury rate plus 90 b.p. For example, if the Treasury rate when the swap is written is 9%, the bid is 9.9% and the asked is 9.7%. Biosoft, the fixed-rate payer, pays Metrobank the asked rate less LIBOR. IC,

EXHIBIT 16.10   An Interest Rate Swap in Practice

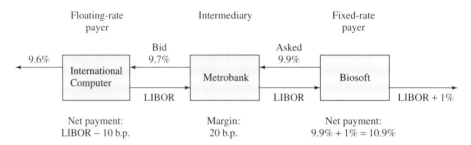

the floating-rate payer, pays Metrobank LIBOR less the bid rate. For example, suppose that on one of the maturity dates LIBOR is 5%. On that date, Biosoft pays (9.9% − 5%) = 4.9% times the notional principal. IC receives (9.7% − 5%) = 4.7% times the notional principal.

The difference between what Biosoft pays and what IC receives—20 b.p.—is Metrobank's margin, and it is equal to its bid–asked spread. The size of the bid–asked spread on swaps is determined by competition among swap dealers. The bid–asked spread covers Metrobank's transactions costs and compensates it for the risk that it bears.

The Risks of Market Making.   The risk that Metrobank bears is replacement risk. It is a party to two separate contracts—one with Biosoft and the other with IC. If one party defaults, Metrobank's contract with the other still stands. To balance its position, Metrobank must find a replacement for the defaulting party. However, if the Treasury rate or the swap spread has changed adversely since the original swap was written, Metrobank will take a loss. For example, suppose Biosoft defaults after a couple of years at a time when the asked is 8%. That means that any replacement Metrobank finds for Biosoft will pay only 8%. Metrobank will have to cover the difference between the 9.8% it pays IC and the 8% it receives from the new fixed-rate payer.

In evaluating and bearing this sort of replacement risk in exchange for a fee, Metrobank is performing much the same functions it does when it makes loans—delegation and credit substitution.

The risks involved in writing swaps have been highlighted by several major failures. Drexel Burnham Lambert failed with $30 billion in swaps outstanding. Other large failures have included Bank of New England, Development Corp. of New Zealand, British & Commonwealth Merchant Bank, and Olympia and York. These failures have made the swap market much more cautious. Some participants are now willing to trade only with counterparties having a rating of AAA or AA. To stay in the market at all, poorer risks now often have to put up collateral.

Some of the dealers themselves have had problems with creditworthiness. Many large banks lack a rating as high as AAA or AA. One solution, adopted by several banks, is to set up a "special-purpose vehicle" to make a market in derivatives. This is a separately capitalized subsidiary with a higher credit rating than the parent.[17]

---

[17] This is rather similar to securitization in that a separate entity is created to isolate certain assets and liabilities from the overall risk of the company. See Chapter 14 on securitization and special-purpose vehicles.

Dealers have sometimes responded to the increased awareness of the risks of intermediating swaps by resorting to "assignment brokering." Under this practice, the dealer still makes a market by being willing to write a swap with a customer at any time. However, as soon as the dealer finds a matching counterparty, the contract is rewritten directly between the two parties. In this way, the credit risk is borne by the parties themselves.

Liquidity in the Swap Market.   As market makers, swap dealers provide liquidity. They stand ready to write a swap at their quoted rates at any time without waiting to match up fixed-rate and floating-rate payers. Indeed, parties to swaps, like parties to futures or options contracts, neither know nor care who ultimately takes the other side of the transaction. As far as the customer is concerned, the contract is with the dealer.

Dealers may also offer liquidity in the sense of being willing to cancel existing swap contracts. In our example, if either IC or Biosoft wants a release from the swap before it matures, Metrobank may be willing to cancel the contract in exchange for an appropriate payment. Metrobank will then find a replacement for the party opting out.

Because they provide liquidity in this way, dealers' net positions will frequently not be balanced. For example, if a dealer's contracts with floating-rate payers add up to more than its contracts with fixed-rate payers, the dealer itself becomes a net fixed-rate payer. This exposes the dealer to interest rate risk. Should interest rates fall, the dealer will take a loss.

interdealer market for swaps
An inside market for dealers in swaps.

A dealer will generally hedge all or part of this risk. It can hedge temporarily in the futures market, or it can balance its position more permanently by doing a swap in the **interdealer market**. The interdealer market in swaps is a brokered market, much like the inside market for government securities or the interbank market for Eurodollars.

Types of Swap

The most common type of swap is the type we have studied in our example—the interest rate swap. There are, however, many other types.

currency swap
Exchange of payments in one currency for payments in another.

Currency Swaps.   In principle, a **currency swap** is much like an interest rate swap. A typical example might involve two corporations in two different countries—for example, IC in the United States and Nagamishi in Japan. IC wishes to build a lab in Japan and Nagamishi wishes to build an automobile assembly plant in the United States. Each company needs funds in the currency of the country in which the investment is to be made. However, each company can borrow *relatively* more cheaply in its own currency because it is better known to investors at home (each company has a comparative advantage in its own currency). A swap enables each to cut its borrowing costs while obtaining the funds in the currency it needs.

This is how it works. IC sells bonds in the United States—for dollars, of course—and Nagamishi sells bonds in Japan for an equivalent amount of yen. The two corporations then exchange the proceeds of the two issues. IC gets the yen and Nagamishi, the dollars. Then, for the life of the two loans, IC pays interest and principal on the yen bonds originally sold by Nagamishi, and Nagamishi pays interest and principal on the dollar bonds originally sold by IC. In this way each company can borrow where its cost is least, while still obtaining funds in the currency it needs.

Just like interest rate swaps, currency swaps allow borrowers to unbundle loans. By using a currency swap, a borrower can separate the decision on where to borrow from the decision on what form to borrow. For example, a currency swap enables Nagamishi to borrow in Japan (the where) but effectively in U.S. dollars (the form of borrowing).

Commodity Swaps.   A commodity swap, too, is much like an interest rate swap. One party makes a periodic fixed payment; the other makes a payment that is pegged to the current price of some commodity. For example, the fixed-price payer on an oil swap might be a public utility that wants to hedge against a possible rise in the price of oil. The floating-price payer might be an oil company that wants to hedge against a possible fall in the price of oil.

Initially, banks were unable to intermediate commodity swaps, because they were prohibited from commodities transactions. However, bank regulators authorized market making in commodity swaps in 1987. In 1990, they allowed banks to hedge their exposure on commodity swaps in commodities futures and options.

Equity Swaps.   Some holders of large positions in particular individual stocks would like to reduce their risk exposure without actually selling the stocks. Reasons not to sell might include liability for capital gains taxes, loss of voting rights, and insider trading restrictions. Equity swaps provide a solution. The notional principal of the swap is the initial market value of the stocks in question. The seller agrees to pay, over the life of the contract, all dividends on the stocks in exchange for LIBOR on the notional principal. At maturity, if the stocks have appreciated, the seller pays the buyer the amount of the appreciation. If the stocks, have declined in value, the buyer pays the seller the amount of the loss. For the seller, this temporarily "converts" the stock into a money market asset, without the disadvantages of a sale. The buyer can hedge the risk, if so desired, by taking a short position in the stock or by purchasing put options.

Credit Default Swaps.   In recent years, a fast-growing segment of the derivatives market has been **credit derivatives**. These include a variety of instruments that allow lenders to hedge credit risk on their loans. The most popular form (40% of the market in 1998) is the **credit default swap**. With this type of contract, the *risk seller* pays annual premiums in basis points of the amount of the loan or loans in question to the *risk buyer*. If a *credit event* occurs, the risk buyer makes a stipulated payment to the risk seller to compensate for the loss on the loan.[18] After some litigation in a number of cases over what exactly constitutes a "credit event," the International Swap Dealers Association (ISDA) has offered a standard definition.[19] This includes such contingencies as failure to pay, bankruptcy, cross-default, restructuring, merger, and downgrading. Each of these happenings increases the probability that the loan will not be repaid and so reduces the market value of the loan.

credit derivative
A derivative instrument that allows the credit risk of a loan to be traded separately from the loan itself.

credit default swap
A swap of a fixed payment in exchange for compensation for a loss on a loan.

---

[18] The form of the payment differs according to the terms of the contract. With "cash settlement" the risk buyer pays the difference between the par value of the loan and the amount recovered. With "physical settlement," the risk buyer takes over the loan in exchange for the par value. With "binary settlement," the risk buyer pays a fixed amount stipulated in the contract.

[19] The ISDA was formed in 1985 to standardize documentation and procedures in the burgeoning market.

VARIETIES OF SWAP

In addition to the basic or "plain vanilla" interest rate, currency, and commodity swaps, there are many more exotic instruments. The following are some examples.

Amortizing or accreting swap. On ordinary swaps the notional principal stays constant for the life of the swap. On amortizing swaps it declines to match the principal on an amortized loan such as mortgage. On an accreting swap it increases over the life of the swap.

Basis swap. Rather than being an exchange of fixed for floating interest payments, this is an exchange of one floating payment for another (for example, LIBOR in exchange for the T-bill rate).

Swaption. An options on a swap. For example, the purchaser of a call swaption gains the right to become a fixed-rate payer at a given rate.

Yield curve swap. This is an exchange of payments linked to a short-term market rate for payments linked to a long-term rate.

Zero-coupon swap. This is an exchange of fixed payments over the life of the swap for a single fixed payment at maturity. It can be used to convert a coupon bond into a zero.

Source: Abken (1991).

For a review of some of the other types of swap, see "Varieties of Swap."

Other OTC Derivatives

Swaps are the most important type of OTC derivative, but banks and securities firms offer a variety of other hedging products.

Forward Foreign Exchange.   As we saw in Chapter 2, there is a forward market in foreign exchange. Companies like Valley Motors (in the example earlier in the chapter) can hedge their foreign exchange positions by buying or selling foreign exchange forward.

The forward market in foreign exchange, like the market for swaps, is an OTC market made by dealers. It was once the case that all the dealers were banks. However, with the globalization of securities markets, securities firms have become increasingly involved in currency transactions, and many have become dealers themselves.

The forward market in foreign exchange is closely linked to the spot market for foreign exchange (see Chapter 8) and to the market for currency swaps. For example, the currency trader who sold the ¥250 million forward to Valley Motors in our earlier example

foreign exchange swap

A combination of a spot transaction in foreign exchange with a forward transaction in the opposite direction.

can hedge the risk in the dealer market by buying a **foreign exchange swap**. This is different from a *currency* swap. A foreign exchange swap is a trade in which a spot transaction and a forward transaction are agreed upon simultaneously (rather like a currency repo). The price of a foreign exchange swap is the difference between the relevant forward exchange rate and the spot rate. Our dealer, to hedge the forward sale to Valley Motors, purchases ¥250 million in the spot market, then uses a foreign exchange swap to sell the ¥250 million spot and simultaneously purchase the same amount forward.

In 2000, the Bank for International Settlements estimated that transactions in foreign exchange forwards and swaps averaged $650 billion *a day*, compared to the daily $450 billion in the spot market for foreign exchange.[20]

forward forward contract

A forward contract for delivery of Eurodollar deposits.

forward rate agreement (FRA)

A forward contract for Eurodollar deposits, settled in cash rather than by delivery.

cap

An option that ensures that floating-rate payments on a loan will not exceed a given limit.

floor

An option that ensures that floating-rate payments from a security will not fall below a given limit.

collar

An option that ensures that floating-rate payments on a loan will be within a given range.

FRAs. There is also an OTC market for hedging products closely related to the Eurodollar market. Banks offer **forward forward contracts**—forward agreements to accept or to deliver Eurodollar deposits. But the most popular instrument is the **forward rate agreement (FRA)**. This is also a forward transaction in Eurodollars, but unlike a forward forward, it is settled in cash rather than with delivery. In our earlier terminology, the forward forward is a forward trade, while the FRA is a derivative.

As an example of a FRA, IC expects to receive a payment of $20 million in 3 months' time and will not need the money for 6 months. It will therefore deposit the $20 million with a Eurodollar bank. IC is worried that interest rates might fall between now and the time that it receives the $20 million. To lock in an interest rate now, IC enters into a FRA with Metrobank. The parties agree on a contract rate of 8%. The payoff depends on the value of 6-month LIBID at maturity of the contract.[21] If LIBID is, say, 7%, Metrobank will pay IC the 1% difference on $20 million (1% on $20 million for 6 months is $100,000). If 6-month LIBID is, say, 9%, IC will pay Metrobank $100,000.

OTC Options. The OTC market also offers a wide variety of option contracts. The most common are options on foreign exchange and various interest rate options.

Interest rate options include *caps*, *floors*, and *collars*. For example, a corporation taking a floating-rate loan at LIBOR can buy a 10% **cap** to ensure that its interest payments will not rise above 10%. If LIBOR rises above 10%, the writer of the option pays the difference (e.g., if LIBOR is 12% the corporation receives 2% on the notional amount). A **floor** guarantees an investor in a floating-rate security that the interest received will not fall below some stated minimum. Purchasers of caps and floors pay a premium, just as they do with exchange-traded options.

A third type of option, the **collar**, requires no premium. The collar combines the purchase of a cap with the *sale* of a floor. For example, a floating-rate borrower might secure a 9%/11% cap from a bank. If LIBOR rises above 11%, the bank pays the borrower; if LIBOR falls below 9%, the borrower pays the bank. That way, the borrower's net interest

---

[20] These numbers were down from 1998, when they were $900 billion and $600 billion, respectively. The main reason seems to be the elimination of foreign exchange transactions involving the currencies of the European countries that have adopted the Euro.

[21] LIBID is the rate at which banks are willing to accept Eurodollar deposits (their borrowing rate). LIBOR is the rate at which banks are willing to make Eurodollar deposits (their lending rate).

cost cannot rise above 11% or fall below 9%. Giving up the possible gain from a fall in interest rate pays for protection against a rise.

Addressing Replacement Risk on OTC Derivatives

Like swaps, these other OTC derivatives all expose dealers to replacement risk. Dealers first of all limit their exposure to this risk by establishing a credit limit for each counterparty, with a higher limit for more creditworthy counterparties. The terms of the relationship with each counterparty, whether an end user or another dealer, are defined by a master agreement—usually a standard form published by the ISDA—which governs all transactions with them.

Dealers try to minimize the risk, at least in the interdealer market, through close-out netting. For example suppose Metrobank owes London Merchant Bank $100 million on swaps and London Merchant Bank owes Metrobank $80 million on FRAs. The exposure of each can be reduced by replacing the two debts with a single debt of Metrobank to London Merchant Bank of $20 million. Such bilateral netting among market participants is increasingly common.

In some cases, dealers will require collateral from a counterparty, usually when replacement risk exceeds an agreed-upon threshold. The collateral is generally in the form of government securities. Even dealers who demand collateral, however, do so in only 10 to 30% of cases. Occasionally, counterparties will agree to marking to market and periodic settlement to eliminate replacement risk. There have also more ambitious attempts to set up clearinghouses that would allow multilateral netting and perhaps guarantees of execution. None of these, however, has managed to attract much business, dealers preferring to rely on bilateral arrangements.

QUESTIONS RAISED BY THE GROWTH OF DERIVATIVES MARKETS

Thirty years ago, financial derivatives did not exist. By 1991, the total notional amount outstanding had reached $8 trillion; in 2002, it had surpassed $100 trillion. The breakdown by type of derivative is shown in Exhibit 16.11.

The explosive growth of the derivatives market raises a number of interesting questions.

- Why did it happen? What changed in the early 1970s to cause this market to emerge and to grow so rapidly?
- Why do both exchange-traded and OTC derivatives exist? They seem to fulfill essentially the same function. Why do we need them both?
- The derivatives markets are constantly inventing new types of derivative. Why do some succeed and others not?

Why Has the Market Exploded?

The demand for financial derivatives was stimulated by a very considerable increase in the volatility of exchange rates and interest rates that took place in the early 1970s. The break-

EXHIBIT 16.11   Financial Derivatives Outstanding, Notional Amounts, Year End 2000 (Billions of Dollars)

Exchange traded			13,522
Futures		8,285	
Interest rate	7,914		
Currency	37		
Equity index	334		
Options		5,237	
Interest rate	3,755		
Currency	22		
Equity index	1,459		
OTC			80,312
Interest rate contracts	50,015		
Foreign exchange contracts	18,011		
Equity-linked contracts	1,488		
Other[a]	10,804		
Total			93,834

[a] Includes commodity contracts and some other nonfinancial instruments.

Source: BIS *(2000).*

down of the Bretton Woods system of fixed exchange rates in the early 1970s led to increasingly wide fluctuations in exchange rates. The loss of control over the quantity of money in the late 1970s and various attempts to regain it led to wide fluctuations in interest rates (see Exhibit 16.12).

The increase in the volatility of exchange rates and interest rates has greatly increased **market risk**. As we saw in Chapter 4, fluctuations in exchange rates and in interest rates cause the values of securities to fluctuate, with corresponding capital gains and losses to their holders.

market risk
The risk of a change in the value of an asset due to changes in market interest rates or exchange rates.

Market makers are particularly vulnerable to market risk. Because they stand ready to buy and sell at quoted prices, market makers must hold substantial inventories of the goods they trade. (A good example is the government securities dealers that we studied in Chapter 12.) By definition, the asset positions of specialized market makers are not well diversified: consequently, fluctuations in market price can cause them large gains or losses.

Financial intermediaries, too, are vulnerable to market risk. Fluctuations in exchange rates and in interest rates may affect their assets and liabilities differently, causing sharp changes in the value of their equity. The massive losses to thrift in the early 1980s as interest rates rose is a good example.[22]

While market risk was a new problem for financial market makers and intermediaries, it was a very old problem for other types of market maker. The volatility of commodity prices and of stock prices had long been a threat to market makers in those markets. Futures and options markets had grown up largely to allow market makers in commodities and in stocks to hedge their positions. When price volatility became a serious problem for

---

[22] See Chapter 19 for a discussion of the thrift crisis.

EXHIBIT 16.12   The Increasing Volatility of Interest Rates and Exchange Rates

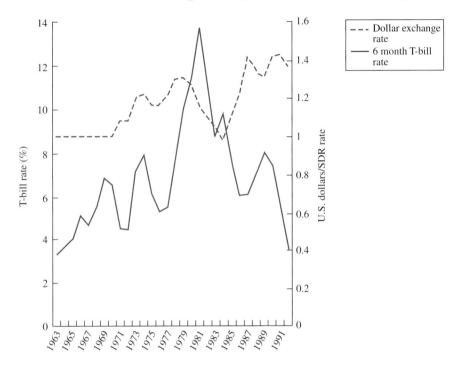

Sources: Economic Report of the President, 1993; IMF, International Financial Statistics Yearbook.

market makers in debt securities. and for financial intermediaries, it was only natural that futures and options market should expand to serve their needs too.

As increasing market risk created a need to hedge that risk; widespread deregulation made it easier to do so. Regulators allowed new instruments to be created, allowed new exchanges to be set up, and allowed financial institutions to use the new hedging instruments.

The creation and the use of new hedging instruments was facilitated by advances in financial theory and in computer technology. Advances in the theory of finance—especially the Black–Scholes option-pricing formula—provided the basis for creating and pricing new instruments. Advances in computer technology provided the rapid calculation required for their use. Computers also made possible the vastly increased volumes of transactions.

Why Are There Both Exchange-Traded and OTC Instruments?

Exchange-traded and OTC instruments serve much the same function. For example, we saw earlier in the chapter that Valley Motors could hedge exchange rate risk by buying foreign exchange forward (an OTC instrument) or by buying foreign exchange futures (an exchange-traded instrument). So foreign exchange futures compete with forward foreign exchange. Similarly, interest rate futures compete with swaps and FRAs; and exchange-traded options compete with OTC options.

Why in each case doesn't competition drive one of the two derivatives out of existence? Why do both alternatives remain available? The answer is that exchange-traded and OTC derivatives differ in important respects. Because of these differences, they largely serve different clienteles, and they can therefore continue to coexist.

How Exchange-Traded and OTC Derivatives Differ.   The two types of derivative differ with respect to liquidity, flexibility, cost, maturity, regulation, and risk.

Liquidity.   Exchange-traded derivatives are much more liquid than OTC derivatives. It is easy and inexpensive to change one's position in exchange-traded derivatives; it is less easy and more expensive to change one's position in the corresponding OTC instruments. For example, if you are hedging interest rate risk in the futures market, it is easy to lift the hedge by closing out your position. If you are hedging with a FRA, you can lift the hedge by taking out another offsetting FRA, but the two agreements do not cancel each other out. You remain exposed to replacement risk on both of them.[23]

Flexibility.   Exchange-traded derivatives, however, are less flexible. As we have seen, because exchange-traded contracts are standardized, they rarely fit the needs of a hedger precisely. The result is basis risk. Dealers in OTC derivatives, on the other hand, are usually willing to tailor the instrument to fit the needs of the customer. If necessary, they will come up with an entirely new type of instrument.

Cost.   Naturally, tailor-made is more expensive. The cost of hedging in exchange-traded contracts is generally lower. Exchange-traded contracts are a commodity, and the market is arm's length and very competitive. The OTC market is more of a relationship market, and this reduces the degree of competition.

Partly offsetting this cost disadvantage, OTC derivatives generally do not require margin. Consequently, there is no inconvenient cash flow before maturity (no daily settlement).

Maturity.   Swaps have an important advantage over exchange-traded derivatives as a hedging instrument: they are available at much longer maturities. Typically, maturity dates on most exchange-traded derivatives go out no more than 2 years. Swaps on the other hand are commonly written for as many as 15 years.

Regulation.   The OTC market has a regulatory advantage: it is essentially unregulated. In contrast, the futures and options markets are quite tightly regulated. This difference is particularly important in the introduction of new instruments. While each new futures or options contract must be approved by regulators—a process that is slow and uncertain—the OTC market is free to offer whatever new instrument it pleases.

---

[23] We have seen that a swap can be canceled. But a customer asking a dealer to cancel a swap is not exactly in a competitive situation and should expect to pay handsomely for the favor.

Naturally, the exchanges feel that the regulatory advantage of the OTC market is unfair, and they have been pressing for more regulation of the OTC market. (Presumably they see little hope of success in pressing for less regulation of exchanges.) Despite this pressure, the CFTC voted in January 1993 to exempt swaps from its regulations, as long as they are not traded on exchanges. This important ruling was welcomed by swap dealers, but not by the exchanges.

Replacement Risk.   Replacement risk is different in the two markets. There is essentially none for exchange-traded derivatives. The combination of broker and exchange guarantees together with the safeguards built into the trading process ensure that promises will be kept. Because replacement risk is not a problem, virtually anyone can participate in the futures and options markets.

In the OTC market, on the other hand, replacement risk is an issue. To a large extent, dealers substitute their own credit, but, as we have seen, their credit is not always beyond question. Because participants are concerned about replacement risk, the OTC market is not open to everyone. It is purely a wholesale market, and only relatively good credits can participate.

Exchange-Traded and OTC Derivatives Serve Different Clienteles. Exchange-traded and OTC derivatives differ, therefore, in their properties. Exchange-traded derivatives are more liquid, are less expensive, and involve less replacement risk. Because they are standardized, they fit the needs of hedgers less precisely, resulting in basis risk. On the other hand, because OTC derivatives can be tailored to fit the needs of the customer, they provide a better hedge. However, they are more expensive, less liquid, and subject to replacement risk. The differing properties of the two types of derivative make each the preferred choice for a different clientele.

The OTC market is much better suited to hedgers who have known and unchanging risks that they wishes to hedge. For example, for nonfinancial corporations that wish to hedge the interest rate risk on their debt or the exchange rate risk on foreign transactions, swaps and forward exchange are ideal. The risks can be hedged more precisely in the OTC market, avoiding basis risk. Since the need for the hedge is not likely to change suddenly, the lack of liquidity is not a problem.

Liquidity is, however, of great importance to market makers. First, they must be able to change the hedge rapidly as the size of their inventory position fluctuates in the normal course of business. Second, they will want to change the extent to which they hedge in response to new market information. Remember that market makers earn a substantial part of their income from position plays—taking unhedged positions in the instruments or commodities that they trade.[24] Market makers therefore find exchange-traded derivatives more attractive.

The market makers who are the main customers for exchange-traded derivatives include not only securities dealers and financial intermediaries but also market makers for OTC derivatives. We have seen that intermediaries, especially banks, make the market in

---

[24] See Chapter 12 for a discussion of how securities dealers operate.

instruments such as swaps and forward foreign exchange. They too need to hedge their inventory positions.

For example, a bank making a market in swaps may agree to become a fixed-rate payer on an interest rate swap with a customer wishing to become a floating-rate payer. If the bank does not immediately have another customer wishing to become a fixed-rate payer, it can hedge its own position in the T-bond futures market. When a suitable customer does come along, the bank can lift the hedge easily and cheaply by closing out its futures position. Catering to this demand, the CBOT announced in July 2001 plans to introduce futures contracts in 10-year and 5-year swap rates that would provide a better hedge than T-bond futures. The better a bank can hedge its own position with futures, the better the service it can provide its customers in the swap market.[25]

Exchange-traded derivatives are also more attractive to speculators (information traders). Exchange-traded derivatives have low transactions costs and good liquidity, making it easy for traders to change their positions rapidly as new information emerges. Because the structure of the market eliminates replacement risk, the market is open to anyone who wishes to play. It is also easier to take a short position in futures. For example, suppose you believe that stocks are going to fall in value. If you wanted to sell short a basket of stocks, any number of restrictions and costs would get in your way. Taking a short position in futures is straightforward.

Because information traders prefer trading on the exchanges, the exchanges dominate the OTC market in price discovery. The exchanges are where the prices are formed. Generally, instruments in the OTC market are priced off the corresponding exchange-traded instrument. For example, to know how much to charge for a FRA or a swap, a dealer checks the corresponding prices on interest rate futures.

Not all "speculators" (those with naked positions in derivatives) are active information traders. Institutional investors, such as pension funds, have been taking increasing interest in adding futures pools to their portfolios for the sake of diversification. Although risky, derivatives have different risk characteristics from stocks and bonds, and so taking a position in them can improve the overall performance of the institutions' asset portfolios. For such investors, too, liquidity and replacement risk are important, while basis risk is not.

Why Do Some Contracts Succeed and Others Not?

Index futures have been a tremendous success. So have Treasury bond and Eurodollar futures. Treasury bill futures were a success to begin with, but they have since declined in importance. Some other contracts never succeeded. For example, a contract in the Consumer Price Index (CPI), intended to provide a hedge against inflation, seemed like a good idea, but it proved to be a flop. Why do some contracts succeed and others not?

For a contract to succeed, there must be trading volume. We have seen that it is the locals who make the market for a given contract. For it to be worth the locals' while to make the necessary investment in information, trading volume must be large enough to repay this investment. If locals are not attracted to the market, it will be illiquid. Also,

---

[25] The increased maturity of Eurodollar futures has improved the liquidity of the swap market because it allows market makers to hedge.

markets have substantial fixed costs that must be covered out of trading fees: with low volume, either the fees must be high or the market will lose money.

To generate trading volume, it is not enough that there be a need to hedge against some risk: there must also be a need to *change* the amount hedged. As we have seen, the principal service that exchanges provide is liquidity. Their two main customers are market makers and information traders. If neither of these have much interest in a given contract, there will be little trading volume, and the contract will not succeed.

We can see, therefore, why the CPI contract was a failure. While there is widespread interest in hedging against inflation, there is little need to change the hedge once it is made. There is no "market in inflation," and so no market makers needing to hedge their positions. Rates of inflation change slowly, so there is little opportunity for information trading. It is not surprising, then, that trading volume never got off the ground, and that the contract eventually died.[26]

APPENDIX: PRICING DERIVATIVE SECURITIES

The pricing of futures, options, and swaps is of great interest and importance. As we have seen, a better understanding of the principles of pricing has played a major role in the development of these markets. A thorough treatment of this important topic is, however, beyond the scope of this book. This appendix is intended only as a summary of the major results.

Futures or Forward Prices

The relationship between the futures or forward price at t for delivery at T, call it $F_{t,T}$ and the spot price at t, P_t, is

$$P_t(1 + r_{t,T} + c_{t,T}) = F_{t,T} \qquad [16.A1]$$

where $r_{t,T}$ is the interest cost of borrowing at t for repayment at T and $c_{t,T}$ is the percentage cost of holding the underlying asset from t to T.

---

[26] Sometimes there are more specific reasons why one contract succeeds and another does not. The T-bill contract, initially a success, was largely displaced by the more attractive Eurodollar contract. There were several reasons for this. First, most money market interest rates (for CDs, commercial paper, etc.) track Eurodollar rates more closely than Treasury rates. Hence, a Eurodollar contract has less basis risk. Second, the T-bill contract is settled by delivery (if not offset beforehand), while the Eurodollar contract is settled in cash: this is more convenient. Finally, because it is traded in Singapore and London as well as in Chicago, the Eurodollar contract trades longer hours. This enables traders to respond immediately to new information, rather than having to wait until Chicago opens.

The contracts in CDs and commercial bills failed because of the heterogeneity of the underlying securities. Under the terms of the contract, delivery could be made in the paper of any one of a list of named institutions. As the credit standing of those institutions varied, the price of their paper varied too. Naturally, traders who had sold the contracts chose to make delivery in the paper that was least expensive on the date of delivery. Understanding that this would happen, other traders were reluctant to buy these contracts, and the market for them died.

For example, suppose the spot price of gold is $300, the interest rate for one year is 5%, and the storage cost of gold is 1% per year. Then the futures or forward price of gold for delivery one year from now must be

$$\$300(1 + 0.5 + 0.1) = \$318$$

To see why this must be so, suppose the futures or forward price is different, say $320. Then it is possible to make a risk-free profit. Here is how. Borrow $300 and buy an ounce of gold. At the same time, sell a futures contract for one ounce or sell one ounce forward for delivery a year from now. At the end of the year you will owe $315 on the loan and $3 for storage—a total of $318. But you will receive $320 in exchange for the gold, a riskless profit of $2.

This sort of arbitrage is called a *cash-and-carry* arbitrage. If the futures price is too low relative to the spot price, it is possible to engage in *reverse* cash-and-carry arbitrage (sell the underlying asset short and lend the proceeds; buy the futures contract). The possibility of these two types of arbitrage ensures that the relationship between spot and futures prices is as shown in Equation 16.A1.

The relationship between the futures price and the expected spot price at the time of delivery, EP_T, is

$$\frac{F_{t,T}}{1 + r_{t,T}} = \frac{EP_T}{1 + r_{t,T} + \beta \times rp_m} \qquad [16.A2]$$

where β is the beta of the underlying asset—a measure of how closely the risk on the asset is associated with the risk on a diversified market portfolio, and rp_m is the risk premium on a diversified market portfolio.

You can see from Equation 16.A2 that the futures price will equal the expected spot price only if the β of the underlying asset is zero.

Swap Prices

As we have seen, swaps are simply bundles of forward transactions. Their price can therefore be determined from the appropriate futures or forward prices.

For example, consider a commodity swap in gold that involves the exchange of fixed payments for whatever the price of gold turns out to be 1 year from now and 2 years from now. The two fixed payments F must therefore satisfy

$$\frac{F - F_{0,1}}{1 + r_{0,1}} + \frac{F - F_{0,2}}{1 + r_{0,2}} = 0 \qquad [16.A3]$$

If F did not satisfy this relationship, it would be possible to undertake a risk-free arbitrage between the swap and the futures markets.

Option Prices

Black–Scholes formula

The basic equation used to price options.

The price at time t of a call option with an exercise price of K, expiring at time T, is given by the **Black–Scholes formula**:

$$C = P_t N(x) - K e^{r_{t,T}(T-t)} N(x - \sigma \sqrt{T - t}) \qquad [16.A4]$$

where P_t and $r_{t,T}$ are as above, $N(\cdot)$ is the cumulative normal distribution, σ is the instantaneous standard error of P_t, and

$$x \equiv \frac{\log(P_t/K) + r_{t,T}(T - t)}{\sigma\sqrt{T - t}} + \frac{1}{2}\sigma\sqrt{T - t}$$

While this formula is not exactly intuitive, some of its implications for the price of an option do make intuitive sense:

- The higher the exercise price, the less valuable the option, because the less likely it is to be in the money.
- The more time that remains before the option expires, the more valuable the option, because the more likely it is to be in the money.
- The more the price of the underlying asset varies (the larger σ), the more valuable the option, because the more likely it is to be in the money.
- The higher the interest rate, the less valuable the option, because the payoff comes in the future.

put–call parity condition

An equation relating the prices of corresponding puts and calls.

The price of a put option, Π, can be derived from the price of the corresponding call (from Equation 16.A4) using the **put–call parity condition**:

$$C - \Pi = P_t - K e^{r_{t,T}(T-t)} \qquad [16.A5]$$

SUMMARY

- There are two types of forward transaction. In a *forward trade*, the parties agree to trade at a specified time in the future, at a price set now. With a *derivative contract*, the two parties agree that they will pay or receive from each other at a set time in the future certain sums of money.
- A futures contract is a wager on the value of a market price at the maturity date. If the market price is above the futures price, the seller pays the buyer a sum proportional to the notional amount. If the value is below the futures price, the buyer pays the seller.
- Because a forward transaction is an exchanges of promises, it is subject to the same credit and liquidity problems as a lending transaction. Organized derivatives markets address these problems.
- Hedging in futures can, at relatively low cost, remove the risk of a long or short position in an underlying asset.
- The futures price is the price at which the market considers the futures contract to be a fair wager. At this value of the futures price, the market believes the expected gain from a rise in price to be just balanced by the expected gain from a fall in price.
- Locals provide the futures market with liquidity, and their trading ensures that new information is integrated into prices rapidly.

- A futures exchange protects traders against replacement risk by guaranteeing fulfillment of contracts. It protects itself through daily settlement, marking to market, and requiring margin.

- A futures contract can be settled before maturity by taking an offsetting position.

- Many types of futures contract are settled at maturity in cash. Older contracts, mainly those for various commodities, were designed to require delivery in the underlying commodity. In practice, most of these are settled by offset rather than by actual delivery.

- To ensure sufficient trading volume to sustain a market, futures contracts are standardized. Standardization creates basis risk.

- Stock index futures allow hedging and speculation on baskets of stocks. Index arbitrage ensures that the price of the futures closely tracks the price of the underlying stocks.

- Options give hedgers protection against adverse price movements, while allowing gains from favorable price movements.

- An option is a one-sided wager on an underlying market price. Consequently, the buyer of the option must pay the seller a premium. The value of the premium is such that the market considers it fair payment for the possible gain to the buyer and loss to the seller.

- Swaps allow borrowers to separate the decision on *where* to borrow from the decision on *what form* the borrowing should take. This allows borrowers to borrow in the market in which they have comparative advantage and so to lower the cost of their borrowing.

- A swap is a series of wagers on an underlying price. Payments depend on the relationship between the underlying price and the swap price and are proportional to the notional principal. A swap is a fair wager: the market determines the swap price so that the expected gains to the two parties are equal.

- A direct swap agreement between two parties involves replacement risk. Therefore, swaps are generally arranged indirectly through financial intermediaries. The intermediaries manage their own replacement risk by limiting exposure to individual counterparties, by bilateral netting, and sometimes by demanding collateral.

- Intermediaries offer interest rate swaps, currency swaps, commodity swaps, credit default swaps, and other types of swap. They also offer forward transactions in foreign exchange and in interest rates.

- The market for derivatives exploded beginning in the 1970s because of the increase in market risk and because of advances in financial and computer technology.

- Exchange-traded derivatives compete with OTC derivatives. Exchange-traded derivatives are more liquid, less expensive, and, because of exchange guarantees, safer. However, they are also less flexible and involve margin requirements and daily settlement, both of which can be inconvenient to traders.

- Exchange-traded and OTC derivatives coexist mainly because they serve different clienteles. The liquidity of exchange-traded derivatives appeals mainly to market makers (including market makers in OTC derivatives) and to speculators. Long-term hedgers, who do not require liquidity, usually prefer OTC derivatives.

- New exchange-traded derivatives succeed when there exists a corresponding clientele of market makers and speculators.

DISCUSSION QUESTIONS

1. What is a local? Why are locals important to the functioning of futures markets?

2. Why is settlement by delivery relatively unusual in futures markets? What are the alternatives?

3. What is basis risk, why does it occur, and why does it matter?

4. a. You have bought an American call option on DM 1 million, with an expiration date of March 15 and an exercise price of 60¢/DM. To what exactly does this entitle you?

   b. You have sold a European put on DM 1 million, with an expiration date of March 15 and an exercise price of 60¢/DM. To what does this oblige you?

5. The price of a 5-year swap is 50 bid and 65 asked. The current rate on 5-year Treasuries is 7%. You become a floating-rate payer on such a swap with a notional principal of $10 million. What will you pay? What will you receive?

6. The swap dealer who sells you the swap of Question 5 does not yet have a matching counterparty. How can it hedge its position in futures or options?

7. Why do there exist both OTC derivatives and exchange-traded derivatives in interest rates and exchange rates?

8. You buy futures contracts for ¥100 million at a price of 0.92¢/¥. If the margin requirement is 20%, how much margin must you put up. Over the next week, the closing price each day is as follows:

Day 1	0.93
Day 2	0.90
Day 3	0.90
Day 4	0.84
Day 5	0.86

For each day, calculate your gain or loss and the balance in your margin account. If maintenance margin is 80% of the original margin, will you receive any margin calls? If so, for how much?

9. Forward transactions are subject to problems. What are these problems? How do futures and options markets deal with them? How does the swap market deal with them?

10. Draw up a table comparing the advantages and disadvantages of hedging with futures, exchange-traded options, and OTC derivatives such as swaps.

11. "The futures market handles forward transactions in the same way the bond market handles direct lending. The swap market is the equivalent of indirect lending." Do you agree? Explain.

12. First National is acting as a swap intermediary. One of its fixed-rate payers defaults on a 7% swap with notional principal of $10 million and with five annual payments remaining. First National replaces the defaulting party with a new fixed-rate payer at the market rate of 6%. What is its loss?

13. Futures exchanges would like to offer swaps. The appeal of exchange-traded swaps is that they would eliminate replacement risk (as illustrated by question 12), because the exchange would guarantee the swap to both parties. What safeguards do you think the exchange would impose to protect itself from the consequent risk? How would these safeguards affect the attractiveness of exchange-traded swaps?

14. Are stock index futures good or bad for the stock exchanges? Is the existence of OTC derivatives good or bad for futures exchanges? Explain your answers to both questions.

BIBLIOGRAPHY

Abken, Peter A. "Beyond Plain Vanilla: A Taxonomy of Swaps." *Federal Reserve Bank of Atlanta Economic Review*, March–April 1991, 12–29.

Bank for International Settlements. *BIS Annual Report.* Basel: BIS, 2000.

Behoff, John P. "Reducing Credit Risk in Over-the-Counter Derivatives." *Federal Reserve Bank of Chicago Economic Perspectives*, January–February 1992, 21–31.

Hunter, William C., and David W. Stowe. "Path-Dependent Options." *Federal Reserve Bank of Atlanta Economic Review*, March–April 1992, 29–34.

Kuprianov, Anatoli. "Money Market Futures." *Federal Reserve Bank of Richmond Economic Review*, November–December 1992, 19–37.

Napoli, Janet A. "Derivative Markets and Competitiveness." *Federal Reserve Bank of Chicago Economic Perspectives*, July–August 1992, 13–24.

Neal, R. S. "Credit Derivatives: New Financial Instruments for Controlling Credit Risk." *Federal Reserve Bank of Kansas City Economic Review*, second quarter, 1996, 15–27.

Smith, Clifford W., Jr., Charles W. Smithson, and Lee Macdonald Wakeman. "The Market for Interest Rate Swaps." *Journal of the Financial Management Association* 17 no. 4 (winter 1988): 34–44.

Stigum, Marcia L. *The Money Market.* 3rd ed. Homewood, IL: Dow Jones-Irwin, 1990.

Wall, Larry D., and John J. Pringle, "Interest Rate Swaps: A Review of the Issues." *Economic Review of the Federal Reserve Bank of Atlanta*, December 1988, 22–40.

KEY TERMS

forward transaction
forward trade
derivative
financial derivative
long position
short position
spot
futures price
notional amount
maturity date
futures commission merchant (FCM)
floor broker
locals
replacement risk
daily settlement
marking to market
margin
margin account
margin call

maintenance margin
settlement by offset
cash settlement
settlement by delivery
basis risk
stock index
index arbitrage
option contract
put option
exercise or strike price
call option
American option
European option
in the money
out of the money
premium
market makers
options on futures
path-dependent option

interest rate swap
fixed-rate payer
floating-rate payer
notional principal
naked position
over-the-counter (OTC) market
interdealer market for swaps
currency swap
credit derivatives
credit default swap
foreign exchange swap
forward forward contract
forward rate agreement (FRA)
cap
floor
collar
market risk
Black–Scholes formula
put–call parity condition

CHAPTER 17

THE ORGANIZATION OF FINANCIAL MARKETS

When you finish this chapter you will understand:

- How organized markets make it easier to trade securities
- Why trading floors are disappearing, increasingly replaced by computer systems
- Why the New York Stock Exchange is losing business to its competitors
- How competition is changing the way that exchanges are organized

We have now studied all the major financial markets—the market for government securities, the mortgage market, the debt market, the equity market, and the market for derivatives. Generally, we have focused on the instruments involved and on the economic issues raised by their use and trading. In this chapter we shall focus on the financial markets themselves and on how they work. We shall see how financial markets are organized, how exactly trading takes place, how financial markets ensure that buyers receive their securities and sellers their money, and how the "market industry" is being rocked by powerful economic forces.

Before we start, let us recall what it is that financial markets do. Remember that markets have two basic functions—*price discovery* and *the provision of liquidity*. Financial markets set a price for the instruments they trade, and they makes it easier for people to trade them.[1] In studying the nuts and bolts of financial markets, we need to keep these functions firmly in mind.

THE NATURE OF ORGANIZED MARKETS

retail market
The market in which the individual investor buys and sells securities.

Let us begin by dividing a financial market into two parts—a retail market and a wholesale market. The **retail market** is the market in which the individual investor buys and sells securities. The **wholesale market** is the market in which professionals, including institutional investors, trade with one another, usually in large amounts. It is in the wholesale market that trading actually takes place. For example, the New York Stock Exchange (NYSE) is a wholesale market. As a retail buyer or seller, you have no direct access to the wholesale market. Rather, you place your order with a retail broker, who sends it on to the wholesale market for execution.

wholesale market
The market in which professionals, including institutional investors, trade with one another.

The retail market is important. It is, for example, where most people in the securities industry work. Moreover, because it involves small investors, it also receives a great deal of attention from regulators. However, it is the wholesale market that we shall be studying in this chapter. That is where the action is.[2]

organized market
A market structured to facilitate trading.

Wholesale markets are **organized markets**. They are structured to facilitate trading. The structure of organized markets can differ along a number of dimensions: they can be exchanges or over-the-counter markets; they can be centralized or decentralized; they can be dealer markets or auction markets. We shall see that a market's structure affects how well it performs its basic functions of price discovery and of providing liquidity as well as the cost of performing these functions.

A Typology of Organized Markets

Exchanges and Over-the-Counter Markets.   There are two basic types of organized market—the exchange and the over-the-counter (OTC) market. Most securities trade in OTC markets: exchanges are the exception. Examples of OTC markets include NASDAQ and the London International Stock Exchange (stocks and bonds), the market for government securities, the money market, the market for mortgage-backed securities, the market for swaps, and the foreign exchange market. Examples of exchanges include the New York, Tokyo, and London Stock Exchanges (stocks and bonds), and the Chicago Mercantile Exchange (futures and options).

You used to be able to tell an exchange from an over-the-counter market by how traders communicated with one another. On an exchange, traders met face-to-face on the trading floor; in an OTC market, they bargained over the telephone. In recent years, as we shall see, this distinction has been blurred by technology. While some exchanges still rely on face-to-face trading, many have switched to automated trading using computer terminals. Many OTC markets now rely on similar automated trading systems.

---

[1] See Chapter 11 for a more extensive discussion.

[2] We talked about the retail market in Chapter 11 when we discussed the brokerage function of securities firms.

The main difference today is in the formality of the structure. With an exchange, participation is more restricted and trading rules more strictly specified. Over-the-counter markets vary in their degree of formality: some are not very different from exchanges; others are very loose structures indeed.

The more structured the market, the more expensive it is to set it up. On the whole, the cost of setting up an exchange is greater than that of setting up an OTC market. The additional cost is worthwhile only if there is sufficient trading volume: much of the cost is fixed, so the cost per trade is high unless the volume is large. On the whole, therefore, bonds, which trade relatively little, tend to trade on OTC markets, and stocks, which trade a lot, tend to trade on exchanges. Similarly, swaps trade in OTC markets, while futures and options trade on exchanges.

In addition, structure is worthwhile only if the number of traders is large. We shall see presently that one of the things that structure does is to make it easier for strangers to trade with one another with confidence. A small circle of traders who know one another well and have a continuing trading relationship will have little to gain from the formal structure of an exchange. As we saw in Chapter 12, government securities trade mainly among a relatively small number of dealers and institutional investors. An over-the-counter market serves them well. The number of traders of stocks is much larger, and stocks generally trade on exchanges.

Dealer Markets and Auction Markets. As we saw in Chapter 11, there are two alternative ways to trade in an organized market—through dealers or by auction. A dealer market is "quote driven": dealers quote bid and asked prices and stand ready to buy and sell at those prices. An auction market is "order driven": it brings together and matches orders from potential buyers and sellers.

In a dealer market, it is the dealers who set the price, responding to new information. In an auction market, the price is set by current supply and demand (we shall see how presently). New information affects the price only through the trading of information traders.

Basic liquidity in both types of market is provided by the traders themselves. On the whole, desired liquidity sales roughly balance desired liquidity purchases. Sometimes, however, there is an imbalance.[3] In a dealer market, it is the dealers who provide backup liquidity—absorbing liquidity imbalances in exchange for the bid–asked spread. In an auction market, it is information traders who provide backup liquidity—absorbing liquidity imbalances in exchange for trading profits.

All OTC markets are dealer markets, but so are some exchanges (the London Stock Exchange was a dealer market until 1997). Most exchanges, however, are auction markets—the futures and options exchanges, most European stock exchanges, and the Tokyo Stock Exchange. Some markets are hybrids, combining elements of both auction market and dealer market. The most notable example is the New York Stock Exchange. There, as we shall see, *specialists* can act either as brokers, matching traders' orders, or as dealers, quoting prices at which they themselves are willing to trade.

---

[3] See Chapter 11 for a discussion of liquidity traders and information traders.

Centralized Markets and Decentralized Markets.   Organized markets differ in their degree of centralization. If you are a trader on one of the Chicago futures exchanges, you see every single trade that takes place. It all happens right there in front of you in the trading pit. On each transaction, you have the opportunity to intervene and to accept a bid or make an offer. This is an example of a **centralized market**.

On the other hand, if you are a trader in the government securities market, you are in contact with some of the other participants but not with others. It is quite possible that trades are taking place somewhere else in the market that you know nothing about. This is an example of a **decentralized market**.

Many markets are "semicentralized." For example, most of the trading in stocks listed on the New York Stock Exchange takes place at the exchange, but substantial trading does takes place elsewhere.[4]

The Advantages of Centralization.   Centralized markets have definite advantages. The process of price discovery–of finding the fair price–works best when all potential buyers and sellers are in contact with one another. Then, when a trade takes place, you can be sure that no one would have bought for a higher price or sold for a lower one. Such a market is described as being a **transparent market**.

Liquidity too is better in a centralized market. The larger the volume of buying and selling that is brought together, the less likely it is that there will be a liquidity imbalance. Moreover, only in a market with a sufficient volume of trading is it profitable for dealers or for information traders to provide backup liquidity.

These advantages of centralization create a natural tendency for trade to become more centralized. Trading volume tends to attract more trading volume. Historically, traders in a particular security tended to meet in a single place; and trading would often be concentrated at a specific time. This tendency towards centralization holds not only for individual securities but also for securities in general. Over time, certain cities have evolved as financial centers where trade in many securities is centralized.

The Disadvantages of Centralization.   Given the advantages of centralization, why are there markets that are not centralized? The reason is that centralization has one serious disadvantage: it creates market power.[5] When trade is concentrated in a single market, those who control access to that market can earn monopoly profits by raising the price of using the market. In practice, that means that trading costs, in the form of commissions and fees, are higher than the cost of providing the service.

As we have seen before, monopoly also means laziness: relieved of competitive pressure, those controlling a centralized market have little incentive to lower trading costs by introducing new technology. Both monopoly profits and technological backwardness can make using a centralized market more expensive.

Decentralized markets are by their nature more competitive. Within a decentralized market, you can shop around for trading partners and make whatever arrangements you

centralized market
One in which all traders have access to the same trading opportunities and all trades are made at publicly announced prices.

decentralized market
One in which prices are quoted and transactions concluded in private meetings between traders.

transparent market
One in which all transactions are visible to all traders.

---

[4] We shall have more to say about this later in the chapter.

[5] A market is, in a sense, a natural monopoly. Market power is the standard problem of natural monopolies.

please. The loose organization of these markets makes collusion to fix the price of services more difficult. Because of the competitive pressure, decentralized markets often offer lower trading costs. Even when they are not as good at price discovery or the provision of liquidity, lower trading costs may make them attractive.

If a centralized market falls victim to the abuse of market power, there is a good chance that centralization will break down. Traders will find alternative ways of trading that lower their transactions costs. We shall see that this is exactly what has happened with stock markets in the United States and Europe.

How Organized Markets Lower Trading Costs

The purpose of an organized market is to trade securities. Trading securities is subject to all the problems of trading in general.[6] First, traders must agree on the terms of a transaction. Then the transaction must actually be completed: securities and money must change hands. All of this involves costs. The lower the cost of trading, the more trading there is. The more trading there is, the better the market performs its basic functions of price discovery and the provision of liquidity. Organized markets lower the cost of trading in a variety of ways.

Restricted Access for Traders.   Traders in an organized market typically execute hundreds or even thousands of trades a day. To be able to do this, they need to know that the people with whom they are trading are reliable. If they had to run a credit check with each transaction, it would take time, cost money, and slow things down intolerably.

One way organized markets address this problem is by restricting access to the market: only authorized traders are allowed to participate. Outsiders can use the market only indirectly through an authorized trader. To be authorized, traders must satisfy certain standards. Typically these include capital requirements, accounting standards, and standards of honesty.

To trade in the New York Stock Exchange, for example, you must be a member. The number of members is fixed at 1,366. So the only way to join is to purchase a "seat" from an existing member (most of the seats belong to securities firms rather than to individuals). The purchase of a seat requires the approval of the exchange. To obtain approval, a potential member must provide full financial disclosure subject to independent audit and meet standards for competence and sufficient capital. Continuing members are subject to the same requirements.

Exhibit 17.1 shows how the average price of a seat on the NYSE has changed over the years. The price declined as stocks suffered during the inflationary 1970s and then revived during the 1980s. The crash of 1987 reduced public enthusiasm for stocks, and so trading volume and commission and the price of a seat declined. The price rose rapidly in the stock market boom of the late 1990s and once again fell when the boom turned to bust.

Rules of Conduct.   Organized markets also have sets of rules governing the conduct of their members. In particular, there are rules to ensure that the market is honest and

---

[6] We discussed these in Chapter 1.

EXHIBIT 17.1   Price of a Seat on the New York Stock Exchange

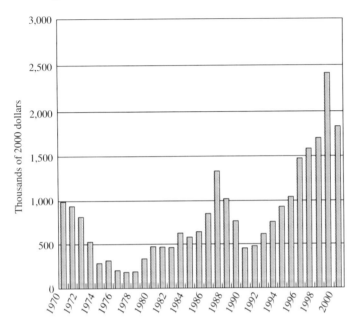

The price shown is the average of the maximum and minimum price for the year.

Source: New York Stock Exchange.

orderly—for example, to prevent price manipulation and insider trading.[7] The market establishes monitoring mechanisms to make sure the rules are upheld. Members who violate the rules are disciplined. Punishments range from nominal fines to suspension of trading privileges to expulsion from the market—the ultimate sanction.

As a result of restricted access and rules of conduct, when you strike a deal in an organized market, even with someone you do not know, you have some confidence in their honesty and in their word. This greatly reduces the cost of trading with them.

Restricted Access for Securities.   In addition to restricting access to traders, organized markets also restrict access to securities. One reason, again, is to lower trading costs. Limiting trading to a relatively small number of securities of known quality makes trading simpler and so less expensive. In addition, many of the costs of setting up a market in a particular security are fixed: they do not depend on the volume of trading. Consequently the cost per trade declines as the volume of trading increases. Moreover, revenue depends directly on volume. So organized markets typically agree to trade only those securities that can be expected to generate a sufficient volume of trading.

---

[7] We shall discuss the regulation of securities markets in Chapter 20.

A second reason to restrict access is reputation. The reputation of the market is tied up in the reputation of the issuers of the securities it trades. A scandal touching an issuer tarnishes the reputation of the market. By being selective in the securities it is willing to accept, a market establishes a reputation for quality. As a result, issuers are willing to pay for the distinction of being admitted to such a market.

listed company
A company whose securities are authorized to be traded in an organized market.

For example, for a company to be **listed** on the NYSE—that is, for its securities to be traded there—it must satisfy a set of **listing requirements**. The company must meet thresholds for earnings history, payment of dividends, and tangible assets or market value. It must provide adequate financial information and be willing to provide "timely disclosure of earnings, dividends, and other information which might materially affect the market." All of these requirements bear on quality. In addition, a company must have a sufficient number of shares held by the public and a sufficiently large number of shareholders. It must also generate a sufficiently large volume of trading. These requirements bear on the potential revenue for the exchange from trading the security. Listing fees are substantial: in total, they add up to about 30% of the revenue of the NYSE.

listing requirements
Standards a company must meet for its securities to be traded in an organized market.

Generally, the thresholds are higher for an initial listing (entry into the market) and less stringent for continued listing (being allowed to stay). However, companies that fail to meet the standards for continued listing are "delisted" (kicked out).

Standardization of Transactions.

In an organized market, transactions are usually standardized and simplified. For example, on the NYSE, stocks are traded in **round lots** of 100 or 1,000 shares[8]; in Chicago, futures contracts are standardized in their terms of delivery. There are also standard procedures for executing transactions—how and when to transfer the securities, how and when to make payment.

round lots
Standardized quantities of shares traded on an exchange.

Standardization makes trading much simpler. Traders need agree only on price and quantity: all the other parameters of the deal are understood and need not be discussed. Standardization also reduces the chance of confusion—of two traders differing in their understanding of the transaction between them.

Conflict Resolution.

Despite these measures, disputes among traders will still sometimes arise. Resolving disputes takes time and is costly, but it is an inevitable part of trading. Organized markets reduce the cost by providing an institutional framework to resolve disputes. Using such a "private court" is much less expensive than litigation in real courts.

This idea has been extended from the wholesale market to the retail market. In the 1980s, brokerages began to ask their clients to agree in advance to resolve any disputes through binding arbitration rather than in the courts. The U.S. Supreme Court ruled in 1989 that such agreements are enforceable. In 1991, the securities industry set up an independent body, the American Arbitration Association, to handle arbitrations.

Guaranteed Completion.

As we shall see later, the completion of a transaction involves a variety of risks. Taking measures to protect oneself against these risks is costly. To reduce these costs, organized markets often guarantee completion of transactions agreed to by its traders. If two traders agree on a transaction, both can be sure that the transaction will be completed as agreed.

---

[8] Special procedures exists for handling smaller transactions.

TRADING IN ORGANIZED MARKETS

How is trading in an organized market actually done? There are several different methods of trading, and each has its advantages and disadvantages.

Methods of Trading

Trading in a dealer market is pretty simple. You go to a dealer and buy or sell at a price the dealer quotes.[9] In large dealer markets, trading among the dealers in an inside market ensures that the quotes of different dealers remain fairly close to one another.[10]

---

[9] Haggling may take place. That is, the dealer may be willing to negotiate better prices or larger limits.

[10] In Chapter 12, we saw how this works in the government securities market.

TRADING ORDERS

While market orders and limit orders are the basic types, there are many variations:

stop order: The broker is to trade when the market price reaches a certain level, but then the order becomes a market order. Sell stops must be entered at a price below the current price.

stop-limit order: A stop order that becomes a limit order when the price reaches a certain level (if the market moves quickly, it may not be executed).

market-if-touched order: A sell order entered at a price above the current price.

fill-or-kill order: The broker is to buy or sell at the specified price or better, but an order that cannot be filled immediately is automatically canceled.

percentage order: The percentage of the order to be activated depends on trading volume in the security.

not-held order: Market order that gives floor brokers permission to delay if they think they can get a better price.

one-cancels-the-other order: Two simultaneous orders, with the remaining one canceled when the first is executed.

specific-time order: An order that must be executed at or by a given time. For example on the close, at the opening, day order (expires at end of day); good 'til canceled. All orders are assumed to be day orders unless otherwise specified.

market order

An instruction to buy or sell at the prevailing market price.

Trading in an auction market is rather more complicated. Buy and sell orders come into the market, and the market brings them together in some way to find a price and to match orders to create trades. There are different ways of doing this, but before we learn about them we need to understand the different types of order.

limit order

An instruction to buy or sell if the price market price crosses a stated limit.

Market Orders and Limit Orders.   The two basic types of order are the market order and the limit order. A **market order** is an instruction to buy or sell at the prevailing market price. An example: "sell 100 shares of IBM at whatever you can get for them." A **limit order** is an instruction to buy, specifying a maximum acceptable price, or an instruction to sell, specifying a minimum acceptable price. An example: "buy 100 shares of IBM if the price falls below 60." There are many variations on these two basic types (see "Trading Orders").

call auction

An auction in which trading takes place only at certain pre-arranged times—the "calls."

The Call Auction.   The simplest way to process orders is to hold auctions or "calls" at certain prearranged times—say once a week or twice a day. This procedure is known as a **call auction**.[11] Many stock exchanges in continental Europe use this procedure. So do most stock exchanges in developing or emerging markets.

The way a call auction works is best understood through an example.

EXAMPLE 17.1

The following orders have been submitted:

Buy	Sell
Market orders	Market orders
1,200 shares	1,300 shares
Limit orders	Limit orders
200 shares at 100.6	100 shares at 100.2
100 shares at 100.5	200 shares at 100.3
300 shares at 100.4	200 shares at 100.4
200 shares at 100.3	200 shares at 100.5

We can plot these orders on a supply–demand diagram as shown in Exhibit 17.2. For example, at a price of 100.3, demand is 2000: market orders for 1,200 shares can be filled at any price, and 100.3 is at or below the limit for all the buy limit orders (800 shares). Supply at 100.3 is 1,600: market orders for 1,300 shares can be filled at any price; 100.3 is above the limit price for the 100 limit orders at 100.2 and at the limit price for the 200 at 100.3. At a price of 100.3, therefore, demand exceeds supply. Similarly, a price of 100.5, demand is 1500 and supply is 2,000: at this price, supply exceeds demand. At a price of 100.4, both supply and demand equal 1,800.

The market-clearing price is therefore 100.4. All orders that can be are filled at this price. Only the buy limit orders at 100.3 and the sell limit orders at 100.5 remain unfilled.

---

[11] Another name for a call auction is *batch auction*.

The Importance of Limit Orders.   What would happen if all orders were market orders? Both the supply curve and the demand curve in Exhibit 17.2 would be vertical, and they would therefore not cross. We would have no way of setting a price to clear the market. It is the limit orders that allow us to form a price: they are essential to the proper working of the market.

Why do some traders enter limit orders rather than market orders? Traders who enter limit orders are essentially information traders. They are taking a position on what they believe to be the *fair price*—what the security in question is really worth.[12] The market prices fluctuates around the fair price as a result of liquidity imbalances. Entering a limit order to buy below the fair price, or a limit order to sell above it will on average get the trader a better execution price: if the market price fluctuates far enough away from the fair price it will hit the limit order and the order will be executed. The greater the volatility, the greater the potential gain from entering limit orders and, consequently, the more that will be forthcoming.

Traders who enter limit orders are providing liquidity to traders who enter market orders (liquidity traders). Limit orders tend to reduce the volatility due to liquidity imbalances. Traders entering market orders "pay" traders entering limit orders for providing liquidity by paying them prices that are worse, on average, than the fair price.

EXHIBIT 17.2   Supply and Demand in a Call Auction

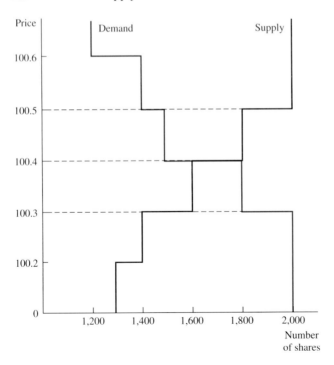

---

[12] See Chapter 11 for further explanation of the fair price.

Why doesn't everyone enter limit orders? Because there is a cost to acquiring the necessary information, and because there are risks involved. If the fluctuation in the market price is due not to a liquidity imbalance but to new information, you can lose. For example, suppose you enter a buy order below what you believe to be the fair price, but new information causes the fair price to rise. Your order will not be executed; and if the fair price continues to rise, you will have to pay more later than you would have paid if you had entered a market order. So to profit from entering limit orders, you need to know what you are doing.

How Well Does a Call Auction Work?   The basic functions that we expect of a call auction are price discovery and the provision of liquidity. How well does the procedure perform these functions? Because calls take place only periodically, orders accumulate over time, and there are many buyers and sellers represented at each auction. Consequently, price discovery is good in the sense that the market price is representative of the opinion of many investors as to the fair price. And liquidity is good in the sense that, with many orders gathered together, pooling works well and a substantial liquidity imbalance is less likely. Moreover, for reasons we shall see presently, limit orders are less risky in a call auction than they are in other types of auction. Consequently, there should be more limit orders, and the price should fluctuate less as a result of liquidity imbalances.

A call auction does have its drawbacks, however. The main one is the gap between the auctions. While price discovery is good *at* the auction, the market provides no price at all between calls. Related to this, there is uncertainty too at the time you submit your order about the price at which your order will be executed and the extent to which it will be filled. Again, liquidity is good *at* the call, but there is no liquidity between calls: you have to wait until the next call (there is a lack of *immediacy*).

The defects of a call auction matter more to information traders than they do to liquidity traders. If you have new information, you want to be able to trade on it immediately, before everyone else hears about it. If you want to arbitrage price differences between markets, you need to trade simultaneously in both.

Many of the defects of a call auction can be overcome with a continuous auction. But, of course, there are trade-offs. As we shall see, the continuous auction has problems of its own.

continuous auction
An auction in which orders are matched, if possible, as they arrive.

limit-order book
A register of currently unfillable limit orders.

The Continuous Auction.   A **continuous auction**, as its name suggests, runs continuously. Rather than orders accumulating to be matched in batches at intervals, they are executed if possible as soon as they arrive. Stock exchanges in North America and in the Far East operate continuous auctions, as do futures and options exchanges.

What makes a continuous auction feasible is the existence of a **limit-order book**—a list of previously submitted limit orders that have not yet been matched. New market orders are executed immediately by matching them with the best limit order available. New limit orders are executed if possible, by matching them with the best order in the limit-order book. If no execution is possible, the new limit order is itself added to the limit-order book. Let us look at an example.

EXAMPLE 17.2

The current limit-order book is

Buy		Sell	
100.2	300		
100.3	200		
100.4	300		
		100.5	200
		100.6	100
		100.7	300

The current market bid price is the buy order with the highest limit—100.4. The current market asked price is the sell order with the lowest limit—100.5.

All the orders in the limit-order book are waiting for the arrival of new orders that would "cross" the existing orders and allow them to be executed. At the moment, none of the orders in the limit-order book can be executed. For the buy orders, there is no one currently willing to sell at a price anyone is willing to pay. For the sell orders, there is no one currently willing to pay a price anyone is willing to accept.

The next order to come in is a buy *market* order for 200 shares—that is, an order to be executed at the best available price. This order is executed by matching it with the sell order with the lowest limit price—100.5.

Next to come in is a sell order for 500 shares at a limit of 100.2. This is matched with the best available "buy" limit orders on the book. The orders with the highest limits are executed first. So the seller receives a price of 100.4 for 300 shares and 100.3 for 200 shares.

Next comes a buy order for 500 shares at a limit of 100.3. There are no sell orders on the book with which this order can be matched, so it is added to the book.

clearing transaction
A call auction at the beginning of a period of continuous trading to clear accumulated orders.

There is no such thing as a pure continuous auction. Markets that operate continuous auctions are open only for certain set hours. When the market is closed, orders accumulate. Usually, each new trading session opens with a call auction—called a **clearing transaction**—to clear orders accumulated since the end of the previous trading session. After that, continuous trading proceeds until the end of the session. Each day may have a single trading session, or it may be divided into two or more sessions with breaks in between. Traders often have a choice of having their orders executed immediately or having them wait for the next clearing transaction.

How Well Does a Continuous Auction Work?   The advantages and disadvantages of a continuous auction are, roughly speaking, just the reverse of those of a call auction. While the price is uncertain between the calls of a call auction, it is always available in a continuous auction (at least during trading sessions). Execution is faster: rather than having to wait for the next call, trades are executed immediately (during a trading session).

However, because orders are executed immediately, the market is inherently "thinner". The number of orders arriving over a short period of time is small relative to the pool of orders that accumulates between calls. Consequently, pooling works less well and, at least potentially, price discovery and liquidity are likely to suffer. With only a few orders determining the market price, it may not be representative of the opinion of investors as a whole. With little offsetting of one order against another, liquidity imbalances are more likely to be a problem. There is less "depth" to the market, so that large orders are likely to have "market impact". For example, a large sell order from a liquidity trader is likely to cause the price to fall, even though in an ideal market it should not.

Backup Mechanisms for Continuous Auctions.   Because of the weaknesses just described, a continuous auction needs a backup mechanism of some kind if it is to function at all well. There are several possibilities.

Information Traders.   One possibility is information traders. By trading to profit from deviations of the market price from the "fair" price, these traders will provide better price discovery and will also provide the market with liquidity. To some extent, this is what the limit orders do. However, placing a limit order in a continuous auction is riskier than it is in a call auction: there is a danger that after the order has been placed, and before it can be retracted, new information will cause the fair price to shift. For example, if the market rises as a result of new favorable information, outstanding "sell" limit orders will automatically be swept up and executed, providing the buyers with a bargain at the expense of those who placed the limit orders.[13] Because placing a limit order is riskier, there will be relatively fewer such orders than there are in a call auction.

An alternative form of information trading that works better in a continuous auction is to have full-time information traders actually present in the market able to intervene (or not) at their discretion as the market fluctuates and as information becomes available. In Chapter 16, we saw that this is precisely what happens in the futures market. It is the presence of the locals there that makes the continuous auction run smoothly.

specialist
A market maker in a stock exchange.

Specialists.   In some exchanges in North America, the role of auctioneer and information trader is combined in the **specialist**. For example, trading on the floor of the New York Stock Exchange is organized around trading posts; each of the listed companies is assigned to one of these. The exchange assigns a specialist to each post to make a market in the securities traded there. The specialist maintains the limit-order book for each security and he also trades on his own account.[14]

The exchange requires the specialist to maintain a "fair and orderly market" for each security. This requirement is not clearly defined, but is understood to include the following:

- *A narrow bid–asked spread.*
- *"Depth" at quoted prices.* Investors should be able to expect that their market orders will be executed at a price near the market price that obtained when they placed their order.

---

[13] This is another example of the "winner's curse" that we encountered when discussing auctions in the government securities market.

[14] The specialists work either for specialized specialist firms or for one of the large securities firms.

- *Stability*. In the face of a liquidity imbalance, specialists should step in and trade on their own account to stabilize the price.
- *Informational efficiency*. The price should adjust rapidly to new information.

In short, the exchange expects the specialist to act as an effective information trader.

The way trade works at a trading post is this. A floor broker arrives with an order and asks the specialist for a price. The specialist quotes bid and asked prices. These may be either the best available prices from the limit-order book or they may be (better) prices at which the specialist is willing to trade on his own account.[15] For example, suppose that to fill a new buy order, the specialist would have to go to a limit order substantially above the current market price (the price of the last trade). If there were no informational reason for such a price rise, the specialist might prefer to provide the shares out of his own inventory at the market price. After receiving quotes from the specialist, the floor broker sees whether any other broker present at the post will offer him a better deal. If none is forthcoming, he may wait or he may accept the price quoted by the specialist.[16]

In this way, the specialist provides depth and stability. The cost of being a specialist is the inventory cost and the risk. Revenue comes from commissions and from trading profits. The source of these trading profits is the superior information that comes from exclusive access to the limit-order book. The exchange rewards specialists who perform their job well by assigning them promising new listings that are likely to generate a lot of volume (and so a lot of commissions). It punishes specialists who perform their job poorly by taking listings away from them.

trading halt
A temporary interruption of trading in a continuous auction when price crosses predetermined limits.

Price Limits and Trading Halts.   Yet another way to deal with the inherent volatility of a continuous auction is to set limits on how far the price is allowed to fluctuate during a trading session. If the price hits the limit, trading is halted for a period of time. It then restarts with a call auction of the orders that have accumulated during the halt. The idea of a **trading halt** is to give potential traders outside the market time to react to the change in the market price, perhaps submitting orders that will stabilize the market. Some stock exchanges, Tokyo, for example, rely primarily on this mechanism to deal with routine liquidity imbalances. Others rely on it only as an emergency measure. For example, trading halts were instituted in U.S. stock markets following the Crash of 1987.[17]

block trades
Large trades in equities between institutional investors.

upstairs market
The market for block trades, conducted off the exchange floor.

Negotiation for Large Orders.   Large orders are particularly disruptive to a continuous auction. Consequently, many exchanges have special procedures to deal with them. For example, in the New York Stock Exchange, orders involving fewer than 10,000 shares go to the specialists. But larger orders, called **block trades**, are sent to the **upstairs market**.

---

[15] Strict rules govern the ability of the specialist to trade on his own account. Basically, he cannot put himself ahead of the limit orders.

[16] The other brokers will include other "commission-house brokers" like himself, executing orders for customers; "two-dollar brokers," working freelance for securities firms with a larger order flow than they can handle or that desire anonymity in trading; and "competitive traders" trading on their own accounts.

[17] We shall discuss these "circuit breakers" in Chapter 20. As we saw in Chapter 16, futures exchanges generally limit how far the price can move during a trading session, but this is mainly to protect the system of settlement and margin.

There, they are matched by brokers called "block positioners." Because of the growing predominance of institutional trading, the upstairs market today accounts for over half the exchange's total trading volume.

To see how it works, suppose Jack, a block positioner, receives a sell order for 500,000 shares. He immediately gets on the phone to his list of institutional clients, negotiating prices at which they would be willing to buy some of the shares. He soon has bids for 450,000 shares at a price only slightly below that quoted by the specialist. He then contacts the specialist to include in the deal all outstanding limit orders down to the price he has set for the deal (he is required to do this) some 10,000 shares. Since this still leaves him with 40,000 shares unsold, he buys the remainder for his own account so that the deal can go through. He expects to be able to sell these later at a profit, or at least without too great a loss. With the deal complete, the whole package goes to the specialist for execution (all trades must go through the specialist to ensure that price information is made public).

The point of this procedure is that, like a trading halt, it mobilizes potential traders not currently active in the market in order to absorb a large order without it having a big impact on the market price.

A Dealer Market as a Continuous Auction Taken to the Limit.   In a sense, if we push these backup mechanisms as far as they will go, we arrive at a dealer market. Dealers are in a way "super block positioners." Block positioners commit some of their own capital to completing a deal for a customer—for example, buying some shares to resell later. Dealers takes this to the limit: they purchase immediately all the shares a customer wishes to sell, and find buyers for them afterwards. Dealers are also in a way "super information traders." Market-making information traders, such as locals and specialists, intervene in the market *at their discretion* to quote prices at which they are willing to buy or sell. Dealers *always* stand ready to buy and sell at quoted bid and asked prices.

By pushing these mechanisms to the extreme, we would expect a dealer market to provide continuous trading with good liquidity and price discovery relative to a continuous auction. On the other hand, by pushing these mechanisms to the extreme, the dealer is taking on greater risk. Dealers need to commit more of their capital than block positioners, and they are sticking their necks out more than locals and specialists. Because the risks are greater, the reward for the market maker should be greater, too. From the point of view of the trader, this means that we would expect the cost of trading in a dealer market to be higher.

An Example of a Dealer Market.   The National Association of Securities Dealers Automated Quotations (NASDAQ) provides an example of a dealer market. On NASDAQ there are no specialists and no limit-order book. Each order is satisfied separately by a single dealer. There are some 500 of these dealers. Each listed stock is quoted by no fewer than two dealers, but on average by about a dozen. To begin quoting a particular stock, all a dealer need do is notify NASD (the organizer of the market) a day in advance.

Some 200,000 NASDAQ screens worldwide display the dealer quotes—bid and asked prices and the amounts dealers are willing to trade at those prices, as well as information on executed trades. Small orders of up to 1,000 shares go to dealers through an electronic Small Order Execution System (SOES) and are executed automatically at the quoted prices. Large orders must be executed over the telephone, and there may be negotiation over price and quantity. Dealers trade with one another on an inside market, using either SelectNet, an interdealer trading system provided by NASDAQ, or Instinet, a private trading system owned by Reuters.

NASDAQ dealers have very different information from specialists on the NYSE. While specialists know immediately of every trade in their stocks (or at least those executed on the NYSE) and can see the backlog of limit orders, NASDAQ dealers do not know the price, size, and direction of orders executed by other dealers until they are reported to NASDAQ and displayed on the screen. On the other hand, dealers are in direct contact with institutional investors, something not allowed to specialists (they receive matched orders from the block positioners). Also many dealers belong to securities firms that have a close relationship with the companies whose stocks they trade. The firm may underwrite new issues or advise on mergers and acquisitions. This provides the dealers with good information on the companies in question.

The Importance of Credit

We have seen that for a market to function properly, market makers (dealers in a dealer market or "locals" or specialists in an auction market) need to take positions in securities. To be able to do this quickly and at the scale required, market makers need access to credit.

Credit and Taking a Position.   For example, if there is a liquidity imbalance in a dealer market, dealers need to buy or sell from inventory to accommodate it. If a liquidity imbalance in an auction market drives the market price away from its fair value, information traders need to buy or sell to right the market. In either case credit is required. To be able to buy securities—to take a long position—dealers or traders must be able to borrow money to finance their purchases. To be able to sell securities—to take a short position—dealers and traders must be able to borrow securities to sell. The lending of securities, then, is no less essential to the proper working of a market than the lending of money.

In the United States, the lending of securities—mainly Treasuries, mortgage-backed securities, and stocks—is a big business. Daily volume runs into the hundreds of billions of dollars. The big lenders are institutional investors, especially pension funds, seeking to earn a little extra on their huge portfolios of securities.

In other countries, securities lending is less common—the worldwide total running only into the tens of billions of dollars, most of it in the United Kingdom. There is less securities lending in other countries because regulations usually prohibit or restrict it.

reciprocal loan
An arrangement whereby two parties simultaneously make each other a loan (one is a loan of money; the other a loan of securities).

Reciprocal Lending.   To be of any use in the securities markets, lending must be quick and inexpensive. But we know that lending is problematic. Dealing with the risks involved in making a loan can be costly and time-consuming. To address these problems, securities markets have developed a kind of loan that greatly reduces the risks and so the costs and the delays. This is the **reciprocal loan**, and we saw an example of it in Chapter 12 in the form of the *reverse repo* in the government securities market.

To understand how a reciprocal loan works in general, let us consider an example. If Leah wishes to finance a $1 million long position in stock, she borrows $1 million from

Harriet and simultaneously lends Harriet the securities she has used the money to buy. Alternatively, if Leah wishes to take a $1 million short position in stock, she does this by borrowing the stock from Harriet and simultaneously lending her trading partner the money she receives from selling the stock. In both cases Leah simultaneously borrows from Harriet and lends to her.

The advantage of the reciprocal loan is that it greatly reduces the potential cost of a default. If Leah defaults on the cash she has borrowed, Harriet can sell the stock to cover the debt. If Leah fails to return the stock, Harriet can use the cash to buy in the open market the stock she is owed. Harriet's exposure to loss, instead of being the full $1 million of the loan, is limited to the possible change in value of the stock.[18] Of course, Leah is similarly protected.

Naturally, both the loan of cash and the loan of the security pay interest. The two rates of interest are determined by supply and demand in the respective markets. Suppose, for example, that a loan of cash carries an interest rate of 8% and a loan of stock carries an interest rate of 5%. If Leah is financing a long position by borrowing cash from Harriet (lending her stock in return), then Leah will pay Harriet the difference between the two rates—3%. If Leah is financing a short position by borrowing stock from Harriet (lending her cash in exchange), then Leah will *receive* 3% from Harriet.[19]

Notice how well reciprocal lending meets the needs of securities trading. In both examples, Leah's goal is to take a position in the stock—long or short. In the case of the long position, she has no use for the stock while she owns it; so lending it to Harriet to secure the loan is no sacrifice. Similarly, in the case of the short position, she has no particular use for the cash proceeds of the sale while she maintains the position.

margin lending
Lending by a broker to finance position of customer.

Brokers will lend to their retail customers to finance a position in securities up to 50% of the value of the securities in question—this is known as **margin lending**.[20] The client agreement for securities purchased on margin generally gives the broker the right to lend the customer's securities. Brokers use the cash they receive from reciprocal lending to fund their margin loans to their retail customers.

Market Information

Those trading securities in an organized market, or thinking of trading, need information. In a dealer market they need to know the dealers' quoted prices. In an auction market, they need to know the prices at which securities are currently changing hands. With a call auction there is no great hurry, since no trading is possible anyhow until the next call; publishing prices in the next day's newspapers is fine. However, for a continuous auction, traders and potential traders need to know what is happening more or less immediately.

Organized markets gather and disseminate information on quotes and on realized trades. On the NYSE, for example, specialists report information on completed trades to

---

[18] Different markets have different arrangements for reducing this risk. In some, the amount of the two loans will differ, so that there is a margin or "haircut". In others, the loan is marked to market each day, so that the amount of the cash loan changes with the value of the security loan.

[19] Any income—interest or dividend payments—received on the securities while they are on loan is due to the original owner and must be paid by the borrower when the securities are returned.

[20] The Fed sets the maximum permissible margin under Regulation T. It has been set at 50% since 1974.

the exchange, which then publishes it on the *Consolidated Tape*. The Consolidated Tape reports trading information from all the stock exchanges in the United States and from the over-the-counter market.[21] Market information is valuable, and the sale of information is an important source of revenue for organized markets.

quote vendors
Providers of market and other information to market professionals.

Markets sell their information to the news media (news agencies, print, TV and radio, and Internet), which distribute it to the public. They also sell it to **quote vendors**, who make it available to market professionals together with other useful information. For a stock price, this might include, for example, the recent history of the price displayed in a chart, information provided by the company itself, and any news likely to affect the value of the stock. The quote vendor provides all of this information on a proprietary screen for which the customer pays a monthly fee of $1,000 to $2,000. The leaders in this $6 billion market are Reuters (with 400,000 screens worldwide in 1998), Bridge (170,000), and Bloomberg (90,000).

Markets face something of a dilemma in the dissemination of information. They have to release enough to potential traders to make trading in the market attractive. However, if they release too much, traders can cut them out entirely and trade outside the market at their published prices. For example, the speedy release of prices on the Consolidate Tape makes it easy for private trading systems to compete with the NYSE and NASDAQ and to offer to execute trades outside these markets at lower cost.

In another example, Instinet, a private trading system, used to identify on its screens the sources of the quotes that it displayed. Traders were therefore able to contact each other directly to execute a trade, saving the commission they would otherwise have had to pay to Instinet. Instinet learned the lesson and made the quotes anonymous.

Another reason to be cautious about the release of market information is that it makes the job of market makers such as specialists and dealers more difficult. It is often only their superior knowledge of what is happening in the market that protects them from losses to information traders.[22]

Automated Trading Systems

automated trading systems (ATSs)
Computer systems that execute orders without direct human intervention.

Today, organized markets are relying more and more on **automated trading systems (ATSs)**—computer systems that executes trades automatically without human intervention (the SOES on NASDAQ is one example we have encountered already). Trading floors where people trade face to face are becoming increasingly rare. Almost all stock exchanges and futures exchanges in Europe have replaced their trading floors with ATSs, and there is increasing pressure on exchanges in the United States to do the same. In the United States there are, as we shall see, dozens of private ATSs that compete with the major exchanges to execute trades.

order routing
Getting orders from customers outside the market to the place of execution.

What Is an ATS?   Of course, not every computer system used by an organized market is an ATS. Any trading system performs three functions. One is **order routing**—getting orders from customers outside the market to the place of execution. Normally, customers

---

[21] Before the consolidated tape was established in 1975, each market released price information separately.

[22] Increasingly, the choice is not being left to the markets. Regulations increasingly impose requirements on the release of information. We shall discuss the implications of this in Chapter 20.

submit their orders to a broker and the broker forwards the order to the market. Today, in almost all organized markets, order routing is computerized—either over a system provided by the market or over one provided by a private supplier (such as Instinet). For example, the NYSE has its SuperDot system that can transmit orders electronically from brokers to specialists.

A second function of a trading system is, as we have seen, the dissemination of market information—information on quotes and on prices of completed trades. Again, this function is universally handled by computer. Computers improve the speed and accuracy of reporting and lower the cost. Computers are also able to calculate instantaneously the value of various market indexes (such as the Dow Jones, the S&P 500, or the FTSE 100) that are essential to various forms of trading in derivatives.

The third function of a trading system is the actual execution of orders—matching orders to create trades. It is only when this third function is computerized that we are talking about an automated trading system. Such a system consists of a host computer with the software to process trades, terminals at which brokers can enter orders, and a network linking them together.

How Well Does an ATS Work?   As we have seen, it can be quite difficult to run a market in a satisfactory way. Can a computer really do this as well as human beings? It depends on the method of trading.

Some types of trading are relatively easy to computerize. For example, executing orders against dealer quotes, as on SOES, is pretty straightforward. It is also easy to match orders at given prices. For example, many private ATSs take their prices from the relevant exchange (typically the average of the published bid and asked prices) and match as many customer orders as possible at these prices. It is pretty easy, too, to computerize a call auction. With a continuous market, however, things become more difficult.

The problem with computerizing a continuous market is not technical. There are many computer systems available, most of them based on CATS, which was originally developed in Toronto. The problem is how, in the context of an automated system, to provide the backup that a continuous market requires. Instituting price limits and trading halts is pretty simple, and these are standard features of most automated continuous auctions. However, meshing the system with information traders—specialists, locals, or dealers—is a bigger challenge.

Locals, for example, have resisted going over to screen-based trading. In open outcry, they are able to observe the other traders and get a feel for the market. This is impossible to duplicate on a computer screen. In addition, in open outcry quotes are valid only for an instant and can be revised rapidly as circumstances change. On an ATS, quotes (limit orders) have to be withdrawn manually, and this may take too much time in a fast-moving market.

Dealers, too, have a problem with leaving quotes out there to be exploited by better informed traders. When trading over the phone, they can tailor their quotes to the circumstances. But when orders are executed against their quotes automatically, they are more vulnerable. To protect dealers on NASDAQ from this problem, for example, orders on SOES are limited to no more than 1,000 shares. The idea is that such trades are too small to be of interest to information traders. However, information traders known as "SOES bandits" get around this restriction by using their computers to fire a rapid stream of 1,000-share orders into the system, sometimes imposing considerable losses on dealers.

We have seen that large orders are disruptive to continuous markets and need to be negotiated separately. No computer can do the work that a dealer or a block positioner does to negotiate a deal for an institutional client with a large order.

So ATSs have been most successful in liquid markets with large volumes of small orders. In such markets, good backup mechanisms are less essential. Many minor exchanges fit this bill and their transition from floor to ATS has generally been successful. For the larger exchanges, the transition is more problematic. For example, after the Deutsche Terminbörse (DTB) derivatives exchange in Frankfurt switched to an ATS, traders complained about the market impact of large orders (for example, a large buy order causing the price to rise significantly). And after London switched from a dealer system to an automated continuous auction, market prices behaved erratically in the early hours of trading when order volume was relatively low.

Hybrid Systems.   The answer to the deficiencies of an ATS is, in many cases, to use some combination of an ATS and human-mediated trading.

Some organized markets handle small orders through an ATS but divert large orders to dealers or block positioners. We have seen that this is the practice on NASDAQ, and it is also the practice on the stock exchanges of Toronto, Tokyo, and London. Small orders for French stocks go to the ATS of the Paris Bourse, but large orders from institutional investors generally go to the International Stock Exchange in London where a dealer market provides better liquidity. In the Chicago derivatives exchanges, small orders are increasingly handled electronically, while large orders are sent to floor traders in the pits.[23]

Some major markets that still rely on face-to-face trading use an ATS for trading after hours. The NYSE operates an after-hours system that matches orders at the exchange's closing price. The Chicago futures and options exchanges have an ATS called Globex for trading after hours.

Some futures exchanges that use open outcry for heavily traded contracts use an ATS for contracts that do not generate a large volume. In such cases, an ATS can actually improve liquidity. Generally, it is not worth a local's time to hang around a market where little trading is going on. However, if the trading is electronic, it is relatively easy for locals to monitor several such markets simultaneously. More attention from the locals means better liquidity.

The Advantages of an ATS.   The uses we have considered hint at some of the advantages of an ATS. The big advantage, of course, is cost. Setting up and operating a trading floor is expensive—not only the space and the equipment, but the costs associated with hundreds of skilled professionals. In comparison, computers are cheap. An ATS with all the trimmings capable of handling 40,000 transactions a day (more than double the number on the Paris Bourse) costs $4 million to $8 million—peanuts. Because it is less expensive, an ATS can charge much lower transactions fees. For example, a round-trip transaction on the nonautomated LIFFE futures exchange in London costs $1.50. A similar transaction on the automated DTB in Frankfurt costs only $0.66.

Because the cost of operating an ATS is low, it is easy to expand trading hours. You do not have to pay a lot of expensive people overtime. It is not clear, however, how useful

---

[23] The rooms full of screens in which electronic trading takes place are known in Chicago as "arcades."

the longer session is. Longer trading hours means an even thinner continuous market, as orders are spread over a longer day. Part of the problem when London switched to an ATS was that the exchange took the opportunity to extend trading hours. After-hours trading systems—Globex, for example—have similarly not been a great success because of the thinness of the market.

A second advantage of an ATS is that it offers remote access. You do not actually need to be there in order to trade. If you are trading from a screen, the screen does not have to be in the exchange. It can be in a broker's office somewhere else in the city, in another city, or even in another country on the other side of the world. So automation has promoted cross-border trading and made it easier to connect exchanges and trading systems to one another.

Automation also improves operational efficiency and reliability. For example, it is much easier to connect an ATS with the back-office systems that process trades after execution (we shall discuss these presently). There is less likelihood of error, for example, in recording trades and transmitting that information to others. On the other hand, computer crashes have been the source of some spectacular messes. For example, when the Super-Dot system of the NYSE crashed on June 8, 2001 (the software had just been upgraded), trading on the exchange had to be halted for over an hour. There had been six similar halts since 1989. The London Stock Exchange was closed for almost 8 hours on April 5, 2000, as a result of a computer crash. That day happened to be the last day of the tax year, and some 12 million investors were unable to trade to minimize their tax bills.

Automation can improve market transparency by making market information more readily available. All the data on trade prices and quantities and on the identity of traders are there in the computer. Easy access to this information makes oversight of the market by the exchange and by government regulators much easier.[24] And it becomes possible to provide traders outside the market with the sort of information available only to brokers on the trading floor in a traditional exchange. For example, it is possible to display the complete limit-order book on trading screens so that everyone can see it.

However greater market transparency does not come without cost. The main advantage specialists have is that only they can see the limit-order book. It is this that gives them the confidence to intervene in the market to even out liquidity imbalances. Without this advantage, this backup mechanism will not be available.

More generally, there are trade-offs between human-mediated and automated trading. Since the two coexist and compete successfully with each other, each must have advantages the other lacks. Human-mediated trading offers better liquidity in a way that cannot (at least yet) be replicated by an ATS. On the other hand, human-mediated trading is much more expensive. When human intervention adds little—for example, in executing a large volume of small orders—it makes no sense to pay the extra cost.

AFTER THE TRADE

We have seen the different ways of organizing trading in a financial market. But trading is only half the story. It is not enough for two traders to agree on the terms of a trade: the trade actually has to be completed. Securities and money need to change hands.

---

[24] We shall have more to say about this in Chapter 20.

Completing a trade is costly, and it involves risks. The lower the cost and the smaller the risks, the easier it is to trade. The easier it is to trade, the better the market will work. So organized markets have developed ways to lower the cost and to reduce the risks. Before we see how they do this, let us see what the risks are.

The Risks of Trade Completion

You are a broker on the floor of the New York Stock Exchange and you have just agreed with A. Smith, another broker, to sell him 10,000 shares of GE at 80. To complete this transaction, you need to transfer ownership of the shares to Smith, and Smith needs to transfer the cash to you. In principle, you could pull the share certificates out of your pocket and hand them over to Smith in exchange for a wad of cash. In practice, this is out of the question. Each of you enters into hundreds of transactions each day and neither wishes to carry around millions of dollars in cash and securities. Moreover, each transaction involves paperwork. If you had to do it all yourself, you wouldn't be able to do much trading.

back office

The part of a securities firm responsible for the completion of trades.

In reality, once you and Smith have agreed on the terms, completion is handed over to others in the **back office**. How long the process takes varies from market to market. In the stock market it takes 3 business days. In the government securities market, completion often takes place the same day. In the market for mortgage-backed securities and in some European stock markets, it may take a month or more to complete the trade.

The delay between agreement on a trade and its completion means that a trade in the securities markets is essentially a *forward transaction*. As we saw in Chapter 1, forward transactions involve promises, and promises may not be kept. There are different kinds of risk, depending on exactly how the promise fails.

principal risk

The risk of default by a counterparty after you have fulfilled your part of a deal.

Principal Risk.   Suppose you handed over the securities, but Smith failed to pay the $800,000. This is much like default on a loan, and unless you can recover something through the courts, your loss is the full value of the deal—the principal. The risk that this will happen is consequently known as **principal risk**. You are exposed to principal risk whenever there is a gap in time between delivery—handing over the securities—and payment—handing over the money.

replacement risk

The risk that a counterparty will fail to execute an agreed transaction, leaving you to find another deal.

Replacement Risk.   Consider a different possibility. You have not yet handed over the securities, so you are not exposed to principal risk. However, before the deal can be completed, Smith backs out. For whatever reason, he cannot or will not fulfill his part of the deal. As a result, you have to find another buyer for your 10,000 shares. If, before you can do so, GE falls to 70, you will lose $100,000. Of course, if GE instead rises to 90, you will actually gain $100,000 as a result of Smith's failure to complete the trade.

The risk that a trade, once agreed upon, will fall through is called **replacement risk**. It is the risk that you will have to replace the counterparty to the original trade with another counterparty. As you can see, unlike with principal risk, there is an upside: you can gain as well as lose. Moreover, the potential for loss is generally much smaller than it is with principal risk.

Liquidity Risk. Suppose now that Smith does complete the trade, but not at the agreed-upon time. He pays, but his payment is late. This creates a problem for you because you were counting on the $800,000 to pay for some other securities you had purchased from someone else. Because Smith's payment is late, either you will have to be late in making payment yourself or you will have to find some other way to raise the money. A similar problem would occur if you had bought securities and the securities were not delivered on time. If you had meanwhile sold those securities to someone else, you would have to be late in delivery yourself or to find securities somewhere else in order to make delivery on time.

In either case, the cost to you of late completion of the trade is the cost of your having to make alternative arrangements—of finding an alternative source of liquidity. The risk that transactions will not be completed on time is therefore called **liquidity risk**.[25] Just as replacement risk is not as serious as principal risk, liquidity risk is not as serious as replacement risk. Nonetheless, it does impose costs, and it can cause serious problems.

Suppose that when Smith fails to pay you on time, you are unable to raise the money elsewhere and you are therefore unable to pay on time yourself. The trader expecting your payment is in a similar bind and is also unable to pay on time. Because traders rely on the completion of one trade to enable them to complete others, problems with one major trader could set off in this way a domino reaction with major consequences throughout the market. The risk of this happening is called **systemic risk**. Systemic risk is not limited to a single market. Traders often trade simultaneously in many markets. Systemic problems in one can easily spill over into others.

Organized markets set up mechanisms of trade completion to address these different types of risk and to reduce the cost of the process.

Understanding Clearing and Settlement

We can divide the process of trade completion into two stages—*clearing* and *settlement*. Settlement is the actual exchange of securities for cash. Clearing consists of all the things that are done before settlement occurs.

Comparison. The first thing that must be done is to make sure that the parties to a trade agree on what it is they have agreed to. A trade in an organized market often involves no more than a few words. For example, your conversation with Smith might have gone as follows:

> You: "GE?"
> Smith: "80 to 80.2" (Bid and asked prices)
> You: "I sell 100!" (You sell 100 round lots of 100 shares each).

Each of you would have jotted down the details on a trade slip and passed it on later to your back-office people for completion.

liquidity risk
The risk that a counterparty will be late in fulfilling his part in a transaction.

systemic risk
The risk that the failure of one trade or trader will cause the failure of others in a domino effect.

---

[25] A common reasons for failure to complete trades on time is a breakdown in the arrangements for completing the trade (about which we shall learn presently). The typical cause is a computer breakdown. The risk of such a breakdown is called *operational risk*.

comparison

Process of con-
firming nature of
trades.

There is potential for misunderstanding and error between you and Smith and between each of you and your respective back offices. Consequently, Smith's back-office people and yours may wind up with different ideas of the nature of the trade to which you have agreed. The first step in clearing a trade, then, is **comparison**—making sure the parties agree on the parameters of the trade. These parameters include the type and quantity of the financial instrument being traded, the transaction date and price, and the identification of buyer and seller. If the parties do not agree, then the differences have to be ironed out before the process can proceed any further.[26]

Most markets have a clearinghouse that is responsible for comparing trades. For example, your trade with Smith takes place on Thursday. That night your back-office people and Smith's each send electronic notification of the trade to the computer of the National Securities Clearing Corporation (NSCC) (see "The NSCC and the DTC"). The NSCC computer checks the two "confirms" against each other. If they match, the trade is "compared," and NSCC confirms to you and to Smith on Friday morning. If the trade does not compare, both parties are notified, and you and Smith have to sort things out and resubmit the trade before the settlement date.

One of the advantages of automated trading systems, of course, is that none of this is necessary. Since all trading takes place on a computer, there is a single definitive record of every transaction. There is no possibility of confusion and no need for comparison.

gross settlement

Settlement of
each trade indi-
vidually without
netting.

Netting.   With the nature of the trade agreed upon, we can in principle proceed to settlement. Indeed, some markets do this, settling each trade individually. This is called **gross settlement**. We saw an example of this in Chapter 12, when we studied the government securities market. In that market, dealers settle most transactions individually over Fedwire.

Bilateral Netting.   Settlement, however, is costly. As we shall see, the actual transfer of securities and of money is expensive. Very few markets have access to a settlement system as good as Fedwire, so the costs can sometimes be much higher than they are in the government securities market. Since a given trader may engage in dozens or even hundreds of trades each day, these costs soon add up. Moreover, since traders do engage in many trades, the need for actual settlement can be reduced considerably by *netting* one trade against another.

For example, suppose you sold the shares to Smith because you expected the price of GE to fall (GE was due to announce its quarterly earnings, and you expected them to be disappointing). Say an hour later the price indeed falls to 75 and you buy the shares back at that price. By coincidence, you buy them from Smith. You and he could save a lot of transactions costs if you net the two transactions—your earlier sale and your later repurchase. Net, Smith owes you $10,000 \times (80 - 75) = \$50,000$. If Smith just pays you this amount, no securities and a lot less money need change hands.

We can extend this idea beyond netting pairs of specific transactions to a general *bilateral netting* arrangement with Smith. You could keep a running tab of your trading in GE shares over a period of time, and just settle your net position at the end of the period. Of

---

[26] In 1999, the increased volume of trading in equities and the shortening of the settlement period from 5 days to 3 days caused the rate of failed comparisons to rise from 5% to 18%.

course, you would save even more if you engaged in *multi-issue netting*—netting your trades in all securities with just one final cash payment.

multilateral multi-issue netting

Netting among all traders and involving all securities.

Multilateral Multi-Issue Netting.   Best of all would be an arrangement for **multilateral multi-issue netting**. A running tab could be kept of your trades with *all* other traders in the market. At the end of the netting period, you would just make or receive a single transfer of money and a single transfer of each security you trade. The saving in transactions costs would be substantial. Multilateral multi-issue netting requires a third party to keep track of all trades and to net them against each other to the degree possible. Generally, this function is performed by the clearinghouse. In the case of the U.S. stock market, it is the NSCC that performs this function.

The Netting Period.   Of course, the benefit of netting will depend on the volume of trades. The larger the volume, the more trades that can be offset against one another and the fewer that will actually have to be settled in securities and money. Volume in turn will depend on the length of the netting period: the longer the period, the larger the total number of trades. For example, in 1993 the Paris Bourse offered two alternative ways to settle—one with a netting period of one day and one with a netting period of a month. With the one-day period, some 13% of transactions netted out and did not require settlement. With the one-month period, 70% of transactions netted out.

The advantage of a long netting period is one reason why completion typically takes so long in low-volume markets. In contrast, in a high-volume market most of the gains from netting can be achieved in a relatively short period. The U.S. stock and futures markets, for example, have a netting period of a single day.

The length of the netting period affects not only the cost of settlement, but also liquidity risk. Because fewer actual deliveries and payments are necessary, and because the parties have longer to make sure they have the securities or cash they need to deliver or pay, a longer netting period makes it less likely that traders will be tardy in meeting their commitments.

Settlement.   Once the trade is cleared—that is, after comparison and possibly netting—the next step is settlement. In our example, you will have to transfer ownership of the securities in question to Smith. And Smith will have to make payment to you in a form that you find acceptable. We shall see that both the transfer of securities and the transfer of money can be costly. Also, it is at the time of settlement that principal risk rears its ugly head. If the transfer of securities and the transfer of money do not occur simultaneously, then one of the parties is exposed to the danger that the other will not come through.

The Transfer of Securities.   The transfer of securities can be complicated, time-consuming, and costly. In some countries, the process can take months and cost hundreds of dollars per transaction. The physical transfer of securities is especially expensive. The securities must be carried from one place to another, with a consequent risk of loss or theft, and the recipient must check them to make sure they are the ones agreed upon in the trade.

If the securities in question are *bearer* securities, once the securities change hands the transfer is done: possession implies ownership. However, for most securities a transfer of ownership requires the new owner to register with either the issuer or with a registrar appointed by the issuer (usually a bank).

The cost of transfer can be reduced enormously and speed and safety correspondingly increased if, instead of transferring physical securities, we transfer title alone. One way to do this, as we saw in Chapter 12 with government securities, is to have the securities issued only in "book-entry" form—as records on a computer. Then transfer merely involves changing a computer record. If the keeper of the "book" is also the registrar, registration is taken care of simultaneously. Doing away entirely with physical securities is called **dematerialization**.

dematerialization
Creation of securities in book-entry form only.

What can we do if the securities already exist, having been issued years or even decades ago? The answer is **immobilization**. Place the physical securities in a **depository**. Then have the depository keep track of who the owner is on a book-entry system, much as the Fed does with government securities. The actual securities stay permanently in a vault at the depository. When securities are "transferred," the record on the computer is simply changed to reflect the change in ownership.[27] If, in addition, the securities are registered in the name of the depository, then the depository can also act as a single central registrar for all the securities it holds. Most U.S. stock is now immobilized at a depository called the Depository Trust Company (DTC) (see "The NSCC and the DTC" for details).

immobilization
Placing of securities in a depository.

depository
An institution that holds physical securities and allows transfer of ownership.

Custodians.   When institutional investors trade securities, there is another layer of complication. To guard against possible malfeasance by the managers of a pension fund, mutual fund, or endowment, the securities it owns are generally held not by the institution itself but by an independent **custodian**. To have the securities released by the custodian, the institution's managers have to follow specified procedures. No one is going to skip town with the pension fund's assets!

custodian
Institution that holds securities in trust for institutional investors.

Custody is a very big business. In 1997, the total value of securities held in custody worldwide amounted to some $40 trillion. For this service, custodians earned over $5 billion in that year. There are enormous economies of scale in custody, and the industry has become quite concentrated. The three largest custodians, Bank of New York, State Street, and Chase, each held around $6 trillion of securities in 2000, and the six largest custodians accounted for most of the business. In addition to holding securities, custodians collect coupons and dividends, vote shares for the owners, and handle the lending of securities. Major custodians offer global service. For example, a U.S. custodian for a U.S. pension fund would handle any German shares the fund owned through a subcustodian in Germany.

Custody can complicate, or simplify, the transfer of securities. Suppose a mutual fund sells some stock to a pension fund. If both institutions use the same custodian, the custodian can simply transfer ownership on its own books from one to the other. The stock is registered with the depository as belonging to the custodian, so no change is required there. If the two institutions use different custodians, then the ownership at the depository has to be changed from one custodian to the other. It is a lot like clearing a check.

---

[27] The idea of a depository is very much like that of the medieval warehouse bank that "immobilized" coins (see Chapter 6).

THE NSCC AND THE DTC

The NSCC was formed in 1977 by combining the clearing operations of the New York Stock Exchange, the American Stock Exchange, and the over-the-counter market (NASD). NSCC currently processes practically all broker-to-broker stock and corporate and municipal bond trades in the United States. Its principal activities are centralized clearance, settlement and posttrade information services for stocks, bonds, mutual fund, and annuity transactions to more than 2,000 brokers, dealers, banks, mutual funds, insurance companies, and other financial intermediaries. In 2000, it processed transactions valued at $105 trillion. Through its Continuous Net Settlement system, it eliminated the need to settle $101.7 trillion, or 97% percent of total obligations.

NSCC has three affiliates: Government Securities Clearing Corporation provides clearing and settlement in the government securities market; MBS Clearing Corporation does the same for mortgage-backed securities; and Emerging Market Clearing Corporation compares and guarantees settlement of cross-border trades of emerging market debt instruments.

The DTC was established as a depository in the late 1960s by the NYSE, AMEX, and NASD. It accepts both bearer and registered securities and if possible registers them in its own name (Cede & Co.). Companies pay their dividends by wiring funds to the DTC account at U.S. Trust; DTC then credits the money account of the security's owner. Securities deposited at DTC can be pledged against loans, pledged to cover written options, or lent to cover fails. DTC had custody of securities worth more than $23 trillion in 2000. It processed an average of over 11 million transactions a day. DTC's network links more than 11,000 broker/dealers, custodian banks, and institutional investors, as well as transfer agents, paying agents, and exchange and redemption agents for securities issuers.

In 1999 NSCC and DTC agreed to combine under a joint holding company, the Depository Trust & Clearing Corporation (DTCC).

The Transfer of Money.   The transfer of money too can be costly and time-consuming. For example, some markets require physical delivery of a certified check in order to settle. Others rely on ordinary checks, but then require a delay until the check clears. To speed the process, some markets require traders to keep an account at one of several banks the market has approved as settling banks.

As we saw in Chapter 8, it is possible to transfer money much faster and at lower expense electronically. The government securities market uses Fedwire, and the foreign exchange market uses CHIPS. However, traders in most securities markets do not have access to an electronic payments system.

The Settlement Period.   Because both the transfer of securities and the transfer of money take time, the deadline for settlement in most markets is set at a date some time after the date of the trade. The length of this settlement period varies from market to market.

It used to be common in many markets to settle on an "account day." For example, all the trades in a given month or quarter were settled on the last day of that month or quarter.

Today, it is more usual to have rolling settlement—settlement at "$t + n$," where t is the date of the trade and n is a number of days later. For example, in most major stock markets today, settlement is at $t + 3$. That is, the trades for each day are netted, and the balances are due 3 business days later. Every business day, there is settlement of the trades made 3 business days previously.

A longer settlement period reduces liquidity risk but increases replacement risk. The longer the time to settlement, the longer the parties have to find the securities and the money they need in order to settle. On the other hand, the longer the time to settlement, the more time there is for circumstances to change and for one of the parties to become unwilling or unable to complete the trade.

To reduce replacement risk, there has been a movement towards shorter settlement periods. In 1989, the Group of Thirty, an international forum for the study of economic and financial issues, drew up standards for clearing and settlement. It recommended rolling settlement at no later than $t + 3$, and most organized markets have since achieved this standard. Indeed, many are working on shortening the settlement period even further. The SEC, for example, has set a goal of $t + 1$ by June 2004.

Addressing the Risks of Trade Completion.   Given the arrangements for clearing and settlement, a certain amount of risk remains. How do organized markets address principal risk, replacement risk, and liquidity risk?

Delivery against Payment.   Principal risk is the result of delay between delivery and payment. If we can eliminate the delay, we can eliminate the risk. If securities and cash change hands simultaneously, there is no principal risk. Such a simultaneous transfer is called **delivery against payment (DAP)**. Unfortunately, only in a few markets is it possible.

delivery against payment (DAP)
Simultaneous execution of both parts of a transaction.

In Chapter 12, we saw that government securities dealers have DAP over Fedwire. This is because Fedwire is at the same time an electronic payments system (for transferring deposits at the Fed) and a system for transferring ownership of book-entry securities held by the Fed. Similar DAP systems are available in government securities markets in several other countries, such as Japan and Switzerland.

There are two difficulties in implementing DAP. First, the participants in most markets do not have direct access to an electronic payments system (access is generally restricted to commercial banks). Of course indirect access is possible through a clearing bank. However, the second difficulty is that even when the securities are in a book-entry system, it is not linked on a real-time basis to the payments system.

A Third–Party Guarantee.   When DAP is ruled out, the usual way to deal with principal risk is to have a trusted third party act as a go-between. Let us see how this works in the case of your trade with Smith.[28] Settlement is due on Tuesday, 3 business days after the Thursday on which the trade took place. On Monday, the day before settlement, the NSCC interposes itself between the two parties to the transaction. That is, the original deal you had with Smith is now replaced with two deals—one between you and the NSCC, and the other between the NSCC and Smith. You now have a deal to sell 10,000 shares of GE to the NSCC at 80 and Smith has a deal to buy them from the NSCC at the same price. You receive a notice to deliver the shares to the NSCC; Smith receives a notice to make payment. By interposing itself in this way, the NSCC guarantees settlement to both of you. Regardless of whether Smith pays up, you will get your money. Regardless of whether you deliver the securities, Smith will get 10,000 shares of GE.

Monday night, the NSCC computer communicates the required transfer of securities to the DTC computer. If you have the shares in your account at DTC, they are transferred to the NSCC account. When Smith pays, the securities are transferred to his account. To pay, Smith must arrange for a Fedwire transfer of $800,000 to NSCC by 3:15 P.M. on Tuesday.[29] Note that DTC handles the transfer of securities, and NSCC the transfer of money.

What happens if either of you fails to settle? If the reason for the "fail" is a liquidity problem, the trade is marked to market and rolled over into the next day's settlement. This is done each day until delivery is made. For example, suppose that you deliver the securities one day late, on Wednesday. If GE was trading at 78 on Tuesday, the day you were supposed to deliver, you will have to pay the NSCC $80 − 78 = $2 a share. The shares will be marked to market this way each day until you deliver.

If the reason for the fail is insolvency of one of the parties, so that settlement will never be made, the NSCC goes into the open market and buys or sells the shares it needs to complete the trade for the nondefaulting party. For example, if Smith's firm goes out of business on Monday night, NSCC will pay you for the securities and resell them on the open market. If there is a loss, NSCC will absorb it.

Protecting the Settlement System.   Clearly, in order to relieve the parties to the trade of principal risk, the NSCC is taking on the risk itself. To cover any potential losses, participants in the NSCC must each post a contribution to the NSCC's reserve fund (the size of the contribution is proportional to the participant's trading volume). If a participant fails, the NSCC can pay its obligations out of this contribution. If that is insufficient, the NSCC uses the contributions of the other participants. If the reserve fund runs out, the NSCC may make an assessment on all remaining participants of up to 25% of their capital. So, ultimately, participants in the settlement system guarantee one another.

To limit the risk to participants of a possible failure, the NSCC is very careful about who it allows to participate in the settlement system. Only firms that meet high standards of capital, liquidity, and operational efficiency are approved as **clearing members** of the

clearing members

Members of an organized market authorized to use its clearing and settlement system.

---

[28] To eliminate any complications from netting for the sake of the example, we are assuming that this was the only trade for either you or Smith that day.

[29] Until recently, Smith would have been required instead to deliver a certified check for the amount in question, with the check payable in Fed funds the next business day. This was called payment in "clearinghouse funds." The switch to payment in same-day funds (over Fedwire) was another recommendation of the Group of Thirty.

stock market. Traders who do not meet these standards have to settle through a clearing member. The clearing member essentially guarantees settlement of trades by the traders who settle through it.

These sorts of arrangement—backup reserves in case of participant failure and restricted access to the settlement system—are typical of settlement systems in most organized markets.

Replacement Risk and Liquidity Risk.   Replacement risk and liquidity risk, too, can be eliminated by substituting the credit of a trusted third party. In Chapter 16, we saw how this is done in the futures market. When A agrees to buy a futures contract and B to sell, rather than each having a deal with the other, each has a deal with the exchange. A has a deal to buy a contract at the agreed price and B has a deal to sell a contract at that price. The exchange plays the role of a **central counterparty**. Since the exchange is pretty reliable, replacement risk and liquidity risk are essentially eliminated for A and B. Of course, the risk is merely transferred to the exchange. But, as we saw in Chapter 16, there are mechanisms in place to protect the exchange—margin, marking to market, and daily settlement.

central counterparty
Trusted third party that interposes itself in all trades.

Notice the difference between the procedure in the futures market and that in the stock market, where the NSCC interposes itself in settlement. In the stock market, traders are exposed to replacement and liquidity risk from the time of the trade until the day before settlement. If a counterparty were to fail, they would be out of luck. In the futures exchange, this is not so: the exchange interposes itself immediately *at the time of the trade*. Traders are never exposed to replacement or liquidity risk.

In most markets, however, there is no central counterparty, and traders therefore have to be careful about choosing their trading partners. Restricted access to the market and to the settlement system provides some assurance, but not enough to relieve traders of the need to monitor their exposure to particular counterparties.

Automated trading systems can be a problem in this respect because trading is typically anonymous. Traders are exposed to loss through the failure of counterparties with whom they would not have chosen to trade had they known who they were. Consequently, a market is unlikely to use an ATS when counterparty risk is a major issue (as is the case with the OTC derivatives market).

Credit and Securities Lending.   Liquidity risk is the risk that a purchaser will lack the necessary funds at the time of settlement or that a seller will lack the necessary securities. With a long settlement period—a month, say—liquidity risk is small. Purchases and sales tend to offset one another over the period, and there is plenty of time for traders to ensure they can settle.

However, as the settlement period becomes shorter, temporary imbalances of purchases and sales can involve traders in large swings in their holdings of securities and cash. If they find themselves having to take temporary delivery of large amounts of securities, they must be able to borrow to finance such holdings. Similarly, if their trading involves temporary negative positions in securities, they must be able to borrow securities in order to settle.

Historical differences in the availability of credit account for many of the differences in trading practices between organized markets. For example, on the New York Stock

Exchange, settlement became much shorter in the latter part of the nineteenth century with the development there of a market for call loans.[30] On the London Stock Exchange, with credit less readily available, the settlement period remained a fortnight. Because of its shorter settlement period, New York long ago developed a market for borrowing securities, something that has appeared in London only recently.

As we saw earlier, securities lending is relatively undeveloped in other countries. However, the push towards uniform and much shorter settlement periods has generated a growing demand for securities lending. Indeed, the recommendations of the Group of Thirty for improving settlement systems included encouraging securities lending and removing any regulatory barriers.

Clearing and Settlement at the Retail Level

The arrangements for clearing and settlement serve the wholesale market—dealers and brokers and large institutional investors.

Retail customers complete their trades through retail brokers. For example, if you, as an individual, own stocks, you will keep them for safekeeping with your broker, say Merrill Lynch. Merrill has its own internal book-entry system in which it records your securities and those of its other customers. When you buy or sell securities, Merrill will complete the transaction for you through the market clearing and settlement system. It will then credit or debit your securities and cash accounts on its book-entry system accordingly.[31]

When Merrill forwards an order from you to the wholesale system, the brokerage house becomes responsible for the completion of that trade. To protect itself, Merrill makes sure that you can cover your trade out of your cash or securities accounts.

ORGANIZED MARKETS TODAY

Now that we understand the different types of organized market and how they work, let us apply what we have learned to today's rapidly changing markets.

Forces for Change

As we saw in Chapter 11, the world's financial markets have felt the pressure of several interrelated trends—the growing importance of institutional investors, globalization, new technology, and changing regulation. We saw that this pressure has transformed the securities industry. We then saw in subsequent chapters that it has had an enormous impact too on the markets for instruments of different types—debt, equities, mortgages, and derivatives. The impact on the organized markets in which these instruments trade has been no less dramatic.

---

[30] See Chapter 6.

[31] From the point of view of the broker, wholesale clearing and settlement is known as "market-side" or "street-side" clearing and settlement. Clearing and settlement with retail customers is known as "client-side" clearing and settlement.

Institutional Investors.   Worldwide, institutional investors such as pension funds and mutual funds hold more securities than individual investors. They also account for most of the trading—over 70% of volume on the New York Stock Exchange, for example. Individuals trade far less. During 1997, for example, only 20% of individuals with brokerage accounts traded six or more times. Some 22% did not trade at all.

Because institutions trade large amounts of securities, they are particularly sensitive to trading costs. Institutional investors have therefore exerted a great deal of pressure to lower trading costs. To this end, they have lobbied regulators and they have supported new trading forums that compete with existing organized markets.

Globalization.   The market for stocks and bonds has become increasingly globalized. Deregulation has removed barriers that prevented institutional investors from acquiring foreign securities. Individuals, too, have taken an increasing interest in foreign securities. In 1998, nearly half of individual stock owners in the United States had some exposure to non-U.S. companies. Between 1979 and 1991, cross-border trade in equities grew at a rate of 28% a year to pass $2 trillion—equal to the total trading volume in U.S. equity markets in that year. Organized markets have competed vigorously for this business.

Increasing Trading Volume.   The volume of trading, particularly of stocks, has increased rapidly. In 1980, the value of shares traded worldwide amounted to 29% of world GDP. By 1998, the value of shares traded amounted to close to 80% of world GDP—a total of some $23 trillion. This increase in worldwide trading volume has been a result of the growing relative importance of institutional investors and of globalization. It has also been a result of the spread of an "equity culture" to countries where it was previously absent—continental Europe in particular.

Regulation.   Regulators of organized markets have generally become procompetition. In most countries, regulators have eliminated the fixed commissions that long allowed brokers to avoid competing with one another. Regulators have also promoted market transparency, forcing organized markets to disclose information promptly, making it easier for others to use the prices they generate to trade outside the market. Some regulations still hinder competition, however, such as the U.S. regulation that requires futures to be traded on a recognized exchange ("board of trade").[32]

Government regulators have also undermined the market power of organized markets by competing with them directly. As we have seen, regulation is a traditional function of organized markets. Organized markets monitor members to prevent manipulation and other abuses. They also monitor listed companies, to ensure that they provide investors with appropriate information. While organized markets continue to perform these functions, they now play second fiddle to government regulators. As we shall see in Chapter 20, government regulators are now the principal enforcers of fair trading in securities mar-

---

[32] Many exchanges in Europe used to be state-owned concerns and had a legal monopoly on trading. However, most were privatized late in the twentieth century.

kets. And government-imposed standards for issuers of publicly traded securities have greatly reduced the importance of listing requirements.

As a result of government-provided regulation, those wishing to trade securities no longer need to go to, say, the New York Stock Exchange, to be sure they will not be taken advantage of. All trading forums are under the watchful eye of the SEC. Similarly, the reputational value of a listing on the NYSE is not what it used to be. Many important companies, such as Microsoft and Intel, now choose not to list in the NYSE even though they meet the listing requirements. Investors feel safe in purchasing the securities of such companies because the SEC monitors their information disclosure, wherever their securities trade.

With the erosion of the regulatory function of organized markets, attention today focuses on liquidity and trading costs. It is therefore almost exclusively along these dimensions that alternative trading forums now compete.

Technology.   Technology, especially information technology, has had a profound effect on organized markets and on the competition among them. First of all, the ATS has drastically lowered the cost of setting up a trading forum. This has made entry into the business of providing a market much easier. Private concerns, mainly brokers and quote vendors, have rushed to set up for-profit ATSs to compete for order flow with existing organized markets. Such **proprietary trading systems (PTSs) or electronic communications networks (ECNs)** have taken over a significant part of the business.

In addition, competition from ECNs has made it harder for established markets to use profits from one type of trading to subsidize another. One example of such cross-subsidization would be for a market to charge small trades above cost and use the profit to subsidize (and so attract) large trades. However, charging small trades above cost makes it easy for an ECN to come in and steal those small trades away by offering them a better deal.

One feature of the ATS is that it offers remote access. Traders no longer have to be physically present on the trading floor in order to participate. This means that it is no longer necessary to limit the number of traders: essentially any number can be accommodated. This again undermines the market power of the exchange and its members. Of course, traders do not even have to be in the same country. With almost all European markets having adopted ATSs, there is no reason today why traders in the United States cannot access those markets directly. Instinet has, in fact, begun offering such access.[33]

Since any number of traders can be accommodated on an ATS, there is no longer any technical reason why investors cannot access the market directly themselves, rather than through brokers. Of course, there are still good reasons to restrict access to the clearing system to those who can be relied upon to complete their trades. However, large institutional investors are often no less reliable than brokers.

Individual traders have increasingly been trading online—accessing their brokerage accounts through the Internet. By 2000, over 40% of trading by individual investors was done in this way. Although this proportion has since declined, the number of online brokerage accounts has continued to climb, reaching some 20 million in 2001. It may be pos-

proprietary trading system (PTS) or electronic communications network (ECN)

A privately operated trading forum using an ATS.

---

[33] Although Instinet is not registered as an exchange, the SEC has turned a blind eye to this in the interest of fostering competition. Because U.S. markets have not generally adopted automated trading, they are not directly accessible to traders overseas.

sible before too long to give retail investors direct access to markets, if a way can be found to guarantee the completion of their trades.

The automation of clearing and settlement has undermined yet another advantage of the traditional organized market. In the days when securities had to be transferred physically with each transaction, a centralized market at a single location reduced the costs of such transfers. With today's electronic systems, traders do not need to be located near the market in order to settle. Moreover, as clearing and settlement systems integrate and become accessible from any market, it is no longer necessary to trade in the traditional market to be able to settle. For example, traders can clear and settle trades in NYSE-listed stocks from any equity market in the United States, since they are all connected to NSCC. In contrast, the fragmentation of settlement in the futures markets is a barrier to competition.

Competition in U.S. Stock Markets

Trading in stocks in the United States is conducted on a number of exchanges as well as over the counter (OTC). The New York Stock Exchange is the largest exchange. The others are the American Stock Exchange, also in New York City, and five regional exchanges—the Chicago, Philadelphia, Pacific, Boston, and Cincinnati exchanges. The principal OTC market is NASDAQ.

Competition for Trading Volume.   Today, little more than half the trading in securities listed on the New York Stock Exchange actually takes place there—down from 80% as recently as 1985. NASDAQ does a little better, capturing 70% of the volume of stocks that it lists.

The Third Market.   Many NYSE-listed stocks are traded on the regional exchanges. Indeed, most of the business of the regional exchanges today is in executing at a lower cost trades in NYSE-listed stocks.[34] The **Intermarket Trading System (ITS)** that allows brokers on one exchange to see prices on other exchanges and to send trades to any other exchange for execution makes it very easy for the regionals to compete.

Access to the ITS is also available to OTC dealers. Consequently, OTC dealers make a market in many NYSE-listed stocks, sending matched trades to a regional exchange for execution (this is called the **third market**).[35] For example, Madoff Investment Securities makes a market in 350 of the S&P 500 stocks and competes with NYSE specialists for small trades. Madoff alone accounts for 2% of total volume in NYSE listed stocks. Its commissions are much lower, and it attracts business from retail brokers by paying them a penny a share for orders. It matches the best price quoted on any exchange, as reported through ITS. Trades are executed through the Cincinnati Stock Exchange.

Intermarket Trading System (ITS)
A system linking trading across U.S. stock markets.

third market
An OTC market for securities listed on the NYSE.

---

[34] In 1935, the regional exchanges accounted for 35% of all listings. Today, very few stocks are listed exclusively on a regional exchange. The importance of the regional exchanges as independent trading centers declined over time as communications improved with the introduction of the telegraph, the ticker, and the telephone and the market became more centralized.

[35] The "first market" is trading in listed stocks on the exchanges. The "second market" is OTC trading of stocks *not* listed on the exchanges.

It is also possible to trade NYSE-listed stocks offshore at the London Stock Exchange. Apart from offering trading when the NYSE is closed, London also allows trades to take place outside the jurisdiction of U.S. regulators. Trading volume in London is about 5% of the volume on the NYSE itself.

fourth market
A number of electronic trading systems for block trading of securities listed on the NYSE.

crossing system
An ATS that matches trades at given prices taken from an organized market.

Proprietary Trading Systems.   There is also a **fourth market**, consisting of proprietary trading systems that match the orders of institutional investors directly without using any exchange. These **crossing systems** mostly operate after the NYSE and NASDAQ close. One such system, Posit (Portfolio System for Institutional Trading), operated by Jefferies & Co., allows whole portfolios of stocks to be traded at the market closing price (NYSE closing price, or mean of NASDAQ bid–asked spread).[36] This is a perfect solution for institutional investors that are passive traders, dealing in indexed portfolios, and unconcerned with the timing of trades. In response, the NYSE began offering its own after-hours electronic trading in 1991. However, it has attracted little business. Traders seem to prefer the existing off-exchange alternatives.[37]

There are, in addition, dozens of proprietary trading systems that set their own prices rather than taking them from the major markets. For example, SPAworks, operated by R. Steven Wunsch, is an after-hours call market. It accumulate orders after the NYSE closes at 4:00 P.M. and, at a predetermined time before the next opening, conducts a computerized call auction for each stock. The largest PTS, Instinet, captured 15% of the trading volume in NASDAQ-listed stocks in 1999, and other PTSs captured a further 15% of NASDAQ trading volume.

The principal advantage of a PTS is the lower trading costs that it offers. One reason for the lower costs is the ability of a PTS to cherry-pick the parts of the order flow that are cheapest to execute. Another is that a PTS can freeload on the price discovery of the major markets. And yet another is lower regulatory costs. A PTS has to register as a broker or dealer or be sponsored by a broker or dealer in order to have access to the clearing system. However, it does not have to register as an exchange, and most do not. They therefore avoid the considerable regulatory costs imposed on exchanges. Not surprisingly, the exchanges complain that this is unfair competition.

Brokers.   Brokerage firms have something of a conflict of interest. As members of organized markets, they benefit from the liquidity created by the order flow brought to the market by other brokers. On the other hand, by keeping most of their own order flow to themselves and executing their customers' orders off the exchange, they can lower their costs. Their ability to do this was greatly enhanced with the repeal in 2000 of Rule 390 of the NYSE, which had required members of the exchange to trade listed stocks on regulated exchanges.

The larger firms have such a large volume of orders that they are able to match many orders in-house and send them for execution to a regional exchange. Brokers have been very active, too, in promoting PTSs. For example, Goldman has invested in Archipelago,

---

[36] Posit also operates during trading hours at specified times.

[37] NASDAQ extended its hours to match the NYSE crossing sessions. The NASDAQ system, however, allows trading at new prices.

a PTS for NASDAQ stocks, in Optimark, a matching system for institutional investors, and in Primex, a PTS jointly owned with Merrill and Madoff.

Competition for Listings.   In addition to facing competition for trading volume, the NYSE also faces serious competition for the listing of stocks. This comes mainly from the NASDAQ OTC market.

NASDAQ began in 1971 as a second-tier market for small companies that did not meet the requirements for listing on the Big Board (the NYSE). It benefited greatly from (and in turn benefited) the rise of private equity investing, providing a market into which companies could be taken public. As these companies grew to the point where they qualified for a listing on the NYSE, many chose instead to remain on NASDAQ. Examples include Microsoft, Intel, MCI, and Apple.

NASDAQ also competes with the NYSE for listings of foreign securities. In some cases, these are actual securities of foreign companies issued in the United States. However, in most cases they are **American Depository Receipts (ADRs)**. ADRs work like this. A commercial bank or securities firm in the United States, acting as a trustee, buys the shares of a foreign corporation in its domestic market and places them in trust accounts with a local custodian.[38] The trustee then issues ADR certificates in the United States backed by these securities. The certificates can be traded and settled entirely in the United States in U.S. dollars (the trustee converts local currency dividends into dollars).

In 2000, U.S. investors held about 40% of their $1.75 trillion holdings of foreign stocks in the form of ADRs. There existed ADRs for the stocks of some 1,900 foreign companies from 78 different countries. Trading in ADRs accounted for about 10% of all trading in U.S. stock markets.

Competition from the Derivatives Market.   A final source of competition for the major stock markets is trading in derivatives. As we saw in Chapter 16, the derivatives markets have developed futures and options in stock market indexes, which institutional investors use to hedge their stock portfolios. In many cases, trading in index futures or options can be a substitute for trading in the stocks themselves. Instead of buying and selling actual stocks in New York, investors can adjust their positions, with lower transactions costs, by buying and selling futures and options in Chicago.

However, the news for the stock markets is not all bad. The existence of stock derivatives can also generate trading volume in the underlying stocks through **program trading**.[39] Computers track stock and derivatives prices and automatically generate buy and sell orders as appropriate. One common strategy is called **index arbitrage**: this exploits pricing anomalies between futures and stock markets. For example, if the price of index futures is above the price of the stocks that make up the actual index, arbitrageurs simultaneously sell the futures and buy the stocks, locking in a sure gain.

Program trading can generate massive trading volume on the exchanges and move prices sharply. This is particularly likely on days when futures contracts expire and the

American Depository Receipts (ADRs)
Dollar denominated claims on foreign securities held by a trustee.

program trading
The use of computers to execute a trading strategy and to generate the necessary orders.

index arbitrage
A form of program trading that exploits pricing anomalies between futures and stock markets.

---

[38] Usually, but not always, this is done in cooperation with the company in question.

[39] A program trade is defined as one involving simultaneously at least 15 stocks and having a total value of at least $1 million.

positions generated by arbitrage plays are "unwound"—the so-called triple witching hours. Overall, program trading accounted for 22% of total trading volume in the NYSE in 2000: a quarter to a third of this was due to index arbitrage. The share of program trading has risen every year for the last decade.

Competition among European Stock Markets

As in the United States, competition has changed the face of stock markets in Europe. The process has been accelerated by policy initiatives of the European Union, which is working to create a fully integrated financial system across its member states. For example, the EU has pressed members to adopt uniform listing and disclosure standards for their publicly traded companies, making cross-border investment easier. Cross-border investment has also been made much easier by the adoption by many European countries of a single currency, the Euro.

Offshore Competition from London.   The United Kingdom first brought competition to Europe with its "big bang" of 1986, when it deregulated its domestic securities markets and opened them to foreign banks and securities firms.[40]

The London Stock Exchange (LSE) began to trade foreign securities on its SEAQ International Exchange. The dramatically lower transactions costs in London attracted a great deal of international business, mainly large orders from institutional investors. In the 1990s, SEAQ International accounted for almost two-thirds of all cross-border trading. It was less regulated and more liquid than many domestic exchanges with which it competed. Half of all trades in French and Italian shares, and a third of all trades in German shares were done on SEAQ International.[41]

The European Exchanges Respond.   Competition from London forced European domestic markets to respond. The result was a wave of deregulation and consolidation. Many countries deregulated their markets and privatized their exchanges, which in many cases had been government-owned monopolies. In 1993, Germany merged its eight regional exchanges into the Deutsche Börse in Frankfurt. Since 1998, the Nordic countries have merged their exchanges into a single exchange, NOREX, with joint membership and a common trading system. The Dutch and the Belgians merged their stock and derivatives markets in 1997 and 1999, respectively, and in 2000 they merged with the Paris Bourse to form Euronext. Today, large companies from all three countries trade in Paris, small companies in Brussels, and derivatives in Amsterdam.[42] In 2000, the London Stock Exchange and the Deutsche Börse announced plans to merge, but negotiations collapsed later in the year.

---

[40] The Eurodollar market, also in London, was already relatively unregulated and open to foreign firms. However, the Eurodollar market had been kept quite separate from the domestic market.

[41] As we have seen, U.S. shares too trade in London.

[42] The small-company market, EASDAQ, was launched in 1996 and has not been a great success. By 2001 it had only 62 listings. It was acquired in 2001 by NASDAQ and relaunched as NASDAQ Europe.

Most European exchanges introduced automated trading systems, with many offering remote access to traders in other countries. The ability of traders in London to trade directly on domestic exchanges helped to undermine the position of SEAQ. In addition, bid–asked spreads on the automated European exchanges fell to 0.1 to 0.15% compared to 0.6% in SEAQ's dealer market. London eventually introduced an ATS of its own (called SETS) in 1997. Costs fell, but performance suffered.

There has been competition in Europe too from proprietary trading systems. Instinet offers trading in many European securities. Posit has opened a European crossing system and faces competition from London-based E-Crossnet and a system operated by Société Générale in Paris.

Problems of Clearing and Settlement.   Integration and consolidation of European markets has been hampered by the difficulty of cross-border clearing and settlement. Initially, clearing and settlement procedures differed widely from country to country. For example, London had a 2-week settlement period with physical delivery of securities, while France had a month-long settlement period. Recently, following the Group of Thirty recommendations, most markets have immobilized or dematerialized their securities and moved to $t + 3$ settlement. Nonetheless, cross-border settlement remains expensive. The cost of clearing and settlement can be 10 times higher in Europe than it is the United States.

Two systems that ease the process are Euroclear in Belgium and Cedel in Luxembourg. Both were set up in the 1970s as depositories and clearing and settlement systems for the Eurobond market (the two systems were linked to allow settlement between counterparties in the two systems). Over the years, they have added other securities, including stocks from most of the OECD countries (held via local subcustodians). They now offer clearing and settlement for some 5,000 stocks. Participants can confirm, net, and settle electronically with DAP in any of 30 currencies. Credit and securities lending are also available.

There has been some integration of clearing and settlement systems in Europe. Cedel has recently merged with Deutsche Börse Clearing to form Clearstream, and Euroclear has merged with Clearnet, the clearing system of Euronext. Crest, the system that serves the London Stock Exchange, is merging with SIS in Switzerland.

Competition among Derivatives Markets

Competition has affected derivatives markets no less than it has stock markets. Derivatives exchanges in the United States, mainly in Chicago, used to have a near monopoly of the worldwide market for hedging instruments. However, since the 1980s, U.S. futures and options exchanges have faced increasing competition from exchanges overseas.

The U.S. markets' share of world trading volume fell from close to 100% at the beginning of the 1980s to 60% by 2000. Europe accounted for 31% and Asia for 8%.[43] Today, the exchange with the largest trading volume in the world in terms of contracts is Eurex,

---

[43] U.S. markets accounted for $84 trillion of notional value traded out of the $140 trillion worldwide total. In terms of number of contracts traded, the U.S. share was considerably smaller.

an electronic exchange created in 1996 out of a merger between the Deutsche Terminbörse in Frankfurt and the Swiss derivatives exchange, SOFFEX. Other exchanges that are comparable to the U.S. exchanges in volume of contracts traded are LIFFE in London, the derivatives exchange of Euronext in Amsterdam, and the KSE in Seoul.

The rapid growth of overseas exchanges is surprising, given the advantages of Chicago. The Chicago exchanges can provide better liquidity than any new exchange because they are already large markets with many experienced locals. Exchanges in Europe and Asia have been able to compete, nonetheless, mainly by offering products designed to meet a specific local need. These are typically derivatives based on local stock indexes or government securities or commodity derivatives of particular importance to the local economy. Of course, these instruments could have been traded in Chicago, but in terms of accessibility of information and trading hours, the local exchanges had an edge that seems to have outweighed Chicago's advantage in liquidity.

In many countries, the development of local derivatives markets was hampered by laws that outlawed derivatives trading as a form of gambling (which of course it is). The result of these restrictions was to move derivatives trading offshore. For example, before derivatives trading was permitted in Germany in 1989, all trading in derivatives based on *bunds* (German government securities) took place on London's LIFFE. And because of regulations that raise the cost of trading derivatives in Japan, SIMEX in Singapore continues to be a center of trading in derivatives based on Japanese stocks.

Competition has spurred exchanges to lower trading costs, extend hours, offer new products, and introduce new trading technology. The trend of commissions has been steadily downwards. For example, commissions on the CBOT fell 20 to 50% in the 5 years up to 1991. In most countries, commissions are negotiable for large customers. Bid–asked spreads have also been shrinking, and trading costs have fallen too at the retail level.

The new overseas exchanges have generally adopted electronic trading. One reason is that it is easier to set up a new exchange with the latest technology than it is to change the technology of an existing one. One advantage of an ATS, as we have seen, is that it makes possible remote access. When, in 1997, the Deutsche Terminbörse in Frankfurt began to offer access to its *bund* market to traders in the United States, its market share went from 40% to 100% within a year. LIFFE, its main competitor for trading in this instrument, almost went out of business but has since made a comeback with new technology and new products.

Exchanges have entered into agreements with one another to offer remote access to one another's markets. The Chicago exchanges, together with Reuters, launched a system called Globex in 1992 to link up exchanges around the world. It allows after-hours trading worldwide when a member exchange is closed. There are also bilateral agreements, such as the one between the CME and SIMEX that offers fungibility of foreign exchange and Eurodollar contracts across the two exchanges. That is, a trading position on one exchange may be transferred to the other or settled by offsetting it against a position on the other exchange. This allows traders, when one exchange closes, to switch easily to the other.

Although U.S. derivatives markets have faced competition from derivatives markets overseas, unlike the stock markets they have not faced competition from alternative trading systems within the United States. The reason is that they have been protected by regulations requiring all trading in futures and options to take place on a registered exchange. While the SEC, in the interest of competition, has been quite permissive in allowing alternative trading systems, the regulator of the futures markets, the CFTC, has shown no such tendency.

The Consequences of Competition

Competition among organized markets has affected their structure. It has affected how they are governed, and it has stimulated consolidation both within markets and between markets.

Market Governance.   We have seen that centralization of trading has significant advantages in terms of price discovery and liquidity. As a result, organized markets have in the past often had considerable market power. This market power posed a potential threat to traders using the market, because the owners of the market could exploit their power to charge traders a monopoly price for access to it. The traditional solution to this problem has been for the traders themselves to own the market. Most exchanges were therefore established as mutual nonprofit organizations controlled by their members, the traders. In much of continental Europe, an alternative solution was for the government to own the exchange.

With competition eroding the market power of organized markets, it is no longer necessary to protect traders from monopolistic exploitation. As a result, the governance structure of organized markets has been changing. Government-owned exchanges in Europe have all been privatized. And member-owned exchanges have been converting into for-profit corporations—a process known as demutualization.[44] In a typical case, half the shares of the new corporation are initially allocated to the members, and the rest are allocated or sold to listed companies and institutional investors. Stockholm began the trend in 1993, and since then all member-owned exchanges in Europe have demutualized. In the United States, NASDAQ has plans to do so, and only the NYSE is holding out. The process has been slower among derivatives exchanges, partly because regulation has preserved more of their market power.

The corporate form has a number of advantages over mutual organization. Decision making is faster when there is no need to reconcile the conflicting interests of members. There is a greater incentive to reduce costs, which is crucial in intermarket rivalry. It is easier to merge and to acquire. And it is possible to raise funds for investment in infrastructure by issuing new stock.

Consolidation

Competitive pressure has led to the consolidation of market-making firms within organized markets. In the more competitive environment, economies of scale can make the difference between a profit and a loss. Large securities firms have been buying up dealers on NASDAQ and specialist firms in the NYSE. Consolidation has reduced the number of specialist firms from 54 in 1986 to 19 in 2001. The three largest specialists (one of which is

---

[44] We saw a similar trend to demutualization in Chapter 6 among mutual thrifts and in Chapter 9 among mutual insurance companies.

owned by Fleet Financial) now account for over half of the business. A similar process of consolidation has been going on among futures commission merchants—the brokers that take orders from customers and convey them to the derivatives exchanges.

There has also been a trend of consolidation among the markets themselves. As we have seen, consolidation in Europe has mainly been within countries, with regional and smaller exchanges merging or being absorbed by larger exchanges. There have also been some cross-border mergers, such as Eurex and Euronext. In the United States, NASDAQ took over the American Exchange in 1998.

Many more deals have been announced than have actually gone through. There are many obstacles to overcome. When the markets in question are still member owned, it is often difficult to obtain the agreement of different member interest groups: demutualization makes mergers easier. In some cases, governments have blocked cross-border deals. And there are usually technical difficulties in merging trading and settlement systems. On the other hand, technology also makes it less necessary to consolidate because it is now relatively easy to link markets without actually merging them.

An important motive for consolidation is to combine order flow and so improve the quality of the market. This brings us full circle. We saw at the beginning of the chapter that centralization tends to create market power. Market power invites competition from trading forums that can offer lower costs. The result of this competition is fragmentation of the market, which leads to a deterioration in price discovery and liquidity. This in turn creates incentives for renewed centralization.

SUMMARY

- Wholesale markets are organized markets. They are structured to facilitate trading.

- Organized markets may be either exchanges or over-the-counter markets. They may be auction markets or dealer markets. They may be centralized or decentralized.

- Markets are natural monopolies: centralization enhances price discovery, improves liquidity, and lowers trading costs. However, centralization creates market power, the abuse of which may more than offset the benefits of a centralized market.

- Organized securities markets lower trading costs by restricting access and setting rules, by standardizing trades, by providing a framework for conflict resolution, and by guaranteeing completion.

- A market order is an instruction to buy or sell at the prevailing market price. A limit order is an instruction to buy, specifying a maximum acceptable price, or an instruction to sell, specifying a minimum acceptable price.

- In a call auction trading occurs only at prearranged times. A price is found to clear as many of the accumulated orders as possible.

- It is the limit orders that allow us to form a price. Traders who enter limit orders are essentially information traders. They provide liquidity to traders who enter market orders.

- In a call auction, pooling of orders provides good price discovery and liquidity at the call, but there is no price or liquidity between calls.

- In a continuous auction orders are filled out of the limit-order book as they arrive.

- With a continuous auction prices are available continuously and trades can be executed immediately. But the thinness of the market necessitates a backup mechanism.

- Possible backup mechanisms include information traders, specialists, price limits and trading halts, negotiation for large orders. In a sense, the limit of these backup mechanisms is a dealer market.

- To function properly, securities markets require credit in both money and securities. Most lending in securities markets is reciprocal.

- Traders and potential traders require information. Organized markets gather, disseminate, and sell information on quotes and on realized trades.

- Organized markets rely increasingly on automated trading systems (ATSs) to execute orders. The main issue with these systems is how to provide the backup that a continuous market requires. Many markets use a combination of an ATS and human-mediated trading.

- The big advantage of an ATS is cost. It also offers remote access and can improve operational efficiency and market transparency.

- Completion of a trade involves principal risk, replacement risk and liquidity risk. In general, the greater the delays, the greater the risks.

- Completion involves clearing and settlement. Clearing precedes settlement and consists of comparison and netting. Settlement is the actual exchange of securities for cash.

- Organized markets have clearinghouses and depositories to facilitate clearing and settlement. The clearinghouse compares and nets trades. The depository immobilizes securities to allow settlement through a book-entry system.

- Principal risk can be eliminated by DAP or by a guarantee from the clearinghouse. To protect themselves, settlement systems generally restrict access to reliable clearing members.

- Replacement risk can be eliminated by use of a central counterparty. Credit and securities lending reduce liquidity risk.

- Organized markets have changed under the pressure of the growing importance of institutional investors, of globalization, of new technology, and of changing regulation.

- Government-provided regulation has largely replaced market-provided regulation, so reducing market power. Technology has made competition easier.

- The NYSE has faced increasing competition from other exchanges and from the third and fourth markets. NASDAQ has competed for listings.

- The markets for index futures and options compete with the NYSE for trading volume. Their existence also results in index arbitrage and in other forms of program trading.

- Competition in European stock markets has led to deregulation, the introduction of new technology, and consolidation.

- U.S. derivatives exchanges face significant competition from exchanges overseas.

- The erosion of market power of organized markets has led to a change in governance from mutual or state-owned to for-profit forms.

- Competition has led to fragmentation, creating incentives for renewed centralization.

DISCUSSION QUESTIONS

1. Compare and contrast the ways that securities markets and financial intermediaries provide liquidity. What are their relative advantages and disadvantages? What can go wrong in each case?

2. Compare and contrast price discovery in dealer and in auction markets. In each case, who decides on what the price should be? What incentives do they have to set the price correctly?

3. Trading costs (as a percentage of price) are much lower in organized securities market than they are in other types of markets. Why? What methods do securities markets use to reduce transactions costs?

What incentives do they have to reduce transactions costs?

4. We saw in Chapter 2 that the basic technology of the financial system consists of delegation, credit substitution, pooling, and netting. What role does each of these play in securities markets?

5. Why is credit important to the proper functioning of securities markets? How would a security market be harmed if no credit were available? What would happen?

6. Why is the New York Stock Exchange under so much competitive pressure? What sorts of competition does the NYSE face?

7. What are the economies of scale and scope in securities markets?

8. What are the advantages of a call market relative to a continuous market? What are the disadvantages?
   a. How do they compare with respect to liquidity, price discovery, and trading costs.
   b. Which makes it easier to trade "off the exchange"?
   c. How does the choice of call vs continuous auction depend on trading volume and size of orders?
   d. Which is better for liquidity traders (those trading for reasons unrelated to the current price)? For information traders (those trading to profit from price movements)?

9. Compare the execution of trades in the government securities market as described in Chapter 12, with execution in the stock market. What are the differences? Why is settlement so much faster in the government securities market? Could the stock market copy the procedures of the government securities market?

10. Shortening the settlement period involves trade-offs. Explain the effect on replacement risk, liquidity risk, and principal risk. How can the trade-off be improved?

11. What are the different ways that corporate stocks are traded in the United States today? What are the advantages and disadvantages of having so many separate trading forums? What do you expect to happen?

12. Increasingly, exchanges are replacing face-to-face trading on the floor with automated trading systems (ATSs) that match orders directly, and they are facing competition from "e-bourses" that offer order matching outside the exchange.
   a. "In e-markets, orders would be matched more quickly and cheaply than can be done by human market makers." How might the lack of human market makers affect a market's performance? What do human market makers do? Can this be automated? Why do you think Posit matches orders only twice a day? How does Primex address the issue?
   b. What are the limitation of an ATS? How well would you expect it to handle small orders vs large? What advantage does Instinet have in this respect?
   c. What are the potential advantages of an ATS?

13. Most exchanges were established as mutual organizations owned by the brokers that trade on them (the remainder were set up and owned by governments).
   a. Why were they set up in this way?
   b. What has changed to make "demutualization" attractive?
   c. What are its advantages?

BIBLIOGRAPHY

Abken, Peter A. "Globalization of Stock, Futures, and Options Markets." *Federal Reserve Bank of Atlanta Economic Review*, July–August 1991, 1–22.

Cybo-Ottone, A., et al. "Recent Developments in the Structure of Securities Markets." *Brookings–Wharton Papers on Financial Services*, 2000, 223–282.

De Long, J. Bradford. "Did J. P. Morgan's Men Add Value? A Historical Perspective on Financial Capitalism." Working paper no. 3426, National Bureau of Economic Research, August 1990.

Domowitz, I., and R. Lee. "The Legal Basis for Stock Exchanges: The Classification and Regulation of Automated Trading Systems." Working paper, Northwestern University, Evanston, IL, 1996.

Domowitz, I., and B. Steil. "Automation, Trading Costs, and the Structure of the Securities Trading Industry." *Brookings–Wharton Papers on Financial Services*, 1999, 33–81.

Jarrell, Gregg A. "Change at the Exchange: The Causes and Effects of Deregulation." *Journal of Law and Economics* 27 (October 1984): 273–312.

Lee, R. *What Is an Exchange? The Automation, Management, and Regulation of Financial Markets.* New York: Oxford University Press, 1998.

McAndrews, James J. "Where Has All the Paper Gone? Book-Entry Delivery-Against-Payment Systems." *Business Review of the Federal Reserve Bank of Philadelphia*, November–December 1992, 19–30.

Macey, J., and H. Kanda. "The Stock Exchange as a Firm: The Emergence of Close Substitutes for the New York and Tokyo Stock Exchanges." *Cornell Law Review* 75 (1990): 1007.

Macey, J. R., and M. O'Hara. "Globalization, Exchange Governance, and the Future of Exchanges." *Brookings–Wharton Papers on Financial Services*, 1999, 1–31.

Michie, R. C. "Friend or Foe? Information Technology and the London Stock Exchange Since 1700."

Journal of Historical Geography 23, no. 3 (July 1997): 304–326.

Pardy, R. "Regulatory and Institutional Impacts of Securities Market Computerization." Working paper, The World Bank, 1992.

Parkinson, Patrick, et al. "Clearance and Settlement in U.S. Securities Markets." Special study no. 163, Board of Governors of the Federal Reserve System, March 1992.

Perold, A. F. "The Payments System and Derivatives Instruments." In *The Global Financial System: A Functional Perspective*. Edited by D. B. Crane et al. Boston: Harvard Business School Press.

Sarkar, A., and M. Tozzi. "Electronic Trading on Futures Exchanges." *Federal Reserve Bank of New York Current Issues in Economics and Finance* 4, no. 1 (Jauary 1998).

Scarlata, Jodi G. "Institutional Developments in the Globalization of Securities and Futures Markets." *Federal Reserve Bank of St. Louis Review*, January–February 1992, 17–30.

KEY TERMS

retail market	block trades	depository
wholesale market	upstairs market	custodian
organized markets	reciprocal loan	delivery against payment (DAP)
centralized market	margin lending	clearing members
decentralized market	quote vendors	central counterparty
transparent	automated trading systems (ATSs)	proprietary trading systems (PTSs)
listed company	order routing	electronic communications
listing requirements	back office	networks (ECNs)
round lots	principal risk	Intermarket Trading System (ITS)
market order	replacement risk	third market
limit order	liquidity risk	fourth market
call auction	systemic risk	crossing systems
continuous auction	comparison	American Depository Receipts
limit-order book	gross settlement	(ADRs)
clearing transaction	multilateral multi-issue netting	program trading
specialist	dematerialization	index arbitrage
trading halt	immobilization	

PART IV

SAFETY AND REGULATION

CHAPTER 18

MANAGING LIQUIDITY AND RISK

When you finish this chapter you will understand:

- How intermediaries manage their liquidity and how things can go wrong
- How intermediaries can make or lose money from movements in interest rates and exchange rates
- How intermediaries can protect themselves against defaulting borrowers

Financial institutions around the world have had undergone a series of disasters in recent years. Some examples:

- In the 1970s, U.S. and foreign banks lent hundreds of billions of dollars to less-developed countries (LDCs). In the 1980s, these loans turned sour and many banks took heavy losses.
- Continental Illinois, in 1984, and Bank of New England, in 1991, both suffered major runs on their deposits. Both were taken over by federal regulators.
- In 1987, Merrill Lynch lost $350 million on its holdings of mortgage-backed securities when interest rates rose suddenly; in 1992, J. P. Morgan lost $200 million the same way when interest rates fell.
- In 1998, the impending failure of a hedge fund called Long Term Capital Management, holding $125 billion in securities and $1 trillion in derivatives, threatened the stability of markets. The New York Fed organized a rescue.

In each of these cases, a financial institution failed in its management of liquidity or risk or both. In this chapter, we shall look at how financial institutions manage liquidity and risk and how and why things can go wrong.

We took a first look at these issues in Chapter 5. That first look was necessarily sketchy, because we knew little about the details of the financial system. Since then, we have learned a great deal. We have studied in depth the different intermediaries, markets, and instruments. We are ready now for a second, more realistic, look at how financial intermediaries manage liquidity and risk.

We begin by examining how financial intermediaries deal with liquidity. We then look at risk—first market risk, then credit risk. We conclude with a closer look at three of the failures just mentioned—the LDC debt crisis, the failure of Continental Illinois, and the collapse of LTCM.

While much of our discussion focuses on commercial banks, an important message of this chapter is that the problems faced by different types of financial intermediary and the techniques they use to deal with them are very similar. Therefore, throughout the chapter, we will be comparing the problems and practices of commercial banks with those of other types of intermediary.

MANAGING LIQUIDITY

Financial intermediaries often promise greater liquidity in their liabilities than their assets can provide directly. As we saw in Chapter 2, the main reason intermediaries can do this is pooling—for example, the offsetting of a bank's withdrawals against its new deposits. However, pooling alone is not enough: withdrawals may sometimes exceed new deposits. Banks and other financial intermediaries must therefore have backup sources of liquidity—ways they can lay their hands on cash whenever they need it.

There is an additional reason that intermediaries need to worry about liquidity. Intermediaries are in the business of lending, and they cannot make new loans unless they have the necessary funds. In some cases, they are contractually bound to make a loan whenever a customer so desires. Such loan commitments account for a large part of commercial lending by banks.[1] Firms rely on these commitments as backup sources of liquidity. So a loan commitment to a customer, just like a deposit, requires a bank to be able to provide liquidity on demand.

Simply holding reserves of cash is an expensive, and therefore unattractive, way to meet liquidity needs. As we saw in Chapter 5, there are essentially two alternatives—*asset management* and *liability management*. The basic idea of asset management is simple: hold assets that can readily be turned into cash as needed. The basic idea of liability man-

---

[1] Under a loan commitment, a bank promises, in exchange for a fee, to lend, at the customer's discretion and at a contracted interest rate. The commitment covers a specified time period and has a prespecified maximum amount. The *prime rate* developed as an index for pricing loan commitments. A bank would commit to lending to its best customers at, or sometimes below, this rate and to others at a markup over prime. More recently, LIBOR has become the more common reference rate, with prime the reference rate mainly for smaller loans.

agement is equally simple: when you need cash, borrow it. Let us see how different types of intermediary apply these ideas to managing their liquidity.[2]

How Large and Small Banks Manage Liquidity

Commercial banks differ widely in how they manage liquidity. The big difference is between small bank and large ones. To understand the reason for the difference, let us look at an example of each. Our example of a small bank is the Ledyard National Bank of Hanover, New Hampshire. On June 30, 2001, it held assets of $204 million. Our example of a large bank is J. P. Morgan Chase & Co. of New York. On June 30, 2001, it held assets of $713 billion.

There are many more banks in the United States like Ledyard than like Chase. As you can see from Exhibit 18.1, over 8,000 of the nearly 10,000 U.S. banks have assets of less than $300 million. However, these small banks account for only one-tenth of the total assets of all banks. There are only 104 banks that, like Chase, have over $10 billion in assets, but together they account for two-thirds of total bank assets.

EXHIBIT 18.1   Size Distribution of U.S. Commercial Banks, 2000

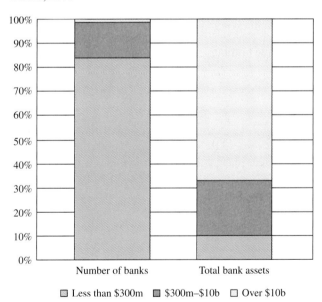

□ Less than $300m   ■ $300m–$10b   □ Over $10b

Source: Federal Deposit Insurance Corp., Statistics on Banking.

---

[2] Simple as these ideas are, they were in their time important innovations. For many years liquidity meant arranging loans so that their repayment at maturity would provide the bank with a steady flow of cash. The idea of using marketable securities as secondary reserves became popular in the United States only towards the end of the nineteenth century. The idea of borrowing to provide liquidity developed with the money market in the 1960s. As a principal source of liquidity, it is quite recent.

EXHIBIT 18.2   Balance Sheet of Ledyard National Bank, June 30, 2001 (Millions of Dollars)

Assets		Liabilities and Net Worth	
Cash and balances due	5.6	Transactions deposits	50.0
Securities	38.1	Time deposits	121.7
Fed funds sold	9.3	Repurchase agreements	11.1
Loans	140.3	Other liabilities	5.5
Other	2.6	Equity	15.4

Source: Statement of Financial Condition.

retail bank
A bank that does business primarily with households and small firms.

deposit-rich bank
A bank that has significantly more funds available than good loan opportunities.

A Small Bank: Ledyard National Bank of Hanover, New Hampshire.
Like most small banks, Ledyard is a **retail bank**: its customers are households and small firms. Consequently, its deposits are small, and its opportunities for making loans are limited. It has no direct access to large creditworthy borrowers.

Exhibit 18.2 shows Ledyard's balance sheet. Ledyard is **deposit rich**: it has significantly more funds available than good loan opportunities.

From Exhibit 18.3, you can see how much Ledyard has left over. The funds it has available include $171.7 million in deposits, $15.4 million in equity, and $16.8 million in other liabilities—a total of $203.8 million. It uses these funds to support $140.3 million in loans, about $5.6 million in reserves and other cash, and $2.6 million in other assets. That leaves **$55.3** million.

Ledyard's situation is typical for a small bank. The successful management of a small bank largely depends on making good use of such leftover funds.

The Basics of Asset Management.   It makes good sense for deposit-rich Ledyard to meet its needs for liquidity through asset management. It therefore invests its leftover

EXHIBIT 18.3   Ledyard National Bank: Sources and Uses of Funds (Millions of Dollars)

Sources of funds		
Deposits	171.7	
Equity	15.4	
Other	16.8	
Total		$203.8
Uses of funds		
Loans	140.3	
Cash	5.6	
Other	2.6	
Leftover funds	55.3	
Total		$203.8

Source: Exhibit 18.2.

funds in two categories of asset that will provide it with liquidity—Federal funds sold and securities.[3]

The Fed funds sold are the more liquid. As we saw in Chapter 6, Fed funds sold for a small bank means correspondent Fed funds—essentially a loan to a correspondent bank. Such loans are mostly overnight. They can be turned into cash at any time simply by not rolling them over.

However, Fed funds sold do have some disadvantages. Because they are an unsecured and uninsured loan to another bank, they are subject to credit risk. They also have an opportunity cost: other alternatives usually offer a higher yield.

Other alternatives usually offer a higher yield because of the shape of the yield curve. We saw in Chapter 12 that the "normal" yield curve slopes upward: long-term rates are usually higher than short-term rates. Since the Fed funds rate is close to the rate on short-term Treasuries, it is generally lower than the yield on longer term government securities. The opportunity cost of Fed funds sold is the yield that could be earned on such longer term securities.

Government securities offer a higher yield than Fed funds sold. They are also free of credit risk and readily marketable. However, they too have their disadvantages. Maintaining liquidity by buying and selling securities does involve transactions costs. Also, if interest rates have risen since the bank bought the securities, the bank will take a loss when it sells them (in Chapter 4, we saw that when interest rates rise, security prices fall). Moreover, the longer the maturity of the securities, the more sensitive they are to a change in market interest rates. So, selecting the maturity of its government securities is an important decision for the bank.[4]

These disadvantages of government securities as a source of liquidity can largely be overcome by using repos (as we saw in Chapter 12, a repo is essentially a loan collateralized by government securities). The bank can hold the securities to maturity and repo them whenever it needs funds. The transactions costs are lower than for actual purchases and sales, and the bank avoids the need to recognize any losses on its books. As you can see from Exhibit 18.2, Ledyard has repoed $11.1 million of its securities.

In terms of asset management, then, Fed funds sold provide the first line of defense, with government securities providing backup when necessary. The art of asset management for a small bank largely consists of balancing the advantages and disadvantages of these two alternative assets and of finding the right proportions between them.

A Money-Center Bank: J.P. Morgan Chase & Co. of New York.   Although Chase, like Ledyard, is a commercial bank, it does a very different kind of business. As a

---

[3] "Securities" generally means U.S. government securities. Before the Tax Reform Act of 1986 took away the tax advantages, banks were large investors in municipal securities. Banks are not permitted to invest in corporate securities.

[4] Of course, the bank takes a loss whether it recognizes it or not. However, for securities held over the long term—in the bank's "investment account"—the loss does not appear on the bank's books unless the securities are actually sold. Since bank officers are rewarded according to the bank's accounting profits, it does matter to them whether the loss appears on the books. Securities held primarily for resale must be listed on the balance sheet in a separate "trading account" at market price, so that their value on the balance sheet does fluctuate with market interest rates. Accounting standards have recently been tightened, making it harder for banks to have the best of both worlds by holding securities in their investment account and selling them only if the value of the instruments increases.

wholesale bank
A bank that does business primarily with large corporations, governments, other financial institutions, and wealthy individuals.

major money-center bank, Chase's business is predominantly **wholesale**: its customers are major corporations, governments, other financial institutions, and wealthy individuals.[5]

In addition to taking deposits and making loans, Chase is very active in the securities markets. A Chase subsidiary is a primary dealer in U.S. government securities. And Chase was the first U.S. commercial bank to be allowed to underwrite corporate debt after Glass–Steagall restrictions were eased in the 1990s. Chase also manages billions in assets for private and institutional clients and sells processing and information services. Chase's income from these various "sidelines" was double its income from taking deposits and making loans. (Its noninterest income was 65% of the total in 2000, compared to 23% for Ledyard.)

Chase's business is also highly international. It has 28 offices overseas. Chase is a leading dealer in government securities in all seven of the world's major economies. It is also a major player in the foreign exchange market.

deposit-poor bank
A bank that has significantly more good loan opportunities than funds available from ordinary deposits.

Exhibit 18.4 shows Chase's balance sheet. In contrast to Ledyard, Chase is **deposit poor**. Its extensive contacts with major corporations, institutions, and governments worldwide provide it with numerous loan opportunities. However, because retail banking is a relatively small part of its business, its access to domestic deposits is relatively limited. You can see the size of the shortfall from Exhibit 18.5. Domestic deposits, equity, long-term debt, and other liabilities add up to some $402.6 billion, well short of the $523.4 billion in loans, cash, securities, and other assets it needs to fund.

While Ledyard can afford to wait for deposits to come in, Chase cannot. Because it wants to fund more assets than it has funds available, it must go into the money market and

---

[5] Some money-center banks, such as such as Citibank and BankAmerica, combine their wholesale business with extensive retail banking.

EXHIBIT 18.4   Balance Sheet of J. P. Morgan Chase & Co., June 30, 2001 (Billions of Dollars)

Assets		Liabilities and Net Worth	
Cash and balances due	24.2	Deposits	
		Non–interest bearing	64.2
		Interest bearing	212.6
Deposits at interest with banks	11.9	Fed funds purchased and securities sold	155.1
Fed funds sold and securities purchased		under repo	
under repo	61.3	Commercial paper	20.0
Securities borrowed	38.3	Other borrowed funds	18.4
Trading assets		Trading liabilities	
Debt and equity instruments	139.1	Debt and equity instruments	53.6
Derivatives receivables	68.9	Derivatives payables	62.4
Securities	68.5	Long-term debt	40.9
Loans	216.2	Other	42.5
Private equity investments	9.9		
Others	74.3	Equity	42.4

Source: Second Quarter Report, 2001.

EXHIBIT 18.5   J. P. Morgan Chase & Co.:
Sources and Uses of Funds (Billions of Dollars)

Sources of funds

Domestic deposits	276.8
Equity	42.4
Long-term debt	40.9
Other liabilities	42.5
Money market[a]	193.5

Uses of funds

Loans	216.2
Cash	24.2
Net securities[b]	198.8
Other	84.2
Money market[c]	73.2

[a] The sum of the categories Fed funds purchased and securities sold under repo, commercial paper, and other borrowed funds.
[b] The sum of the categories securities borrowed, trading assets, and securities, less trading liabilities.
[c] The sum of the categories deposits at interest with banks and Fed funds sold and securities purchased under repo.

Source: Second Quarter Report, 2001.

borrow actively. It borrows some $120.2 billion net in the money market—its $193.5 bil-lion in money market liabilities less its $73.2 billion in money market assets.

If Chase needs to borrow in the money market, why does it also lend there? Partly it is a matter of timing: funds sometimes come in when loan opportunities are not immediately available. Partly it is to accommodate customer needs. Mainly, though, as we shall see later in the chapter, it reflects Chase's overall strategy to make profit and to control risk. Chase is a typical money-center bank both in the business it does and in its reliance on the money market to provide it with the funds its needs.

If the big question for a small bank is what to do with its excess funds, the big question for a large money-center bank is how to manage its borrowing. How it does this is crucial both to its profitability and to its management of liquidity and risk.

The Basics of Liability Management.   Since it is deposit poor, Chase finds asset management an unappealing way to satisfy its needs for liquidity. Asset management would require it to borrow funds, use them to purchase assets, and then sell the assets to provide funds as needed. This would be silly. It makes much more sense simply to borrow funds directly as needed. That is, of course, the essence of liability management.

Banks like Chase that rely on liability management to meet their needs for liquidity must decide on what form their borrowing should take. In particular, should the bank borrow overnight or longer term (term funds)?

Overnight funds usually cost less. Because the yield curve normally slopes upward, the shorter the term, the lower the cost. But relying too heavily on overnight funds has its dangers. As we shall see, it increases the exposure of the bank to interest rate risk. In addi-tion, overnight funds are the least stable source of borrowing: if the bank gets into diffi-culties, these funds can literally be gone tomorrow. Options for overnight borrowing include Fed funds purchased, overnight Eurodollars, repoing government securities, and borrowing from the Fed (about which more presently).

Term funds are more stable. If the bank matches the maturity of its liabilities to the maturity of its assets, there is no liquidity risk. However, longer term funding is usually more expensive. Options for term borrowing include selling NCDs, deposit notes, or bank notes, having the bank's holding company sell commercial paper or medium-term notes, selling acceptances, and borrowing term Eurodollars.

Successful liability management involves balancing the advantages and disadvantages of overnight and term funding to find the right proportions between them. As we shall see, however, there are also considerations of risk.

Evaluating a Bank's Liquidity Position.   Both for Ledyard and for Chase, the first step in managing liquidity is knowing the bank's position. What are its funding needs? What are the chances it will have problems in meeting them?

To answer such questions, banks follow certain standard procedures. Exhibit 18.6 shows one way this is done. The bank evaluates, over differing time horizons, the likely cash flows in and out.

The bank knows when certain assets and liabilities are due to mature, when certain commitments to lend will be called upon. Of course, none of this is absolutely certain: loans may be prepaid or rolled over at maturity; time deposits may be withdrawn before maturity or rolled over. There are other predictable cash flows. Interest payments will be coming in and going out. There will be seasonal changes in deposits that are fairly pre-dictable from year to year.

In addition to these relatively predictable cash flows are others less predictable. Some deposits, like checking deposits, have no specified maturity and can be withdrawn at any

EXHIBIT 18.6   "Cash Flow" Liquidity Evaluation

Cash Flow In	Cash Flow Out
Actual	
Maturing assets[a]	Maturing liabilities and firm commitments to lend[a]
Interest from nonmaturing assets	Interest on nonmaturing liabilities
	Seasonal changes in deposits
Potential	
Salable nonmaturing assets	Deposits with unspecified maturity
Established credit lines[b]	Optional commitments to lend and other off-balance-sheet activities

[a] Long-term relationships may cause some assets and liabilities to be automatically rolled over, reducing the actual cash flows in and out.

[b] The availability of these lines are sometimes affected by material adverse change clauses. Also if credit lines require collateral, their use can limit the use of asset sales.

Source: Federal Reserve Bank of New York, 1990.

EXHIBIT 18.7   Calculating the Funding Gap

Funding gap = Funds required − funds available

Funds Required	Funds Available
Assets to be funded	Equity
Percent of unused commitments	Long-term liabilities
Less: marketable assets	Stable short-term liabilities
Less: short-term discretionary assets	Proven unused funding capacity

Source: Federal Reserve Bank of New York, 1990.

time. Some loan commitments and off-balance-sheet guarantees may be called upon unexpectedly. In addition, as we saw in Chapter 8, banks are exposed to enormous variations in intraday cash flow as a result of their participation in clearing systems such as Fedwire and CHIPS. To balance all these unpredictable cash flows, banks have assets they can sell and credit lines they can draw on.

funding gap
New money a bank must raise to cover new assets and liabilities that need refunding.

An additional tool used in assessing liquidity needs is an index called the **funding gap**. Exhibit 18.7 shows how this is calculated. The "gap" represents new money the bank must raise to cover new assets and liabilities that need refunding.

Of course, applying these procedures is difficult, and a great deal of judgment is necessarily involved. However, they do provide at least a rough picture of the bank's overall position and a warning of potential problems.

The Problems of Liability Management

Liability management is inherently a much more dangerous strategy than asset management. A small bank that gets its asset management wrong will lose some potential income; a large bank that gets its liability management wrong will fail.

The key to liability management is always being *able* to borrow. A bank's credit must be beyond question because most of its borrowing is unsecured. If there is any doubt about its credit, lenders can switch to another, safer bank at no cost. With the slightest suspicion of trouble, the rate a bank pays to borrow rises rapidly. If its credit is seriously in doubt, it will be unable to borrow at any rate, and it will go under.

These dangers became painfully clear with the collapse of Continental Illinois in 1984 (we will study this in detail at the end of the chapter). After Continental Illinois, banks looked for ways to reduce their vulnerability.

Lengthening the Maturity of Liabilities.   One way to reduce vulnerability is to rely more on term funding. But this is expensive: banks do not want to pay higher longer term rates. The trick then is to borrow long term for stability, but to pay short-term rates for lower cost.

maturity of a loan
The time until repayment.

To do this banks, needed to separate the maturity of a security from its repricing period. **Maturity** is the time until repayment. A security with shorter maturity is more liq-

repricing period
The length of
time for which the
interest rate re-
mains fixed.

uid for the lender, but it is a less stable source of funds to the borrower. The **repricing period** is the length of time for which the interest rate remains fixed.

The distinction is illustrated in Exhibit 18.8. For a three-year, $1 million deposit at a fixed rate, both the maturity period and the repricing period are 3 years. On this deposit, the bank pays the 3-year rate of 6%. The bank could obtain the same $1 million for 3 years by rolling over 1-year deposits. The advantage is that it pays the lower 1-year rate (which varies from year to year); the disadvantage is that it must repay the $1 million each year and borrow again. A 3-year deposit with yearly repricing gives the bank the best of both worlds: it has the $1 million for 3 years, and it can pay the lower 1-year rate.

The problem, of course, is that lenders will not be interested in such a deposit. If they give up the liquidity, they expect to get the higher rate.

The solution is a swap. A swap allows the bank to separate the maturity of the deposit from the repricing period. The bank issues a 3-year deposit note, so ensuring itself a stable source of funds. It then becomes a floating-rate payer on a corresponding swap, effectively converting the fixed-rate deposit into a floating-rate one. Banks have taken advantage of this method of lengthening the maturity of their liabilities, increasingly relying on medium-term borrowing.

Other Ways to Improve the Stability of Funding.   Banks can improve the stability of their funding in several other ways. One is to rely more on **core deposits**—transactions deposits and retail time deposits. Although these are often payable on demand, pooling keeps the total amount quite stable. Large banks have made considerable efforts in recent years to increase their core deposits and so reduce their reliance on borrowed funds. The easing of restrictions on interstate banking has made it easier for large banks to acquire core deposits by buying out-of-state retail banks.

core deposits
Transactions de-
posits and retail
time deposits.

Another way to improve the stability of funding is to strengthen relationships with major lenders so that they are less likely to withdraw their funds in a crisis. For example, if GM knows it can borrow from Citibank whenever it needs to, at a lower rate than it would pay elsewhere, it will be less likely to pull its deposits if Citibank's credit rating is downgraded. GM is willing to help Citi because Citi is valuable to it. To buy this kind of loyalty, a bank must be less aggressive in squeezing the last penny out of every deal.

EXHIBIT 18.8   Different Ways for a Bank to Borrow

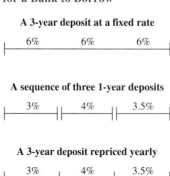

A 3-year deposit at a fixed rate

6%   6%   6%

A sequence of three 1-year deposits

3%   4%   3.5%

A 3-year deposit repriced yearly

3%   4%   3.5%

A third way to improve the stability of funding is to diversify sources. This means borrowing from different lenders, but it also means borrowing in different markets. Because of a desire to diversify, a bank may be reluctant to rely too heavily on any one source even if it is the least expensive.

Reducing Reliance on Liability Management.   Although liability management remains their principal method of managing liquidity, large banks have been making increasing use of asset management. The recent risk-based capital standards have made it relatively more attractive for banks to hold liquid assets such as government securities, interbank deposits, and mortgage-backed securities. Notice in Exhibit 18.4 that Chase is holding a relatively large amounts of securities: a few years ago this number would have been much smaller.[6]

Another way to reduce the dependence on liability management is to take assets off the balance sheet altogether. That way there is no need to fund them and so no liquidity problem. A bank can keep loans off its balance sheet by helping customers issue commercial paper rather than making them direct loans. It can take loans already on its balance sheet off by securitizing them. Securitization should not, however, be seen as a form of asset management: it takes too long to put a deal together for this method to be useful as a tool of short-run liquidity management. It is also especially hard to securitize loans when a bank is in trouble and its need for liquidity is greatest.[7]

Using all these methods, the major banks have considerably improved their liquidity position and have reduced their reliance on potentially unstable sources of funds.

Managing a Bank's Reserves

For small banks, this is not a big problem: in many cases, the amount of cash they hold in their ATMs exceeds their required reserves. However for larger banks, reserve management is more complicated. To understand the issues, put yourself in the shoes of the reserve manager at a large bank.

Calculating Reserve Requirements.   Reserve requirements set the *average* reserves your bank must hold given the *average* amount of its deposits over a given period. The calculation is quite complex.

Each day, at the close of business, you fill out a report listing the amount the bank has of each of the following:

- Vault cash
- Checking deposits subject to reserve requirements
- Deposits at the Fed

Each week, you send this report to the Fed so that it can monitor your compliance with reserve requirements.

---

[6] We will discuss the new capital standards in Chapter 19.

[7] See Chapter 14 on securitization.

computation period
The period over which average deposits determine a bank's required reserves.

maintenance period
The period over which average reserves must cover average deposits over the computation period.

The period over which you calculate your reserve requirement is called the **computation period**. Each computation period lasts 2 weeks—from Tuesday to the Monday 2 weeks later. When one computation period ends, the next one begins. The period over which you must meet the requirement is called the **maintenance period**. The average amount of reserves you must hold during the maintenance period depends on the average amount of your deposits during the corresponding computation period. The maintenance period begins on the Thursday after the beginning of the corresponding computation period and runs through the Wednesday after the end of the computation period.

Meeting your reserve requirements requires some finesse. At the start of the maintenance period, you know the amount of your deposits for only the first 2 days of the computation period. More information comes in each day, and you will have all the information you need by Monday afternoon 2 days before the end of the current maintenance period. Until then, you must estimate the amount of checking deposits for the remainder of the computation period and adjust your reserves accordingly.

We saw in Chapter 6 that banks are able to reduce the amount of reserves they need to hold. They do this by "sweeping" balances out of the checkable deposits of their wholesale customers into bank repos and overnight Eurodollars, liabilities that do not require reserves to be held against them. Since 1994, banks have been allowed to do the same for their retail customers, sweeping balances into nonreservable money market deposit accounts. As a result, banks have been able to reduce considerably the reserve balances they hold at the Fed.

Adjusting Reserves.   Achieving your reserve target day by day is not easy. Your balance at the Fed fluctuates wildly during the day as large wire payments come in and go out. For much of the day you are in overdraft. Towards the end of the day, you must make or receive a payment to settle on CHIPS. To end the day with the balance you want, you must anticipate incoming and outgoing payments, and make sure you have enough to cover your daylight overdraft plus your target level of reserves.[8]

There are a number of ways you can add to your balance at the Fed, most obviously by borrowing Fed funds or borrowing from the Fed.[9] But borrowing Eurodollars or selling or repoing securities is just as good, since in each case you will receive the funds in your account at the Fed the same day over Fedwire. If your balance at the Fed is too high, all these methods can be used, in reverse, to reduce it.

If you need to increase your balance at the Fed, you will naturally try to do so at the lowest possible cost. Timing is important. You can achieve your target level of reserves by having more early in the maintenance period and less later or vice versa. Which strategy you choose will depend on whether you think interest rates are going to rise or fall towards the end of the current maintenance period. Of course, the reserve managers at the other large banks are in a similar position. They too are trying to guess which way interest rates will move.

---

[8] See Chapter 8 on payments and daylight overdraft.

[9] The latter is known as "borrowing at the discount window." We shall have more to say about it in Chapter 19. Although this used to be an important source of liquidity for reserve adjustment, banks rarely use it for this purpose today.

If everyone is gambling on a fall in rates, it may happen at the end of the maintenance period that everyone is short of reserves. If so, everyone will try to borrow simultaneously and the Fed funds and related rates will go up sharply. Or the opposite may happen: all parties may have more than they need, and the Fed funds rate will drop as everyone tries to unload funds. If you have guessed right, you will make some money for your bank. If not, your bank will take a loss.

How Other Intermediaries Manage Liquidity

Intermediaries other than commercial banks do not have to hold required reserves, but they do face a similar need to manage their liquidity. Looking at the differences among the different types of institution will give us a deeper understanding of liquidity management.

Eurodollar Banks. Eurodollar banks differ from U.S. commercial banks both in their assets and in their liabilities. Their loans are relatively long term and they fund them mostly with relatively short-term time deposits. Given this structure, Eurodollar banks must manage their liquidity carefully.

Eurodollar banks rely largely on the interbank market for liquidity—both for liability management and for asset management. For this reason, and for others that we shall see presently, the amount of interbank Eurodollar deposits is enormous.

If deposits are not rolled over, or if new deposits fail to come in fast enough to refund maturing deposits, a Eurodollar bank can turn to the interbank market to borrow. However, relying entirely on liability management is dangerous. If, for some reason, a bank's creditworthiness comes into question, its cost of borrowing may rise sharply, or it may be unable to borrow at all.

Consequently, Eurodollar banks rely quite heavily on asset management. They hold substantial secondary reserves in the form of deposits that they place with other banks through the interbank market. They call on these interbank deposits as necessary in managing their liquidity.

Thrifts. The typical balance sheet of a thrift—long-term mortgages funded with short-term time deposits—is uncomfortable from the point of view of liquidity. Liquidity problems were common under Regulation Q. Because it set a maximum rate that thrifts would pay, a rise in market interest rates would cause a loss of deposits that thrifts had difficulty in accommodating.

The Federal Home Loan Banks were set up to address this problem. They would issue bonds and lend the proceeds to thrifts against mortgage collateral. In this way, loans from the Home Loan Banks would replace the lost deposits on the thrifts' balance sheets.

Two developments have greatly reduced the thrifts' liquidity problems and so the need for assistance from the Home Loan Banks. The first is the abolition of Regulation Q. This put an end to disintermediation: now when interest rates rise, thrifts are able to raise the rates they pay on their deposits.

The second development is mortgage securitization. Increasingly, thrifts originate mortgages and then sell them in the secondary market. As a result, they no longer need to fund them. Hence, no liquidity problem. Thrifts also buy securitized mortgages as investments. Mortgage-backed securities, unlike actual mortgages, are very liquid. If they need cash, thrifts can readily sell their mortgage-backed securities in the secondary market.

Insurance Companies, Pension Funds, and Mutual Funds.

The liabilities of insurance companies, pension funds, and mutual funds are such that, in general, liquidity is not a major concern.

Life insurance companies have liabilities—life insurance and retirement products—that are long term and involve fairly predictable cash outflows. We saw in Chapter 9 that liquidity has sometimes nonetheless been a problem: policy surrenders and an increased demand for policy loans have at various times caused difficulties. The range of products that lifes offer today, more closely linked to market rates, make such problems less likely in the future.

Pension plans, like lifes, have very long-term liabilities with highly predictable cash flows and little need for liquidity. The only demands on liquidity come from plan terminations as a result of participant separations. These are not normally a problem. Pension plans take a long time to "mature." In their early years, they collect contributions but do not yet pay benefits: cash flows in continually, but little flows out. This inflow of cash is usually more than enough to cover any plan terminations. There is little need to hold reserves, let alone to liquidate long-term assets.

For property–liability companies, however, liquidity is a concern. Natural disasters—hurricanes in Florida or earthquakes in California—can mean large and unpredictable outflows of cash. Property–liability companies ensure their ability to meet such outflows by investing mainly in marketable short-term assets—that is, through asset management.

Mutual funds generally invest only in highly marketable securities. To redeem shares, they simply sell the corresponding amount of securities. When shareholders are basically long-term investors and when the market for the securities is liquid, redemptions are not a problem.

Securities Firms.

Securities firms, acting as underwriters or market makers, have traditionally relied on secured borrowing to finance their holdings of securities. This took the form either of call loans from banks or, more recently, of repos. Liquidity was generally not a problem. It was usually easy to expand or contract borrowing as holdings of securities fluctuated.[10]

This picture has changed somewhat as the business done by securities firms has changed. Securities firms are increasingly investing in securities themselves as well as making a market in them. They are also engaging in various forms of lending—for example, bridge loans to LBOs and merchant banking.[11] As a result of these new activities, their balance sheets have ballooned. They now rival in size those of the largest commercial banks. To finance their expanded, and less liquid, portfolios of assets, securities firms have had to go beyond traditional secured borrowing. They have become large issuers of commercial paper and medium-term notes and large borrowers of Eurodollars.

---

[10] Firms with significant retail business also had a source of "free" funding in the form of credit balances owed to their customers. However, with stiffer competition, these balances now pay market rates of interest and many have been converted into expensive (to the broker) cash management accounts.

[11] See Chapter 11.

As a result of these changes, liquidity management at large securities firms, like liquidity management at large banks, relies heavily on liability management. Like banks, securities firms have been worried about this reliance on liability management. They too have been trying to increase the stability of their funding. One way they have done so is by diversifying their sources of borrowing. Where once a security firm would have relied on a line of credit from a single "lead bank," today it relies on lines from many different banks. Of course, this diversification has its cost in terms of the banking relationship: there is no longer the kind of loyalty that can be relied upon in times of trouble.

MANAGING MARKET RISK

Having seen how intermediaries manage liquidity, we now turn to the management of risk. To understand the risks that financial intermediaries faces, it is best to begin with a balance sheet.

book value

The value of an asset or liability calculated according to accounting conventions.

In setting up a balance sheet, accountants use a variety of conventions to place a value on assets and liabilities: such values are called **book values**. For our purposes, however, we need to assess assets and liabilities at their **market value**. For an asset, the market value is the price for which it could be sold now.[12] For a liability, the market value is the price that would have to be paid now to be freed of it.[13] The market value of equity is the residual—what is left over. It is defined by the relation

$$\text{equity} = \text{assets} - \text{liabilities}$$

market value

The market price of an asset or liability.

For example, in the following balance sheet, a bank has assets worth $100 million at market prices and liabilities worth $90 million. Its equity is worth $10 million.

Assets	$100m	Liabilities	$90m
		Equity	$10m

Because equity is a residual, any change in the value of assets or liabilities will change the value of equity. There are two reasons the value of assets or liabilities might change.

The first reason is changes in market prices—mainly interest rates and exchange rates. Such changes may affect the value of assets and liabilities differently, so causing a change in the value of equity. For example, in the foregoing balance sheet, a rise in market interest rates might lower the value of assets to $95 million and lower the value of liabilities to $89 million; this would lower the value of equity to $6 million (we shall see why this might happen presently). The risk of a change in the value of the intermediary due to changes in market prices is called **market risk**.

market risk

The risk of a change in market value as a result of changes in market prices.

---

[12] Since many assets are not readily marketable, calculating their market value can be difficult. What we want is the "fair" value: for an illiquid asset this might be considerably higher than what could be realized from a forced sale. We shall have more to say about this in Chapter 19.

[13] This might be the price that would have to be paid to the creditor to be released from the liability (for example, the market price of a bond or, if it is currently callable, the call price, whichever is lower). It might also be the price that would have to be paid to someone else to assume the liability.

specific risk
The risk of a change in market value as a result of changes specific to the asset or liability.

The second reason the value of assets or liabilities might change lies in factors specific to individual assets or liabilities. We will call the risk of this happening **specific risk**. For most intermediaries, the principal source of specific risk is borrower default. We will call the risk of this happening, **credit risk**.

We begin our study of risk management by looking at how intermediaries manage market risk. We then go on to look at how they manage credit risk and other specific risks.

The Nature of Interest Rate Risk

credit risk
The risk that a borrower will default on a loan.

For most financial intermediaries, the most important type of market risk is *interest rate risk*. To see why, let us look at a simple example.

First National Bank has a portfolio of $100 million in loans—half are for 1 year at 6%; half are for 2 years at 7%. It funds its loan portfolio by borrowing in the Eurodollar market. The maturity at which it borrows determines the nature of the *interest rate* risk that it faces.[14]

Taking a Refinance Position.   Suppose 1-year LIBOR is 4%, and 2-year LIBOR is 5%. Then the least expensive way to fund the loan portfolio is to rely entirely on 1-year deposits:

Loans		Eurodollar deposits	
1-year at 6%	$50m	1-year at 4%	$100m
2-year at 7%	50m		

After a year, the 1-year loans are repaid, and the Eurodollar deposits come due. Repayment of the loans covers $50 million of the Eurodollar deposits. On these loans, First National has made a margin of 2%.

To obtain the funds it needs to pay off the rest of its Eurodollar deposits, First National borrows $50 million in new 1-year Eurodollar deposits. That is, First National must refinance its 2-year loans in their second year. Consequently, this way of funding a portfolio is called taking a **refinance position**.

refinance position
A situation in which the maturity of an asset is longer than the maturity of its funding.

What First National earns overall on its portfolio depends on the interest rate it has to pay when it refinances. If LIBOR is unchanged, it pays 4% on the new Eurodollar deposit, and its margin on the 2-year loan is 3%. If LIBOR falls, its margin is higher; if LIBOR rises, it is lower. If LIBOR rises enough, the bank may take a loss on financing the loans.

Taking a Reinvestment Position.   An alternative way to finance the loan portfolio is with 2-year Eurodollar deposits:

Loans		Eurodollar deposits	
1-year at 6%	$50m	2-year at 5%	$100m
2-year at 7%	50m		

---

[14] We have already seen that the maturity of its borrowing also affects its liquidity.

After a year, the 1-year loans are repaid. Since none of the Eurodollar deposits are due yet, First National can use this money to fund new 1-year loans. That is, First National can reinvest the funds. Therefore, this way of funding a portfolio is called taking a **reinvestment position**.

reinvestment position

A situation in which the maturity of an asset is shorter than the maturity of its funding.

On its 2-year loans, First National earns a sure margin of 2%. What it earns overall on its portfolio depends on the interest rate at which it can reinvest. If interest rates are unchanged, it can make new 1-year loans at 6%, and its margin on the sequence of 1-year loans is 1%. If interest rates fall, and it must lend at less than 6%, its margin is lower. If interest rates fall enough, it may even take a loss. If interest rates rise, its margin is greater than 1%.

Comparing the Two Alternatives.   The relative merits of a refinance position and a reinvestment position depend on the relationship between long-term rates and short-term rates. The difference between short-term rates and long-term rates is called the **term premium**. That is, we can think of the long-term rate as being equal to the short-term rate plus the term premium. When a bank is in a refinance position, because it borrows short term and lends long term, it is earning the term premium. When a bank is in a reinvestment position, because it borrows long term and lends short term, it is paying the term premium.

term premium

The difference between short-term rates and long-term rates.

We know that the normal yield curve has an upward slope. That means that the term premium is normally positive. So a refinance position offers a positive average return. Therefore, we would expect banks generally to be in a refinance position.

While a refinance position gives a higher return on average than a reinvestment position, the returns from both are uncertain. If interest rates should rise, a bank in a refinance position will take a loss, while one in a reinvestment position will make a gain. If interest rates should fall, a bank in a refinance position will make a gain, while one in a reinvestment position will take a loss.

Therefore, if a bank expects interest rates to fall, a refinance position becomes even more attractive. However, if it expects interest rates to rise, a reinvestment position may be the more attractive, even though it yields a lower margin on average.

Avoiding Interest Rate Risk

As a rule, banks will tailor their position depending on their expectations of future interest rates. They will not, however, wish to take too large a gamble. There are a number of ways they can reduce their exposure to interest rate risk.

Matching Maturities.   First National can avoid interest rate risk completely by **matching maturities**. It can fund its portfolio with Eurodollar deposits that match precisely the maturities of its loans:

matching maturities

A situation in which the maturity of an asset equals the maturity of its funding.

Loans		Eurodollar deposits	
1-year at 6%	$50m	1-year at 4%	$50m
2-year at 7%	50m	2-year at 5%	50m

Now, whatever happens to interest rates, First National's margin is unaffected. It will continue to make a sure 2% on all its loans.

Matching Repricing Periods.   If loans and deposits have fixed interest rates, then it is their maturities that we need to look at. However, if they have floating rates, it is the *repricing period* that matters. The **commitment period** is the time until the loan is to be repaid. The **repricing period** is the interval after which the bank is allowed to adjust the interest rate.

commitment period
The time until a loan is repaid.

For example, suppose First National funds its loan portfolio entirely with 1-year deposits. It can eliminate interest rate risk entirely by charging a floating rate rather than a fixed rate on its 2-year loans:

repricing period
The time until the interest rate on a loan may be changed by the lender.

Loans		Eurodollar deposits	
1-year at 6%	$50m	1-year at 4%	$100m
2-year at LIBOR + 2%	50m		

The rate on the 2-year loans is set at 2% above LIBOR, to be repriced after a year.

For the first year, First National makes a margin of 2% on all its loans. At the end of the year, it must borrow new Eurodollar deposits to refinance its 2-year loans. For example, suppose LIBOR has jumped to 10%. With fixed-rate loans, this would have meant a loss. With floating-rate loans, the bank simply passes on the increased cost to its borrowers. It raises the rate on its floating-rate loans to 2% over the cost of its Eurodollar deposits, 12%.

Although the loans still have a maturity of 2 years, in terms of interest rate risk they are equivalent to 1-year loans that are rolled over. It is the repricing period, not the maturity, that determines the interest rate risk.

Hedging Interest Rate Risk

Floating-rate loans eliminate interest rate risk for the bank, but only by passing it on to the borrower. This transfer of risk may not be as much of a bargain for the bank as it first appears.

The floating rate protects the bank from an increase in the market interest rate only to the extent that the borrower is actually able to pay the higher rate. If the borrower is forced to default, all the bank has achieved is a transformation of interest rate risk into credit risk.

Indeed, borrowers generally prefer not to bear the interest rate risk, and they are willing to pay to avoid it. The amount they are willing to pay is the term premium: the premium by which the average long-term rate exceeds the average short-term rate.

By lending at a fixed rate the bank is essentially selling a forward contract in interest rates. It is providing protection against interest rate risk in much the same way that it provides protection against exchange rate risk through the forward sale of foreign exchange.

The way for the bank to cope with the risk, of course, is to hedge. We saw in Chapter 16 that the market for derivatives now offers a wide array of hedging instruments.

What is the advantage to the bank of hedging over simply matching maturities? Bank liabilities are short term: it is easier for a bank to borrow short term and hedge than it is for it to borrow long term.[15] Also, the hedge is easier to adjust to changing circumstances: loans may be prepaid, or the bank may want to be in a position to profit from an expected change in interest rates.

---

[15] European and Japanese universal and investment banks are issuers of long-term liabilities.

Let us see how the various hedging instruments can be used to provide protection against interest rate risk.

Hedging with Futures.   Suppose that First National has a portfolio of $100 million of 2-year, fixed-rate loans funded with 1-year Eurodollar deposits:

Loans		Eurodollar deposits	
2-year at 7%	$100m	1-year at 4%	$100m

The bank is in a refinance position. The loans pay 7% interest at the end of the first year, and the bank pays 4% interest on its deposits. This gives it a certain return at the end of the first year of

$$\$100m \times (0.07 - 0.04) = \$3m$$

At the same time, the bank must take in $100 million of new Eurodollar deposits to repay the $100 million in deposits that mature. The rate it will pay on the new deposits and its return on the second year of the loan depend on LIBOR at that time.

Let us consider three possible scenarios for the interest rate in the second year

Scenario 1. LIBOR remains the same. The bank must pay the same rate on the new Eurodollar deposits as on the old (4%). At the end of the second year, the bank's return is again

$$\$100m \times (0.07 - 0.04) = \$3m$$

Scenario 2. LIBOR rises to 12%. The bank must pay 12% on the new deposits. At the end of the second year, the bank's return is

$$\$100m \times (0.07 - 0.12) = -\$5m$$

That is, the bank loses $5 million on the loan in the second year.

Scenario 3. LIBOR falls to 2%. At the end of the second year, the bank's return is

$$\$100m \times (0.07 - 0.02) = \$5m$$

From these three scenarios, it should be clear that a one-percentage-point rise in LIBOR means a reduction in return to First National of $1 million.

Suppose now that First National decides to hedge the interest rate risk by taking a position in Eurodollar futures. The Eurodollar futures contract in question is a wager on the Eurodollar rate at the end of year one.[16] The notional amount of a single contract is $1 million. The price of each contract is

$$\frac{100 - \text{Eurodollar futures rate}}{100}$$

[16] In reality, Eurodollar futures are based on the 3-month Eurodollar rate rather than the 1-year rate, and they have a maturity of 3 months rather than 1 year. We are using a year rather than 3 months to simplify the arithmetic.

If the current Eurodollar futures rate is 6%, then the contract price is 0.94. What position should First National take (buy or sell), and how many contracts should it enter into? Let us see the payoff from buying a single contract in each of the three scenarios.

Scenario 1. LIBOR remains the same. Since 1-year LIBOR is 4%, the payoff to a purchaser of one contract is

$$(\text{actual price} - \text{futures price}) \times \text{notional amount}$$

$$= \left(\frac{100 - \text{LIBOR}}{100} - \frac{100 - \text{Eurodollar futures rate}}{100} \right) \times \$1\text{m}$$

$$= (0.96 - 0.94) \times \$1\text{m} = \$20,000$$

Scenario 2. LIBOR rises to 12%. In this case, the payoff is

$$(0.88 - 0.94) \times \$1\text{m} = -\$60,000$$

Scenario 3. LIBOR falls to 2%. In this case, the payoff is

$$(0.98 - 0.94) \times \$1\text{m} = \$40,000$$

In general, then, if First National takes a long position in a single contract, it will lose $10,000 for every percentage point that LIBOR turns out to be above the current Eurodollar futures rate of 6%.

First National takes a loss on its underlying loan financing position if LIBOR rises. So, if it wishes to hedge this risk, it needs to take a position in futures that will provide a *gain* if the interest rate rises. That means that it should *sell* futures: that is, it should take a short position in futures. Selling a single contract will provide it with a gain of $10,000 for each percentage point rise in LIBOR. Since it needs to offset a $1 million loss on its underlying position, it should sell 100 contracts.

Exhibit 18.9 summarizes the effect of the hedge. Notice that the gain or loss on the futures position is incurred at the end of the *first* year. It therefore has to be carried forward as a future value to the end of the second year to be added to the loss or gain on the underlying loan financing position which is incurred then (the future value is calculated at LIBOR). As a result of the hedge, First National's net return is less variable and therefore less risky than it otherwise would have been. The hedge is not perfect, however, because

EXHIBIT 18.9   Net Return from a Balance Sheet Hedged with Futures

Scenario	LIBOR at End of Year 1 (%)	Return from Unhedged Underlying Position at End of Year 2	Net Return on Hedged Position at End of Year 2
1	4	$3m	$3m − (1.04) × $2m = $0.92m
2	12	−$5m	−$5m + (1.12) × $6m = $1.72m
3	2	$5m	$5m − (1.02) × $4m = $0.92m

the timing of the gain or loss on the futures position does not match the timing of the gain or loss on the underlying position.

Problems with Hedging with Futures. Large banks, because of their extensive trading and market making, face substantial market risk. They are therefore major users of hedging instruments. Small commercial banks are less exposed to market risk. They also lack trained personnel with the necessary expertise to make proper use of hedging instruments. Consequently their use of hedging instruments remains minimal.

Hedging with futures is subject to some regulatory problems. In some countries banks are simply not allowed to trade in futures: these instruments are considered too "speculative." Even in the United States, bank regulators remain suspicious of their use, not least because they find them difficult to understand.

The regulatory problems are reinforced by inconsistencies in accounting rules. Generally, gains and losses on futures must be recognized immediately. At the same time, gains and losses on balance sheet assets and liabilities are not recognized until they are realized (when the asset matures or is sold). For example, if a bank hedges a refinance position with futures, and interest rates fall, the loss on the futures position is recognized while the gain on the balance sheet is not. Consequently, it looks as though the bank has taken a loss. In reality, of course, there is no loss: the whole idea of hedging is that losses on one position and gains on the other will automatically offset each other. However, regulators and boards of directors often react to accounting gains and losses rather than to the true situation.

In 2001 the Financial Accounting Standards Board (FASB), the body that sets accounting standards in the United States, adopted new rules for accounting for derivatives. These rules require companies to report on their balance sheets the fair market value of their derivative positions and to report on their earnings statements changes in value that do not exactly cancel out losses or gains on the underlying position.[17] The new rules are a result of almost a decade of negotiations between the FASB and companies, but they remain highly controversial.

Hedging with Options. Instead of hedging with futures, First National could hedge its position by buying put options on Eurodollar futures. As we saw in Chapter 16, options protect against a loss *without* ruling out a gain.

First National buys 100 put options on Eurodollar futures with an expiration date at the end of year 1 and an exercise price of 0.94 (equivalent to a Eurodollar rate of 6%). If it chooses to exercise these options, the payoff will be the same as if it had sold 100 futures contracts at a futures price of 0.94. As we saw in Chapter 16, the purchaser of an option must pay a premium. The premium in this case is $13,000 per contract for a total of $1,300,000.

Exhibit 18.10 shows how hedging with options would pay off under our three interest rate scenarios:

Scenario 1. LIBOR remains the same. At the end of year 1 the options are not "in the money," so First National does not exercise them. Its return is just the return from its

---

[17] The European Union plans to adopt similar rules.

EXHIBIT 18.10   Net Return from a Balance Sheet Hedged with Options

Scenario	LIBOR at End of Year 1 (%)	Exercise Options?	Gain from Options at End of Year 1	Cost of Options Start of Year 1	Net Return on Hedged Position at End of Year 2
1	4	No	0	$1.3m	$3m − $1.3m × (1.05)² = $1.57m
2	12	Yes	$6m	$1.3m	−$5m − $1.3m × (1.05)² + $6m × (1.12) = $0.29m
3	2	No	0	$1.3m	$5m − $1.3m × (1.05)² = $3.57m

underlying position (see Exhibit 18.9) less the future value of the options premiums brought forward to the end of the second year[18]:

$$3m - \$1.3m \times (1.05)^2 = \$1.57m$$

Scenario 2. LIBOR rises to 12%. At the end of year 1, the options *are* in the money, so First National does exercises them. Its return from exercising the puts is what it would have made from selling futures at 0.94 (see Exhibit 18.9)—$6 million. Its net return is the return from its underlying position less the cost of the options plus the gains from exercising the options:

$$-\$5m - \$1.3m \times (1.05)^2 + \$6m \times (1.12) = \$0.29m$$

Scenario 3. LIBOR falls to 2%. Once again, the options are out of the money, and First National does not exercise them. Its return is

$$\$5m - \$1.3m \times (1.05)^2 = \$3.57m$$

How does hedging with options compare with hedging with futures? You can see by comparing Exhibits 18.9 and 18.10 that the bank does worse with options when interest rates rise. It is still protected by the hedge, but the hedge is more expensive. On the other hand, the bank does better when interest rates fall. While the futures hedge eliminates the gain, the options hedge leaves it intact—less the cost of the options, of course.

Hedging with Swaps.   A third way for First National to hedge its balances sheet is to use a swap. First National could become a fixed-rate payer on a 2-year swap with a notional principal of $100 million.

Suppose the swap rate is 5%, and that 1-year LIBOR at the beginning of the first year is 4%. Then, at the end of year 1, First National pays

$$(0.05 - 0.04) \times \$100m = \$1m$$

---

[18] The appropriate rate is the 2-year rate at the time the puts are purchased, which we have assumed to be 5%. The bank could have financed payment of the premiums by borrowed for 2 years. The rate on 2-year deposits is 5%.

At the end of year 2, First National pays or receives a payment that depends on LIBOR at the *beginning* of year 2. Let us see what that means under our three scenarios (the results are summarized in Exhibit 18.11).

Scenario 1. LIBOR remains the same. At the end of year 1, First National must pay $1 million. At the end of year 2, since LIBOR did not change, it once again pays $1 million. Its net return is

$$\$3m - \$1m - \$1m \times (1.04) = \$0.96m$$

Scenario 2. LIBOR rises to 12%. At the end of year 1, First National pays $1 million. At the end of year 2, it receives

$$(0.12 - 0.05) \times \$100m = \$7m$$

Its net return is

$$-\$5m + \$7m - \$1m \times (1.12) = \$0.88m$$

Scenario 3. LIBOR falls to 2%. At the end of year 1, First National pays $1 million. At the end of year 2, it pays

$$(0.05 - 0.02) \times \$100m = \$3m$$

Its net return is

$$\$5m - \$3m - \$1m \times (1.02) = \$0.98m$$

Measuring Overall Exposure

In our example, First National's balance sheet is very simple, and it is easy to see the extent of its exposure to interest rate risk. A real bank has a far more complex balance sheet (as well as off-balance-sheet commitments). To manage its interest rate risk, it needs to know its exposure, not just on a particular loan–funding combination, but for its position as a whole.

EXHIBIT 18.11   Net Return from a Balance Sheet Hedged with Swaps

Scenario	LIBOR at End of Year 1 (%)	Swap Return at End of Year 1	Swap Return at End of Year 2	Net Return on Hedged Position at End of Year 2
1	4	−$1m	−$1m	$3m − $1m − $1m × (1.04) = $0.96m
2	12	−$1m	$7m	−$5m + $7m − $1m × (1.12) = $0.88m
3	2	−$1m	−$3m	$5m − $3m − $1m × (1.02) = $0.98m

duration gap
Measure of the
sensitivity of the
value of a bank's
balance sheet to
changes in market
interest rates.

Defining the Duration Gap.   To gauge their overall exposure to interest rate risk, banks use an index called the **duration gap**. In Chapter 4 we saw that the sensitivity of the value of a security to a change in the interest rate could be described in terms of its duration. The duration is a weighted average of the maturity of the elements of a security's cash flow. We can apply the same principle to the bank's entire balance sheet.

We can think of the bank's portfolio of assets as being a claim to a stream of payments due at different times in the future. For example, $500 million might be due in 1 month, $2 billion in 3 months, $5 billion in 6 months, and so on. Similarly, we can think of the bank's liabilities as being a stream of payments that the bank is due to pay. We can calculate the duration of these two streams of payments. Let us call them d_A and d_L respectively.

If the market interest rate changes by Δi, then, using Equation 4.19 from Chapter 4, the percentage change in the value of the bank's assets is

$$\frac{\Delta_A}{A} = -d_A \frac{\Delta_i}{(1 + i)} \qquad [18.1]$$

the percentage change in the value of the its liabilities is

$$\frac{\Delta_L}{L} = -d_L \frac{\Delta_i}{(1 + i)} \qquad [18.2]$$

We can use these equations to find out how much the market value of the bank's equity will change as a result of a change in the market interest rate. The change in the market value of the bank's equity, ΔE, is the just the change in the market value of its assets, ΔA, less the change in the market value of its liabilities, ΔL:

$$\Delta E = \Delta A - \Delta L \qquad [18.3]$$

In Equation 18.3, divide and then multiply ΔA by A and ΔL by L:

$$\Delta E = \frac{\Delta_A}{A} A - \frac{\Delta_L}{L} L \qquad [18.4]$$

Next, use Equations 18.1 and 18.2 to substitute for $\Delta A/A$ and $\Delta L/L$:

$$\Delta E = \left(-d_A \frac{\Delta_i}{(1 + i)}\right) A - \left(-d_L \frac{\Delta_i}{(1 + i)}\right) L \qquad [18.5]$$

or

$$\Delta E = -(d_A A - d_L L) \frac{\Delta i}{(1 + i)} \qquad [18.6]$$

or

$$\Delta E = -D_{gap} \times A \times \frac{\Delta_i}{(1 + i)} \qquad [18.7]$$

where

$$D_{gap} = d_A - d_L \frac{L}{A}$$

If we know a bank's duration gap, we can use Equation 18.7 to calculate how much it will gain or lose from a change in market interest rates. Exhibit 18.12 shows how a rise in interest rates from 5% to 6% would affect different banks with different duration gaps.

You can see from Equation 18.7 and from Exhibit 18.12 that a positive duration gap means that the market value of the bank's equity will *fall* when interest rates rise. This corresponds to a refinance position for the bank's balance sheet as a whole. A negative duration gap means that the market value of its equity will *rise* when interest rates rise. This corresponds to a reinvestment position for the balance sheet as a whole. If the gap is zero, the market value of equity will be *unaffected* by changes in interest rate. This corresponds to a maturities-matched position for the balance sheet as a whole.

Using the Duration Gap.   Calculating the duration gap in practice is no easy task. The timing of cash flows from different assets and liabilities is not always clear. Loans may be prepaid; deposits may be withdrawn. So, at best, the duration gap is an educated guess. An alternative method, not necessarily more reliable, is computer simulation. A computer program is used to assess the effect on the bank's position under a variety of interest rate scenarios and under a variety of assumptions.

In calculating its duration gap, or using any other method, a bank needs to take into consideration all of its operations. For example, Chase will take into account all of its dollar assets and liabilities—those of its securities dealer subsidiary and of its Eurodollar branches and subsidiaries overseas, as well as those of its domestic commercial banking operations. It would be a mistake to calculate the duration gap for any single part of the company, since a positive gap there might be offset by a negative gap somewhere else. It is the overall gap that matters.

Using duration gap, a bank can hedge its overall exposure to interest rate risk rather then hedging specific loan–funding combinations individually. For example, suppose a bank with $10 billion in assets has a duration gap of 2. That means that a 1% rise in interest rates will cause it a loss of roughly $200 million. To hedge this risk in futures, it needs to sell enough contracts so that a 1% rise in interest rates will give it a gain on the futures of $200 million. Hedging overall exposure in this way minimizes the need to trade in hedging instruments and so minimizes cost.

Value at Risk.   Duration is really only of much use in measuring sensitivity to relatively small fluctuations in interest rates. It can be quite misleading with respect to larger

EXHIBIT 18.12   The Effect of a Rise in Interest Rates on Different Banks

Bank	Assets	D_{gap}	Change in Value of the Bank
A	$100 million	2	$-2 \times \$100m \times \dfrac{0.01}{1.05} = -\$1.9m$
B	$20 billion	0.5	$-0.5 \times \$20b \times \dfrac{0.01}{1.05} = -\$95.2m$
C	$70 billion	-0.5	$-(-0.5) \times \$70b \times \dfrac{0.01}{1.05} = \$333.3m$

value at risk (VAR) analysis
A computer model that uses data on past prices to predict the extent of possible losses from a position.

fluctuations. Since larger fluctuations do occur, financial institutions have tried to develop methods to assess their vulnerability to them. These methods are known collectively as **value at risk (VAR) analysis**. A VAR model uses historical data on interest rates and some combination of statistical estimation and simulation to make probability statements about possible losses. For example, for a given position, "The chance of interest rate movements over the next week causing a loss greater than $5 million is less than 1 percent." The best-known VAR model is RiskMetrics, developed by J. P. Morgan and made available free of charge on the Internet.[19]

Of course, VAR has its limitations too. Because it depends on historical data, it works best for instruments for which such data is abundant. It is not much help with new instruments and those traded infrequently, nor is it very useful in predicting the likelihood of rare but potentially damaging events. For this reason, it is only of limited use in assessing an institution's overall vulnerability to interest rate risk. In addition, VAR models have to make assumptions about the statistical behavior of interest rates. Since these assumptions are often questionable, VAR models do not work very well for horizons longer than a week or two.

Exchange Rate Risk

Much of what we have said about interest rate risk applies equally to exchange rate risk. Changes in exchange rate can affect the market value of a bank's assets and liabilities differentially, causing a change in the market value of its equity.

Consider the example illustrated in Exhibit 18.13. First National has yen-denominated loans outstanding for a total amount of ¥37.5 billion. It has yen deposits of ¥25 billion. (Of course, it also has assets and liabilities denominated in dollars and in other currencies.)

The value of the yen falls from 0.80¢/¥ to 0.77¢/¥ (125 ¥/$ to 130 ¥/$). As you can see, in dollar terms, the assets fall in value from $300 million to $289 million—a loss to the bank of $11 million. At the same time, the deposits fall in value in dollar terms from $200 million to $193 million—a gain to the bank of $7 million. The loss exceeds the gain by $4 million, and that is the fall in the value of the bank's equity as a result of the change in the exchange rate. Had First National had more liabilities than assets denominated in yen, it would have gained from a fall in value of the yen.

Borrowing and lending denominated in a foreign currency is not the only source of exchange rate risk. Another major source is a bank's foreign exchange trading. If the bank

EXHIBIT 18.13   An Example of Exchange Rate Risk

Exchange Rate	Yen Assets	Value of Yen Assets in Dollars	Yen Deposits	Value of Yen Deposits in Dollars
0.80¢/¥	¥37.5b	¥37.5b × 0.0080 = $300m	¥25b	¥25b × 0.0080 = $200m
0.77¢/¥	¥37.5b	¥37.5b × 0.0077 = $289m	¥25b	¥25b × 0.0077 = $193m

---

[19] http://www.riskmetrics.com/ RiskMetrics was spun off as an independent company in 1998.

has more yen assets than liabilities, it will lose from a depreciation of the yen. Similarly, if the bank has bought forward more yen than it has sold, it will take a loss.

Avoiding Exchange Rate Risk. The ways to avoid exchange rate risk parallel exactly the ways to avoid interest rate risk. The equivalent to matching maturities is called **running a matched book**. This requires the bank to keep the value of its assets and forward purchases in a given nondollar currency equal to the value of its liabilities and forward sales in that currency. If it runs a matched book, changes in exchange rates have no effect on the value of the bank's equity.

running a matched book
The practice of matching the amounts of assets and liabilities in a given currency.

As is the case with interest rate risk, banks can avoid exchange rate risk by passing it on to their customers. That means doing business exclusively in dollars. Customers who wish to make deposits or accept loans in foreign currency are generally foreigners. The reason they want to transact in their own currency rather than in dollars is precisely to avoid exchange rate risk. If, for example, they borrow from the bank in dollars and the dollar rises in value, they will have to repay more in terms of their own currency. As was the case with interest rate risk, passing the exchange rate risk on to borrowers may not be a very good solution. Exchange rate risk is merely converted into credit risk.

Hedging Exchange Rate Risk. Banks can use a variety of hedging instruments to hedge exchange rate risk—forward trading, futures, options, and swaps. These instruments are used in essentially the same way to hedge exchange rate risk as they are to hedge interest rate risk.

Currency swaps are particularly useful to banks because they enable banks to make loans and take deposits in whatever currency their customers want, without having to worry about exchange rate risk. For example, if IC goes to First National Bank for a Euromark loan, First National will fund it by borrowing interbank Eurodollars and swapping them into marks. Or if a Japanese company wants to make a Euroyen deposit, First National will immediately swap the yen into dollars and lend the dollars on the Eurodollar interbank market. In fact, many banks keep their balance sheets entirely in dollars, automatically swapping into dollars all foreign currency deposits and loans.

How Much Market Risk?

We have treated market risk as though it were strictly something to be avoided. This is not the case. Fluctuations in interest rates and in exchange rates present opportunities for gain as well as for loss.

If a bank expects interest rates to fall, then increasing its duration gap will increase the potential gain. If the bank expects interest rates to rise, then a negative duration gap is indicated. The same can be said for changes in exchange rate. If the dollar is expected to appreciate, the bank should be short foreign currencies (more foreign currency liabilities than assets); if the dollar is expected to depreciate, the bank should be long foreign currencies.

There is, of course, the usual trade-off between risk and return. By playing it safe—by avoiding or hedging market risk—a bank can earn a secure but modest return. To do better, it must bear some risk. Presumably, large banks enjoy the benefits of good market information, so they are relatively well placed to make trading profits. Indeed, successful plays on movements of interest rates or exchange rates are among the few ways a bank can make extraordinary profits. The real question, then, is not whether to bear market risk, but *how much* to bear.

Of course, too much risk is always a possibility. There are some famous examples of banks that gambled and lost:

- In 1973, Franklin National faced large losses on its loan portfolio. In an attempt to recoup, it bet on a continued fall in interest rates and a continued rise in the dollar. It borrowed short term, lent long term, and took a short position in foreign currencies. However, in 1974 interest rates rose steeply and the dollar plummeted 10%. Franklin collapsed.
- Foreign exchange speculation played a major role in the Herstatt failure that shook the Eurodollar market in 1973.
- The rise in interest rates in 1979 sank First Pennsylvania, which had been funding a large bond portfolio with short-term money; the bailout cost the FDIC $1.5 billion.

Notice that these failures occurred quite a long time ago, when the volatility of interest rates and exchange rates was a relatively new phenomenon. Partly as a result of these failures, banks have learned to be more cautious.

Market Risk and Nonbank Intermediaries

Other financial intermediaries employ much the same methods as banks in dealing with market risk.

Thrifts.   We have seen in previous chapters that thrifts used to be dangerously exposed to interest rate risk. Long-term, fixed-rate mortgages and short-term deposits left them with a horrifying duration gap. When interest rates rose in the late 1970s, their losses were staggering.

Since then, thrifts have done much to reduce their exposure. Mostly, they avoid interest rate risk rather than hedging it. Today, thrifts rarely carry fixed-rate mortgages on their balance sheets. They sell the fixed-rate mortgages they write in the secondary market. The mortgages they do carry on their balance sheet are usually ARMs, with a floating interest rate.

Thrifts were first allowed to hedge in futures in 1981. To hedge their positive duration gap, many thrifts took a short position in futures. When interest rates fell in the early 1980s, they of course took large losses on their futures position. These losses were balanced by corresponding gains on their balance sheets. However, the latter were not recognized on their books, and the thrifts wound up looking bad.[20] As a result of this unhappy experience, thrifts largely abandoned the use of futures.

Swaps would seem to be far better suited. By becoming a fixed-rate payer on a swap, a thrift can convert its receipts from fixed-rate mortgages into floating-rate payments that

---

[20] Franklin Savings and Loan, a large and highly successful institution and a sophisticated user of hedging instruments, found the book value of its equity severely reduced. Regulators simply did not understand what Franklin was doing and, in an excess of zeal, closed it down.

match the rates it pays on its deposits. The snag, however, is prepayment risk. If interest rates fall, mortgages will be prepaid. The thrift will then be left high and dry with the swap, paying high fixed payments in exchange for low floating payments.

The best way to hedge against prepayment risk is with options. By allowing the borrower to prepay, the lender implicitly writes an option. This implicit option becomes valuable if interest rates fall. The best way to hedge is to buy actual options on financial futures. Then, if interest rates fall, the value of the actual options will rise and will offset the loss due to prepayment. The OTC market offers special options tailored to the needs of mortgage lenders.

Since 1987 regulators have provided thrifts with an incentive to reduce or to hedge their interest rate risk. When calculating a thrift's required capital, regulators now take interest rate risk into account. If the duration gap is smaller or if it is hedged, the thrift faces a lower capital requirement.

Insurance Companies. Historically, the liabilities of life insurance companies were largely long-term, fixed-rate whole life policies. Lifes could, and did, avoid interest rate risk by investing in long-term, fixed-rate assets.[21]

Interest rate risk became more of a problem when whole life policies were replaced by variable life and by GICs (see Chapter 9). These products have a much shorter repricing period, and lifes have correspondingly been investing in floating-rate assets, such as commercial mortgages.

The GIC is a fairly complicated product including a number of implicit options that expose the issuer to considerable interest rate risk. For such a product to be profitable, it is essential that it be properly priced: the price must reflect the value of the implicit options. However, lifes generally underpriced their GICs. When interest rates rose in the early 1980s, lifes did well. But when interest rates fell, they took substantial losses. For example, Equitable Life, with $15 billion in GICs outstanding, lost about $2 billion after 1983.

Pension Funds. Pension funds have well-defined long-term liabilities. To avoid interest rate risk, they need to hold long-term assets with no reinvestment risk. As pension funds have grown, the increasing demand for such assets has brought forth a variety of innovations to satisfy it—zero-coupon bonds, Treasury strips, GICs, and CMOs.

Another innovation that has responded to a particular need of pension plans is **dynamic hedging** or **portfolio insurance**. The sponsor of a pension plan is liable for any shortfall if investments fail to cover liabilities but receives only a part of the surplus if investments more than cover liabilities. As a result, sponsors try to earn a higher return, but they want to be sure that funding does not drop below 100%. Investment in stocks provides them with the higher return; portfolio insurance provides them with the necessary hedge.

dynamic hedging (portfolio insurance)
Hedging a stock portfolio by continuous adjustment of a position in index futures.

---

[21] Even this was not so simple. One problem, to which zero-coupon bonds provided a solution, was reinvestment risk. Another problem was that lifes promised a fixed rate, not only on existing reserves, but also on premiums yet to be paid. A way to avoid the consequent risk is to borrow with a maturity matched to projected premiums and invest in zeros matched to expected payouts. The risk then is that policies will be surrendered, as would happen if market interest rates were to rise. These problems go some way to explaining the low promised rates on whole life policies. The purchaser is paying for a variety of implicit options written by the life insurance company.

The direct way to hedge a stock portfolio against a fall in value is to buy put options. For example, suppose a pension fund holds a stock portfolio with the same composition as the S&P 500. If the index is at 1,000, the value of the portfolio is such that the plan is fully funded. If the fund buys puts on the S&P 500 with an exercise price of 1,000, it is guaranteed that the plan will never be underfunded. If the index falls, its options will rise in value to compensate for the fall in the value of its stocks. However, if the index rises, the fund can tear up the options and keep the gain. The problem, of course, is cost: as we have seen, options are expensive. Portfolio insurance promises the same protection as options, but at lower cost.

The idea of portfolio insurance is simple. If the fund sells index futures equal in value to its stock portfolio, it is as if it had sold the stock forward at the futures price. It cannot lose from a fall in the index or gain from a rise. If it sells futures covering only a fraction of the value of its portfolio, it is partially protected. Portfolio insurance requires the fund to increase the fraction of the portfolio covered if the index falls and to decrease it if the index rises. If this is done just right, it precisely replicates the effect of buying put options on the whole portfolio. However, as we shall see in Chapter 20, portfolio insurance is not without its problems.

Mutual Funds.   Mutual funds are not subject to market risk. A mutual fund's liabilities are equity shares in the value of its assets. Its assets and its liabilities are therefore perfectly matched. Since the fund's managers have no residual claim on its assets, they are not at risk.

Conceivably, a mutual fund might wish to hedge its assets against market risk as a service to its shareholders. The problem is that different shareholders will have different attitudes to risk and will want different degrees of protection. It makes more sense, therefore, for shareholders concerned about market risk to do their own hedging.

Securities Firms.   Securities dealers and underwriters are very much exposed to interest rate risk. Their funding is usually short term, often overnight. The securities they hold are of longer maturity.

Consequently, securities firms have been major users of hedging instruments. Since their positions in securities are constantly fluctuating, the liquidity of the hedge is particularly important. They are, therefore, big users of exchange-traded derivatives, particularly futures.

Like banks, securities firms see their exposure to interest rate risk as an opportunity as well as a danger. Like banks, securities firms should have good market information and will wish to trade on it. Falling profits in their traditional lines of business in the 1980s (retail brokerage and underwriting), spurred them to take greater risks in their trading positions. As interest rates fell from 1984 to 1986, they did well. When interest rates rose sharply in 1987, they took substantial losses. The virtues of hedging were reestablished.

MANAGING CREDIT RISK AND OTHER SPECIFIC RISKS

While market risk provides opportunities for profit as well as loss, credit risk can result only in loss. Indeed, the most common reason by far for the failure of financial intermediaries is loan losses. Of course, the assessment and bearing of credit risk is an important part of what financial intermediaries do. So there is no question of avoiding it entirely. The key is to manage it carefully and to keep it under control.

A financial intermediary has four lines of defense against credit risk. The first line of defense is care. Careful assessment of the risks and realistic pricing are essential. The second is diversification: don't put all your eggs in one basket. The third is hedging: pass off some of the risk to others. The final line of defense is capital. If losses do occur, adequate capital protects the intermediary from insolvency.

In addition to credit risk, intermediaries face other types of specific risk. Insurance companies face uncertain claims: an increase in the value of their liabilities is as much a danger to them as a decrease in the value of their assets. Securities firms face trading risks. Intermediaries in the OTC market for derivatives face replacement risk. Intermediaries protect themselves against other types of specific risk in much the same way they do against credit risk—care, diversification, hedging, and capital.

Care in Lending and Realistic Pricing

Borrowers generally intend to repay their loans. Fraud does occur, but it is relatively unusual. So most defaults are the result of an *inability* to repay. A realistic assessment of the borrower's ability to repay is, therefore, the essence of care in lending.

Commercial Lending.   With commercial lending, as we saw in Chapter 14, such an assessment involves analysis of the firm's business situation, of its financial situation, and of its credit record. Some information is available from external sources such as Dun & Bradstreet, which publishes reports on the financial history and current credit status of many businesses. However, the prospects for the firm's future are more important than the record of its past. A lender's continuing relationship with a firm may provide it with superior information on the firm's prospects and so reduce the risks of lending to it.

Large banks generally use an internal credit rating system—much like the systems used by public credit rating agencies—to rate the loans they make.[22] This helps them manage their exposure to credit risk on their tens of thousands of commercial loans.

Consumer Lending.   With consumer loans, less information is readily available. Lenders rely to some extent on consumer credit bureaus that collect and make available credit and employment information on individuals. They also often rely on credit scoring to evaluate a loan application. The applicant receives points for current income, years in current job, net worth, demographics (for example, married people are better credit risks than singles), and so on. If the total score is high enough, the loan is approved. This procedure may seem mechanical, but the sums involved are usually small (from the bank's point of view), and a more "personalized" treatment would be too costly.[23]

Lending to Other Intermediaries.   Lending to other financial intermediaries is also a source of credit risk. Because of the peculiar structure of U.S. banking, small banks

---

[22] On rating agencies, see Chapter 14.

[23] As we saw in Chapter 6, the same credit scoring has recently begun to be used for small business loans.

and thrifts lend large amounts to regional and money-center banks.[24] There is also an enormous amounts of interbank lending in the Eurocurrency market.

Lending among intermediaries takes the form of Fed funds sold, correspondent deposits, Eurodollar deposits, and the purchase of wholesale deposits. Fed funds sold and Eurodollars are not covered by deposit insurance. Domestic deposits are covered only up to $100,000.

As a result of these interbank loans, the failure of a large bank can bring down dozens of other institutions. Some spectacular failures in the 1980s made the risks very obvious and led banks to become much more careful in their dealings with one another.

sovereign risk
The risk of loss from the default of a sovereign borrower due to an inability to collect through the courts.

Lending to Governments.   Lending to national governments involves a special type of risk—**sovereign risk**. Since the "sovereign" cannot be sued in his own courts, a lender has little recourse if a sovereign borrower defaults. Default on sovereign loans has often been a source of serious problems for banks ever since the fourteenth century, when sovereign default sank the great Florentine banks, the leading international lenders of the day. In the 1980s, as we shall see later in the chapter, it came close to sinking such banks as Chase and BankAmerica.

Reducing Risk with Collateral and Guarantees.   As we saw in Chapter 14, the potential loss from default can be reduced by demanding collateral—some specific item of value that becomes the property of the lender in case of default. Most consumer lending is collateralized—specifically, home mortgages, automobile loans, and installment credit. Most lending by banks to securities firms is collateralized.

Sometimes, though, the security provided by collateral is illusory. Periodically, banks and insurance companies take major losses on loans to developers of commercial real estate, even though such loans are collateralized. The problem is that the value of the collateral falls in precisely those circumstances in which the borrower is likely to default—in a real estate slump.

We saw in Chapter 14 that credit risk can be reduced, too, by guarantees. Governments often provide guarantees for foreign borrowing by domestic companies. The U.S. government provides a wide range of guarantees—for mortgage loans, for student loans, for foreign trade, for farm loans, for loans to small business, and so on. There are also private guarantees. Parent firms often guarantee the borrowing of their subsidiaries. Private insurers guarantee the borrowing of municipalities.[25]

The Importance of Pricing and Its Limitations.   It has been said that there is no such thing as a bad risk, only bad pricing. The implication is that lenders who charge the appropriate rates on the loans they make should be compensated fairly for the risks they take. If the rate can be set at the appropriate level, then there is no such thing as a "bad risk."

---

[24] See Chapter 7 for a discussion of the correspondent relationship.

[25] In the oldest form of bank lending—the discounting of commercial bills—the payee guaranteed the loan in case the payer defaulted: see Chapter 6.

What is the appropriate level? The expected return on a loan is given by the following equation:

$$\begin{matrix}\text{expected}\\\text{return}\end{matrix} = \begin{matrix}\text{contractual}\\\text{rate}\end{matrix} \times \begin{matrix}\text{probability}\\\text{of repayment}\end{matrix} - (1 - \text{recovery rate}) \times \begin{matrix}\text{probability}\\\text{of default}\end{matrix} \qquad [18.8]$$

risk premium
The difference between the expected return on a risky loan and the rate on comparable government securities.

Clearly, the expected return on a risky loan should be higher than that on a risk-free loan. The difference is called the **risk premium**. We can therefore break down the expected return on a risky loan as follows:

$$\text{expected return} = \text{risk-free rate} + \text{risk premium} \qquad [18.9]$$

To price a loan properly, the lender should assess the probability of repayment, the probable recovery rate in case of default (which depends on collateral and guarantees), and the appropriate risk premium. The lender should then use Equations 18.8 and 18.9 to solve for the appropriate contractual rate.

Unfortunately, there are some serious obstacles. As we saw in Chapter 5, the main obstacle is *adverse selection*. Lenders have imperfect information about the risks of a loan. Even if they get it right on average, they will sometimes set the contractual rate too high and sometimes too low. Borrowers always have better information about the risks of a loan than do lenders. Consequently, when a lender sets the rate too high, the borrower will refuse the loan; when the lender sets the rate too low, the borrower will be happy to take it. As a result of adverse selection, realized returns on loans will be lower than expected. Raising contractual rates further does not help, because it merely leads to more adverse selection.

What this means is that proper pricing is important, but it is not by itself enough. Lenders must also monitor borrowers to control the risks. And they must refuse loans when the risks are hard to assess or the borrower is difficult to monitor.

usury ceilings
Legal limits on the rates a lender can charge.

A second obstacle to proper pricing, especially when market interest rates are high, is **usury ceilings**. These are legal limits on the rates a lender can charge. When market interest rates rise significantly, as they did in the early 1980s, usury ceilings can become a problem. Usury ceilings prevent banks from lending to their most risky borrowers. For example, banks may be forced by them to restrict their credit card lending.

Diversification

Care in lending is essential, but there will always be mistakes. The best defense is diversification. If individual loans are small relative to the size of a lender's capital, the danger of insolvency will be small.

Lenders will therefore limit their exposure to individual borrowers. For example, banks will set lines for their exposure to other banks to which they extend credit and will monitor their exposure to make sure those lines are not exceeded.

Limits on lending to individual borrowers are not enough to ensure adequate diversification. Default risks may be correlated across classes of borrowers. For example, difficulties in an industry are likely to affect all firms in that industry. Consequently, cautious lenders will set limits not only on individual loans but also on classes of loan—by industry, by country, and so on.

Diversification vs Specialization.   The need for diversification can come into conflict with the desire for specialization. To make efficient use of information, lenders often specialize in particular industries or in particular geographic areas. Specialized information lowers the cost of lending for a given degree of risk. But specialization undermines diversification.

One solution to this problem is size. A really large lender can capture the informational efficiencies of making many loans to the same class of borrower without the total amount of such lending becoming a dangerously large proportion of its total lending.

Regulation of Diversification.   Regulators often attempt to enforce diversification by setting limits on the size of individual loans and on the proportion of assets in particular classes. For example, a U.S. bank may not lend to any single borrower an amount greater than 15% of its equity (25% if the loan is collateralized). Since bank equity is usually no more than 8% of total assets, this restriction implies that no single borrower can account for more than 1.2% of a bank's loan portfolio. Even a large bank like Chase, with $5 billion in equity, is limited to lending no more than $0.15 \times \$5$ billion $= \$750$ million to any one borrower.

This regulatory maximum can be a problem. In some cases, borrowers require substantially more than even the largest U.S. bank can lend. For example, an LBO might require 10 times Chase's limit.

Canadian regulators impose no limit on the size of loan a bank can make. So, for many years, the regulatory limit on U.S. banks handicapped them in their competition with Canadian banks for the financing of very large deals. However, in the 1980s, a number of Canadian banks took massive losses on such large loans. As a result, Canadian banks have imposed on themselves a voluntary limit of 15%, much like the regulatory limit imposed on U.S. banks.

loan syndication
Lending by a group of banks that come together to negotiate and to make a loan.

loan sale
The sale of a loan, or part of a loan, to a third party by a bank that continues to service the loan.

Participations, Syndications, and Securitization

An obvious solution when the advantages of specialization or the need for large loans conflict with the principle of diversification is to sell off some of the loans or part of the loan to other banks. In a **loan syndication**, a lead bank puts together a group of lenders, each committed to taking a part of a large loan. With a **loan sale**, a single bank makes a loan and then sells a part of it to others.[26] As we saw in Chapter 14, an increasingly important variation on the selling of loans is securitization. Rather than selling loans directly to others, a bank sells them to an SPV, which issues securities backed by the loans (asset-backed securities).

---

[26] There are two types of loan sale. In a *participation*, the contract between the borrower and the original lender remains unchanged, but an additional contract is written between the original lender and the loan buyer (the borrower need not even know about this). In an *assignment*, the contract between the borrower and the original lender is replaced by one between the borrower and the loan buyer.

Participations, syndications, and securitizations improve the trade-off between specialization and diversification. Banks gain the informational benefits of originating loans in an industry or geographic area they know well. But they avoid the lack of diversification by selling to other banks the loans they originate. Rather than earning a lending spread, they earn fees for originating and servicing the loans.

Among the purchasers of participations, syndications, and asset-backed securities are small and medium-sized banks. As we saw earlier in the chapter, small banks lack loan opportunities and large banks lack funds. The sale of loans by large banks to small banks improves the situation of both. Purchased loans generally improve the diversification of small banks, which are often overly dependent on loans to local borrowers.

Buying loans from other banks is not without risks of its own. In both participations and securitizations, the purchaser is relying on someone else to assess the credit risk. There is a danger that the seller of the loan will not exercise sufficient care. Syndicators and sellers have a legal obligation of full disclosure, much like an underwriter, and they may be sued if they fail to fulfill it. This does not, of course, relieve the members of the syndicate or the buyers of the loans from the responsibility of performing due diligence.

sale without recourse
The sale of a loan without explicit or implicit guarantee by the seller against default by the borrower.

Typically, with a loan sale, the seller does not guarantee the loan (the loan is said to be sold **without recourse**). A guarantee would make little sense, since the whole point is to reduce the seller's own credit exposure. However, the seller often retains part of the loan, and it does have a reputational interest in selling only good loans. Any seller that does not will see little repeat business. The reputational incentive does not work, however, if the seller is already in serious trouble. Repeat business is of little interest if there is a high probability that you will not be around to benefit from it. So the credit of the seller is important, even thought the seller does not guarantee the loans.

Hedging Credit Risk

An alternative to selling the loan is selling the risk. We saw in Chapter 16 that credit derivatives offer a way of doing this. Instead of transferring the loan together with the credit risk to someone else, a bank can keep the loan on its books and become a risk seller on a credit default swap. By paying a third party to take on the risk of the loan, the bank "converts" it into a risk-free asset. The risk buyer (the seller of the protection) earns a return in exchange for taking on the risk. Consequently, buying risks through credit derivatives offers the same possibility of diversification as does the purchase of syndications or the purchase of asset-backed securities.

Banks are the biggest sellers of credit risk (63% of the total outstanding at the end of 1999), but they are also buyers (47% of the total. Securities firms sell and buy about the same amount (18 and 16%, respectively). Insurance companies buy much more risk than they sell (23 vs 7%).

An advantage of selling the risk rather than the loan is that it is less likely to upset the borrower. Indeed, the borrower need not even know about it. Credit derivatives are particularly popular in Europe, where banks often have agreements with their borrowers that prevent them from selling their loans to third parties.

Credit derivatives are, of course, subject to the same information problems as syndications and loan sales. In general, only major banks can sell the risks on their loans and only on loans to well-known credits. Small and medium banks and borrowers need not apply. There is an extra measure of risk with credit derivatives, because they are a new instrument and as yet untested. How legally and financially robust they will prove in a major economic crisis remains to be seen.

Capital

The final line of defense against credit risk—and against market risk—is equity capital. An intermediary with substantial capital can absorb occasional losses without becoming insolvent.

However, as we saw in Chapter 5, there is a cost to this protection: a higher ratio of equity to assets means a lower return on equity. So a financial intermediary will try to hold no more capital than it has to.

How Much Capital?   The amount of capital that is necessary depends on the nature of the business. As you can see from Exhibit 18.14, equity ratios vary widely across different types of financial institution. The differences reflect differences in the risks they face. For example, property–liability insurance companies have such high equity ratios because of the risk inherent in their liabilities.

You can see that banks have relatively low equity ratios. This is largely because of the existence of deposit insurance. Without deposit insurance, equity ratios would be higher.

EXHIBIT 18.14   Equity-to-Asset Ratios for Different Financial Institutions (Median Equity Ratios, as of Year End 1989)

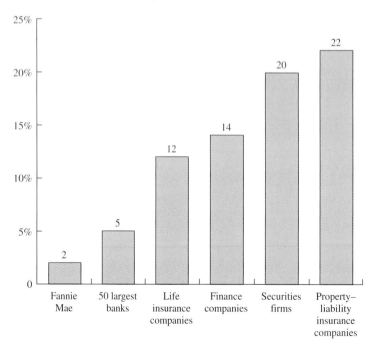

Source: U.S. Department of the Treasury (1991).

Regulators have recently been trying to compensate for this distortion by imposing stricter capital requirements.[27]

A financial intermediary has two ways to ensure that the amount of capital is suited to the risks it faces. The first is to ensure that risks are not excessive given the capital. The second is to ensure that capital is adequate given the risks.

One tool that intermediaries use to decide how much capital they need to protect themselves against the risk of a given position is the VAR models that we encountered earlier in the chapter. For example, suppose a bank has a futures position with a notional value of $100 million. Its VAR model shows that there is less than a 1% chance of a loss in excess of $10 million on this position in the next month. So, if the bank wishes to be 99% safe, it needs to allocate $10 million of its capital to cover the risk of this position.

The bank can also use this result to calculate the expected profitability of the position. Suppose the bank expects to make a $500,000 gain on the position over the next 3 months. Then, dividing by the necessary $10 million in capital required, the expected ROE is 5% for 3 months, or 21.5% per annum. By comparing the expected ROEs on different positions and activities, the bank can select the most profitable and eliminate those that do not meet its target ROE.

Ways of Increasing Capital. Intermediaries can increase their capital in either of two ways. Assuming they are profitable, they can retain profits rather than paying them out as dividends. And intermediaries that are publicly traded can increase their equity by issuing new stock.

Public issue is not an option for small institutions or for institutions in difficulty. As we have seen, the public issue of equity is both problematic and expensive. It is an option only for companies that are sound and relatively large. The need to improve equity ratios, together with the difficulty of a public issue, have been among the driving forces behind the wave of mergers and acquisitions among financial institutions.

Public issue is not an option either for institutions that are not corporations. We have seen that many thrifts and insurance companies are organized as mutual associations. Mutual associations cannot issue stock. Neither can they be a party to a merger or an acquisition. The need on the part of such institutions to increase their capital has motivated a large number of conversions from mutual to corporate form.

It is possible to raise equity externally without a public issue. If the institution in question is a subsidiary of another corporation, it can raise capital from its parent. The advantage of this way of increasing capital is that avoids many of the problems of asymmetric information that make a public issue so difficult.

CASE STUDIES IN THE MANAGEMENT OF LIQUIDITY AND RISK

We will now apply the principles of liquidity and risk management to understanding what went wrong in three notorious examples of mismanagement.

---

[27] We shall discuss the connection between deposit insurance and equity ratios in Chapter 19.

Case 1: The LDC Loans

As a result of sharp increases the price of oil in 1973 and again in 1979, many members of the Organization of Petroleum Exporting Countries (OPEC) found themselves with large amounts of cash. The Eurodollar banks took in the OPEC billions as deposits and lent them out again to the countries that needed to borrow to pay their oil bills. They called this "recycling petrodollars."

The borrowers were mainly less-developed countries (LDCs). By 1982 U.S. banks had made some $107 billion in loans to non-OPEC LDCs. Banks in other countries had lent equally large amounts. The U.S. banks had lent $72 billion to Latin American countries, principally to Mexico, Brazil, and Argentina.[28]

Many small and medium-sized U.S. banks, eager to enter the lucrative Eurodollar market, participated in these loans through syndications arranged by the big money-center banks. In 1982, some 1,500 U.S. banks were holding LDC debt acquired in this way.

The loans were considered to be relatively safe. Most of them were to governments or to government-sponsored companies. So the credit risk was thought to be small. The loans were thought to be well protected from market risk. They were floating-rate, eliminating interest rate risk. And they were denominated in dollars, eliminating exchange rate risk.

In 1980, in an attempt to control inflation, the Fed drove up interest rates to record heights. The rising interest rates drove up the exchange value of the dollar. They also brought on a severe recession that quickly spread to the other economies and sharply reduced the demand for the raw materials that were a large part of LDC exports.

The rising interest rates increased the interest payments due on the floating-rate LDC loans. Since interest payments had to be paid in dollars, the rise in the value of the dollar made the burden even greater. With their exports down, the LDCs found it impossible to meet their payments. In August 1982, Mexico became the first debtor country to suspend payments on its debt.

Between a third and a half of the amount outstanding in 1982 has since been written off as unrecoverable. The loss seriously weakened the capital position of the money-center banks that were the most active lenders. The smaller banks that participated in the syndications took losses too, but LDC loans were a much smaller fraction of their assets.

The "debt crisis," as it came to be known, illustrates a number of the points we have discussed:

- Shifting interest rate risk or exchange rate risk to borrowers only transforms it into credit risk.
- Sovereign lending is hazardous. The banks had no way to collect the bad debts.
- Relying on others to assess the risks of lending is not a good idea. The small banks taking part in the syndications had no idea of the risks involved.
- Diversification protects lenders against mistakes. The smaller banks were not seriously hurt by the debt crisis: LDC loans had never been a large part of their assets. Many money-center banks, however had lent several times their own capital, and some of them remained weakened by their losses for many years.

---

[28] Mexico was an oil exporter, rather than an importer. However, it wished to borrow against its expected future income.

Case 2: Continental Illinois

Roger Anderson took over as CEO of Continental Illinois of Chicago in 1973. His great ambition was to have Conti grow larger than its local archrival, First Chicago. Conti's loan officers were urged to lend at all costs. They offered bargain rates to lure borrowers away from other banks. They accepted every syndication and participation they could lay their hands on. By 1983 Conti had $42 billion in assets and had passed First Chicago to become the seventh largest bank in the United States.

The same rise in interest rates that precipitated the LDC debt crisis started Conti's decline. As the recession worsened, the poor quality of its loans became evident. Default followed default. When Penn Square Bank of Oklahoma City failed in July 1982, it transpired that Conti was holding $1 billion of its energy loan participations. Conti's loss on these alone was $220 million.

These losses were particularly serious because of Conti's heavy reliance on liability management. Because its home state of Illinois did not then allow bank branching, Conti had only a single office in downtown Chicago. Consequently, core deposits made up only 25% of its funds. The rest came from the money market. Some 16% of its funds were borrowed from U.S. banks and some 40% were Eurodollars. As its financial situation worsened, Conti found it progressively harder to roll over its NCDs, and it was forced to rely more and more on overnight funds.

Conti's condition deteriorated further over the next year and a half. In April 1984 Conti announced an additional $400 million of problem loans, bringing the total to $2.3 billion, an amount greater than its equity. On Friday May 11, as a result of rumors that it was about to be closed, Conti was unable to roll over its overnight borrowing, and it was forced to borrow $3.5 billion from the Chicago Fed.

A week of efforts by the Fed and by the other major banks to prop up the failing bank proved fruitless. On May 17, the FDIC announced that it would guarantee *all* of Conti's liabilities (not just its insured deposits). In July, after it proved impossible to arrange its acquisition by another bank, Conti was taken over by the federal government.

The failure of Continental Illinois illustrates the following points:

- Heavy reliance on borrowed funds (liability management) is undesirable.
- A bank that does rely heavily on borrowed funds must be very careful about the safety of its assets. Borrowed funds are much more volatile than core deposits and can evaporate if the bank gets into trouble.
- Rapid expansion of a loan portfolio is not a good idea. It is much easier to find bad loans than good ones.
- Conti knew nothing about the oil business and was rash, to say the least, to accept the participations from Penn Square.

Case 3: Long Term Capital Management

In 1991, John Meriwether had to leave Salomon Brothers because a trader in his department had been caught attempting to corner a Treasury auction (see Chapter 12). In 1994, together with a group of academics and traders who had worked with him at Salomon, Meriwether set up a hedge fund called Long Term Capital Management (LTCM).

The core strategy of the new fund was "convergence arbitrage," a play on the difference between interest rates on similar instruments. For example, 10-year corporate bonds might have a yield of 9%, while the corresponding Treasuries had a yield of 7%. LTCM would take a position on the risk premium—the 2% differential between the two types of bond—by going long the corporate bonds and short the Treasuries. If the risk premium shrank, the firm's long position would appreciate with no change in its short position, and it would make a profit.[29] If interest rates as a whole rose or fell, the gains and losses on the firm's long and short positions would cancel each other out: for this reason LTCM's position was described as being "market neutral."

Initially, LTCM was extremely successful. Its play on the convergence of interest rates in the Euro zone earned its investors a healthy return, raising its capital from an initial $1 billion to $7 billion by 1997. As it became harder to find good profit opportunities, the return it paid to its investors declined. LTCM decided to compensate for the lower yields by increasing its leverage. While maintaining or increasing the size of its positions, it returned $2.7 billion of capital to its investors.

LTCM leveraged its $125 billion of assets (its long positions) largely with repos. Because of the stellar reputations of its partners, lenders were willing to take a near-zero "haircut" (overcollateralization) on these repos, and LTCM could support these assets with less than $5 billion in capital. The firm also had a huge position in derivatives, totaling some $1 trillion. This included positions in swaps, futures, and options.

To calculate the risks of its position, and the adequacy of its capital, LTCM relied on a VAR model. Based on recent historical experience, this model predicted that there was less than a 1% chance that LTCM would lose more than $50 million of its capital in a single month. In this light, nearly $5 billion in capital seemed quite adequate.

In 1997, the Asia crisis had shaken investor confidence and, as a result, risk premiums had increased significantly. LTCM bet that this was an overreaction and that risk premiums would gradually fall back to more normal levels. However, by May 1998 risk premiums were still stubbornly high and LTCM started to sustain losses. Then in August, Russia defaulted on its debt and risk premiums skyrocketed. LTCM lost $1,710 million of its capital in a single month—an event that according to its model should have happened only once in 800 trillion years (40,000 times the age of the universe). Perhaps the model was wrong.

LTCM's losses continued in September, and it had trouble meeting margin calls on its repos and derivatives. Because of the illiquidity and the size of its position, it could unload its bonds only at a significant loss.

The New York Fed feared the effect of a default by LTCM on markets. If LTCM defaulted, the holders of its repos would be forced to dump tens of billions of dollars of securities onto the market, and its brokers would have to close out hundreds of billions of dollars in derivatives. The Fed therefore quickly put together a consortium of LTCM's lenders to take over the fund—providing $3.6 billion in new capital in exchange for a 90% stake. This was essentially equivalent to a bankruptcy.

---

[29] As the two bonds approached maturity, the risk premium would have to shrink and eventually disappear unless the corporate bonds defaulted.

The failure of Long Term Capital Management illustrates the following points:

- Leverage is dangerous: it brings higher returns, but only at the cost of higher risk.
- Statistical models such as VAR must be used with caution. Especially if they are built only on recent history, they will underestimate the likelihood of extreme events.
- Large trading positions in illiquid securities are dangerous because it is very difficult to undo them in an emergency without significant loss.
- Know your borrower or your counterparty. The banks and securities firms that lent to LTCM and entered into derivative contracts with it had very little idea what the firm was doing or how highly leveraged it was. They relied too much on the star quality of its personnel.

SUMMARY

- The business of small banks is mostly retail. They are therefore deposit rich. Consequently it makes sense for them to rely on asset management for their liquidity.

- The business of money-center banks is mostly wholesale. They are therefore deposit poor. Consequently it makes sense for them to rely on liability management for their liquidity.

- To assess their needs for liquidity, banks use tools such as cash flow liquidity evaluation and the funding gap.

- Liability management is inherently a more dangerous strategy than asset management. The key to liability management is always being able to borrow.

- Banks can reduce the danger by lengthening the maturity of their liabilities. Keeping the repricing period short avoids the consequent increase in the cost of funds. Swaps are particularly useful for separating maturity and repricing period.

- Large banks have also been trying to reduce their reliance on liability management in other ways—by increasing core deposits, by holding more liquid assets, by increasing off-balance-sheet activity.

- A complicating factor in managing a bank's liquidity is the need to meet reserve requirements. Banks adjust their reserves mainly by borrowing or lending in the overnight market.

- Intermediaries other than banks must also manage their liquidity.

- Intermediaries with assets and liabilities imperfectly matched with respect to maturity and currency denomination face market risk. Differential changes in the market value of assets and liabilities can cause changes in the institution's equity capital.

- Intermediaries also face specific risks from changes in the value of individual assets and liabilities unrelated to movements in market interest rates or exchange rates.

- A bank in a refinance position will take a loss if interest rates rise. One in a reinvestment position will take a loss if rates fall. Because the yield curve has a positive slope, banks tend to take a refinance position. By doing so, they earn, on average, the term premium.

- Banks can reduce their exposure to interest rate risk by matching maturities (of fixed-interest rate assets and liabilities) or by matching repricing periods. The latter approach transfers the risk to the borrower, so increasing the bank's credit risk.

- Banks can also hedge their interest rate risk with futures, FRAs, options, or swaps. Hedging with futures involves basis risk and can lead to difficulties with accounting and with regulators.

- A bank can measure its exposure to interest rate risk by estimating its duration gap and by using VAR analysis.

- Market risk has the potential for gain as well as for loss, and banks do take positions to profit from expected interest rate or exchange rate movements. The trick is not to overdo it.

- Other intermediaries, too, face market risk. The case of the thrifts is notorious. Pension funds use portfolio insurance to hedge the risks of holding stocks.

- To deal with credit risk, intermediaries must exercise care in lending (collateral and guarantees are desirable when possible), must price appropriately, and must diversify. Recently, they have been able to hedge credit risk with credit derivatives.

- Intermediaries must make sure that their risks and their capital are appropriate to one another. VAR models provide one way of assessing how much capital is necessary.

DISCUSSION QUESTIONS

1. Explain the dangers of a refinance position. Why do banks usually take a refinance position nonetheless?

2. What are the different ways a bank can reduce its exposure to interest rate risk? What are the advantages and disadvantages of each?

3. "There is no such thing as a bad risk, only bad pricing." Discuss.

4. How does the correspondent relationship affect the risk and liquidity of the banks involved?

5. Suppose you were managing risk for a bank with the following balance sheet:

Loans	Eurodollar deposits
1-year at 7% 100m	2-year at 5% $100m

   a. Calculate your profit under the three interest rate scenarios used in the chapter (assume you can lend at LIBOR + 3%).
   b. How would you hedge using futures or FRAs? Calculate your profits under the same three interest rate scenarios.
   c. How would you hedge with options?
   d. How would you hedge with swaps?

6. How do the balance sheets of large and small banks differ? How does this affect the way they manage liquidity?

7. A German bank has made a loan in U.S. dollars for $100 million, and it has $50 million in U.S. dollar deposits.

   a. What is the change in the value of the bank if the exchange rate goes from 1.60DM/$ to 1.40DM/$?
   b. If it goes from 1.60DM/$ to 1.80DM/$?
   c. How could the bank protect itself against a change in the exchange rate?

8. The market value of a bank's assets is $20 billion and the market value of its liabilities is $17 billion. The duration of its assets is 2.5 years and the duration of its liabilities is 1.5 years.

   a. What is the bank's duration gap?
   b. Suppose market interest rates fall from 7% to 6%. What is the change in the value of the bank's equity?
   c. If the bank were expecting such a change in interest rates, what should it do?

9. For property–liability insurance companies, liquidity is an important concern. Such insurance companies, even large ones, do not generally rely on liability management as a source of liquidity. Why not?

10. What are dangers of reliance on liability management? What are the different ways a bank can reduce its reliance on liability management?

11. Make up a table listing all the intermediaries we have discussed in previous chapters. For each one, explain how its liquidity and risk problems differ from those of a commercial bank.

12. Banks are highly regulated but have low equity ratios. Finance companies are not regulated much at all, yet they have much higher equity ratios. How do you explain this?

BIBLIOGRAPHY

Belongia, Michael T., and G. J. Santoni. "Hedging Interest Rate Risk with Financial Futures: Some Basic Principles." *Economic Review of the Federal Reserve Bank of St. Louis*, October 1984, 15–25.

Bodie, Zvi. "The Lender's View of Debt and Equity: The Case of Pension Funds." In *Are the Distinctions Between Debt and Equity Disappearing?* Edited by R. W. Kopcke and E. S. Rosengren. Boston: Federal Reserve Bank of Boston, 1989.

Federal Reserve Bank of New York. *Funding and Liquidity: Recent Changes in Liquidity Management at Commercial Banks and Securities Firms.* New York: FRBNY, 1990.

Kimball, R. C. "Failures in Risk Management." *New England Economic Review*, January–February, 2000, 3–12.

Kopcke, Richard W. and Richard E. Randall, eds. *The Financial Condition and Regulation of Insurance Companies.* Boston: Federal Reserve Bank of Boston, 1991.

Neal, R. S. "Credit Derivatives: New Financial Instruments for Controlling Credit Risk." *Federal Reserve Bank of Kansas City Economic Review*, second quarter 1996, 15–27.

Parkinson, P., and P. Spindt. "The Use of Interest Rate Futures by Commercial Banks." In *Financial Futures in the U.S. Economy*. Washington, DC: Board of Governors of the Federal Reserve System, 1986.

Simons, K. "Value at Risk—New Approaches to Risk Management." *New England Economic Review* September–October, 1996, 3–13.

U.S. Department of the Treasury, *Modernizing the Financial System: Recommendations for Safer, More Competitive Banks.* Washington, DC: The Treasury, 1991.

Wall, Larry D., John J. Pringle, and James E. McNulty. "Capital Requirements for Interest Rate and Exchange Rate Hedges." *Economic Review of the Federal Reserve Bank of Atlanta*, May–June 1990, 14–28.

KEY TERMS

retail bank
deposit-rich bank
wholesale bank
deposit-poor bank
funding gap
maturity of a loan
repricing period
core deposits
computation period
maintenance period
book value

market value
market risk
specific risk
credit risk
refinance position
reinvestment position
term premium
matching maturities
commitment period
repricing period
duration gap

value at risk (VAR) analysis
running a matched book
dynamic hedging (portfolio insurance)
sovereign risk
risk premium
usury ceilings
loan syndication
loan sale
sale without recourse

CHAPTER 19

BANK SAFETY AND REGULATION

When you finish this chapter you will understand:

- Why governments need to regulate banks
- Why bank runs and banking panics happen
- What can be done to prevent them

B anking problems—failures, runs, and panics—can do serious damage to an economy. A sharp reduction in bank credit can leave many small and medium-sized businesses without working capital and therefore unable to function. The damage to the payments system can bring normal economic activity to a halt. For these reasons, banks have always been a concern of public policy, and governments have always been involved in their regulation.

We saw in Chapter 3 that government intervention in banking can be justified on the grounds of a kind of market failure called an externality. Externalities occur whenever individuals do not bear all the costs of their actions. Two types of externality occur in banking. First, because bank failure can be so damaging to the economy, bankers taking risks that seem reasonable from their own point of view may be taking too much risk from the point of view of society. Consequently, it may make sense for government regulators to limit banks' risk taking. Second, as we saw in Chapter 3, the composition problems that underlie runs and panics involve a kind of externality. When I withdraw my deposit from a bank, I do not consider the effect on others. Here, too, then government intervention to assure the stability of the banking system may be justified.

PRUDENTIAL REGULATION

prudential regulation
Government regulation and monitoring of the banking system to ensure safety and soundness.

The regulation of banks to protect depositors and to limit their taking of risk is called **prudential regulation**. At a minimum this takes the form of chartering and disclosure requirements. Setting up a bank requires a government charter, which is granted only to those considered "fit and proper." In addition, banks are generally required to disclose financial information to the public, and they are inspected by government supervisors to make sure that their disclosure is accurate. Beyond this minimum, regulations may limit the types of asset banks can hold and the activities in which they can engage. Regulations may require a level of reserves or capital. And since competition encourages risk taking, regulations may restrict competition among banks in various ways—for example, by setting caps on deposit rates. Typically, each new banking crisis elicits new legislation that imposes additional restrictions. We shall see the most recent examples later in the chapter.

Prudential regulation is not a new idea. There has been prudential regulation as long as there have been banks. To open a bank in the Middle Ages, a banker had to obtain a license from the city and to provide guarantees. In fourteenth-century Bruges, after a number of bank failures had led to serious friction with foreign merchants, the city supplemented private guarantees with a form of deposit insurance. In some European cities, the authorities tried to limit the risk exposure of banks by restricting their assets. Venice had a long history of such restrictions, adding new ones after each banking crisis. In the 1370s, it banned investment in most commodities (especially bullion); in the early fifteenth century, it limited investments in commercial ventures to one and a half times the personal wealth of the banker. In general, bankers had unlimited personal liability for their deposits. In 1360, when a Barcelona banker, Francesch Castello, failed to pay up, he was beheaded in front of his bank.[1]

Prudential Regulation in the United States

In the United States too, prudential regulation goes back to the beginning of banking. U.S. bank charters of the nineteenth century imposed disclosure requirements, restrictions on permissible assets, and equity requirements.[2]

dual banking
The U.S. system of regulation, involving regulation at both state and federal levels.

Today, U.S. banks are monitored by a multiplicity of regulators at both the state and federal levels. This is a legacy of the historical battle over banking jurisdiction between state and federal governments. This system of regulation is known as **dual banking**.

A Multiplicity of Regulators.   There are currently four categories of banks and thrifts from the point of view of regulation[3]:

1. *Banks with a national charter.* The Office of the Comptroller of the Currency (OCC) grants charters, approves mergers and new branches, examines these

---

[1] Usher (1943), p. 242.

[2] For example, the state of New York passed a law in 1827 requiring annual reports and setting a required equity ratio. Louisiana passed a law in 1842 that, among other things, required banks to match maturities! The Louisiana banking system was a model until the Civil War.

[3] Legislation in the 1980s largely did away with separate regulators for thrifts, and these institutions became subject to essentially the same regulators as banks. Credit unions are an exception, being regulated by the National Credit Union Administration (NCUA).

banks, and, if necessary, closes them. These banks must be members of the Federal Reserve System, and they must be insured by the FDIC. They are subject to all federal laws and regulations.

2. *State-chartered banks that are members of the Fed.* State regulators grant charters, approve mergers and new branches, and, if necessary, close these banks. They are examined by the Fed and sometimes also by the state. They must be insured by the FDIC.

3. *State-chartered banks that are not members of the Fed but are insured by the FDIC.* Regulated as in category 2, except that examination is by the FDIC.

4. *State-chartered banks not insured by the FDIC.* Regulated as in category 2, except that examination is by state regulators.

In addition to the foregoing categories, the Fed has jurisdiction over all bank holding companies—granted to it by the Bank Holding Company Act of 1956—and all financial holding companies—granted to it by the Gramm–Leach–Bliley Act of 1999.[4] It also has the authority to set reserve requirements for all institutions offering transactions accounts. This was granted to it in 1980.

The balance of power has generally shifted towards federal regulators in recent years. After runs on state-insured thrifts in Ohio, Maryland, and Rhode Island in the 1980s, state-sponsored deposit insurance has withered. Most banks and thrifts are now insured by the FDIC. The lax regulation of state-chartered thrifts was an important factor in the S&L crisis, and this has further reduced the authority of the states in bank regulation.[5]

Is a Multiplicity of Regulators Good or Bad?   The overlapping patchwork of bank regulation has been criticized for its duplication and lack of clear lines of authority. For example, although the FDIC examines state-chartered nonmember banks, if such a bank is found to be insolvent, the FDIC cannot close it itself and must turn to state regulators to close the bank.

There seem to be significant differences in the quality of supervision, even at the federal level. The Fed conducts on-site examinations of 97% of the banks under its supervision, the FDIC 64%, and OCC 36% (21% for banks with less than $1 billion in assets). One study found that banks examined by the Fed had the lowest failure rate and that those examined by OCC had the highest. Although the latter group made up only 33% of all banks, they accounted for 73% of the losses to the insurance fund over the preceding five years.

race for the bottom
Alleged lowering of standards by regulators to attract business.

Dual banking is also criticized for encouraging regulators to compete with one another by offering less strict rules—often described as a **race for the bottom**. Banks are allowed to change their charters from state to federal or vice versa, and they have done so to benefit from differences in the regulatory burden. For example, before the Fed imposed its reserve requirements on all banks, state-imposed reserve requirements on nonmember banks were substantially less stringent. As a result, many banks switched to state charters and Fed membership declined. Regulators care about "losing" banks because any such "loss" affects their budgets and their importance. For example, when Chase switched

---

[4] See Chapter 6 on the Gramm–Leach–Bliley Act.

[5] We shall discuss both the runs on the state-insured thrifts and the S&L crisis later in the chapter.

from a federal to a state charter in 1995, the fees lost to the OCC equaled 2% of its total budget.

On the other hand, for those who believe that regulation is excessive, dual banking does have its attractions. Regulators prefer not to work too hard. They also fear being blamed for allowing banks to do things that lead to trouble. As a result, when asked to authorize new products, procedures, or activities, they would rather say no. However, faced with competition, the possible loss of business balances this selfish conservatism. Competition among regulators has therefore opened the way for many important innovations. A good example is provided by the Massachusetts state thrift regulators, who were the first to allow NOW accounts. State regulators also led the way towards interstate banking. Without competition from state regulators, federal bureaucrats might be less flexible and responsive.

Regulation of Offshore and Multinational Banking

The prudential regulation of offshore and multinational banks is a particular problem because jurisdiction is often uncertain. Who is responsible for a Japanese bank operating in U.S. dollars in London? Is it the Bank of Japan, because the bank is Japanese owned? Is it the Bank of England, because the bank is located in London? Is it the Fed, because the bank is taking deposits and making loans in the U.S. currency?

Offshore banking began with very little regulation or supervision. That was the whole point. The division of responsibilities was ill defined. It was not clear which authorities were supposed to monitor which banks or who was supposed to clean up the mess if a bank collapsed. The division of responsibilities has become progressively clearer as the result of a series of crises.

The Herstatt Crisis and the Basel Concordat.   In 1974, Bankhaus Herstatt, a medium-sized German bank heavily involved in Eurocurrency banking, failed. As a result, depositors, particularly those from the Middle East, withdrew large sums from non-U.S. Eurodollar banks and redeposited their money with the largest and safest U.S. Eurodollar banks. A serious liquidity crisis was avoided only because the U.S. Eurodollar banks turned around and lent the money back to the banks that were losing deposits.

In response to the Herstatt crisis, central bankers got together in Basel in 1974 to draw some lines of responsibility. They reached an agreement that came to be known as the **Basel Concordat**. Under that agreement each central bank is supposed to be responsible for the foreign branches and subsidiaries of its own banks.

This arrangement is not entirely satisfactory because of the peculiar nature of offshore banking. If a German bank faces a loss of domestic deposits in Euros, it can find the funds by borrowing from other European banks. If that proves insufficient, it can borrow from the European Central Bank, which can create as many Euros as are needed. However, if a German bank faces a loss of dollar deposits, other German banks will not be able to help, and U.S. banks—not sufficiently familiar with its credit—may be unwilling to lend to it. The European Central Bank has reserves of dollars, but unlike the Fed it cannot create them.

As a result, most Eurocurrency banks set up their own safety nets. They usually establish lines of credit with U.S. banks on which they will be able to draw if necessary. The

U.S. bank in question will act as a lender of last resort. Often the foreign bank will "pay" for the dollar line of credit by providing the American bank with a reciprocal line of credit in its own currency. That way, the American bank is covered too if it faces a run on its foreign currency deposits. The number and scope of such arrangements increased dramatically after the Herstatt crisis.

Banco Ambrosiano.   The adequacy of the Basel Concordat came into question as a result of another crisis in 1982. Banco Ambrosiano, a large Italian bank, had a Eurodollar subsidiary—Banco Ambrosiano Holdings, S.A., in Luxembourg. The subsidiary was not formally a bank; rather, it was a financial holding company. Banco Ambrosiano Holdings failed after it was revealed that it had lent some $1.4 billion to Panamanian companies controlled by the chairman of Banco Ambrosiano. It had also borrowed over $500 million from various Eurodollar banks.

The Bank of Italy supported Banco Ambrosiano itself but refused to pay the debts of Banco Ambrosiano Holdings on the grounds that it was not a bank and not in Italy. Luxembourg also denied responsibility on the grounds that Banco Ambrosiano Holdings was not a bank.

As a result of the Banco Ambrosiano scandal, there was great unease in the Eurocurrency market, but no panic. Nonetheless, the central bankers made another trip to Basel in 1983. They set up the **Basel Committee on Banking Supervision**, consisting of regulators from 11 major nations, to propose new international standards. The committee put together a plan to impose uniform capital standards on all banks in all the major countries.[6]

BCCI.   The next crisis involved a multinational rather than an offshore bank. The Bank of Credit and Commerce International (BCCI) was founded in 1972 by a Pakistani financier with Gulf Arab backers. By 1991 it had branches in 69 countries with over $20 billion in deposits and 1.2 million depositors. Blocked by suspicious regulators from entering the United States directly, BCCI used fronts to acquire First American Bancshares of Washington, D.C., and several other U.S. banks. BCCI consisted of a complicated international network of holding companies and subsidiaries. The whole complex was controlled by a Luxembourg holding company, but its operations were run out of London.

In 1991, BCCI was closed in a coordinated sweep by regulators in seven major countries. Its operations elsewhere were soon halted too. The regulators had acted in response to accumulating evidence of widespread fraud and corruption. The bank had provided banking services, and others, to spy agencies, to organized crime (especially the drug trade), and to terrorists. It had been plundered by its officers. And, to keep regulators at bay, it had been lavish with bribes to politicians around the world. The bank's losses were expected to exceed $5 billion, with corresponding losses to depositors.

The collapse of BCCI brought renewed pressure for tighter regulation of international banks. The Basel Committee issued new standards in 1992 for the supervision of international banks. These standards mandate a "dual-key" approach. Home and host country regulators are each to assess the quality of the other's supervision.[7] If the host country finds

---

[6] We shall learn more about these capital standards later in the chapter.

[7] The standards do require that the bank have a home country responsible for supervising it. BCCI managed to slip between the cracks.

the home country's supervision inadequate, it should exclude the bank in question from operating in its territory or impose special restrictions. If the home country finds the host country's supervision inadequate, it should discourage the parent bank from operating the office in question.[8]

LIQUIDITY CRISES

Government intervention in banking has progressed well beyond the sort of prudential regulation that we have examined so far. The reason is an inherent contradiction in the structure of a bank. On the one hand, most of its assets are illiquid loans. On the other, most of its liabilities are liquid deposits payable on demand or at short notice. A bank "manufactures" liquidity mainly through pooling: new deposits largely offset withdrawals. In addition, as we saw in Chapters 5 and 18, a bank has a variety of backup mechanisms to provide additional liquidity when pooling proves insufficient. Sometimes, however, the demand for liquidity can be great enough to completely overwhelm these backup mechanisms, so that the bank is unable to provide the funds its depositors demand. Such an overwhelming demand for liquidity is called a bank run.

Bank Runs and Banking Panics

There were a number of bank runs in the United States as the twentieth century drew to a close, the most serious being the New England banking crisis of 1991 and the run on Continental Illinois in 1984.[9] Why do people run on a bank? The best way to understand is to imagine how you yourself would behave in the same circumstances.

How Would You Have Behaved during the Conti Crisis?   Put yourself in the shoes of a Eurodollar banker lending to Continental Illinois in 1984. Being a banker yourself, you know that "Conti" relies principally on liability management for backup liquidity: when it needs extra cash, it borrows it. All this is well and good, as long as Conti remains solvent. However, Conti has suffered a series of large losses in recent years, and there is some danger of its equity being wiped out. If that happens, there will not be enough to pay off all the deposits, and you will stand to lose some of your money.

But what about deposit insurance? Doesn't the federal government guarantee Conti's deposits. Yes, it does. But it guarantees a maximum of $100,000 per depositor. You have a deposit of $20 million. Moreover, Eurodollar borrowings are not covered by deposit insurance. Naturally, you are quite concerned.

---

[8] In response to the BCCI scandal, the United States passed the Foreign Bank Supervision Enhancement Act of 1991. This requires any foreign bank wishing to establish a branch or subsidiary in the United States to obtain approval from the Fed and a license from state or federal regulators. The Fed will withhold permission unless it is persuaded that the bank's worldwide operations are adequately supervised by the bank's home government. Foreign banks must also obtain the Fed's permission before acquiring an equity stake of more than 5% in a U.S. bank. To accept insured deposits, a foreign bank must create a separately capitalized subsidiary (foreign banks already accepting insured deposits are exempt from this requirement). The Fed hired 250 new bank examiners just to work on foreign banks.

[9] We shall discuss the reasons for these crises presently.

As Conti's situation has deteriorated, you have continued to roll over your deposit, albeit at an increasing rate of interest. But now things look bad enough to make you decide not to roll over. Why take the chance? It is so easy to move your money to another bank whose solvency is not in doubt. All you need do is call your Eurodollar broker. Congratulations, you have just participated in a bank run.

Why Depositors Run on a Bank.   Let us analyze your decision to withdraw your funds. Partly, it was the result of uncertainty. Conti's solvency is unknown. It is hard, even for Conti itself, to know what its loan portfolio is worth. Bank loans are generally not marketable, so there is no market price to go by. There is uncertainty, too, about the extent of government guarantees. We shall see later in the chapter that the government often covers uninsured deposits like yours. However, at the time, in 1984, there was considerable uncertainty about what the government would do in the event that Conti failed.

Suppose you personally are confident that Conti is solvent. Because of your close connections with the bank, you have good information that Conti is solidly in the black. Will this affect your decision to withdraw your deposit? Not necessarily. You know that *other* depositors are uncertain about the bank's solvency. They may well withdraw their funds. Since Conti relies on liability management to deal with excess withdrawals, doubts about its solvency may be fatal. The bank may be unable to borrow what it needs to replace the deposits it loses. If so, it will fail.

If the bank fails, it may be liquidated—its assets sold to pay off its liabilities. This process of liquidation may destroy enough value to leave depositors with a loss, even though the bank was solvent before it failed. Assets sold off in a hurry may fetch only fire-sale prices, well below their true worth.

Consequently, you are concerned not only about the true state of Conti's solvency, but also about what others *believe* that state to be. If you think that others, however misguidedly, are going to run on the bank, you had better get your money out fast. There is, therefore, an element of self-fulfilling prophecy about a bank run. A rumor of insolvency, well founded or not, can trigger a run that causes the bank to fail and leaves it insolvent.

It makes sense for you to get your money out fast for another reason, too. When depositors withdraw their money from a bank, the rule is "first come, first served." As long as it can, the bank will pay off all deposits in full. Therefore, the *last* depositors to attempt to withdraw their money from an insolvent bank will bear *all* the loss. This gives you a strong incentive to be among the first.

Contagion: From Bank Run to Banking Panic.   Given the way bank runs work, there is a tendency for a run on one bank to precipitate runs on others. There is always uncertainty about the true value of a bank's assets. There is also a certain similarity between banks in the types of loan they make. For example, when LDC lending was fashionable in the late 1970s, most large banks were involved. Likewise with commercial real estate in the late 1980s. So, when you hear of one bank in trouble, it is not unreasonable to assume that it is not alone—that others will turn out to have similar problems.

In addition, a failure or a run on a single bank can heighten awareness of potential problems, causing depositors to jump ship more readily, just as drivers are more careful after passing an accident. For example, the collapse of BCCI in 1991 led to runs on a number of unrelated banks in Hong Kong.

contagion

The tendency of a problem to spread from one place to another.

Banks are very concerned about this tendency of problems to spread from one bank to another—a phenomenon known as **contagion**. For this reason, they are usually willing to lend a hand to a sister bank in trouble. For example, the major banks tried, unsuccessfully, to prop up Continental Illinois.[10]

In the worst case, there can be a loss of confidence in *all* banks and a general desire on the part of the public to convert its bank deposits into cash. Such a **banking panic** can have severe consequences for the economy.

Why Do Bank Runs and Banking Panics Happen?

Bank runs and banking panics do have an internal dynamics that drives them along. There is a large element of self-fulfilling prophecy. However, they do not just happen at random. There are various factors that will make a liquidity crisis more likely. Let us look at some of them.

Financial Crises and the Business Cycle.   Bank runs and banking panics usually happen against a background of financial crisis. As news accumulates of more and more bad loans, depositors become increasingly nervous. In this atmosphere, any small event can trigger a bank run.

The most common reason for a financial crisis is the business cycle. A period of general economic prosperity comes to an end, and investments that looked promising in good times turn out to be unprofitable in bad. Moreover, as the economy slows down, prices stop rising and may even fall. Borrowers, who expected to repay in devalued dollars, find the real burden of repayment unexpectedly large and many default.

This was the typical scenario for many banking panics in the nineteenth and early twentieth centuries. More recently, the worldwide recessions of 1980–1982 and 1990–1991 contributed significantly to loan losses and created financial crises in many countries.

Industry Cycles.   Financial crises can also be the result of cycles in a specific sector of the economy. Agricultural cycles were a common cause of financial crises in the nineteenth and early twentieth centuries. An agricultural cycle in the 1970s led to the failure of many small banks.

Cycles in commercial real estate are another common cause of loan losses—perhaps the most common. Banks lend to developers, who build on speculation in a booming commercial real estate market. The boom turns to bust, the borrowers default, the collateral is worth much less than the outstanding loans, and the banks take major losses. This has been the story at one time or another in most countries. It was the story in the banking crises in the United States in the 1980s and 1990s. And this was a major part of the story in the Asian banking crises of the late 1990s.

The Strains of Increasing Competition.   Another common reason for financial crisis is heightened competition within the financial system. When there is little competi-

---

[10] The run on Continental Illinois happened on a Friday. Over the weekend, a group of 16 major banks, led by Morgan, put together a $4.5 billion line of credit to restore confidence in the troubled bank. The crisis at Continental was making it harder for all the major banks to borrow in the money market, and the stocks of most of them were falling in value.

tion and profits are easy, banks generally play it safe. But when competition heats up and profits are thin, they often begin to take chances. This happened in the 1920s, and it happened again in the 1970s and 1980s.

Deregulation of interest rates and easing of restrictions on geographic expansion meant increasing competitive pressure. In the rush to capture economies of scale, expansion became a condition for survival, and access to the money market made it possible to fund growing loan portfolios. The pressure to expand led to a lowering of lending standards. For example, Bank of America, with a strategy of expanding its loan portfolio by 10% a year, rewarded its loan officers according to the amount of new loans they wrote—quality did not seem to matter. First Chicago tripled its lending between 1969 and 1974 to become the ninth largest bank in the United States; in 1976 bank examiners found that its problem loans amounted to double its equity.

While financial crises are more or less inevitable, it is not inevitable that they lead to liquidity crises. It is quite possible for banks and other intermediaries to take losses without there being a panic. There are a number of factors that affect how well banks can weather a financial crisis.

Banking Industry Structure and Stability

Fragmentation and Interdependence.   Different banking systems, with different structures, seem to differ widely in their susceptibility to problems. Fragmented banking systems consisting of many small banks have historically been much more susceptible to runs and panics than have integrated banking systems made up of a few large banks.

Why does fragmentation reduce stability? First, the individual institutions themselves are much weaker. Being small, they forfeit natural economies of scale. They are less well diversified, making insolvency more likely. Because their pooling is less effective, small banks also have poorer liquidity. This makes them more vulnerable to a run if one does occur.

The second reason that fragmentation increases instability is interdependence. As we saw in Chapter 7, the small banks of a fragmented banking system try to capture economies of scale through interbank connections. Deposits of one bank held at another contribute to the vulnerability of the system to runs and to panics.

Banks themselves make very skittish depositors. Interbank funds constitute "hot money"—money ready to take flight at the least hint of trouble. Banks are also more likely than ordinary depositors to hear about possible trouble.

Interbank connections also reduce stability by spreading problems from one bank to another. The failure of a bank with large interbank deposits can cause serious losses to many of the banks holding deposits with it. These losses may cause the depositors of those banks to run on them.

Historical Evidence on Fragmentation and Instability.   The correspondent system of U.S. banking in the nineteenth century was notoriously liable to panics. Small country banks held reserve balances with larger city correspondents; these in turn kept reserve balances with banks in the financial centers, particularly in New York. This "pyramiding" of reserves turned small local problems into national ones. A run on a few small country banks would result in large withdrawals from the small banks' city correspondents.

Other country banks, fearful of the safety of the city banks, would also withdraw their balances. Under this pressure, the city banks, in turn, would withdraw their deposits from the money-center banks.

The fragmented British banking system also suffered frequent runs and panics in the first half of the nineteenth century. However, as it underwent consolidation towards the end of the century, problems became less frequent and eventually disappeared entirely. Increasingly, a bank in difficulty would simply be taken over by one of the other large banks, usually before the public had any idea there was a problem.

The importance of banking structure for stability is illustrated by the record of the Great Depression. As we have seen, the U.S. banking system collapsed. But not everywhere. In California, with unrestricted statewide branching, only one bank failed. In contrast to the United States, Canada had unrestricted nationwide branching. No banks failed there.

New Methods of Managing Liquidity and Risk

The way banks manage liquidity and risk have important implications for the stability of the system. There are two basic approaches to the management of liquidity and risk—internal and external.

internal methods of managing liquidity and risk Methods that rely on the rearrangement of an institution's balance sheet.

Internal and External Methods of Managing Liquidity and Risk. **Internal methods** rely on the rearrangement of an institution's balance sheet to provide protection. In terms of liquidity, this means asset management—the holding of cash and secondary reserves. In terms of risk, it means matching the maturity and currency denomination of assets and liabilities, diversification, and the holding of substantial equity capital.

External methods of liquidity and risk management rely on resources outside the institution itself. In terms of liquidity, this means liability management. Rather than relying on its own liquidity, the institution relies on its ability to borrow cash from others. In terms of risk, it means hedging with derivatives. Rather than reducing the risk of its own position, the institution pays others to bear the risk.

external methods of managing liquidity and risk Methods that rely on resources outside the institution itself.

How External Methods Increase Efficiency. External methods increase efficiency. They allow liquidity to be shared and risk to be spread. By borrowing cash from one another as needed, institutions share their reserves. Each, indirectly, has access to the reserves of all. In this way the system as whole can economize on costly reserves.

There are two ways in which external hedging makes it easier for the financial system as a whole to bear risk. First, if one institution has a positive duration gap and another a negative duration gap, each one can reduce its risk by trading derivatives with the other. The derivatives allow both institutions to exploit the fact that their *combined* balance sheet has a better maturity match than either balance sheet separately.

Second, by hedging externally, the risks are spread more widely. Trade in risk, like any trade, is beneficial. Rather than being exposed to all the risk of its own position, each institution is exposed to a fraction of the risk of the combined position of everyone. Sharing the risk with others in this way, each institution can take an individually riskier, and therefore more profitable, position.

How External Methods Reduce Stability.   While they do increase efficiency, external methods of liquidity and risk management can also reduce stability. This is because these methods rely on a form of pooling, and pooling can break down.

External methods of liquidity management rely on the pooling of reserves. Rather than relying on its own reserves, in times of need each institution calls on the pooled reserves of all. This is very much like the pooling of deposits at a bank by individual depositors.

When there are demands, however, not on a single institution, but on the system as whole, pooling will break down. For example, in a banking panic *all* banks are under liquidity pressure: there aren't any "other" banks from which to borrow. For the banking system *as a whole*, there can be only asset management: the system must rely on internal sources of liquidity.

composition problems

Problems that arise out of behavior that is sensible for a single individual but harmful if pursued by all individuals.

The same sort of breakdown can occur with the external management of risk. Perhaps the best example is the failure of portfolio insurance during the stock market crash of 1987. The essential idea of portfolio insurance is to avoid losses by selling when prices fall.[11] This can work for a single institutions or for a few, but it cannot work for everyone. If everyone wants to sell, there is no one to buy.[12]

These breakdowns are the result of **composition problems**. What works for a single individual does not necessarily work for all individuals taken together.

PRIVATE SOLUTIONS FOR LIQUIDITY CRISES

Having seen what liquidity crises are and why they occur, let us now see what can be done about them. Before we see what governments can do to protect the economy from this sort of problem, let us see what private initiative can achieve. Since banks themselves are the primary victims of runs and panics, they have a strong incentive to find a solution. Historically, banks have done much to reduce the chances of runs and panics and to minimize the harm if they do occur.

The Clearinghouse Associations

The failure of one bank, because it reduces confidence in banks in general, can trigger runs on other banks. Such contagion gives banks a strong incentive to organize into an association that will monitor the behavior of individual members. Indeed, before government regulation replaced it, such self-regulation was common among banks.

clearinghouse association

An association of banks in a city, formed to facilitate clearing.

The vehicle for this self-regulation was generally the **clearinghouse association**. As we saw in Chapter 2, clearinghouses were set up for quite a different purpose. Once in existence, however, they provided a natural framework for self-regulation.

A bank could join the clearinghouse only by satisfying certain standards. Membership in the clearinghouse increased public confidence in a bank and made it easier for the bank

---

[11] Simple "stop-loss" strategies, sometimes called "closet portfolio insurance" achieve much the same goal.

[12] In 1987, portfolio insurers were far from being "everyone": the amount of stock in portfolio insurance programs was $60 billion to $90 billion—only 2 to 3% of the total. However, this seems to have been a large enough proportion to cause problems.

to attract deposits. This advantage, plus the advantage of actual clearing, made the costs of membership worthwhile.

The first U.S. clearinghouse was established in New York City in 1854. To become a member, a bank had to have a minimum capital of $500,000 (a large sum in those days), and it had to open its books to the clearinghouse for scrutiny. The success of the New York Clearing House led to its imitation in most major cities: by 1913, there were 162 clearinghouses in the United States.

Mutual Aid and the Provision of Liquidity.   The clearinghouse did more than just monitor its members. In a crisis, it would organize mutual aid. If the problem was local—a run on one or a few banks—the clearinghouse would arrange for other members to lend reserves to the bank or banks under pressure. Because of the fear of contagion, the other banks were more than willing to help.[13]

If the crisis developed into a full-fledged panic, the clearinghouse would act to defend the system as a whole. Its first step would be to substitute the credit of the association as a whole for the credit of individual banks. Information about individual banks would be suppressed (individual banks were not permitted to publish their balance sheets). Instead, the balance sheet of the whole association would be made public to indicate both the system's soundness and its unity.

If this failed to restore confidence, the clearinghouse would increase the liquidity of member banks by means of **loan certificates**. Issued to member banks against collateral, these certificates could be used in place of cash to clear payments between banks.[14] Their use freed the banks' cash reserves for payment to the public. Some certificates were even issued in small denominations and used by the public as currency. During the panic of 1907, some $500 million in cash substitutes was created by the clearinghouses, a significant addition to the $3,000 million of currency then in existence.[15]

loan certificates
Certificates issued by clearinghouse association to be used in settling interbank payments.

Suspension of Convertibility.   In severe panics, the measures just described proved inadequate. The loss of reserves continued to the point that banks were no longer able to convert their deposits into currency. In such a situation, the clearinghouse would declare a partial **suspension of convertibility** for all banks in the association. Cash withdrawals by depositors would be restricted to a certain amount per day (except for employers who needed cash to pay wages).

Despite the suspension, payments by check could be made in the normal fashion, and the clearing process proceeded normally. During a suspension bank deposits usually traded

suspension of convertibility
A temporary refusal by banks to convert deposits into cash on demand.

---

[13] The Herstatt crisis in the Eurodollar market (see Chapter 7) provides a more recent example of mutual aid. When Herstatt failed, depositors rushed to withdraw funds from the smaller Eurodollar banks and to redeposit them with larger banks. The latter immediately lent the money back to the smaller banks through the interbank market. This prevented any liquidity problems for the banks facing large withdrawals.

[14] In the event that a bank failed, the other members of the clearinghouse would be required to cover any losses on the certificates issued to it. So collateral was scrutinized carefully. The interest rate on loan certificates was set high enough to encourage banks to repay as soon as possible.

[15] The idea of loan certificates was extended by the Aldrich–Vreeland Act of 1908. This authorized groups of 10 or more national banks to form national currency associations that could issue actual currency in an emergency. This arrangement forestalled a panic in 1914.

at a discount against currency. That is, if you paid by check, you had to pay more than if you paid in cash.[16]

The suspension of convertibility was certainly harmful. It reduced public confidence in the banking system by casting doubts on its ability to provide liquidity when liquidity was most needed. However, it was the lesser of evils. Without a suspension, the banking system would have been wiped out, doing much greater harm.

Private Guarantees

Of course, prevention is better than cure. Rather than dealing with runs and panics when they occur, it is better to prevent them from happening in the first place. One way to do this is to guarantee depositors against loss. If depositors know they are protected, they will have no reason to take part in a run.

State Deposit Insurance Systems.   To this end, the State of New York organized a Safety Fund for its banks in 1829. Banks were to make contributions that would be used to guarantee creditors if a member bank failed. In essence, banks were to provide a mutual guarantee of one another's liabilities.[17] The fund initially performed well, weathering the nationwide panic of 1837. But some large failures in 1841 wiped out most of its reserves, and it was gradually phased out.

Similar schemes were tried in several other states, with varying success. In Vermont and Michigan they failed; in Indiana, Michigan, and Ohio, they performed reasonably well. With the establishment of national banks in 1863, guarantee schemes sponsored by the states largely died out.

Problems with Private Guarantees.   Private guarantees suffer from three serious problems. The first is that they are not sufficiently credible: the guarantees are backed by limited reserves, which people know can easily be wiped out by a large loss. This was demonstrated with the New York Safety Fund and again more recently, with state-sponsored insurance in several states.

The Ohio deposit insurance agency covered $4.1 billion in deposits with a reserve fund of $123 million. In 1985, the failure of a single Ohio thrift, Home State Savings of Cincinnati, wiped out the fund. In Rhode Island, a $14 million loss from the failure of a single $25 million bank, Heritage Loan and Investment Co., wiped out the insurance fund. Seeing the guarantee funds were insolvent, depositors ran on the other banks the funds covered, even though these banks were sound.[18]

---

[16] In the national banking era, 1863–1914, three major panics ended in suspensions (1873, 1893, 1907–1908). In 1884 and 1890 the clearinghouses succeeded in containing panics without a suspension.

[17] The designer of the Safety Fund, Joshua Forman, modeled it on the practice of Hong Kong merchants, who provided a mutual guarantee of one another's debts. It is because state-sponsored plans generally rely on this principle of mutual guarantee that we include them here among "private" solutions.

[18] Home State failed as a result of losses on repos with E.S.M. Government Securities: see Chapter 12. See box in Chapter 3 ("The New England Banking Crisis of 1991") for more on the Rhode Island crisis.

The second problem with private guarantee funds is that they cannot guarantee liquidity. When a bank fails, depositors do not usually lose a large part of their money. Typically, the loss is no more than 5% to 10%. The real danger for depositors is the potential loss of use of their deposits while the bank is liquidated. When failures are widespread, private guarantee funds lack the resources to pay off depositors quickly. Even if the state stands behind the fund and pays losses out of tax revenue, the process takes time. For example, depositors in Rhode Island did eventually get most of their money back, but some had to wait years.

The third problem with guarantees—whether private or public—is our old friend moral hazard. If an institution's liabilities are guaranteed, its creditors have little reason to monitor it. Its owners can therefore take on greater risk without penalty. Their doing so increases the rate of failure and, ultimately, can bankrupt the guarantor. Moral hazard problems played a significant part in the failure of state insurance funds. We shall have much more to say about moral hazard when we discuss federal deposit insurance later in the chapter.

A LENDER OF LAST RESORT

In addition to its role in regulation and supervision, the government can create institutions designed to enhance stability. We have seen that private attempts to create such institutions face three problems—credibility, liquidity, and moral hazard. The government has a significant advantage with respect to the first two problems but not, as we shall see, with respect to the third.

What gives the government its advantage is its almost unlimited ability to create money. If a government's liabilities are acceptable as money, then its promise to provide money is totally credible. Because the government can create as much money as it needs, it will never run out. Liquidity is not a problem either. The government can create as much money as necessary as quickly as necessary.

The government can use its ability to create money to provide the banking system with liquidity in a crisis. The institution that does this is known as a **lender of last resort**.

lender of last resort
A government-sponsored agency that provides liquidity to the financial system in a crisis, usually by creating money.

The Origins of the Lender of Last Resort

The idea of a lender of last resort developed in Britain in the nineteenth century.[19] Britain experienced a series of banking panics in the first half of that century. On several occasions the crisis was worsened by the reaction of the Bank of England.

The Bank of England, although then a private institution, had a privileged position. It acted as underwriter for government debt, and most of its assets were government bonds. In return for these favors to the government, it had been granted a monopoly of note issue in London and its vicinity, as well as other privileges. The size and safety of the Bank led other banks to hold a large part of their gold reserves with it. However, in times of crisis,

---

[19] In 1797, Sir Francis Baring described the Bank of England as a "dernier resort" to which all other banks should have recourse in an emergency.

rather than helping other banks by lending to them, the Bank of England had acted to protect its own reserves.

Following a particularly bad episode in 1866, Parliament passed new legislation that required the Bank of England to accept the responsibility of providing liquidity in a crisis. After this, there were no further panics in the United Kingdom. The Bank's actions stopped the development of panics in 1878, 1890, and 1914.[20]

Other countries soon adopted similar arrangements. By the end of the nineteenth century, most advanced economies had a central bank that played the role of lender of last resort.

What a Lender of Last Resort Should Do

The principles of operation of the Bank of England and other lenders of last resort were molded by the principles suggested by two British economists, Henry Thornton and Walter Bagehot. We can summarize these principles as follows:

1. The lender of last resort should lend only against good collateral.
2. It should accept all good collateral.
3. It should charge a penalty rate of interest on its loans.
4. These policies should be made known to the public.

Principle 1 makes it clear that the lender of last resort will help *illiquid* banks and not *insolvent* ones. A bank that is solvent has assets that are worth more than its deposits. It can therefore use these assets as collateral with the lender of last resort and borrow enough to pay off all its liabilities. A bank that is insolvent has assets worth less than its liabilities. It will therefore be unable to borrow enough to pay off all its liabilities. It will fail and its depositors will take a loss.

Principle 1 protects the lender of last resort against moral hazard. In the absence of the requirement for good collateral, a bank in trouble could always borrow enough to pay off its depositors. Its debt to its depositors would simply be replaced by a debt to the lender of last resort. Consequently, when the bank failed, it would be the lender of last resort rather than depositors that took the loss. Because depositors would never take a loss when a bank failed, they would have no reason to monitor their banks. Relieved of the need to reassure depositors, banks could take on more risk in the pursuit of higher returns and pass on the cost to the lender of last resort. The collateral requirement rules out this sort of behavior.

Principle 2 ensures that no solvent bank will be allowed to fail for lack of liquidity. Rather than having to liquidate its assets at fire-sale prices, a solvent bank will be able to borrow against them at their fair market value. Realizing this, depositors who know a bank is sound have no reason to withdraw their deposits, even if uninformed depositors do so. This makes a run less unlikely. Moreover, if there is a run on a sound bank, no harm will be done.

---

[20] We have already seen that consolidation of the banking system in the United Kingdom was simultaneously making it less subject to panics. Consolidation also made the job of the lender of last resort easier. It had to deal only with a few large institutions, with which it was well acquainted.

Principle 3 ensures that the lender of last resort really is a last resort. We have seen that managing liquidity is costly. If liquidity is readily available at low cost from the lender of last resort, why bother with expensive alternatives? If banks were to rely entirely on the lender of last resort for their liquidity, they would hold fewer liquid assets, and the inherent liquidity of the system would be reduced. If borrowing from the lender of last resort is expensive, banks will rely on their own resources for normal liquidity management; only banks with no other choice will go to the lender of last resort for a loan.

Principle 4 recognizes that to maximize the benefit of having a lender of last resort, the public needs to know it is there. Knowing that the lender of last resort is ready to provide support increases public confidence and lessens the chance of a panic. Any doubt about the lender of last resort's intentions or commitment reduces its value.

The Fed as Lender of Last Resort

By the end of the nineteenth century, the United States was the only developed country without a lender of last resort.[21] While banking panics had become a historical curiosity is most other countries, they continued to occur with some frequency in the United States. The panic of 1907 and the ensuing recession were particularly bad and led to an outcry for reform.

The Founding of the Federal Reserve System. After protracted debate and lengthy political bargaining, Congress passed the **Federal Reserve Act of 1913** to create the Federal Reserve System. What emerged was not created in the image of a strong European-style central bank. There was too much political opposition from populists fearful of concentrated power and from thousands of small banks fearful of stronger regulation. Rather, the Federal Reserve System was something much weaker and less centralized.

The Fed was created essentially as a network of government-run correspondent/clearinghouses. Twelve Federal Reserve Banks were set up across the country, with a coordinating Federal Reserve Board in Washington. The regional Banks were meant as safe repositories for the deposits of country banks. They were to replace the wicked New York correspondents that used the deposits of country banks to finance stock market "speculation."

Within the system, the regional Banks were given most of the power: the Board in Washington was weak. National banks were required to join the system, and it was hoped that state banks would become members voluntarily.[22]

The Fed was charged with providing an "elastic currency"—one that would satisfy the public's demand for converting bank money into currency in times of panic.[23] To help achieve this goal, the Fed was authorized to issue a new form of currency—Federal

---

[21] The first Bank of the United States, 1791–1811, and, even more so, Nicholas Biddle's second Bank, 1816–1836, had acted as central banks in terms of regulating the banking system. They had not, however, acted as lenders of last resort.

[22] The state banks were, however, unenthusiastic. Membership was expensive. It was also restrictive in terms of reserve requirements and allowable assets. Moreover, the correspondent system continued to provide a viable alternative for clearing and for the holding of liquid reserves.

[23] The elastic currency was also expected to help country banks meet the seasonal demand for currency associated with the harvest cycle: farmers liked to be paid for their crops in cash. The Fed was expected to accommodate this demand for currency by lending to farm banks.

Reserve notes. These notes were to replace the existing mixture of national bank notes and greenbacks. While Federal Reserve notes were convertible into gold on demand, it was hoped that backing by the "full faith and credit of the United States" would make them nearly as acceptable as gold itself.[24]

Member banks could borrow from the Fed against collateral. However, the only acceptable collateral was commercial bills.[25] The Fed's ability to lend was further restricted by reserve requirements imposed upon it. It had to hold gold reserves of at least 35% against its deposits and 40% against its notes (the rest could be either gold or commercial bills).[26]

The Fed's First Test.   The first serious test of the new system came in 1929, when the stock market crash set off a series of banking panics. The Fed failed this test dismally. While it did expand its lending to relieve the pressure, this expansion was far less than was needed. The Fed's failure was partly the result of confusion and inexperience. The division of authority between the regional Federal Reserve Banks and the Federal Reserve Board in Washington was unclear, and Fed officials lacked experience in managing a central bank during a crisis. However, the main reason for the Fed's failure were the restrictions on its inability to lend.

The linkage to gold was one problem. When Britain took the pound off the gold standard, there were fears the United States would follow. Foreigners rushed to convert their dollars into gold. To protect its gold reserves, the Fed raised interest rates (at higher interest rates, foreigners were more willing to leave their deposits in the United States). But the higher interest rates made it harder for banks to borrow.

The restriction of acceptable collateral to commercial bills was an even greater problem. Since commercial bills made up only a small part of many banks' assets, banks were unable to borrow as much from the Fed as they needed.

With the establishment of the Fed, the private arrangements that had moderated previous crises had been dismantled. When the Fed failed to provide the necessary support, banks failed in unprecedented numbers. Faith in the banking system sank to an all-time low.

Between 1929 and 1933 the public increased its holdings of currency by 50%, while checking deposits shrank by about a third. Banks responded to this pressure on their liquidity by increasing their own reserves from 15% of deposits in 1930 to 22% in 1932. The resulting contraction in the quantity of money led to falling prices and tight credit. The economy plunged into depression.

A Second Try.   The collapse of the banking system, and the failure of the Fed to arrest it, led to a wave of new banking legislation in the 1930s. The structure of the Fed was

---

[24] During the banking panics of the national banking era, the public had demanded conversion of deposits, but not of banknotes. Its confidence in the notes of national banks, backed as they were by government securities, had never been shaken.

[25] This restriction had its origin in the *commercial bills doctrine*: see Chapter 6.

[26] Not being run for profit, the Fed was expected to have, in normal times, significant excess reserves. It was therefore expected to be able to expand its lending in times of crisis.

altered. A new Board of Governors was set up in Washington and given clear control. The definition of acceptable collateral was expanded to include government securities and a broad range of bank assets. Convertibility into gold was suspended temporarily and then reestablished in a more limited form.[27]

Subsequent to these reforms, the Fed has performed its function of lender of last resort admirably. Whenever the liquidity of the banking system has been threatened, the Fed has lent freely.

For example, in 1974, Franklin National failed with a large amount of NCDs out-standing. As a result, the NCD market dried up: the premium over T-bills increased from 45 basis points to 470 b.p., and there was a danger that some banks would not be able to borrow at all. The Fed immediately increased its own lending to replace the funds that banks were temporarily unable to borrow in the money market. Similarly, in the failures of Continental Illinois and the Bank of New England, the Fed acted quickly and decisively to provide the needed liquidity.[28]

The Discount Window

As lender of last resort, the Fed stands ready to lend against suitable collateral to banks in trouble. In addition, it also makes a variety of nonemergency loans. **Adjustment credit** is available to banks having temporary difficulty in meeting their reserve requirements; such loans are usually for only a few days. **Extended credit** is available for longer periods to small institutions with seasonal demands for credit and poor access to the money market—for example, small agricultural banks and small banks in regions of tourism. Extended credit is also available to banks in trouble. For example, after the initial crisis was resolved, the Fed continued to lend to Continental Illinois for several months in the form of extended credit.

Borrowing from the Fed is called borrowing at the **discount window**. The rate the Fed charges is called the **discount rate**. As we saw in Chapter 6, banks used to lend by dis-counting commercial paper—buying it at a discount below its face values. A central bank would lend by *re*discounting such paper—buying it from the banks at a further discount. Today, most lending by the Fed is in the form of an *advance*—a straightforward loan secured by collateral. Despite the change in form, it is still called discount lending.

As collateral, banks today usually offer U.S. government securities: the book-entry system makes them particularly easy to transfer back and forth.[29] However, the Fed will accept almost any asset if necessary—including overseas assets and even a bank's build-ings. Generally, discount loans are overcollateralized.

adjustment credit
Short-term loan from the Fed to help a bank meet reserve requirements.

extended credit
Longer term loan from the Fed to help a bank having a seasonal need for credit or to a bank in trouble.

discount window
Borrowing from the Fed is called borrowing at the discount window.

discount rate
The rate charged by the Fed on discount loans.

---

[27] The official price of an ounce of gold was raised from $20.67 to $35.00, and only foreign central banks had the right to convert their dollars into gold (currency held by residents of the United States was no longer convertible into gold). At the same time, private individuals and institutions were required to sell any gold coin or bullion they owned to the government. The external convertibility of the dollar was ended in 1971. Since 1975 U.S. residents have again been allowed to own gold.

[28] As we shall see in Chapter 20, the Fed has also responded to crises in the securities markets.

[29] See Chapter 12 on the book-entry system.

Access to the discount window used to be restricted to banks that were members of the Federal Reserve System. However, in 1978 the right to borrow was extended to foreign banks operating in the United States, and in 1980 it was extended to all depository institutions.[30]

Discount loans are made by the individual Federal Reserve banks. Formally, each bank's board of directors sets its own discount rate, subject to approval by the board of governors. In reality, the board sets the rate, which is the same for all banks. The basic rate applies to all adjustment credit and to seasonal extended credit. The Fed usually charges more for emergency extended credit.[31]

The Fed generally sets the discount rate at a level that trails market rates, but with a lag. Contrary to the third of our four principles for a lender of last resort, the discount rate is usually below market rates. To prevent the borrowing of large amounts at this bargain price, the Fed rations the amount banks can borrow. It sets guidelines for maximum borrowing, and a bank that exceeds these guidelines can expect unwelcome attention from bank regulators.

GOVERNMENT GUARANTEES OF BANKS

The failure of the Fed in the 1930s, besides leading to reform of the Fed itself, also opened the door to a proposal that had been around since the turn of the century—federal deposit insurance.

The Introduction of Federal Deposit Insurance

Because of the dismal experience with state deposit insurance in the 1920s, the federal scheme faced considerable opposition. The Roosevelt administration and many legislators were deeply concerned about moral hazard. No other country had ever had deposit insurance: none had thought it necessary or desirable.

The large banks, too, were solidly opposed to deposit insurance. They saw it as a political scam designed to make the sound banks (them) pay the losses of the unsound (the small banks).

Given these obvious flaws, who supported federal deposit insurance? Its supporters were mainly those who wished to preserve the existing banking structure. They understood that federal deposit insurance was the only way to prevent the disappearance of the small unit bank.

Because of economies of scale, large banks are safer than small ones. This gives them a substantial competitive advantage in attracting deposits. But deposit insurance makes safety irrelevant for depositors and nullifies this competitive advantage. Since safety is no

---

[30] Access to the discount window was extended to these institutions as compensation for making them subject to the Fed's reserve requirements. Before 1980, S&Ls relied on the Federal Home Loan Banks for emergency credit and credit unions relied on the Central Liquidity Facility. Since neither of these institutions can itself create money, ability to help in an emergency ultimately depends on ability to borrow from the Fed. Both institutions continue to exist, but they are now somewhat redundant.

[31] There is a 1% premium after the first 60 days and a 2% premium after 150 days. For longer periods, the Fed usually charges a floating rate at a markup over a market rate.

longer a concern, depositors are just as happy placing their money with a small bank as with a large one.

Between 1886 and 1933, some 150 separate proposals for federal guarantees or deposit insurance came before Congress. All failed. However in 1933, deposit insurance finally passed. Its passage partly reflected the desperation of the times. But it also reflected the political skill of its main supporter, Representative Steagall of Alabama, chairman of the House Committee on Banking and Currency.

Federal Deposit Insurance Corporation (FDIC)

The federal agency set up to insure bank deposits.

The new legislation set up a **Federal Deposit Insurance Corporation (FDIC)** to insure deposits at banks. Legislation in 1934 established a parallel institution, the **Federal Savings and Loan Insurance Corporation** (FSLIC—pronounced "fizlik") to insure deposits at savings and loans.

Were the Opponents of Deposit Insurance Right?

Federal Savings and Loan Insurance Corporation (FSLIC)

The federal agency set up to insure S&L deposits; replaced by the SAIF in 1989.

The opponents of deposit insurance argued that it would encourage bad banking and that ultimately it would prove a burden to the taxpayer. Yet for many years it seemed they were wrong. For the first time in the history of American banking, there were no bank runs and no banking panics. Few banks failed, and insurance premiums fell steadily in the light of favorable experience.

Then, in the 1980s and 1990s, all the dire predictions of the opponents of deposit insurance came true. Bank failures rose to epidemic proportions. In some ways, these failures surpassed those of the Great Depression. While many more banks failed in the 1930s, the *magnitude* of failures was much greater in the 1980s and 1990s. This is true both in terms of the absolute size of the failed banks' assets and in their size relative to total bank assets. And the troubles of the commercial banks, serious though they were, were small compared to those of the savings and loan industry. Of the 4,000 S&Ls that existed at the start of the 1980s, almost half had failed by 1992. The cost to the taxpayer of the S&L bailout came to some $220 billion.

Clearly, deposit insurance has some serious problems. But before we can understand what went wrong with deposit insurance, we need to understand how it works. What does deposit insurance cover? What does it cost? What happens when a bank fails?

Bank Insurance Fund (BIF)

The section of the FDIC that insures deposits at commercial banks and savings banks.

How Deposit Insurance Works

In 2000, the Federal Deposit Insurance Corporation insured deposits at some 10,000 depository institutions. The FDIC manages two insurance funds. The first, the **Bank Insurance Fund (BIF)**, insured deposits at some 8,600 commercial banks, savings banks, and insured branches of foreign banks; these institutions held some $2.3 trillion of insured deposits. A second fund, the **Savings Association Insurance Fund (SAIF)**, insured deposits at some 1,300 S&Ls; these held some $700 billion in insured deposits. SAIF is the successor agency to FSLIC, which, as we shall see, became insolvent as a result of the S&L crisis.[32]

Savings Association Insurance Fund (SAIF)

The section of the FDIC that insures deposits at savings and loans.

---

[32] A separate federal agency—the National Credit Union Share Insurance Fund (NCUSIF)—insures deposits at credit unions.

Individual depositors are insured up to a maximum of $100,000 in principal and accrued interest.[33] This provides complete coverage to 99% of all depositors. However, it covers only three-quarters of the amount of total deposits. This is because large deposits, only partly covered by insurance, account for a large fraction of the total. Most large deposits are held at large banks. Consequently uninsured deposits account for 50% of total deposits for banks with more than $5 billion in assets, but less than 10% of total deposits for banks with less than $100 million in assets.

Insured institutions pay a premium on *all* their deposits, even those that are not covered by insurance. This means that large banks, which have a large proportion of uninsured deposits, pay significantly more for their insurance per dollar of insured deposit. As we shall see, this is not as unjust as it seems, since uninsured depositors at large banks do receive a measure of protection.

The deposit insurance agencies are required to accumulate out of premiums a reserve fund equal to no less than 1.25% of the deposits they insure. In 2000, the two reserve funds totaled some $42 billion—more than meeting this requirement. The level of premiums banks must pay depends on the size of the reserve fund: once it reaches the required level, premiums are reduced.

risk-related premiums
Deposit insurance premiums based on regulators' assessment of an institution's risk of failure.

Given the overall level of premiums, the premium an individual bank pays is **risk related**. In 2001, a well-capitalized bank in the safest supervisory category was paying no premium at all: there were roughly 9,000 such banks. In contrast, an undercapitalized bank in the riskiest supervisory category was paying a premium of 27¢ per $100 of deposits: there were only six such banks.

What Happens When a Bank Fails?

To understand what happens when a bank fails let us consider a fictitious example—Jefferson Savings Bank. Jefferson's balance sheet is as follows (assets are listed at market value)[34]:

Assets	$100m	Deposits	
		Insured	$40m
		Uninsured	80m

Jefferson is clearly insolvent: the market value of its assets, $100 million, is less than the total $120 million of its deposits.

The FDIC monitors the banks and thrifts that it insures. Examiners visit each institution periodically to go over its books. Seeing Jefferson's balance sheet, the FDIC examiners decide it must be closed.[35] Once an insolvent institution is closed, there are two

---

[33] The ceiling applies to the total of all deposits held by an individual at a given bank. Coverage may be increased in various ways, by using joint accounts, trust accounts, IRAs, and so on.

[34] See Chapter 18 for a discussion of the distinction between market and book value.

[35] They cannot do this themselves, however. The authority to close an institution rests with the entity that gave it a charter. In Jefferson's case this is the state. So the FDIC asks the state banking commissioner to close it down.

Ordinary corporations that are insolvent can continue to operate. Only when their obligations come due and they actually default can their creditors force bankruptcy. Banks can be closed by regulators as soon as they become insolvent: actual default is not necessary.

alternative ways for the FDIC to proceed—by payout or by purchase and assumption.[36] Let us see how each of these would work in the case of Jefferson.

payout
Resolution of a failed bank by paying off insured depositors and liquidating the bank's assets.

A Payout.   In a **payout**, Jefferson is liquidated and ceases to exist. The FDIC pays off its insured depositors, up to the insurance limit, for a total of $40 million. It then sells the bank's assets and uses the proceeds to pay off the bank's uninsured creditors. These include the owners of uninsured deposits and the FDIC itself. The FDIC has become a creditor by "purchasing" the $40 million in insured deposits.

The $100 million realized on the assets is divided *pro rata* among the creditors: everyone receives

$$\frac{\$100 \text{ million}}{\$120 \text{ million}} = 0.83$$

of the amount owed, or 83¢ on the dollar.

The FDIC itself receives 0.83 × $40 million = $33.3 million. Therefore the cost to the FDIC of resolving the failure through a payout is $40 million − $33.3 million = $6.7 million.

purchase and assumption (P&A)
Resolution of a failed bank by arranging its purchase by a healthy bank.

A Purchase and Assumption.   If Jefferson is worth something as a going concern, that value is lost in a liquidation. If another bank is willing to pay something for Jefferson's "franchise"—its customer base, its location, its trained personnel—then that payment will help the FDIC offset the costs of the failure. In a **purchase and assumption (P&A)**, the FDIC arranges for another bank to purchase Jefferson and to *assume* (take over) its liabilities. Banks interested in purchasing Jefferson submit bids to the FDIC. It accepts the highest bid, for $10 million, from Hamilton National Bank.

Hamilton takes over Jefferson's assets as well as its liabilities. The FDIC pays Hamilton the value of the liabilities, $120 million, less the market value of those assets, $100 million, less the purchaser's bid, $10 million, for a total of $10 million. Since the true value of Jefferson's assets is uncertain, the FDIC guarantees Hamilton against further losses on these loans.[37]

The cost to the FDIC is higher here than in a payout, and this is typically the case with a P&A. However, the overall loss is less ($10 million vs $20 million), because the value of the bank as a going concern is preserved. The beneficiaries are the uninsured depositors, who now avoid a loss altogether.

Which Method to Use?   How does the FDIC decide which method to use to resolve a bank failure? A payout is generally the less expensive route for the FDIC because the lost

---

[36] There is actually a third, less common alternative, a "bridge bank." This is a temporary solution in which the FDIC essentially takes over the bank. In the end, this usually results in a payout or a purchase and assumption. Occasionally, the banks may return to normal operation.

[37] This is known as a "whole-bank" P&A. In a "clean-bank" P&A, Hamilton would take over only Jefferson's liabilities, with the FDIC paying it their cash value, $120 million, less the amount of Hamilton's bid, $10 million, for a total of $110 million. The FDIC would then liquidate Jefferson's $100 million in assets and keep the proceeds. Although the net cost to the FDIC is the same in both versions, the whole-bank version ties up less of its resources because the FDIC does not have to take on and liquidate a $100 million of loans.

value of the failed bank's "franchise" is usually less than its uninsured liabilities. In a P&A, all liabilities of the failed bank are covered—uninsured deposits as well as insured, and nondeposit liabilities (Fed funds bought, for example) as well as deposits.

Cost, however, is not the only consideration, or even the main one. The purpose of deposit insurance is to protect the banking system. If the FDIC feels that liquidation, and the consequent losses to uninsured depositors and creditors, would shake public confidence in the banking system, it may prefer to bear the greater cost of a purchase and assumption.

Of course, a P&A is much more popular politically. Depositors and other creditors of the bank are delighted not to lose any money, and the taxpayer does not feel the cost as long as the reserve fund holds up. Even when the taxpayer does start to feel the cost, the pain is diffuse and it is not felt directly or immediately.

During most of its history, the FDIC has shown a preference for purchase and assumption. Of the 2,097 insured banks that failed between 1934 and 2000, only 603 were payouts.

THE U.S. DEPOSIT INSURANCE CRISIS

The remarkable thing about U.S. deposit insurance is how well it worked initially. The reason was that for 40 years after the establishment of federal deposit insurance, banking was a very safe business.

It was the period of "3-6-3" banking: bankers paid 3% for deposits, charged 6% on loans, and were out on the golf course by 3 P.M. Interest rates and exchange rates were stable, so there was little market risk. Because of branching restrictions, interest rate limits, and the segmentation of the financial system, there was little competitive pressure. In this stable and profitable environment, protected from competition, there was little reason to take chances. Banks played it safe, and very few failed.

Why Banks Became Riskier

All this began to unravel when the inflation of the late 1960s drove up interest rates. The restrictions that had protected banks from competition now put them at a disadvantage relative to the money market and other types of intermediary. As Regulation Q crumbled, banks' cost of funds rose steadily.

In the newly competitive environment, growth was essential: economies of scale became the key to survival. Growth was also easier than it had been, since banks could now tap the money market for funds.

As we saw in Chapter 18, the imperative to expand and the higher cost of funds led many banks to lower their lending standards. Large banks lent heavily to a variety of high-risk borrowers—LDCs, the energy industry, developers of commercial real estate, and LBOs. Small banks were eager to buy participations.

Increasing credit risk was matched by increasing market risk. When interest rate and exchange rate volatility rose sharply in the 1970s, many institutions were vulnerable and unprepared. Balance sheets—particularly those of the thrifts—had long been exposed to market risk. But, because actual fluctuations had been small, the danger had remained hidden. Bankers were often unaware of the risks and ignorant of methods of risk management.

Of course, increased volatility was not only a danger, it was also an opportunity. As banks saw their traditional business of intermediation become less profitable under the pressure of competition, they turned increasingly to trading profits as a way to boost their earnings.

As we saw in Chapter 18, Franklin National tried in 1974 to recoup its loan losses with a gamble on interest rates and exchange rates. The gamble was unsuccessful, and Franklin failed—the largest bank to fail since the Depression. The rise in interest rates in 1979 caught another large bank, First Pennsylvania, that had been funding a large bond portfolio with short-term money. That bailout cost the FDIC $1.5 billion.

The Moral Hazard Problem

Risk Taking without Deposit Insurance.   Deposit insurance played a key role in this increase in risk taking by banks. When a bank takes on more risk without deposit insurance, its deposits become riskier. Naturally, depositors expect to be compensated for the increase in risk. If they are not, they withdraw their funds. Consequently, if the bank takes on more risk, the cost of its funds increases in proportion. It is left no better off than it was before.[38]

Risk Taking with Deposit Insurance.   *With* deposit insurance, however, the story is very different. Since deposit insurance protects them from loss, depositors are not concerned by the bank's risk taking. As far as they are concerned, the bank's deposits are a risk-free liability of the government. As a result, the bank does not need to compensate depositors for the increased risk. Therefore, increased risk taking raises the bank's (risk-adjusted) profits.

The loser of course is the FDIC and, ultimately, the taxpayer. By taking on more risk, the bank increases the expected cost to the FDIC of the deposit insurance, but it does not pay a higher premium. This is the moral hazard problem that lies at the heart of deposit insurance.

The Importance of the Method of Failure Resolution.   The severity of the moral hazard problem depends on how the FDIC resolves failures. With a payout, uninsured depositors and other creditors stand to take a loss. With a purchase and assumption, they do not. If uninsured depositors and creditors expect a payout, they have every incentive to monitor the bank's risk taking. If they expect a purchase and assumption, they have no incentive to monitor.

The FDIC Cracks Down

Until the late 1970s, the FDIC had largely resolved failures with purchases and assumptions. Depositors rarely took a loss. For example, no depositor at Franklin or First Pennsylvania lost a cent. However, as failures increased and the FDIC's losses mounted, it became alarmed. Citing the need for greater "market discipline," it increasingly resorted to

---

[38] This is, essentially, an application of the Modigliani–Miller theorem (see note 12 in Chapter 5).

payouts. Depositors did indeed take losses in the failures of several small banks. The big question, of course, was, What would the FDIC do if a large bank failed?

Penn Square.   The answer came with the collapse of Penn Square of Oklahoma City in July 1982. Penn Square was a typical product of its times. In 5 years, its assets had grown from $30 million to over $500 million. Some 80% of its loans were energy related. In addition to its own lending, Penn Square had sold $2.1 billion of participations to other banks—over $200 million to Chase, $400 million to Seafirst, and $1 billion to Continental Illinois. Regulators had detected problems with Penn Square's loans (possibly involving fraud) as early as 1980, but it had taken 2 more years for extensive defaults to drive the bank under. Most of its participations also proved to be bad.

Rather than arrange a purchase and assumption, the FDIC decided on a payout.[39] Uninsured depositors—among them small banks, savings and loans, and credit unions—took a substantial loss. Losses to uninsured depositors, who held over half the bank's deposits, were estimated at over $38 million. The lesson was well learned. As a result of Penn Square, large uninsured depositors became much more nervous.

The Run on Conti.   The consequences of the new market discipline were felt 2 years later in the run on Continental Illinois (see Chapter 18). Conti was unusually dependent on uninsured deposits and liabilities: they amounted to 75% of its funding. Conti had been accumulating losses for several years (Penn Square's participations were among the largest).

When rumors spread on May 11, 1984, that the bank was about to succumb, there was a "quiet run." Overnight lenders declined to roll over their lending. The Fed had no alternative but to convert Conti's $3.5 billion daylight overdraft into a discount loan.[40] Conti continued to lose deposits as the depositors remained uncertain about what would happen if the bank were closed. Even the FDIC's declaration that it would guarantee all liabilities failed to reassure depositors. The FDIC's declaration was vague on specifics. For example, would interest be covered as well as principal? In July, unable to find a purchaser, the FDIC took over the bank.

Too Big to Fail.   The "get-tough" policy had proven a failure. First, increased market discipline had a cost—a greater chance of a bank run. This defeated the main purpose of deposit insurance, which is to prevent bank runs. Second, when it came to the crunch, regulators did not carry through on their threat. Whatever they had said in advance, when a really large bank failed, they did bail out all its creditors.[41]

The Comptroller of the Currency, the principal regulator of national banks, accepted defeat. In testimony to Congress in September 1984 he declared that the 11 largest banks

---

[39] The FDIC may have had little choice. Oklahoma's branching restrictions made it hard to find a purchaser, and possible liability in lawsuits arising from alleged criminal violations made the future costs of a purchase and assumption highly uncertain.

[40] See Chapter 8 on daylight overdraft.

[41] This is an example of a problem called *time inconsistency*. A threatens B that if B does X, A will do Y. Y hurts B, but is also costly to A. If B does X anyhow, A will not gain anything from carrying through on the threat: it will be too late to influence B and it will be costly to A. Since B knows this, the threat is not credible.

too-big-to-fail doctrine

The doctrine under which very large banks are not allowed to fail because of the potential damage to the national economy.

would not be allowed to fail. In the event of insolvency, the FDIC would bail them out, and no depositor or creditor would take a loss. This policy came to be known as the **too-big-to-fail doctrine**.

Despite its capitulation on large banks, the FDIC continued to be tough in resolving the failures of small banks. It essentially set up a double standard. Predictably, deposits flowed out of small banks and into the large banks, where they implicitly enjoyed 100% insurance.

The S&L Mess: Moral Hazard at Its Worst

While the FDIC faced rising losses from bank failures, its problems were soon dwarfed by those of FSLIC. Mortgage lending had been heavily concentrated in the hands of thrifts, which had funded these loans primarily with short-term time deposits. When interest rates rose steeply in 1979, the industry took a beating.

Deregulation and Forbearance.   There were two regulatory responses to these losses. The first was *deregulation*. In an attempt to improve their diversification and reduce their exposure to interest rate risk, S&Ls were allowed to invest in a broad range of non-mortgage assets. The second response was **regulatory forbearance**. Thrifts that were in fact insolvent were allowed to continue in operation in the hope that somehow they would recover.

regulatory forbearance

A policy that allowed insolvent thrifts to continue to operate in the hope that they would recover.

Regulatory forbearance was essentially an attempt to brush the problem under the rug. Closing down all insolvent thrifts in 1982 would have bankrupted FSLIC. The $20 billion estimated cost was more than it had in its reserve fund. FSLIC's insolvency would have raised awkward questions about the competence of its administrators and of its overseers in Congress.

To put off the evil day, insolvent thrifts were allowed to continue in business, accumulating losses. By 1988, when the problem was finally addressed, the cost of closing all insolvent thrifts had risen to $70 billion, and it was still rising at the rate of $15 billion a year for each year of further delay.

When is a Bank Insolvent?   Since regulators are required by law to close an insolvent bank, forbearance required some creative accounting. Of course, insolvency, like beauty, is in the eyes of the beholder. It all depends on how you value assets and liabilities. The most sensible way is to use market values. However, accountants tend to rely on book or historical values. Even so, there are different accounting measures of a bank's capital.

The choice of method of accounting makes a big difference. One study estimated that in 1982 the net worth of the S&L industry was 3.7% of its assets according to the accounting method used by regulators. However, according to the most stringent accounting method the number was –12%.

Deregulation and Brokered Deposits.   If delay in closing insolvent thrifts provided the motive to gamble, deregulation provided the opportunity. The Garn–St Germain Act of 1982 allowed thrifts to take on commercial as well as residential mortgages, to make direct investments in real estate, and to invest in junk bonds. The problem was worst in states like Florida, California, and Texas, where state-chartered thrifts had almost unlimited freedom to invest in any asset they pleased.

Of course, permission to invest is not much use without the funds to finance the investment. No problem. Money brokers provided the funds. When deposit rates were deregulated in 1980, depositors began to look around for the best rates. With a large number of institutions and with rates constantly changing, the informational demands were substantial. This situation created a profit opportunity. For a commission, **money brokers** (usually securities firms) placed depositors' funds at the best available rate. In addition, to ensure coverage by deposit insurance, they broke up large sums into packages of no more than $100,000, which they then placed with different banks.[42]

money brokers
Brokers that place bank deposits for customers at the highest available yield.

brokered deposits
Deposits placed by money brokers.

Such **brokered deposits** proved a boon to small banks wishing to expand their lending. While they lacked the credit standing to borrow funds in the money market, they could borrow as much as they wanted through money brokers. All they had to do was offer a high enough rate. Empire Savings and Loan of Mesquite, Texas, provides a particularly dramatic example of the abuse of brokered deposits. Empire's deposits grew from $17 million to $309 million in the 2 years before it failed in March 1984. At the time that it failed, 85% of its deposits were brokered. Most of its loans involved real estate speculation in the Dallas market. Many of them were fraudulent. Empire's failure cost FSLIC over $160 million.[43]

Arbitraging Deposit Insurance. While outright fraud of this type was not infrequent, it accounted for a relatively small part of the total cost of the S&L debacle.[44] Most managers of S&Ls were honest. Some were incompetent, simply unable to deal with the complexity and risk of the new environment in which they found themselves. Others were all too competent. They exploited to the maximum the arbitrage possibility provided by federal deposit insurance: they borrowed at the risk-free rate and invested in high-return, high-risk assets.

Columbia Savings and Loan of Beverly Hills provides an extreme example. Between 1983 and 1989, Columbia grew from $1 billion in assets to $12 billion. Less than a sixth of its business was traditional mortgage lending funded by time deposits. The rest involved borrowed funds and marketable securities. A third of its assets consisted of junk bonds; a third of its liabilities, brokered deposits. This strategy proved highly profitable: its return on equity in 1986 was 46.3%. However, the collapse of the junk bond market wiped out most of its capital, and Columbia was seized by regulators in 1991.

Clearly, moral hazard was out of hand, and the resulting losses were casting doubt on the viability of federal deposit insurance. Before we look at the actions that were taken to resolve the crisis, let us take a look at how deposit insurance has worked in other countries.

---

[42] In 1984 the FDIC announced that in future payouts it would regard all deposits placed by the same broker as belonging to a single depositor. For example, if Merrill had placed $5 million at a failed bank (50 packages of $100,000, each belonging to a different client), the $100,000 limit would apply to the whole $5 million, rather than to each individual package. But the courts found this practice illegal, and the FDIC was forced to back down.

[43] When Penn Square failed, 25% of its deposits were brokered.

[44] S&L consultant Ely & Co. attributed about 3% of the loss to fraud.

DEPOSIT INSURANCE IN OTHER COUNTRIES

For many years the United States was the only country with formal deposit insurance. However, in recent decades most other developed economies have introduced it.[45] Exhibit 19.1 summarizes the features of various national schemes. Some are voluntary; others are compulsory. Some are administered by the government; others, by the banking industry. Some levy a fixed premium in advance; others levy an assessment after the event, based on losses. The members of the European Community are trying to standardize their deposit insurance as they integrate their banking systems (see Chapter 7); some have recently introduced deposit insurance for this reason.

As you can see, the United States has one of highest levels of fixed coverage and the highest premium. It also has the highest ratio of reserves to insured deposits, the most intensive government supervision, and a relatively large number of institutions licensed to offer insured deposits.

EXHIBIT 19.1   Deposit Insurance in Various Countries

Country	Year Established	Voluntary or Compulsory	Run by	Maximum Covered	Premium per $100 of Deposits
United States	1933	Compulsory	Government	$100,000	23–31¢ for all deposits
Canada	1967	Compulsory	Government	$52,000	10¢ for insured deposits
Japan	1971	Compulsory	Industry	$66,000	1.2¢ for insured deposits
Germany	1966	Voluntary	Industry	30% of bank's liable capital per depositor	3¢ for all deposits
United Kingdom	1982	Compulsory	Government	75% of deposit up to $43,000	Variable, up to 30¢ for all deposits
Italy	1987	Voluntary	Industry	100% of first $130,000; 75% of next $520,000	Assessment as needed
France	1980	Voluntary	Industry	$72,000	Assessment as needed, based on deposits
Switzerland	1984	Voluntary	Government	$21,000	Assessment as needed

Source: Congressional Budget Office (1990).

---

[45] It was not the first however. Czechoslovakia introduced deposit insurance in 1924, and this remained in effect until the country was invaded by Germany in 1938. Cuba introduced deposit insurance in 1952 to stop a flight of deposits to U.S. banks. However, most countries have introduced deposit insurance only relatively recently.

The Relative Merits of Different Schemes.   There is little evidence on which to assess the relative merits of different designs of deposit insurance scheme. Most schemes are relatively new. The only one to have experienced serious difficulties is that of Canada. When deposit insurance was introduced there in 1967, Canada had a highly concentrated banking system, consisting of a few very large banks. None had failed since 1923. Deposit insurance changed this structure by allowing small banks to compete for deposits, and several small banks were chartered in the 1970s. Between 1985 and 1989 most of these either failed or were absorbed by larger institutions.[46] Canada also experienced a "thrift crisis" in the early 1980s that paralleled that in the United States. The combined losses wiped out the insurance reserve fund.

The Danish system is often held up as an example. It relies on aggressive marking to market, high required equity ratios, and rapid closure if these cannot be met. Directors face criminal charges if they fail to report promptly any fall in value of the bank's assets. The banking system in Denmark, like others in Scandinavia, underwent a crisis in the 1990s. However, in Denmark the losses fell mainly on bank owners rather than on taxpayers as happened elsewhere.

The Minor Importance of Deposit Insurance in Most Countries.   Deposit insurance schemes in countries other than the United States play a relatively minor role in protecting the stability of the banking system. Runs and panics had ceased to be a problem in most developed economies by the end of the nineteenth century. This was largely the result of two developments. The first was consolidation of the banking system: the relatively few large banks were safer and, having more to lose, more willing to sacrifice for the good of the system. The second development was the establishment of an effective lender of last resort in these economies.

Deposit insurance agencies in most countries other than the United States play only a secondary role in resolving a banking crisis. In countries with concentrated banking systems, the doctrine of "too big to fail" applies to all or most banks. When a bank is in trouble, regardless of whether there is deposit insurance, the central bank and the other banks step in to prevent depositor losses.[47] As a result, banking problems rarely get to the point at which deposit insurance would have to come into play.

Given the minor role of deposit insurance in most countries, why have they bothered to introduce it? The motive seems largely to have been consumer protection rather than protection of the banking system. For example, British depositors lost money in the collapse of a number of small banks in 1979 and German depositors lost money in the Herrstat collapse in 1974. Both countries introduced deposit insurance soon after these episodes.

Why Deposit Insurance Has Mattered More in the United States.   Other countries managed without deposit insurance for so long and even now rely on it much less than the United States because their banking systems have been inherently much less unstable. The main reason for the greater instability of the U.S. banking system has been

---

[46] Most of these were in Alberta, which went through an energy slump much like that in Texas.

[47] In a fashion similar to the Continental bailout in the United States.

its structure. Fragmentation created instability by keeping banks small, by impairing diversification, and by leaving banks overly dependent on volatile sources of funding. Deposit insurance was introduced to prop up this inherently unstable structure. This worked for a while, but eventually the system collapsed under the pressure of moral hazard.

REDUCING THE COST OF MORAL HAZARD

The response to the deposit insurance crisis in the United States was twofold. The first response was structural reform of the banking system to reduce its inherent instability. The second was changing bank incentives to control moral hazard.

Structural Reform

A Treasury study, presented to Congress in February 1991, proposed removing both the restrictions on the geographic expansion of banks (allowing full interstate banking) and those on the range of bank activities (repeal of Glass–Steagall). As we saw in Chapters 6 and 7, these restrictions were in fact largely removed during the 1990s. As a result, the banking system of the United States has come to resemble much more those of other countries.

Of course, reforming the structure of U.S. banking is not a new idea. It came up in 1913 in the discussions that preceded the founding of the Fed. And it came up again in the debate over deposit insurance in the 1930s. However, on both occasions, Congress decided to bolster the safety net rather than reform the structure. In 1991, however, Congress finally bit the bullet.

Changing Bank Incentives

Although structural reform reduces the likelihood that banks will fail, the problem of moral hazard remains. As long as depositors know that they are guaranteed against loss, they are willing to lend to banks at the risk-free rate (a little higher if there is uncertainty about the guarantee), and they have little incentive to monitor. The bank, knowing this, can exploit the guarantee to take a higher risk, higher return position. While government guarantees of banks in other countries are less formal than they are in the United States, guarantees of any kind create the same problem of moral hazard.

Government Guarantees and Bank Capital. By the 1980s it was clear that governments had to protect themselves against the moral hazard problem. If we see this as an insurance problem, the basic method insurance companies use to control moral hazard is to make sure that the insured participates in the loss. For example, if you have to pay the first $500 of the cost of an accident, you will drive more carefully. Applying this idea to government guarantees, the more the owners and managers of a bank bear the losses themselves, the less likely they will be to take on excessive risk.

The exposure of the owners of a bank to loss is measured by the bank's equity ratio. As we saw in Chapter 5, reducing the equity ratio (increasing leverage) increases ROE. However, in the absence of government guarantees, reducing the equity ratio also has a cost. It makes depositors nervous. They demand a higher return on deposits and are more likely to run on the bank.

With government guarantees, any increased risk is borne by the government, so depositors stop caring about a bank's equity ratio. Not surprisingly, then, banks respond to government guarantees by lowering their equity ratios. For example, after deposit insurance was introduced in the United States in the 1930s, equity ratios fell steadily: see Exhibit 19.2. In principle, the government can compensate for this tendency by requiring banks to raise their equity ratios. Bearing more of the losses themselves, banks will be more careful. This should reduce the exposure of the government to losses.

The Problem of the "Level Playing Field."   As the condition of the banks in many countries deteriorated in the 1980s, regulators became alarmed and began to pressure banks to raise their equity ratios. However, with increased international competition among banks from different countries, there was some worry that a country imposing stricter capital standards would put its own banks at a competitive disadvantage.

EXHIBIT 19.2   Commercial Bank Equity Ratios

Source: Historical Statistics of the United States; Statistical Abstract of the United States.

As a result, regulators from the United States and 12 other major countries came together to frame uniform capital standards that would apply to all their banks. These standards were formulated under the auspices of the Bank for International Settlements (BIS), an international clearing bank for central banks, and were adopted in November 1988. Originally intended only for internationally active banks in the major economies, the BIS standards have since been adopted by bank regulators in most countries throughout the world.

The BIS Capital Standards

BIS standards
International capital standards adopted under the auspices of the Bank for International Settlements.

The **BIS standards** set requirements for two categories of capital—Tier 1 capital and total capital. The categories are defined as follows

- **Tier 1 capital** is the book value of stock plus retained earnings.
- **Tier 2 capital** is the sum of loan-loss reserves and subordinated debt.
- **Total capital** is Tier 1 capital plus Tier 2 capital.

Tier 1 capital
The book value of stock plus retained earnings.

Subordinated debt is long-term debt that, in the event of insolvency, is paid off only after depositors and other creditors have been paid. It therefore provides depositors and other creditors with the same sort of protection against insolvency as does equity.[48]

The requirement for each category of capital is based on the amount of a bank's **risk-weighted assets**. This is a weighted sum of the value of different types of asset, each weighted according to its credit risk. The less risky an asset, the lower its weighting. From January 1, 1993, banks were required to have Tier 1 capital of at least 4% of risk-adjusted assets and total capital of at least 8%.

Tier 2 capital
The sum of loan-loss reserves and subordinated debt.

Exhibit 19.3 shows the weights for some typical assets and the amounts of Tier 1 and total capital that would be required for each $100 million of the asset.

Total capital
The sum of Tier 1 capital and Tier 2 capital.

Off-balance-sheet commitments are included in the total of risk-adjusted assets. Each off-balance-sheet item is converted into a "credit equivalent" of an on-balance-sheet item. For example, a standby letter of credit (SLC) is counted in full on the grounds that it exposes the bank to the same default risk as a loan of the same amount.

subordinated debt
Long-term debt that, in the event of insolvency, is paid off only after depositors and other creditors have been paid.

EXHIBIT 19.3 Risk-Weighted Capital Requirements on Some Assets

Asset	Risk Weight	Risk-Weighted Value of $100m of the Asset	Tier 1 Capital Required	Total Capital Required
Cash	0	0	0	0
Loans	1.0	$100m	$4.0m	$8.0m
Government securities	0	0	0	0
Mortgages	0.5	$50m	$2.0m	$4.0m
Interbank deposits	0.2	$20m	$0.8m	$1.6m

risk-weighted assets
An index of the value of a bank's assets, weighting each category by a risk weight between 0 and 1.

---

[48] Some S&Ls sold $1,000 subordinated notes over the counter to their retail customers as a kind of high-yield "savings account" without making clear that the notes were not deposits and that they were not insured.

The Leverage Requirement.   In addition to the BIS requirement, U.S. regulators impose a separate **leverage requirement**. This is based on total assets. Total assets are simply the unweighted sum of all balance sheet assets: off-balance-sheet items do not count. Regulators require a minimum ratio of Tier 1 capital to total assets of 3%. Depend-ing on asset quality, regulators they may impose a higher requirement, ranging from 4% to 6%. There is no leverage requirement for total capital.[49]

A bank must meet whichever of the two standards—BIS or leverage—is the more stringent.

An Example of Calculating Capital Requirements.   To see how the standards work, consider the assets of First National Bank:

Cash	$100m
Federal funds sold	200m
Government securities	500m
Loans	1200m

First National also has $1 billion of SLCs outstanding to issuers of commercial paper.
Using Exhibit 19.3, the contribution of the balance sheet to risk-adjusted assets is

$$(0 \times \$100m) + (0.2 \times \$200m) + (0 \times \$500m) + (1 \times \$1,200m) = \$1,240m$$

The SLCs have a weight of 1.0, just like commercial loans, and therefore we add another $1 billion to the total. Total risk-adjusted assets therefore is $2,240 million.
First National must have at least

$$0.04 \times \$2,240m = \$89.6m$$

in Tier 1 capital and at least

$$0.08 \times \$2,240m = \$199.2m$$

in total capital.
To calculate First National's leverage requirement, we need to add up its total assets:

$$\$100m + \$200m + \$500m + \$1,200m = \$2,000m$$

Off-balance-sheet items do not count, so First National's $1 billion in SLCs adds nothing to the total. Suppose regulators set First National's leverage requirement at 4%. This means it must have Tier 1 capital of

$$0.04 \times \$2,000m = \$80m$$

---

[49] Responding to pressure from the FDIC, which is concerned that the standards are not tough enough, the Fed has proposed that only the healthiest banks (about one in five of all banks) be allowed a leverage requirement of 3%.

For First National, the BIS requirement is more stringent than the leverage requirement—$89.6 million vs $80 million—so it must have $89.6 million of Tier 1 capital. It must also have $199.2 million of total capital (only the BIS standards matters for total capital).

THE CONSEQUENCES OF TIGHTER REGULATION

Government guarantees of the banking system have created a moral hazard problem. To protect themselves from moral hazard, governments have introduced tighter regulation, mainly in the form of capital standards. These new capital standards have in turn created a whole new set of incentives. In response to these new incentives, banks have changed the way they do business. And, because banks are so important, this change has affected the structure of the entire financial system.

Banks Respond to the New Capital Requirements

Of course, the whole point of the capital requirements was to change bank behavior. The intention was to push banks towards safer assets—those with a lower risk weighting. And this is what happened, at least initially.

A Shift to Low-Weighted Asset Categories.   For example, the risk weights increase the attractiveness of government securities relative to commercial lending. In our example, if First National replaces $250 million of its loans with the same amount of government securities, its risk-adjusted assets fall to $1,990 million. This reduces required BIS Tier 1 capital to $79.6 million and total capital to $159.2 million. The leverage requirement is unaffected by the change in asset composition and remains at $80 million. Since the leverage requirement is now the more stringent, First National must hold at least $80 million of Tier 1 capital.

Banks responded to this incentive. They lowered the amount of their loans and increased their holdings of government securities. While this did have the desired effect of reducing the risk of bank asset portfolios, it also reduced the supply of credit to firms. This reduction contributed to the **credit crunch** that played an important role in the 1990–1991 recession.[50]

credit crunch
A situation in which credit is difficult to obtain.

As you can see from Exhibit 19.2, equity-to-asset ratios rose steeply as the new capital standards were imposed, and the ratio of equity to "risk assets" (principally business loans) rose even more steeply.

Of course, by shifting towards safer assets, banks were earning less. This reinforced the effect of the capital requirements themselves in lowering their return on equity. Not surprisingly, banks sought to minimize the damage to their bottom line. They looked for ways of satisfying the regulations that would be least costly, or most profitable, for them—that is, they looked for loopholes. And of course they found them.

---

[50] Because the demand for commercial loans falls, it is normal for investments to rise and loans to fall during a recession. However, the shift in 1990–1991 was much larger than normal.

Exploiting the Loopholes.   One major loophole comes from the assignment of risk weights to broad categories of asset. For example, the BIS standards give the government securities of all OECD countries the same weight of zero, and they give all commercial loans the same weight of 100%. A bank can therefore increase its ROE by shifting towards riskier assets within each category. For example, in the category of government securities, it can hold Portuguese or Greek government bonds rather than those of the United States. Or in the category of commercial lending, it can provide financing for LBOs rather than lending to the most creditworthy corporations. Or in consumer lending, it can seek out "subprime" borrowers (borrowers with poor credit histories). In each case, by accepting greater risk, it can earn a higher rate.

A second major loophole comes from considering only credit risk. As we well know, there are other forms of risk. A bank that finds its ROE falling because of a switch from commercial loans to government securities can raise it back up by taking on more interest rate and exchange rate risk. It can become more aggressive in trading to profit from expected changes in interest rates and exchange rates. It can also take on more risk as a forward intermediary.[51]

Additional minor loopholes abound. For example, before the imposition of the BIS standards it was common for banks to issue one-year lines of credit. However, the risk weighting of a one-year line of credit is 50%, while the risk weighting of a line of less than one year is only 20%. Consequently, today, all "one-year" lines are written for 364 days rather than 365 in order to quality for the 20% weighting.

Going Off-Balance-Sheet.   We saw in Chapter 6 that, because of regulatory costs, banks can often satisfy their customers' borrowing needs at lower cost by helping them issue debt directly rather than by lending to them. The banks make up in fee income some of what they lose in spread, and they reduce their exposure to credit risk and liquidity risk. For this reason, even before the imposition of capital requirements, banks were syndicating loans and helping their customers issue commercial paper. The new capital requirements significantly increased the regulatory costs of bank intermediation and so accelerated the trend towards off-balance-sheet banking. They also stimulated the development of new techniques of off-balance-sheet banking such as securitization and credit derivatives.[52]

The Effect on the Structure of the Financial System

We saw in Chapter 6 that one consequence of the increasing regulatory burden on banks has been a steady decline in the relative importance of bank lending in financing the economy. Of course, as bank lending has declined in relative terms, other forms of lending have expanded and emerged to take its place. As a result, the entire financial system has been distorted by the pressure of regulatory costs falling disproportionately on one part of it—on banks. In response to this pressure, *the financial system has restructured itself to mini-*

---

[51] A 1996 amendment to the Basel standards did impose an additional capital requirement related to the market risk inherent in a bank's trading positions.

[52] See Chapter 14 on securitization and Chapter 16 on credit derivatives. Both of these techniques can be seen as ways of leveraging a bank's capital and so defeating the intent of the capital requirements.

mize the regulatory burden. We can think of this restructuring as involving two main mechanisms—disintermediation and reintermediation.

Disintermediation is the replacement of indirect lending through banks with direct lending through financial markets. One example of this is a company that issues commercial paper instead of borrowing from a bank. Another example is the securitization or syndication of various types of bank loan. While banks originate the loans in these cases, and perhaps service them, the loans are rapidly converted into securities and sold to investors through the financial markets.

In most cases, however, the securities created by disintermediation—the commercial paper, the syndications, and the asset-backed securities—do not wind up in the portfolios of individual investors. Rather, they are sold to nonbank intermediaries. As a result, indirect lending through banks is replaced by indirect lending through some other intermediary or sequence of intermediaries. This in **reintermediation**.

reintermediation
Loss of deposits by financial intermediaries because alternative types of indirect lending become more attractive.

The process is illustrated for the money market by Exhibits 19.4 and 19.5. Traditionally, firms and households kept their liquid reserves in bank deposits, and banks used these funds to make various types of short-term loans. This pattern is shown in Exhibit 19.4

Today, the regulatory burden on banks makes this an expensive way of doing business. In its place, there is some disintermediation as large firms purchase money market paper directly from the issuers. But most of the action is in reintermediation, as the "deposits" of small firms and households find their way to borrowers through money market mutual funds.

However, as we know, only low-risk borrowers are able to borrow by issuing paper in arm's-length financial markets.[53] For higher risk borrowers another type of intermediary is needed to provide the necessary element of relationship—the finance company. Money market mutual funds purchase the paper of finance companies, which use the proceeds to lend to higher risk borrowers such as small firms and households.

So rather than ultimate lenders lending to ultimate borrowers through banks, such lending takes place either through money market mutual funds or through a sequence of money market mutual funds and finance companies.

EXHIBIT 19.4   Traditional Channels of Short-Term Lending

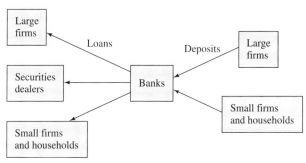

---

[53] As we saw in Chapter 14, banks have found ways to extend access to some higher risk borrowers through guarantees and securitization.

EXHIBIT 19.5   Short-Term Lending through the Money Market

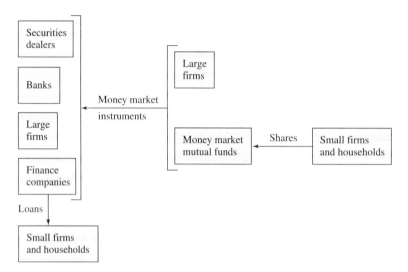

In a similar fashion, a great deal of securitization and syndication is financed by pension funds, insurance companies, hedge funds, and mutual funds. For example, *The Wall Street Journal* of July 23, 2001, reported that the share of syndicated loans to non-investment-grade companies held by mutual funds and other institutional investors had risen from about 20% in the early 1990s to about 50% in mid-2001.

WHERE DO WE GO FROM HERE?

The new regulations that were intended to protect governments from the problems of moral hazard have, at best, been only partially successful. Banks have found all sorts of ways around them, and the regulations have had unanticipated and unintended effects on the nature of banking and on the structure of the financial system.

More Regulation?

Regulators are, of course, well aware of the banks' attempts to circumvent the BIS capital standards. Naturally, they would like to block these attempts with further regulation. In 1999, the BIS published proposals for new regulations intended to repair the deficiencies of the original capital standards.

Basel 2, as the proposal has come to be known, adopts a broader approach to regulation in which capital standards constitute only one of three "pillars." Capital standards are to be refined to deal with the "within-category" problem, with risk weights assigned to assets based on rating. The rating can either be provided by a rating agency, or by a bank's own internal rating system if that system is approved by regulators.[54]

The second pillar is a switch in the focus of regulation. Rather than just examining a bank's balance sheet and checking compliance with a fixed set of rules, regulators are to assess the soundness of the bank's management practices in controlling risk. This is intended to be more forward looking and to head off problems before they occur. The Fed adopted such a "process-based" approach in 1995 in its regulation of the largest, most complex banks.

The third pillar of Basel 2 is a greater reliance on market discipline through greater transparency and through the issuing of subordinated debt. Disclosure is essential, since market discipline is possible only if the market knows what banks are doing. New Zealand provides an example of heavy reliance on disclosure alone. It requires from its banks a comprehensive financial statement every quarter and the prominent posting in all branches of ratings from credit agencies. Bank directors have unlimited liability for its losses if, in the event of problems, the financial statements prove to have been falsified (beheading outside the bank may be the next step!).

The idea of requiring a bank to issue subordinated debt is that it creates a group of investors with a strong interest in monitoring the bank. If a bank fails, the holders of subordinated debt are repaid only when all debts to depositors and to all other lenders have been settled. Argentina adopted this device after the "tequila crisis" of 1994. It strengthened disclosure rules and introduced a requirement that banks issue subordinated debt each year equal to 2% of their deposits. Implementation has been problematic, since in times of crisis it is hard to find buyers for this subordinated debt.

The BIS proposals have overall been very controversial, and many of the details remain to be worked out. As of mid-2001, the new program was due to be adopted by late 2002, with a gradual phasing in by 2005.

A More Fundamental Rethinking

However, before continuing down the path of ever tighter and more intrusive regulation, we should pause and take stock. Is this really the direction we want to go?

Can Regulators Win?   The first reason for not moving towards increased regulation is that, in this contest between regulators and banks, regulators are unlikely ever to win. When restrictions stand in the way of profits, banks will always find ways around the restrictions. For every move, there is a countermove. Of course, regulators will eventually catch on to each clever trick, and they will add new regulations to cover it. But by that time the banks will have found other clever tricks.

Regulators are at a disadvantage in this contest. They are fewer: for each ill-paid regulator, there are thousands of well-paid bankers. They are also less motivated: the banker who finds a new loophole makes a fortune; the bureaucrat who plugs it gets a pat on the head.

---

[54] Neither the banks nor the ratings agencies have been enthusiastic about bringing the agencies into the process. Moreover, internal models for evaluating credit risk are much less reliable than the value-at-risk models used for market risk. So the implementation risk weighting for individual assets remains highly problematic.

How Big Is the Problem Anyway?   The second reason for not wishing to continue with this rather unequal struggle is that it may not really be necessary. Banking systems today, at least in the advanced economies, may not be all that vulnerable. Historically, the problems of the U.S. banking system, the one most liable to problems, were largely the result of regulations that distorted the structure of the banking industry. Of the 3,000 bank failures between 1865 and 1936, the most common reason cited was local economic conditions. Local conditions were so important because branching restrictions left banks geographically undiversified. Bank runs, on the other hand, were cited as a cause of failure in fewer than 5% of cases. The losses of the S&Ls, too, were more the result of misregulation than of any inherent vulnerability of banks. Now that the distorting regulations have largely been removed, and the U.S. banking industry has become more "normal," banks are much less vulnerable.

One of the main arguments for regulation is systemic risk—the risk that the failure of one bank will bring down others in a sort of domino effect However, a recent study has cast doubt on the importance of this phenomenon.[55] One simulation showed that if the biggest borrower in the (uninsured) Fed funds market were to fail with a loss of 40% of its assets, it would bring down two to six other banks with a total of less than 1% of all bank assets. If the failing bank lost a more typical 5% of its assets, no other banks would fail. When Continental Illinois became insolvent in 1984, it was the largest correspondent bank in the country, holding deposits from some 2,300 other banks. If Conti had been allowed to fail and if it had lost 60% of its assets (10 times the actual loss), 27 of those banks would themselves have become insolvent, with total losses of $137 million. At the actual level of losses, no banks would have become insolvent.

Does Government Intervention Help?   Even supposing that banks are particularly vulnerable to problems, does government intervention make banking systems any safer? A recent study by the World Bank suggests that it does not.[56] Based on data on government regulation of banking in over a hundred countries, researchers found that stringency of capital requirements and intensity of supervision were not associated with greater stability. Restricting bank activities, barriers to foreign entry, and deposit insurance were associated with greater *instability*. Measures that were positively associated with stability were those that facilitated market control, such as disclosure requirements and improvements in corporate governance of banks.

The Cost of Government Intervention.   While tighter regulation may not buy us very much, it does not come free. In addition to the administrative costs borne by governments, regulations impose costs on banks. A study by Crédit Suisse estimates that implementing the Basel 2 regulations would cost each bank about $7.5 million. With some 30,000 banks worldwide affected, this would make the total cost about $2.25 *trillion*.[57] Whatever the accuracy of this estimate, it is clear that the cost of Basel 2 would be substantial.

---

[55] Kaufman (2000).

[56] Barth et al. (2001).

[57] *The Economist* (2001).

But out-of-pocket costs are not the only, or perhaps the most important, costs. As regulation is piled on top of regulation, it becomes more and more difficult for bankers to go about their business of assessing and bearing risks. The damage to the economy is less than it might otherwise be because the financial system can find ways around obstructive regulation. As we have seen, banks can be replaced in their traditional lending function, and they are being replaced, by markets and by other institutions. Money markets, finance companies, mutual funds, and other institutions—unencumbered by the regulations imposed on banks—can provide many of the same services. However, these workarounds perform the task that banks could have performed only at higher cost: otherwise they would have been adopted in the first place. So financing is more expensive and less available than it would have been without the regulation.

Perhaps then, rather than continuing the regulatory arms race, we should back off. Market discipline alone might work quite well.

SUMMARY

- Government intervention in banking can be justified on the grounds of a kind of market failure called an externality. Bankers take risks that seem reasonable from their own point of view but may be excessive from the point of view of society. The composition problems that underlie runs and panics involves a kind of externality.

- The regulation of banks to protect depositors and to limit their taking of risk is called prudential regulation.

- U.S. banks are monitored by a multiplicity of regulators at both the state and federal levels (dual banking). This encourages competition among regulators. Some argue that dual banking causes a race for the bottom, but others believe that it causes regulators to be more balanced in weighing the pluses and minuses of regulation.

- The prudential regulation of offshore and multinational banks is a particular problem because jurisdiction is often uncertain. The Basel Committee has issued standards to try to clarify the situation.

- Banks provide depositors and borrowers with liquidity. In a bank run or panic, an overwhelming demand for liquidity can overwhelm the banks' ability to provide it.

- Factors that cause depositors to run on a bank include uncertainty (about the bank's solvency or the coverage of deposit insurance), fear that withdrawals by others may lead to insolvency, and the advantage of being first in line.

- Liquidity crises exhibit contagion: they spread from intermediary to intermediary.

- Liquidity crises often occur as a result of a general financial crisis. Increased competitive pressure on banks can lead to increased risk taking and a greater chance of bank runs.

- Fragmentation and interdependence increase the instability of the banking system. External methods of managing liquidity and risk increase the vulnerability of the financial system to instability because of composition problems.

- Banks organized in clearinghouse associations to deal with bank runs and panics. The associations created liquidity by issuing loan certificates and, if necessary, organized a temporary suspension of convertibility.

- Private guarantees of bank deposits were tried in various forms in the nineteenth and twentieth centuries, generally with poor results. Private guarantees lack credibility; they cannot guarantee liquidity; and (like public guarantees) they suffer from moral hazard.

- The operation of a lender of last resort should satisfy the following principles: lend only against good collateral; lend against all good collateral; lend at a penalty rate; make the policy public.

- The Fed was created as a lender of last resort, but its design was flawed, and it failed its first serious test during the Great Depression. The Fed's structure was then redesigned, and the system now performs its intended function well.

- Deposit insurance was introduced in 1934, despite serious misgivings about potential moral hazard problems, to save the system of small banks in the United States. The misgivings became reality in the 1980s and 1990s.

- The FDIC insures deposits at banks and savings banks (through the BIF) and at S&Ls (through the SAIF). Institutions pay premiums based on regulators' assessment of their risk of failure.

- The FDIC can resolve a bank failure through a payout, a purchase and assumption, or a bridge bank. The methods differ in their cost to the FDIC and in how much depositors and other creditors of the bank stand to lose.

- Banks took on more risk because of increasing competitive pressure. Deposit insurance allowed them to do so without a corresponding increase in their cost of funds.

- The FDIC's attempt to "get tough" resulted in the run on Continental Illinois and, subsequently, the too-big-to-fail doctrine.

- The S&Ls originally got into trouble because of their exposure to interest rate risk. Regulatory forbearance and deregulation magnified the problem.

- The design of deposit insurance in other countries offers few lessons. However, the absence of problems elsewhere suggests that difficulties in the United States have more to do with the structure of the country's banking system than with the design of deposit insurance.

- The response to the deposit insurance crisis in the United States was twofold: structural reform of the banking system to reduce its inherent instability, and changing bank incentives to control moral hazard.

- The BIS international capital standards set minimum capital requirements for a bank based on the credit risk of its assets and its off-balance-sheet commitments. In addition, U.S. regulators impose a leverage requirement.

- The capital standards have created a whole new set of incentives. In response, banks have changed the way they do business. They have found ways of satisfying the regulations that are least costly, or most profitable, for them.

- And, because banks are so important, this change has affected the structure of the entire financial system. Through disintermediation and reintermediation, the financial system has restructured itself to minimize the regulatory burden.

- There are proposals for new standards to eliminate loopholes, but this does not seem to be a war that regulators can win. Given the recent structural improvement of banking, the problem may no longer be as great. Market discipline alone might work quite well.

DISCUSSION QUESTIONS

1. Explain the distinction between internal and external methods of managing liquidity and risk. How does the choice between internal and external methods affect system stability?

2. Compare private and government methods of protecting banks against a liquidity crisis. What are the merits and limitations of the different methods?

3. Compare federal guarantees of defined benefit pension plans with federal deposit insurance. What are the similarities in terms of the function they serve and the problems to which they are subject? What are the differences?

4. In what ways are money market mutual funds and finance companies like banks? In what ways

different? How do they manage to compete successfully with banks?

5. Adams National Bank has the following balance sheet (at market values):

Assets	$1b	Deposits	
		Insured	$300m
		Uninsured	400m
		Nondeposit liabilities	400m

The bank's "franchise" is worth $50 million. Would a payout or a purchase and assumption be less expensive for the FDIC?

6. Transactions between financial intermediaries increase efficiency, but they reduce stability. Discuss, giving as many examples as possible.

7. In what ways has government intervention reduced the stability of the U.S. financial system?

8. "Deregulation has been the cause of the deposit insurance crisis. Reregulation is the solution." Discuss.

9. Mountain National Bank has the following balance sheet:

MOUNTAIN NATIONAL BANK

Cash	$10m	Checking deposits	$100m
Loans	200m	Time deposits	250m
U.S. securities	190m	Fed funds	
Fed funds sold	20m	purchased	50m
		Equity	20m

a. Mountain National's leverage requirement for capital is 4%. Does it meet this requirement?

b. There is a $40 million loss on Mountain National's loans. Who bears this loss? (Assume

that all the bank's deposits are insured and that the bank is liquidated in a payout).

10. Third National has the following assets:

Cash	200m
Eurodollar deposits	100m
Government securities	300m
Mortgages	200m
Loans	600m

Third National is also guaranteeing $500 million of participations that it has sold to other banks. Calculate Third National's capital requirements (risk-based and leverage requirement).

11. The importance of banks as lenders (relative to other financial intermediaries and financial markets) has steadily declined in the United States in recent decades.

   a. To reverse this trend, some have suggested extending to other financial institutions the regulations that currently apply to banks. What are the justifications for such a move? What would be the likely consequences for banks? For the economy?

   b. What do you believe to be the reasons for the declining importance of banks? What remedies, if any, would you suggest?

12. Suppose that to prevent stock market crashes, which are a threat to the retirement savings of working Americans, the government sets up the Federal Stock Insurance Corporation to guarantee the value of stocks. What sorts of problems would you anticipate? Explain carefully.

BIBLIOGRAPHY

Alfriend, Malcolm C. "International Risk-Based Capital Standard: History and Explanation." *Federal Reserve Bank of Richmond Economic Review*, November–December 1988, 28–34.

Barth, J. R., et al. "Bank Regulation and Supervision: What Works Best?" World Bank, May 2001.

Bordo, Michael D. "The Lender of Last Resort: Alternative Views and Historical Evidence." *Federal Reserve Bank of Richmond Economic Review*, January–February 1990, 18–29.

Bovenzi, John F., and Arthur J. Murton. "Resolution Costs of Bank Failures," *FDIC Banking Review*, fall 1988, 1–13.

Calomiris, Charles W. "Regulation, Industrial Structure, and Instability in U.S. Banking: An Historical Perspective." In *Structural Change in Banking*. Edited by M. Klausner and L. J. White. Homewood, IL: Business One Irwin, 1992.

Carey, M., et al. "Does Corporate Lending by Banks and Finance Companies Differ? Evidence on

Specialization in Private Debt Contracting." *Journal of Finance* 53, no. 3 (June 1998), 845–878.

Congressional Budget Office. *Reforming Federal Deposit Insurance*. Washington, DC: Government Printing Office, 1990.

DeFerrari, L. M., and D. E. Palmer. "Supervision of Large Complex Banking Organizations." *Federal Reserve Bulletin*, February 2001, 47–57.

Dwyer, Gerald P., Jr., and R. Alton Gilbert. "Bank Runs and Private Remedies." *Economic Review of the Federal Reserve Bank of St. Louis*, May–June 1989, 43–61.

The Economist, June 30, 2001.

Friedman, Milton, and Anna Jacobson Schwartz. *A Monetary History of the United States 1867–1960*. Princeton, NJ: Princeton University Press, 1963.

Golembe, Carter H. "The Deposit Insurance Legislation of 1933: An Examination of Its Antecedents and Its Purposes." *Political Science Quarterly* 76, no. 2 (June 1960), 181–200.

Kaufman, G. G. "Does Bank Regulation Retard or Contribute to Systemic Risk?" Stanford Law School, December 2000.

Keeton, William R. "Small and Large Bank Views of Deposit Insurance: Today vs the 1930s." *Federal Reserve Bank of Kansas City Economic Review*, September–October 1990, 23–35.

Mayer, Martin. *The Greatest-Ever Bank Robbery: The Collapse of the Saving and Loan Industry*. New York: Scribner's, 1990.

Mishkin, F. S. (2000). "Prudential Supervision: Why Is It Important and What Are the Issues?" National Bureau of Economic Research, September 2000.

Parthemos, James. "The Federal Reserve Act of 1913 in the Stream of U.S. Monetary History." *Economic Review of the Federal Reserve Bank of Richmond*, July–August 1988, 19–28.

Rosen, R. "Do Regulators Race for the Bottom or for the Quiet Life? The Relationship Between Regulators and the Regulated in Banking." Kelley School of Business, Indiana University, January 2001.

Sylla, Richard. "The United States 1863–1913," In *Banking and Economic Development*. Edited by R. Cameron. New York: Oxford University Press, 1972.

Tallman, Ellis. "Some Unanswered Questions About Bank Panics." *Federal Reserve Bank of Atlanta Economic Review*, November–December 1988, 2–21.

Usher, A. P. *The Early History of Deposit Banking in Mediterranean Europe*. Cambridge, MA: Harvard University Press, 1943.

White, E. N. *The Regulation and Reform of the American Banking System, 1900–1929*. Princeton, NJ: Princeton University Press, 1983.

White, Lawrence I. *The S&L Debacle: Public Policy Lessons for Bank and Thrift Regulation*. New York: Oxford University Press, 1991.

KEY TERMS

prudential regulation
dual banking
race for the bottom
Basel Concordat
Basel Committee on Banking Supervision
contagion
internal methods of managing liquidity and risk
external methods of managing liquidity and risk
composition problems
clearinghouse association
loan certificates
suspension of convertibility

lender of last resort
Federal Reserve Act of 1913
adjustment credit
extended credit
discount window
discount rate
Federal Deposit Insurance Corporation (FDIC)
Federal Savings and Loan Insurance Corporation (FSLIC)
Bank Insurance Fund (BIF)
Savings Association Insurance Fund (SAIF)
risk-related premiums
payout

purchase and assumption (P&A)
too-big-to-fail doctrine
regulatory forbearance
money brokers
brokered deposits
BIS standards
Tier 1 capital
Tier 2 capital
Total capital
subordinated debt
risk-weighted assets
leverage requirement
credit crunch
reintermediation
Basel 2

CHAPTER 20

SECURITY MARKET REGULATION AND STABILITY

When you finish this chapter you will understand:

- How regulation protects small investors
- Why market transparency may not be as good as it sounds
- Why stock markets crash and what can be done about it

Securities markets face two major problems—cheating and instability. As we shall see, there are many ways to cheat investors, and regulators have been increasingly active in protecting them. In the first half of this chapter, we shall examine securities regulation and ask whether it is effective.

No one who lived through the Internet bubble can be in any doubt that stock markets are highly volatile. In the late 1990s, Internet stocks rose to stratospheric values, only to collapse a few years later. The decline in stock prices was rapid, but not as rapid as it was in the Crash of 1987, when the S&P 500 lost 20% of its value in only a couple of days. How harmful is this volatility and what, if anything, can be done about it? We shall address these questions in the second half of the chapter.

THE REGULATION OF SECURITIES MARKETS

Of course, cheating is not a problem only in securities markets. It is a problem in all markets. In most markets, however, we rely primarily on *caveat emptor*—let the buyer beware! There are general laws against fraud. But these provide consumers with limited protection and only against the most flagrant types of cheating. In some markets, there are more specific consumer protection laws. But mostly, we expect consumers to watch out for themselves. Why are we more worried about cheating in securities markets?

Why Regulate Securities Markets?

To some extent the regulation of securities markets is merely an extension of fraud laws and consumer protection to the particular circumstances of the securities market. However, the concerns of securities regulation really go beyond this.

Why Does Cheating Matter?   Behind securities regulation, there is a concern not only for the consumer, but also for the market.[1] A well-functioning securities market is important for the health of the economy. Widespread cheating can threaten its viability. Cheating raises transactions costs, because participants must devote resources to protecting themselves. Increased transactions costs and the fear of being cheated reduce the scope of the market. Investors stay away, and honest issuers find the cost of funds prohibitive. Because of the large element of fixed cost in dealing with the problem, it is a particularly great obstacle for smaller investors and smaller issuers.

Is Government Intervention Necessary?   Cheating is essentially an incentive problem. Of course, honesty is a moral issue, but individuals will be most reliably honest when "honesty is the best policy." This will be so whenever the cost of a bad reputation is greater than the potential gain from cheating.

The problem in the securities market is that, for an individual, the gain from cheating can easily exceed the cost of loss of reputation. However, there is an additional cost that the individual does not bear or take into account—a "reputational externality." Not only will the reputation of the individual cheater be harmed, but so too will the reputation of the market.

The existence of this externality suggests a need for intervention. But do we really need *government* intervention? There is an alternative: **self-regulation**. Since other market participants suffer from the reputational externality created by individual cheating, they have an incentive to police. Of course, in order to police they have to organize, and for their policing to be effective, they have to be able to punish cheaters.

In fact, because of the nature of securities markets, these conditions for self-regulation are easily satisfied. We have seen that securities trading tends to centralize in organized markets. The governance of organized markets provides the necessary organization for

self-regulation
Enforcement of fair, ethical, and efficient practices by an organization of market participants.

---

[1] This is much like the motivation for the regulation of banking—more a concern for the banking system than a concern for depositors.

policing. The ability to exclude cheaters from the market provides the necessary punishment. And of course it helps that the reputational advantage of good policing is captured by the market: a well-regulated market attracts more trading.

The Government Takes Over.   Historically, self-regulation has indeed been the rule. Exchanges policed both traders and issuers. However, as we saw in Chapter 17, governments have usurped this role, weakening the authority of exchanges in the process.

In the United States, it was the Great Crash of 1929 and the ensuing Depression that brought about this change. There was a general feeling that regulation by the exchanges had been inadequate, that cheating of various forms had been widespread, and that these factors had contributed both to the boom and to the crash. Popular assertions included the following:

- That exchanges lacked the will or the power to get issuers to disclose sufficient information to investors
- That members of the exchange manipulated prices at the expense of the public
- That excessive margin lending by banks and brokers had exacerbated the boom
- That members had sold short to deliberately precipitate a panic (a 'bear raid')

Although subsequent research has failed to substantiate any of these charges, they were firmly believed at the time, and they provided the motivation for the government to take over the regulation of securities markets.

Who Needs Protection?   Not all participants in securities markets are in equal need of protection. Arm's-length investors need protection more than relationship investors. Small investors need protection more than large investors.[2]

While relationship investors have both the incentive and the means to look after themselves, arm's-length investors do not. For relationship investors, monitoring is part of the package. They have access to private information, and they usually possess the means to make their voices heard. Arm's-length investors lack the incentive, the means, or both. They are unable to protect their own interests effectively.

One class of arm's-length investor—small investors—by definition, has little incentive to take the trouble to monitor. If in doubt, get out! Large arm's-length investors—institutional investors and the wealthy—have a stronger incentive to protect themselves because they have much more at risk. They usually hire professional money managers to do the work for them. Small investors can do this too by entrusting their money to mutual funds, pension funds, or insurance companies rather than trying to go it alone. In 1998, some 84 million individuals in the United States owned stocks—34 million directly and 50 million indirectly through pension plans and mutual funds. Among those who held stock directly, ownership was highly concentrated in the hands of the wealthy—some 10% of individual stock owners held about 80% of the stock directly held by individuals.

Another class of arm's-length investor—foreign investors—may have the incentive, but it is at a significant disadvantage with respect to the means. "Public information" is less

---

[2] See Chapters 14 and 15 on the distinction between arm's-length and relationship investors.

home market bias

The preference of investors for securities of their own country.

accessible if it is in a foreign language. A great deal of "soft information" may be unpublished but well known to locals. Time zone differences may mean that things are happening while foreign investors are asleep. It is not surprising, therefore, that despite a great deal of progress in globalization, there is a strong **home market bias** in investment. Investors have a strong preference, other things equal, for investing in their own securities markets.

Investors are not the only ones in need of protection. Another vulnerable group is market makers. In a dealer market, dealers are vulnerable to information traders with privileged information (inside traders). In an auction market, the information traders who provide price discovery and liquidity are vulnerable to market manipulation. If these problems are sufficiently great, market makers will withdraw their services and the quality of the market will suffer.

Now that we understand the reasons for securities market regulation, let us see how it is done. We begin by looking at the regulatory structure—at how regulation is organized. We then look at the substance of regulation. We shall focus initially on regulation in the United States and then discuss how regulation differs in other countries.

The Structure of Regulation

The structure of regulation of the principal securities markets is summarized in Exhibit 20.1. Notice the fragmentation of this structure. Closely related securities are regulated by different agencies. In particular, the stock market is regulated by the SEC, while the market for stock index futures is regulated by the CFTC.[3] Notice, too, that markets that are mainly wholesale markets with few small investors, like the money market and the market for mortgage-backed securities, largely escape regulation. The market for municipal securities is not regulated by the federal government because of federal–state issues.

EXHIBIT 20.1   The Regulation of U.S. Securities Markets

Market	Self-Regulation	Government Regulators
U.S. and agency securities	None	Treasury, the Fed, SEC
Money market	None	None
Mortgage-backed securities	None	None
Corporate stocks and bonds	NYSE and other exchanges, NASD	SEC, the Fed (margin requirements)
Municipal securities	Municipal Securities Rule-Making Board	None
Financial futures	National Futures Association	Commodity Futures Trading Commission
Financial options	Options Clearing Corporation	SEC (futures options regulated by CFTC)

---

[3] The division of jurisdiction between the SEC and the CFTC was agreed in 1981. The SEC regulates options on securities; the CFTC regulates futures on securities and options on futures. After the crash of 1987, there were calls to unify the regulation of these markets, but nothing has yet happened.

EXHIBIT 20.2   The Securities Act of 1933 and The Securities Exchange Act of 1934

Securities
Exchange
Commission
(SEC)
The federal
agency that regu-
lates U.S. finan-
cial markets and
securities firms.

- The **Securities Exchange Commission (SEC)** is established to administer the securities laws
- Issuers of new securities must register with the SEC, filing statements that disclose fully all relevant information. A prospectus containing this information must accompany all solicitations of sales.
- Issuers whose securities are listed on a stock exchange must file annual reports and other periodic statements with the SEC.[a]
- Any trading system that is a "securities exchange" must register with the SEC. It must be owned by its members (those who trade on it), and it must set up a system of self-regulation.[b]
- Company insiders must file a report of any trading in a company's securities.[c]
- Various forms of market manipulation, including the disclosure of false and misleading information, are prohibited.

---

[a] The Securities Act Amendments of 1964 extended this requirement to OTC securities.
[b] The Maloney Act of 1938 extended the registration and self-regulation requirements to OTC markets; the NASD is the only OTC market that has registered. The Securities Reform Act of 1975 established the Municipal Securities Rule Making Board for self-regulation of the municipal bond market. The Government Securities Act of 1986 required all dealers in U.S. government securities not otherwise regulated to register with the SEC.
[c] The law on insider trading was strengthened by the Insider Trading and Securities Fraud Enforcement Act of 1988 and extended in 1991 to trading in derivatives related to a company's securities.

The Securities Acts.   The legal basis for securities regulation was established by two acts—the **Securities Act of 1933** and the **Securities Exchange Act of 1934**. Their main provisions are listed in Exhibit 20.2.

As you can see, the securities laws involve a mixture of the government *policing* self-regulation and of the government *replacing* self-regulation. In the regulation of trading and of the market, the role of the government is largely limited to overseeing self-regulation by exchanges. In contrast, in the regulation of issuers, the government has largely taken over the role that had previously been played by the exchanges.

As is often the case, regulation entrenches monopoly. Protected from outside competition by the securities laws, exchanges adopted rules that limited competition within the exchange and therefore provided members with monopoly profits. The outstanding example was fixed commissions: members were required to charge customers commissions according to a schedule set by the exchange. These practices were authorized and supported by the SEC. In the 1970s, these practices came under increasing criticism. In response Congress passed the **Securities Acts Amendments of 1975**. This abolished anti-competitive exchange rules, especially those regarding fixed commissions. It also directed the SEC to promote competition in the securities markets and to establish a "national securities market."[4]

Regulation of Futures and Options.   The first federal legislation for the regulation of futures and options was the Grain Futures Act of 1922, amended and renamed the **Commodity Exchange Act (CEA)** in **1936**. This act required trading to take place on designated exchanges and established licensing and regulation of exchanges, traders, and brokers.

---

[4] See Chapter 17 for a discussion of the impact of this on the stock market.

Commodity Futures Trading Commission (CFTC)

The agency created by Congress in 1974 to regulate exchange trading in futures in the United States.

The **Commodity Futures Trading Commission (CFTC)** was established in 1974 to administer futures and options legislation. It took over from the Commodity Exchange Authority (established in 1934), a small agency in the Department of Agriculture, which was no longer equal to the task of regulating the mushrooming markets. The CFTC monitors futures markets and traders and must grant its approval before a new type of futures contract may be traded.

The regulation of securities markets can be divided into a number of categories—regulating issuers, regulating trading, regulating markets and market makers, and regulating money managers. We take up each in turn.

Regulating Issuers

Offering Securities to the Public.   Securities regulation polices the primary market. Its main concern is to prevent issuers from exploiting asymmetries of information to mislead investors.

Historically, as we saw in Chapter 11, there was a private solution to this problem— the underwriter. The underwriter could acquire the necessary information, regardless of whether it was made public, and vouch for the honesty of the issuer. A credible underwriter would lower financing costs for issuers and so attract future business.

disclosure requirement

A requirement that companies release all information pertaining to their business activity.

Government regulation supplements the work of the underwriter with a public **disclosure requirement**. Companies wishing to offer securities to the public must register with the SEC, disclosing all relevant information. Note that the requirement goes beyond a negative injunction against fraud or misrepresentation. It constitutes an affirmative requirement to reveal all relevant facts.

Not all issues of securities have to be registered with the SEC. Important exemptions include the following:

- Issuers of less than $1.5 million of securities per year
- Private placements—offerings to small groups of private investors experienced or informed enough not to require such disclosure
- Corporate securities with original maturity of 270 days or less and most other money market securities
- Securities of the U.S. government and most municipal securities (although state laws often require disclosure for the latter)

Continuing Disclosure.   In the secondary market, too, there is a concern that issuers may mislead investors, with the result that investors will buy and sell securities at prices that do not reflect their true value.

As we saw in Chapter 17, the solution to this problem too used to be nongovernmental, in the form of exchange listing requirements. Listing requirements continue to be important. Exchanges typically require listed companies to file quarterly reports that reveal all "material information."

Government regulation supplements this with a requirement to file a variety of reports with the SEC, to be made available to the public (these days on the Internet). The basic reports are an annual report on Form 10-K, a quarterly report on Form 10-Q, and a current report on Form 8-K for any month in which certain specified events occur. Enforcement largely depends on investors' right of legal action: the law makes those responsible for preparing these reports liable for any losses caused to investors through misrepresentation or omission.

Disclosure requirements are not without their critics. One objection is that companies can be put at a competitive disadvantage by having to reveal commercially valuable information. However, there is little evidence that this is so. Another objection, with more substance, is that disclosure requirements distort manager incentives, leading to much wasteful manipulation of numbers and "**window dressing**." Moreover, meeting disclosure requirements is not without cost, and it is possible to go too far if the cost exceeds the benefits to companies and to investors.

What are those benefits? Apart from helping to ensure that securities trade at prices that reflect their true value, disclosure plays an important role in corporate governance. As one manager noted, "People who are forced to undress in public will presumably pay some attention to their figures." In addition, the need to meet disclosure requirements provides an incentive for managers to develop a good internal information structure, and this can only help to raise the quality of management. Good disclosure makes a lot of substantive regulation unnecessary. For example, self-dealing is impractical if the deal has to be disclosed.

Of course, for disclosure to be of any value it must be based on sound accounting practices. The SEC delegates the task of setting accounting standards to a professional body, the **Financial Accounting Standards Board (FASB)**. The FASB is constantly trying to improve standards—to address "window dressing," for example, and to catch new abuses. Standard setting is a process of give and take involving the FASB, accounting firms, and companies. The resulting standards therefore tend to take into account both the benefits *and* the costs, addressing the concern that requirements may be excessively costly.

Investors not only need information, they also need to know what it means. Fortunately, there is a whole industry of security analysts and financial media processing the numbers and peddling their insights to the public.

State Laws.   Federal securities laws were imposed on top of a web of existing state securities laws. These laws remain in place and are generally known as "**blue sky laws**," because their purpose was once described as being to prevent "speculative schemes which have no more basis than so many feet of blue sky." Typical state laws contain provisions against fraud in the sale of securities and require the registration of securities to be sold in the state.

Investors are also protected by corporate law. Corporate law is provided by the states rather than by the federal government, and there is vigorous competition among state legal systems for companies to incorporate in their jurisdictions. It is corporate law that provides much of the legal protection to equity investors that we discussed in Chapter 15. And corporate law also sets the rules for corporate restructurings (mergers, acquisitions, and so on) to protect the interests of arm's-length shareholders.

Regulating Trading

Securities regulation monitors the trading of securities with the purpose of ensuring that trading is fair. One reason trading might not be fair is that traders with privileged access to

"window dressing"
Activity near the end of a quarter or fiscal year that is designed to improve the appearance of a balance sheet to shareholders.

Financial Accounting Standards Board (FASB)
A board composed of independent members who create and interpret Generally Accepted Accounting Principles (GAAP).

"blue sky laws"
State laws covering the issue and trading of securities.

information might sell securities for more than they are worth or buy them for less than they are worth. For example, insiders, knowing a company is doing better than generally believed, might buy its securities from uninformed investors for less than the securities are really worth. The prevention of such **insider trading** is one goal of securities regulation.

Another reason that trading might not be fair is manipulation of the market. We know that market price responds both to new information and to imbalances of liquidity. It can be manipulated through either channel. Misleading information can be released with the deliberate aim of causing the price to rise or fall. For example, **"painting the tape"** involves publishing false trading information to create an impression of activity in a stock.[5] Or a trader can buy up a large part of a particular issue to create an artificial scarcity (a liquidity imbalance) that drives up its price: this is called a "**squeeze**" or "**corner**."[6] The prevention of such **market manipulation** is another goal of securities regulation.

Insider Trading.   Since 1961, the SEC has interpreted the antifraud provisions of the securities acts as prohibiting trading by insiders based on information not generally available to the public. "Insiders" are taken to be the directors and officers of a corporation as well as professional advisers such as investment bankers, lawyers, and accountants. To facilitate enforcement, insiders are required to report all trading in the shares of the corporation. Violators are subject to fine and imprisonment and are liable to be sued for damages in civil court by investors.

The argument for insider trading laws is that insider trading harms the investors who buy from insiders or sell to them at unfair prices. Insider trading can also harm market makers. The risk of insider trading may therefore reduce the supply of market making and so impair the liquidity of the market. Insider trading is also a corporate governance issue: the use of corporate information by insiders for private gain can be seen as a form of theft from the corporation and from arm's-length shareholders.

There are those, however, who argue that insider trading can also be beneficial because it results in more rapid and accurate adjustment of the market price to new information. As long as inside information is withheld from the market and no one trades on it, the market price will be "unfair" even if no insider benefits. It will be "unfair" because it does not reflect all the available information. If insider trading is allowed, insiders will have a strong incentive to trade on that information as rapidly as possible, and the market price will quickly adjust to reflect the new information.

In addition, restrictions on insider trading reduce the benefits and increase the costs of being an insider. Large shareholders who are represented on the board—which makes them insiders—are constrained from trading their shares for fear of prosecution. This makes their position much less liquid. This is one reason why institutional investors are reluctant to become active shareholders. For them, the potential loss of liquidity is too great a sacrifice. In this way, restrictions on insider trading tend to discourage concentrated shareholding and so undermine corporate governance.

There is, as always, a trade-off. It is unclear whether on balance insider trading laws do more good than harm. Enforcement is a problem, and actual prosecutions are rare. It is

---

insider trading
Trading by officers, directors, major stockholders, or others with information not available to the public.

"painting the tape"
Manipulating the market by buying and selling a security to create the illusion of high trading activity.

"squeeze" or "corner"
Creation of an artificial scarcity in the market for a commodity or security to drive up its price.

market manipulation
Illegal activity designed to influence the price in a market.

---

[5] It can be detected by matching trading reports with settlement reports.

[6] We saw an example of cornering in the government securities market in Chapter 12.

also relatively easy for insiders to get around insider trading laws—for example, by trading the stocks of competitors or of suppliers rather than of their own company. Moreover, evidence of increased trading volume before the publication of important inside information suggests that insider trading continues despite the prohibition. Indeed, because insider trading laws increase the market impact of announcements, they actually make insider trading more lucrative.

Market Manipulation.   While market manipulation is prohibited in all securities markets, it is not a major issue in the markets for equities and debt. In contrast, in the markets for futures and options, preventing market manipulation is the main objective of regulation.

From their beginnings after the Civil War, markets in commodities futures and options were viewed with suspicion by the public and by government authorities. They were often seen as disreputable gambling dens that destabilized the prices of commodities. This perception was only reinforced by the frequent attempts by speculators to corner various commodity markets. During 1868, there was an attempted corner once a month on average. The most famous case was in 1869. Jay Gould and Jim Fisk attempted to corner the gold market and were thwarted only when President Ulysses S. Grant ordered the federal government to sell gold.

harm-based regulation
Regulation that relies on prosecution of violations after the fact.

In regulating against market manipulation, there are two possible approaches—"harm based" and preventive. **Harm-based regulation** monitors the market for manipulation, and if it is detected punishes the manipulator. **Preventive regulation** seeks rather to establish rules that make manipulation impossible or at least difficult.

preventive regulation
Regulation that attempts to prevent violations from taking place.

While regulation in the stock market relies on the harm-based approach, regulation of the futures and options markets is principally preventive. There are regulations that limit the size of speculative positions. The CFTC reviews the terms of new contracts and can require changes to reduce the possibility of manipulation. If the CFTC suspects manipulation, it can even intervene in the market to impose a price at which traders must settle or to force traders to liquidate outstanding positions.

Regulating Markets and Market Makers

front-running
Trading on his or her own account by a broker with advance knowledge of a block transaction that will influence the price of the underlying security.

The next category of regulation is regulation of the markets themselves. Such regulation attempts to prevent abuses by the securities firms that make the market, and it sets rules for organized markets with the intention of improving their performance.

Securities Firms.   Brokers working for securities firms can misbehave in a variety of ways. One example is **front-running**. This occurs when a broker, receiving a large order and anticipating the resulting change in price, trades on his own account *before* executing the customer's order. Another example is **churning**, when a broker trades a customer's account excessively to generate commissions.

churning
Excessive trading of a client's account to increase the broker's commissions.

The first line of defense against the misbehavior of security firms is registration—both with state regulators and with the SEC (there are similar requirements for futures commission merchants). Registration may be suspended or revoked if the broker or dealer is found guilty of abuses. In addition, the securities laws specifically prohibit certain kinds of behavior, such as front-running and churning, and require certain management practices. The latter include detailed record keeping and reporting of trades and the clear separation of customer assets from a broker's own assets.

To protect customers against the failure of a securities firm, regulations require a minimum level of capital. The Securities Investor Protection Corporation Act of 1970 set up the **Securities Investor Protection Corporation (SIPC** or "sipik") to insure customer accounts. SIPC insures the accounts of customers of securities firms for up to $500,000, including $100,000 insurance on cash accounts. All registered brokers and dealers must join SIPC, which is financed out of an assessment on member firms. From the time it was set up through December 2000, SIPC paid out $391 million to 443,000 customers of securities firms that failed (this amounted to about 10% of the value of the accounts in question). Many securities firms provide their customers with additional private insurance, bringing the total coverage to as much as $10 million per account.

Securities Investor Protection Corporation (SIPC)
A nonprofit corporation that insures customers' securities and cash held by member brokerage firms against the failure of those firms.

Organized Markets.   Regulation of organized markets is largely self-regulation—left by the SEC to the organized markets themselves. Securities exchanges must register with the SEC and set up a system of self-regulation. Such a system might include, for example, rules establishing **trading priority**—for instance, that higher bids and earlier bids be executed first.

trading priority
Rules that determine which orders coming into an auction market are to be executed first.

Market Transparency.   One matter that the SEC does not leave to self-regulation is **market transparency**. A market is transparent to the extent to which trading information is made public on a real-time basis. A market is perfectly transparent if all relevant information—prices, volume, quotes, order flow, trader identification—is instantly available to all. Since the Securities Acts Amendments of 1975 gave the SEC a mandate to establish a "national securities market," the SEC has pushed to make markets more transparent, and in particular it has required organized markets to publish promptly price and quantity information on completed trades.

market transparency
The extent to which complete trading information is available to investors in real time.

Transparency certainly sounds like something that one should be in favor of, and it does have its virtues. Transparency makes it easier for investors to monitor the quality of execution of their brokers. This keeps brokers honest and stimulates competition among them. Increasing investor confidence and lowering transactions costs should encourage more trading and improve the liquidity of the market. Transparency also facilitates the integration of markets by making it easier to arbitrage across different trading venues. In these ways market transparency makes it easier to ensure that traders obtain **best execution**—that is, that their trades are executed at the best prices available anywhere.

best execution
Execution of orders at the best price currently available.

But of course there are trade-offs. Enforcing greater transparency has complex effects on the structure of securities markets. If price is available instantly and at no cost, why incur the expense of trading on the exchange? As we saw in Chapter 17, transparency undermines organized markets by making it easier to trade "off-market." The result is fragmentation, with a negative impact on liquidity and price discovery. Since off-market trading is unregulated, the result may also be less effective regulation. Greater transparency also exposes market makers to increased risk of loss to information traders. It may therefore reduce the supply of market making, once again harming price discovery and liquidity.

Organized markets compete for order flow. Each offers traders a basket of services—execution and settlement, dispute resolution, liquidity, *and* price discovery. Given a choice of organized markets, issuers and traders can pick the one that suits them best. For some, trading costs will be decisive, and they will look for best execution and low fees and commissions. Others may care less about cost and more about quality. They will look for the best liquidity and price discovery. Left to themselves, organized markets will publish trading information—enough to attract business, but not so much that market makers will be harmed or that it becomes unnecessary to use the market at all. It is not clear why organized markets, in drawing the line, will provide too little transparency or why regulators will be able to improve on their decisions.

Regulating Money Managers

So far, we have focused on how regulation can protect individual investors who trade securities in organized markets. Individuals can, however, avoid the dangers and the costs of choosing, holding, and trading securities by delegating some or all of the task to financial intermediaries or money managers. With intermediaries such as life insurance companies, pension funds, and mutual funds, the individual purchases the liabilities of the intermediary and leaves investment to the intermediary. Indeed, as we have seen, an increasing fraction of securities are held and traded by such institutional investors. With money managers such as bank trust departments, private bankers, and investment advisers, the securities belong to the individual customer, but the investment decisions are delegated to the money manager. Delegation makes sense because of economies of scale and specialization, and intermediaries offer the additional advantage of intermediation.

The problem with these arrangements, however, is how to protect the customer from the delegate. Intermediaries can deceive their customers or fail. Money managers can defraud or steal (outright or through churning) or cause the customers losses through incompetence and negligence.

In the regulation of intermediaries, much the same considerations apply as in the regulation of banks (see Chapter 19). To a large extent, economies of scale should lead to a market dominated by large institutions with a strong reputational interest in satisfying (rather than cheating) their customers. However, it seems reasonable to supplement this safeguard with prudential regulation that requires licensing or registration and imposes disclosure requirements. The states are responsible for the prudential regulation of lifes, and the Department of Labor regulates pension funds. The SEC regulates mutual funds under the Investment Company Act of 1940.[7]

The SEC is responsible for the regulation of money managers under the **Investment Advisors Act of 1940**, which requires that investment advisers register with the SEC and regulates their relationship with their clients. With this type of regulation, too, there are trade-offs. Tighter regulation is likely to lead to a higher quality of service, but by restricting entry, it also favors cartelization and a higher price for that service. This may harm those who care more about cost than quality. On the other hand, less stringent regulation eases entry and promotes competition. This leads to cheaper, but not necessarily better, service. Good service is costly, and it is hard for customers to know when they are getting it. Consequently bad service may drive out good.

---

[7] For the details of regulation, see Chapter 9 on lifes and Chapter 10 on pension funds and mutual funds.

Regulation in Other Countries: Two Different Approaches

Broadly speaking, the regulation of securities markets in different countries can take one of two overall approaches. The approach taken in the United States, in other English-speaking countries, and in a few others is to seek to reinforce market mechanisms. The approach taken elsewhere—for example, in most continental European countries and in Japan—relies on more direct government control. We shall call the former approach the **"Anglo" approach** and the latter the **"Continental" approach**.

The "Continental" approach relies on close oversight to prevent problems from happening. For example, new issues of securities require permission: officials judge whether or not they are "appropriate" for investors (this is called the "merit" system). In contrast, the "Anglo" approach sets standards and then focuses on detecting and punishing abuses. For example, new issues require registration and disclosure rather than permission. If the disclosure turns out, *ex post*, to be deceitful or inadequate, violators are prosecuted. Otherwise, there is no attempt to prevent investors, once they are fully informed, from making foolish decisions.

Of course, disclosure requires good accounting procedures, and these tend to be more characteristic of the "Anglo" countries. For example, in one "Continental" country, Germany, financial accounting is mixed up with tax reporting. This confusion allows companies to understate earnings when they are high and so to conceal losses when they are in trouble. It is therefore hard to know how a company is doing or to compare its performance to that of others. In Japan, another "Continental" country, accounting tends to report only good news.

"Continental" countries generally have civil-law legal systems. The basic principle of civil law is that anything the law does not specifically allow is prohibited. Financial innovation is therefore difficult because anything new requires regulators' permission. "Anglo" countries generally have common-law legal systems. The basic principle of common law is that anything the law does not specifically prohibit is allowed. There is consequently no restriction on financial innovation that does not violate existing laws. Not surprisingly, most financial innovations originate in "Anglo" countries.

"Continental" countries tend to rely on direct control or management of markets by officials. "Anglo" countries tend to build on existing self-regulation by supplementing it with regulatory oversight. The closer regulation of the "Continental" approach limits entry and tends to favor larger institutions because they are easier for officials to deal with. It therefore frequently creates or reinforces market power. The looser regulation of the "Anglo" approach is more conducive to entry and to competition.

Under the "Continental" approach, because the government is more directly and obviously responsible if anything goes wrong, government bailouts and coverups are more common. However, as we saw in Chapter 18, they do occur in "Anglo" countries too.

Few countries are purely "Anglo" or "Continental" in their approach to regulation. Actual systems tend to be a mixture that favors one approach rather than the other. In the United States, for example, regulation of the stock market by the SEC fits the "Anglo" pattern, while regulation of the derivatives market by the CFTC tends more towards the "Continental."

"Anglo" approach to regulation

An approach to regulation characteristic of English-speaking countries and a few others.

"Continental" approach to regulation

An approach to regulation characteristic of continental Europe and Japan.

Because the U.S. financial system is widely perceived as a great success, there has been a tendency for other countries to imitate the U.S. approach to regulation. Since the 1980s, a number of "Continental" countries have switched from merit for new issues to registration and disclosure, and from direct regulation of markets to supervising self-regulation. Also following the U.S. lead, many countries, including some "Anglo" ones, have abolished fixed commissions and introduced insider trading laws.[8]

However, as we have seen, not all U.S. regulation works well even in the United States. It is not surprising, therefore, that in other countries, with different regulatory traditions and legal systems, not all the transplants have been successful.

Globalization and Regulation

Globalization and the resulting increase in cross-border trading have created some additional problems for regulators. First, the ability to issue and to trade securities offshore increases opportunities for cheating because issuers and traders are out of reach of domestic regulators. Second, differences in standards between countries are an obstacle to cross-border investment: investors may be leery of buying securities in another country if they lack confidence in the fairness of its markets. Third, cross-border trading in securities raises the question of jurisdiction. Should cross-border trading be subject to the rules of the home country, of the host country, or of some shared regulatory body?

harmonization
Resolution of cross-border differences in regulation by trying to make rules the same.

One solution to these problems is **harmonization**—making regulation the same everywhere. The International Organization of Securities Commissions was formed in 1984 with this purpose. The Fédération Internationale des Bourses de Valeurs, a Paris-based organization of stock exchanges, is working towards the same goal. At the same time, the London-based International Accounting Standards Committee (IASC) has been working towards harmonization of accounting rules and disclosure standards. None of these efforts has so far borne fruit.

mutual recognition
Resolution of cross-border differences in regulation by one country recognizing the rules of the other.

An alternative solution is **mutual recognition**—a reciprocal agreement that regards compliance with foreign law as compliance with domestic law. The United States and Canada have such an agreement for new issues and for acquisitions. The countries of the European Union have such an agreement for most securities regulation. Mutual recognition has some advantages over harmonization. Unlike harmonization, it does not stifle regulatory competition (we discussed the benefits of regulatory competition in Chapter 19). In addition, mutual recognition is much easier to achieve politically because it does not require any sacrifice of sovereignty.

Trends in Regulation

As we saw in Chapter 11, changes in regulation have been a response to, and have in turn contributed to, some important trends in securities markets—globalization, innovation, and the increasing importance of institutional investors. As we saw in Chapter 17, globalization and innovation have tended to undermine regulation by providing issuers and

---

[8] The European Union issued an Insider Trading Directive in 1989.

investors with alternative trading venues. The increasing importance of institutional investors has been a force for deregulation—for example, the abolition of fixed commissions and the removal of barriers to cross-border trading. There has also been increasing recognition, as with the introduction of Rule 144a, that institutional investors do not need the same degree of protection as small investors.

Not all of the pressures, however, have been towards less regulation. Innovation, in some cases, has helped regulation. Automated trading systems make market surveillance much easier. For example, regulators can detect insider trading quickly by matching the identity of traders with lists of company insiders. Computer technology also makes market transparency much easier to achieve, which may be one reason why it has become a regulatory goal. And institutional investors, mainly from the United States, have been a powerful lobby for investor protection laws in foreign countries.

We have completed our review of regulation that is aimed at eliminating, or at least reducing, cheating in securities markets. Let us now turn to the second problem of securities markets—instability.

THE STABILITY OF SECURITIES MARKETS

Securities markets, principally stock markets, have a distressing tendency to experience booms and busts. A stock market may take off and rise rapidly for a period of time, as during the recent "Internet bubble" in the United States. Then the market declines no less rapidly. In some cases, the decline is rapid enough to constitute a **market crash**. For example, in October 1987, an avalanche of selling caused a crash in stock prices around the world.

It is such crashes that are the principal concern of policy because of the potential danger they pose to the economy and to the market itself. Before we ask what, if anything, can be done about them, we need to understand how crashes happen and what their underlying causes might be.

What Happens in a Crash?

The first step in understanding crashes is to understand how securities markets provide liquidity and how market liquidity can break down.

How Securities Markets Provide Liquidity.   Securities markets provide liquidity in a very different way from financial intermediaries such as banks. Intermediaries provide liquidity by redeeming their liabilities in cash. Security markets provide liquidity by helping investors to sell their securities to other investors for cash.

As we saw in Chapter 11, a market should absorb liquidity-driven sales with no change in price. The price in an ideal security market should change only in response to new information about future cash flow. As long as liquidity sales and purchases are random and unrelated, they tend to offset one another with little impact on price. We can think of this as a form of pooling. The larger and the more concentrated the market, the better the pooling, and the less the market price is affected by liquidity trading.

Nonetheless, there will inevitably be occasional imbalances of desired liquidity sales and purchases. Security markets have various ways of handling these. In dealer markets, designated market makers absorb liquidity imbalances by trading for their own account. In auction markets, specialized traders jump in to buy and sell if liquidity imbalances drive prices away from their "fair" values.[9]

Sometimes, however, the mechanisms that provide a market with liquidity can be swamped by a rush of selling. The result is a crash. The best way to understand what drives such a rush of selling is to imagine how you yourself would behave in the same circumstances.

What Would You Have Done in the Crash of '87?   Put yourself in the shoes of the manager of a large pension fund in October 1987. Your basic problem is uncertainty about the long-term value of securities. The stock market has been rising rapidly for several years—especially in the past 12 months. Does this reflect an increase in long-term value or is it just a bubble that may soon burst?

The upward march of prices has slowed recently. So just to be safe, you decide to sell part of your stock portfolio and invest in short-term securities. Because you are not alone in doing this, prices fall. Worried about further declines, you sell more.[10]

Suppose that you are confident that high stock prices *do* indeed reflect long-term value. Will this stop you from selling? Not necessarily. While long-term value is important, you must also pay attention to what others believe that value to be. If others believe that stocks are overvalued, they will sell and prices will fall. Even if you think others are wrong to sell, it makes sense for you to sell before prices drop. So a securities market crash, like a bank run, can be the result of self-fulfilling expectations.

Why Market Makers Do Not Absorb the Decline.   The mechanisms that provide liquidity to the market may be unable to handle such a concerted rush of selling. One reason is simply volume. Market makers provide liquidity by buying up securities when there is an excess of sell orders. To be able to do this, they need credit to finance their purchases: the availability of credit is not unlimited. During the 1987 crash, banks became nervous about brokers' rapidly increasing borrowing and were reluctant to lend more.

Volume also strains the clearing and settlement process. In 1987, back offices lagged further and further behind trading, creating significant delays in completion. Differences in settlement procedures between stock markets and futures markets and delays in settlement left brokers with huge demands for payment in one market while they waited for payment in another.[11]

---

[9] See Chapters 11 and 17 for further discussion of liquidity in securities markets.

[10] If you were managing an index fund (see Chapter 10), you might well sell index futures rather than the stocks themselves. This is called "portfolio insurance" (see Chapter 18). The sale of index futures by you and by others will drive their price below the price of the underlying basket of stocks. This will cause index arbitragers to sell stocks short to profit from the discrepancy (see Chapter 16). Both portfolio insurance and index arbitrage are examples of program trading—the use of computers to follow a trading strategy and to generate the appropriate trading orders.

[11] This is an example of operational risk (see Chapter 17).

A second, more fundamental, reason why liquidity backup mechanisms will not halt the decline is that this is not what they are there for. The excess of selling in this case does not constitute a liquidity imbalance. Rather, it reflects a change in sentiment—a change in the fair price. While market makers are willing to absorb liquidity imbalances, they are not in the business of taking a position on long-term value. If they believe—justifiably or not—that the market is about to collapse, they have as much reason as anyone else to bail out. In 1987, rather than buying to offset the excess of sell orders, several specialists on the NYSE unloaded their own inventories, adding to the downward pressure on prices.

Contagion in Market Crashes.   Crashes in securities market exhibit the same sort of contagion that bank runs do, presumably for the same reasons. Evidence that securities in one market may be overvalued can suggest that the same is true in other markets. A collapse in one market heightens awareness of danger in others, making investors more inclined to hit the panic button. As you can see from Exhibit 20.3, the 1987 crash in the United States spread rapidly to stock markets elsewhere.

An Important Difference between a Bank Run and a Market Crash.   As you can see, there are important similarities between the bank runs that we discussed in Chapter 19 and market crashes. However, there is also an important difference. It makes no sense to sit out a bank run: if you do not withdraw your deposit, you will regret it. Things are a little different in a market crash.

Suppose that you, as a pension fund manager, had decided to sit out the 1987 crash without selling any of your stocks. How would you have fared? Not too badly, as it turns out. Within a couple of years, the market regained and even surpassed the level it had reached before the crash. In fact, the overwhelming majority of investors did sit it out. Trading volume on Monday, October 19, extraordinary as it was, represented only about 1% of listed stock.[12]

EXHIBIT 20.3   Change in Stock Market Prices in October 1987

Country	Decline in Price (%)
United States	21.5
Australia	44.7
Canada	22.2
United Kingdom	21.7
France	18.6
Germany	17.7
Italy	12.3
Japan	7.5

Source: Greenwald and Stein (1988).

---

[12] Recovery after the crash of 1929 took much longer. But even then, an investor who had purchased stock before the crash would have done quite well in the long term.

While sitting out the crash without selling would have been good, *buying* stock would have been even better. A crash can be an excellent time to buy. If panic selling by other investors causes market prices to drop below fair value, you should be able to pick up some bargains. As the price falls, buyers will come in to buy and so arrest the fall. Of course, this may take time, as investors wait for the market to "bottom." So a securities market in a liquidity crisis, unlike a bank in a similar situation, is to some extent self-righting.

Understanding the Behavior of Traders

Behavior during a crash does not fit easily into either of the two categories that we have used until now in describing trader behavior—liquidity trading and information trading.

Liquidity Trading and Information Trading. Liquidity trading is trading that is unrelated to the current price—for example, when a retiree sells some stock to finance current expenditures. Information trading is trading to profit from a discrepancy between the current market price and the "fair" price—for example, when locals respond to a liquidity imbalance or trade on new information. To function properly, a market needs both liquidity traders and information traders.

A market with only information traders would not work. First, responding to liquidity imbalances provides information traders with their basic income: no liquidity traders, no liquidity imbalances. Second, if you were an information trader and another information trader wanted to sell to you, would you buy? If he did not think the security was overvalued, he would not be selling. What if he knows something that you do not know? Information traders want to trade with liquidity traders, not with each other.

A market with only liquidity traders would not work either. At what price would liquidity traders trade with one another? Without information traders, there would be no price discovery. Moreover, without information traders, there would be no way to deal with a liquidity imbalance.

Noise Trading. Trading that is neither liquidity trading nor information trading is called **noise trading**. It is driven not by information, but by "noise"—factors unrelated to the fair price of the securities in question.

noise trading
Trading that is driven neither by information nor by liquidity considerations.

Trading during a crash is one example of noise trading. It is a kind of herd behavior—motivated primarily by trying to anticipate what other traders will do. If others are selling, they may have good reason. Or even if not, it is better to sell before they drive the price down. The buying that propels a stock market boom is similarly a kind of herd behavior. If others are buying, they may have good reason. Or even if not, it is better to buy before they drive the price up. Various "nonrational" strategies also fall into the category of noise trading. One such strategy involves plotting charts of stock movements and identifying characteristic shapes such as "shoulders" and "resistance levels."

The traditional view of noise trading is that it is a losing proposition. Over the long run, noise traders should lose money to information traders and be driven out of the market. Of course, even if true, there is no reason why new noise traders could not come in to replace them (there is one born every minute!).

The more recent view, however, is that noise traders "create their own space" by increasing uncertainty in securities markets. For example, during a market crash, or even a significant downturn, would information traders necessarily step in to buy? They might be confident that current market prices were below long-run value. However, they would have no idea how long this situation might persist. Indeed, market prices might well continue to fall. The reason for this uncertainty is the unpredictable behavior of noise traders themselves.

By increasing uncertainty, noise traders protect themselves from extinction, but they also degrade the quality of the market. The increased risk will reduce the supply of information trading, resulting in worse price discovery and impaired liquidity.

Factors That Contribute to Market Instability

Basically, stock markets are so unstable simply because there is so much uncertainty about the long-run value of stocks. However, several things can exacerbate this natural instability.

Uncertainty, Limits on Short Selling, and Noise Traders.   Particularly when there is something new like the Internet, there is enormous uncertainty about long-run value. There is no single rational valuation, and opinions differ widely. Some investors are optimistic, while others are skeptical. The optimists favor a long position; the skeptics, a short position. However, if it is more difficult, costly, or risky to take a short position, then the market tends to express the views of optimists more than it does those of skeptics. As a result, prices will rise.

When the market rises, there is a rush of "noise traders" wanting to get in on the action. Noise traders care little about long-term value and are simply betting that the rising trend will continue. Their buying can drive prices up further, providing them with the capital gains that they had hoped for. This in turn, spurs more buying, and so on. The phenomenon of a rapid rise in prices followed by a sudden collapse is known as a **bubble**.

bubble

A sustained price movement in a securities market driven by self-fulfilling expectations.

Quality Cycles.   The inflation and collapse of a bubble is reinforced by changes in the quality of the investments themselves, which often experience a **quality cycle**. Something new proves to be very successful, or at least very promising. This creates a hunger on the part of investors for more of the same. The market feeds this hunger, but only at the expense of ever declining quality.

quality cycle

A cycle in a security market in which initial success spurs the issue of lower quality securities.

The recent Internet bubble provides a good example. The early IPOs of Internet companies proved enormously successful, with shares trading at astronomical multiples of earnings. This created a hunger for more such IPOs that was satisfied by companies with progressively vaguer business plans and weaker prospects. Because of the enthusiasm for new deals was outweighing long-run reputational considerations, a lot of money could be made up front just from putting a deal together. Eventually, the lack of actual results caused investor confidence to falter and then collapse, and share prices fell back to earth with a thud.

Other examples of quality cycles associated with bubbles include the Japanese stock market and real estate bubble of the late 1980s, the South Sea and Mississippi bubbles in the eighteenth century, and the U.S. stock market boom of the late 1920s. In many cases, the rise and fall associated with a quality cycle are less dramatic. This was the case with LBOs and biotech companies in the 1980s and with railroads in the nineteenth century.

The Importance of Institutional Investors and Foreign Investors. Institutional investors are a more serious threat to stability than individual investors. Institutional investors are more active traders: they account for the bulk of trading volume. They are generally better informed than individuals, and they are quicker to react. When they do react, because of their size, the impact of their actions is much greater.

As we saw in Chapter 11, institutional investors are becoming increasingly important in securities markets. Rather than holding stocks themselves, individuals now hold the liabilities of intermediaries that hold stocks—pension funds, mutual funds, and insurance companies. The increasing importance of institutional investors in the U.S. stock market has increased its susceptibility to crashes. In the crash of 1987, selling by institutions played a major role.

If domestic institutions are a source of increased volatility, foreign institutions are even worse. Foreigners are generally less confident in their knowledge of domestic conditions and therefore especially quick to bail out if there seem to be problems. With increasing globalization, cross-border holdings of securities, especially by institutions, have steadily increased. The increasing importance of foreign institutional investors is likely to exacerbate volatility.

Portfolio Insurance. Some of the selling by institutions in 1987 was related to portfolio insurance. Portfolio insurance programs require the sale of stock index futures as the value of the index falls. The initial fall in stock prices triggered large sales of futures on the part of these programs. Index arbitrage transferred the selling pressure from the futures market to the stock market itself.[13]

While the actual volume of sales by portfolio insurance programs in 1987 was modest, the problem was that it was predictable. Other traders had learned from experience how portfolio insurance affected the market. Anticipating a wave of sell orders from the programs, and a consequent sharp dip in prices, other traders rushed to sell first. This "defensive" selling in response to the programs was of far greater magnitude than the sales of the programs themselves.

So portfolio insurance and program trading have increased instability in two ways. They have increased it directly, through their own effects on the market. They have also increased it indirectly, by inducing a reaction on the part of other traders.

What Can Be Done to Reduce Instability and Prevent Crashes?

Can anything be done to reduce the instability of securities markets or to prevent crashes? A number of policies have been suggested and tried.

Restricting Credit to Traders. Traders are able to increase the size of their positions, and so their potential profits (and losses), through leverage. That is, they can finance their positions by borrowing on margin rather than by relying on their own funds alone. Because such margin credit increases buying in a boom, it may help to drive up prices

---

[13] See Chapters 16 and 18 on portfolio insurance.

faster. When prices fall, leveraged investors may be forced to sell in order to meet their margin calls. These forced sales may accelerate the collapse in prices.

So it seems reasonable that restrictions on margin borrowing should reduce volatility. This was certainly the belief of U.S. legislators when they included such restrictions in the Securities Exchange Act of 1934 "for the purpose of preventing the excessive use of credit for the purchase or carrying of securities."[14] Unfortunately, there is no evidence that margin restrictions do reduce volatility. Empirical studies that have looked for such an effect have failed to find one.

Moreover, as we saw in Chapter 17, credit is essential for the proper functioning of securities markets. It is necessary to lubricate the settlement process, and it is necessary to finance the positions of information traders. Indeed, since information traders stabilize markets in the face of liquidity imbalances, restricting their credit will reduce stability in this sense.

Restricting Short Sales.   Short sellers often get the blame for falling prices and crashes. Certainly, short sellers do sell, and selling does drive down prices. As a result, securities market regulators in many countries (but not in the United States) restrict or ban short selling. Because short selling is particularly risky, regulators of financial institutions often limit or prohibit it to those institutions.[15] Since institutions are so important in the market, this has the effect of limiting the amount of short selling.

As we have seen, however, restrictions on short selling introduce a bias towards optimism in market behavior that helps to get booms and bubbles started. So restrictions on short selling may restrain price falls, but they may also reinforce price rises. Whether they reduce volatility overall is therefore far from clear.

Reducing Trading.   Another approach to reducing volatility is to reduce trading. The idea is that it is trading—especially "speculative" (short-term) trading—that is responsible for excessive volatility.

The way to reduce trading is to increase its cost, mainly through taxes. Such taxes are known as "**Tobin taxes**," after an economist of that name who suggested them as a way of reducing volatility. One possible tax is a tax on transactions, which falls especially heavily on trading for short-term gains. Another possibility is a tax on capital gains that applies to short-term gains but not to long-term gains.

Again, there is no empirical evidence that reducing trading in this way reduces volatility. And of course, as we know, "speculation" is an important stabilizer of markets. Tobin taxes penalize not only the potentially harmful trading of noise traders, but also the beneficial trading of information traders. In this way, they harm liquidity and price discovery.

Circuit Breakers.   Rather than just reducing trading, we can stop it altogether. As we saw in Chapter 17, continuous auctions often rely on price limits and trading halts as a backup mechanism to deal with routine liquidity problems. The idea is that by halting trad-

"**Tobin taxes**"
Taxes on transactions designed to reduce the amount of short-term trading.

---

[14] The restrictions are administered by the Fed.

[15] The loss on a long position is limited to the value of the securities held: their price cannot fall below zero. The loss on a short position is in principle unbounded: there is no (logical) limit on how high the price can rise.

ing temporarily, we allow traders that are not currently active to come forward and submit orders that will stabilize the market.[16]

The same mechanism can be mobilized to deal with market crashes. In these circumstances, the halt in trading not only allows other traders to come forward, but it also relieves the pressure on market infrastructure, allowing back-office functions to catch up with the volume of trading.

circuit breakers

Automatic trading halts triggered by a fall in securities prices of a given magnitude.

The presidential task force that investigated the 1987 crash recommended that such automatic trading halts—called **circuit breakers**—be instituted, to be triggered when the market had fallen by a preannounced amount. The recommendations were embodied in the Market Reform Act of 1990. This gave the SEC emergency authority to halt trading and to restrict such practices as program trading during periods of extreme market volatility.

Critics of circuit breakers argue that they actually exacerbate volatility. Seeing prices approaching the limit, traders rush to sell to get their orders in before the halt and so avoid being caught with open positions. This certainly seems to have happened in the crash of 1997. Also, where markets are linked through arbitrage—as is the case with the stock market and the index futures market—closing one market while leaving the other open can cause chaos. Finally, as we saw in Chapter 17, there are today many alternative trading forums. A trading halt on the New York Stock Exchange, for example, will simply divert trading to other forums. Overall, then, it is unclear whether circuit breakers really help.

In all, none of the various devices that have been introduced in the hope of reducing market instability seem particularly promising. It is not clear that any of them work, and all of them seem to have undesirable side effects. Given the great uncertainty about the long-run value of stocks, instability may be unavoidable. Instead of trying to prevent market crashes, perhaps we should focus on surviving them.

Surviving Market Crashes

Crashes as a Threat to the Economy. Crashes, however dramatic, seem to do less harm to the economy than banking panics. Historically, crashes that were not accompanied by simultaneous banking crises seem to have had relatively little impact. Of course, the Great Crash of 1929 is associated in popular memory with the Great Depression. But economists who have studied the period do not generally attribute an important role to the crash itself, as opposed to the subsequent collapse of the banking system and monetary mismanagement by the Fed. Indeed, although the crash of 1987 was more severe than that of 1929, it had little impact on the economy.

Crashes as a Threat to Market Makers. While crashes do not seem to pose a threat to the economy as a whole, they do pose a threat to the market itself. A precipitous fall in securities prices exposes market makers to huge capital losses on their inventories of securities. It also exposes them to enormous replacement risk from customer defaults. Because of this increase in risk, it becomes difficult for market makers to borrow. As a result, they may be forced to sell the securities they hold in order to repay loans they cannot roll over. This worsens the crisis and can wipe out the market makers themselves.

---

[16] The continuous auction is halted and restarted, after a delay, with a call auction (see Chapter 17 on continuous and call auctions).

In 1987, the Fed played a vital role in preventing this from happening. It pressured banks to resume their lending to specialists and to securities firms, and it promised to provide the necessary liquidity. Again in the minicrash of 1989 the Fed announced it would provide ample credit to banks to enable them to lend to brokerage firms and to other large investors wishing to buy stocks.

These actions are consistent with a more general policy of the Fed of acting as a lender of last resort not only to banks but to the financial system as a whole. For example, when the Penn Central railroad failed in June 1970 with over $200 million in commercial paper outstanding, the commercial paper market dried up. Worried about the effect on companies that relied on commercial paper for their working capital, the Fed encouraged banks to take up the slack by expanding their lending. The Fed increased its own lending to banks to make this possible.

Strengthening Market Infrastructure. A crashing market also places a great deal of strain on market infrastructure. Trading volume during the crash of 1987 was two to three times its normal level. Difficulties in executing orders and in completing trades were widespread and contributed to the general feeling of panic. It is important to strengthen the operational capacity of trading and settlement systems so that they can withstand the pressure of a crash. U.S. markets have learned the lessons of 1987, and systems today are much more robust.

Fragmentation of the settlement system was also a problem in 1987 because it greatly exacerbated liquidity risk. Futures and options markets settled the next day, while equity trades then settled after 5 days. Consequently, traders with large offsetting positions in equities and futures found themselves having to pay enormous sums to settle their futures trades, long before they received settlement on their equities trades. Settlement time in the equities market has since been reduced to $t + 3$ and will eventually be brought down to $t + 1$. Actually integrating settlement systems, so that the positions of traders in different markets can be netted, would also do much to reduce potential problems.

So we find that with securities markets, as with banking, government intervention is a very mixed blessing. Not every problem requires government intervention, and not every government intervention helps.

SUMMARY

- Cheating raises transactions costs in securities markets and so reduces their scope. Because of the element of fixed cost, it is a particular obstacle for smaller investors and smaller issuers.

- Cheating involves a reputational externality that creates incentives for group action (self-regulation).

- Governments have largely superseded self-regulation—either policing it or replacing it. In the United States, this government takeover dates from the crisis of the 1930s.

- Regulators police the primary market. Issuers must satisfy disclosure requirements. Standards for disclosure are set by the FASB.

- Regulators monitor the trading of securities to ensure that trading is fair. Insider trading and market manipulation are prohibited. However, insider trading laws are hard to enforce, and they have costs as well as benefits.

- Brokers and money managers are regulated to protect investors. Organized markets are regulated with the intention of improving their performance.

- A major goal of regulators is market transparency. However, transparency has costs as well as benefits, and it is not clear that government intervention here is necessary or beneficial.

- The "Continental" approach to regulation (associated with civil-law legal systems) relies on close oversight to prevent problems from happening. The "Anglo" approach (associated with common-law legal systems) sets standards and then focuses on detecting and punishing abuses. Innovation is easier under common-law systems.

- Globalization of markets is hindered by differences in regulation. There are two approaches to resolving the problem—harmonization and mutual recognition.

- Securities markets are subject to crashes. Crashes are similar in some respects to bank runs and banking panics—a breakdown of liquidity mechanisms, a degree of self-fulfilling expectations, and contagion. However, crashes, unlike runs and panics, are to some extent self-righting.

- Trading that is neither liquidity trading nor information trading is called noise trading. Trading during a crash is one example of noise trading.

- Factors that contribute to market instability include uncertainty about long-run value, limits on short selling, and noise trading. Quality cycles also play a role.

- Policies to reduce instability include limiting buying on margin, restricting short sales, "Tobin taxes," and circuit breakers. There is little evidence that any of these improve matters.

- Rather than trying to prevent crashes, policy should focus on limiting the damage when they do occur.

DISCUSSION QUESTIONS

1. Why is cheating harmful to securities markets? Is government intervention necessary to prevent it?

2. What are the benefits of disclosure requirements for the public issue of securities? What are the costs (whom might they harm)? What would happen if there were no such requirements? Would there be disclosure? How much? How could small investors manage without government protection?

3. What are the arguments for and against insider trading laws? How is it possible to get around the law?

4. What are the costs and benefits of market transparency? How transparent would markets be

in the absence of government intervention? Would investors be worse off?

5. Make up a table showing the differences between "Anglo" and "Continental" approaches to securities regulation. What are their relative advantages and disadvantages?

6. Is harmonization or mutual recognition a better approach to resolving cross-border differences in regulation?

7. Why do markets crash? What are the respective contributions of investors, market makers, and market institutions? What are the parallels with bank runs and banking panics?

8. What policies have been tried to reduce market instability? Discuss their benefits and costs.

BIBLIOGRAPHY

Blume, M. E. "The Structure of U.S. Equity Markets." The Wharton School, the University of Pennsylvania, October 2000.

De Long, J. Bradford, Andrei Shleifer, Lawrence H. Summers, and Robert J. Waldmann. "Noise Trader Risk in Financial Markets." *Journal of Political Economy* 98, no. 4 (1990): 703–738.

Greenwald, Bruce, and Jeremy Stein. "The Task Force Report: The Reasoning Behind the Recommendations." *Journal of Economic Perspectives* 2, no. 3 (summer 1988): 3–23.

Lee, R. *What Is an Exchange? The Automation, Management, and Regulation of Financial Markets.* New York: Oxford University Press, 1990.

Mahoney, P. G. "The Exchange as Regulator," working paper no. 97-5, University of Virginia Law School, Spring 1997.

Shleifer, A., and L. H. Summers. "The Noise Trader Approach to Finance." *Journal of Economic Perspectives* 4, no. 2 (spring 1990): 19–33.

Stout, L. "Why the Law Hates Speculators: Regulation and Private Ordering in the Market for OTC Derivatives." *Duke Law Journal* 48 (1999): 701–786.

KEY TERMS

self-regulation

home market bias

Securities Exchange Commission (SEC)

Securities Act of 1933

Securities Exchange Act of 1934

Securities Acts Amendments of 1975

Commodity Exchange Act (CEA) of 1936

Commodity Futures Trading Commission (CFTC)

disclosure requirement

"window dressing"

Financial Accounting Standards Board (FASB)

"blue sky laws"

insider trading

"painting the tape"

"squeeze" or "corner"

market manipulation

harm-based regulation

preventive regulation

front-running

churning

Securities Investor Protection Corporation (SIPC)

trading priority

market transparency

best execution

Investment Advisors Act of 1940

"Anglo" approach to regulation

"Continental" approach to regulation

harmonization

mutual recognition

market crash

noise trading

bubble

quality cycle

"Tobin taxes"

circuit breakers

NAME INDEX

SUBJECT INDEX

Marginal glossary terms and the page on which they are defined appear in **boldface** type.